Reconstructing American Historical Cinema

RECONSTRUCTING
American Historical Cinema

From *Cimarron* to *Citizen Kane*

J. E. Smyth

THE UNIVERSITY PRESS OF KENTUCKY

Publication of this volume was made possible in part by a grant
from the National Endowment for the Humanities.

Scholarly publisher for the Commonwealth,
serving Bellarmine University, Berea College, Centre College of Kentucky,
Eastern Kentucky University, The Filson Historical Society, Georgetown College,
Kentucky Historical Society, Kentucky State University, Morehead State University,
Murray State University, Northern Kentucky University, Transylvania University,
University of Kentucky, University of Louisville, and Western Kentucky University.
All rights reserved.

Editorial and Sales Offices: The University Press of Kentucky
663 South Limestone Street, Lexington, Kentucky 40508-4008
www.kentuckypress.com

10 09 08 07 06   5 4 3 2 1

Library of Congress Cataloging-in-Publication Data

Smyth, J. E., 1977-
  Reconstructing American historical cinema : from Cimarron to Citizen Kane / J. E.
Smyth.
     p. cm.
  Includes bibliographical references and index.
  ISBN-13: 978-0-8131-2406-3 (alk. paper)
  ISBN-10: 0-8131-2406-9 (alk. paper)
  1. Historical films–United States–History and criticism. 2. Motion pictures and history.
I. Title.
  PN1995.9.H5S57 2006
  791.43'658–dc22   2006020064

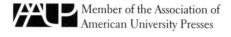 Member of the Association of
American University Presses

For Evelyn M. Smyth and Peter B. Smyth

and for K. H. and C. G.

You might say that we grew up together.

There's a lot of words we haven't covered yet. For instance, do you know what this means, "I'll get you on the Ameche"? Of course not! An Ameche is the telephone, on account of he invented it. . . . Like, you know, in the movies.

—Sugarpuss O'Shea (Barbara Stanwyck)
in *Ball of Fire*, 1941

Contents

List of Illustrations . . . xi
Acknowledgments . . . xiii

Introduction: Toward a Filmic Writing of History
    in Classical Hollywood . . . 1

One: Traditional and Modern American History

  1. The New American History: *Cimarron*, 1931 . . . 27
  2. Contemporary History in the Age of *Scarface*, 1932 . . . 57

Two: Resolving Westward Expansion

  3. Competing Frontiers, 1933–1938 . . . 89
  4. The Return of Our Epic America, 1938–1941 . . . 115

Three: Civil War and Reconstruction

  5. Jezebels and Rebels, Cavaliers and Compromise, 1930–1939 . . . 141
  6. The Lives and Deaths of Abraham Lincoln, 1930–1941 . . . 167

Four: Veterans of Different Wars

  7. War in the Roaring Twenties, 1932–1939 . . . 197
  8. The Last of the Long Hunters, 1938–1941 . . . 225

Five: Hollywood History

  9. Stars Born and Lost, 1932–1937 . . . 251
10. A Hollywood Cavalcade, 1939–1942 . . . 279

Conclusion: From *Land of Liberty* to the Decline and Fall
    of *Citizen Kane* . . . 307

Appendixes . . . 341
Notes . . . 367
Selected Bibliography . . . 413
Index . . . 435

Illustrations

Cimarron's multiethnic, racial, and gendered West . . . 36

Estabrook's projected text titles . . . 38

A white merchant-pioneer tells the Indians to get out . . . 39

Estabrook's annotated copy of *Cimarron* . . . 40

The vulture's eye view . . . 43

Sabra's frontier rhetoric elicits a sad smile from Yancey . . . 46

LeBaron, Ree, and Estabrook receive Academy Awards . . . 50

Darryl F. Zanuck at Warner Brothers, ca. 1930 . . . 58

Rico alters the clock . . . 64

Small-time crook Rico reads the headlines for Diamond Pete . . . 67

Little Caesar makes the headlines . . . 67

Rico checks his press coverage . . . 67

Establishing the period in *The Public Enemy*, 1931 . . . 69

Documentary shots of Chicago: State Street . . . 70

The Union Stockyards . . . 70

War is declared, but Tom and Matt are oblivious . . . 70

Mummifying the gangster . . . 72

Al Capone handles the commissioner . . . 75

Who killed Big Jim in 1920? . . . 79

Courting "press-tige" . . . 79

Writing history with a new instrument—the machine gun . . . 79

Happy Valentine's Day from Tony Camonte . . . 81

Mae West in *She Done Him Wrong*, 1933 . . . 94

Text foreword for *The Last of the Mohicans*, 1936 . . . 101

Twentieth Century–Fox research library, ca. 1939 . . . 102

DeMille's historical staff in the late 1930s . . . 109

Close-up of Geronimo . . . 123

The final chase in *Stagecoach* . . . 124

Opening credits of *The Plainsman* . . . 132

Julie and her maid share a similar taste in dresses . . . 155

The color of the dress is red, but what is the color of the heroine? . . . 157

Julie sings with "her children" . . . 157

The politics of race and dress . . . 159

Scarlett and the South rise again . . . 161

The oath . . . 161

"Reconstructed" southern woman . . . 161

Trotti's foreword for *Young Mr. Lincoln*, 1939 . . . 177

An uncertain hero's first speech . . . 180

Mastering Blackstone's *Commentaries* and the common laws of *Poor Richard's Almanac* . . . 184

Raymond Massey's swearing in . . . 190

Tray full of pawned war medals . . . 200

The Great War splits the couple in *The Story of Vernon and Irene Castle*, 1939 . . . 214

Ginger Rogers as Irene Foote Castle in *Patria* . . . 215

Overdetermined images . . . 219

Mark Hellinger's modern history . . . 220

Sergeant York reads *The History of the United States* . . . 232

Alvin York: a twentieth-century Lincoln . . . 232

Revisiting old "texts": the Daniel Boone connection . . . 233

Clara Bow in *Call Her Savage*, 1932 . . . 252

David O. Selznick with his father, Lewis J. Selznick . . . 253

A Star Is Born: introducing the "text" . . . 270

John Gilbert and Greta Garbo in *Queen Christina*, 1933 . . . 271

Jean Harlow's memorial at Grauman's Chinese Theatre . . . 273

John Bowers, ca. 1924 . . . 275

Esther tries stepping into Norman Maine's footsteps . . . 276

Esther is stopped in her tracks by the past . . . 276

Norman Maine's slab . . . 276

Facing custard pies from the past . . . 292

Opening shot: someone else presents George M. Cohan . . . 302

Independence Day, 1878 . . . 302

Remembering "Over There" . . . 302

Remembering the Great War . . . 328

Kane's declaration . . . 329

The "vault" of the Thatcher library . . . 330

Thompson reads Thatcher's journal . . . 331

Reading from the text of history to the cinematic West . . . 332

Historical completion and "the Union forever" . . . 332

Acknowledgments

Many people assisted in the shaping and production of this book, but none of it would have been possible without the help and patience of dozens of film archivists and librarians. My thanks to the staff at Indiana University's Lilly Library, the University of Southern California's Cinema-Television Library and Warner Brothers Archive, the Warner Brothers Corporate Archive, UCLA's Arts Library Special Collections and Special Collections, Yale University, the Huntington Library, Brigham Young University, Boston University, the Harry Ransom Research Center at the University of Texas, and the Academy of Motion Picture Arts and Sciences. I am especially grateful to Leith Adams, James D'Arc, Lauren Buisson, J. C. Johnson, and Jenny Romero. But above all, I want to thank the invaluable Ned Comstock, Noelle Carter, and Barbara Hall.

Yale University, the Huntington Library, and Indiana University all supported this project with generous grants and fellowships.

I want to thank Dudley Andrew, Charles Musser, Michael Denning, and Alan Trachtenberg for their help when this project was emerging as a doctoral dissertation at Yale. My colleagues and students at the University of Warwick provided me with a new forum for my ideas, and I am grateful for their support and friendship. David Culbert, Peter Rollins, and Robert A. Rosenstone published my early writings on history and film, and some of that work has become part of this book. Robert witnessed my first challenge to mainstream American historiography, and I'll always be grateful for his rigorous editing and unflagging enthusiasm for Lamar Trotti and Darryl F. Zanuck. I am deeply indebted to my editor, Leila Salisbury, for skillfully guiding this project to completion.

Some of the pleasantest days of my life were spent discussing Cecil B. DeMille with Mickey and Patrick Moore. I'll always remember them with affection and awe. Noel Taylor is another who made my many visits to Los Angeles unforgettable. But I owe five ladies debts for their support and kindness, which I hope someday to repay, if only in part: Olivia de Havilland, Katharine Hepburn, Marsha Hunt, Ann Rutherford, and Janet Leigh. And, as always, my love to Evelyn, Peter, Rose, and Lillie.

Introduction

Toward a Filmic Writing of History in Classical Hollywood

> We believe that we have as much right to present the facts of history as we
> see them . . . as a Guizot, a Bancroft, a Ferrari, or a Woodrow Wilson has
> to write these facts in his history.
>   —D. W. Griffith, *The Rise and Fall of Free Speech in America*, 1916

When D. W. Griffith published his defense of historical filmmaking in
1916, there was little doubt why he believed that filmmaker-historians
needed a spokesman. Public controversy had yet to subside over his Civil
War and Reconstruction epic *The Birth of a Nation* (1915). Although
Griffith had already filmed eleven southern period pictures, including
The Honor of His Family (1909), *His Trust* (1910), and *The Battle* (1911),
he had never before made such lengthy, complex, and controversial use of
American history. Griffith's decision to venture into major American historical filmmaking was undoubtedly prompted by the success of Thomas
Ince's *The Battle of Gettysburg* (1913), released on the fiftieth anniversary
of that engagement.[1] However, Griffith not only scripted the heroic sacrifices of Confederate and Federal soldiers and the national reconciliation
of Abraham Lincoln's leadership; he also pursued American history into
the postwar era. The second half of *The Birth of a Nation* was an adaptation of Thomas Dixon's Reconstruction novel *The Clansman* (1905).

Griffith's choice to film one of the most racially transfiguring and
socially contested periods in national history from what many of his contemporaries considered a blatantly racist, white southern perspective out-

1

raged much of black and white America.[2] Even before its release, the National Association for the Advancement of Colored People (NAACP) campaigned to suppress and censor the film, and after its release, critics accused Griffith of "capitalizing race hatred" and of making an "aggressively vicious and defamatory" film.[3] Curiously, one of his most prominent critics, Francis Hackett of the *New Republic*, felt that the projected text "titles" were as offensive and incendiary as the most violent images of blacks attacking white women and profaning the Senate chamber and of Klansmen riding to the rescue "in defense of their Aryan birthright." "My objection to the drama," he wrote, "is based partly on the tendency of the pictures but mainly of the printed lines I have quoted. The effect of these lines, reinforced by adroit quotations from Woodrow Wilson and repeated assurances of impartiality and good will, is to arouse in the audience a strong sense of the evil possibilities of the Negro and the extreme propriety and godliness of the Ku Klux Klan."[4]

Moving Picture World's W. Stephen Bush also noticed that the film's "controversial spirit" was "especially obvious in the titles."[5] Griffith had chosen to intensify the historical discourse of his film with projected text. Intertitles, though derivative of early slide lecturers and onstage narration of nonfiction films, introduced the unique combination of projected text and images; Griffith's historical "narrative" fused two seemingly distinct discourses on screen. But his text did not simply give continuity to the visual narrative or compound the historical prestige associated with Civil War cinema; it provided historical detail and arguments about slavery and Reconstruction that were lightning rods for national controversy.

Having to watch a Civil War and Reconstruction film that was at times reminiscent of Mathew Brady's poignant photography was one experience, but having to *read* a film's historical perspective interspaced with Woodrow Wilson's *History of the American People* was another.[6] Griffith's images and text forced the audience to take sides. When the director-screenwriter defended his film, he took the offensive, claiming, however erroneously, that the entire narrative was "authenticated history."[7] Although scholars have since pointed out that African Americans did not overrun Congress or the senates of southern states during Reconstruction and that the Klan served purposes other than keeping black people under control,[8] Griffith was interested in projecting a final image of white solidarity. Showing abrasive Yankees annexing old plantation lands and over-taxing the impoverished inhabitants would not have helped his vision of white unity any more than images of Klansmen going after carpetbaggers and white Federal soldiers would have. "History" may have translated as conflict to Griffith, but the unresolved struggle between white and black Americans overshadowed the Civil War heroics of the Camerons and the Stonemans.

Although Griffith understood that traditional writers of history were influenced by their own personal view of the past, and that objectivity was difficult to achieve, he asserted repeatedly that *The Birth of a Nation* was "accurate" and more objective than previous written histories of the era. Actress Lillian Gish would recall Griffith justifying the elaborate production in order "to tell the truth about the War between the States. It hasn't been told accurately in history books. Only the winning side in a war ever gets to tell its story."[9] As historians have since pointed out, the initially polarized and polemical early histories of the war were superseded by massive attempts at conciliation that avoided overtly "northern" or "southern" perspectives.[10] But by the first two decades of the twentieth century, historians such as Ulrich Phillips were laying the foundations for the rise of white southern history. Griffith was part of a larger revisionist movement bent on reclaiming a regional historical perspective in Civil War and Reconstruction discourse.

Griffith attributed his capacity for historical objectivity to his status as a filmmaker. Shortly after the film's release in April 1915, he was interviewed by Richard Barry in the *Editor* and predicted that filmmakers would eventually replace writers as historians. In his imagined film library, "There will be no opinions expressed. You will merely be present at the making of history. All the work of writing, revising, collating, and reproducing will have been carefully attended to by a corps of recognized experts, and you will have received a vivid and complete expression."[11] Griffith had an almost pristine faith in the camera's exceptional status as an interpretive tool of history, its recording apparatus providing filmmakers with advantages in objectivity that traditional writers of history lacked. But the following year, his perspective in *The Rise and Fall of Free Speech in America* changed, focusing instead on the continuities between historical filmmaking and traditional historiography. What prompted this new outlook? Perhaps the censorship storm over *The Birth of a Nation* had chastened him. What is more likely is that Griffith recognized that his power as a director and historian was vested in his interpretation of history. Merely recording facts from the past was documentation; the projection of history involved active engagement with historical evidence.[12] Filmmakers had every right to be historians, he wrote, and to "present the facts of history as we see them."

Although late-twentieth-century film historians have dismissed

Griffith's view of history as a simple, pernicious, but potent national myth influenced by the triumphant chauvinism of George Bancroft, the Whiggish equation of history and progress, and violent racism,[13] Griffith himself embraced the connection with Bancroft and the American historical tradition. Bancroft, the premier American historian of the nineteenth century, was a scholar possessing both academic and popular respect.[14] Griffith's claim of professional ties was his way of legitimizing filmmaking as a powerful form of historiography in 1916.[15] Although *The Birth of a Nation* endorsed national unity and strength through clearly defined racial and cultural conflicts, Griffith compromised Bancroft's historical trajectory of inevitable progress and development. After all, *The Birth of a Nation* is a monument to the historical crisis of war and disunion. Griffith was driven by two competing historical visions of America: the reassuring, triumphant nationalism intoned by Bancroft, and his own desire to contradict, to correct, and to narrate the South's struggle against northern "progress," making a history of rebellion and opposition to the traditionally construed forces of history the central narrative of nineteenth-century America. His film did more than simply record or document history with the camera's capacity for reenacted realism.

Although filmgoers and critics had long been astounded by cinema's capacity to record events in the present, President Woodrow Wilson was the most prominent spectator to recognize Griffith as an intermediary between American history and 1915 America, remarking that *The Birth of a Nation* was "history written in lightning."[16] Griffith agreed, seeing himself and his peers as historians, and claimed that "the motion picture is at least on a par with the spoken and written word."[17] More than any other filmmaker of his generation, he exploited cinema's potential to write and rewrite the text of American history, to compete with and even exceed the scope, complexity, and audience of traditional writings about the past. Historical cinema was more than a recording apparatus, an instrument of reenactment, or the passive handmaiden of historical writing. By allying himself publicly with the great writers of history and absorbing the discourse and iconography of historiography through projected text and documents, Griffith proved that filmmaking could engage traditional historical discourse on fundamental and multivalent levels. Griffith offered the possibility of a filmic "writing" of American history.

But when filmmakers chose to become historiographers—literally, "writers of history," whether in ink, in celluloid, or in lightning—Griffith found that they were often subject to professional historians' contempt and public controversy. *The Birth of a Nation* set the standard for Hollywood's future historical work (the preliminary research and the publicized if contested claims to historical authenticity; the adaptation of the discourse of traditional historiography through projected text inserts, documents, and historical characters; the transformation of a period novel into a more historically assertive film, linking fictional protagonists to visually and textually documented historical events; the massive cost; the public adulation and outrage), yet few filmmakers dared or wanted to equal its mammoth cost and public controversy. Instead, from 1916 to 1927, American historical feature filmmaking became a prestigious but only occasional part of Hollywood's A-feature output. This ranged, in the silent period, from biographies (*Davy Crockett*, 1916; *The Dramatic Life of Abraham Lincoln*, 1924) to reenactments of famous events in history (*America*, 1924; *The Iron Horse*, 1924; *Old Ironsides*, 1926) to adaptations of historical novels (*The Last of the Mohicans*, 1920; *The Scarlet Letter*, 1926) to more modern historical events (*The Big Parade*, 1925; *The Rough Riders*, 1927). Unlike American attempts at narrating European history (*Orphans of the Storm*, 1922; *The Sea Hawk*, 1924; *The Patriot*, 1928), these films, regardless of star power, attracted a larger and more informed national audience, particularly westerns such as *The Covered Wagon* (1923) and war epics such as *The Birth of a Nation*. Critics such as Robert Sherwood did not rhapsodize about lavish sets and costumes but quarreled with or praised the filmmakers' narrative choices and presentation of historical events and conflicts.[18]

Although many of these films were extremely popular and attracted critical praise,[19] they were only a small part of Hollywood's annual output. At this time, studio research departments were tiny, and their duties did not affect the content of screenplays. Instead, directors like Griffith often dictated the historical script, which revolved around well-known historical events (*The Rough Riders*) or people (*The Dramatic Life of Abraham Lincoln*) or general historical periods (*The Covered Wagon*). After the public reaction to Griffith's racist historical position in *The Birth of a Nation*, these films more cautiously celebrated naval victories over Britain and freelance pirates, courageous pioneers, wartime heroics, and saintly presidents. Potentially critical narratives such as Paramount's *Vanishing American* (1925) were very rare, and the scenes of government abuse of Native Americans were tempered by the noble Navaho hero's decision to enter World War I and assimilate as a patriot.[20] The use of text inserts in silent American historical films mainly praised national achievements and noted dates and locales. In spite of the necessity for intertitles and projected text, screenwriters had little power when it came to choosing historical material and constructing the narratives. Although directors James Cruze and George B. Seitz did not achieve Griffith's total autho- rial control over their scripts, screenwriters during the silent era were not accorded recognition or respect as the writers of filmed history.[21]

With the advent of sound, what had been an occasional expensive practice became the industry's most innovative, prestigious, and contro- versial form of feature filmmaking. American historical features were a significant chunk of the A-feature output from RKO, Paramount, Warner Brothers, MGM, and later Twentieth Century–Fox from 1930 to 1941, and by 1939–1940 they easily outnumbered any other genre or cycle.[22] Filmmakers focused more exclusively on the national past, and research libraries, historical experts, original screenplays, publicity campaigns, and critical attention became part of the craft of American historical film- making. Suddenly Hollywood's greatest need was capable writers. New producers such as Darryl F. Zanuck and David O. Selznick began to work closely with teams of writers and researchers on individual film projects.[23] Screenwriters read both traditional and revisionist historiography, reevalu- ated accepted interpretations and arguments, and often pursued modern or popular subjects ignored by historians. Original screenplays competed with adaptations of history, biography, and old press headlines. Silent American period films such as *Ramona* (1910, 1916, 1928) and *The Last of the Mohicans* (1909, 1920) were remade with greater historical atten- tion. Historical novels were scripted with prominent historical intertitles, documents, and reenactments unknown in the original fiction.

During the 1930s, the most respected screenwriters were even al- lowed to develop and complete their own historical projects without significant studio interference. Twentieth Century–Fox mogul Darryl F. Zanuck had started his career at Warner Brothers as a lowly hack writer churning out dozens of treatments (including the Rin Tin Tin series); as head of his own studio, he allowed his writers more autonomy in the selection and day-to-day development of film projects. Writers were paid better at Fox, too. In 1938 Twentieth Century–Fox's top salaries belonged to Shirley Temple ($110,000) and screenwriter-producer Nunnally John- son ($100,000).[24] In contrast, MGM gave its writers the least power and opportunity to develop original scripts; in spite of its wealth, the studio did not pioneer films about American history, as did the smaller RKO, or consistently dominate the cycle in the 1930s, as did Warner Brothers, Paramount, and Twentieth Century–Fox.[25] But MGM was adept at ap- propriating other studios' historical innovations. For example, in 1937 it hired Edward G. Robinson to star in *The Last Gangster*; both the title and the star evoked memories of the controversial historical gangster cycle Zanuck had helped create at Warner Brothers in the early 1930s. However, MGM's film was safe fiction. *New York Times* film critic Frank S. Nugent, mindful of Warner Brothers' high-profile historical and biographical productions, wrote, "Had Warners been doing it, it would have read: 'Mr. Edward G. Robinson in *The Life of the Last Gangster.*'"[26] Beginning in the early sound era, Warner Brothers became one of the most prominent producers of historical cinema. As part of its constant search for historical novelties, forgotten events, and contemporary historical figures, the studio also developed one of the most impressive and well-publicized research libraries in California. Its head, Dr. Herman Lissauer, not only advised on major features but also helped create Warner's Academy Award–winning educational shorts *Give Me Liberty* (1936), *The Man without a Country* (1937), *The Declaration of Independence* (1938), and *Sons of Liberty* (1939).

The advent of sound coincided with and even fostered the rise of the studio research libraries, but it had the greatest impact on the role of the historical screenwriter. Sound films enabled screenwriters to literally "write" a historical film, and for the first time since Griffith's commentary in 1915–1916, the word gained ascendancy in film production. Zanuck's dictum "Put it in writing," inscribed on the studio stationery at Warner Brothers and Twentieth Century–Fox, applied to every aspect of film production but had its greatest resonance with the emerging American historical films that he produced. Sound's transformation of film production arguably affected historical filmmaking more than any other feature film genre or cycle, but paradoxically, these new sound-era screenwriters owed their most obvious structural debt to the mechanics of silent filmmaking. Projected words did not disappear with the introduction of talking pictures. Although sound had rendered intertitles and projected text obsolete, historical films retained and embellished their textual content as a means of lending their narratives historical credibility and prestige. Historical forewords introduced their subjects, dates punctuated the narratives, and text inserts "chapterized" these new film texts. In an age of mesmerizing screen images, the use of text deliberately drew attention to the constructed nature of the film. Audiences saw neither unmediated reality nor seamless studio fantasies, but rather images organized by the words of new Hollywood historians. Beginning in 1930 and continuing for a dozen years, the Hollywood studios released an unprecedented number of these films, and filmmakers, critics, and audiences responded to the industry's pursuit of American history.[27]

The Myth of Classical Cinema

Although the films discussed here all fall within the critical boundaries of the period known to academe as "classical Hollywood" (roughly 1920 to 1960), the term *classical Hollywood cinema* and its critical heritage have seriously constricted previous historical scholarship on pre–World War II Hollywood filmmaking. The term originally signified French film critic André Bazin's praise for a beautifully balanced stage of American film narratives, a moment in the late 1930s when the visual structures and seamless continuity of Hollywood film production were blended with an overpowering narrative unity.[28] Over the next thirty years, professional film historians and theorists recast Bazin's appreciation for prewar aesthetic balance and narrative resolution with an overdose of economic determinism. According to this view, aided by totalizing structuralist and post-structuralist discourses on film language and ahistorical psychoanalytic theories about the ideological function of the film apparatus, studio-era Hollywood was a massive industrial machine producing a standardized cinema that supported the nation's overarching capitalist ideology.[29] In addition, Hortense Powdermaker's 1950 study of the Hollywood "dream factory" inspired film theorists and historians to decipher and describe the "mythic discourse" of classical Hollywood cinema.[30] The Hollywood system's genre formulas, binary narrative system of good and evil, conflict and resolution, fixed dramatic patterns, hidden and insidious ideological apparatus, passive spectator, and resolution of dominant national ideology are all recognized as trademarks of myth.[31]

Traditional views of Hollywood genre presented by Robert Warshow and Will Wright claimed that classical Hollywood genres consistently resolved timeless conflicts within fixed dramatic patterns.[32] More recently, Rick Altman attempted to replace the traditional transhistorical concept of film genre with a more historically specific approach, but most criticism over the past thirty years has intoned classical Hollywood's unconscious reflection of dominant ideologies and the monolith of classical Hollywood genre.[33] Occasional anomalies in the genre were considered just that—occasional—and they were often attributed to a maverick director-auteur. Good films were made in spite of the system and in spite of producers, although film historians Thomas Schatz and George Custen did much to restore Irving Thalberg's, David O. Selznick's, and Darryl F. Zanuck's reputations as the authentic geniuses of the Hollywood system.[34]

In *The Classical Hollywood Cinema* (1985), leading film scholars David Bordwell, Kristin Thompson, and Janet Staiger reinforced the concept of the Hollywood system as never before. In measuring Hollywood's slow and predictable change as a form of industrial and stylistic adaptation, they concluded that money and technology were the supreme catalysts of Hollywood cinema.[35] The mammoth structure of mainstream filmmaking easily overcame potential idiosyncrasies, and although subject matter and characterization reflected contemporary trends and cultural beliefs, Bordwell, Thompson, and Staiger created a Hollywood that grew within an enclosed, deeply structured world outside the boundaries of American history and culture. In fact, one might argue that in their account, the words *classical* and *mythic* are interchangeable. The Bordwell-Thompson-Staiger formula has led film scholar Miriam Hansen to charge Bordwell (and his methodology of neo-formalist poetics and cognitive psychology) with using the term *classicism* to transcend history, enabling a mythic, totalizing, and reductive view of Hollywood production and style.[36] Curiously, Bordwell's formulation of classical Hollywood resembles the structuralist–post-structuralist accounts of the 1970s that he allegedly intended to revise. Although Hansen's "historicizing" of classical Hollywood cinema examined Hollywood's potential for modernism in its representation and dissemination of the conditions of modernity rather than in films' capacity for narrative critique and stylistic innovation, her intervention is crucial in recovering a historically nuanced understanding of Hollywood film practice in the 1930s.

Certainly there were quota quickies, serials, predictable genres, fantasy, glamour, and narrative formulas that producers and screenwriters could easily adapt and communicate to carefully measured target audiences. But the seemingly transhistorical, mythic discourse of classical Hollywood genre cannot be applied to historical filmmaking, where the subject matter deliberately reached beyond the borders of the film industry, contemporary culture, and Depression-era audiences. Perhaps this is why so few film historians have bothered to look closely at the production and discourse of historical films from the classical era.[37] Rather than following the patterns of myth, dissolving historical specificity within symbols and resolving all cultural contradictions in a reassuring narrative pattern, American historical films in particular had to be responsible on some level for things beyond the consideration of a good story.

The developing iconography of historical cinema departed from the seamless continuity and insularity of classic narrative. Frequent text inserts literally separated viewers from the visual narrative, offering a disjunctive visual experience that forced them to read as well as see and hear. Although in the late 1920s, Sergei Eisenstein and other Russian filmmakers hoped that sound would obliterate the "uncinematic" use of intertitles,[38] more recently, film theorist Pascal Bonitzer praised the use of projected text in late 1960s documentaries as a means of distancing the audience from the totalizing ideological powers of the voice-over narrator. The "fragmentary, discontinuous" presence of text on screen "appeals to the 'consciousness'" and creates a direct means of interrogating what an audience sees and hears.[39] Although Bonitzer was referring to post-1968 documentaries, the use of text in classical Hollywood history films draws films outside the confines of Eisenstein's "cinematic" essence and Bordwell-Thompson-Staiger's conception of Hollywood narratives. The text of American history had other conventions and anomalies that, when interpreted through film, altered the basic iconography and narrative practices of the Hollywood cinema.

Although both traditional historiography and film production depend on narrative form, the writing of history involves argument, evidence, and multiple perspectives—things that are often in conflict with Hollywood studios' need to get films made on schedule and within budget. Throughout this period, filmmakers added major historical events to adaptations of period novels like spectacular digressions; close-ups of historical documents competed with close-ups of the protagonists. Although contemporaneous critics appreciated the spectacles of massive battles, balls, and conventions and the details of letters, newspapers, and government documents, others would point out that these historical concerns overwhelmed traditional fiction film narratives.[40] History often had a jarring way of breaking the seamless continuity of protagonist-driven narratives. The presence of text, spectacles, and competing narratives of history were disjunctive, eye-popping, and distractingly complex. One might even be tempted to term history as the ultimate cinematic *attraction*, fracturing the traditional sense of a good film narrative that tells its story quickly and clearly.[41] But these films are not variations of the counternarrative tradition that Tom Gunning noticed in early "historical" attractions of the silent era; instead, they present an *excess* of narratives: the fictional, filmic narrative and the historical narrative. Hollywood filmmakers' adaptation of historical discourse resulted in a foregrounding of style and iconography to a degree unknown in other genres (text, document inserts, historical digressions), and it generated historical narratives that fractured the insular world of fictional film. Instead of masking the traces of history, these classical Hollywood historical films showed the evidence of their own historical construction, and even the most spectacular images of the past did not obey the formulas of narrative and continuity editing enumerated by Bordwell and others. And although many American historical films relied on heroic fictional protagonists and epic struggles to form their narratives, Hollywood's eclectic and challenging collection of historical facts and faces did not necessarily support an assembly-line historical argument.

Many of these American historical films also blurred the division between fiction and documentary cinema codified in the 1930s by filmmaker and critic Paul Rotha.[42] Films such as *The Public Enemy* (1931), *The World Moves On* (1934), *The Roaring Twenties* (1939), and *Citizen Kane* (1941) all used documentary footage to sharpen the historical context of their narratives. Several years later, Darryl Zanuck would use feature fiction films as historical evidence, appending old footage from *Jesse James* (1939) and *The Jazz Singer* (1927) to *The Return of Frank James* (1940) and *Hollywood Cavalcade* (1939) as a means of legitimizing his most recent historical productions. In almost every case, these past images were inscribed within the narratives by projected written historical commentary. In *Citizen Kane*, the oral narration of the "documentary" *News on the March* is superseded by the power of the text in the Thatcher Library sequence. Taking a cue from Bonitzer's work on text versus voice in documentaries, one could argue that Hollywood historical films' appropriation of the more ambivalent textual discourse (also the hallmark of historiography) rather than the more ideologically determining voice-over sacrificed the authority of one voice for a greater narrative complexity. But American historical films' most basic connection with documentary cinema lay in a shared sense of authenticity. In simplest terms, the cinema's illusion of movement and researchers' and screenwriters' painstaking efforts at detailed verisimilitude made American history "live" again. Nevertheless, despite their historical content and similar iconography (text, voice-overs, document inserts, and the like), all historical films, since they are "reenactments," have been classified as "fiction."[43] Written history is itself an exercise in analytical reenactment, but few historians would countenance being labeled fiction writers.

The Burden of Historical and Film Scholarship

Professional historians have rarely admitted the possibility that Hollywood films could serve as a new and comparable form of historiography. When historian Michael Isenberg read Griffith's defense of filmmaker-historians, he ignored both Griffith's call for equality among traditional historians and filmmaker-historians and his underlying challenge of historical objectivity, instead dismissing Griffith as merely feeling "the burden of the truths of history." For Isenberg and countless other historians, filmmakers could never achieve the status of true historians because of "the necessary oversimplicity of the cinematic approach to history, coupled with the desire for dramatic effect," which has led to "a gross overemphasis on Great Men and Great Events."[44] According to Isenberg, Hollywood's view of the past was not only hopelessly inaccurate but also compromised by an otiose approach to historiography, one that stressed a nineteenth-century view of grandiose progress and historical change dependent on the actions of a few remarkable people.[45] Although contemporary professional historians like Isenberg were the guardians of objectivity and "real" history, when they were not working on serious history, they would occasionally deign to look at films as interesting historical artifacts.

Since the 1960s, the work of Michel Foucault, Jacques Derrida, Michel de Certeau, and Hayden White has subjected the ideal of historical objectivity to a massive interdisciplinary assault. In recent years, even professional historians have realized the fallibility of revised grand narratives and have turned their attention to histories of race, ethnicity, gender, and sexuality. But curiously, post-structuralism was not America's first taste of historical critique and doubt. Frederick Jackson Turner, arguably America's most influential academic historian, acknowledged that no historian could prevent contemporary concerns from affecting his or her historical perspective. In his 1891 essay "The Significance of History," he insisted, *Each age writes the history of the past anew with reference to the conditions uppermost in its own time."*[46] During the late 1920s and early 1930s, Turner's student Carl Becker and others, such as Charles Beard, explored the darker implications of Turner's inherently changing historiography. Relativism, founded on the instability and impossibility of attaining the "objective" ideal, was particularly prevalent in the years following the Great War and often found fullest expression in revisionist histories that criticized themes of national triumph and progress inherent in traditional, positivist American historiography.[47] In 1931, in his address to the American Historical Association, Becker argued that history was not a perfectly transcribed reality but the historian's "imaginative reconstruction of vanished events." According to Becker, professional historians had no monopoly on objectivity and truth; the process of researching, revising, and reconstructing the historical past through documents and analysis was one that the average American, Mr. Everyman, went through on a daily basis. Historical interpretation was not a ritual known and practiced by the chosen few, and in the postwar era, popular history—"the history of Mr. Everyman"—was far more powerful than anything he and his colleagues would write.[48] Becker also recognized that in the age of the modern mass media, Mr. Everyman no longer formulated his historical interpretations from books alone but also from newspapers, advertising, radio programs, and films.

Although Allan Nevins was no relativist, he too was frustrated with academic historians' inability to reach a public audience. In 1939 he developed a strand of Becker's argument but addressed a more public audience than the American Historical Association. His query, "What's the Matter with History?" appeared in the *Saturday Review of Literature*.[49] Nevins knew that his popular apostasy would anger his colleagues, but in the eight years since Becker's address, Nevins perceived no change in the professional historian's approach to the past. In fact, he drew attention to the fissure between popular biography and serious, "scientific" history and castigated professional historians for their intolerance of other forms of historiography. This intolerance was resulting in a notable drop in the audience for "serious" works of history. According to Nevins, "Vitality, in history as in every other field of letters, means variety." Unlike Becker, Nevins's methodological diversity applied only to written histories and did not suggest the potential equality of visual (painting, photography, film) and verbal history. Nevertheless, his endorsement of the popularity and historical richness of biography and "literary" historical styles mirrored the Hollywood studios' prevailing perspective on what constituted worthwhile American history.

More recently, film historian George F. Custen explored the classical Hollywood cinema's reliance on biography as a means of presenting and constructing public history (both American and European), arguing that the eulogistic, ideologically conservative studio system and biographical tradition are uniquely suited vehicles of historical interpretation. However, films about the American past, especially those released from 1928 to 1942, were by no means confined to what Custen termed the narrative constraints of "the great [male] life."[50] Hollywood scripted the lives of real (Annie Oakley, Lillian Russell) and fictional (Ramona Moreno, Scarlett O'Hara) American women, reconfiguring the traditional notion of biography and confronting the problematic performance of femininity and race. In spite of mainstream narrative cinema's obvious dependence on one protagonist, biography competed with many historical approaches in the classical era. Popular history, historical novels, famous cinematic epics, old news headlines, and even legends of Hollywood's silent past all contributed to the studios' American historical repertoire. And while the "professional" historical community forced female scholars to the margins, women reclaimed their historical voice by dominating the realm of historical fiction. America's most influential and popular historical novelists during the late 1920s and early 1930s were Edna Ferber (*Cimarron,*1929; *Show Boat,* 1926) and Margaret Mitchell (*Gone with the Wind,* 1936). And while academic historians like Nevins were quarreling over what constituted "history," popular historians such as Albert Beveridge, Walter Noble Burns, and Fred Pasley; historical novelists such as Ferber and Mitchell; and filmmakers such as Zanuck and Selznick were dominating the nation's historical consciousness.

Many of these popular historians (most notably Mitchell, Burns, and *Scarface* screenwriter Pasley) began as journalists or continued to write for the newspapers after they achieved success as historians. These writers fractured the boundaries separating historians, historical novelists, and journalists and redetermined what constituted historical material. Burns (later immortalized in Howard Hawks's 1940 "tribute" to the newspaper business, *His Girl Friday*) wrote about the nineteenth-century West and Billy the Kid, as well as postwar Chicago and Al Capone. Zanuck would also manage these historical transitions, producing both *Alexander Hamilton* and *The Public Enemy* in 1931, within a few months of each other. Focusing on twentieth-century events and figures, Hollywood filmmakers would redefine not only the tenuous border between historical writing and filmmaking but also that allegedly separating history and journalism.

Over a fifteen-year period, these filmmakers presented alternative views of traditional historical events, filmed unconventional biographies of famous figures and little-known Americans, tackled the divisive years since the Great War, and even examined their own history. Great men and women and great events in American history dominated the narratives, but these were often critical views (*Cimarron, Ramona, Young Mr. Lincoln*) or popular biographies (*Scarface, Jesse James*); they dealt with controversial historical issues (miscegenation and interracial relations in *Call Her Savage, Jezebel,* and *Gone with the Wind*) and revelations of things that traditional American history overlooked (*The Prisoner of Shark Island, Hollywood Cavalcade*). Respectable historians of that generation either ignored the presence of historical films (like Nevins) or criticized their accuracy. After seeing *The Scarlet Pimpernel* (1935), Louis Gottschalk wrote to Samuel Marx, "No picture of a historical nature ought to be offered to the public until a reputable historian has had a chance to criticize and revise it."[51] But Hollywood filmmakers had become their own historians; they not only read, researched, and cited traditional and contemporary historical works but also presented text and documents in the film narratives. While historians attempted to separate the worlds and capabilities of filmmakers and historians, Hollywood was actively breaking those boundaries.

Yet decades later, historians continued to dismiss Hollywood's attempts at filming history even as film scholars tended to ignore such films as aberrations within the system. Twenty years ago, Isenberg wrote that professional historians lacked a methodological vocabulary with which to categorize bad film history. At one time, historians were actually hesitant about using the concepts of myth and symbol to describe film history.[52] Unfortunately, since then, historians have more than made up for lost time, and in their self-righteous pursuit of inaccuracies they have drained whatever scholarly dynamism was originally associated with this form of cultural analysis.[53] Myth, as cultural historians such as Richard Slotkin reminded us, is the simple binary language of cinema—a mode that reflects the national mood and resolves any historical conflicts within a blissful visual opiate.[54] Film theorists and historians, unsure and even suspicious of their American history but acquainted with Claude Lévi-Strauss's *Structural Anthropology* and Roland Barthes's *Mythologies*, have acquiesced to professional historians' denigrating view of Hollywood "epics." Ironically, Barthes believed all cultural productions to be mythic, the writing of history among them, a concept that has strained relations between film critics and historians who still cling to the "noble dream" of objectivity and verifiable facts. Yet film scholars and historians found themselves agreeing about studio-era historical cinema. Hollywood marketed not only traditional and comforting myths but also inaccurate (mythic) views of historical events. History was simply beyond Hollywood's intellectual capabilities or professional values, and filmmakers were certainly not historians.[55]

Cahiers, Lincoln, and the Fight against Film History

Cahiers du cinéma's influential essay on the 1939 film *Young Mr. Lincoln*, although rarely acknowledged by historians writing about film, argued that this landmark Hollywood production exemplified classical Hollywood cinema's reflection of overarching national myths and ideology.[56] Perhaps more than any other Hollywood film of its era, *Young Mr. Lincoln* has been forced to carry the burden of late-twentieth-century criticism of classical Hollywood cinema. Among these film critics and historians, *Young Mr. Lincoln* is, for better or worse, the definitive Lincoln film. Historians writing within the past ten years have decided that it is for the worse, dismissing the film as a historical travesty and an inaccurate, folksy perversion of Lincoln's most famous legal case: the 1858 William "Duff" Armstrong murder trial. This criticism reflects historians' entrenched suspicion of cinema, and Hollywood cinema in particular, as a historical medium.[57] By privileging printed words over moving images and books over films, historians have condemned *Young Mr. Lincoln* as a flawed historical text, capable of eliciting aesthetic pleasure but incapable of presenting a sophisticated historical argument.

For *Cahiers du cinéma*, a classical Hollywood film's historical content was less important than its support or subversion of an underlying capitalist ideology. But the article, rarely if ever cited by American historians or film historians, has great consequences not only for *Young Mr. Lincoln* but also for any American historical film produced in the classical era. *Cahiers* superseded the belief that cinema merely reflects its cultural context and instead argued that certain Hollywood films made by directors such as John Ford are texts notable for their complicated and often subversive engagements with the dominant capitalist ideologies that supported Hollywood. Even though *Young Mr. Lincoln* was a product of the ruling power structures operating in Hollywood and American politics in the late 1930s, they claimed that a close Lacanian psychoanalytic reading of Lincoln's presence in the film revealed the oppressiveness of both the Lincoln figure and the American capitalist system.

Cahiers asserted that this Marxist-psychoanalytic subversion was unconsciously expressed by the filmmaker. In particular, *Cahiers* reduced director John Ford's role to that of a gifted but helpless and unconscious mythmaker whose complicated film discourse was truly revealed only by the *Cahiers* editors' critical methodology. To deny Ford agency as a critic of the capitalist order, the editors had to disable the role of history within *Young Mr. Lincoln*. They therefore claimed that within the film, history is "almost totally reduced to the time scale of myth with neither past nor future," since there are no direct references to politics, conflict, or the Civil War.[58] Their argument depends on viewing the filmed Lincoln as an idealized mythic hero presented without any historical-political context. Ford's Lincoln is seen as an expression of a long-term, uncontested cultural investment rather than a historical figure subject to the filmmaker's deliberate critical analysis.

Many film historians have silently (or unconsciously) consented to the implications of the *Cahiers du cinéma* essay, stating that Hollywood films generally reflect a mythic view of the past that resolves timeless cultural contradictions rather than exploring the complexities within histori-cally specific terrain.[59] Additionally, the narrative processes of classical Hollywood cinema, classified as genres or formulas, depend on a process of symbolization that drains its mythic subject of historical reality. Even those still under the spell of auteur criticism and the popular legend of John Ford have focused on Ford's independent later work as the epitome of his historical consciousness rather than his more intense collaborations with Lamar Trotti, Dudley Nichols, and Darryl F. Zanuck at Twentieth Century–Fox during the classical era.[60]

Young Mr. Lincoln is not the only American historical film that has been yoked to the theoretical projects of film criticism and historical re-proach. *Scarface* (1932) has become an integral part of the gangster genre, while its historical subject and discourse are ignored; *Annie Oakley* (1935) and *Ramona* (1936) have been forgotten; *Gone with the Wind* (1939) has become Selznick's magnificent and flawed "moonlight and magnolias" epic;[61] *Sergeant York* (1941) has become the ultimate propaganda fea-ture;[62] *Stagecoach* (1939) was represented as the return of the great myth-ic western genre epitomized by *The Covered Wagon*.[63] Perhaps because of their importance as tools for Marxist, psychoanalytic, and genre film criti-cism, as whipping boys for historians, and as the epic fantasies of film fans, I focus on these very productions as the industry's most complex and con-spicuous examples of American film historiography. Their self-conscious historical voices, their constructed manipulation of text and image, their deliberate confrontation of controversy, all thwart the critical agendas of previous scholarly interpretations.

Foundations of Film Historiography

Although this study revises traditional approaches to the discourse of clas-sical Hollywood cinema and films about American history, its methodolo-gy and conception of film historiography owe debts to the work of Warren Susman, Robert A. Rosenstone, Philip Rosen, Donald Crafton, and Pa-mela Falkenberg. Susman was perhaps the first historian to acknowledge cinema's complex relationship with history. Cinema, he wrote, not only was capable of reflecting and documenting historical eras but also was important "as an interpreter of history."[64] For Susman, "the filmmaker, simply because he operates directly in terms of the actual manipulation of time and space, because in his editing he makes arrangements of time and space that shatter simple chronology," functions like a historian, "faced with the same problem of finding the proper arrangement of materials to provide a view of the process that is his history."[65] Susman was the first to notice structural similarities between the construction of filmed history and written history.[66] Although Hayden White has been vocal in his defense of film as a mode of historical interpretation, like his associate Robert A. Rosenstone, he separated the verbal and visual historical discourses of historical writing (historiography) and historical cinema.[67] Its system, address, and values were essentially different from those of writing; the word was separate from the image.

Although, according to Marc Ferro, "a filmic writing of history" does not exist, he argued that certain European directors such as Andrei Tarkovsky and Luchino Visconti were capable of producing "an original contribution to an understanding of the past."[68] However, Ferro denied Hollywood filmmakers a similar capacity, claiming that they merely reflected dominant ideological views of history. In recent years, Rosenstone, Robert Burgoyne, Steven C. Caton, and Natalie Zemon Davis have proposed that isolated Hollywood films are capable of making serious historical arguments and contesting entrenched cultural ideologies, yet their examples are films that were made after the classical studio era and under the influence of post-structuralist discourse.[69] Evidently, without the example of postmodern, post-structural teleologies, cinema lacked the self-reflexive historical capacity of critique. In his exploration of the interrelations between cinema and historiography, Philip Rosen perceived a capacity for modernism and critical distance in the work of British documentary filmmaker John Grierson,[70] but in *Change Mummified*, he did little to rethink this possibility for classical Hollywood cinema.[71] His view of modern American historiography, epitomized by the work of Frederick Jackson Turner, mirrors his conception of classical Hollywood cinema's historical reach. Both are relics of an era devoted to national encomiums and the documenting of period details. Rosen's perspective has changed little from a 1984 essay in which he showcased the allegedly pretentious, institutionalized, and assertive historical voice of *The Roaring Twenties* (1939).[72] His view of modern American historiography neglects the critical revisionism existing in both historical writings and films of the interwar period.

Although Donald Crafton viewed the classic British historical epic *The Private Life of Henry VIII* (1933) as a self-conscious lampoon of traditional history,[73] he distanced himself from debates about film's continuities with traditional historical discourse and its potential to interpret the past. Instead, Crafton saw Korda's work as historical fiction's leveling and undercutting of history rather than as part of the modern historical revisionism flourishing in the 1920s and 1930s. For Crafton, as for White, Ferro, and Rosenstone, cinema does one thing, the tradition of written history another. The word and the image continue to have a separate but equal status in studies of Hollywood cinema.[74] Only the work of Pamela Falkenberg has addressed classical Hollywood cinema's capacity for a deliberately constructed, written discourse on the past. Although her research was confined to the cinema's subversion and reaffirmation of the system of corporate capitalism that produces it (via *Cahiers*), Falkenberg was the first to notice projected text and its ambivalent historical connotations in Cecil B. DeMille's epic of western development, *Union Pacific* (1939).[75]

The New American Film Historiography

In the following pages, I argue that a filmic writing of American history flourished in Hollywood from 1931 to 1942.[76] Rather than force-fitting classical Hollywood films into an industrial-artistic formula or deconstructing their mythic discourses, this book aims to reconstruct a critical understanding of classical Hollywood's American historical cycle and its engagement with professional and popular history, traditional and revisionist historical discourse, and modern history. Although my earlier work on *Cimarron, Young Mr. Lincoln,* and *The Public Enemy* addressed classical Hollywood cinema's capacity for deliberate, critical writing of American history, its claims were necessarily narrower and applied to individual films.[77] Here I have expanded these arguments for film historiography to include a pan-studio, fifteen-year period to examine Hollywood filmmakers' changing attitudes toward traditional and contemporary American historical writing.

Hollywood filmmakers' attitudes toward history survive in production memos, research notes, reviews, and, of course, the development of scripts. More than any other production group of this era, American historical films were products of careful scripting and continual attention to the text. Indeed, in order to argue for a classical Hollywood filmic writing of history, I have focused on the most fundamental manifestation of film historiography: the script. Actors simply could not override the script and delete a scene, and when censors demanded revisions and cuts, they often met with vigorous resistance. During the 1930s, the Production Code lost its most public censorship campaigns over historical films (*Scarface* and *Gone with the Wind* are two of the more prominent cases). Although the Production Code was vigorous in its suppression of themes of miscegenation, *Call Her Savage, Ramona, Jezebel,* and *Gone with the Wind* all managed to challenge traditional discourses of race and sexuality and escape rigorous censorship. History was often protection against censorship and a means of making controversial films. Screenwriters have traditionally been seen as the least powerful contingent in Hollywood, but even before the Screen Writers' Guild was certified by the National Labor Relations Board in August 1938,[78] individual writers at several studios had an unusual independence and autonomy over their work. Historical screenwriters often did their own research, wrote original screenplays, and had the power to work alone and make their own revisions. Often their story sense overpowered their producers. These writers were more respected than others, particularly at Twentieth Century–Fox, where Zanuck made Lamar Trotti and Nunnally Johnson some of the most powerful writers in Hollywood. Trotti and Johnson and RKO writers Howard Estabrook (*Cimarron*) and Dudley Nichols (*The Arizonian, Stagecoach*) would eventually become producers and directors. But if screenwriters briefly exerted power in this one area of Hollywood filmmaking, it was due to producers such as Zanuck, Selznick, William K. LeBaron, Hal Wallis, and George Schaefer.

The following pages not only recover a neglected film cycle crucial to classical Hollywood filmmaking but also call for a fundamental revision in the way scholarship considers classical Hollywood cinema and film history. In the past, film histories looked at Hollywood in isolation from the rest of the country; one of the most deeply cherished beliefs in American film history is that Hollywood producers paid attention solely to box-office returns.[79] However, where American historical filmmaking was concerned, producers actually paid attention to what the New York newspapers and other national publications said about their "prestige" films.[80] At RKO, producer Kenneth Macgowan even tried to convince Selznick to hire critics Richard Watts and Gilbert Seldes as screenwriters for their new prestige productions.[81] When preparing to write a script about American history, screenwriters compiled and consulted a bibliography, not just past film successes. Researchers traveled to national libraries; publicity agents worked with local families and museums. Hollywood's relationship with American historical filmmaking took film production *outside* the studios.

Although some were the most successful films of their eras (*San Francisco* and *The Great Ziegfeld,* 1936; *A Star Is Born,* 1937; *In Old Chicago,* 1938; *Gone with the Wind,* 1939; *Sergeant York,* 1941),[82] many more American historical films consistently lost money for the studios (*The Big Trail,* 1930; *Cimarron,* 1931; *The Conquerors, Scarface,* and *Silver Dollar,*

1932; *The Mighty Barnum,* 1934; *So Red the Rose,* 1935; *Sutter's Gold,* 1936; *Wells Fargo,* 1937; *The Girl of the Golden West,* 1938; *Young Mr. Lincoln* and *The Story of Alexander Graham Bell,* 1939; *Northwest Passage,* 1940; *Citizen Kane,* 1941; *Tennessee Johnson,* 1942).[83] But in social historian Leo Rosten's imaginary day in the life of a producer, everything is reducible to money: "The 'screwball' pictures are packing them in; Mason's *Wives on Leave* is cleaning up, and Wolf's *Alexander Hamilton,* a fine historical dramatization, stands to lose $200,000. The New York office and the exhibitors say that anything 'heavy' is murder at the box office."[84] This smug shorthand had a historical sting; although the other films were imaginary, Rosten was not making up *Alexander Hamilton.* It did lose money at the box office, as did many "heavy" historical films. But a number of Hollywood producers, possibly encouraged by film critics, continued to make these expensive highbrow films until wartime production and shrinking budgets finally curtailed the cycle. This goes glaringly against the grain of traditional studies of Hollywood film production, in which every filmmaking decision can be reduced to financial considerations. So in this study, box office–audience reception is of negligible importance compared to the production history and critical reception of these films.

In his history of Hollywood production from the Great Depression to the advent of full-scale European war in 1939, film historian Colin Shindler argued that Hollywood's "golden age" emerged at a time of national and international crisis.[85] Although it is certainly tempting to see Hollywood's complex and contradictory engagement with American history from *Cimarron* to *Citizen Kane* as a response to the growing popular awareness of historical relativism, revisionism, and modern America, or as a massive mythic manifestation of national nostalgia in the face of contemporary uncertainty, these explanations are too simplistic. Rather than simply contextualizing these interwar or Depression-era American historical films as reflections of their cultural milieu or cultural artifacts,[86] *Reconstructing American Historical Cinema* foregrounds these films' continuities with traditional historical writing and interpretation and explores their self-conscious interpretation of American history.

The American historical films in this study cut across studio genres popularized by film studies, such as the gangster, western, biopic, musical, and melodrama genres; they cut across studio-named cycles such as the woman's picture, the action film, the epic, the crime drama, the superwestern, and even the Astaire-and-Rogers cycle. Filmmakers often referred to these films as "historical epics," "costumers," "prestige dramas," or "biographies." They were all linked by their historical subject matter and self-conscious references to American history; their projected historical commentary, documents, portraits, and tableaux; their use of text; their research and publicity; their expense; the critical attention given to screenwriters and historians; and their critical responses and awards.[87] Together, they formed a diverse body of film historiography ranging from the struggles of early pioneers and the machinations of the expanding government to the contested careers of Chicago gangsters and Hollywood's silent stars.

Far from being a linear film history, this book travels in an arc negotiated by several key films and filmmakers. The study begins in 1930, a year of crisis for American historical cinema. Many autocratic silent directors and their writers could not adapt to the possibilities of the new medium. Studios seemed hesitant to involve themselves in expensive epics that now demanded accurate and sophisticated speech. However, with the release of *Cimarron* and *The Public Enemy* in 1931, Hollywood reclaimed the historical cycle. *Cimarron* not only revisioned the nation's frontier past but also became the industry's standard for historical perfection. The product of a risk-taking, impoverished studio and an innovative screenwriter, RKO and Howard Estabrook's masterpiece would be Hollywood's most influential American historical film. That same year, *The Public Enemy* confronted postwar modern history and national decline and redefined the canon of national heroes. The film's producer, Darryl F. Zanuck, would become Hollywood's most versatile force in American historical filmmaking and one of the first filmmakers to fight censorship with the talisman of history. Zanuck began the 1930s by exploring veterans of other wars, unknown heroes from forgotten western fronts, corruption, greed, and the nation's loss of a sense of its past, whether in modern biopics (*I Am a Fugitive from a Chain Gang*) or in musicals (*The Gold Diggers of 1933*). As head of Twentieth Century–Fox, he returned to the nineteenth century's rebels (*The Prisoner of Shark Island, Jesse James*) but also rethought Selznick's work on Hollywood's history (*Hollywood Cavalcade*).

Cimarron's multiracial and feminist West would inspire *Ramona* and *The Last of the Mohicans*; its iconography would serve as a template for films as diverse as *Wells Fargo* (1937) and *Hollywood Cavalcade* (1939). Sabra Cravat would be a powerful antecedent for Julie Marston and Scarlett O'Hara, and Yancey's biracial ancestry would color these southern heroines' own subversive histories. In 1939 Warner Brothers would expunge *Cimarron*'s critical historical attitudes and rework its setting in *The Oklahoma Kid* (1939). But in 1940, Orson Welles and Herman Mankiewicz would return not only to RKO but also to *Cimarron* and the national legacy it created. I argue that *Citizen Kane*'s pompous *News on the March* and its visualization of a filmic writing of American history through the life of a degenerated "western" hero completed the arc of American film historiography generated between 1930 and 1941. The film's cinematic excavation of both Hollywood and the nation's past brings this critical film history full circle, back to the small, risk-taking studio and maverick filmmakers.

Unlike Thomas Schatz, I do not argue that each studio had a "house style" or a particular historical attitude or viewpoint adhered to from film to film. Instead, I found that a small group of producers and directors deliberately turned their backs on traditional views of the past and a canon of American heroes, while other filmmakers presented a competing historical discourse, perhaps more spectacular and lavish, but ultimately uncritical and traditional. This dialectic animates the history of the West, the Civil War, the Great War, the Roaring Twenties, and even Hollywood. But sometimes Hollywood's most challenging American historians had misgivings about the cycle; Zanuck, most notably, changed his attitude in late 1939. Selznick would pioneer innovative histories of the Civil War and early Hollywood but avoided the controversy of the nineteenth-century West and the Reconstruction era. Warner Brothers was responsible for both the subversive southern period film *Jezebel* and what critic Frank Nugent would term the "dog-eared scripts" of *The Oklahoma Kid* (1939) and *The Fighting 69th* (1940). Cecil B. DeMille may have generated more American historical box office than any other filmmaker, but it was the perennially bankrupt RKO that produced Hollywood's most critically respected historical films, *Cimarron* and *Citizen Kane*.

Orson Welles, echoing D. W. Griffith in 1915, once defended *Citizen Kane* as a historical film. He wrote, "It was impossible for me to ignore American history."[88] This must also be the reason for the shape and argument of this book. Although some film historians may object to the unusual prominence given to projected text, screenwriters, and written history, historians will doubtless react adversely to my claims for visual history. Film theorists may sniff at the undue credit given to trade-paper reporters, national critics, and exhibitors and my occasional thrusts at canonical film theory. Contemporary historians may dislike the greater emphasis placed on the work of historians Carl Becker, Walter Noble Burns, and even Edna Ferber and Margaret Mitchell and my pointed refusal to focus on and valorize more recent historical contributions to these areas. They will undoubtedly shudder to see Ferber, Mitchell, Welles, and

Zanuck defined as "historians." These were all deliberate and necessary choices intended to question the canons of film studies and American history. This approach is intended as a comparative historiography, and it attempts to combine both the historical critiques and the narrative synthesis employed by Hollywood-based American historians from 1928 to 1942. Although film scholars and historians continue to argue that modern and postmodern eras have witnessed advances in film form and historiography, this book reveals a critical revisionism, if not a protomodernism, at the heart of interwar classical Hollywood cinema.

PART ONE

TRADITIONAL AND MODERN AMERICAN HISTORY

1

The New American History: *Cimarron*, 1931

There's been nothing like it since Creation!
—Yancey Cravat, *Cimarron*, 1931

In April 1929, film critic and playwright Robert E. Sherwood predicted that Hollywood's adaptation to sound cinema would improve the overall quality of motion pictures and, more particularly, increase the power of screenwriters. Convinced that "the writer will now be boosted into a position of importance that is equivalent, at least, to that of the director," Sherwood could look back on the American cinema's silent past without regret.[1] His colleagues, critics Gilbert Seldes, Rudolf Arnheim, and Béla Bálazs, were not so sanguine and gloomily prepared for the word's tyranny over the image.[2] The studios' 1929 season did little to dispel their prognostications; photographed Broadway musicals (*Show Boat*, *Glorifying the American Girl*), verbose and static plays (*The Last of Mrs. Cheyney*, *This Thing Called Love*), and even stories about Broadway (*Gold Diggers of Broadway*, *Broadway*) dominated the box office. Though film executives hired an indiscriminate number of Broadway playwrights and writers in the late 1920s, few of them were capable of adapting to the screen. Even though Sherwood envisioned a new age of screenwriting in the sound era, executives were slow to acknowledge the primacy of a good script in film production or to recognize the qualities that differentiated cinematic writing from eastern highbrow pap. No studio was willing to go to the expense of making a D. W. Griffith out of a screenwriter; perhaps some

27

even feared the day when the writer would "have a great deal to say about the preparation and production of a picture, [when] his remarks won't all be variations of the affirmative yes."[3]

Nowhere was the crisis in screenwriting more evident than in the production of American historical films. Curiously, while the studios had staved off potential box-office instability with fluffy musical comedies for the past two years, they hesitated to pursue the type of film that had earned the American film industry its first critical acclaim during the silent era. By early 1930, the sound equivalents of the prestigious American historical features *The Birth of a Nation* and James Cruze's *The Covered Wagon* had failed to materialize. American historical films required more than lavish spectacle and stunning sets to capture critics and audiences; Americans were familiar with the historical text of the Civil War and the "winning of the West" and would notice too much "poetic license." Were the demands of written history too complex for American cinema? If, as Sherwood claimed, screenwriting was key to a regeneration of the film industry, under what circumstances could a screenwriter achieve the prestige and power of a traditional historian?

The Question of American History in 1930

In early 1930, D. W. Griffith began filming a sound biography of Abraham Lincoln. Although he was arguably the father of American historical cinema, it was not certain whether Griffith could reclaim Hollywood's past artistic and economic feats. For the past few years, the director's box-office potential had slipped. Although his last American historical production, the romantic Revolutionary War narrative *America* (1924), had been popular, some critics found his film treatment as dated as the subject matter.[4] In planning *Abraham Lincoln*, he still maintained his taste for period stories but wisely hired a professional "historical" screenwriter to sharpen his lengthy treatment.

Hiring Stephen Vincent Benét, author of *John Brown's Body*, was a public-relations coup for United Artists, but Benét was not all that different from a slew of other New York writers who came to Hollywood in the early sound era. He thirsted for Hollywood money but had an equal contempt for filmmaking and its artistic values. Also, as Benét freely admitted, he knew nothing about screenwriting and left Griffith and his secretary to handle the mechanics.[5] Though he claimed that his script, an edited version of Griffith's original, was detailed, accurate, and "playable," executives, perhaps relishing the chance to chasten the uppity New Yorker, forced him to write five versions before agreeing on the final one, which was episodic, epigrammatic, and sentimental. Although Benét complained about the "sheer waste, stupidity, and conceit" of Joseph Schenck and the front office, Griffith allowed the producers to rework the script.[6]

Variety advertised the film in August as "Griffith's biggest contribution to the exhibitor" and a "masterpiece . . . [without] a line of dialog that would offend race, color, creed or belief," while Richard Watts of the New York Herald Tribune commended its "dignified" treatment of Lincoln's life.[7] However, most critics were appalled by its sentimentality and old-fashioned, static treatment of history. Mordaunt Hall of the New York Times preferred the livelier Dramatic Life of Abraham Lincoln (1924) and wrote that the sound film failed "to give the details of the scenes that were so ably told in the mute work." Hall also complained that Griffith was guilty of "prognosticating too often in the course of scenes."[8] Instead of portraying the events in Lincoln's life as part of a complex and evolving process, crucial events were given in their mythic totality in a series of tableaux: the young Lincoln was never an immature, uncertain youth but always the hero. Above all, Lincoln's heroic presence stabilized both personal and national conflicts in a monotonous, schoolbook narrative. The most famous, emblematic moments of Lincoln's life were strung together in a collection of static scenes and deliberately enunciated epigrams (Lincoln reading by firelight, the death of Ann Rutledge, the coming of the Civil War, the Gettysburg Address, the assassination). Harry Alan Potamkin of the New Masses was more direct in his criticism of the sentimentalized eulogy, which he dismissed as "a mooning idyll." According to Potamkin, Griffith's callow sense of American history portrayed "a Lincoln that any child beyond the fifth grade in school would disown."[9] Curiously, Potamkin did not imply that the sound medium was at fault, but rather that the silent aesthetic standards Griffith had perfected years before were no longer any match for an innovative new art form. A film about Lincoln required an astute historical perspective conveyed through language and argument, not the folksy images and symbols of silent cinema, the mawkish scenes of rail-splitting and sickbed moments with Rutledge. Rather than reviving the American historical cycle he had helped create fifteen years before, Griffith's work on Abraham Lincoln proved that silent techniques lacked the historical complexities and sophistication demanded by sound-era critics. And yet, critics in Hollywood and New York justified the film's serious subject matter as a way of elevating the American cinema and its audiences.

That same year, other Hollywood filmmakers tried to revisit American history through another traditional route. The western had long been the American cinema's most consistent contribution to historical filmmaking and had been a mainstay of the industry long before Griffith's *The Battle at Elderbush Gulch* (1913). In 1929 and 1930, both Paramount and MGM experimented with different varieties of sound westerns, but rather than commissioning screenwriters to construct new narratives, they relied heavily on remakes of silent classics. Owen Wister's novel *The Virginian* had been adapted for stage and screen shortly after its publication in 1902. The 1914 and 1923 film versions were still fresh in Hollywood's memory when Paramount decided to remake the story as a partial sound feature in 1929. Wister's tale, with its silent southern cowpoke, its vast landscapes, its romantic narrative unmarked by historical events, and its numerous remakes, epitomized the mythic West. Always popular with filmgoers, the story had comforting box-office potential in the unstable early sound era. Director Victor Fleming clung to more than the narrative conventions of silent cinema; although advertised as "all talkie," the film made little use of the medium beyond the sound of cattle and gunfire. After all, the mystique of the hero lay in his silence. Fledgling screenwriter Howard Estabrook kept to the western tradition. He did not insert any main text titles or introductory allusions to the time period or locale, and while the script synopsis stressed "epic atmosphere," the film possessed little of the epic historical pretension associated with a silent western such as John Ford's *The Iron Horse* (1924).[10] Unlike Ford's early epic, *The Virginian*'s landscape was unmarked by the historical consequences of the railroad; instead, the West was identified with the open range. As expected, *The Virginian* was a hit, in part because it clung to what Jerry Hoffman of the *Los Angeles Examiner* called "the good old days" of storytelling and filmmaking.[11] But the panoramic silences and laconic hero were not things that the studios could duplicate indefinitely. Unfortunately, MGM took Hoffman's praise for the "resurrection of the much-mourned western" literally by resuscitating two other western narratives. Paramount and Warner Brothers followed suit with Rex Beach's *The Spoilers* (1930) and David Belasco's *Girl of the Golden West* (1930), which were equally old-fashioned westerns patterned after *The Virginian*'s success. By 1930, however, critics were complaining, among other things, that the narratives "dawdled."[12] Perhaps *The Virginian*'s partial silence was in its favor. In 1929, with the cacophony of talking drawing-room comedies, Gary Cooper's silence was a throwback to a more confident past. In 1930, however, critics were demanding something new.

Later that year, MGM experimented with a new sound western—a screen story of Billy the Kid, loosely based on Chicago reporter and popular historian Walter Noble Burns's *The Saga of Billy the Kid*.[13] Burns's biography had the requisite dates, the details of cattle baron feuds, and the stories of William Bonney's fame, but his biography had an entertaining immediacy; it used present-tense dialogue and historical scenes that were immensely popular with the public and familiar to filmmakers who wrote and read scripts in the present tense. Burns's re-creations of historical moments matched the cinema's own capacity to make the past present, and he viewed Billy's life and western history as a dramatic pageant akin to the cinema.[14] Burns also recognized that the myth of Billy the Kid was inseparable from his place in history. "Less than fifty years after his death, it is not always easy to differentiate fact from myth," he wrote. "Historians have been afraid of him, as if this boy of six-shooter deadliness might fatally injure their reputations if they set themselves seriously to write of a career of such dime-novel luridness."[15] Burns feared neither Billy's status as a popular icon nor his dramatic, cinematic life and legacy.

Burns developed a democratized view of American history, and it appealed to MGM's story department. Although the studio kept Billy's name in the title, the screenwriters altered everything else, taking Burns's inclusive attitude toward western history and myth over the brink. Tunstall became Tunstan, and a romantic interest in Tunstan's fiancée complicated Billy's killings. Historical detail simply did not seem to matter. Like *The Virginian*, the film faded in on an expository shot of a wagon train amidst a herd of cattle.[16] While critics had appreciated *The Virginian*'s unpretentious, archetypal gunfights, they reacted with condescension or hostility to MGM's irresponsible treatment of history, its distortions and fabrications, and its idea of a western as "a composite of gunshots and gooey romance."[17] In fact, the *Hollywood Reporter* condemned the film for betraying not only the historical challenge of Burns's biography but also the expectations of American audiences who wanted better films: "It seems as though the title had been bought to attract the customers and instead of making a really great epic picture of one of the best loved and most dashing characters that ever roamed the West of pioneer times, the producers have succeeded in making just another western."[18]

A few months later, Fox Studios tried a different approach to filming western history, hiring screenwriter Hal G. Evarts to construct an original story, a talking equivalent of the expansionist epic *The Covered Wagon*. *The Big Trail* was planned meticulously as a chronicle of westward expansion along the Oregon Trail in the mid-nineteenth century. Evarts and director Raoul Walsh proclaimed in the opening title that the film honored "the men and women who planted civilization and courage in the blood of their children." Although it too failed at the box office, critics took its historical content more seriously. Although *Variety*'s Sime Silverman called it "a noisy *Covered Wagon*," a poor relation of the silent western epics, he did praise *The Big Trail*'s historical aspects as the "single interesting part."[19] But it was precisely the heavy history that some felt overwhelmed the flimsy romance and fictional film narrative.[20] There was a subtle awareness on the part of some contemporary film critics that history's multiple associations and complex narratives competed with and even counteracted the power of a traditional, clearly defined, and uncomplicated cinematic narrative.

While ticket sales for *Abraham Lincoln* and *The Big Trail* floundered and Hollywood recoiled from the economic shock and criticism, RKO executives held their breath. For the past few months, their small studio had shouldered the mounting costs of their own American historical epic, a film that fit into no recognizable historical category or film genre. It was neither exclusively a western nor a biopic. Founded only in 1928, after the financial instability of its parent companies necessitated its consolidation by the Radio Corporation of America, Radio-Keith-Orpheum was the youngest of the major American studios.[21] It emerged with the technological revolution of sound and grew slowly in the midst of the Depression. The studio had the least capital resources of all the major studios and the most invested in the as yet unperfected new film form.[22] It was symbolically fitting and even more financially imperative that the young sound studio produce the definitive sound feature. Now, as the end of 1930 approached and postproduction and retakes wrapped, the studio's publicity department prepared the way for its new prestige film and studio image. The studio's annual advertisement in *Film Daily* heralded "Mightier shows . . . Mightier plans . . . Mightier progress. The radio titan opens the curtains of the clouds and a new and greater year dawns for the most spectacular show machine of all time! A new and mightier pageant of the titans is forming . . . and marching irresistibly to leadership of the modern show world!"[23] RKO was staking its future economic and artistic credibility on a new type of American historical film: the production of Edna Ferber's *Cimarron*.

Revisioning the Historical Film in 1931

Edna Ferber was one of America's most financially successful novelists.[24] She had a decided proclivity for writing generational narratives set in

America's past, such as *So Big* (1924) and *Show Boat*, and for constructing semibiographical stage hits with George S. Kaufman such as *The Royal Family of Broadway*, a barely concealed portrait of America's greatest theatrical family, the Barrymores. All these works became successful films, and by 1930, Ferber was one of the most bankable names in Hollywood. While preparing for *Show Boat*, she had researched the lives of nineteenth-century southern performers, but southern history served only as a colorful background for the Hawks family odyssey. *Cimarron* was different. Ferber decided to write a chronicle of a couple's marriage over several decades, but she spent months researching her historical context—Oklahoma history from the birth of the territory to 1929—in the State Historical Library in Oklahoma City. She mentioned these preparations in her preface but deliberately distanced her work from the academic world of professional historians. Ferber was certainly no pedant; she belonged to the smart set of New York's literary and dramatic world and was proud of it. Nevertheless, *Cimarron*, in many ways Ferber's first self-consciously historical novel, bears consideration with contemporary western historiography.

By 1930, a few professional historians had begun to question the traditional historical interpretations of Frederick Jackson Turner, but the criticism tended to dispute individual aspects of Turner's "frontier thesis" rather than to generate an organized alternative.[25] Turner's postwar professional critics, among them Charles Beard, John C. Almach, and Carey McWilliams, contradicted Turner's proclamation that the frontier had closed in 1890, deprecated his magisterial tone, and focused on his unjustifiable neglect of eastern values in molding the American character.[26] Few professional historians were capable of synthesizing a developed alternative to dominant western historiography. Arguably, the first widely read revisionist history of the West was written not by an accredited academic but by a popular novelist. When Ferber published *Cimarron* in early 1930, she acknowledged in the preface that although the novel was "no attempt to set down a literal history of Oklahoma," it chronicled the experience of a fictional pioneering couple from 1889 to the present day and was supported by extensive research.[27] Although Ferber later claimed that *Cimarron* was a revisionist account of the American West, depicting Oklahoma's multiethnic and multiracial settlement and development, she concentrated her historical critique within her fictional protagonists, Yancey and Sabra Cravat. Ferber felt that in her scathing portrait of Sabra, a bigoted pioneer woman, she was denouncing the essential bourgeois capitalism of American society and its sentimental view of the female pioneer.[28] "It contains paragraphs and even chapters of satire," she said.

Yet academics were not willing to credit a Broadway-Hollywood success like Ferber with historical sensitivity. Writing in 1931, literary critic Percy Boynton understood the novel only as a popular reconfirmation of Turner's 1893 frontier thesis, as a culmination of twentieth-century western nostalgia.[29] Other reviewers were more pointed in their criticism of Ferber's romantic history. Dorothy Van Doren's review for the *Nation* was tellingly entitled "A Pioneer Fairy Story," and she concluded that although Ferber's highly colored western novel was poor history and trite literature, it might be the basis for an exciting film.[30] If Van Doren and other critics took a dim view of popular historical novelists such as Ferber, their artistic expectations of motion pictures were even lower. Popular historian E. Douglas Branch was particularly anxious to separate his written historical territory from the encroachments of Hollywood. He believed that whereas he and other "serious" historians chronicled complex historical events and movements, the glorious evolution and repetition of the frontier experience, popular films were interested only in flashy individuals. "Calamity Jane, Simon Girty, Kit Carson, Sam Bass, make good melodrama," he sniffed. "Billy the Kid is now in the photoplays, where, so far as I am concerned, he belongs."[31]

The Hollywood motion picture community's expectations for *Cimarron* could not have been more different. Critics anticipated that RKO would transform Edna Ferber's best-selling novel into innovative American historical cinema, not a run-of-the-mill western or bandit biopic.[32] RKO was initially enthusiastic, spending an unprecedented $125,000 on the story,[33] but regardless of the success of *So Big, The Royal Family of Broadway,* and *Show Boat, Cimarron* was something different.[34] It was not a musical, and it was based on relatively unexplored historical material. RKO knew the risks in producing an expensive historical film, but in spite of its ominous economic situation and the recent criticism leveled at both sound films and historical productions by leading national critics, the studio hired William K. LeBaron to oversee the production and then former Broadway stage producer and writer Howard Estabrook to create *Cimarron's* screenplay. Estabrook was not a disdainful eastern import like Benét; he was comfortable with Hollywood. Like Ferber, Estabrook had a decided predilection for historical subjects and had garnered his greatest successes writing historical material into Paramount's Great War love story *Shopworn Angel* (1928), *The Virginian,* and Howard Hughes's wartime aviation epic *Hell's Angels* (1930). He seemed the ideal choice to transform *Cimarron.*

Not everyone at the studio shared this enthusiasm. RKO story editor

Paul Powell still worried about his studio's gamble with another historical epic. If the wealthier and more established United Artists, MGM, and Fox had failed, so could RKO. Even after the completion of Estabrook's adaptation and first script, Powell fretted, "Although the characters are fictitious, this is essentially a historical novel . . . I believe that it is a matter of experience that historical novels have not, as a rule, proven to be good picture material, and I fear this is no exception."[35] Although *Cimarron* had sold well as a historical novel, he and others feared that the history Estabrook transferred to the screen would not be palatable to a popular motion picture audience. The specter of *The Big Trail* hung over the studio. Yet Estabrook refused to minimize the historical elements in favor of the fictional story; like Ferber, he did extensive research on traditional and contemporary western history. Although Estabrook included his fair share of Walter Noble Burns's and Courtney Ryley Cooper's popular histories in his bibliography, and even reread Emerson Hough's fictional *The Covered Wagon*, he was not going to pattern *Cimarron* after the triumphant chronicle of white westward expansion. Estabrook was one of the few people to read William Christie MacLeod's *The American Indian Frontier* (1928), a rare view of the white settlement of America from the Native American perspective.[36] For MacLeod, "Every frontier has two sides. . . . To understand why one side advances, we must know something of why the other side retreats." The frontiersman was no hero, but the scum of the eastern settlers. According to MacLeod, historians were equally guilty of romanticizing the pioneers: "In the little red schoolhouse it is a sacrilege to intimate that the pioneers suffered from ordinary human frailties. . . . But the masses were no better than the masses of any society."[37] MacLeod's book was unnoticed, even in academic circles, but Estabrook was certainly influenced by the maverick historian's approach.[38]

Estabrook also refused to emulate the one major Hollywood precedent for Oklahoma history—W. S. Hart's *Tumbleweeds* (1925), which used the 1893 opening of the Cherokee Strip merely as a backdrop for a cowboy-pioneer romance. Whereas both Hal Evarts's historical novel and Hart's film sublimated the Indian perspective to focus exclusively on the impending dispossession of the Strip's free-range cowboys, Estabrook retained Ferber's revisionist picture of a multiracial and ethnic West, a dynamic space inhabited by Native Americans, mestizos, black and white southerners, Jews, and Anglo-Saxon northeasterners. But then, with the support of director Wesley Ruggles, Estabrook completely transformed and emphasized *Cimarron*'s projection of history, moving Ferber's acknowledged site of historical contention from Sabra Cravat to a broader

Cimarron's
multiethnic, racial,
and gendered West:
Young Isaiah imitates
the biracial Yancey
as his stunned wife
looks on.

critique of the construction of western history. It was an unusual step away from character-oriented narratives (*The Virginian*) and biographies (*Billy the Kid*) and even familiar historical eulogies (*The Big Trail*). Estabrook and Ruggles introduced the ideas of re-creating the 1889 land rush (which Ferber had only alluded to in her novel), of inserting historical expositions, dates, and documents within the diegesis, and of introducing the film with an extensive opening title, or text foreword.[39]

Titles were an indispensable component of silent films, essentially articulating dialogue and giving continuity to changes in time and place. The opening titles had the greatest length and importance, however, particularly in silent historical films. Some of the most elaborately planned, constructed, and marketed silent films—*The Birth of a Nation, The Covered Wagon*, and *The Vanishing American*—made extensive use of opening titles or text prologues to lend historical authenticity and complexity to their fictional narratives. With the advent of sound, one might have expected titles to disappear, since they were merely continuity crutches for an obsolete art form.[40] By and large, text did vanish from sound features—with one considerable exception. History films still retained titles as a recognizable visual attribute, thereby self-consciously allying their narratives with the more traditional and respectable forms of written history. Filmmakers compounded the relationship, referring to the opening text insert as a "foreword." More than any other filmmakers in the early sound era, those of *Cimarron* were responsible for inaugurating this structural practice. They even included a footnote after the credits; like Ferber's historical novel, Estabrook and Ruggles acknowledged a memoir as an invaluable resource.[41]

Estabrook's vision for wedding text and image was an original component of his adaptation: he integrated an elaborate opening foreword and a continuous series of text inserts and documents within his first treatment and script. With Ruggles on board by August 1930, the two then layered a series of dated superimpositions to punctuate the shooting script.[42] Remarkably, almost all the elaborate text and document inserts survived postproduction and exhibition. Text was an essential component of the historical narrative, not a postproduction afterthought used to unify a disjunctive narrative such as that of MGM's *The Great Meadow*. The latter film, based on a historical novel by Elizabeth Madox Roberts,[43] was a eulogy to the eighteenth-century women pioneers of Virginia and would be *Cimarron*'s historical competitor in early 1931. Like many silent epics, Charles Brabin's scripts had no interest in the historical material beyond its weak support of the fictional romantic melodrama, but late in postproduction, MGM hired dialogue writer Edith Ellis to add a historical dedication to the "women of the wilderness" and a few text inserts chronicling the stages of the grueling journey to Kentucky.[44] The foreword was undoubtedly added to dress up what the producers feared was a floundering production, but Ellis's text inserts were modeled on *The Big Trail*. That Hal Evarts–Raoul Walsh epic had used several text inserts, but only to summarize the protagonists' moods or to cite unspecified passages of toil and time. In this sense, the use of text in both *The Big Trail* and *The Great Meadow* was still based on the silent technique of elucidating the fictional narrative. In contrast, *Cimarron*'s filmmakers established the use of text as the medium for conveying and questioning an established view of American history.

Text versus Image

Cimarron's two-shot foreword reads as follows:

A NATION RISING TO GREATNESS

THROUGH THE WORK OF MEN

AND WOMEN . . . NEW COUNTRY OPENING . . .

RAW LAND BLOSSOMING . . . CRUDE

TOWNS GROWING INTO CITIES . . .

TERRITORIES BECOMING RICH STATES . . .

IN 1889, PRESIDENT HARRISON OPENED

THE VAST INDIAN OKLAHOMA LANDS

FOR WHITE SETTLEMENT . . .
2,000,000 ACRES FREE FOR THE
TAKING, POOR AND RICH POURING IN,
SWARMING THE BORDER, WAITING
FOR THE STARTING GUN, AT NOON,
APRIL 22ND . . .

This text prologue expresses the dominant academic and popular view of western expansion derived from Theodore Roosevelt's *Winning of the West* (1885–1894) and particularly Turner's "The Significance of the Frontier in American History." *Cimarron*'s given history stresses that the nation's progress and greatness are dependent on an organic westward expansion. It is a history of egalitarian white settlement sanctioned by

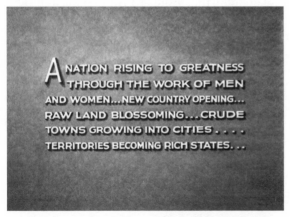

Estabrook conceived *Cimarron*'s projected text titles in his preliminary draft.

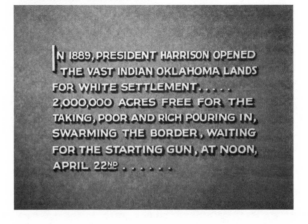

the authority of the president, a panegyric to the government and the people who transformed "raw land" into a great nation. As in Turner's view, the previous occupants, the Indians, have been almost entirely written out of the history of the West. The "vast Indian Oklahoma lands" are free, opened up to white settlers by the government; there is no mention of broken treaties and territorial displacement. The past wars with "the weaker race" that Roosevelt documented in *The Winning of the West* have given way to triumphant settlement.[45] The late-nineteenth-century generation descends from the "distinctive and intensely American stock who were the pioneers . . . the vanguard of the army of fighting settlers."[46] According to the film's prologue, as Oklahoma grows from territory to state, *Cimarron's* settlers fulfill Roosevelt's prophecy of national expansion. Also inscribed within the text is Turner's belief that "American social development has been continually beginning over and over again on the frontier" and that the "true point of view in the history of the nation . . . is the Great West."[47] Both Turner and Roosevelt shared a faith in the western frontier as the definitive source of American national identity and history, and *Cimarron's* prologue, containing the rhetoric of progress and supplemented by presidential decree and the historical specificity of the date, 22 April 1889, appears to arrogate historical authority to the film narrative and to legitimize the established histories of Roosevelt and Turner.

Following the text prologue, *Cimarron* dissolves to shots of the settlers preparing for the land rush. Two Indians approach a tradesman's wagon. Seeing them reach for his wares, the white merchant attacks them, yelling, "Hey, drop that, Indian, and get out!" Rather than supporting the text,

Cimarron: A white merchant-pioneer tells the Indians to get out.

Cimarron's opening images work in counterpoint to the chauvinism of the written history and add poignancy to the unspoken dispossession and rampant racism on the frontier that were all but invisible in dominant, early-twentieth-century American histories. This initial contrast between text and image, between a triumphant view of American history that stresses homogeneous white settlement and the more complex reality of racism, dishonorable government policies, and brutality contained within the filmed images, is a strategy repeated throughout the film's narrative.[48] *Cimarron* pushes still further when it narrates Yancey Cravat's role in the land rush and his recounting of the events to his southern in-laws in Wichita. Yancey may praise the expansion as "a miracle out of the Old Testament," but his rhetoric is ironic. Yancey is a mixed-blood Cherokee.

By the late 1920s, Hollywood had produced a few westerns with Indian or mixed-blood protagonists, including *The Vanishing American* (1925) and *Red Skin* (1929), both starring Richard Dix. George Seitz's production of Zane Grey's *The Vanishing American*, released to great popular and critical acclaim by Paramount, may have paved the way for *Cimarron*.[49] One might speculate that RKO's decision to film *Cimarron* with Dix was evidence of a cycle of Native American westerns and Hollywood's recognition of the Native American perspective. But although *Cimarron*'s hero is not the archetypal, pure-blooded Anglo gunfighter cleansing the West of Indians, neither is he a noble, equally pure-blooded Indian con-

CIMARRON

ing about and talking as he strode. His step was amazingly light and graceful for a man of his powerful frame. Fascinated, you saw that his feet were small and arched like a woman's, and he wore, even in this year of 1889, Texas star boots of fine soft flexible calf, very high heeled, thin soled, and ornamented with cunningly wrought gold stars around the tops. His hands, too, were disproportionate to a man of his stature; slim, pliant, white. He used them as he talked, and the eye followed their movements; bewitched. For the rest, his costume was a Prince Albert of fine black broadcloth whose skirts swooped and spread with the vigor of his movements; a pleated white shirt, soft and of exquisite material; a black string tie; trousers tucked into the gay boot-tops; and, always, a white felt hat, broad-brimmed and rolling. On occasion he simply blubbered Shakespeare, the Old Testament, the Odyssey, the Iliad. His speech was spattered with bits of Latin, and with occasional Spanish phrases, relic of his Texas days. He flattered you with his fine eyes; he bewitched you with his voice; he mesmerized you with his hands. He drank a quart of whisky a day; was almost never drunk, but on rare occasions when the liquor fumes bested him he would invariably select a hapless victim and, whipping out the pair of mother-o'-pearl-handled six-shooters he always wore at his belt, would force him to dance by shooting at his feet—a pleasing fancy brought with him from Texas and the Cimarron. Afterward, sobered, he was always filled with shame. Wine, he quoted sadly, is a mocker, strong drink is raging. Yancey Cravat could have been (in fact was, though most of America never knew it) the greatest criminal lawyer of his day. It was said that

[10]

CIMARRON

he hypnotized a jury with his eyes and his hands and his voice. His law practice yielded him nothing, or less than that, for being sentimental and melodramatic he usually found himself out of pocket following his brilliant and successful defense of some Dodge City dance-hall girl or roistering cowboy whose six-shooter had been pointed the wrong way.

His past, before his coming to Wichita, was clouded with myths and surmises. Gossip said this; slander whispered that. Rumor, romantic, unsavory, fantastic, shifting and changing like clouds on a mountain peak, floated about the head of Yancey Cravat. They say he has Indian blood in him. They say he has an Indian wife somewhere, and a lot of papooses. Cherokee. They say he used to be known as "Cimarron" Cravat, hence his son's name, corrupted to Cim. They say his real name is Cimarron Seven, of the Choctaw Indian family of Sevens; he was raised in a tepee; a wickiup had been his bedroom, a blanket his robe. It was known he had been one of the early Boomers who followed the banner of the picturesque and splendidly mad David Payne in the first wild dash of that adventurer into Indian Territory. He had dwelt, others whispered, in that sinister strip, thirty-four miles wide and almost two hundred miles long, called No-Man's-Land as early as 1854, and, later, known as the Cimarron, a Spanish word meaning wild or unruly. Here, in this strange unowned empire without laws and without a government, a paradise for horse thieves, murderers, desperadoes it was rumored he had spent at least a year (and for good reason). They said the evidences of his Indian blood were plain; look at his skin, his hair, his manner of walking. And

[11]

Estabrook's annotated copy of *Cimarron*. (Courtesy of the Academy of Motion Picture Arts and Sciences)

demned, like Nophaie (the "vanishing American"), to extinction in a changing nation. He is neither a noble anachronism nor a casualty of national expansion. Yancey Cravat, also known as "Cimarron," is of mixed blood, and he is the first of these new heroes to dominate and adapt to historical events and change.[50] When Estabrook first read Ferber's novel, which hinted more than once that Yancey was half Indian, he heavily underlined and annotated the passages, determined to focus on them "in dialog."[51] In the scripts, Estabrook emphasized both Yancey's ancestry and his active sympathy with his people. Yancey even has a voice in writing the history of the West; he is a news editor, and the headlines from his aptly named newspaper, the *Oklahoma Wigwam*, play an integral role in narrating *Cimarron*'s written history of the West.

Cimarron's Counterhistory

The film's next text insert occurs after the land rush as Yancey, Sabra (RKO's recent acquisition, Irene Dunne), and son Cimarron arrive in Osage, Oklahoma. The title reads, "The boomer town of Osage—a population of 10,000 in six weeks." Again, a series of images follows that questions the progress and optimism inherent in the town's population growth. A "half-breed" shoots a man in front of a saloon, a lawyer rooks his clients, and a pioneering husband and wife work through the night to get their frame house up. Later, after the Cravats have moved into their new house, young Cimarron is chastised by his mother for accepting a present from one of "those dirty, filthy Indians." Following this sequence, Sol Levy, the town's Jewish merchant, is abused by a group of saloon-loafing white trash. Yancey plays an ironic role in both these scenes. Sabra's vitriolic attack on the Indians also denigrates Yancey and young Cimarron's mixed blood—even Cimarron's name. Sol is pushed against a grain scale by one of the town bullies, and when his arms lock around the balance, he resembles a crucified Christ. Yancey saves Sol and gently extricates him. The film presents two scenes of violent racial hatred—the mother teaching the son to hate, and anti-Semitism—which, although part of Ferber's historical novel, were rarely if ever acknowledged in written histories of the West.

Soon after "1890" fades in and out over a long shot of the growing town, the film introduces a new text insert: the front page of Yancey's newspaper. The headlines of the *Oklahoma Wigwam* are prominently displayed and announce ex-President Grover Cleveland as Benjamin Harrison's possible successor, Otto von Bismarck's resignation from the

German Chancellery, the coming of the World's Fair to Chicago, and, barely visible on the margins of the frame, Congress's decision to preserve the buffalo now that they have been slaughtered to near extinction. In spite of the seriousness of some of the articles, the male voice-overs discussing the paper only joke about the editor's note at the top of the page—Yancey and Sabra have just had a second child. The paper documents a traditional view of American expansion concurrent with European political events, while undercutting the effects of that growth with the announcement of the near annihilation of the buffalo and the public's preoccupation with trivialities. The film juxtaposes the text insert with the more critical social history revealed in the images. Soon after the glimpse of the headline news, Osage witnesses another historic event. The famous outlaw known as "the Kid," a former free-range cowboy who lost his job in the wake of the developing railroad, returns to Osage. When his gang tries to rob a bank, Yancey, the Kid's former associate, shoots and kills him. During the battle, the townsfolk cower in their houses, and only after the Kid is killed do they emerge from their doorways. Ruggles's unusual high-angle shot transforms the citizens into vultures crowding a carcass.

Although violence was an integral part of Roosevelt's West, the bank robber, the gunfighter, and the street duel were not part of either Roosevelt's history or Turner's agrarian visions; they belonged to another past. This scene in *Cimarron* references hundreds of Hollywood westerns since their appearance at the turn of the century, and certainly Estabrook's scripted confrontation between the Virginian and Trampas two years before. Is *Cimarron*'s gunfight merely a repetition of the ahistorical genre conventions enumerated by film theorists Will Wright, John Cawelti, Jim Kitses, and Richard Slotkin?[52] These codifiers of the western genre have always been uncomfortable with *Cimarron* and quickly dismissed it as an expensive failure. But the reason that *Cimarron* is mentioned in western film criticism as a historical marker is precisely because it thwarts the mythical, transhistorical structures of genre adapted from the work of Claude Lévi-Strauss.

According to this critical heritage, the western is composed of visual codes and themes, a recognizable iconography and a series of refined narrative structures. These genre structures have a tendency to operate transhistorically.[53] Therefore, even though westerns are set in the past, they present generalized images evoking frontier nostalgia. The films do not question American history. Through genre's powerful visual symbolism, the structures dramatize the dominant cultural ideology. As with all myths, the western is said to lack a self-reflexive relationship toward its

Cimarron: The vulture's eye view.

subject matter; it passively mirrors national myths rather than deliberately confronting and contesting those discourses. Yet *Cimarron's* engagement with the text of traditional history fractures this insular, mythic world of the western genre. This western actively engages the structure and process of history—even the archetypal scene of the shoot-out is a specific moment prefaced by a date, 1890, and a series of documented events.[54] After Yancey shoots the Kid, the townsfolk plan to put the outlaw and his gang on display in a storefront window! Although the gunfighter may be a heroic abstraction in western film criticism, he is documented, on view in a makeshift museum, and deliberately contained as a historical artifact in *Cimarron's* narrative.

The next inserts occur in 1893. Again, a group of men studies the headlines, which now read, "August 17, 1893: Cherokee Strip Opening. President Cleveland Expected to Sign Proclamation on Saturday of This Week. Rush of Settlers Will Exceed 1889. Long Awaited News Stirs Country." Sabra, returning from her women's club speech, has just put Oklahoma's pioneer heritage in safe, historical perspective. She, like Turner, views the frontier as closed and sees a new, settled era beginning. She is therefore stunned when news of further land rushes inspires her husband first to criticize the government for its trickery and then to confound his criticism by cavorting off to the Strip with a group of white, gun-toting cronies. This sequence is critical to *Cimarron's* historiography because it challenges Turner's idea of a closed frontier in 1890 by showing yet another land rush about to happen in 1893. Oklahoma history proves that the frontier is still viable and that the lure of its rhetoric still blinds the nation to its own racism. But Sabra, as historian, refuses both to acknowledge her husband's need to go to the Strip and to amend her view of the past. She remains trapped in her version of western historiography while the frontier, her husband, and the film's history rush onward.

More significantly, while the headline and documents proclaim the size and import of the expansion, Yancey's participation in that "new empire building," that perennial last frontier, is scripted not as a national necessity or as a triumphant part of the American past but as a white man's lark and an escape from town life. The fused argument of the newspaper and Yancey's search for new territory constitutes its own critique of the impulses that drove the country to expand. Historian Gerald Nash would write years later that the mythic West represented an escape from the real West, and he considered Hollywood cinema to be an unconscious expression of this need to elude the burdens of history.[55] Yet decades before Nash and other historians began to fathom the mythic rhetoric of western history, *Cimarron* implied that the history of the West was a conscious retreat into myth. Each historically specific title in *Cimarron* is superimposed over an expanding urban landscape, and throughout the second half of the film, it is a West from which the mythic figure, Yancey, flees.

Yancey's disappearance, the passing of the Cherokee Strip, and the coming of the Spanish-American War in 1898 are united in the text of the next intertitle. The film cuts to the front page of Osage's newspaper (now run by Sabra), and male voice-overs discuss its headlines regarding the peace settlement. Yet Sol Levy and Sabra talk only of the elusive Yancey. As Sol remarks, Yancey has become "part of the history of the great Southwest." Indeed, his frontiersman type has been written into the historical record epitomized by the text inserts and Sol's projected histories. Ironically, this historicizing implies Yancey's passing as a living force while he still lives in the film narrative. In fact, Yancey has made the transition from Southwest frontiersman to Roosevelt Rough Rider: for the past few years, he has been fighting in Cuba. The titles' institutional history makes a similar analogy, noting the end of the Cherokee Strip expansion and the coming of the Spanish-American War as if they were natural progressions in American nationhood. The headlines that once reported the opening of the Cherokee Strip now praise military victories abroad. In this sequence, Estabrook and Ruggles's juxtaposed text and images introduce one of the consequences of territorial expansion: American imperialism. With the conquest of the American West achieved, the frontier expanded beyond national borders.

Yet *Cimarron*'s structural contrast between these two events is not the straight linear progression implied by the text inserts; rather, it is confounded by the screen images. It is important to remember what is not shown in this sequence. One never sees that other frontier. *Cimarron*'s historical narrative remains within Osage, and there is no narrative progression from the American West to Cuba and the Philippines. The diegesis circulates within the racial prejudices of Oklahoma. The actions of Sabra and Yancey Cravat also thwart any imagined narrative conflation of territorial expansion and imperialism. Although Sabra's dislike of the "lazy" Indians' neglect of the land appears to sanction a Manifest Destiny view of continental expansion, she stays within her western sphere and is no advocate of imperialism. Yancey, as a Rough Rider, executes the letter of American imperialism in Cuba, but he is not motivated by Sabra's racial prejudice or chauvinism. It is his childish love of adventure and personal glory that motivates his expansionist acts.

Yancey's conflicting thoughts and actions, his sympathy and kinship with the Indians, and his own lust for frontier adventure may embody what Richard Slotkin has called the "ideological ambivalence" of the American frontier, most vividly expressed in the mythic forms of classical Hollywood cinema.[56] Yancey is the frontiersman who makes the journey to Oklahoma, watches the town of Osage grow, and then leaves when civilization stifles him—the archetypal "hunter-hero" who destroys the wild frontier he inhabits and who embodies America's conflicted attitude toward expansion.[57] By killing the Kid, Yancey unwittingly condemns his world and himself to the past. He understands the Native Americans but goes on the Cherokee run.

Slotkin's assertion of mythical complexity is misleading. In his analysis, myths disarm critical investigation,[58] their narratives are simple, and

Sabra's frontier
rhetoric elicits
a sad smile
from Yancey.
(*Cimarron*)

the language of myth is written with no greater complexity than as a series of binary oppositions and resolutions contained within the dominant, triumphant view of American history and the bland, happy endings of Hollywood films. Yet *Cimarron*'s self-conscious historical structure proposes that traditional texts on western history present a bombastic and reductive version of the past. Yancey's exaggerated last frontier rhetoric and Sabra's mimed use of his words to historicize Oklahoma's early years are both parodies. At one point during the 1893 sequence, as Sabra strikes a pose and mimics her husband's initial speech about Oklahoma's miraculous history (in a suitably deep voice), Yancey smiles, both genuinely amused and wistful. In Estabrook and Ruggles's film, Turner's rhetoric defining the essential national character and Roosevelt's faith in American expansion are not the foundations of another heroicized tale of the American past; they are the imperfect means by which people justify themselves. *Cimarron* confronts America's myths rather than memorializing them.

The next series of titles begins in 1907, announcing Oklahoma's statehood, and then cuts to a close-up of Roosevelt's grim portrait and signature on the document. This unusual series of images recalls Roosevelt as president and as historian. Both affected Oklahoma's history. Yet Roosevelt's histories of the West celebrated the industrial progress and unproblematic, racially justified expansion that Estabrook and Ruggles's film contests. Roosevelt's evolving West sanctioned the eventual extinction of the Indians and the triumph of the white race, and it certainly did not admit the immigration of non-European ethnic groups.[59] Osage's oil-rich Indians and immigrant Chinese would not fit into Roosevelt's West. Within the film, the president's endorsement of Oklahoma statehood brings no great changes to Osage. Roosevelt's belief that the frontier had to end as a natural step in the industrial progress of the United States is contrasted with the film's visualizing of the persistence of class and race prejudice, government corruption, and the obsolete Yancey's refusal to disappear entirely from the history of Oklahoma.

Scripting Modern American History

By 1929, skyscrapers obliterate Osage's view of the western horizon. Even amid this modernity, the age has become self-consciously historical. Sabra reprints Yancey's famed 1907 editorial excoriating the government for its mistreatment of the Osage Indians. The nation, on the verge of the Great Depression and a deflation of the shibboleth of expanding national success, looks back with a distinctly sentimentalized attitude toward the past. Sabra's racism has been transformed by comfortable success into nostalgic regret. Her eulogy to her husband as a liberal man ahead of his time honors the power of an individual to influence his government's policy. As Sabra remarks proudly, the government has done exactly what he wanted in the end, and Native Americans are now U.S. citizens. But are the Osage better off? Since oil was discovered on their land, they have become some of the state's wealthiest inhabitants, driving around Osage in Packards and Rolls-Royces, the women wearing tribal blankets and jewelry over their Paris gowns. Are they assimilated U.S. citizens or a self-determining Osage nation? Estabrook and Ruggles deliberately created a conflicted visual place for Native Americans in modern society.

In that same sequence, Sabra also remembers that the last time she had any news of her husband was when a soldier reported seeing him fighting at Chateau-Thierry, his hair dyed black to disguise his age. Has America's involvement in the First World War (1917–1918) become an extension of the frontier in the American mythic consciousness? The border skirmishes, repossession of territory, bloody conflict, and racialized propaganda are a bitter genealogy for a mere escapist frontier myth. In 1926, Lewis Mumford drew a deliberate connection between the sterile myths of the West and the devastating realization of the new frontiers in France and Flanders. Because of the pervasiveness of the frontier idea, "One finds that the myth of the Pioneer Conquest had taken possession of even the finer and more sensitive minds: they accepted the ugliness and brutalities of pioneering, even as many of our contemporaries accepted the bestialities of war.[60] Historian David Kennedy would later connect the frontiers of the West and the Great War, alluding to Willa Cather's *One of Ours* (1922) as contemporary evidence of this feeling.[61] Edna Ferber's decision to make Yancey a war veteran may be a reflection of Cather's frequent frontier doughboy protagonists (Tom Outland in *The Professor's House* is yet another), but *Cimarron's* filmmakers deliberately transformed Ferber's passing narrative mention of the world war into dialogue between Sabra and her printer.[62] Yancey's participation in the Great War is perhaps, as far as Sabra is concerned, just another crusade of her errant husband, but it may be the filmmakers' indirect critique of an aging frontier myth whose ideas of noble conquest locked the nation into the bitterest of wars. The bloody and ironic descent of Yancey's frontier heritage seems to overshadow Sabra's growing historical consciousness.

The final text insert occurs in 1930, when Sabra, now a congresswoman at a political banquet, again echoes Yancey's overblown expansionist rhetoric as a historical explanation for Oklahoma's past. However, she radicalizes her speech by emphasizing female pioneers, noting at the beginning of her address: "The women of Oklahoma have helped build a prairie wilderness into the state of today." This feminist tone came at a time when traditional values and the authority of the pioneer patriarch were in dispute. By 1930, the citizens of Oklahoma were some of the first Americans to experience the pinch of the Great Depression. Month by month, the reality of unemployment and poverty materialized, but Estabrook and Ruggles made no direct allusion to the crisis. Perhaps in omitting defeat, *Cimarron* ultimately resolves its conflicted early history and sanctions a myth of American progress. One could also speculate that when Ferber wrote *Cimarron* in 1929, the Depression had not happened, and that Estabrook and Ruggles merely stuck to the book. Yet *Cimarron's* filmmakers deliberately took the diegesis beyond the stock market crash to 1930. Did they believe that they were creating a usable past and a mythic narrative conclusion that would help the nation deal with economic defeat? These are difficult questions; no conference memos exist detailing RKO's feelings about the ending. Yet the feast is a political celebration for Sabra. The fact that she was elected during the Depression may signify the country's imagined need for pioneers to lead it, but it also suggests that male pioneers have failed to extricate the state from its present economic crisis. If Sabra is one of those who oversaw the growth of Oklahoma from prairie wilderness to statehood, perhaps she is also the one to rebuild the demoralized state.

Shortly after Yancey's death in an Oklahoma oil field, the film concludes at the unveiling ceremony for a statue commemorating the Oklahoma Pioneer. Naturally, the subject is a colossus of Yancey in his broad-brimmed hat and Prince Albert coat. His hand rests on the butt of his gun, and a young Indian crouches behind him, as if seeking shelter in Yancey's enormous shadow. *Cimarron's* projection of Oklahoma's elegy to the pioneer, a mythic symbol, is ironic. Yancey, a historic figure in the narrative, has become an abstract hero, a larger-than-life, flawless statue embodying society's perception of the passing of an age. The man who repeatedly dispossessed the Oklahoma tribes of their land and even denied his own mixed Native American heritage, while still acting as a friend to the oppressed, has become by the end of the film the savior of the weak. Popular history has written him as a hero. The final shots of the unveiled monument are not simply the filmmakers' patriotic coda; rather, Yancey's heroic statue belongs to a narrative structure that consistently draws attention to the present generation's transformation of the past.

RKO and the Perils of Critical Success

RKO's gamble with a sophisticated historical film paid off. Estabrook and Ruggles produced an American historical film that dominated every major poll of the year's best films.[63] *Cimarron* would even win the Academy Award for Best Picture and Best Screenplay. If the Academy's recognition could be considered a marker for a film's "seriousness" as art, then surely *Cimarron* succeeded. For the next sixty years, it would be the only western to garner such accolades, despite the genre's accelerating popularity. Although some of the film's reviewers recalled the uneasy reception of *The Big Trail*, the majority understood *Cimarron's* rigorously historical structure and content as an advance in the history of American cinema, rather than as a narrative flaw.[64] Robert Sherwood was ecstatic: "The excellence of *Cimarron* is further proof that the movie is the national art of America."[65] In his column, Richard Watts Jr. introduced the idea that the film was far better as history than Ferber's historical novel or, potentially, any written history. If he had any criticism of the film, "it is only because the genuine brilliance of the production makes the slight dissatisfaction aroused by the photoplay both puzzling and worthy of careful consideration."[66] Ferber's fictional romance and bowdlerized West, which Dorothy Van Doren pictured as ideal for a large-scale motion picture, were actually, for Watts, the least appealing qualities of the historical film. For Watts, *Cimarron's* complex use of western history made it a success. It was certainly a rare moment when a New York film critic believed that history could take the place of the conventional Hollywood narrative.

Ironically, the newest medium for representing the past, and one

Producer William K. LeBaron, art director Max Ree, and screenwriter Howard Estabrook (far right) receive Academy Awards from presenter and U.S. Vice President Charles Curtis. (Author's collection)

denigrated and resented by traditional writers of history, was projecting a reading of western history that challenged both the credibility of traditional historiography and revisionist historians' inability to synthesize the past. Carl Becker was the most prominent academic historian to recognize professional history's need to reconcile itself to a popular audience. His 1931 address to the American Historical Association occurred several months after *Cimarron*'s release. He asserted, "The history that lies in unread books does no work in the world. The history that does work in the world, the history that influences the course of history, is living history, that pattern of remembered events, whether true or false, that enlarges and enriches the collective specious present, the specious present of Mr. Everyman."[67] Although Becker said little of cinema, undoubtedly this ultimate form of popular history would be Mr. Everyman's choice. Yet with *Cimarron*, cinema had penetrated the realm of academic history and led its popular audience away from the cultural comfort of myths and into a complicated and hitherto uncharted historical territory. While contemporary academics picked away at the isolated inadequacies of Turner's thesis and traditional western historiography, a popular novel and an even more popular film articulated a persuasive new way to look at the past. Curiously, the film's structure and historical concerns seem to have anticipated the "New Western History" of the late twentieth century.[68] In 1931, *Cimarron* presented a multiracial and ethnic West; it elevated minorities to positions of power within the narrative; and it gave Native Americans a voice in creating the historical record. The film also articulated a thorough and prolonged critique of the accepted historiography; it interrogated the rhetoric of traditional written history with images that counteracted and even denied the omniscience of the written word. Yet unlike much of the late-twentieth-century historiography that echoed the divisive rhetoric of post-structuralism and the postmodern suspicion of narrative historiography, *Cimarron* managed to retain a historical complexity without sacrificing a coherent synthesis of historical change. It could tell one story with many voices, combining a critical historical viewpoint with a lucid historical synthesis.

Years later, documentary filmmaker and historian Paul Rotha would remember the film as "the American cinema's one accurate study of social history."[69] Rotha responded to both *Cimarron's* social richness and its historical accuracy, qualities that recall the documentary tradition he helped create and historicize. Although he said nothing about the historical film's potential as a nonfiction, documentary mode, Rotha's rare praise certainly raises questions about historical films' potential for documenting history outside the realm of classical Hollywood fiction filmmaking. As film critic Thornton Delehanty concluded in 1931, "*Cimarron* has set a mark for pictures of its kind which, it is not hard to believe, may never be hit again."[70] Unfortunately, Delehanty's remark would haunt American historical filmmaking. At the end of the decade, film historian Lewis Jacobs credited the film with inaugurating a long-term cycle of American historical films, and as time passed, Hollywood executives and trade papers tried to justify big-budget historical and western films by invoking *Cimarron's* memory.[71] The film's name became a sort of talisman for artistic achievement in an industry traditionally credited with a short memory, although it is arguable whether these ensuing films approximated *Cimarron*.

Certainly the circumstances surrounding the film's production were unique. Estabrook and Ruggles were responsible for *Cimarron's* unusual union of narrative coherence and historical complexity, but RKO could not afford another artistic success. In spite of the fact that *Cimarron* made $1.38 million for RKO in the worst industrial year of the Great Depression, the studio had spent $1.5 million to produce it.[72] Executives replaced William LeBaron with David O. Selznick, son-in-law of Metro-Goldwyn-Mayer mogul Louis B. Mayer. Wesley Ruggles left RKO to direct Mae West and Carole Lombard vehicles; it would be nine years before he made another historical western, Columbia's *Arizona* (1940).

Estabrook, meanwhile, remained at RKO, collected his Oscar, and tried to write his next project, *The Conquerors*, without interference. But his days as the sole author of a film script were limited. Estabrook had experienced what few screenwriters ever attained: extensive and unusual power in creating a prestigious and influential film. With *Cimarron's* release, the press concentrated almost exclusively on Estabrook as the film's author. London's *Graphic* did an in-depth interview with him entitled "Writer's Gold in Hollywood." Estabrook wrote articles for the *Hollywood Reporter* that credited the film with generating a renewed interest in American history.[73] "In almost every city where *Cimarron* has been exhibited," he wrote, "the interest aroused in its historical theme has been reflected in a demand for volumes dealing with this page of American history." He was suddenly the most prominent screenwriter in Hollywood and an influential American historian with the widest public imaginable. He had become Mr. Everyman's historian. But *Cimarron* was also his nemesis. Having adapted and subtly transformed other people's work, Estabrook now wanted to write his own historical screenplay. His next script, *The March of a Nation* (later retitled *The Conquerors*), was loosely based on a series of *Saturday Evening Post* articles about America's nineteenth-century financial history. Perhaps the deepening Depression affected him, or perhaps the surge of public recognition altered his critical judgment, but Estabrook now wanted to get a message across to the public. *The March of a Nation*, conceived as an episodic story of a New York financial family, focused on the American people's historic triumphs over a series of financial crises (1873–1929).[74] History would now serve the needs of contemporary events. As he wrote in an early draft in December 1931, "There was a severe financial panic in each period. . . . By simply portraying personalized history through the daily lives of our characters, we show that the reverse is always true . . . the nation always sweeps forward with strides of new prosperity, new developments, new inventions, to greater heights than ever—the record of history proves it." Estabrook even planned to film each episode, or historical "transition," with shots of a man perusing an enormous history book. For example, a shot of a venerable old book with the date "1873" would be followed by a close-up of a relevant engraving.

This was just the type of historical pomposity that Selznick despised. His response a week later was simply, "Flat!" Hack writers Robert Lord and Humphrey Pearson were hired to change Estabrook's pet epic. Eventually, Selznick and cranky action director William Wellman revamped Estabrook's epic antidote to the Depression into a cheaper and more pugnacious version of *Cimarron*. Estabrook's multiracial West and hero were gone, as were the ironic text inserts and the precise use of dates. Instead,

Czech émigré Slavko Vorkapich was hired to make a series of newspaper montages to cover holes in the narrative. Vorkapich, with possibly less interest in American history than Selznick, replaced most of the projected text with a series of images displaying rising and falling columns of money.[75] Even with Richard Dix playing the lead, the film failed. Both Selznick and the young Wellman had a conventional view of the West; triumphant white "conquerors" interested them more than America's "Cimarron" past.

Cimarron's impact on American historical cinema was not confined to the crude reworking of its national historical framework, one depicting the development of one place's transformation from territory to state. In 1932, Clara Bow made a comeback in sound features in Call Her Savage, playing an illegitimate half–Native American heiress whose struggle against the social and sexual conventions of the white world drives her back to her Indian roots. Also at Paramount, Cecil B. DeMille's story department moved away from ancient history and began to generate treatments of Benjamin Franklin and Wild Bill Hickok's careers. And at Warner Brothers, producer Darryl Zanuck began to experiment with modern American biographies and histories. In 1932 he supervised both The Mouthpiece, a screen biography of famous New York mob lawyer William Fallon, and Silver Dollar, a biography of nineteenth-century frontiersman and miner H. A. W. Tabor. In the latter film, based on a popular biography by David Karsner, Zanuck had originally planned to use the real historical names, but fresh from legal trouble with Fallon's daughter over The Mouthpiece's alleged slanderous portrayal, he grudgingly decided to change the names, since "the central figure does desert his wife and child and live with another woman for fourteen years before finally marrying her." "Haw" Tabor was an obscure figure, neither a Lincoln nor a Billy Bonney, and the alteration would not be noticed.[76] It was one of Hollywood's first conflicts between censorship and historical truth in the sound era. Harvey Thew wrote the majority of the script, mixing historical detail and text superimpositions with a complex and frequently satirical portrayal of Tabor (renamed Yates Martin). Paul Green also worked on early versions but complained to assistant producer Lucien Hubbard that Thew's treatment was too critical of their hero's pompous frontier rhetoric. He saw Silver Dollar as a eulogy, "symbolic of a great movement which opened up the last American frontier," and Tabor (Martin) as a great hero, honored by the major politicians and businessmen of his day. Green believed that it was "poor grace in us who try to tell his story to make a fool and charlatan out of him and his followers."[77]

But Zanuck thought that this antihero's flaws—his brash self-motivation, his strident Americanism and comparisons between himself and Lincoln, his capacity to make mistakes and to be defeated by historical events beyond his control—made his story worth telling on screen. At one point, Martin strides in front of an ornately framed portrait of a famous American, temporarily upstaging and replacing this traditional hero with his overblown, living image. Of course, Martin "frames" himself only temporarily as a hero; shortly afterward, he embarks on a personal and professional decline, figuratively "framing" himself when he takes Lily as his mistress. Zanuck also liked the man's cultural iconoclasm, his hostility to the wealthy intellectual elites. Zanuck and actor Edward G. Robinson suggested a scene in which Martin would survey his newly constructed Denver Opera House and stare with blank incomprehension at the fancy busts of Shakespeare and Socrates lining the walls. "Ask them who in hell they are and what did they do for Denver!" he roars, commanding the workmen to replace them with busts of Ulysses S. Grant and Edwin Mc-Masters Stanton, American figures.[78] Zanuck and his team of filmmakers seemed to enjoy adding scenes of historical import: Martin's second marriage, with President Chester A. Arthur in attendance; the date of the opera house opening; and the announcement of his brief tenure as senator. *Silver Dollar* took several months to complete—an unusual occurrence at the thrifty Warner Brothers—and after an October preview, it opened in December.

Warner Brothers' major historical prestige picture of 1932 received a great deal of critical praise, much of it evocative of *Cimarron*. Thornton Delehanty said that it had "true historical sense," Richard Watts called it an "admirable screen contribution to the current nostalgic rediscovery of the old America," and Mordaunt Hall of the *New York Times* saw an emerging pattern of Hollywood production, naming *Silver Dollar* part of a new "cycle" in Hollywood.[79] In fact, *Silver Dollar* was only the beginning of the American historical cycle; a surge of prestigious historical cinema followed *Cimarron*'s release, and those films made during the next ten years would practice its techniques of the foreword, the projected text insert, the use of extensive research, and the employment of one dominant screenwriter. The industry and national critics would repeatedly honor these films, but their box-office appeal was erratic. Some were successes, but all were expensive, often failing (as critics predicted) to make up their costs even with good attendance.

Such was *Silver Dollar*. When the film failed to retrieve its losses in the holiday season, Zanuck was irritated with the public. In 1929 Robert

Sherwood had predicted that prestige pictures created by the sound-era "Renaissance" in Hollywood would enable producers to "thumb their noses at the rabble."[80] By 1932, Zanuck was realizing the cost of such gestures. Two years later he could joke to John Huston that "*Silver Dollar* made the artistic and box-office mistake of taking itself too seriously. It was the Great Drama, the great baloney picture of the rise of a great American character."[81] But the producer still maintained his business-risk devotion to American history in the face of public apathy or stupidity. Sometimes he was on the side of history and film art, and sometimes he was with the rabble. But in the early 1930s he adapted to historical filmmaking. As traditional American history, pioneers, and frontiers returned to the theaters in a new and vigorous form, Zanuck and others found that this historical style could be applied to the less stable topics of modern history—the Great War, urban crime and corruption, Prohibition, the Depression, gangsters, and veterans. When Zanuck made *The Mouthpiece* in 1932, he was well acquainted with the pitfalls of filming events and lives of the twentieth century. Slander suits were often the least of his problems.

2

Contemporary History in the Age of *Scarface*, 1932

Sounds like a typewriter, eh? I'm goin' to write my name all over Chicago
with this, in capital letters.
                    —Tony Camonte (Al Capone) in *Scarface*, 1932

Darryl F. Zanuck began working for Warner Brothers in 1924, and by 1929
he had moved from writing Rin Tin Tin scripts to overseeing George Arliss reprise his stage success as Benjamin Disraeli. According to Arliss and
Warner Brothers' publicity department, *Disraeli*'s historical content was
intended to "increase the prestige of talking pictures."[1] Critics agreed and
were pleasantly surprised that a major studio was not always interested
in that classic oxymoron, the "public taste." *Variety* praised the film and
sniggered, "Some of the peasants won't get the smartness or appreciate the
subtle shades of the Arliss technique, not to mention a plot that concerns
the diplomatic imperativeness of possessing the Suez Canal."[2] The fact
that *Disraeli* was so obviously not intended as standard box-office fare
intrigued reviewers, who could now act as cultural intermediaries for "the
peasants." With more prestige productions such as *Disraeli*, film criticism
also had a new cachet. Back in Hollywood, the film embellished Zanuck's
reputation, and in early 1931 he began to plan Arliss's *Alexander Hamilton*, another play that the actor had coauthored with Mary Hamlin.[3]
    This would be Arliss's first role as an American in a Hollywood film.
The play and the script were painstaking endorsements of Hamilton's
sense of moral and political honor, a personal code at odds with that of his

Darryl F. Zanuck
at Warner Brothers,
ca. 1930.

invidious and rabble-rousing colleague Thomas Jefferson. Shot in a series
of static tableaux, *Alexander Hamilton* was released in September 1931.
Whereas *Disraeli*'s old-fashioned "starring vehicle" prestige had succeeded in 1929, by 1931, neither critics nor audiences were impressed. Although many noted its pretentious, epigrammatic historical tone, the film
contained few text inserts and instead gave most of the historical commentary to Arliss in excruciatingly long speeches. The *New York Sun's*
John S. Cohen Jr. and Richard Watts of the *New York Herald Tribune*
compared the film's retelling of historical events to Claude G. Bowers's
recent biography of Jefferson and his colleagues, but the comparison was
not flattering. The critical consensus was that the Arliss biography was
"lifeless and slow-moving," its historical perspective "conventional" or
mere "melodrama." Watts's review echoed Potamkin's criticism of *Abraham Lincoln* the summer before: "A study of the film's dialogue suggests
that, if the Arliss work is true to history, our forefathers were somewhat
given to talking in copy-book maxims in Colonial days."[4] The filmmakers had failed to manipulate language as a means of engaging with history. Even *Variety*, known to be more charitable to the industry's attempts
at highbrow filmmaking, was disgusted with its historical pretensions.[5]
Though Arliss would make a few more biographical films for Zanuck at
Twentieth Century–Fox, he never again ventured into American history.

   Alexander Hamilton was one of the few conspicuous failures that Zanuck produced while at Warner Brothers. Because of Arliss's dictatorial
control over his scripts, the producer was prevented from getting involved
in the literary process he enjoyed so much: editing. But Zanuck, who

would later become famous at his own studio for monitoring every aspect of a film's production, had his mind on other projects while *Alexander Hamilton* was slowly developing in early 1931. At that time, he was deeply involved in overseeing the production of John Bright and Kubec Glasmon's novel *Beer and Blood. The Public Enemy*, as it was soon retitled, would be Zanuck's first major American historical film. With its depiction of Prohibition, gangsters, and crooked cops of the Roaring Twenties, the producer did not have to worry about unfortunate comparisons between his film and more established, respectable forms of historiography. In fact, with an eager national audience, matchless publicity venues, and a group of "historical experts," he could effectively control the development of modern American historiography.

Can *The Public Enemy* be called a historical film? Few scholars have been willing to consider the gangster as a historical figure and the classic sound-era gangster films (*Doorway to Hell*, 1930; *Little Caesar*, 1931; *The Public Enemy*, 1931; *Scarface*, 1932) as deliberately constructed interpretations of postwar American history.[6] Such an admission would violate two major traditions in film scholarship and cultural history: that early gangster films were strictly modern genre subjects, and therefore could not be historical films; and that classical Hollywood filmmakers were unconscious mythmakers, their work lacking the necessary textual depth, historical evidence, argument, and critical distance that more traditional writers of history possessed.[7] For the past half century, academic and popular criticism of the classical Hollywood gangster film has followed the guidelines of Robert Warshow's "The Gangster as Tragic Hero."[8] Warshow's emphasis on gangster cinema's mythic narrative formula, its inescapable modernity, and its paradoxical reflection and subversion of the American Dream has become the organizing principle of classical Hollywood genre studies, film and cultural histories, and investigations of censorship and ethnicity.[9]

Although many film historians have recognized that the gangster film "questioned the very foundation of American society," film studies preferred to regard the gangster in classical Hollywood cinema as part of a genre formula and an inescapable reflection of modern life.[10] His "subversion," however modern, represented merely the opposing force in the binary paradigm of myth. Garth Jowett, Carlos Clarens, Richard Maltby, and Jonathan Munby each contextualized the gangster film's representation of ethnic heroes and the resulting public controversy and censorship campaigns, but within their interpretive framework, these remain inescapably modern battles in which the gangster serves as a reflective site of contemporary social antagonism.[11] Curiously, even as a controversial figure destabilizing "the myth of America," the gangster has remained an uncharacteristically passive and nameless figure, a set of mirrors between public life and public culture of the interwar years.[12]

In addition, these modern narratives of crime and corruption may seem irreconcilable with the reverential trajectories of Western progress and American biography, and they may seem too recent for Zanuck's generation to consider them as legitimate subjects of history. But as early as the 1930s, a variety of American historians considered the impact of the gangster—in particular, Al Capone—on the construction of American history. Academic and popular historians struggled to exclude and to place postwar America and its major figures within the grand narrative of American history, but Zanuck, John Bright, Ben Hecht, and Howard Hughes prominently engaged with twentieth-century history in their attempts to structure events of ten, five, or even one year earlier within the discourse of an emerging historical cinema.

Modern History's Doorway to Hell

Films about contemporary crime and fictional gangsters had been popular since D. W. Griffith's *Musketeers of Pig Alley* (1913), but it was only in the late 1920s, and with the conversion to sound, that high-profile gangster films began to script the historical trajectory of crime and advertise the lives of real gangsters and bootleggers. This desire to capture and document the real aspects of Chicago and other postwar elements of American life grew as the public recognized their impending obliteration by the law. Capone's era was ending. Many of the more famous gangsters were dead, in jail, or in court. The 1920s had passed so quickly that already its most famous newspaper personalities were becoming relics. Journalists such as Walter Noble Burns, Fred Pasley, and John Bright had spent so many years covering Chicago crime stories that they now transformed them into histories (Burns's *The One-Way Ride*) and biographies (Pasley's *Al Capone* and Bright's *Hizzoner Big Bill Thompson*).[13] Even an academic like Preston William Slosson was willing to write a history of the postwar era.[14] But Zanuck's first historical gangster films, *Doorway to Hell* and *Little Caesar*, were not merely reflections of more traditional historians' awareness of a passing era. Instead, they were the most powerful part of this first wave of postwar historiography, engaged directly with questions of objectivity, the boundary between journalism and history, and the subversive recognition and portrayal of national heroes.

Professional historians seemed far less comfortable with the postwar era. Slosson's *The Great Crusade and After* (1930) was one of the few "serious" modern histories, and it claimed that America's path since the war had been transformed, if not scarred, by the forces of modernity. Editors Arthur M. Schlesinger and Dixon Ryan Fox both commented on the difficulty facing any historian attempting to write a "'contemporary history,'" and they praised Slosson's detachment and style, which "he would use in chronicling the life and way of any previous generation." Yet the postwar era and its people were *not* like any previous generation. Despite the modern generation's unprecedented access to news, Slosson sadly remarked that the American press and public talked with more animation about the "crime wave" than the political scandals of the Harding administration.[15] As a historian, he claimed to grapple with "the outstanding problems" of the postwar era—Prohibition, immigration, and the speedy transformation of modern life to modern history—but he went to great lengths to expunge the embodiment of these ills, the gangster, from his narrative. Slosson's historiography, patterned after the work of Charles Beard, arranged American history as a conflicting equation of economic and political forces unhampered by individual action.[16] In a postwar modern age marked by mechanized massacres and Fordian efficiency, the heroic individual had ceased to exist as a historical factor.

Popular historians had another perspective. These writers, more connected with a public audience, were aware of the crucial role that mass culture played in defining contemporary history. Academics wrote of a series of impressive forces and events that controlled postwar American history: modernity, Prohibition, wealth, crime. Popular historians located the figure who manipulated all these factors and shaped the decade, satisfying a public need for both hero and villain: the gangster. Frederick Lewis Allen's *Only Yesterday* (1931) not only identified the gangster as the definitive force in postwar life but also adopted a different historical approach to creating contemporary history. Films, music, fashion, crime biographies, college life, leisure, and literature dominated Allen's episodic historical account. As he acknowledged in his preface, "A contemporary history is bound to be anything but definitive . . . [but] half the enjoyment of writing it has lain in the effort to reduce to some sort of logical and coherent order a mass of material untouched by any previous historian."[17] Like his academic counterparts, Allen addressed the major political, economic, and social forces of the decade, but he located them within the dynamic career of the gangster, best exemplified by Al Capone.[18] Allen's own style paralleled his historical attitude toward the postwar era: fast, vivid, kaleidoscopic, image driven, and stopped only by the Depression.

Allen's brand of historiography, though unique to written history, was already a part of Darryl F. Zanuck's work at Warner Brothers. *Doorway to Hell* (1930) was his first gangster film to focus on the exploits of one Chicago protagonist.[19] Although known for introducing James Cagney to Warner Brothers, *Doorway to Hell*'s star was Lew Ayres, who had just come from the set of Universal's *All Quiet on the Western Front.* In transferring from Universal's set to Warner Brothers', Ayres went from one modern battlefield to another. The casting may have been a coincidence, but the metaphor was powerful for audiences in 1930. In a country marked by postwar disillusionment, the gangsters of this generation were often real or pretended war veterans. Capone, for instance, was famous for claiming that the scars on the left side of his face had come from fighting on the Western Front. Capone's biographer, *Chicago Daily News* reporter Fred D. Pasley, believed that Capone's war experience introduced him to the machine gun and determined his dominant role in the Chicago underworld. Walter Noble Burns, however, was more skeptical of Capone's eight months in the "Lost Battalion," dryly commenting that in Capone's later testimony before a grand jury, he admitted that the scars were the result of a New York saloon brawl in his youth.[20] Yet other gang leaders such as Samuel J. "Nails" Morton were well known as decorated vets.[21] Zanuck, a Great War veteran himself, had a growing penchant for ransacking newspapers for prospective screen stories, and he would have been familiar with the many postwar journalists who explicitly connected the rise of the gangster with Great War violence. *Doorway to Hell*'s subtle awareness of these historical connections predated Burns's use of this material by over a year.[22]

Were these various writers commenting on the legacy of the corruption of heroism, a variation of "the great crusade and after"? Or were the gang wars of Chicago a natural result of the displacement and neglect of the American veteran? The veteran, once a powerless doughboy at the mercy of machinery and possible massacre in no-man's-land, was now literally behind the machinery of crime. By 1926 he carried his own machine gun, often gave his own orders, started his own wars, and fought for his turf with the tools and training he had learned on another front.

Crime boss Johnny Torrio was not a veteran, but Roland Brown's original story, "A Handful of Cloud," loosely followed Torrio's rise and fall and formed the basis of *Doorway to Hell*.[23] Zanuck was obviously fascinated with the idea of adapting modern history for the screen, but even though

Torrio's story was torn from the headlines, they were yesterday's headlines. By 1930 Capone had replaced him as head of South Side vice; Torrio was now part of Chicago's past. Zanuck could not resist alluding to this development by incorporating images of historiography into the script. When Louie Ricardo (Lew Ayres) attains a certain status as a public gangster, he gets a contract to write his memoirs. The film's last shot is a close-up of the last page of his autobiography, a modern historical record. The roar of machine guns announces the protagonist's murder, even as the film and historical text reach the last page of the final chapter. The film thus becomes a visual biography of Ricardo, and it inaugurated Zanuck's use of projected historical texts in his gangster cycle. Like any good historian, he also cared about advertising his historical acumen. He directed Warner Brothers' publicity team to promote the film's authenticity, even claiming, as Universal had for *Underworld* (1929), that the film was a biography of New York gangster Lou "Legs" Diamond. Soon studio press sheets boasted that Zanuck had hired real gangsters to act as consultants on the set.[24]

Doorway to Hell attracted a great deal of critical notice as an innovative talking gangster film; critic Creighton Peet even claimed that it was "the first real 'motion' picture the Warner Brothers have made this year, what with punk operettas and photographed stage plays."[25] Under Zanuck's leadership, sound cinema had finally achieved something new. But it was the release of Zanuck's next gangster picture, *Little Caesar*, that witnessed a new engagement with contemporary history and the boundary between journalism and history. It was also the first gangster film to be mentioned by both *Film Daily* and the *National Board of Review* in their annual lists of the best feature films.[26] Usually these organizations honored more traditional historical epics and prestigious literary adaptations, such as *Disraeli* (1929), *All Quiet on the Western Front* (1930), and *Cimarron* (1931). Perhaps it made sense for *Little Caesar* to be part of this group. During the early 1930s, studio publicists and critics were echoing and amplifying films' historical allusions and prestigious links to traditional historical cinema.[27]

Robert N. Lee adapted W. R. Burnett's novel *Little Caesar* for Zanuck in 1930. Although there were many similarities between Al Capone and Burnett's Sicilian hood Caesar Enrico Bandello, the book could in no way be considered a biography of Capone. Burnett went out of his way to defend the novel's fictional subject matter.[28] The screenplay, however, emphasized the "documented" nature of Rico's career and retained many of the elements associated with the historical film, including the text foreword. On film, Rico first demonstrates his cleverness by surreptitiously

Little Caesar:
Rico alters
the clock.

altering the hands of a lunchroom clock in order to secure an alibi for
a robbery he has committed. Rico's manipulation of time and historical
events is in many ways analogous to the filmmakers' transformation of
Chicago gang wars and modern history. Operating under an increasingly
repressive censorship system that would have attacked any attempt at the
biographical glorification of a real gangster-hero like Capone,[29] the filmmakers obscured the historical details to suit their immediate needs. Yet
this parallel manipulation does not fool the audience. The film offers the
audience a more complete view of events—one that is denied to its participants (and to the censors). Rico is a version of Capone; he is real and
has committed the robbery.

Rico's destabilization of truth would motivate popular historians' accounts of postwar America and its preeminent figure, Al Capone. He and
his colleagues became the major historical figures of postwar America,
and they changed not only what appeared in print but also the way it was
written. The assassination of crime lord Big Jim Colosimo in 1920 introduced a new historical uncertainty to the era, an uncomfortable mixture
of fact and fiction. No one ever discovered the identity of Colosimo's killer
or the motive, although both Torrio and Capone, emblematic of the new
underworld order, were suspects. According to popular historian Walter
Noble Burns, no one knew for certain whether Capone was directly responsible for ordering the deaths of Dion O'Bannion, Hymie Weiss, John
Scalisi, Alberto Anselmi, Franky Uale, Bill McSwiggin, John Duffy, and
Jim Doherty.[30] It was a world where nothing could be proved, where truth

was occluded by contradictory tales, where no one saw what happened, where police, judges, newspapermen, and, by implication, popular historians all told lies.

Capone and his colleagues simply defied the tools of historiography, and popular historians of this era cited written documents in mockery of traditional historians and their approaches. In his history of the Chicago gangs, Burns cited two conflicting versions of Capone's alleged role in killing Assistant State's Attorney William McSwiggin in 1926.[31] In Fred Pasley's popular 1930 biography of Capone, he cited official documents and news copy only to point out their fallibility. In Capone's first newspaper appearance, the reporter spelled his name "Alfred Caponi" and got the story wrong.[32] Later, Pasley quoted the findings of the inquest following the murder of small-time hoodlum Joe Howard. Although witnesses saw Capone shoot him, they later had a "change of heart," and the intimidated jury refused to indict him.[33] This conflicted relationship between the expectations of traditional history and the untold, elliptical, often vague and contradictory modern history embodied by the gangster was epitomized by *The Finger Points* (Warner Brothers, 1931). W. R. Burnett and John Monk Saunders confronted this historical disruption by scripting the semidisguised career of Chicago reporter Jake Lingle. Lingle, killed by unknown persons in June 1930, was discovered to have been in the employ of both the "upper world" and the underworld. A reporter who was, it turned out, pursuing everything but truth, Lingle represented the ultimate corruption of the printed word by municipal government, law enforcement, and gangsters. Just as in *Little Caesar*, the film's omniscient presentation of the protagonist's increasing corruption contrasts with the press's bathetic manufacturing of headlines claiming nationwide mourning for a "martyr."

Although many professional historians were disillusioned by wartime propaganda and the government's successful impressment of formerly respected historians as wartime "writers," few were willing to choose the relativism of Carl Becker's and Charles Beard's antiheroic revisionist history, where historical objectivity was an impossible ideal.[34] But Burns and Pasley realized that writing about twentieth-century Chicago left few opportunities for traditional research and definitive conclusions. Their work ignored footnotes and bibliography, quoted word of mouth, presented multiple perspectives on a single event, admitted gaps and unknown information, and mixed facts with metaphors. Pasley concluded, "The Capone picture is never in focus with the realities. They merge into it to lose their factual identities and regularities of form as in a side-show distortion mirror, then to leer back in preposterous travesty, hoaxing reason and mocking the data of common sense. The picture is theatrical."[35]

Early in Burnett's *Little Caesar* script, Rico reads a news account of Diamond Pete's glamorous "underworld" party, and in his mind, he revises the news headlines and photographs. Later in the film, "Little Caesar" Bandello will replace Diamond Pete in the headlines and go down in the city's "history." Throughout both the final script and the film, Rico consults the papers, checking their documentation of his career, their accuracy, and the amount of ink he gets in each issue. Shots of newspaper inserts punctuate the narrative,[36] and although the paper is immediate, a reminder of contemporary life, it is also a printed document, a text insert within the film narrative; it is the postwar equivalent of contemporary historiography, since the major postwar historians and Capone's principal biographer were also reporters. Rico's constant reappraisal of the news is also the filmmakers' reappraisal of the history (text) of the 1920s. For Rico, the importance of the printed word lies not only in its ability to publicize his career and feed his vanity; it also provides a mark of permanence, of being "somebody" who is documented and a maker of history. The newspapers can make heroes. Naturally, Rico is never satisfied with what he reads. The papers and the historical record are always wrong. At one point in the script, he reads about the murder of McClure, a crime commissioner he shot at a nightclub. According to the papers, Rico was not recognized (even this notoriety would have pleased him), but the report describes the unknown murderer as "a small, unhealthy-looking foreigner." Rico reacts angrily, claiming indignantly that he is no foreigner, just as Capone once did when told that nativists condemned his career and linked his crime-ridden life to his Italian background.[37] Later, when a reporter asks Rico how he liked the paper's most recent story on him, Rico counters, "Where do you get that 'Little' Caesar, Scabby? There ain't nothing little about me." Rico's relationship to the text, the document, the stand-in for history, is one of both collaborator and critic. He determines what they see, but he never reads the truth. Even his death results from a dispute over a cop's printed interview about the rise and fall of Little Caesar.

The Risks of Filming Modern History

John Bright was one of the first historians to use the term *revisionist* in his satirical biography of William "Big Bill" Thompson. For Bright, the revisionist school was born in the postwar era, when Thompson and Capone would become some of the country's most public figures.[38] The law,

Small-time crook
Rico reads the headlines
for Diamond Pete.
(*Little Caesar*)

Little Caesar makes
the headlines.

PRISONER-JUDGE
IN BARGAIN

"LITTLE CAESAR" BANDELLO
GIVEN TESTIMONIAL BY
FOLLOWERS

FIVE ARE KILLED
AS TRAIN HITS
DERAILED CAR

Rico checks his
press coverage.
(*Little Caesar*)

official histories, and unbiased public information achieved comic deaths during Thompson's rule. Although Bright's historical perspective was not appreciated in Chicago,[39] in Hollywood, under Zanuck's direction, he would become one of the most prominent screenwriters of the postwar era. Warner Brothers' press book and advertising for *The Public Enemy* announced that the script, based on Bright and Glasmon's unpublished novel *Beer and Blood*, dramatized the lives of Terry Druggan and Franky Lake, two inventive brewery businessmen who shot to fame as associates in Al Capone's liquor empire.[40] *The Public Enemy* took the form of a double biopic, positioning the careers of "Tom" and "Matt" within the trajectory of twentieth-century American history.

Bright's second chronicle of Chicago carefully disguised the names of the two principal characters. Lake and Druggan had survived the 1920s, and neither Bright nor Zanuck wanted a slander suit. While Harvey Thew adapted their work, Zanuck was very cautious with regard to the Production Code. The narrative's violence, open defiance of the law, legal corruption, sex, and rough language all gave the censors something to carp about. In response to the numerous demands for revisions, Zanuck wrote to Code henchman Jason Joy, defending *The Public Enemy*. He promised that naturally the picture would prove the moral that "crime doesn't pay," but then he took the intellectual and artistic high ground, claiming, "Our picture is going to be a biography more than a plot."[41] Zanuck attempted to protect the film's artistic integrity from the censors by asserting *Public Enemy*'s historical content and accuracy, thereby linking it to the artistic and intellectual prestige of traditional historical filmmaking and justifying whatever potentially objectionable content the Production Code Administration (PCA) found. It was a strategy he would practice throughout his career. Although the film would not emerge unscathed, the PCA adopted Zanuck's attitude toward the subject matter, deeming it a "more or less correct account" of Chicago history.[42]

However, this deepening historical consciousness may have triggered the PCA's growing criticism of gangster films. *The Public Enemy* was subject to far more scrutiny and demands for censorship than Zanuck's earlier efforts, *Doorway to Hell* and *Little Caesar*. The PCA undoubtedly forced Zanuck and his script polisher, Thew, to alter many of the historical characters populating Bright and Glasmon's book; Al Capone was removed as a potential character in the film narrative, as were O'Bannion and Weiss.[43] Yet Zanuck's faith in the historical elements of this film was not mere camouflage for the PCA. Zanuck invested the script with a historical consciousness that the novel conspicuously lacked. In spite of *Beer and Blood's* historical cast, it had no historical exposition or analysis, and conversations were unmarked by time, place, or detail. As film historian Henry Cohen remarked, it was "personal encounter in dialogue and incident."[44]

Under Zanuck's supervision, *Beer and Blood* became a historical film, containing a textual structure of inserts and superimpositions to bolster the narrative. The structure of its biography is punctuated, or "chapterized," by a series of text inserts superimposed over shots of Chicago consisting of years in the city's history: 1909, 1915, 1917, and 1920.[45] Even the first shot of the film is an enormous insert of "1909," followed by archival footage of the city, the Loop, State Street, and the Union Stockyards. Although RKO had pioneered the sound-era use of multiple text inserts and date superimpositions in *Cimarron*, released in January, that film was in many ways the ultimate traditional American historical film—a chronicle of westward expansion and pioneers from 1889 to 1930. Zanuck's appropriation of this structure for *The Public Enemy* indicates that he placed postwar gangsters and crime within a historical process. Most important, for a twentieth-century "historical" narrative, archival film footage has the same status of historical documentation as the text of a newspaper or a superimposed date. But this period footage is almost indistinguishable from Wellman's "fictional" footage; there is no difference between the shots of early-morning commuters and the Loop and the shots of Tom (James Cagney) hustling beer. In the text of the film, both are part of Chicago's history.

The press noticed Zanuck's transformation of Hollywood's gangster cycle. *Variety* wrote, "It's low-brow material given such workmanship as to make it high-brow."[46] The gangster picture had entered the prestige

Establishing the period in *The Public Enemy*, 1931.

Documentary shots of
Chicago: State Street.
(*The Public Enemy*)

The Union Stockyards.
(*The Public Enemy*)

War is declared, but Tom
and Matt are oblivious.
(*The Public Enemy*)

league of the historical film. The reviewer drew attention to the historical structure of the film, listing the historical progression and the use of
date inserts. The last two inserts (1917 and 1920) specifically referred to
major events in American history and the main characters' rejection of
their import: American entrance into the First World War, and ratification of the Volstead Act sanctioning Prohibition. Tom and Matt ignore
and then scorn the patriotism of the war and make a killing off their defiance of the government during Prohibition. Significantly, after Tom and
Matt consolidate their beer industry and participate in a full-blown beer
racket run by Nails Nathan and Paddy Ryan, the inserts, emblematic of
the constraints of historical narrative and the boundaries of time and history, disappear. At the height of Prohibition and the Chicago gang wars,
time and the traditional structural trappings of historical cinema simply
vanish in the glare of the postwar era.

Late in *Public Enemy*'s production, Zanuck, in collusion with Thew,
Bright, and Glasmon, added one more element: a projected text foreword
resembling those beginning more traditional historical and biographical
film subjects of that era (*The Great Meadow, Cimarron, Alexander Hamilton*). These text inserts not only justified the films' historical significance
and accuracy but also lent the narratives a historical prestige and structural parity with traditional written history. Even though *Public Enemy*'s
foreword asserted the film's accuracy, it was unusually cautious. It testified
that the plot depicted a particular phase and "environment" in American
life and did not intend to glorify the life of the criminal, but then it continued, "While the story of *The Public Enemy* is essentially a true story,
all names and characters appearing herein, are purely fictional."[47] Again,
American film, like its gangland subjects, was under the censorious eye
of the government. Filmmakers, now under the stricter surveillance of
Will Hays—president of the Motion Picture Producers and Distributors
of America (MPPDA), author and enforcer of the Code—had to be careful that their historical accuracy did not glorify crime. Ironically, the only
recourse filmmakers had was to remove the original explosive historical
content or at least modify it. But the foreword's halfhearted concession to
the censors, stressing the film's status as contemporary fiction, was completely subverted by its claims to truth and the opening shot—the looming
specificity of "1909." Savvy film reviewers saw through the Code-imposed
subterfuges. Critic William Boehnel commented, "Anyone who has read
of Chicago's underworld will recognize characters and incidents immediately."[48] Boehnel also noticed that the film narrative contained a plethora
of historical details, such as the famous shooting of Nails Morton's horse,

Mummifying
the gangster.
(*The Public
Enemy*)

that were not strictly necessary to the story but added to the audience's
identification of Chicago's recent past.[49]

Like many of the popular histories of the Prohibition era, *The Public
Enemy* makes an analogy between America's involvement in the Great
War and the Volstead liquor wars that followed. Tom and his older brother Mike embody this connection. After "1917" is superimposed over the
screen and fades, Tom is first bewildered and then contemptuous when
he learns that his sanctimonious brother has joined up to fight in the
war for democracy. Tom stays home and gets rich linking up with Paddy
and Nails, while his veteran brother comes home from the war, still pale
and priggish, to plug away at a small job. Earlier, Tom had sneered that
by attending night school after work, his brother is "learning to be poor."
Yet Mike retains one thing from his war experience that will help him in
Chicago: grenades. In the final minutes of the film, Tom is shot and killed
by a rival gang, evidently paying for his crime (unlike the real Terry Druggan, who lived in luxury through the wars), and his murderers drop off his
body at the front door. When Mike opens it, Tom's body, mummified in
bandages—a visual relic and a stunning metaphor for the film's historical
transformation of the gangster—topples forward to the floor. Mike stares at
the corpse, his eyes filling with rage, and then he rises mechanically and
marches off past the camera. Here, contemporary release prints of the film
ended with a fulsome and incongruous text condemnation of the gangster
and his world, but Wellman's final shooting script and original shot footage

followed Mike to his room, where he opened a case of grenades brought home from France.[50] Wellman then planned to fade out on Mike's hands as he stuffs the grenades into his worn army trousers, intent on avenging his brother's death. The veteran thus becomes another criminal.

Evidence suggests that the filmmakers attempted to sneak the controversial conclusion past the censors; it was added late to the final script and then shot and reshot toward the end of February. However, the PCA's Jason Joy caught Zanuck and demanded that the scene be cut in order to end on an unequivocal condemnation of violence.[51] This scene also may have hit too close to the historical nerve for the censors, for here the filmmakers explicitly link the veteran with the gangster. Other studios would ponder the connection, particularly Columbia's *The Last Parade* (1931), in which the veteran protagonist turns to crime after the war.

Other contemporaneous historians wrote about the displacement of veterans and their manipulation by the government. Burns's 1931 history of Chicago's gang wars, *The One-Way Ride*, was the most comprehensive. Like *The Public Enemy*'s use of text and date superimpositions, Burns sought to give the disturbing stories and images of Chicago gangland some reassuring historical continuity. Known for his popular history of Tombstone and *The Saga of Billy the Kid*,[52] Burns framed Chicago and its gangsters as the natural inheritors of the Wild West.[53] The gangster was America's new lone hero, the Chicago rackets the new American mother lode, and Chicago the wildest and most lawless of the western cities. Burns began his study by comparing Colosimo to a pioneer striking a gold mine: "His pick was sunk up to the hilt in the lode of bootleg treasure."[54] Even those who despised gangsters as foreign, pleasure seeking, and effeminate could not resist the traditional lawless metaphor. Yet Torrio and Capone displaced the old-fashioned Colosimo as the preeminent gunmen of the new West, and with this new phase in gangland history, Burns could not avoid introducing analogies between the old West and the deadlier Western Front of recent memory. Just as Burns saw the old-style gangster Colosimo tied to the romanticized, violent heritage of the old West, so he likened the new, colder, more efficient generation of heroes to the bloodshed on the Western Front.[55] These gangsters lacked "the natural bravado of the outlaws of the western plains," and their perceived relevance to American history was measured not by frontier images of independence and exhilarating conflict but by distorted memories of the Great War. Rather than functioning as agents of national continuity, the modern gangster was a product of a war that had fractured an understanding of a unified and progressive past.[56]

Burns framed much of his gangland history with chapters alluding to Great War events and parlance, such as "Opening Guns of the War" and "The Western Front." Pasley named Capone's push to gain total dominance in the Chicago rackets "The Bootleg Battle of the Marne." This war began with the Capone gang's run-ins with the O'Donnell faction and ended with the St. Valentine's Day massacre; it was marked by frequent and often meaningless scraps accompanied by the press's screaming headlines, "This Is War!"[57] It is almost as if the war never ended for many veterans, and the Volstead Act and the ensuing public passion for liquor and lawbreaking only provided the battlefield for these modern heroes. Capone, Weiss, O'Bannion, Torrio, O'Donnell, and Morton were the postwar era's new heroes; displaced by one war, they were now arbiters of a new wartime "theater" with unstable historical boundaries.

Whereas Zanuck, Pasley, and Burns unequivocally set the gangster within the trajectory of America's past, social historian John Landesco rejected the notion of the gangster's continuity with American history. Hired by the Illinois Association for Criminal Justice, he published a meticulously researched social history of Chicago crime that claimed that the gangster and the law-abiding citizen "have been reared in two different worlds" and belong to separate cultures. Although his social history attempted to depict the gang environment from the "criminal" perspective, he cut off the gangster from the nation's values and history.[58] Landesco ignored the connections among the general postwar decline, the government's abuse of veterans and marginalized groups, and the rise of the gangster; if he had not, then men like Al Capone and Nails Morton would have been the natural outcome of America's "law-abiding" culture. Landesco's book quickly passed out of print when the Illinois Crime Commission disbanded.

In contrast, Zanuck, Pasley and Burns, who stressed the historical continuities between the gangster and mainstream American history, had an eager public. They placed Al Capone and his colleagues within the traditional framework of heroic American biography. Pasley's book is famously subtitled *The Biography of a Self-made Man*, likening Capone to Benjamin Franklin, Abraham Lincoln, and Andrew Carnegie.[59] He defined Capone as "Chicago's monument to civic thrust" and compared the underworld entrepreneur repeatedly to John D. Rockefeller.[60] By the late 1920s, Pasley claimed that Capone was not only the definitive "life" of his era but also a hero in the same category with Henry Ford, Charles Lindbergh, Mary Pickford, and Douglas Fairbanks. He quoted one Chicago official on Capone: "If he had only been honest, what a hero he would have made for a Horatio Alger tale."[61] But the days of Alger were gone; for many Americans, the Great War relegated these narratives to quaint anachronisms.

The Life of Al Capone

While Zanuck was in the process of organizing *The Public Enemy,* Howard Hughes was developing his own idea for a modern biopic. A multimillionaire and son of a Texas industrialist, Hughes began investing in motion pictures in the mid-1920s. In 1928 he produced his first gangster picture. *The Racket* began in 1927 as a Broadway hit by former Chicago crime reporter Bartlett Cormack and featured Edward G. Robinson in his only stage gangster role.[62] The character of Nick Scarsi was loosely based on Al Capone, but Cormack refrained from depicting real events in Chicago history or Capone's life, marginalizing Scarsi's role in favor of an incorruptible cop, McQuigg. The film script, directed by Lewis Milestone, also avoided condemnation by focusing on the tribulations of the honest cop and killing the magnetic Scarsi in the final scenes. It was successful, but Hughes wanted to produce something more daring—something with more basis in history. In his first sound film, *Hell's Angels* (1930), he turned to the exploits of fliers in the First World War but soon became interested in a different kind of battlefield. He was not coy about

Al Capone handles
the commissioner.
(Author's collection)

it; he planned his subject to be the life of Al Capone, thereby confronting the two battlegrounds of modern American culture: Chicago gangland history and Hollywood's Production Code Administration. Hughes hired maverick film director Howard Hawks for the inflammatory project. Although Hawks shared Hughes's renegade filmmaker status and contempt for Louis B. Mayer and the rest of the studio moguls, he had never made a historical film set in America. Hughes's most crucial production decision was the choice of the principal screenwriters: W. R. Burnett (author of *Little Caesar*), Fred D. Pasley (Capone biographer), and ex–Chicago reporter Ben Hecht. Whereas *Little Caesar*'s narrative structure manipulated the traits of early sound-era historical cinema, and *The Public Enemy* described many incidents recognizable within Chicago's gangland history, *Scarface* would take its engagement with modern history one step further. More than the other two critically acclaimed gangster pictures, *Scarface* was a biopic. It was also one of the most highly censored films in Hollywood's history, mostly due to its alleged glorification of the life of Al Capone. Like Zanuck, *Scarface*'s producer hired "historical experts" on Chicago's early Prohibition era to supervise production. *Scarface*'s principal screenwriter was, in a sense, part of this category.

Ben Hecht, a former reporter for the *Chicago Daily News*, had left the New York literary world a few years earlier, based on the advice of successful Hollywood screenwriter Herman J. Mankiewicz, who told him that huge money could be made working for the film industry. Hecht's first effort, *Underworld* (1927), an early silent gangster film, drew loosely on his knowledge of Thompson and Capone in Chicago, but it had no historical elements or recognizable references to the alleged character templates. The antiheroes were merely urban types. But by 1931, sound had transformed the gangster film. Film historian Jonathan Munby recently emphasized the revolutionary aspect of hearing ethnic speech, but more significant to film producers at the time was the talking gangster's authenticity. Urban speed and accent made him more real than his silent predecessors, and in the early 1930s, when the artistic viability of the talkies was still in contention, the added authenticity of sound film was a major argument in its favor. Inevitably linked to the industry's new pursuit of authenticity was the emerging cycle's appropriation of history. The gangsters not only looked and talked like real gangsters; they *were* real gangsters. But Hecht's next gangster script, *Scarface*, had more than *Underworld*'s perfunctory interest in real incidents and people.

Burnett, Pasley, and Hecht based their material on Armitage Trail's pulp novel, *Scarface*.[63] Although Howard Hawks later claimed that

Hughes's Caddo Company had paid Trail only for the use of the suggestive title,[64] Trail's novel, like Bright and Glasmon's *Beer and Blood,* provided a lurid and powerful historical background from which to project
a gangster biopic. Trail named his hero Tony Guarino and provided him
with a crooked cop for a brother, but the urban pulp novel still resembled
a popular biography of Capone.[65] He dramatized Capone's hazy New
York career, his small-time beginnings as an assassin in Chicago, and his
partnership with and eventual displacement of Johnny Torrio. Most curious is Trail's explanation of his protagonist's nickname and the book's
title. Hounded by the police and bored with his fractious moll, Tony goes
to a movie alone. As Trail relates: "America had entered the World War
but a few days before and the screen flashed an appeal for volunteers to
join the army for immediate overseas service. Tony wondered what sort
of saps would fall for that. Not he. What did he owe the country? What
had the country ever done for him?"[66] Tony Guarino, like Tom in *The
Public Enemy,* initially scoffs at patriotic appeals. Yet after killing a pair
of thugs, he enlists—in a machine gun company. Like Nails Morton, he
acquires his scar, wins the Croix de Guerre, and returns to Chicago an
anonymous doughboy. The war and the government have taught him
"the fine art of murder" and provided him with the tools and strategy to
fight another war.[67] Trail novelized Capone's own imaginative autobiography, but it would take the gritty speech of Hecht's Chicago, Paul Muni's
ethnic toughness, and a vigorous press and censorship campaign to reify
the controversies of filming contemporary history.

The screenwriters retained the novel's reference to Capone and reconstructed a biopic along the lines of Pasley's *Biography of a Self-made
Man.* Up until that point in his eclectic and prolific literary career, Hecht
had never attempted to write a popular history, and Burnett, far more experienced with gang and historical scripts, would later claim that Hecht
only polished their efforts. However, Hecht knew both Burns and Pasley
from his Chicago newspaper days and sought their historical knowledge
in framing his script.[68] Burnett, Pasley, and Hecht's script, later rewritten and doctored by writers John Lee Mahin and Seton I. Miller, loosely
followed Pasley's popular biography. In fact, it introduces Scarface (Paul
Muni) in a Twenty-second Street barbershop shortly after Colosimo's assassination. As the barber crosses out the dead gangster's name from his
shaving mug, a cop asks, "Where's Scarface?" The script then describes
the young protagonist as he sits in the barber's chair. He removes the
towel covering his face. His scars gleam in the light. It is Capone.

Unlike *Little Caesar* and *The Public Enemy,* *Scarface* does not begin with an epigraph or foreword (neither on paper nor on the screen). Dated newspaper inserts are used sparingly, and there are no superimposed dates or historical intertitles to textually guide the audience through Scarface's public and private life. And yet, like its predecessors, the film does begin with a text shot linking it to its historical referent. The first scripted shot fades in on a Chicago street sign, Twenty-second Street and Wabash Avenue, perhaps the most notorious intersection in America during the Prohibition era. This corner was at the heart of Capone's South Side and the site of many of his most sensational alleged crimes. The narrative outlined in the script then follows the pattern established by the major histories of the Chicago gangs: The affable and aging Colisimo (Colosimo) is gunned down in his own cabaret by a shadowy, "unknown" gunman. The cold businessman Johnny Lovo (Torrio) takes over his rackets with the assistance of his loud-mouthed, fancy-dressing, scarfaced lieutenant, Tony Camonte (Capone). But Camonte, unlike Lovo, is a glutton for press coverage and loves seeing his name in print. When Camonte later commandeers power, he boasts that his machine gun is a new instrument for writing history: "I'm goin' to write my name all over this town." His machine gun, like Hawks's camera, will rewrite Chicago's history.

Although *The Public Enemy* maintained a cast of recognizable Chicago hoodlums, Zanuck was forced to change their names in all but one case ("Nails" Nathan). *Scarface's* extant scripts reveal that the team of screenwriters used the historical names and sites, only occasionally altering the spelling: Colosimo became Colisimo, O'Bannion became Bannon, Moran became Doran, and Capone became Camonte.[69] Although this evidence suggests that the screenwriters were under the impression that they were writing a traditional biopic or souped-up history of the 1920s Chicago gang wars, by the time production began, Hawks had become more cautious about the excessive historical details. His copy of the script contains multiple penciled annotations calling for the changing of names and Chicago locales. Early on page three, he told Miller and the other dialogue writers to "change everything identifying locale as Chicago and everything identifying characters."[70] Evidently, the film endured a gradual screening process to dilute its historical character. Historical scholarship would doubtless attribute this effacement to Hollywood's overmastering mythic discourse and lack of historical accuracy, but this view only explains why a film would ignore historical aspects from the beginning. *Scarface* began as a rigorously historical film but was subsequently altered.

Who killed Big Jim
in 1920?
(*Scarface*)

Courting "press-tige."
(*Scarface*)

Writing history with a
new instrument—the
machine gun.
(*Scarface*)

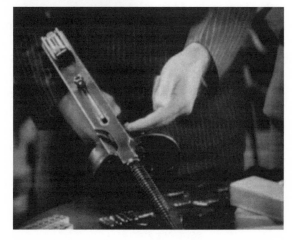

The reasons lie with the PCA and the fear of screening an unapologetic Capone biopic without even the obvious ruses of *The Public Enemy*. In March 1931, Jason Joy of the PCA noted that Hughes and Hawks were in the process of making a film "to be based on the life of Al Capone and to be called 'Scarface.'"[71] Already the censors worried about what a few facts could do to the reputation of the film business and, most embarrassingly, to the government. In a letter to Hughes dated 1 May 1931, Joy fretted: "The motion picture industry has for a long time . . . maintained its right to produce purely fictional underworld stories . . . *but has, on the other hand, admitted the grave danger of portraying on the screen actual contemporary happenings relating to deficiencies in our government, political dishonesty and graft, current crimes or anti-social or criminal activities.*"[72] When gangster films were contained by fiction, the censors knew they were harmless, but historical gangster pictures were dangerous. According to Joy, Capone was the worst possible subject for a biopic, since he was the most dangerous of these evil forces. Censors kept an unrelenting watch on the film's progress for months, complained that it glorified Capone's life, and demanded that the script show Camonte to be a "yellow rat" in the final police battle and that he be tried and hanged. Hays and his associates were particularly maddened by the title and its obvious reference to Capone. They pressured Hughes to change the title to either "Yellow" or "Shame of the Nation." Hughes fought for his title and its historical specificity, undoubtedly angered by the censors' suggestion to drop the Capone angle and instead add a foreword that described the film's subject more generally as "the gangster."[73] He was even more incensed when Hays demanded an additional foreword narrated by the police commissioner of New York condemning all crime. But in late 1931, there was little Hughes could do. Faced with the prospect of Hays's refusal to grant *Scarface* a license, he reshot the ending and promised to make all the changes specified by the PCA.

Yet the PCA's attempts to write Capone out of the film's historical record failed on two counts. When the New York and Chicago censor boards still rejected the revised *Shame of the Nation*, Hughes felt betrayed by Hays and Joy; he was also convinced that MGM's Louis B. Mayer, a close friend of Hays, was attempting to prevent successful innovations by independent competitors with the use of extreme censorship.[74] Hughes, a rich renegade, was a minority but a potential threat to Mayer's more mundane production line. In an unprecedented decision, Hughes and his press director Lincoln Quarberg engineered a press showing of the original *Scarface* in Hollywood and New York. The critics' extravagant praise and uniform condemnation of Hays and Joy encouraged him to chance the repercussions of state censorship and release the film in different national markets without all the alterations stipulated by the PCA. He began to recall and destroy all the tainted, censored prints and stocked theaters with the real version.[75] Hays, reeling from the press's criticism, tried to claim that the original *Scarface* was the censored version he had approved in late 1931. Few listened.

Scarface remained *Scarface*, and soon audiences recognized the high points of Capone's historic career: the O'Donnell and O'Bannion beer wars, the assassination of O'Bannion and Weiss, the fall of Torrio, the St. Valentine's Day massacre. But the unprecedented campaign by the censors to remove the historical aspects of the narrative also failed because of the national publicity and scorn it attracted in the press. The public read about the many attempts to repress the Capone screen biography, and at the theaters, audiences associated Lovo with Torrio and Camonte with Capone with ease. The major national reviewers referred to *Scarface* as the "Capone film," often quoting the historical allusions the censors had taken such pains to suppress.[76] But screenwriter, playwright, and critic Robert E. Sherwood's "Moving Picture Album" review in the *Hollywood Citizen-News* expressed the wrath of many filmmakers toward the censors. Hughes's people had approached Sherwood in the early stages of Hays's campaign to destroy the film, and after seeing the original version in New York, Sherwood became *Scarface*'s champion: "The possible merits of 'Scarface' as entertainment, or its importance as a sociological or historical document, are of no particular consequence in the argument that should be made for its free release. All that matters is that an utterly

Happy Valentine's Day
from Tony Camonte.
(*Scarface*)

inexcusable attempt has been made to suppress it—not because it is obscene, not because it is corruptive, or libelous, or blasphemous, or subversive—but because, like 'Public Enemy,' it comes too close to telling the truth."[77] As one of America's most astute and respected film critics, Sherwood recognized that *Scarface*'s greatest danger was that it came too close to being a historical film. The perils of filmmakers dealing with modern history, of becoming modern historians with the modern historiographical tool of film, were too much for many people outside the industry. Although the life of Abraham Lincoln[78] or Alexander Hamilton might safely bore people in the theaters, placing Capone and his cohorts in the same category and using the same tools for historical filmmaking was simply, as Sherwood put it, "too close to telling the truth" about what had happened to history and heroes in modern America. *Scarface* may have earned only a modest run in theaters, but its near destruction and controversial subject easily made it the most discussed film of 1932.

Although film scholarship would later cite these classical Hollywood gangster films' inherent "modernity" as the source of their subversive narratives and the PCA's censorship campaigns, reviewing them as historical films rather than Hollywood fantasies or modern myths reveals far more dangerous elements. As their production histories and reception attest, these films, in particular *The Public Enemy* and *Scarface*, were constructed as histories of postwar America, reinterpretations of the nationalist tendencies of traditional historiography and the canon of American "heroes." The structures of historical cinema could narrate the lives of both Abraham Lincoln and Al Capone. As veterans became indistinguishable from gangsters, so journalism became only the first stage of historiography, and filmmakers became historians. The Great War, Prohibition, and the criminal empires of Al Capone, Dion O'Bannion, Terry Druggan, Franky Lake, and Johnny Torrio were their historical material; *Doorway to Hell, Little Caesar, The Public Enemy,* and *Scarface* turned the text of America's postwar history into a script.

The End of an Era

MGM's *Manhattan Melodrama* (1934) was arguably the last of the "historical" gangster films of the early 1930s. It references historical events such as the Arnold Rothstein killing, and it contains newspaper inserts and superimposed dates. Since it was a period gangster film, the PCA reacted with its characteristic aversion to representing contemporary history.[79] For once, Jason Joy had nothing to worry about. Like MGM's other gangster picture, *The Secret Six* (1931), the filmmakers were out to put the criminal behind bars. In fact, *The Secret Six*, a bowdlerized story of Eliot Ness's hunt for Capone (the crime lord Scorpio), was the first crime film passed by Chicago's censorship board without cuts.[80] In preparing *Manhattan Melodrama*, MGM attempted to make its historical content and allusions as banal and uncontroversial as possible. Set in New York, Oliver H. P. Garrett's narrative avoided dramatizing the lives of the more infamous Chicago gangsters and therefore did not arouse the widespread historical recognition of the press and public. Only its exhibitors' advertising manual linked the film to other historical gangster successes such as *Scarface* and *Little Caesar*, which "were based on the life and career of Al Capone."[81] Initially, Garrett linked his heroes Blackie and Jim Wade to Zanuck and Hughes's historical gangsters by giving their war experiences textual prominence. Later versions of the script, doctored by Joe Mankiewicz, eliminated the connection between the gangster and the veteran.[82] Although the film was punctuated by dated text inserts, MGM's use of historical structures was merely an attempt at prestige gloss.

However meager its internal commitment to representing historical events, following one Chicago screening, *Manhattan Melodrama* unwittingly became an event in the final chapters of gangster history. With Capone's conviction for income tax evasion in 1931, John Dillinger, a smaller-scale but charismatic bank robber, became the public's favorite lawbreaker for a short time. Dillinger was also an avid movie fan, and in 1934 he was murdered by federal agents shortly after seeing *Manhattan Melodrama* at Chicago's Biograph Theatre. Ironically, Dillinger's death provided the screen censors with ammunition to end the cycle. Although studios were eager to film Public Enemy Number One's biography, the censors anticipated the resurgence of gangster films, and in 1935, Hays imposed a moratorium on their production.[83]

Although gangster films continued to appear until 1935, even those based on historical events, such as Twentieth Century–Fox's *Now I'll Tell* (1934) and Warner Brothers' *Dr. Socrates* (1935), were mostly low-budget endeavors, indifferently marketed by the studios and indifferently received by the critics. *Now I'll Tell* was scripted from the memoirs of Mrs. Arnold Rothstein and attracted some industrial attention as an "authentic" document of Rothstein's career and his infamous love of racing and baseball.[84] Like *The Public Enemy*, Mrs. Rothstein's script began with a text foreword and a 1909 setting. But Zanuck's interest in recording the real events of gang history had waned. The film's sloppy marketing and rapid disappearance from the theaters indicated that the producer had found more lucrative historical ventures.

A few months after producing *The Public Enemy*, Zanuck released his safer, more traditional American biography *Alexander Hamilton*, which caused no run-ins with the Production Code. Zanuck's bloody, disjunctive, elliptical, and troubling modern histories gave him unprecedented control over the direction of an evolving cycle balanced precariously between objectivity and distortion, journalism and history, heroes, veterans, and villains. But by 1935, the costs of confronting the nation's violent postwar heritage, its ambivalent heroes, and the uncertain evidence were too high. As head of Twentieth Century and later Twentieth Century–Fox, Zanuck took fewer obvious risks with modern American history and honed his historical acumen with biographies of Samuel Mudd (1936), Jesse James (1939), Alexander Graham Bell, Abraham Lincoln, Stephen Foster, Lillian Russell (1940), and Belle Starr (1941). Although he continued to explore marginalized historical events, government injustice, and ambivalent national heroes, he would avoid historicizing criminal figures of his own generation.

At Warner Brothers, *Dr. Socrates*, based on a country surgeon's secret operation on John Dillinger and written by W. R. Burnett (*Little Caesar*), shared a similar fate. Original scripted references linking Jesse James to the modern gangster were minimized.[85] There were no more historical references to Chicago or textual trappings, and the press releases tended to disguise their historical approximations rather than to capitalize on them.[86] It was Paul Muni's last gangster film, but significantly, he did not play the Dillinger stand-in, "Red Bastion." He, like Zanuck, soon turned to safer biographical roles (*The Life of Emile Zola*, 1937). Undoubtedly, censorship and the 1935 moratorium crippled the cycle. In fact, Hays and the censors did their best to write the historical gangster out of film history. Jack Warner and Hughes were repeatedly denied the right to rerelease *Little Caesar*, *The Public Enemy*, and *Scarface* in theaters after 1935.[87]

Instead, Hays permitted New York cop Johnny Broderick to get star treatment from Edward G. Robinson in the Warner Brothers action biopic *Bullets or Ballets* (1936). It was moderately successful, and *New York Times* film critic Frank S. Nugent dutifully noted the main character's similarities to Broderick,[88] but the film did not receive the attention and critical acclaim of Robert E. Sherwood's filmed Broadway hit *The Petrified Forest* (1936), which allegorized the life and career of Dillinger. By 1936, Warner Brothers had to look to Broadway for the challenging modern biographies it had once pioneered. Although Humphrey Bogart's performance as Duke Mantee electrified Hollywood, the film narrative existed in a timeless world unmarked by the textual references of the former historical gangster films. The setting, after all, is a desolate roadhouse in the petrified forests of the Arizona desert, far from the documented world of Chicago and the well-publicized details of Dillinger's career. A few years later, when Zanuck filmed John Steinbeck's "history" of the early 1930s Oklahoma dustbowl, *The Grapes of Wrath* (1940), Nunnally Johnson, perhaps the most famous historical screenwriter at Twentieth Century–Fox, removed Steinbeck's analogy between Tom Joad and the well-known Dust Bowl bandit and associate of John Dillinger, Pretty Boy Floyd. The producer and his top screenwriter had learned a lesson regarding film and contemporary history and resisted the temptation to make *The Grapes of Wrath* a historical film documenting the early 1930s exodus to California.[89] Instead, Zanuck moved back to the more traditional fields of entertainment biographies and Civil War history.

Warner Brothers, though, had not quite finished filming the Roaring Twenties. In 1937, the studio tentatively remembered its gangster past in the opening sequence of the contemporary melodrama *That Certain Woman*, with a shot of the headstone of a former Chicago crime lord. "Al Haines" had been killed in 1929 in Capone's St. Valentine's Day massacre, but his memory still haunted Bette Davis's young widow Mary. She, and Warner Brothers, could not escape their past.

Part Two

Resolving Westward Expansion

3

Competing Frontiers,
1933–1938

The moving picture has entered into a new phase of development. It has outgrown the small clothes of theater and fiction. Producers are beginning to realize at long last that they must not go to "proved" sources so much as to original sources of material.

—Frances Taylor Patterson, *North American Review*, 1937

While censorship dismantled the production of historical gangster films, from 1932 to 1935, the studios were equally unable to produce another *Cimarron*. For Hollywood, 1931 and 1932 were the worst years of the Depression, and the studios produced few expensive American historical films. Prestige westerns such as *The Big Trail, The Great Meadow,* and *Cimarron* gave way to more modest gunfighter adaptations such as *Destry Rides Again* (1932), *Law and Order* (1932), and *Frontier Marshal* (1934). Decades later, film and cultural studies of the western claimed that the genre disappeared with the conversion to sound.[1] Due to the financial "disasters" of *The Big Trail* and *Cimarron*, studios supposedly handed the worn genre to Poverty Row and Gene Autry. According to historical tradition, it was only in 1939 with the release of John Ford's *Stagecoach* that the western returned.

This powerful myth has thrived over the years on a very narrow but highly structured definition of the western genre pushed by Robert Warshow, John Cawelti, Will Wright, and John Tuska in the 1970s. The classic western, though roughly reflecting widespread cultural beliefs about

America's frontier past, was supposedly incapable of a critical interpretation of western history. Even more than the Hollywood gangster genre, the western was said to dramatize the definitive national myth. Rigidly constructed, it employed set binary oppositions (cowboy versus Indian, white versus red, civilization versus savagery), predictable conflicts and resolutions, and simple formulas unsullied by the course of time. Film historian Peter Stanfield recently corrected the fallacy of the "empty" decade of the 1930s,[2] but like his predecessors, he defined the essence of the western as the frontier cowboy-and-Indian paradigm. Though recovering part of the "lost trail" of 1930s westerns, Stanfield's conservative definition excludes much of the studios' historical development and remixing of the genre.

It is true that the powerful western myth, hallowed in the silent era, disappeared from major film production during the Great Depression, but the western did not. Filmmakers such as Darryl Zanuck, Edward Small, and Cecil B. DeMille did not develop a film genre or cycle within the circumscribed structuralist rules of late twentieth-century film history. Instead, they spent much of the 1930s reinventing the western, trying different approaches and historical topics and mixing cycles and genres. *Cimarron's* eclectic, conflicted, multiracial, feminist West provided a rich and unfamiliar historical approach to the American cinema's most enduring genre. For filmmakers who remembered *The Covered Wagon* or *The Iron Horse*, *Cimarron* meant both a redemption of the prestigious silent westerns and a transformation of their mythic discourse of heroic progress into a more self-conscious presentation of American history. Between *Cimarron's* release and the explosion of the "superwestern" in 1939, Hollywood tested the borders of major western filmmaking as never before. Between 1933 and 1938, the historical western was a rich and contested frontier where issues of racial instability, the myths of gender and heroism, and national narratives of progress fought within conflicting strategies of film production. There were western musicals, Mae West vehicles, frontier epics, critiques of frontier epics, narratives about mixed-blood Americans, and biographies of frontier women.

Many of the films discussed in this chapter descended from authors who scorned traditional views of history and chose to write their revisionist accounts of the American frontier as historical novels. Like Edna Ferber, James Fenimore Cooper (*The Last of the Mohicans*, 1826) and Helen Hunt Jackson (*Ramona*, 1884) sought more accurate views of the past, often courting controversy and the disdain of professional historians. But their more accessible historical novels also captured the wider popular audience denied to their colleagues' moldering texts. Their conviction to articulate a new historiography, both in form and in content, and to reach a larger audience significantly influenced screenwriting's impact on the production of American historical cinema. It also drove filmmakers John Balderston, Lamar Trotti, Darryl Zanuck, Frank Lloyd, and Howard Estabrook in many irreconcilable ways.

Who Was "Andy" Oakley?

Despite the failure of *The Conquerors* in 1932, RKO continued to adapt and produce films set in the national past. But the period melodramas *Little Women* (1933) and *The Age of Innocence* (1934) were relatively low-maintenance narratives, requiring no grandiose on-location shots or epic battle scenes or the lengthy preliminary research needed for an original historical screenplay. Although lacking forewords and superimposed dates, the narratives relied on a period setting and the passage of years, in which women either determined the course of the narrative or destabilized its settled traditions. Jo March and Ellen Olenska dominated their nineteenth-century worlds, but unlike Sabra Cravat, they lacked the prepossessing historical structures and support of *Cimarron's* account of American history from 1889 to 1930. Warner Brothers and Twentieth Century–Fox had taken the lead in writing impressive if dull biographies of men, whereas American women seemed to operate within the confines of popular fiction.[3] As George Custen noted in his study of classical Hollywood biographical films, filmed American history seemed the conventional province of "great men."[4]

Once again, RKO redeemed women in American history with its 1935 production of *Annie Oakley*. According to the RKO story department, the Oakley biopic was based on a "semi-historical biographical romance" by Joseph A. Fields and Ewart Adamson.[5] It is likely that the Fields-Adamson story and much of the narrative detail were culled from the recently published popular biography of Oakley by Courtney Ryley Cooper.[6] Hard times had befallen RKO since *Cimarron's* release. The studio could no longer afford to invest in a prestigious historical tale by Edna Ferber, but it found the virtually copyright-free field of history a cheaper means of appropriating material. But the studio had also cut its most experienced screen historian. Howard Estabrook's once enormous research resources and salary had been pared down to fit hack writers Joel Sayre and John Twist, and the whole production of *Annie Oakley* cost less than $320,000.[7] Despite the script's preoccupation with Annie's shooting rivalry and romance with "Toby Taylor," *Annie Oakley* retained vestiges of RKO's historical prestige. Although there were no intertitles or date superimpositions, Annie's illustrious career was documented in a series of newspaper headlines and articles. Eventually, as production wrapped, the filmmakers added a suitably impressive text foreword: "No fiction is stranger than the actual life of Annie Oakley who came out of a backwoods village half a century ago to astonish the world."[8]

Yet, the filmmakers were hesitant to present a screen biography of a woman popularly recognized as the greatest shot in the world. When the hastily arranged shooting match with the renowned Toby Taylor is announced, the spectators assume that the mysterious challenger "A. Oakley" must be Andy Oakley. No one has ever heard of *him*. When Taylor discovers the identity of his opponent, he refuses to compete with her. Annie asks, "Just because I'm not a man, you won't let me try?" He finally agrees. With the first shot, it is obvious that she is the better marksman. This scene is the first of many scripted questionings of the veracity of the printed word. Here, as in *Cimarron* and *Little Caesar*, one has to trust what is seen, not read, just as filmed history, by implication, is more interesting and accurate than traditional texts. Yet RKO's screenwriters were uncomfortable with the historical truth. Although Annie wins her match in the first draft, in subsequent scripts, she thwarts her own skill, first claiming that Taylor let her win, and then deliberately missing her last shot to assuage his ego. The original estimating script planned for Annie to win the match, but not from her own efforts. Instead, Taylor was supposed to do the chivalrous thing and generously allow her to win the last shot. An accompanying newspaper insert would reinforce Taylor's actions by describing his gentlemanly deference to a lady, but a country musician would scoff at the story, saying, "Nobody believes newspaper talk," thus adding to the untrustworthy nature of textual histories within historical film.[9] These early scripts confronted not only the construction of history by the press but also the distortions of dime novelists. When Buffalo Bill decides to make Oakley a shooting legend in his Wild West Show, he promises that soon her "life" will be documented in the dime novels. But later the filmmakers dispel any assumption of text "prestige" when a close-up shows Bill chortling over a "Buffalo Bill" novel's inaccuracies and excesses.[10] Film's essential capacity to represent the "real" Buffalo Bill scoffing over his "biography" (rather than resorting to the ludicrous textual constructions of the dime novels) acknowledges visual history's superiority over printed accounts.

Originally entitled "Shooting Star," late in production the filmmakers decided to lend Annie Oakley's screen life some additional historical clout by identifying it specifically as a biography. They added a text foreword, and the publicity department focused on the film's historical aspects. Publicists even claimed that Annie Oakley was "a gold mine to the great showmen who sponsored her miraculous career a half century ago and she will prove another box office bonanza to the showmen of 1935 as she lives again in the picture that bears her name."[11] Oakley's life certainly had advantages as a film biopic, in that she was first constructed as a show business star; this paralleled the rise of actress Barbara Stanwyck, who played Annie, from Brooklyn foster child to Broadway showgirl to Hollywood star. To a certain extent, *Annie Oakley* functioned as a double biography of Oakley and Stanwyck, with one life reinforcing the other for 1930s audiences.[12] Annie Oakley was both a show-woman and part of the showmanship of public history (Buffalo Bill's Wild West Show). Although the history of her life was fascinating, even more magical was her life in Buffalo Bill's public forum of revived western history. "His wild west shows, still alive in the recollections of many, established a towering monument to a brilliant period in American showmanship and did more to immortalize a fierce period of history than did the harrowing events themselves," claimed RKO's publicity department.[13] It was a subtle way of insinuating the superiority of performed histories over the actual or written event. But of course, film "historiography" trumps all its predecessors. Even Buffalo Bill's Wild West Show, a famous early visual history later credited with codifying many myths of the West,[14] is demystified by a film biography that shows Oakley's life before and behind the tents.

Many films in the early sound era would explicitly link a powerful and disruptive woman with the development of the West. She was often a glamorous show-woman, her songs and performances destabilizing the predetermined and comparatively dull historical record. *Belle of the Nineties* (1934), *Klondike Annie* (1936), *Naughty Marietta* (1935), *San Francisco* (1936), and *Girl of the Golden West* (1938) are undoubtedly the most prominent of these films, and although Mae West's hip swinging and Jeanette MacDonald's singing often upstaged the scripted period frontier locale, the character often engaged in a dynamic relationship with the Wild West. West and MacDonald were two of Paramount's and MGM's biggest stars, and their greatest successes were in period films. Mae West's first starring vehicle at Paramount was in an adaptation of her own Gay Nineties play *She Done Him Wrong* (1933). Later, West's disruptive presence revitalized the myth of western history and the frontier experience in *Klondike Annie*.[15] Although she continued to appear in period stories un-

Mae West in *She
Done Him Wrong*
(1933): resisting
ties to history.

til 1940, West refused to play an identifiable historical character. She told
historian and sometime-screenwriter Stuart Lake, who offered to write
her a role as Lillian Russell or Lillie Langtry, that real historical roles were
not right for her screen persona.[16] West preferred to avoid the demands
and expectations of historical cinema.

Jeanette MacDonald's career followed a similar route. In the early
1930s she changed studios, leaving Paramount's contemporary love stories for MGM's period glamour. Although she never played a recognizable historical figure, MacDonald's characters always fled to the American
frontier and changed it. In *Naughty Marietta*, she and Nelson Eddy shun
France, colonial New Orleans, and the rule of law and disappear into the
wilderness. In Anita Loos's *San Francisco*, country girl Mary Blake arrives
in the music halls of the Barbary Coast and eventually becomes "Queen
of the Coast." She sings the city's anthem at the annual Chickens' Ball,
and the 1906 earthquake brings down the house, purging San Francisco
of its unruly past. Yet in spite of the sense of historical period structured
throughout the text,[17] major Hollywood studios such as Paramount and
MGM continued to sublimate history to the wills of their most prominent stars. And although RKO's *Annie Oakley* challenged traditional film
biographies of great men, the other major studios had yet to present a
fully developed historical western along the lines of *Cimarron*, one that
engaged the complex problems of national origins, the displacement of
Native Americans, and the articulation of a series of events.

But in 1936, several studios, perhaps gathering momentum from the
growth in adaptations of literary classics and historical films, tackled the

problems of national history, the frontier, and racial identity. Studio executives developed two methods of producing historical westerns. Some returned to classic historical novels that had achieved prior success in silent pictures, and others turned to popular histories, a new approach that was still in keeping with Hollywood's new self-imposed role as creator of serious historical cinema. The relative success of, and the historical research and attitudes articulated by, *The Last of the Mohicans* (1936), *Ramona* (1936), and *Wells Fargo* (1937) not only offer surprising insights into *Cimarron's* legacy but also reveal the conflicting paths that western film historiography would take after 1937.

James Fenimore Cooper's American History

In March 1935, screenwriter John Balderston was convinced that James Fenimore Cooper's novel *The Last of the Mohicans* (1826) would make a great "historical 'epic' picture." He wrote to independent producer Edward Small, "What I mean by 'epic' is a picture that deals with a vaster and more important theme of general and permanent historical significance than is involved in the fortunes of the human being whose stories are involved." Balderston's distinction between history, which elucidates complex and widespread historical events, and biography, which focuses on one cinematic life (such as George Arliss's set of biopics), created an intellectual and financial hierarchy in American historical cinema. The screenwriter acknowledged the rarity of true epic films, quoting the pure line started by *The Birth of a Nation*, continued by *The Covered Wagon*, and culminating in *Cimarron*. He predicted that Cooper's *Last of the Mohicans* could be the next in line. Its narrative, he believed, could provide the basis for an epic precisely because of its historical content, the 1757 massacre at Fort William Henry.[18]

It was curiously appropriate that Cooper's *Last of the Mohicans* was expected to inherit *Cimarron's* mantle as the next great American historical film. Both Edna Ferber and Cooper were historical novelists with a jaundiced view of traditional American historiography. Both eschewed the pedantry of historians but conducted rigorous research on their subjects. Both explored the role of the mixed-blooded American in their work and, through these biracial protagonists, succeeded in producing an alternative view of a formative period in American history. More recently, late-twentieth-century academics described their work as part of a foundational American mythic discourse. As a film, *Cimarron* has been imprisoned in the late-twentieth-century critical framework of the western genre, one that denied the film's representation of historical arguments and complex events and insisted that it was part of a pattern of mythic western archetypes. Cooper's novel also suffered from this criticism. Cultural historians such as Richard Slotkin considered *Last of the Mohicans* to be the definitive national myth.[19]

In Slotkin's trilogy on the frontier myth in American culture, *The Last of the Mohicans* serves as a bridge linking early American captivity narratives to the nineteenth-century imagination of a unique American character and later to the twentieth-century genre of western films. According to Slotkin, elements of American culture (such as Cooper's novel) are myths reflecting the country's deep ideological investment in a romanticized view of its past. These myths dramatize history, simplify it, and reduce it to "a constellation of compelling metaphors."[20] Although historical events may generate a novel like *Mohicans*, the novel is not historical. Slotkin's argument for the novel's mythic status, like his later work on the Hollywood cinema, depends on Cooper's (and his text's) lack of a self-conscious and critical attitude toward American history.[21]

However, Cooper's first preface to the novel deliberately constructs his role as a historian. He defines his book as a "narrative" and dismisses a potential audience anticipating fantasy: "The reader, who takes up these volumes, in expectation of finding an imaginary and romantic picture of things which never had an existence, will probably lay them aside, disappointed."[22] He continues with an abbreviated ethnography of the native peoples indigenous to the New York frontier of his narrative and even punctuates his wholly fictitious account of the Munro daughters' adventures in New York with footnotes on the accuracy of the text.[23] Although scholars have questioned Cooper's vaunted historical accuracy,[24] the novelist's deliberate historical construction of the narrative remains. Over the years, however, that historical structure has been severely compromised. The first American edition gave equal weight to the two parts of Cooper's complete title: *The Last of the Mohicans: A Narrative of 1757.*[25] Following Cooper's death, editions began to minimize and even exclude the historical subtitle, thereby emphasizing the elegiac, mythic character of the book.

Within the text, Cooper's critical attitude toward the past takes many forms. His omniscient historical asides impugn both the presence of the European armies in America and Britain's own impending imperial decline.[26] Yet during his description of the massacre at Fort William Henry, he condemns not only the course of historical events but also the extant historiography. Late-eighteenth- and early-nineteenth-century historians

noted General Montcalm's callous inaction during the massacre of the
British garrison, but they often bowdlerized or dismissed the gruesome
eyewitness accounts.[27] Cooper scorned these deficiencies and, after recounting his history of the massacre, set his role as a historical novelist
above that of a "professional" historian. "The bloody and inhuman scene
. . . is now becoming obscured by time; and thousands, who know that
Montcalm died like a hero on the Plains of Abraham, have yet to learn
how much he was deficient in that moral courage . . . and, as history, like
love, is so apt to surround her heroes with an atmosphere of imaginary
brightness, it is probable that Louis de Saint Véran will be viewed by posterity only as the gallant defender of his country, while his cruel apathy
on the shores of the Oswego and the Horican will be forgotten."[28] Cooper
directed his most searing critique at historiography's heroicized rhetoric
and imaginative memory, thereby attacking the very mythic discourse of
professional history that Slotkin would later claim as innate and unquestioned within *The Last of the Mohicans*.

Even Cooper's fictional protagonists are ambivalent toward the European practice of writing history. Hawkeye's assaults on the truthfulness of
books and written history are most frequent. During a conversation with
Chingachgook, the scout compares the European or white way of recording the past to that of the Indian: "My people have many ways, of which, as
an honest man, I can't approve. It is one of their customs to write in books
what they have done and seen, instead of telling them in their villages,
where the lie can be given to the face of a cowardly boaster, and the brave
soldier can call on his comrades to witness for the truth of his words."[29]
Hawkeye's contrast prefigures the novel's historical form. The narrative
preceding the massacre at Fort William Henry exemplifies the European
practice of writing history. The novel's fictional narrative evolves from
established events in the French and Indian War and British imperial history. Cooper's opening chapter begins by recounting the history of those
events, but rather than creating a dichotomy between the bloody legacy
of European history and the mythic lack of history on the American continent, Cooper places America and Native Americans directly within the
forces of history: "There was no recess of the woods so dark, nor any secret
place so lovely, that it might claim exemption from the inroads of those
who had pledged their blood to satiate their vengeance, or to uphold the
cold and selfish policy of the distant monarchs of Europe."[30] America is
not a mythic space innocent of history, and the Native Americans do not
merely exist outside the forces of western history. They act within it.[31]
Magua not only acts but also recounts a Native American perspective on

the European invasion of America and the progress of the French and
Indian War.[32] As there is no known written account of the wars by a Native
American, Cooper's perspective is the first historical narrative of its kind.

Late-twentieth-century studies of Cooper's novel may have revolved
around questions of myth and history, but even those interested in recovering the historical aspects of *Mohicans* have ignored events following
the massacre.[33] Once the massacre is over and the British army has been
obliterated, the landmarks of European civilization and history disappear.
Magua leads his captives into the wilderness. Did Cooper intend for history to disappear in the world of the Indian? In one sense, the massacre at
Fort William Henry does separate the world of traditional European history from the mythic world of the Indian. Cooper's first American edition
consisted of two volumes and split the narrative along the massacre. Yet
the structure of *The Last of the Mohicans* is not that of a historical narrative succeeded by a mythic narrative; instead, Cooper, contrasts two ways
of telling history. Cooper cited his Native American sources in his preface, and in 1861, his daughter Susan cited the full extent of his historical
research—not on the events of Fort William Henry, but on native history
and character.[34] However, Cooper found the "professional" histories inadequate for the task and was frustrated by the lack of Native American
perspectives on their own history. In part two of *Mohicans*, he extends his
self-conceived identity as a new historian. His European style, including
his repeated use of footnotes and historical asides, virtually disappears, in
favor of a dramatic narrative. Indian histories are told orally before the
whole community. Magua, Chingachgook, Uncas, and Tamenund are the
principal historians after the massacre. Magua is the dramatic historian of
his people, but Cooper does not quote Magua directly. Instead, Cooper
places rhetorical distance between the white reader and the events that
he, as a historian, mediates and interprets.[35]

Yet Cooper does not impose a rigid racial separation between the two
modes of historiography. Just as Native American tribes participated in the
bloody European history of the French and Indian War and told their version of events in the midst of the struggle, so the white protagonists cross
the boundaries to the realm of Indian history. In the hope of saving the
captives, Duncan assumes multiple identities, including that of a mixed-
blood French ally and even Hawkeye, thereby temporarily renouncing his
British identity in a hostile environment. Yet it is the biracial Cora Munro
who recounts the only true "mixed" oral history of events, as she tells the
Delaware elder Tamenund of her capture.[36] Whereas Hawkeye and Magua present irreconcilable perspectives on the abductions, Cora admits

the cruelty of her European people while appealing to the superior justice of Tamenund to free her sister. Ironically, her history of the events acts as a counterpoint to those of Hawkeye and Magua, and she introduces yet another version of the same events told by Uncas. Cooper's deliberate use of multiple histories is a crucial development in his conception of American historiography. In part one, his view of the massacre at the fort conflicts with that of the accepted historiography, but by the end of the novel, he has created multiple perspectives on the past. Although the mixed-race Cora and Uncas die, eliminating racial amalgamation in the New World, Cooper's mixed historical structure survives.[37] Cooper's construction of himself as a historian, his recognition of the inadequacy of traditional historiography, and his own attempt to render alternative forms of history persist throughout the narrative. Viewed in this context, Cooper is not simply the creator of an American frontier myth founded on racial exclusion and rigid binary oppositions or an imaginative historical novelist. In *The Last of the Mohicans: A Narrative of 1757*, Cooper creates the structure for a new American historiography—one that Hollywood historians would easily adapt.

Independent Historical Production

Hollywood filmmakers had the potential to represent the historiographical and racial complexities of Cooper's American history without sacrificing the drama or what screenwriter John Balderston perceived as its qualities as a historical epic. *Cimarron* alluded to Yancey's mixed status in several key scenes. Early in the narrative, Isaiah, a young black boy who stowed away with the Cravats en route to Oklahoma, copies Yancey's outfit and comes to church dressed as a pint-sized version of his hero. Yancey laughs when he sees his youthful mirror image, but Sabra, schooled in the South, does not find the implications of this "cimarron" mixing amusing. By foregrounding Cora's mixed ancestry, the filmmakers had the opportunity to do something similar. Yet Balderston considered the Native American aspects of the narrative a "subplot," thereby distancing Edward Small's film from two large-scale silent versions made by D. W. Griffith (Biograph) in 1909 and Maurice Tourneur and Clarence Brown (Associated Producers/Universal) in 1920 that had concentrated on the poignant interracial love story of Cora (who is of West Indian extraction) and Uncas. Balderston wanted his film to be an "epic." To achieve this, the new film had to avoid racial ambiguity and focus on "serious" history, the massacre, and "the Anglo-American victory which determines the future of the continent for all time."[38] He was so taken with the theme of British-American union that he planned to add his own historical coda to the *Mohicans* script.[39] He envisioned the end of the film culminating in Wolfe's rout of Montcalm's French forces on the Plains of Abraham. Although he planned to retain the Native American characters and Magua's abduction of the Munro girls, these sequences would be subservient to the "serious" historical episodes, the documented history that would earn the film epic prestige.

Balderston had aimed his screen treatment at independent producer Edward Small, who hoped that a successful film would keep his Reliance Studios in business. In 1935 Small decided that Balderston's vision of American historical epics would be the surest way for him to garner financial stability and critical praise, so he hired Balderston. The screenwriter was conscious of his role as a historian and began his treatment with a suitably impressive text foreword. It was three paragraphs, and therefore three shots, long, recounting the court intrigue and jealousies between France and England, the perspicacity of Prime Minister William Pitt, and his vision for the North American continent.[40] Balderston's ensuing narrative concentrated overwhelmingly on the first half of Cooper's novel, which dramatizes and comments on the actual events of the war and massacre at Fort William Henry. Hawkeye is still Cooper's Anglophobic, colonial huntsman, but Balderston has him admit the error of his ways at the end of the film: Hawkeye joins the British army as a legitimate soldier. In many of the early versions of the script, Hawkeye actually helps Wolfe find a way up the cliffs of Quebec and defeat the French forces.[41]

Screenwriter Philip Dunne read Balderston's material at Small's request and soon wrote his own version, but he still emphasized the novel's historical context. Dunne also maintained a pompous three-paragraph foreword that focused on the European political forces controlling the war, and he even opened his version with a superimposed date, 1757. With the assistance of a script polisher, the text foreword had been cut to only one paragraph by October. Still, the filmmakers continued to cling to *The Last of the Mohicans* as a legitimate historical epic, and well into 1936, they projected a text foreword that would set the stage for 1757. Balderston's dream of concluding his French and Indian War epic on the Plains of Abraham foundered, however, when Small's company deleted it from the script in June 1936.[42] It is likely that they abandoned this historical coda only because of the prohibitive cost of staging yet another "epic" battle. Nevertheless, *Mohicans* remains a tribute to the British or-

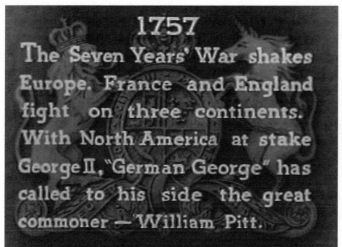

1757

The Seven Years' War shakes Europe. France and England fight on three continents. With North America at stake George II, "German George" has called to his side the great commoner — William Pitt.

Text foreword for *The Last of the Mohicans* (1936).

deal and triumph in North America and the colonials' union with the mother country. Hawkeye's reconciliation with the British cause and his decision to join the army in the final sequences of the film overshadow any potential consideration of the Native American perspective. Whereas the structure of Cooper's historical novel argues for a juxtaposition of the European and Indian worlds and their ways of recording the past, Small's production concentrates almost exclusively on the institutional history of the French and Indian War. Whereas *Cimarron*'s text inserts were set to work in counterpoint to the complex social history of an evolving Oklahoma, *Mohicans*'s text foreword establishes a European historical struggle that it then resolves through the cinematic narrative. The images support the text.

Small based his film's historical quality on the accuracy of the sets, costumes, and language. To this end, he hired independent researcher E. P. Lambert in the fall of 1935 to research the period of the French and Indian War, to correct any errors in the script, and to produce a dossier of pictures and excerpts of primary texts for the set designers. Lambert had provided a similar service for Darryl F. Zanuck in preparation for *Cardinal Richelieu* (1935), but while working at Fox, he had access to the studio's expanding research library, under the direction of Frances Richardson, as well as the Los Angeles and Huntington Libraries. Reliance Studios lacked the impressive resources of the major studios, but at the time, it was standard practice for studios to share their research facilities and finds with other screenwriters and production staffs.[43] This may have been the

Twentieth
Century–Fox
research library,
ca. 1939.

only area where Warner Brothers and Paramount would cooperate rather
than compete with each other.

Lambert's research log and bibliography constituted a second crucial
process in the construction of American historical cinema. The first involved the screenwriter's personal research for the treatment and script,
undertaken either in the studio's own research library or at the Los Angeles Public Library or the Huntington Library in nearby San Marino.
Lambert remained on Small's payroll throughout the production, but
his attitude toward historical research was curious. He wrote to Small in
October 1935, "Film fans do not mind a little margin for history to work
loosely in when it is part of a story, especially as in good histories there
are conflicting accounts of the same occurrence. The producer has the
same right as a painter to make history picturesque and events occur in
the order they should have happened for best dramatic effect . . . we must
not be too considerate of inconvenient truth when dramatizing history."[44]
Lambert knew from his research that history was often conflicted and
incomplete. To him, cinema was entertainment, and few members of the
audience were likely to recognize departures from the historical record.

Yet his comments emphasize the paradox of American historical filmmaking. If the facts themselves were often obscure, and historians were
unreliable, how could filmmakers resist the lure of their own dramatic alterations? In making historical films, screenwriters used the same tools as
historians, often covering the same ground. Somewhere along this path,

they were confronted by conflicting loyalties. Before the advent of sound, few writers or studio producers worried about these discrepancies and the construction of history, but now, screenwriters often devoted as much time to preparation and research as they did to writing. Studio libraries and research departments began to grow, and by the latter half of the 1930s, studios were advertising their research libraries in periodicals such as the *Library Journal* and the *Wilson Bulletin for Librarians*.[45] Critical attention focused on a film's accurate "look," but it was equally sensitive to a film's projected attitude toward history and its use of historical events. Although Small's researcher may have questioned the need for and advisability of historical accuracy, his misgivings were not necessarily shared by the principal filmmakers. The fact remains that Small wanted to make a successful American historical epic. To do so, his screenwriters focused on the documented historical events in Cooper's novel and developed a historical foreword with which to contextualize their film, while Small hired a full-time research assistant to document visual detail. Yet in focusing on the historically verifiable elements of the story—namely, the Anglo-American struggle against the French and Indians—Small avoided what *Cimarron* chose to do in 1931: present multiple perspectives on America's multiracial past and engage the rhetoric of its founding myths of national history.

The "True History" of Ramona

It was left to Lamar Trotti and Twentieth Century–Fox to attempt the next critique of institutional American history and the notion of frontier conquest. Again, the foundation for the historical critique was not the work of a professional historian but that of a novelist interested in publicizing the darker side of the American past. And, as with Cooper, Helen Hunt Jackson focused on the experiences of a mixed-race woman to destabilize traditional triumphant narratives of the West. The history of *Ramona* began in 1881 with the publication of Jackson's history of the U.S. government's policy toward Native Americans, *A Century of Dishonor*.[46] It was the first attempt to indict the government's Indian policy with the tools and rhetoric of a thoroughly researched and argued history, but in spite of her eloquence, Jackson's book was largely ignored by the public. Jackson had hoped that her history would change the current government attitude toward Native Americans. She turned away from traditional history and adopted the form of the novel in order to capture her audience.[47] As she wrote to her friends Antonio and Mariana Coronel in November 1883, "I am going to write a novel, in which will be set forth some Indian experiences to move people's hearts. People will read a novel when they will not read serious books."[48]

Yet in writing her novel, Jackson adhered closely to a number of personal histories in Southern California's recent past. In 1883 she was in the Los Angeles area at the behest of the Commission of Indian Affairs to investigate the living conditions of the California mission Indians. Later that year she visited the Guajome Rancho of Senora Ysobel Coutts near the San Luis Rey Mission, as well as the Camulos Rancho in the Santa Clara valley. Her friends the Coronels supplied her with many stories of Doña Ysobel del Valle and her son, ex-senator Reginald del Valle, and the del Valles' ward, the little Indian daughter of a Piru chief. She also heard the sad history of Juan Diego, a Cahuilla Indian who had been shot for alleged horse stealing by Sam Temple in October 1877. The Indian had a small farm in the San Jacinto mountains, where he had lived with his wife and baby. At the trial, Temple claimed that Juan Diego had attacked him with a knife. The protestations of Diego's wife were not recorded by the court; since she was an Indian, her testimony was not valid.[49] And Jackson also heard rumors of the elopement of Ramon Corralez and a half-breed Indian girl, Lugarda Sandoval. Based on these events, Jackson chronicled the life of the half-Indian Ramona, ward of the rich Moreno family. When Senora Moreno tells Ramona of her heritage, the girl leaves the ranch and the love of the Moreno's only son for a life with her Indian people. She marries Alessandro, a chief's son; she sees their land taken by white settlers, her people killed by those same "Americans," and her husband shot by a white man for horse stealing.

Ramona's life succeeded in capturing the attention of an American public that was indifferent to traditional histories and exposés of government abuse.[50] Surprisingly, that same audience eagerly sought historical confirmation of Ramona's life on the Moreno ranch and in Temecula. Over the years, news articles, books, and photographs accumulated a history and an annotated bibliography for Jackson's novel. The fact that Jackson's characters were composites of real people and that her tale of Alessandro's death was an attempt to preserve some of the sad history of Juan Diego only fueled the American public's curiosity. Jackson was a historian, and Ramona's narrative reflected her background. As C. C. Davis wrote in his *True Story of Ramona*, "It is doubtful if an author ever before had taken such pains as had Mrs. Jackson to prepare for the production of 'Ramona.' . . . She felt that public criticism would be merciless, and fully realized the importance of unquestioned correctness in every position taken."[51] In 1881 Jackson had written a counterhistory of American expansion, a lone counterpoint to George Bancroft's glorious purge of the continent,[52] but it was only when her arsenal of facts was bound to the power of a marginal personal history that the public took notice and clamored for facts.

Sometimes this market for history took an amusing turn. One historian complained, "There is scarcely a settlement south of the Tehachapi that is not pointed out to the traveler as the 'home of Ramona.' She was married at every mission station from San Diego to San Luis Obispo, if one could credit local legend." Many of these same skeptics joined in the search to pin down the real Ramona, dismissing one woman's claim because she was just a "common Indian."[53] Jackson's tragic history and the public's desire to make Ramona "real" fused each year in the Ramona pageants held at the foot of Mount San Jacinto. There, in the actual landscape Jackson wrote about, actors re-created her characters. Programs proclaimed that their mission was "instrumental in preserving a bit of California history," and they chronicled Jackson's historical sources, even providing an abbreviated history of Native American culture from ancient times to the coming of Catholicism and the English. The subject of the pageant was, of course, the last chapter in the Indians' tragic story, and the programs identified late-nineteenth-century California history as "the Ramona period."[54]

Ramona was also screen material and was filmed unobtrusively in 1910, 1916, and 1928, the last a silent version starring Mexican actress Dolores Del Rio.[55] Although Hollywood whitewashed Cora Munro's mulatta identity, filmmakers were evidently less worried about mixed-blood mestiza heroines. What distinguishes the 1936 version from the other silent efforts is the underlying historical impulse driving filmmakers Darryl F. Zanuck and Lamar Trotti. From the inception of Twentieth Century–Fox in 1936, Zanuck planned a diverse set of American historical films. *Cimarron* had proved that mixed-race American protagonists could survive at the box office. *Ramona* would be a less flashy and more serious counterpart to wild New York life in *The Bowery* (1935), and by April 1935, Zanuck had assigned Lamar Trotti to write a treatment of Jackson's material.

Trotti, like many other screenwriters of the early sound era, was a former journalist, trained to get the story down on paper concisely and before the deadline. An ex-reporter from Atlanta, Trotti became Fox screenwriter Dudley Nichols's protégé in 1933. Throughout the early 1930s, they would work together with John Ford on Will Rogers's Americana pieces.

They also collaborated on a semibiographical script about Chicago mayor Anton Chermak (*The Man Who Dared*, 1934), who had recently taken an assassin's bullet intended for President Franklin Roosevelt. Trotti liked Ford and would work with him again at the close of the decade, but Zanuck shaped his day-to-day experiences at the studio. It would be one of the most prolific and rich partnerships in screenwriting history. Under Zanuck's supervision, Trotti would produce, both on command and on spec, a series of American historical screenplays that subtly grasped the nuances of American historiography and the counterpoint of text and image.[56] *Ramona* was the first of these independent projects at Twentieth Century–Fox.

Although Helen Hunt Jackson's novel begins without a historical apologia or an introduction citing her sources and argument, Lamar Trotti's story outline, written in April 1935, does.[57] He begins by contextualizing life in California during the middle of the nineteenth century and then sets a historical tone for the picture closely akin to Jackson's *Century of Dishonor*: "This is the period just following the acquisition of California by the United States. . . . Heretofore the Red Man has been under the domination of the missions; and while injustices may have been done, the Indian at least has been clothed and fed, and his spiritual needs attended to. The early American pioneer, however, has little or no sympathy for the native whom he proceeds to rob of his land, his cattle, and his dignity."[58] Trotti's outline adheres to Jackson's novel and the major conflict between Ramona's ancestry and the racial prejudices of Senora Moreno. Trotti emphasizes the moment when Ramona discovers who she is and what her ancestry makes her; Ramona accepts her mixed Indian identity with pride and joy, not shame, as Moreno would have it.[59] When Ramona and Felipe elope and are married by Father Gaspara, Trotti plans Gaspara's denouncement of the U.S. government's treatment of the California Indians. Trotti later outlines the destruction of native villages, American settlers' theft of Alessandro and Ramona's farm, and John Farrar's murder of Alessandro.

Trotti's first draft of the screenplay replicated his outline, but strangely, it lacked the original opening title. Script polisher Paul Hervey Fox, under Zanuck's direction, reproduced a suitably sympathetic foreword: "Slowly the first American settlers came to drive out the picturesque tribes of Indians . . . many of whom had been educated in the early missions." This foreword drew attention to the "historical background" and Ramona's status as a person of mixed blood. Later drafts by Fox and Trotti reworded it to sharpen the critique of the American pioneers, who were "driving everything before them."[60] Although the rest of the script remained the same, the tone of the foreword was reworded and changed half a dozen times before shooting began in the late summer of 1936. Zanuck himself established the opening title and continued to include some kind of historical exposition, but as shooting time drew near, he cut Trotti and Fox's criticism of American settlers in California and references to the "historical background" of Jackson's novel. Zanuck's experience with *The Public Enemy*'s inflammatory foreword and the censors' sensitivity to historical critiques had made him equally aware of text's capacity for direct and provocative address. Ramona's racial history thus became "a pastoral background" for "her immortal romance" and was accompanied on screen by bucolic shots of California orange groves and sheep.[61] Although Zanuck retained the telltale historical attribute of a text foreword, he erased any trace of a historical point of view from the text. Instead, the brutality of the American pioneers was shown only in the images taken from Jackson's narrative. Zanuck's action, undoubtedly intended to dispel Jackson's anti-American overtones, transferred the potential means of critique from text to image. Whereas *Annie Oakley*'s sly jokes about newspapers and dime novels had been built into the screenplay, Zanuck's more arbitrary cut conveyed a similar historical critique of text through images. But from the beginning, Trotti deliberately constructed *Ramona* as a historical film and called attention to its historical nature with the use of text.

Zanuck made the unusual decision to film *Ramona* in Technicolor. Experimental and notoriously expensive, the Technicolor process was chosen by a studio only for its most prestigious films. Many of the most prominent were adaptations of historical novels, such as *Becky Sharp* (1935). But in *Ramona*, color reveals the problematic dimensions of racial history in the American West. Actress Loretta Young's alabaster skin belies Ramona's mixed-blood heritage. Thus, with no physical mark to identify her inherent racial difference, she dresses the part when she discovers and adopts her heritage. Race is therefore depicted as something to be performed in costume, as an essentially unstable visual and historical construct. *Ramona*'s sense of racial injustice is heightened by the very visual ambiguity of race. Without the justification of "color" difference, the discourse of Manifest Destiny falls apart, and the vicious expansion in California is revealed for what it is: capitalist theft. Critics were initially uneasy about Zanuck's decision to cast Young as Ramona. As Zanuck wrote to attorney Neil McCarthy, "I was severely criticized by my associates as well as by the newspaper columnists . . . for imagining that Loretta Young could play a half-Indian."[62]

Zanuck's compelling version of *Ramona*'s history confronted the deep consequences of America's dishonorable Indian policy and, in foregrounding the experience of a mixed-race woman on the western frontier, projected an alternative Hollywood western. In the classic western genre, the division between white and red is as stark as that between civilization and savagery. The interracial western hero or heroine transgresses not only racial barriers but also the traditional categories of genre. And like Yancey Cravat, Ramona is no tragic mestiza or vanishing American—she survives. Although many film reviewers rhapsodized about the classic bucolic romance, one of *Time*'s film critics caught the social critique: "Ramona herself is half historical, half fictional, half white and half Indian, but there is nothing half-way in the manner in which Twentieth Century–Fox has handled her biography. It has used the simple framework as a bitter disquisition on the traditional white methods of dealing with Indians, civilized or raw."[63] Yet for all its subversive hybridity, most labeled the film a "quiet classic." After all, neither Jackson nor Trotti and Zanuck gave Ramona an active role in writing her own history and criticizing government policy toward Native Americans. Unlike Edna Ferber's mestizo news editor Yancey Cravat, Ramona has no access to text and the instruments of historiography. Only white, educated Helen Hunt Jackson could give the mixed-race woman a place in the American past.

Selling History at Paramount

By 1935, Howard Estabrook's policy of consulting multiple historical sources in constructing a historical screenplay was an established practice, and by the end of the decade, a small group of screenwriters headed by Lamar Trotti and Nunnally Johnson were known almost exclusively for their historical work. Like the novelists whose writings served as the basis for so many historical films in the early sound era, these screenwriters often rebelled against the traditional views of historical events and attitudes cherished by professional historians. Historians, for their part, often publicly criticized the accuracy of Hollywood films or studiously ignored the invention of motion pictures. Hollywood, in turn, did not seem to need them. As long as there were libraries, screenwriters did their own research. Yet the growing interest in manufacturing American historical films caused executives at Paramount to take a chance with popular historians.

At Paramount, Cecil B. DeMille proposed another view of the epic historical western. In 1935 he and Jeannie Macpherson, his principal screenwriter and research analyst, turned away from biblical, ancient, and medieval history and went back to the American frontier. DeMille had been associated with the western since the early days of his career. He was the first to film *The Squaw Man* (1914 and 1918), *The Virginian* (1914), and *The Girl of the Golden West* (1915). He made these definitive versions at a time when the wild landscape and lifestyle associated with the frontier were still present. These "westerns," all recent Belasco stage hits set in the immediate past, were handled with lavish locations but little of the text and visual historical consciousness found in Griffith's *The Birth of a Nation* and *Intolerance* (1916). DeMille would remake his first success, *The Squaw Man*, a third time as a sound film in 1931, but neither he nor his screenwriters showed any interest in converting the tale into a prestigious historical film along the lines of *The Big Trail*, *The Great Meadow*, and *Cimarron*. Instead, he focused his epic talents, researchers, and writers on the decline of the Roman Empire in *The Sign of the Cross* (1932), the affair of Antony and Cleopatra in *Cleopatra* (1934), and *The Crusades* (1935).

But in September 1935, DeMille and Macpherson returned to the epic West. *The Plainsman* (1936) may have been inspired by the successes of *Cimarron* and *Annie Oakley* (both books were included in the research bibliography), but DeMille was not interested in multiracial or feminist views of western history.[64] DeMille's production company ultimately decided to cull the work of popular historians who had written about the lives of William F. "Buffalo Bill" Cody and James Butler "Wild Bill" Hickok.[65] *The Plainsman* had all the trappings of a prestigious historical film (text inserts, battles, historical figures), but in the text fore-

DeMille's historical staff in the late 1930s. Jeannie Macpherson is at the far right. (Author's collection)

word, DeMille wrote: "The story that follows joins together the lives of many men and widely separated events. It is an attempt to do justice to the resourcefulness and courage that characterized the Plainsman of our West."[66] DeMille and his team of writers implied that the historical details were subservient to the present generation's need to honor their courage. In order to serve historical memory, *The Plainsman* had to disregard its principles as a historical film. It was a significant admission coming from DeMille, an impressive and direct statement of his historical position, whereby basic historical concerns of chronology, accuracy, and objectivity were exorcised in the interests of a cinematic eulogy.

Whereas other filmmakers had used forewords to arrogate historical authority to filmmaking, DeMille used the foreword as a screen against the demands of history. After all, the narrative used major historical characters in a wholly fictitious account of Calamity Jane and Hickok's love affair against a backdrop of Indian wars. *The Plainsman* was a panegyric to Cody and Hickok, splashy gunmen who fought wicked and bloodthirsty Indians in a simple, binary racial clash for a new empire. The plainsmen, whose impoverished, anonymous, blighted push westward may have evoked a more nuanced account of the post–Civil War West and the Native American perspective, were written out of the story. After all, the filmmakers had originally wanted Roosevelt's *Winning of the West* as the film's title and had to settle for *The Plainsman* when DeMille learned that Columbia owned the rights to the title. However, the film did mark an alliance among popular historians, filmmakers, and big-budget historical films: Courtney Ryley Cooper and Frank J. Wilstach received film credit for their work. It is still debatable whether the partnership and the result were happy ones.

But Paramount was impressed with DeMille's use of popular historical material, and in 1936 the studio hired Frank Lloyd to adapt Stuart Lake's unpublished (and unfinished) history of the Wells Fargo Company. Like many other screenwriters of this era, Lake had worked as a reporter, freelance writer, and popular historian. Lake believed that he possessed a historical connection to the West that no historian could match: he had spoken with old-timers Bat Masterson and Wyatt Earp, who cleared up a lot of "frontier mysteries."[67] He proclaimed that his entry into the historical world would replace western myths propounded by historians with firsthand accounts and research. He would cleanse history and have a best seller on his hands. But when he wrote to Frank Lockwood of the University of Arizona about his work on Earp, Lockwood, like many professional historians, dismissed Lake's efforts, saying, "I think entirely too much stress has been laid upon the bloody aspects of Tombstone. However, that is what people want, and I have no doubt that your book will bring in an enormous sale."[68] Lake's rapid style, with its present-tense narrative and extensive use of Earp's interviews, was in many ways reminiscent of Walter Noble Burns's work on Billy the Kid.[69] The book sold well, and Lake immediately tried to sell the rights to Hollywood.

Studio correspondence and letters from Lake's agents predicted that when he put the book on the market in late 1931, Cimarron's success would only help *Frontier Marshal* become a successful film.[70] In fact, both Lake and Mrs. Earp wanted RKO to make *Frontier Marshal*, considering the fantastic job it had done with *Cimarron*. RKO, however, did not want to make another expensive western and did not consider Wyatt Earp a serious historical subject. As the months passed, all the other studios came to agree.[71] It seemed that *Frontier Marshal* would never make it to the screen. When *Frontier Marshal* eventually sold to Fox for only $7,500, Lake made it clear to his agents and to the studio that he wanted to be part of the package. He wanted a job that would enable him to oversee the authenticity of the script and the picture from start to finish.[72] The studio ignored him. Fox initially hired its two top screenwriters, Dudley Nichols and Lamar Trotti, to write the script, apparently intending to make *Frontier Marshal* a top historical project. But Nichols and Trotti were soon reassigned, and two studio hacks took over the job.[73] Lake's frequent demands to be made a technical adviser were studiously ignored. Perhaps people knew of his lack of skill as a screenwriter and his reputation as a troublemaker. Or perhaps the executives read the book and realized that it was not the type of material from which serious historical films were made. *Frontier Marshal* was no scholarly biography; it was a shoot-'em-up story of a western hero, and that is how it was filmed in two low-budget productions in 1934 and 1939.[74]

A few years later, Lake sent Paramount a ten-page synopsis of a fictional story loosely based on the history of the Wells Fargo organization.[75] Paramount recognized its potential and, leery of Lake's tendency to threaten studios with plagiarism suits, paid him $9,000 for the outline, but it did not hire him. After all, screenwriters with little or no historical background had proved themselves capable of historical research and writing. Lake, however, believed that he had a professional edge, boasting that if he stood for anything in Hollywood, it was as the preserver of "good taste and the eternal fitness of things." His self-appointed job was to keep screenwriters from making superficial, formulaic history films because, when left to their own devices, they only "horsed the thing around."[76]

Lake's copies of his numerous "treatments" still exist, including his *Wells Fargo* opus. These treatments reveal that he never departed from the most staid and pedestrian screenwriting formulas, often prefacing his work with pompous prose ("It is the age old conflict between the man and nature, or man and woman, who must inevitably sacrifice her wishes").[77] Lake's historical wisdom resembled intertitles from short films of the early 1910s.

Lake thought that if he passed off this story outline and advertised his historical expertise, he would be indispensable to the studio as "the only man who knows what he's doing on the project."[78] His agents warned him that Paramount, like all studios, had an extensive research library and many resources at the disposal of experienced screenwriters. The implication was that Hollywood had no need to import historians to write historical films; instead, through research and reading, screenwriters were capable of becoming historians themselves. Needless to say, Lake paid them no attention and went straight to director Frank Lloyd and producer William LeBaron, who had produced *Cimarron* four years earlier. His epistles, sometimes two and three a day, served only to antagonize everyone. Lake's claims that the screenwriters knew nothing about Wells Fargo history became even more ridiculous when Howard Estabrook was hired to write the screenplay. Lake persisted, though, and soon he had to obtain news of the production from the trade papers. Eventually he was hired but was kept off the set by a series of ploys. When Lloyd gave Lake a copy of the script to read and comment on, Lake's only emendation was to change "over the Pecos" to "across the Pecos"[79] (perhaps this is what historical experts are for). *Wells Fargo* was a moderate success in 1937, and Lake took all the credit, telling Lloyd and LeBaron that they had been "dutiful little pupils of Professor Lake."[80] There is no record of any response to this letter.

It is hardly surprising that, after Paramount's experience with Lake, filmmakers were reluctant to include historians in the production of historical films. In spite of his vision for elevating historical cinema with his fiery prose and expertise, Lake's own view of filmmaking was low. He referred to westerns, even those he wrote and attempted to sell to the studio, as "oaters" or "horse operas." Frank Lloyd, William LeBaron, and Howard Estabrook had loftier ambitions for *Wells Fargo*. Both LeBaron and Estabrook undoubtedly recalled the success of *Cimarron* and tried to emulate it. Estabrook would doctor the script, add a foreword, and punctuate the narrative with several text inserts. LeBaron spent lavishly on the production and even produced educational pamphlets on the film that included an extensive bibliography.[81] Yet for all their efforts, film production had changed. Estabrook no longer had control over his properties and writing. Wesley Ruggles had adhered to Estabrook's script in 1931, but Lloyd was a different sort of director, an aspiring C. B. DeMille autocrat. Whereas much of *Cimarron*'s production publicity had revolved around Estabrook's role, Lloyd took all the credit for making *Wells Fargo*. Yet Lloyd evidently learned something from working with LeBaron and Estabrook—a historical distance with which to curb his chauvinism. Publicizing the film, Lloyd wrote: "No two men can agree on what history should be. To some it is falsity, to others a record of crimes; some will make it a chronicle of doings by men in high places; some will make it the essence of innumerable biographies. Who shall be the hero? Shall the tale be written by the iconoclast, or by a Carlylean hero-worshipper? Shall a pedestal be put up, or a hammer be brought down on the feet of clay?" But this was mere strategic equivocation; Lloyd knew what type of history he preferred: "I like to regard history as a pageant—a very brave pageant, but with struggles and turmoil behind the music and waving banners. I wanted a pageant set in the United States, but with a universal theme." He continued with an elaborate description of *Wells Fargo*'s theme: "a struggle for a great western empire" from the Mexican War through the Civil War. Lloyd even went so far as to say that he hoped the film would be seen as a contribution to the history of this era and a tribute to the Wells Fargo Company.[82]

The Hollywood critics acknowledged the film as Paramount's historical follow-up to *The Plainsman*.[83] The *Hollywood Reporter* called the film "a cavalcade of early American transportation" and noticed the historical structure Estabrook had given to the film, with its ten episodes and text inserts.[84] Another reviewer responded to the historical structure but disliked the heavy-handed manner in which Lloyd drew attention to himself as a historian, particularly when his narrative had little regard for the historical facts. "The screen is dominated throughout the 115 minutes of the unveiling by the unseen but constantly felt personality of Lloyd the storyteller, the historian, the weaver of vast tapestries and spinner of tremendous tales."[85]

The memory of *Cimarron*'s massive production values overcame *Wells Fargo*'s filmmakers. Lloyd suffered the presence of a popular historian, spent a year on his script, and bolstered it with massive production features, historical inserts, and tableaux. It had all the structural attributes of a prestigious historical film, but as its reviewers noted, the historical iconography seemed to operate independently of a rather weak narrative. The *New York Times* reviewer was bewildered by the encyclopedic, history-laden plot, "too preoccupied with great events to bother about sound characterizations and too hurried with his great events to give any one of them its proper due."[86] The film lacked *Cimarron's* counterpoint of visual social history and written history, of images and words, of Yancey and Sabra. The Wells Fargo Company with its white troubleshooting hero shoved everything (Indians, Confederates, wife, saboteurs) from its inexorable path. Estabrook could take and apply the historical structures he had reinvented with *Cimarron*; however, *Wells Fargo's* narrative of financial success and empire had been developed by a director who shared none of *Cimarron's* multiethnic perspectives and self-critical view of historiography. Lloyd shared DeMille's view of American history, and DeMille, equally impressed with Lloyd, applied *Wells Fargo's* tale of transportation expansion, troubleshooters, and even star Joel McCrea to *Union Pacific* (1939).

By the mid-1930s, many studios had attempted to produce prestigious historical films that, in different ways, responded to the revolution of structure and subject matter introduced in 1931. As historian Frances Taylor Patterson wrote in the *North American Review* in 1937, cinema finally achieved original scripts with the development of the historical film, "a type of film which probably captured the imaginations of audiences for the very reason that it threw off the claustrophobia induced by the drama and the printed word. Staff writers were sent scurrying to libraries to consult old newspaper files, to dig into obscure biographies, or even into the current volumes of *Who's Who*."[87] For Patterson, the American cinema achieved prestige and independence from theatrical and literary adaptations only through the rise of the historical film. Even the historical novel was transformed by the new film historiography. The cycle had given screenwriters a prominence in the selection, research, and construction of historical scripts they had never possessed, and film historiography involved an exercise of independent judgment unknown in faithful adaptations of Broadway hits. But the most prestigious American historical films, among them *Annie Oakley, The Last of the Mohicans, Ramona, The Plainsman,* and *Wells Fargo,* all involved complex adaptations and emendations of traditional and revisionist historical texts. Each emerged from its author's desire to revise, embarrass, emulate, or add to the work of traditional historians. The films continued to present the attributes of written history and the adopted structure of historical cinema, but they maintained an uneasy relationship with historians and historiography. Their different inabilities to sustain a critical view of the American past indicated a moment of crisis and doubt for historical filmmaking.

4

The Return of Our
Epic America, 1938–1941

History is not just a matter of names and dates—dry facts strung together.
It is an endless, dramatic story, as alive as the news in the morning's paper.
That's why I feel for the sake of lively dramatic construction, I am justified
in making some contractions or compressions of historical detail, as long
as I stick to the main facts.

—Cecil B. DeMille, 1939

For two weeks in February 1939, *New York Times* film critic Frank S.
Nugent focused on *Stagecoach*. He began, "In one expansive gesture . . .
John Ford has swept aside ten years of artifice and talkie compromise and
has made a motion picture that sings a song of the camera." The following
week, he amplified Ford's artistry with the western: "In simple terms, he
has taken the old formula . . . and has applied himself and his company
to it with the care, zen, and craftsmanship that might have been accorded
the treatment of a bright new theme. It is as though the picture had been
made ten or fifteen years ago."[1] Although Nugent did not mention it, it
had been ten to fifteen years since Ford had made his last two westerns
for Fox, *The Iron Horse* (1924) and *Three Bad Men* (1926).[2] According to
Nugent, with Ford's return to the genre he once dominated, the western
was cleansed of its sound-era "artifice."

More than any other film critic, Nugent stressed John Ford's role as
the exclusive creator of *Stagecoach*. His praise would serve him well; only
a few years later, Nugent would replace Dudley Nichols as Ford's principal

writer.[3] But his review had a more lasting effect on film history. Nugent's praise created the impression of a silent "golden age" of the western followed by a talking drought, with the implication that only Ford's artistry was capable of returning the western to the magnificence it had achieved in the silent era. On this foundation lay future film scholarship's creation of the pure western genre, the empty decade of A-level production, and Ford the auteur's responsibility for its renaissance in 1939. In fact, *Stagecoach* is one of the most lionized of westerns largely because film theorists, film historians, John Ford biographers, frontier historians, and cultural historians universally considered the film to be the epitome of the western myth and a template for the genre.[4] The film's cast of characters was a collection of western archetypes: the tough but boyish-faced cowboy out for revenge, the whore with the heart of gold, the crooked banker, the snobbish southern gambler, the drunken Irish doctor. The landscape existed in lyrical counterpoint to the timeless conflict between civilization and savagery, between whites and Native Americans. The narrative moved within the mythic boundaries of the western genre world. Although historical events may have generated the film, it was not historical.

After "westerns" such as *Annie Oakley; Klondike Annie; Go West, Young Man; The Last of the Mohicans; Ramona;* and *San Francisco,* Nugent must have seen *Stagecoach* as a welcome return to the less baffling, classic, cowboy-and-Indian westerns known since at least D. W. Griffith's *The Battle at Elderbush Gulch* (1913). *Stagecoach's* narrative must have seemed like an escape from the wordy historical era of the sound film. Decades later, the highly structured and confined concept of the western genre codified by Will Wright, John Cawelti, and others ignored the more eclectic, disruptive, and unclassical historical westerns of 1935–1938 and emphasized the genre's repetitive and transhistorical narratives.[5] In fact, by amplifying the concept of the "empty" decade and expounding on the mythical purity of the western genre, these film scholars pursued their own ethnic cleansing and true lineage of the western. It is true that *Stagecoach* lacks the self-conscious historical trappings of text forewords, historical documents, recognizable historical figures, and superimposed dates. But even though the film lacks the textual pretensions of a *Wells Fargo,* Nugent's praise of *Stagecoach's* visual splendor did not imply a concomitant transhistorical, mythic power. Nugent's focus on *Stagecoach's* references to silent western cinema suggests that Hollywood's long-term dominance as the popular historian of the West was also an important part of American history. Hollywood's West and the actual West had fused in American consciousness, and John Ford, like historians Francis Parkman or Frederick Jackson Turner or Frederic Paxson, was writing a new narrative—with a camera. Nugent's criticism pointed to a subtle reinterpretation of the variety and capacity of historiography. According to Nugent, *Stagecoach* was a powerful form of self-conscious film historiography, not a myth.

Although Nugent pointedly ignored talking historical westerns that violated the classical purity of the western genre, a closer look at *Stagecoach*'s production history and contemporary reception reveals the film's connections to the historical innovations of the past few years. Screenwriter Dudley Nichols was responsible for scripting *Stagecoach*'s historical perspective and its deliberate connection to the cycle of sound-era historical westerns.[6] But in 1939, historical screenwriters' early independence and experimentation with western history were solidifying into a cycle known to critics as the "superwestern." Nichols's waning influence over *Stagecoach*'s production of American history, the critical outcry over Nunnally Johnson and Darryl Zanuck's re-creation of Jesse James's life, and Robert Buckner and Hal Wallis's consolidation of western history at Warner Brothers all indicated escalating conflicts between aberrant American voices and the growing power of a historical filmmaking establishment.

Dudley Nichols's History of the Old Southwest

When Dudley Nichols (a former *New York World* reporter) and John Ford began to edit the script of *Stagecoach* in October 1938, they were perhaps the most respected filmmaking partnership in Hollywood. Since *Men without Women* and *The Seas Beneath* (1931), they had developed a reputation for taut adventures and popular success. In 1935 the industry honored them with separate Academy Awards for their work on the critical success *The Informer*. In subsequent years they continued to work together, but with the merging of Twentieth Century and Fox, Ford became Zanuck's property, while Nichols remained at RKO. In spite of Ford's legendary status (even in 1930s Hollywood), ensuing film scholarship has emphasized Ford the auteur and ignored the inherently collaborative artistry behind his work.[7] But from the early sound era until the early 1940s, Nichols and Ford shared equal reputations as filmmakers. Indeed, as president of the Screen Writers' Guild and his studio's preeminent prestige writer, Nichols may have possessed even more autonomy at RKO than Ford enjoyed under Zanuck's meticulous eye. In a 1939–1940 poll conducted by the Screen Writers' Guild, Nichols was voted the industry's most admired writer.[8]

During the 1930s, many Hollywood insiders acknowledged that screenwriters had more autonomy and power over film production than directors did. At the time, the power of a writer was often connected to his or her status as a historical screenwriter. In addition to Nichols, Lamar Trotti, Nunnally Johnson, Sonya Levien, Ben Hecht, Norman Reilly Raine, Seton I. Miller, John Bright, Robert Buckner, John Huston, and Jeannie Macpherson made their reputations during the sound era on historical scripts. Veteran Anita Loos, who had begun writing intertitles for Griffith on *Intolerance* (1916), maintained her independence at MGM with her period film *San Francisco*. Loos's independent achievement was remarkable at a studio notorious for its mistreatment of writers and its constant, expensive, and often unhappy collaborations. Often when critics praised a prominent director's skill, others realized that the credit was due to the writer. In his 1941 study of Hollywood, Leo Rosten quoted Gilbert Seldes: "Ninety percent of the judgments delivered on the quality of directors is really concerned with the thoughts and ideas presented ready-made for the directors to work with."[9]

Although Ford was highly regarded in the press, with the exception of *The Informer*, he had not distinguished himself with a film comparable to *The Iron Horse*. Zanuck assigned him to a wide variety of productions. His only American historical "prestige" picture, *The Prisoner of Shark Island*, fascinated critics with its unusual historical narrative but owed its success more to its original screenwriter, Nunnally Johnson, and to Zanuck. Curiously, for a filmmaker who would eventually dominate the western genre, it was Ford's competitors, Ruggles, Seitz, DeMille, and Lloyd, who had proved the continued draw of the American West in major Hollywood productions. Even Nichols had written a historical western, the Wyatt Earp–based *Arizonian*, in 1935. Ford, eager to return to western filmmaking, bought Ernest Haycox's short story "Stage to Lordsburg" in 1937, but he had difficulty selling the idea to producers.[10] Although film historian Edward Buscombe and others have cited this resistance as evidence of Hollywood's belief that westerns were "lower order, with small budgets, mass-produced in series," this was simply not the case.[11] Hollywood invested in the West, but only when the scripts were connected with prestigious historical topics, such as the lives of Annie Oakley, Buffalo Bill, and Wild Bill Hickok; the settlement of California; and the development of stage transport. Haycox's brief story, with no historical characters or references, was not attractive as a potential film. Zanuck, although he respected Ford, did not want to spend the money on the slim property. He was already in the midst of planning a historical western with Nunnally Johnson, *Jesse James*. David O. Selznick also rejected the property, not simply because it was a western but because it was "some uncommercial pet" of Ford's. Selznick had disliked the West ever since he had been forced to edit *The Conquerors* for RKO, but he also felt that Ford was not a good enough director to save the poor story. He wrote, "I see no justification for making any story simply because it is liked by a man who, I am willing to concede, is one of the greatest directors in the world, but whose record commercially is far from good."[12] But Ford persisted, and he wanted the author of all his smashes and failures, Dudley Nichols, to write the script. Independent producer Walter Wanger eventually agreed to hire them, and *Stagecoach* went into production in late 1938. Outside of the supervision of a major studio, Ford at last found himself directly involved with the screenwriting process.

Nichols's first self-appointed task was to transform the thin narrative that producers had dismissed into a commercial prestige western. By November 1938, he had completed his final shooting script.[13] Although Nichols maintained the skeleton of Haycox's fictional narrative, he lengthened and transformed "Stage to Lordsburg" into *Stagecoach* largely by augmenting its historical context and setting the narrative in New Mexico and Arizona during the devastating Apache wars of the 1880s. Like many of his peers, Nichols consulted traditional and contemporary historical perspectives when reconstructing the background of the stagecoach attack and adding the legendary Apache warrior Geronimo to the script's cast. Studio research departments during this period were extensive, but many top writers such as Nichols, Estabrook, and Trotti would do their own preliminary research for historical scripts. Although Nichols's research notes no longer exist,[14] it is likely that he turned to the growing number of popular histories and memoirs published in the late 1920s and early 1930s about Geronimo and the Apache wars of the 1880s. Paul Wellman's *Death in the Desert: The Fifty Years War for the Great Southwest* (1935) was typical of the literature condemning Geronimo's resistance to the U.S. government's Indian policy.[15] The memoirs of cavalry officers Britton Davis (1929) and Anton Mazzanovich (1931) offered other perspectives.[16] Both had fought against Geronimo in the 1880s and wrote detailed, personal accounts of life in the Southwest.

While Mazzanovich portrayed Geronimo as cold-blooded and cruel,[17] Davis, an army officer who had been personally acquainted with Geronimo, wrote a revisionist history of the Apache wars that was more in line with William Christie MacLeod's 1928 account of race in the West. In the preface, Davis's editor even stated that the book was intended to contradict the popular conception of Geronimo and the Apaches as vicious barbarians. Like Mazzanovich, Davis described his account as "the truth about Geronimo," but he directed his anger at those "whose knowledge [of the Apache] was gained from barroom talk."[18] Whereas Mazzanovich, an Austrian immigrant, responded to the West like an effusive tourist, Davis, with his insistence on eschewing "romantic embellishment or poetic description," possessed the tone of a revisionist historian.[19] According to Davis, Geronimo's raids had been provoked by a legacy of white treachery and interference in Apache culture. Davis's self-styled role as a historian would add Geronimo's perspective to contemporary western history.[20]

In spite of Geronimo's prominence in traditional and revisionist popular western histories, professional historians writing in the 1920s and 1930s ignored the Chiricahua leader, just as they considered Billy the Kid, Calamity Jane, and Wyatt Earp trivial subjects suitable only for popular history and the cinema. Only in the late 1980s and 1990s did professional historians reassess the racial dynamics of western history and puncture white establishment historiography with the many Native American, female, black, Chinese, and Mexican voices participating in or opposing the "development" of the nation.[21] But in the 1920s and 1930s, popular history and cinema had already developed an audience for marginal and aberrant westerners, whether they were Native American leaders, women pioneers, or working-class gunfighters. Nichols's conception of *Stagecoach* as an Apache war drama reflects contemporaneous trends in popular western history, but his and Ford's visual engagement with the past surpassed the texts of both popular and professional historiography.

Dudley Nichols's concern with writing a historical western was not confined to the expansion of Haycox's pedestrian narrative. Like his screenwriting colleagues, he planned an impressive historical foreword, a textual invocation of the past to lend credence to Ford's visual narrative. The final script begins with a projected text foreword:

> Until the Iron Horse came, the Stagecoach was the only means of travel on the American frontier. Braving all dangers, these Concord coaches—the "streamliners" of their day—spanned on schedule wild, desolate stretches of desert and mountainland in the Southwest, where in 1885 the savage struggle of the Indians to oust the white invader was drawing to a close. At the time no name struck more terror into the hearts of travelers than that of Geronimo—leader of those Apaches who preferred death rather than submit to the white man's will.[22]

His foreword details the white invasion of the Apaches' land and contextualizes the narrative with a specific date and time. The titles do not refer to a simple, mythic time dominated by a white conflict with nameless "Indians"; instead, they describe a specific tribe and a historic Apache leader, Geronimo. Nichols significantly altered his final shooting script's attitude toward the Native Americans' plight in the face of white expansion. An earlier draft, which also began with a text foreword, had conveyed an uncomplicated image of nameless Apache savagery:

> Until the Iron Horse came, the stagecoach was the only means of travel on the American frontiers. . . . Braving all perils, these coaches traversed desert and mountain in the untamed Southwest of 1885, when the savage struggle of the Apache Indians to oust white settlers was drawing to a close.[23]

Here, the stagecoach, a symbol of civilization in the desert, is the hero of the frontier. Geronimo is not mentioned, and the Apaches have no fearless leader. Instead of refusing to "submit" to "the white invader" as they do in the final script, these Apaches merely attempt to fight the white settlers. Evidently, John Ford worked with Nichols on the script from late October to early November as they got ready for preliminary shooting. The result was a longer and more historically nuanced foreword, or opening title.

Since *Cimarron's* manifold deployment of text inserts eight years before, text had become the definitive feature of historical filmmaking. Whether conveying an attitude of eulogy, criticism, or irony toward its historical subject, the projection of text on screen was an immediate trigger to filmmakers' and audiences' sense of a historical film. Considering all its connotations in terms of the established documentation and reputation of traditional written history, text had the potential to lend cinema a new and serious historical dimension. For Nichols and Ford to begin *Stagecoach* with a text foreword suggests components of the film's history hitherto unrecognized by late-twentieth-century film criticism: the filmmakers' approach to the West connected *Stagecoach* to a legacy of historical westerns and to a self-conscious preoccupation with questions of history.

But for some reason, this text foreword was cut before the film's national release. Without the prologue, *Stagecoach's* attitude toward history is not directly or textually constructed in relation to the accepted vocabulary of historical filmmaking in the early sound era. In the screenplay, the conquest of the West, the dispossession of the Indians by the "white invaders," and the refusal of Geronimo and his people to "submit" are all directly stated from the outset, complicating any simple view of the film as a violent racial myth that denies an Indian perspective. Did Ford cut this foreword in early 1939 before he finished shooting or before the film's release, perhaps because he wanted to avoid creating a history-book western? This seems unlikely for several reasons. Although Nichols created the text foreword for the rough draft before Ford involved himself in the script, the text survived their intensive work sessions in October and November. Ford not only liked Nichols's foreword but even expanded it; the text prologue in the final shooting script is twice its original size. The prologue was thus a long-term component of the planned film.

Ford did, however, delete Nichols's opening sequence that described Geronimo's rampage in the southwestern territories and foregrounded his fearful effect on the townspeople and the stagecoach passengers. In the final shooting script, when the sheriff warns the passengers that Geronimo is on the rampage and advises that they travel at their own risk, the pedestrians overhear and whisper the Apache's name in a fearful crescendo.[24] Ford evidently cut this shot, or series of shots, that would have contextualized Geronimo's reputation as a threat to both established settlements and isolated outposts.

Ford did not cut Nichols's specific provision in the script for a stunning close-up of Geronimo.[25] Ford actually shot Geronimo full face as he looked directly into the camera—one of only two such close-ups in the film (the other is the first shot of Ringo). Geronimo's direct confrontation with the camera and his look of concentrated menace, intensified by a low-angle shot, fracture the insularity of the classical western narrative and the spectator's distance from the film's historical narrative. Geronimo's stare implicates the white audience in his 1885 response to the white "invasion" of the Southwest. Chief White Horse's thin, scarlike mouth; deep cheek furrows; narrow, close-set eyes; and piercing stare are all recognizable attributes of Geronimo. The Chiricahua leader sat for his likeness many times after his surrender in 1886.[26] Indeed, the film's close-up is its "photograph" of Geronimo, taken not in captivity but when the Apache's feared name and reputation coexisted with his defiant features. The shot also provides a closer view of Geronimo than any contemporary photographic portrait. Most, like the famed A. Frank Randall photograph, are full- or half-length portraits taken from a distance. In one sense, *Stagecoach*'s close-up seems to present, if only momentarily, a better sense of Geronimo and of history.

Close-up of Geronimo.
(*Stagecoach*)

In a famous article on the dinner-table sequence in *Stagecoach*, Nick Browne demonstrated Ford's deliberate distance from the formal, identifying, point-of-view structures of classical Hollywood cinema.[27] Although the sequence shows society's ostracism of Dallas, Browne argued that Ford's presentation of Ringo's reaction, his close sympathetic shots of Dallas, and a reestablished distance from the scene all cause the audience to reject the dominant view of society embodied by the proper soldier's wife, Lucy Mallory. But Ford truly subverted traditional forms of audience identification in his presentation of Geronimo and the Chiricahua perspective. In the film's final battle, as the white passengers fight the Apaches, Ford integrated multiple shots of the moving stagecoach. Most of these show the stagecoach moving forward to the left of the frame, with the Indian riders gaining on the right. Audiences are closely aligned with the stagecoach passengers or positioned in front of the coach (like a Lordsburg citizen or cavalry officer looking out onto the desert). Yet at one point, Ford crosses the 180-degree line of action, "violating" the conventions of Hollywood editing. In that shot, the stagecoach is shown under attack in the distance, moving forward left to right. Ford's choice, long understood as a mistake in editing by late-twentieth-century film historians, was no mistake.[28] Although, as in the case of Lucy Mallory's point of view, we may be led to reject this structure of identification, we are still seeing the stagecoach *from the Apache point of view*.

Stagecoach's unusual if abbreviated portrayal of the Apache perspective and the visual and verbal power of Geronimo's name and figure give him a cinematic presence throughout the film. It was the only major film

The final chase in *Stagecoach:* Whose side is Ford on?

in 1939 that even acknowledged the Native American point of view in this supposed return of the western myth. But Native Americans were not the only "aberrant" groups invested with their own perspective. Southerners Hatfield and Lucy Mallory, though nominally society's arbiters of manners and privilege, are marginal enemies in the West. En route to Lordsburg, Doc Boone gloats over his status as a former Union officer serving under General Philip Sheridan (who later became an infamous Indian killer). It was Nichols who decided to make Haycox's anonymous army wife and gambler southerners. Nichols's and Ford's attitudes toward the South were highly ambivalent throughout their careers—unlike that of most of their colleagues, who tended to lionize southern qualities as they traveled west—but *Stagecoach* disparages the hoity-toity cultural trappings of Hatfield and Mallory. In both the final shooting script and the film, the South is the epitome of the civilization from which Ringo and Dallas happily escape at the end. Nichols took this attitude toward the South even further in his final script. During the last stagecoach battle with the Apaches, Doc Boone shouts as he kills an Apache, "Got ya, Johnny Reb!" thereby conflating the former Confederate rebels with the Apache rebels.[29] Both these rebel forces were essentially destroyed by the assault of a new wave of white civilization. Ford may have thought that Nichols went too far here; the line was cut.

Although Ford's transformation of the opening narrative sequence, his deviations from Nichols' script, and his deletion of Doc Boone's line in the last sequence all suggest an effort to curb Nichols's complex historical allusions, many critics focused on the screenwriter's role.[30] After the premiere and reviews, Nichols, perhaps worried that his acclaim was souring a future working relationship with Ford, soothed his old friend with a letter. "If there was ever picture that was the director's picture," he wrote, "it was that one, and I tried to make that clear to everyone who complimented me in New York." He continued, "It seemed to me in some of the notices I received undue mention and I tried to set it straight."[31] Curiously, in both major prints of *Stagecoach*, the credits placed Nichols's name as screenwriter beneath that of Ernest Haycox, who wrote the original short story. This reversed the etiquette of motion picture crediting, which always gave precedence to the screenwriter. As one detects from Nichols's letter to Ford, many speculated that the director might have done this deliberately to diminish Nichols's role in authoring the film. Although this surprising postproduction attack may have initially irritated Nichols, he hastened to defend Ford in the same letter and even professed what "a very happy collaborator" he had been and still hoped to be. Ford was soothed, if only temporarily. He and Nichols would work together on only one more film during that period, *The Long Voyage Home* (1940). Although it earned Nichols another Academy Award nomination, it was not then considered one of Ford's great achievements.

In spite of Ford's resentment and possible invidious behavior, the screenwriter's project for *Stagecoach* succeeded. Reviewers praised Nichols's script, but even more prevalent was their emphasis on *Stagecoach*'s historical underpinnings. According to these reviews, *Stagecoach* revived American history in films by re-creating the Southwest during Geronimo's last raid.[32] *Stagecoach* was true to both western history and the Hollywood history of the West. *Life* magazine highlighted *Stagecoach* as the movie of the week in late February, before the film's general release, but instead of summarizing the fictional plot, the article began with an expanded version of Nichols's prologue: "The railroad came to Arizona in 1878, but as late as 1885 you traveled overland to Lordsburg by stage." It continued with a detailed account of the hardships a passenger encountered on the two-day, 170-mile run. "But the real menace of the Arizona Overland," *Life* reminded its readers, "was the Indians. The very name of Geronimo made the passengers blanch with terror."[33] *Life*'s review is further testimony not only that the screenwriter's prologue was included in the original film version but also that it made a powerful if somewhat skewed impression on audiences in 1939.

Of course, contemporary reviewers did not attribute the film's success merely to Nichols's historical influence. Ford received an incredible amount of critical and popular praise for *Stagecoach*. But ironically, considering the auteur's legendary reputation as an artist, his decision to cut the prologue and many of the obvious historical elements seems to have been based on a need to assert control over the production at the expense of the high-profile screenwriter, rather than on an aesthetic desire to reinvent the western or connect *Stagecoach* with the mythic past of silent film. Nichols's partial defeat on *Stagecoach* may have symbolized a turning point for both the power of the screenwriter and the construction of western cinematic historical discourse. In late 1942, after he had parted company with Ford, Nichols would comment that the studio compromised cinema's potential by disempowering the writer. Both he and Twentieth Century–Fox writer-producer Nunnally Johnson would sense the waning power of the Hollywood writer and attempt directorial careers in the 1940s.[34] Nonetheless, in 1942, Nichols looked back on his work and concluded, "I devoutly believe it is the writer who has matured the film medium more than anyone else in Hollywood."[35]

In 1943, Nichols and the head of the Theatre Guild, John Gassner, published a collection of twenty of Hollywood's best sound-era screenplays for popular consumption. Gassner's praise for *Stagecoach* centered on Nichols's sophisticated reconsideration of the nation's western past. He wrote:

> The representation of American history and ideals has, in fact, added not a little weight to the screen's output, and can add a

great deal more. . . . A realistic examination of our past, as well as of the present in relation to our past, is imperative, and an impressive beginning was made by Dudley Nichols' *Stagecoach*. . . . The "western," regardless of its superficiality and naiveté, represented the American dream of independence and virility—but on a juvenile level. As *Stagecoach*, as well as a number of other screen stories like *The Plainsman* and *Wells Fargo*, demonstrate, the story of the West is not inherently wedded to puerilities.[36]

Rebels against the Railroad

One of the most prominent writers in Hollywood, and one directly connected to the rise of the American historical film, was former Georgia and New York reporter Nunnally Johnson. When Johnson moved from Paramount to Fox, he and Darryl Zanuck embarked on a massive American historical cycle. In fact, Johnson was so closely associated with Zanuck's vision that in their first major American historical film, the Reconstruction-era account of Dr. Samuel Mudd's trial and imprisonment, *The Prisoner of Shark Island*, Johnson was the film's associate producer. He would later act in a similar capacity on *Slave Ship* (1937) and *Jesse James* (1939). Released a month before Wanger premiered *Stagecoach*, *Jesse James* was Zanuck and Johnson's major prestige picture of 1939. It was also the first important film of the year, and Fox had prepared audiences for its arrival with a spate of publicity that focused on the film's notorious heroes.[37]

In the December 1938 issue of *Liberty* magazine, journalist Helen Gilmore asked Johnson why gunfighters were coming back to A-feature Hollywood productions. Johnson answered that although gunfighters had never really gone out of style, *Jesse James*'s major audience pull would be its history. He then proceeded to read what would be the entire text of the opening frames. His foreword narrated American history following the Civil War, when "the eager, ambitious mind of America turned to the winning of the West." According to Johnson, the railroad was the symbol of this new industrial age, but it was not an era of unalloyed progress: "The advance of the railroads was, in some cases, predatory and unscrupulous. . . . Whole communities of simple, hardy pioneers found themselves victimized by an ever-growing ogre—the Iron Horse." Johnson explained Jesse and Frank James's rise to fame as part of the climate of lawlessness, the dissatisfaction with American "development," and the victimization of the pioneers.[38]

After his dramatic reading for the press, Johnson supposedly shut his

script with a flourish and assured Gilmore that the studio was not glorifying the James brothers but presenting important facts about an era
previously neglected by the screen. Johnson had been scripting historical
films since 1934, and he knew the value of injecting impressive historical
iconography and research into a period narrative. The textual background
of the Reconstruction era and the rise of industrialization gave depth to
legendary characters such as Frank and Jesse James and invested the film
with an aura of prestige. *Jesse James* represented a sublimation of Zanuck's
gangster cycle, where history had been too close for the censors' comfort.
But as Johnson reminded readers in 1938, nineteenth-century gangsters
could not possibly be bad examples subject to censorship, since "those
times have passed forever."

Johnson's lengthy prologue, which would eventually involve three
text superimpositions in the final film, introduces many conflicts between
America's past and future. The text foreword and the James brothers' lives
begin after the Civil War has ended. The Union is restored, but with the
advance of the railroads, a new lawless age develops. The massive foreword, first outlined in 1937 by writer Hal Long, concentrated on the un-
derside of progressive business, as "the ruthless railroads pushed forward
to new frontiers." The emphasis was on industrial corruption. "Hoodlums,
abetted by crooked politicians and financed by avaricious robber barons,
capitalized on the development of the fertile valleys which lined the Mississippi for miles. Simple, hardy and God-fearing pioneers, real owners
of the land from which all manner of life and sustenance sprang, found
themselves victimized by the ever-growing ogre, The Iron Horse."[39]

What the foreword does not state is that these unscrupulous indus-
trialists and their agents are northerners, and the victimized farmers, like
the James family, are former Confederates. So has the Civil War really
ended? Isn't Jesse and Frank's decision to rob their first train a direct result of an ongoing guerrilla war between industrialism and agrarianism?
Aren't they self-styled Confederates, violently pushing the past and the
Lost Cause of southern independence into Missouri's troubled future?
This is what Jesse James Jr.'s biography of his father and the myth of Jesse
James stated.[40] But as biographer T. J. Stiles recently pointed out, it was a
self-conscious identity construction created not only by James's frequent
letters to local newspapers but also by editorials written by his friend and
fellow Confederate veteran John Newman Edwards.[41] Historians did not
create the James mystique. Claims of historical objectivity or a search to
find the "real" Jesse James are therefore lost causes, because so much of
his life was a public performance of Confederate values. Eyewitnesses to

his first robberies even attested that he and his men wore Ku Klux Klan masks.[42] The persistence of the James legend depended on creating and retaining a unified southern identity; only then could James's robberies and murders be justified and admired as patriotic acts.

Surprisingly, Johnson and Zanuck excised the James brothers' self-conscious presentation of their work as a continuation of Confederate resistance. The filmmakers suppressed Missouri's endurance of martial law, the relocation of southern families, the enforced oath of allegiance that barred Confederate sympathizers from voting, as well as the barbarous crimes committed against Unionists by the James brothers and their bushwhacking associates during Reconstruction. Instead, Johnson started Jesse James's career after railroad agents had killed his mother for not selling her farm. It was not the first time that Reconstruction would be written out of Hollywood's history of nineteenth-century America, nor would it be the last. Only the vestiges of the James family's doomed agrarian resistance survived the filmmakers' historical transformation of America from a nation at war to a nation bent on expansion.

Zanuck and Johnson bolstered their critique of postwar industrialization with text forewords, dates, and details linking the careers of the James brothers to the ruthless path of the railroad. The titles note "April 8, 1872," as the day the workers drove in the last spike of the St. Louis Midland Railroad, and the images and text then chronicle the rise of the James's careers. These historical trappings gave Jesse and Frank James a historical prestige bestowed on other famous Americans, and Zanuck and Johnson zealously relied on assumptions of historical accuracy and the participation of James's granddaughter Jo as a technical adviser to support the film. Critics reacted with amusement to the studio's "apocryphal" and "purified" Jesse James, and Nugent wistfully noted that "movies frequently would be better if they didn't try to draw a lesson." Besides criticizing the film's refusal to portray "Jesse James as he was, or even as we had thought him to be," Nugent scoffed at the filmmakers' portrayal of James as an anti-industrialist. "As a member of the capitalist press," he sniggered, "we must condemn this obstructionist policy. As a vicarious member of the James gang, as every former reader of the nickel thrillers must be, we rather resent this moralistic lesson." But Nugent overlooked the way James had manipulated the media and been reinvented by the Missouri press, dime novelists, biographers, and historians. It was facile to hope for a picture of James "as he was." As *Time*'s film critic pointed out, the dime novel *Jesse James, the Outlaw* and its sequels portrayed Jesse as "a morally delinquent crook."[43] In their historical film, Zanuck and Johnson were attempting to place two outlaws' criminal exploits within a more complex historical framework.

But Johnson and Zanuck also surpassed any simple historian's approach to find the "truth" about Jesse James. Johnson included a version of John Newman Edwards (played by the fiery Henry Hull), who editorialized James's career and directed public understanding of his acts. After James's murder, the editor fittingly gives a eulogy and disperses James's individual criminality within the more sinister forces of government and industry. Zanuck connected the outlaw to a crucial period in American history: "His death marked the end of an era where such-and-such happened." Zanuck continued, "He did many things wrong but he was not entirely to blame—laws—railroads—and all that—so we have a feeling that there was a *point* to the whole thing."[44] A biography of a gunfighter, however legendary, had to have historical overtones as narrative support. Johnson concurred, but he also portrayed James's mythmaking as an ongoing process by the press. Nugent may have had tongue in cheek when he sputtered about capitalist resentment of Johnson's historical premise, but the film is still remarkable for its presentation of a devious establishment and its acknowledgment of America's desire for aberrant heroes.

Jesse James was not a classic western in the silent tradition as Frank Nugent understood it. As a Twentieth Century–Fox film, it retained a deliberate textual component and overarching historical argument that linked it to the core of sound-era prestige pictures. Although some prominent critics objected to its historical peccadilloes, by siding with the James brothers, Zanuck's film stood against establishment history, government control, and national pursuit of expansion. *Variety* quoted the film's foreword as historical justification, and *Motion Picture Herald* reviewed the film as "Twentieth Century–Fox's Biography of an Outlaw," linking the new film to audiences' more recent memories of gangster Al Capone.[45] The film's declared and structured discourse was historical, not a hazy western myth. For all its deviations from strict accuracy, *Jesse James* belonged to a historical tradition established in the sound era.

Other films released in the ensuing months would claim in projected and printed text that they dealt with issues in western history, but their historical approach no longer sided with the rebels against the oppressive will of national expansion. Instead, the majority of historical westerns shown during and after 1939 justified the glory of America's progressive history. But for a while, in the midst of a surge in American historical films, *Jesse James* proved that filmmakers were not always on the side of government-backed industry.

Converting the Critics of Expansion?

Later in the year, Cecil B. DeMille's *Union Pacific* was released as the antidote to Zanuck's critique of industrialization. DeMille had begun working on another historical western after the success of *The Plainsman* in 1937 and Lloyd's ambitious *Wells Fargo*, but he had no particular historical event, person, or neglected historical topic in mind. Instead, he began with an idea of national expansion and completion. Over lunch one day in February, he and Jeannie Macpherson worked it out: "*Union Pacific* is going to bind together two sides of the continent—Senators screaming 'we don't want the West. It can't be done. It's a madman's dream.'—Dreams of a few men who believed it could be done.—President Lincoln believed that it must go through—without it the West would fall into foreign hands.—The drive to do the superhuman task."[46] Macpherson could not have been surprised when DeMille decided on the railroad as his heroic protagonist and the Indians and train-robbing outlaws as his villains.

Jesse Lasky, one of DeMille's screenwriters for the project, skimmed through the popular history collected from neighboring libraries and chose Ernest Haycox's semihistorical novel *Troubleshooter* as his source. Lasky was frankly contemptuous of Haycox's story but believed that, with the appropriate historical groundwork, the fictional characters might work. He also looked at Trottman's *History of the Union Pacific* before deciding on the Haycox work. He wrote to DeMille that the worthwhile element of the book "is lost in the stupid flamboyant style of its writing. There are the seeds of a good style underneath a bad 'western' literary style."[47] After the script was completed in September, producer William LeBaron read it and stressed the need for DeMille to include a truly impressive foreword emphasizing the national import of the Union Pacific. He suggested having Abraham Lincoln say, "This is not just important to the Middle West and the coast—but is important to the world." Although DeMille added Lincoln to the visual prologue, he was uncertain about the foreword. Perhaps thinking that a national historical connection was too small for him, he toyed with comparing the Union Pacific with the Pyramids and the Great Wall of China. Luckily, one assistant producer thought that this type of foreword would be a bit too esoteric.[48] DeMille may have tried to ease his historical discomfort by constructing a text foreword that identified *Union Pacific* as "a legend." But as Pamela Falkenberg pointed out, even DeMille's fabrications cannot be taken lightly. "This title," she wrote, also ascribes to the depiction a particular status: what we are about to see is neither historical nor factual (that is, not a true representation), but a legend. A legend is both "an unverified popular story handed down from earlier times" and "a romanticized or popularized myth of modern times." There is a certain ambiguity here. To the extent that *Union Pacific* is the legend, it is a myth of modern times that romanticizes the Union Pacific of the past. . . . To the extent that *Union Pacific* simply quotes the legend of the Union Pacific, it hands down a fictional past from earlier times.[49]

DeMille's legends may be self-conscious transcriptions of historians' own romantic views of nineteenth-century expansion and capitalist enterprise. And as Falkenberg reasoned, the opening credits are arranged to recede into the distance, becoming more historically illegible as time progresses. It was an approach DeMille had pioneered with *The Plainsman* in 1936. Although the titles deliberately inscribe this uncertainty, this sense that all history is based on recycled legends and elusive text, according to Falkenberg, DeMille's narrative also exposes capitalism's and American history's own contradictions. When the evil capitalist Barrows turns around and funds the railroad that he once planned to destroy, capitalism is momentarily subverted, but not for long. The Union Pacific is completed; thus, "capitalism negates itself in order to maintain itself."[50]

Yet no contemporary film critic was willing to credit DeMille with

Opening credits of *The Plainsman* illustrate the theme of the recession of history.

an unconscious discourse on corporate capitalism or any self-conscious historical subtlety. Nugent was cutting: "For Mr. DeMille spares nothing, horses or actors, when he turns his hand to western history." The narrative was an "encyclopedia of frontier adventure." Hollywood trade papers called it "a significant addition to the roster of historical melodramas" but neglected to specify what it added, save epic size and over $1.4 million of productions costs.[51] Historical filmmaking in the late 1930s had become an overarching business that became more and more adept at masking its historical qualities and subversive text.

DeMille still believed in stressing the importance of American history—when it served his cinematic purpose. When critics complained of historical inaccuracies in *The Plainsman*, he had quoted his foreword as a disclaimer. When Reverend Shiuhushu of the Indian Association of America condemned *Union Pacific*'s "rotten" portrayal of Native Americans as a "savage race," DeMille countered, "We were making pictures based on historical facts," without specifying whose facts he relied on.[52] He claimed utter objectivity in his films, yet Frank Calvin, a nephew of the head of the Union Pacific Railroad, headed *Union Pacific*'s research department. Surely there was a conflict of interest. Speaking with Bosley Crowther of the *New York Times* in May 1939, DeMille defended his historical vision: "History should be honestly and diligently respected. But, also I'd maintain that its teaching should be done more naturally, too. History is not just a matter of names and dates—dry facts strung together. It is an endless, dramatic story, as alive as the news in the morning's paper."[53] Unfortunately, DeMille's main facts were his constant faith in heroic national expansion, the purity of the white race, the sacredness of industry, and his stock of cinematic images and sequences that he could recycle at will. These were not facts but attitudes and legends, which, as Falkenberg argued, perversely turned on themselves for sustenance. Like the opening credits of DeMille's film, history itself seemed to disappear, leaving only its main argument formed by the thrust of the Union Pacific's tracks. Spurred on by DeMille's example, Hollywood filmmakers pursued the "superwestern"[54] but left the wreckage of historical experimentation in their wake.

Warner Brothers and the Winning of the West

Although Warner Brothers had been releasing American historical productions during Darryl Zanuck's era, it was only in 1936 that the studio created the Warner Research Library and appointed Dr. Herman Lissauer to head it.[55] Warner Brothers was preparing to compete with Zanuck, and though it would soon possess one of the most impressive research libraries in California, it still lacked the historical screenwriters with whom Zanuck worked so closely. By 1938, Robert Buckner emerged as Warner Brothers' most prominent writer of American historical films. His first collaboration on such a script for Warner Brothers was the rather stodgy *Gold Is Where You Find It* (1938), a history of the clash between California's emerging hydraulic power industry and the agricultural economy. A few months after the release of *Gold Is Where You Find It*, the studio library collected Thornton Delehanty's article "Westerns—The Last Word in Safety."[56] The noted critic said that westerns were cheap and satisfying to the nation and predicted that 1939 would be dominated by Americana. The studio had already made its own prediction several months before.

Under the supervision of Hal Wallis, Warner Brothers took as few financial risks as possible and decided on a remake of a successful historical period—the opening of Oklahoma's Cherokee Strip in 1893. The event had figured prominently in *Cimarron*, and even eight years after its release, the film still possessed an aura in Hollywood. Its scale and expense had deterred remakes, but by 1939, with the overall economic situation in Hollywood improving and with a different script, Warner Brothers decided to make *The Oklahoma Kid*. The researchers even dug a copy of Ferber's *Cimarron* out of the studio's library and studied it.[57] Originally, writers Wally Klein, Edward E. Paramore, and Warren Duff opened *The Oklahoma Kid* with a highly critical historical prologue beginning with a shot of the Indian Territory and the title quoting the government treaty, "Theirs as long as the grass grows and the water flows."[58] They then planned a quick dissolve to the White House in 1893, when President Cleveland broke the treaty. Buckner cut this potentially embarrassing prologue and planned to open with a voice-over extolling "the five and a half million acres of virgin land." Duff agreed to replace the original critical treatment with Buckner's positive spin on the imperial proclamation and decided to combine the endorsement of the new land rush with the original shot of the White House.[59] The writers studied *Cimarron*, both the book and the film, and although the time span and prologue were significantly diminished, they still maintained a protagonist, the Oklahoma Kid, who publicly sneered at "empire building" and remembered that the land had prior owners—the Cherokees.

However, unlike Yancey Cravat, the Oklahoma Kid (James Cagney) is neither of mixed blood nor a journalist-historian. The Kid is just on the wrong side of the law. Although he initially criticizes the government's expansionist policies before and during the land rush, his antiexpansion rhetoric disappears as the narrative progresses. The filmmakers were evidently worried about any antiestablishment comments, and in the final stages of film production, they began to add a number of temporizing text inserts to the first half of the film. Their impressive intertitles render the Kid's individual critique of the government even more marginal: "Out of the wilderness sprouts an empire. Pioneers, their eyes fixed on the future, build a town—one day to be a city . . . Tulsa."[60] In constructing *Cimarron's* history of Oklahoma, Estabrook had incorporated a counterpoint of overblown rhetoric with multiethnic, multiracial, feminist, and antifrontier images; in contrast, Buckner and Warner Brothers' team of writers used text as a means of restraining aberrant film images. After the land rush, these historical structures vanish, and the Kid's conflict with crooked saloon-keeper Whip McCord (Humphrey Bogart) dominates the narrative. In fighting the men who killed his father, the Kid becomes a good American citizen again, one who supports law and order and expansion. Screenwriter Norman Reilly Raine explained the new goal of the script: "Whatever he does against the McCord crowd would be lifted out of the status of the personal and would become the act of a patriot . . . and would provide a legitimate reason for stressing largeness of vision in the settling of the country and the onward march of civilization."[61] Zanuck had suggested something similar when expanding the historical significance of Jesse James, but Raine, Buckner, and Wallis did not share his valorization of critics of American empire. The Oklahoma Kid's opening criticism of the government's treatment of Indians and his own contempt for the government and expansion are transformed in the course of the narrative. Curiously, as traces of history and text disappear from the film and the scenes develop exclusively along the personal story, Cagney's character becomes a figure for law and order. He absorbs the discourse of the projected text. Buckner had originally planned to solidify the Kid's national devotion in a final speech that praised the settling of the West and claimed that it had been his father's dream, and was now his own, and would belong to future generations.[62] But this was too much for the studio. The film ended on a kiss.

Released in March, *The Oklahoma Kid* was a mild popular success. The critics thought otherwise. Nugent wrote, "Mr. Cagney doesn't urge you to believe him for a second; he's just enjoying himself." After starting off the year and a new western cycle with *Jesse James* and *Stagecoach*, *Variety* was appalled by this "small-time western" masquerading as a *Ci-*

marron, and it blamed the clichés on the writers.[63] Howard Barnes of the *New York Herald Tribune* also attacked the script. Critics of historical films usually focused on the accuracy of the narrative, but Barnes took the filmmakers to task for their pretensions in adding prestigious touches and intertitles to a western. "The direction falters to the point of having to substitute subtitles at points where a bit of significant action or dialogue might have knit the continuity together. . . . If you care to pigeonhole the photoplay, call it the latest example of the glorified westerns, which are rapidly assuming the proportions of a major screen cycle."[64] For nine years, the use of projected text in film had been the most recognizable iconography of the historical film. Critics unfamiliar with the period or with the nuances of historiography used to quote or paraphrase the film-makers' forewords. Often they became the keynotes for a critic's review. But in 1939, Barnes reacted to text in *The Oklahoma Kid* as though he had noticed it for the first time: text had become so obvious and disjunctive that the visual narrative fell apart.

In spite of the film's mediocre reviews, Warner Brothers seemed determined to control the production of historical westerns. After a huge premiere and fancy national promotions, it released its next installment, *Dodge City,* in April 1939.[65] Prestige, historical trappings, and the making of "glorified" westerns all seemed to be the surest method to rescue a hidebound Hollywood genre from its own repetitive anonymity and mediocre profits. But critics recognized that, unlike *Cimarron,* these "splashy" films increasingly explored history and conflict as a means of concealing mediocre scripts. Warner Brothers, Paramount, and MGM, in their mad dash to surpass RKO and outdo Zanuck, had a surfeit of major actors and a dearth of scripts. Since Buckner worked on all of Warner Brothers' efforts, time constraints forced him to repeat impressive historical formulas. At Warner Brothers, scripts became films at a breathless pace, and it was tempting to repeat narrative formulas from James Cagney's last feature to support Errol Flynn's latest adventure. Historical intertitles and details could patch only so much; Barnes's criticism may have hit its mark. *Dodge City*'s antecedents were undistinguished, and Buckner realized it, so his solution was to add some historical filler. Aeneas MacKenzie had done some preliminary research on Wyatt Earp and Doc Holliday in early 1938.[66] The studio had wanted to make another picture about Earp in Tombstone, but Twentieth Century–Fox owned the rights to *Frontier Marshal* and the only major biography of Earp by Stuart Lake. It did not want to risk a lawsuit from the irascible Lake or the pugnacious Zanuck. But, as Walter MacEwan wrote, the studio could always do a film about

Earp's experiences in Dodge City, Kansas, and fictionalize everything by making "a swell big western."[67]

Jack Warner was intrigued by this inexpensive suggestion and sent MacKenzie to the research library to read popular history, hoping that this precaution would save them from the pitfalls of plagiarism. Buckner had an even simpler solution: make it up and treat it like history. He knew nothing about Earp's life and even asked the research department if there *was* such a place as Tombstone, Arizona. He wrote, "Reduced to its actual elements, Dodge City was a dynamic, wide-open cattle town — that and only that. Any other reasons for its colorful existence would be an absolute falsification of historical facts. The result is a 'western' picture, if a label must be applied; but a formula which we have attempted to improve and distinguish within the natural limitations of the material."[68] The old "western" formula lacked prestige at that time, as Buckner's almost embarrassed hesitation indicated; during the heyday of the sound-era historical western, critics preferred to dress up westerns with terms such as "historical melodrama," "history," "semibiographical," and "period adventure."

Buckner attempted to cover the genre's plebian past with the gloss of the Civil War. It was a solution he and the studio would return to in *Virginia City* (1940), *The Santa Fe Trail* (1940), and *They Died with Their Boots On* (1941). Both his first draft and final script of *Dodge City* begin with text superimpositions and prologues opening during the Civil War.[69] Wade, the fictional protagonist (though modeled on Earp), is actually a southern officer at Gettysburg. Buckner eventually restrained his enthusiasm for history, however, and had the script begin after the war, when "the soldiers of both armies put aside their guns and consecrate themselves to the rebuilding of a great nation." The railroad becomes the new plow. Wade's southern origins are barely noticeable, and although tensions with Yankee saloon-keeper Surette flare, Wade's real preoccupation is the rebuilding of the nation out west. He has none of the Oklahoma Kid's scruples but is a full-blown cattleman and sheriff.

Even more than *Dodge City*, *Virginia City* protected its western narrative with the impressive rhetoric of Abraham Lincoln and epic battles of the Civil War.[70] Buckner and Wallis also enlisted the resources of the research department to bolster the narratives, but by 1940, critics were not impressed. Barnes and Nugent both dismissed the stories as "conventional horse operas" trying to be "glorified westerns" but projecting only "well-worn" and "hackneyed views of the West."[71] Behind closed doors, the filmmakers openly acknowledged that these historical gestures were meaningless. Actors were changing their own lines, and Wallis predicted that when "everyone becomes a writer," the script would fail.[72]

In a major break with the structure of historical filmmaking, Darryl Zanuck's production of *The Return of Frank James* (1940) used actual footage from *Jesse James*, and the original film functioned like the traditional text foreword. Film history became the structural equal of historiography. Producer Julian Johnson was thrilled with the idea, and Zanuck, with some misgivings, agreed.[73] With the exception of serials and the use of documentary footage, it was one of the first times that a major A feature used old fiction film footage as historical evidence. In Vera Dika's analysis of the postmodern "nostalgia" film of the 1970s and 1980s, she defines the postmodern impulse as a potentially critical view of the past lodged in the disjunctive return of past images.[74] Although Dika limits these self-reflexive moments to postclassical Hollywood, Zanuck's reuse of his old footage points to a self-conscious use of film as a historical document and to the symbolic decay of the historical genre. Remakes of historical films such as *The Oklahoma Kid*, Fox's *Frontier Marshal* (1933, 1939), Universal's *Destry Rides Again* (1932, 1939), and MGM's *Billy the Kid* (1930, 1941) testified to the studios' occasional experimentation with historical structures and iconography, but critics saw only repetition. Even the *Hollywood Reporter* complained, "It doesn't seem to matter what you do to a western; it still comes out as a western, and whether you spend $50,000 or $500,000 or even more to make one, they all seem to wind up with about the same story that has the same entertainment values."[75] By 1939, as these struggles between historical innovation and mass-produced spectacles resulted in more and more western formulas, the memory of Hollywood's pioneering sound-era westerns faded into the distance.

PART THREE

CIVIL WAR AND RECONSTRUCTION

5

Jezebels and Rebels, Cavaliers and Compromise, 1930–1939

Do you know, you're the only reviewer who has picked up the diaries and memoirs out of my background? Of course, I used everybody from Myrta Lockett Avary to Eliza Andrews and Mary Gay and Mrs. Clement Clay and Miss Fearn and Eliza Ripley and the Lord knows how many unpublished letters and diaries. And I'm glad, with your Southern background, that you noticed and maintained that Tara wasn't a movie set but a working plantation.

—Margaret Mitchell to Stephen V. Benét, 1936

When Macmillan published Margaret Mitchell's *Gone with the Wind* in June 1936, reviewers compared the author to Tolstoy, Hardy, and Thackeray.[1] Mitchell, usually the soul of courtesy, replied a little starchily that although her mother used to pay her to read serious literature as a girl, even the lure of a quarter had never tempted her to pick up *War and Peace* or *Vanity Fair*. In fact, she read Thackeray only after her own novel was completed and an automobile accident left her with some spare time. In his review for the *New York Evening Post*, Hershel Brickell felt that *Gone with the Wind*'s closest antecedents were not literary but historical. He concluded, "I can only compare it for its definitiveness, its truthfulness and its completeness with Douglas Southall Freeman's *R. E. Lee*, and I know of no higher praise that can reasonably be bestowed upon it than

141

this."[2] This was the type of review that Mitchell enjoyed, and Brickell would soon become her close friend. He had recognized an affinity between Mitchell's and Freeman's work that went deeper than their shared southern heritage and backgrounds in journalism. Freeman's 1934 biography of Robert E. Lee was immensely popular with both academia and the public, and by 1939, he was certainly America's most respected popular southern historian.[3] Mitchell's *Gone with the Wind* remains the most widely read American novel. And yet, as her correspondence reveals, she was less interested in comments about her literary style and impact than in an appreciation of her historical acumen.

Freeman also recognized a historical kinship with Mitchell and struck up a correspondence with her soon after the publication of her book. A few years later he began *The South to Posterity*, a survey of southern historiography, with a brief reference to *Gone with the Wind*'s influence on the growing public interest in southern history.[4] Yet Freeman was careful to separate Mitchell's popular novel from the realm of "legitimate" history, where his work belonged. In his chapter "Yet to Be Written," Freeman focused on Confederate women. He wrote, "Least of all has the part played by southern women in the War been presented. . . . Those who did most to maintain the morale of the South during the war, and to preserve spiritual ideals after the hostilities, are those of whom least is known and least written."[5] He also complained that the only good biography of a Confederate woman was that of Varina Howell Davis, the First Lady of the Confederacy. Freeman ignored the huge bibliography of published diaries and autobiographies of southern women,[6] thereby denying women the right to compose their own history—a privilege he gave to Confederate generals, statesmen, and advisers in an earlier chapter. Mitchell's novel, an avowed narrative of many of these women's experiences, pointedly had no place in Freeman's study of southern history. In fact, it appears that Freeman attempted to damn Mitchell with faint praise; he politely mentioned Mitchell's success in publicizing southern history but then drew attention to its proper arena, masculine public history and memoir. He wrote, "With the fullest admiration for Miss Mitchell . . . and other contemporary writers on the Confederacy, I have to confess that I am not sure I understand all the reasons for the steady increase in the number of those who read deeply of the South's four-year struggle."[7]

Almost from the moment of its publication, *Gone with the Wind* began a voluble, contradictory, and often acrimonious debate about its historical content and voice. The most enduring wail of disgust came from

Malcolm Cowley in the *New Republic*, who began with the impressive pronouncement, "'Gone with the Wind' is an encyclopedia of the plantation legend," initiating a prevailing academic aversion to the work's glorification of white-columned plantations, cotton and magnolias, white-haired "gentlemen" drinking mint juleps, and black "retainers" with appalling accents.[8] More recent cultural studies of the historical novel have partially revised Cowley's criticisms, acknowledging that Mitchell's construction of the maverick belle, Scarlett O'Hara, subverts much of the plantation mythology.[9] But despite interest in recovering a more nuanced understanding of the novel's tempestuous heroine, scholars have persisted in viewing *Gone with the Wind*'s historical background as myth, an imaginative if somewhat conflicted retelling of American history reflecting the twentieth century's longing for a safe Victorian past.[10]

Historical examinations of Mitchell's work have been confined to minute disputations on its historical points, which ultimately claim that Mitchell merely fabricated a romantic myth of the Civil War and Reconstruction eras ideal for classical Hollywood cinema. Scholars Gerald Wood, Kenneth O'Brien, and Richard King all claimed that in this "woman's narrative" (a book by and about women) history is irrelevant, while historians Elizabeth Young and Catherine Clinton have concentrated on *Gone with the Wind* as a complex reinscription of racism, dismissing Mitchell's historical claims as a way of "whitewashing" the novel's problematic racial stereotyping.[11] Tara McPherson's most recent cultural "reconstruction" of Mitchell's work, though acknowledging Scarlett's sexual aberrations, concludes that the heroine's subversion "is possible because it is situated within a scenario that romanticizes the Old South, revamping plantation mythologies."[12] In *Blood and Irony*, Sarah Gardner focuses on southern women's narratives of the Civil War from 1861 to 1937, but her interpretation of *Gone with the Wind* emphasizes its "simple" and "nostalgic" historical perspective.[13]

Although Mitchell has been consistently excluded from the patriarchal realm of historical writing, charged with replicating a racist myth of the Lost Cause, the following pages reconstruct her role as an innovative, influential popular historian responsible for engaging questions of gendered historical interpretation and racial hybridity. Historians have been equally dismissive of classical Hollywood's interpretations of American history, but even David O. Selznick's 1939 adaptation of *Gone with the Wind* confronts Mitchell's complex mixture of race and gender and, as I argue, projects the possibility of a biracial history of the reconstructed southern woman.

Margaret Mitchell's Revisionist Southern History

Mitchell and her friends enjoyed reading the spate of *Gone with the Wind* reviews in the summer of 1936, but Cowley's generated by far the most mirth. Had he even read the book, they wondered? His waspish indictment of the myth of southern life in American culture may have had its validity, but not when leveled at *Gone with the Wind*. The novel was an obvious assault on the myth of moonlight, magnolias, and passive, pretty women from the opening description of its willful and rebellious heroine. Scarlett O'Hara was unconventional, to say the least, preferring the company of the black children on the plantations to her aristocratic girlish contemporaries.[14] The O'Haras were not Anglo-Saxon gentlefolk but poor Irish immigrants; Tara had no white columns but was a rambling, unplanned, and undignified homestead. Later in her life, Scarlett would be bored and then disillusioned by the southern cause, viewing it not as "a holy affair, but a nuisance that killed men senselessly and cost money and made luxuries hard to get."[15] All four of Mitchell's protagonists—Scarlett, Melanie Hamilton Wilkes, Ashley Wilkes, and Rhett Butler—criticize the fire-eating politicians for starting the war, and her narrative confronted the widespread Confederate disunion, divisiveness in the cabinet, and mounting army desertion.[16] Drew Gilpin Faust's *Mother of Inventions: Women of the Slaveholding South in the American Civil War* (1996) chronicled women's gradual antagonism toward the war effort and its effect on Confederate defeat. But it was Mitchell who first intimated that women (and soldiers) did not wholeheartedly support the war. Although, as Sarah Gardner has pointed out, many of Scarlett's contemporaries are loyal to the cause, Mitchell gives readers access only to Scarlett's resentment, privileging it above others' blind devotion.[17]

Fellow southerner and *New Republic* writer Stark Young, whose more romantic Civil War novel, *So Red the Rose*, was filmed by Paramount in 1935, told Mitchell that in selecting the rugged background of north Georgia for her novel, she contradicted much of the genteel Virginia–Greek Revival nonsense written about the South. He wrote, "a part of the freshness of your choice lay in your choosing that upstate region, far less elaborated than the places like Charleston, Savannah, Natchez, etc." Mitchell agreed but wrote to Young, "I wish some of them [the critics] would actually read the book and review the book I wrote—not the book they imagine I've written or the book they think I should have written."[18]

Historian Henry Steele Commager understood Mitchell's passion for historical re-creation over novelistic imagination. Appreciating the dramatic authenticity of her setting and characters, Commager wrote that her story was "woven of the stuff of history," and her choice of mid-nineteenth-century melodramatic form gave *Gone with the Wind* the status of a true "dramatic recreation of life itself."[19] In both subject matter and style, Mitchell re-created her historical era. Yet Commager fell short of the next analytical step—of describing *Gone with the Wind* as a work of historiography. However brilliantly the novel may have reflected its historical era, Commager did not credit Mitchell with developing a new historical perspective on the war. Her work bore no comparison to his historical world, and as scholar Darden Asbury Pyron later pointed out, male reviewers often conflated her novel's complex and "ambiguous" historical position with her identity as a woman writer.[20] Because her perspective on the Civil War and Reconstruction eras did not conform to Whiggish historiography, equating history (and the defeat of the South) to progress, her book lacked "direction."

Mitchell's worry that critics would ignore her darker southern view of the war and Reconstruction, replacing it with their own simplistic view of how history should be written, was sadly justified. Many disparaged her lack of "literary style" and her melodramatic characters and plot, not realizing, as Commager did, that the elements of period melodrama were intended to support the historical accuracy of a Georgia woman's life from 1861 to 1873. In her letters, Mitchell also defended her style on historical grounds, stating that in order for her to transcribe historical events and meld them with the thoughts of her characters, she had to adopt a spare, unpretentious, even documentary tone.[21] Mitchell's construction of her stylistic choices served two purposes: on the one hand, her flare for melodrama gave her fictional romance narrative a feeling of historical accuracy; on the other hand, her careful research techniques were supported by a documentary tone intended to connote the authority of a historian.

Mitchell's glowing thank-you notes to Freeman and Commager for their praise were not merely extensions of good southern manners. She once admitted that she had initially wanted to write a history of Georgia during the Civil War and Reconstruction eras; however, she knew that it would never sell or be read beyond her circle of friends. "If I had my way the whole book would have been about that running fight [Johnston's retreat toward Atlanta in 1864]," she wrote to one of her admirers, "but I realize the reading public does not care for military campaigns as much as my family do, so I cut prodigiously . . . in an effort to keep it from being too heavy."[22] Like D. S. Freeman, she had worked as a news reporter, often combining her historical and literary interests by writing Civil War ar-

ticles for an Atlanta paper. But unlike Freeman, she had little money and
no university degree. She was also a woman. The worlds of the public and
academic historian were closed to her. Thus, she did her best to please
herself and her potential public by constructing a fictional narrative to
support her historical knowledge. Ironically, it was that fictional "wom-
en's" narrative of the war, Mitchell's substitute for her beloved traditional
military history, that captured the public's imagination and anticipated
the trend in women's social histories of the war era by half a century.

In her letters to friends, colleagues, and fans, Mitchell emphasized
the amount of historical research involved in writing her novel, her inter-
minable bibliography, and her own historical perspective articulated in
the book.[23] Like any professional historian, she went through old newspapers, campaign records, memoirs, government documents, biographies,
and histories. She interviewed survivors of the siege of 1864 and veterans
of Johnston's and Hood's armies. She revisited the old battlefields and
plantations where she had once walked with her father. And she wrote
about the period not only because her background and personal research
qualified her to do so but also because she was tired of reading and hearing about plantation myths, sentimentalized history, and Virginia's traditional dominance in the fields of Civil War and military history. In a letter
to Donald Adams she explained, "The more I dug into the back history of
the town, the more I realized how important it was during those days. But
for all that's known about it, the war might have been waged in Virginia.
And I got pretty sick and tired of reading about the fighting in Virginia
when for sheer drama the campaign from [the] Tennessee line to Atlanta
has no equal."[24]

There were other omissions in the standard historiography that irritated her. Mitchell had a great love and respect for history, but like James
Fenimore Cooper, Helen Hunt Jackson, and Edna Ferber, she had an un-
disguised contempt for historians who allowed contemporary economic
and political discourses to direct the retelling of events. Her explanation
of the South's defeat in Gone with the Wind paralleled that of noted historian James G. Randall in Civil War and Reconstruction, emphasizing
the lack of a cohesive southernness, economic underdevelopment, and
divisive political rhetoric.[25] Although her novel contained a sustained examination of the historical forces that accounted for the southern defeat,
Mitchell disliked histories by the likes of Charles and Mary Beard, who
viewed the Civil War's outcome as no more than a demonstration of the
triumph of industrialism over agrarianism. She was appalled when some
reviewers from Left-leaning periodicals complained that her book had

too little of these contemporary economic and political "isms," thereby implying that she should write a historical novel that complemented the Beards' *Rise of American Civilization* (1927). Even Mitchell's apparent belief in economic determinism was not a contemporary critical philosophy grafted on Civil War history but a historical response from one of the many Civil War diarists she came across in her research, Georgian Eliza Frances Andrews.[26] Mitchell was a dedicated and meticulous historian, not a tendentious social critic. For her, however crucial the historical theory, the historian's rhetoric must be contained by the actual war experience of white southern women.[27]

Yet in re-creating what an eyewitness to the war in Georgia would have seen, she drew furious protests from northern readers. Particularly controversial was the alleged desecration of the Atlanta cemetery by Sherman's troops in the fall of 1864. When Frank Kennedy and some other Confederate soldiers arrive unexpectedly at Tara for Christmas, the family asks for news of Atlanta. Frank tells them that although the Confederates and later the Yankees burned the town, many of the buildings are still standing, including Aunt Pittypat's house. He then pauses, for "he could not tell them what the army saw when they marched back into Atlanta, the acres and acres of chimneys standing blackly above ashes. . . . He hoped that the ladies would never hear of the horrors of the looted cemetery. . . . Hoping to find jewelry buried with the dead, the Yankee soldiers had broken open vaults, dug up graves. They had robbed the bodies, stripped from the coffins gold and silver name plates, silver trimmings, and silver handles. The skeletons and corpses, flung helter-skelter among the splintered caskets, lay exposed and pitiful."[28] Northern readers were affronted by this pro-southern distortion, and even *Time* magazine expressed doubt about the validity of the account. Mitchell, furious that her historical research had been questioned, wrote back to *Time*, stating that the military war records contained extensive passages about the desecration and that many respected studies of the war, including Avery's *History of Georgia, 1850–1881*, wrote of it.[29] Frank Kennedy's reminiscence almost duplicated W. P. Howard's report to Governor Joseph Brown in December 1864 when Confederate troops reentered the abandoned city.[30]

Mitchell would have many similar disputes with a public unused to such persuasive criticism of the Federal army. Some attacked Mitchell's chronicle of the depredations of Sherman's army without realizing that her fictional narrative was based on eyewitness testimony from both sides, including, most infamously, Sherman and his aide, Henry Hitchcock, who boasted proudly about his army's feats in "straggling" and "foraging."[31]

Although Randall's history, published in 1937, mentions the "shocking amount of downright plunder and vandalism," the historian was careful to avoid reprinting the vivid testimonies of 1864 and skimmed over assaults on southern men and women and the theft of private property that left many country folk to starve that winter.[32] Randall, perhaps with an eye toward healing disunion, wrote a well-tempered and fairly impersonal national synthesis of events from 1860 through 1876. Mitchell had no interest in mitigating the conflicts of the period or in editing history to suit a current mood of national reconciliation. Although it was certainly in her interest as a novelist to emphasize the violent drama of that era, Mitchell's commitment to chronicling Georgians' war experience was just as deep. It was this personal element in her historical novel that angered so many.

Mitchell's chronicle of southern women's struggle in 1864 was a modern woman's assessment of historical occurrences remembered and written by women. The war, as Faust would later comment, was an unprecedented period of feminine liberation in the South.[33] Women ran the plantations, hoed, planted, picked cotton, fended off starvation, and watched their houses looted and burned. Women recorded the Yankees' pillaging and violence in biographies (LaSalle Corbell Pickett), diaries (Eliza Andrews), and novels (Ellen Glasgow) and for decades attempted to shape public memory of the war.[34] Almost certainly, the gender of these historians influenced Randall to pass over their details of the March to the Sea and made university professors Francis Butler Simkins and James Welch Patton react with indulgent condescension to their reliability as historical sources. Their *Women of the Confederacy*, published in 1936, tempered southern women's impassioned accounts with objective, "professional" historical judgment. They used phrases such as, "After making due allowances for the inevitable exaggerations which are found in the feminine accounts of the behavior of the invaders. . . ."[35] Far from crediting these women with writing the first social histories of the Civil War, the authors charged them with having an anachronistic and subjective view of the past that prevented the South from advancing with the rest of the nation: "The hatred of Northerners . . . continued to glow in the feminine heart long after the Veterans of the Blue and the Gray were bridging 'the bloody chasm' through demonstrations of fraternity. Thousands of the women of the post-bellum South never tired of instilling into their young the vivid tales of bygone cruelty and wrongs."[36] Just as Freeman gently but firmly put Mitchell in her historical place, so contemporary historians (and their late-twentieth-century peers) continued to disparage and doubt the objectivity of southern women diarists and historians. Mitchell's novel gave them a voice and a public that no historian could hope to match.

Mitchell's women do not merely endure deprivation; they fight against it. One of *Gone with the Wind*'s more controversial passages is a Federal soldier's attempted rape of Scarlett in the autumn of 1864. Although *Gone with the Wind* contains several incidents of Yankee soldiers ravaging the countryside, looting homes, and attempting to burn Tara, Scarlett's first meeting with a Yankee is her most violent and empowering.[37] Armed with her dead husband's pistol, she shoots the uniformed intruder full in the face. With the help of Melanie, she loots his corpse and finds enough money and trinkets stolen from other southern families during his march with Sherman to support her family through the winter. She feels no remorse, only retribution. Many contemporary readers reacted stridently to the idea of a soldier wearing an American uniform looting and then attempting to rape a southern woman. Later, during the Reconstruction era, Scarlett is nearly raped by a white-trash vagrant and a freedman in Atlanta. Although late-twentieth-century historians have allowed that Federal troops did commit a bit of vandalism in the South, many have questioned or discounted the rape of white southern women by Federal soldiers or blacks, speculating that the rape of black women was far more credible.[38] Faust alleged that the rape of white women was almost nonexistent, citing the few cases ever brought to trial during Reconstruction. Mitchell's comments sixty years earlier provide an illuminating explanation for this absence. According to Mitchell, if a white woman were raped in the South, it would be too shameful to display in a public court. The victim's father, brother, or husband would consider it his duty to kill the rapist before a trial and thus avoid the stigma.[39] Mitchell's claim was supported by Civil War diarist Mary Chesnut, who described her husband's own reluctant revelation of the vicious rape and murder of a white South Carolina girl by seven of Sherman's men. The victim's name was not mentioned out of respect for her family, who had been forced to witness the crime.[40] Mitchell stood by her research, which included testimony from Federal and Confederate officers, but she also paid heed to the voices of southern women—even those voices that could not or would not speak.

Southern Women in Hollywood, 1930–1936

Mitchell's detailed confrontation of the darker history of the Civil War was something that few professional historians wished to address, but in the early stages of film production, Selznick glossed over any impending controversy and stated that he wanted changes to the novel kept to a minimum: "I find myself a producer charged with recreating the best loved book of our time and I don't think any of us have ever tackled anything that is even comparable to the love that people have for it."[41] After purchasing the film rights, Selznick despaired about how to script the thousand-page historical novel. He appealed to Mitchell, but she was one of the few successful American writers who refused to involve herself in the creation of *Gone with the Wind*'s screenplay. Selznick and assistant Katharine Brown made several attempts to lure her to Hollywood as a co-screenwriter and production assistant to oversee the historical authenticity of the film, but Mitchell was wary of what the group of Southern Californians would do to southern history. Early on, she wrote to Brown that she hoped Lamar Trotti, a native Georgian and authority on the Civil War era, would write the screenplay.[42] Trotti was under contract to Darryl Zanuck, however, and Selznick was not about to ask to borrow him. Instead, he assigned one of his own studio writers, Sidney Howard, to the project. When Mitchell learned that the New England–born Broadway playwright would be writing the screenplay, she lost interest. Howard wrote to her, asking for her help, but she politely declined to offer any suggestions or advice.[43]

Why did Mitchell refuse all active involvement in the film project? Her attitude toward the film industry seems to have been extremely cautious. As she explained to Sidney Howard, her book was her people's history, and she did not want to be held accountable for Hollywood's chronic distortions of the truth: "Southerners have been wonderful to my book and I am grateful indeed that they like it and are interested in the forthcoming picture. Not for worlds or for money would I put myself in the position where if there was something they didn't like in the picture, they could say, 'Well, you worked on the script. Why did you let this, that and the other get by?'"[44] Although an avid filmgoer and undoubtedly pleased with the $50,000 Selznick paid for the screen rights, Mitchell felt that Hollywood's representation of the Civil War since the advent of sound was not encouraging.

Griffith's controversial *Birth of a Nation* was still circulating in national theaters in the mid-1930s, but Hollywood's most recent sound films on the war tended to focus on the northern war experience and view of the conflict. Gary Cooper's portrayal of a Yankee soldier-turned-spy in *Only the Brave* (Paramount, 1930) is one example. When Captain James Braydon is forced to go behind enemy lines, the patriotic Union hero is faced with a more insidious opponent than southern cannons; belle

Barbara Calhoun (played by Mary Brian) is the embodiment of seductive southern romanticism. But the steadfast Captain Braydon is churlish to Calhoun and, most impoliticly for a spy, refuses to drink a toast to the Confederate States of America at a plantation ball. Eventually, though, Grant and Lee are reconciled in the final sequence, and James and Barbara are married. *Only the Brave* avoids any overt historical iconography or commentary within a standard establishment view of the war. There is no imposing opening foreword in Agnes Brand Leahy and Edward E. Paramore Jr.'s script—instead, text is confined to scattered dates. The one document insert gives a Union general the power to write and therefore control history: a close-up of General Grant as he writes his famous letter to General Halleck, "I'll fight it out on this line if it takes all summer."[45] There is no attempt to explain the war beyond a set military conflict and a personal battle between seductive, passive femininity and masculinity. The reasons behind the Confederate rebellion remain a mystery.

In 1933, RKO's prestigious remake of *Little Women* was also set during the Civil War, and it presented the New England March family as exclusively female. The South was even more foreign here than in *Only the Brave*; the region never entered *Little Women*'s narrative or mise-en-scène. Other than accounting for Mr. March's absence in the early sequences, the war is barely felt by the family. Even Sarah Y. Mason and Victor Heerman's early scripts, though reinforcing the narrative with text inserts from Jo's manuscripts, do not contain historical forewords or textual allusions to the war.[46]

As shooting commenced on *Little Women*, MGM planned Marion Davies's next star vehicle, *Operator 13* (1934). Studios were recognizing the power of historical settings in garnering critical and box-office "prestige," and Davies's role as Gail Loveless, a northern actress-turned-spy, was obviously modeled on the role Cooper had played three years before. Like James Braydon, Gail Loveless can experience the South only as a foreign country and an enemy. Though romantically involved with Confederate officer-spy Jack Gailliard (Cooper), she firmly believes in national union. But Loveless never really experiences the war; everything—even her role as a master spy—is an extension of her acting career, an exciting fiction. Throughout most of the film, she repeatedly plays on the weaknesses of southern manhood. Whereas Loveless is, as she says, "man enough" to be a successful spy, Gailliard is feminized; he is attracted and duped by Loveless as both a black-faced laundress and a Copperhead belle. Only when she falls in love with him does she realize that her role-playing has deadly consequences. It is Gailliard, a Confederate, who reminds her that real people suffer and die in war. Only after she is confronted by the reality of war does the film include a montage of recognizable dates and battles. Yet in the final moments of the film, the two romantic leads demand that everyone "forget war, forget hate, forget division."[47]

The film consistently distances the audience from the past. *Operator 13* was based on Robert W. Chamber's serial in *Cosmopolitan*, and the film made no attempt to disguise its fictional antecedents. The credits unfold over shots of a feminine hand turning the pages of the magazine. There is no foreword; the opening war montage shows soldiers sword fighting and singing rather than shooting rifles and loading cannons. An early script planned to acknowledge how the present informs our memories of the past, showing the aged Loveless remembering her career of wartime espionage as a 1933 Civil War parade passes her bedroom window, but the scene was cut.

Universal's 1936 adaptation of Edna Ferber's *Show Boat* was set after the Civil War and resonated with many studios' historical reworkings of silent "classics" (Twentieth Century–Fox's *Ramona*, United Artists' *Last of the Mohicans*). However, in spite of the historical specificity of Ferber's novel and her attempt to dramatize the horror of racial prejudice and miscegenation laws (both topics usually excised from Hollywood films by the Production Code), the film presents the South as a mythic playground. The final number of Kim Ravenal's Broadway show is a crinoline, moonlight-and-magnolia dance sequence in which scores of white-clad, hoop-skirted chorus girls hum black spirituals while blacks stay very much in the background. Broadway's crude view of nineteenth-century southern life commercializes a myth, just as Chicago nightclub owners turn Magnolia's talent for singing "Negro songs" into "coon shouting."

While Stark Young was telling Margaret Mitchell Hollywood horror stories about the adaptation of his novel *So Red the Rose*, Darryl Zanuck's latest vehicle for Shirley Temple, the Civil War tearjerker *The Littlest Rebel*, was playing in theaters. Although Zanuck was appalled by one of his screenwriter's historical inventions ("If you even suggest that Shirley Temple was the inspiration for the Gettysburg Address, they'll throw rocks at us"),[48] the film was concerned not with portraying southern history but with presenting Fox's most popular star, and the Civil War South functioned well as a sentimental background. If this was Hollywood's view of southern history, it is no wonder that Mitchell wished to disassociate herself from Selznick and Howard.

However trite *The Littlest Rebel*'s view of the South's Civil War experience, Zanuck's decision to cast the country's leading box-office star as a staunch Confederate child represented a significant departure from Hollywood's early Federal sympathies. And for all its sentimentality and lack of historical credentials, *The Littlest Rebel* employed many of the themes uniting southern historical cinema in the late 1930s—the strong women running the plantations, the kinship between black servants and white mistresses, the confrontation with violent northern invaders, the woman as the principal rebel against the government, the aberrant voice telling Confederate history in defiance of northern "national" histories. Scarlett O'Hara's pint-sized predecessor succeeded with audiences, and in 1935, Virgie proved the attraction of a strong southern woman as a rebellious figure, both destabilizing and then healing the course of national union in the final frames.

Jezebels and Rebels

With the publication of *Gone with the Wind* in the summer of 1936, Hollywood was faced with the possibility of confronting not only traditional histories of the war but also the racial and sexual discourses silently structuring those narratives. The American film industry's true problematization of race and history occurred in Warner Brothers' antebellum epic *Jezebel* and in *Gone with the Wind*. For years, critics of Mitchell's novel and Hollywood's Depression-era "plantation epics" have claimed that these texts preserve racist discourses and color barriers.[49] A closer look reveals their ambiguous presentation of the southern belle's sexual and racial identity—one that the cinematic medium amplified in startling ways.

Although in her correspondence Mitchell asserted that women historical novelists such as Mary Johnson (*Cease Firing, The Long Roll*) had the greatest influence on her work, she was a public admirer of the work of Thomas Nelson Page. Page's Reconstruction novel *Red Rock* (1898), far from anticipating the racism in Thomas Dixon's *The Clansman* (1905), actually projects a view of a multiracial southern family and region both before and after the war. Whereas Dixon envisioned American identity through white solidarity in the North and South, excluding blacks from the new nation, Page's blacks are true family members of the southern community and unite against the threat of white northern intervention.[50]

Mitchell would bring Page's multiracial family to a new level, emphasizing both the cultural and the blood ties between black and white southerners to such an extent that her heroine embodied this hybridity.

It is more than Scarlett's "black Irish" ancestry echoing the black slaves around her;[51] Scarlett is actually part of their family. In fact, Mitchell's Scarlett is closer than family to Mammy, Pork, and Dilcey. Though short-tempered with everyone else while she struggles for survival at Tara in the winter of 1864, Scarlett treats the stoic and courageous Dilcey, a mixed-race Cherokee and African American woman, or "mustee," as an equal. While Mammy is in despair over the death of Scarlett's mother, Dilcey and Scarlett grimly endure. With her father insane, Scarlett may identify herself as the "head of the family," but it is Pork, Dilcey's husband, who becomes the man of the house. Scarlett and Dilcey share Pork in a make-shift southern household where traditional patriarchal roles and familial control shift among the three of them. Later, when Scarlett gives her dead father's watch to Pork (a man more worthy of inheriting the token symbol than Scarlett's own son), Pork tells her, "'Ef you wuz jes' half as nice ter w'ite folks as you is ter niggers, Ah spec de worl' would treat you bet-ter.'"[52] Scarlett is both a sexually and a racially transgressive force in *Gone with the Wind,* and her kinship with and understanding of blacks embody blood and cultural ties that in many ways make her the most powerful biracial heroine in American historical literature.

Mitchell's racial mixing of Scarlett is metaphorical, but it is not unique in contemporary southern period literature. Owen Davis's play *Jezebel,* produced on Broadway in 1933, hinted that the emotional kin-ship between Julie Marston and black folks was more than skin deep. Race, gender, and rebellion are fused in the character of Julie, who is more at home with her black servants than with white folks. They even favor the same clothes. From the moment she sees that red dress in the New Orleans shop, Julie wants it, causing her fiancé to remark in horror, "Why, it's more fit to be seen at the Quadroon Ball."[53] She wears a dress that only a black woman or a prostitute would wear. She defies her fiancé and, in the play, is quite at home watching a cockfight with mulatto and black riverfront "trash." Later, when she returns from a trip abroad, Julie visits her servant Mammy Lou and her new twins before seeing her white family. The cinematic medium makes Julie's racial border-crossing even more evocative; on screen, Julie's red dress has become black.

Jezebel was set not in the Civil War period but in antebellum New Or-leans, a time that nonetheless showed the growing economic and cultural tensions between North and South. When Jack Warner refused to buy *Gone with the Wind* for Bette Davis, he bought Owen Davis's play for her instead. Screenwriter Robert Buckner brought the time period forward from 1830 to 1852 to emphasize the impending crisis. The similarities

Julie and her maid share similar taste in dresses. (*Jezebel*)

between Davis's Julie and Mitchell's Scarlett, violent and powerful heroines who control the films' narratives, were extreme, but ironically, when David O. Selznick wrote to Warner objecting to *Jezebel's* plagiarism of his forthcoming production of *Gone with the Wind,* he cited the film's use of southern history. "There is one scene of the men around the dinner table which actually is a slow spot in your picture. . . . I refer to the dialogue scene dealing with the difference between the North and the South, the discussion of imminent war, and the prediction by the Southerner that the North will win because of its superior machinery, etc. This scene is lifted bodily from *Gone with the Wind* [and] has nothing to do with either the original play *Jezebel* or with your adaptation."[54] Warner's brief and courteous reply was a rebuke, and he enclosed copies of the scenes replicated from Davis's play. The producers' dispute over historical argument, over the reasons for the South's defeat, indicated how important history had become in film: these weren't just money-making costume romances. In fact, its association with Mitchell's novel led Selznick to believe that *Gone with the Wind's* national popularity gave him a copyright on this part of American history.

But southern history was also crucial to *Jezebel*; the narrative was useless without it. Buckner wrote in the first draft of the script, "For many years, in fiction and pictures, the South has been presented in the same fashion—until the whole scene and all the characters have become typed and familiar *ad nauseam*. But New Orleans, perhaps the most truly southern in spirit and history of all locales, has been strangely neglected."[55]

Buckner's comments recall Mitchell's reasons for revising Civil War history and writing about Georgia. The difference is that screenwriters were also aware of the historical cachet of innovation and argument—of writing something new, a part of southern history that had been neglected by traditional historians. Buckner noted that the immediate antebellum years had greater potential than Owen Davis's original 1830 setting. But Davis's controversial heroine represented Warner Brothers' greatest historical challenge.

Warner Brothers handled *Jezebel* as its major American prestige effort of 1938.[56] It had all the structural credentials of a major historical film, including Warner Brothers' massive research bibliographies and background for both screenwriters and set designers. Studio publicity took two forms. On the one hand, it emphasized the filmmakers' historical research. *Jezebel's* research "bible" was extensive, with references to everything from Charles Gayarre's *History of Louisiana* (1866) to Lyle Saxon's more recent popular history, *Fabulous New Orleans* (1928).[57] Set designers and costume designers were not the only ones to consult the library or ask questions of the research department. Screenwriters' and directors' queries filled pages of the log. Warner Brothers, more than any other studio, prided itself on its historical apparatus. On the other hand, advertising in the press book indicated that the publicists were wary of marketing the film as a full-blown, serious historical film. To avoid any highbrow historical complications that might keep the average filmgoer away, they stressed the contemporary nature of the story, the heroine's modern outlook, and the up-to-date love scenes. "She's a modern miss in an old-fashioned setting," wrote one of Bette Davis's Julie.[58] These studio publicists had an ally in Owen Davis, who had introduced his published play as follows: "An attempt has been made that the facts and social customs of the period should be authentic, but the principal effort had been toward presenting the characters of this story as human beings; writing of them as though they lived today rather than as though they were dim figures of a ghostly past."[59]

So Warner Brothers followed two paths, emphasizing both the historical content and relevance and the heroine's modern appeal. But in combining Julie's modern sexual rebellion with the premise of historical accuracy, Warner Brothers made Julie, the embodiment of southern rebellion, the character with whom most people identified. *Jezebel* placed the seductive and transgressive power of the South in the character of Julie Marston. Her personal rebellion thus becomes emblematic of the South's rebellion against northern economic repression. Because she flouts sexual conventions by wearing a dress only a black woman or a prostitute would wear, Julie is a true spokeswoman for all southern women. Her impassioned descriptions of the South and her bewitching attempts to lure Preston Dillard, the southern-born Boston banker, back home to her are some of the film's most persuasive sequences. When Julie and Preston stand alone in the moonlight, she sees him waver in his devotion for his northern wife and northern bank and cries triumphantly, "We're in your blood, and you'll never forget us." For Julie, black blood is part of her too. When she plays the southern belle for Dillard's northern wife, she gathers the plantation's black slave children on the porch, and she is the only white to join in their songs. Her violently white dress not only

The color of the dress is red, but what is the color of the heroine? (*Jezebel*)

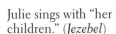

Julie sings with "her children." (*Jezebel*)

contrasts with the skin of the slave children but also darkens her own skin. Eventually, Dillard rejects this appeal of tainted southern womanhood, even when it is deceptively clad in white. But his rejection of Julie's South, his choice of a pure, untainted northern woman, signifies his faith in racial purity and industrial order and his rejection of the past. It is a decision that nearly costs him his life at the end of the film.

Hal Wallis originally assigned Edmund Goulding to direct *Jezebel* before replacing him with William Wyler. Goulding recorded his view of the film in some production notes, believing that it told the tale of the perils of "petticoat government."[60] Goulding ignored the fundamental elision of southern history and the dangerous female historian that John Huston's final script and Wyler's direction bring out. Julie is dangerous, impure, combative, obsessed with memories of her southern childhood and the love of Preston Dillard, but she has a power that is impossible to exorcise. It is she who walks out, resolute, fearless, and healthy, to face the pestilence of yellow fever. The film's racially transgressive heroine was virtually unknown to 1930s historiography. William Dunning, Ulrich Phillips, Claude Bowers, and Thomas Dixon still dominated professional and popular historical opinion on race and slavery. W. E. B. DuBois's *Black Reconstruction* (1935) presented a radically different view of American race relations, but it was not until C. Vann Woodward's *Tom Watson: Agrarian Rebel*, published within months of *Jezebel*, that mainstream American historians began to challenge traditional racial history.[61] However, Woodward dealt with Populist challenges to segregation; he did not question the white symbol of antebellum southern womanhood.

The Black Irish of *Gone with the Wind*

Like Julie, Scarlett O'Hara was closer to her black servants than to her white family. Although Scarlett's mother never perceived her rebellious character, Mammy saw and understood it. During the impoverished, agonizing months after her return to Tara, Mitchell has Scarlett doing tasks that slaves consider beneath "house niggers." *She* captures and ties up a cow to provide milk for Melanie's baby, *she* goes to Twelve Oaks to gather food, *she* hunts for the animals in the swamp, *she* hoes and plows and picks cotton. In the process, she even begins to look like Mammy, Dilcey, and Prissy. On screen, her skin darkens from sunburn and exposure, her thick, black hair frizzles in the heat, her clothes are patched and filthy. She even wears Mammy's sunbonnet in the fields. Occasionally, Selznick and his team of filmmakers show an awareness of this racial transforma-

The politics of race and dress: Scarlett and Prissy. (*Gone with the Wind*)

tion. Walter Plunkett, famed costume designer specializing in historical films, made Prissy's and Scarlett's post-siege dresses out of the same cheap fabric. Melanie wore an apron made out of a burlap sack, and Suellen and Careen wore cotton print dresses that had obviously once belonged to slaves.[62]

Sidney Howard's decision to eliminate cracker Will Benteen and slave woman Dilcey from the script may indicate his and Selznick's desperate efforts to streamline *Gone with the Wind's* complex narrative, but also to mask Scarlett's close, sympathetic friendship with two racial and class hybrids—the poor white and the Cherokee–African American. The fact that Scarlett's only unguarded relationships are with Will and Dilcey marks her own status as a racial and class hybrid after 1864. But traces of Scarlett's hybridity remain in the film. Undoubtedly, the most powerful scene in both the novel and the film involves Scarlett's and the Old South's rebirth on the Negro soil in the slave quarters. In Mitchell's novel, Scarlett has just returned home to Tara and realizes that she must run the plantation, care for her family, and save them all from famine and the destruction of Sherman's invading army. The ghosts of her ancestors and the memory of their struggles in Europe and the New World lull her into a dreamless sleep, but in the morning, she is still haunted by hunger and the ruin of the old world that she loved but took for granted. Scarlett walks to John Wilkes's Twelve Oaks in search of food and sees southern history in charred ruins at her feet: "There towered the twelve oaks as they had stood since Indian days, but with their leaves brown from fire and the branches burned and scorched. Within their circle lay the ruin of John Wilkes' house, the charred ruins of that once stately home which had crowned the hill in white-columned dignity. . . . Here was the Wilkes pride in the dust at her feet."[63] Twelve Oaks, more than the rambling, immigrant-built Tara, exemplified the powerful racial myth of the antebellum South. Scarlett gets no sustenance there but finds food in the slave gardens near the ruins. She pulls a radish from the earth, eats it, and then vomits, falling in the dirt. While lying there, memories of a dead age assault her. When she rises at last from the slave earth—a purged and grim southern phoenix rising from the ashes—she swears an oath, showing no loyalty to principle or memory but only to herself and her family's salvation. The new South is literally born from the ashes of the old; Scarlett draws new life from the soil of her former slaves. She has worn their clothes, eaten their food, slept on their earth, and her kinship is now total.

Howard and Selznick recognized the overarching importance of this sequence, and Scarlett's oath (restaged at Tara) concludes the first half of the film. Ironically, the first time one sees the mythical southern moonlight is when it illuminates for Scarlett the ruins of Twelve Oaks and the ravaged facade of Tara. Director Victor Fleming and cameraman Ernie Haller turned the full force of American cultural myth on the devastation of Sherman's march. Scarlett finds death and madness inside her home, and as she staggers outside, she sees the ravaged expanse of slave gardens and houses that once held life. Haller shot into the harsh red light of predawn, turning Scarlett into a near-black silhouette, a symbol of all struggling southern women, regardless of color, in 1864. With her dark, frizzled hair and ragged, hoopless dress, Scarlett looks not only poor white but black as she limps toward the slave gardens. In one of the longest unbroken close-ups in classical Hollywood cinema,[64] Fleming and Haller followed her descent to the slave earth and her extraordinary and brutal refusal to bow to defeat before tracking out on her rigid silhouette, echoed by the remains of a charred oak. Here, in this allegory of the course of southern history (defeat, purge, recovery, revenge), the filmmakers recast the iconic image of southern rebellion as an almost biracial woman.[65] Their violation of the norms of classical Hollywood filmmaking amplified another larger historical transgression in standard plantation narratives of the Civil War South.

This was the pivotal moment of historical transition for both Mitchell and Selznick, one that confronted the myth of southern history and the shadowy future of the reconstructed southern woman. In its pursuit of

Scarlett and the South rise again.
(*Gone with the Wind*)

The oath.
(*Gone with the Wind*)

The "reconstructed" southern woman.
(*Gone with the Wind*)

controversial historical fiction, Hollywood did not forget the role of the biracial woman in American history, her subversive past acting in counterpoint to traditional history's accepted racial categories and biography's patriarchal canon of heroes. Although Selznick and Howard feared historicizing the Reconstruction era in part two,[66] replacing the projected text and other historical iconography of the Civil War sequences with a melodramatic romance, *Gone with the Wind* was not a traditionally racist narrative that defined black and white Americans through rigid genre typologies and binary oppositions. Instead, through film's historiographic tool—cinematography—racial mixing left its trace on the historical narrative.

Ignoring Reconstruction

Hollywood's previous attempt to film American history in the antebellum South through Reconstruction had resulted in one of the most controversial box-office attractions. D. W. Griffith's *The Birth of a Nation* could still give Selznick heartburn in 1937. Howard immediately sensed the peril of re-creating the historical period synonymous in Hollywood with that 1915 film. In his "preliminary notes on a screen treatment," dated 14 December 1936, he began, "Our chief difficulty will come from the lack of organization in the second half of the novel." Perhaps he already envisioned repetitions of the race riots and public condemnation that had dogged Griffith's film—and Griffith had not had the Hays Office to deal with. Howard felt that in transforming Mitchell's historical novel into a film, he and Selznick should "think of the book as Scarlett's story" and focus on the main thrust of the book, namely, "what she conceives to be the tragedy of an unrealized love." Howard wanted to downplay the historical content and make the film a compelling love story, and he criticized Mitchell for allowing "other themes" to disrupt and overwhelm the simple love narrative. Howard was certain that the historical "forces" would create "difficulties" in the second half of the narrative when "a whole new series of forces," Reconstruction and racism, had to be explained.[67]

Mitchell's interest in her novel's historical background extended beyond 1865. She described the major events of the postwar era in Georgia, the repressive (if one was a white southerner) Reconstruction government, the fall of the southern aristocracy, and the rise of the Ku Klux Klan as a refuge for disenfranchised white men and a means of "protecting" southern women. In contrast, Selznick and Howard avoided treating the Reconstruction era with the same deference accorded to the war. Early in preproduction, Howard and Selznick agreed that Scarlett's killing of the Yankee cavalryman "was one of the most exciting and dramatic scenes in the book" and had to remain in the script.[68] A number of diatribes from Union veterans' groups demanded the removal of all scenes of Federal soldiers looting and burning southern homes,[69] and although Selznick compromised, cutting several violent encounters with Union soldiers at Tara and their final attempts to burn the place to the ground, he kept Scarlett's shooting of the Yankee.

No such historical disputes animated the construction of *Gone with the Wind's* second half. Their withdrawal of text from the second half of the film suggests the filmmakers' distinct uneasiness with this period and all the structural historical ceremony accorded to the wartime Confederacy. This full-blown retreat into the purely fictional romance might indicate that black and white Georgia, as a conquered territory, was effectively silenced by the Reconstruction government and was simply written out of the country's official history. Far more likely, though, is that Selznick and Howard wanted to avoid any racial incidents linking their film to Griffith's *Birth of a Nation*. It was not that Mitchell's novel echoed Thomas Dixon's strident racism; her own view that "the scourge of war had been followed by the worse scourge of Reconstruction" was far less virulent than historian Claude G. Bowers's *The Tragic Era* (1929), which referred to Reconstruction as an atrocity.[70]

The Reconstruction era was not entirely unexplored in Hollywood cinema. In 1936, Twentieth Century–Fox's *Prisoner of Shark Island* vividly depicted the mob hysteria and violent national antagonism toward the white South following the assassination of Lincoln (while masking the era's more remarkable if abbreviated attempts to improve the lives of black southerners). But Sidney Howard was not Nunnally Johnson. In his outline to Selznick, Howard confessed that when the narrative reached Reconstruction, he was "a little shaky . . . largely because I want if possible to avoid telling the audience that Georgia had refused to ratify the vote, on the grounds it is a little dry dramatically."[71] But this excuse was ingenuous; far more dangerous was the potential negative press. Selznick worried about alienating black viewers, but he seemed even more concerned about the growing fascism in Europe and America. Since the 1920s, the Klan had become even more eager to attack Jews than blacks. As he wrote to Howard, "I personally feel that we should cut out the Klan entirely. It would be difficult, if not impossible, to clarify for audiences the difference between the old Klan and the Klan of our times. . . . I, for one, have no desire to produce any anti-negro film either. . . . I do hope that you will agree with me on this omission of what might come out as an unintentional advertisement for intolerant Societies in these Fascist-ridden times." Later in the letter, Selznick concluded that "our great problem is going to be to get the background in unobtrusively while we concentrate on the personal story."[72] Here he reveals his attitude toward history in *Gone with the Wind*: it was an uncomfortable narrative component he wanted to avoid as much as possible, particularly with regard to the Reconstruction era and racism. Selznick had many letters from black organizations warning him to make an "acceptable" film or face their boycott, even though, as film historian Thomas Cripps pointed out, the book and film were not violently racist and even undercut racial stereotypes.[73] The film in particular created a greater engagement between Hollywood films and black audiences and gave actors such as Eddie Anderson, Oscar Polk, Butterfly McQueen, and Hattie McDaniel unprecedented control over what they would say and do on the set.

Selznick's legendary fiddling with the script and the parade of screenwriters throughout 1937 and 1938 did little but waste time. After several frenetic months with Oliver H. P. Garrett, Ben Hecht, and F. Scott Fitzgerald, he would return to Sidney Howard's original outline and adherence to Mitchell's narrative and dialogue. Although Howard planned the foreword and titles for Gettysburg and Sherman's march at an early stage, their exact wording was left until after shooting was completed. Howard's final script outlined the opening title but made no attempt to word it beyond "a comment on the southern aristocracy."[74] Selznick hired high-profile script doctor Ben Hecht to write the titles toward the end of production.[75] The producer's final touch was to establish the film's tone and intent with a staple component of historical films, but rather than emphasizing time and place, the impending war, and the end of a way of life, Selznick retreated from the historical period and refrained from introducing *Gone with the Wind* as Mitchell had: by emphasizing the heroine's complete subversion of southern myths. Instead, after three years in production, *Gone with the Wind* was introduced as Selznick's fantasy of the Old South: "There was a land of cavaliers and cotton fields called the Old South. . . . Look for it only in books, for it is no more than a dream remembered. A civilization gone with the wind." Although Hecht hinted that *Gone with the Wind* had been taken from history books, the film's representation of the past was articulated as only a myth, America's lost paradise.

Selznick staged the premiere in Atlanta, no doubt attempting to recapture the film's southern antecedents.[76] Mitchell was in attendance, and surviving Confederate war veterans paraded once more down Peachtree Street. Although Mitchell did not publicly disown the film, neither did she regret her severance from the filmmaking process. If the pudgy militiamen and brand-new uniforms made her cringe, Twelve Oaks's three-story white columns made her laugh as hard as she had at Malcolm Cowley's review.[77] The book Cowley claimed she had written was epitomized in Hecht's foreword. Although Selznick's unintentional moments of southern burlesque may have made Mitchell snigger, and the last-minute foreword revealed a fainthearted attempt to dehistoricize the transgressive voices of southern women, Selznick, Howard, Plunkett, Fleming, and Haller maintained the legacy of Eliza Frances Andrews, Mary Chesnut, Margaret Mitchell, and Julie Marston. Although Selznick may have retreated from the ongoing racial battles of Reconstruction, at the heart of his film, a dark-skinned, ragged woman with frizzled dark hair pushed herself up from the slave earth of Tara and swore to forget the past. Nearly ten years later, she would stand in almost the same place and realize that forgetting was impossible.

6

The Lives and Deaths of Abraham Lincoln, 1930–1941

Lincoln should be treated as a symbol. The two men who personify
forgiveness in the history of the world are Jesus Christ and Abraham
Lincoln. . . . It will have the most powerful effect when the picture fades
out on the tableau of Abraham Lincoln, the Negro, and the little girl, and
a military band playing "Dixie."

—Darryl F. Zanuck, 1936

Although, between 1933 and 1939, fictional southern women enabled
Hollywood filmmakers to reinscribe and valorize a persistent historical
rebellion within national narratives, Civil War and Reconstruction biographies were almost exclusively the province of men. For a while, Darryl
Zanuck had considered Missouri outlaw Belle Starr as the southern people's
"idol, their symbol of revolt" during Reconstruction. Cameron Rogers's early story outline in September 1938 built on the southern woman rebel tradition: "In a day when the West was a man's province and the frontiers were
sown with the graves of masculine individuals who had gone into action a
loud second too late, Belle put herself on an equal footing with the coolest
of the so-called dominant sex."[1] But while Zanuck believed that Belle had
the screen potential to be another Scarlett O'Hara or a Jezebel, he nonetheless advised screenwriters to constrict her independence as a guerrilla
leader.[2] By 1940–1941, the movie version of Belle Starr had become a
passive if patriotic member of her husband Sam's band. He was the brains
and the catalyst for revolt; she became his glamorous subordinate.

Zanuck's decision on *Belle Starr* reflected his considerable investment in American men as the arbiters of history. Where the Civil War and
Reconstruction were concerned, like so many of his colleagues, Zanuck
concentrated on Lincoln and his legacy. Abraham Lincoln's presence in
Civil War films symbolized the studios' supreme effort to counter the racial
and sexual disunion created by the Jezebels and Scarletts of the American
cinema. He was the homespun man of the people, a hardworking, self-
educated lawyer and politician who managed to stay honest, an impressive head of state who held the nation together yet could still tell an off-
color joke. His working-class humanity made him a good cinema character,
whereas George Washington's unapproachable heroism and Robert E. Lee's
gracious dignity did not seem to photograph well. In many ways, Lincoln
had been the industry's stock historical character since he first appeared
in Edwin S. Porter's *Uncle Tom's Cabin* in 1903. In the ensuing century,
Lincoln obligingly read by firelight, split rails, debated Stephen Douglas,
wrote and rewrote the Gettysburg Address, stared off into space with pro-
phetic solemnity, and got himself shot over and over again.[3] Throughout
the 1930s, filmmakers deployed Lincoln's image with an unprecedented
regularity, a habit shared by academics and popular historians.

The persistence and variety of Lincoln scholarship were so overwhelming that James G. Randall headed his 1934 address to the American Historical Association "Has the Lincoln Theme Been Exhausted?"
Although Randall believed that, given the number of new Lincoln documents surfacing (principally Robert Todd Lincoln's collection), professional historians still had opportunities for new Lincoln research, he had
to admit that nonprofessionals had long dominated the field. "Lincoln is
everybody's subject," he wrote, and "the hand of the amateur has rested
heavily on Lincoln studies." As a result, Lincoln was perhaps the most
manipulated subject in American history, his life and thoughts used by
"the propagandist, the political enthusiast, the literary adventurer."[4] In his
efforts to separate the realms of popular and professional history, Randall
did not conceal his contempt for Carl Sandburg and Albert J. Beveridge,
his generation's most famous Lincoln biographers. According to Randall,
their form of biography was mere hagiography. Despite their popular appeal, he claimed that their work made no original contribution to Lincoln
scholarship. Few outside the academy paid any attention. But a few short
years later, even Sandburg and Beveridge were superseded by the popular
historical work of Darryl Zanuck, Lamar Trotti, and Robert Sherwood. In
a decade dominated by countless Lincoln cameos and reenactments of
the Lincoln myth, two major biographical films would redefine the his-

torical values and rhetoric of American biography, challenging Randall's view of American history and myth in ways he never dreamed.

Early Supporting Roles

Just as Randall complained that Lincoln's presence sanctified whatever theme or subject the "historian" chose, for most of the 1930s, Lincoln generously supported whatever period film a studio happened to create. He lent authenticity to insignificant scripts; he healed any divisive tale of the Civil War; he was a prestigious touch added to secure that elusive critical and box-office appeal. In 1930 Lincoln had been D. W. Griffith's choice to reinvigorate his filmmaking career. In the following years, filmmakers borrowed many of *Abraham Lincoln's* emblematic historical moments. Lincoln myths were applied like historical details. From 1934 to 1938, he and his wartime speeches became the American cinema's favorite historical props. When Charles Laughton's English butler went west in *Ruggles of Red Gap* (1935), he reminded the lawless frontiersmen of their national heritage by reciting Lincoln's Gettysburg Address to a rowdy saloon. That same year, Shirley Temple sat on Lincoln's knee and shared an apple with him in *The Littlest Rebel*. It was Lincoln who saved little Virginia's Confederate father from a charge of espionage. His kindness to her and her doting servant (Bill Robinson) softens her heart toward the Union, and after the war, she is reunited with both her father and her Yankee officer friend. In both cases, the screenwriters added *Ruggles's* Gettysburg Address and Virginia's meeting with Lincoln at late stages of production, indicating that they were imagined as ways to enliven otherwise pedestrian scripts.[5] Zanuck, in particular, saw Lincoln "as a symbol" and planned the historical tableau as a means of giving "the complete picture of the Civil War—the Negroes that he freed, and the rebels whom he is going to forgive."[6] History was the ultimate guarantee of prestige, and Lincoln was a safe, uncontroversial means of attaining it. He was also good for some extra publicity, since these added Lincoln touches garnered critical attention in the trade papers. The *Hollywood Reporter* wrote that the recitation of Lincoln's words was *Ruggles of Red Gap's* "most memorable" moment, while *Daily Variety* called Temple's scene with Lincoln (Frank McGlynn Sr.) "the picture's high spot."[7]

Of all the studio production companies, Zanuck and his team of screenwriters at Twentieth Century–Fox were perhaps the most committed to American historical filmmaking, and they seemed particularly prone to insert references to or shots of Lincoln into their nineteenth-century period films. One of the many works in progress that Zanuck inherited when Twentieth Century and Fox merged in 1935 was *The Farmer Takes a Wife*. Based on Frank B. Elser and Marc Connelly's successful Broadway play, it was a nonspecific character study of the lives of Erie Canal freight workers during the conversion to railroad transport in the mid-nineteenth century. At that time, Zanuck had several other historical scripts to develop, including *The Bowery, The Mighty Barnum,* and *Captain January,* and he was not particularly impressed with Elser and Connelly's charming script or its callow star, Henry Fonda (who, despite Zanuck's low expectations, would become the producer's most popular actor). Zanuck and screenwriter Edwin Burke, who worked together on *The Littlest Rebel,* fiddled with the folksy play and managed to insert some impressive long shots of covered wagons, craggy pioneers, political arguments, and predictions of industrial development. The preparation succeeded, and reviewers noted that Zanuck had given the material the "prestige" treatment, not only in terms of director Victor Fleming and established stars Janet Gaynor and Charles Bickford but also in terms of its revamped script.[8]

Burke was largely responsible for introducing Lincoln into the latest Shirley Temple vehicle and, building on his popularity with Zanuck, added Lincoln to the text of *The Farmer Takes a Wife*. Freight workers Molly (Gaynor), Klore (Bickford), and Fortune (Slim Summerville) are accustomed to meeting all kinds of people on their travels to and from the Erie Canal, and one morning they agree to take on some temporary passengers—celebrity actor Junius Brutus Booth and his sons. Molly, Klore, and Fortune are impressed and discuss the events of the day with their guests. As they are chatting, Fortune reads a newsprint speech by an up-and-coming politician, Abe Lincoln, whom he identifies as "a man out west. He don't want any more states to be slave states." Fortune calls him a great man, but one of the boys interrupts pugnaciously, "I never heard of him." When Fortune, smothering a smile, asks for *his* name, the boy gives it: "John Wilkes Booth. I bet he'll hear of me when I grow up. I'm going to be famous too."[9] This was just the sort of historical vignette Zanuck liked to add to undistinguished period scripts, but critic Thornton Delehanty found the film too "episodic," a common criticism of period films that ignored narrative for the sake of historical touches. Delehanty dismissed the Booth scene as "irrelevant" to the sentimental romance.[10] Zanuck's historical production values were becoming dangerous excesses. Delehanty was not unappreciative of historical films; he had once admired *Cimarron,* but he despised self-conscious historical tricks used to divert his attention from an otherwise bland narrative.

Several months later, Zanuck and Nunnally Johnson would revisit Lincoln and John Wilkes Booth when they developed *The Prisoner of Shark Island*. Filming the life of Dr. Samuel Mudd was a watershed in American historical cinema; it was the first biographical film of a man victimized by the federal government and unjustly vilified by the public. But it was also the first film to represent the darker side of American hero worship. Here, Lincoln was not needed to generate historical authenticity and national reconciliation; instead, he became the means of introducing the lost potential of national unity. In the opening sequence, after the historical titles and tableaux announce the end of the Civil War, Johnson introduces Lincoln as a potential healer. On his first visit to Richmond in April 1865, he asks the band to play "Dixie." It is a gesture that wins the grudging respect of the predominantly Confederate crowd, for Lincoln's temperate political principles and plans for Reconstruction are not widely known in the region devastated by five years of war. Booth soon assassinates Lincoln, and though his death indirectly causes Mudd's misfortune, Johnson's script stresses its broader effects. With Lincoln gone, Secretary of War Edwin Stanton, Congress, and the American public have no one to restrain their vicious demands for revenge. Lincoln's apotheosis is the crucible for the abuse of absolute power.

The Prisoner of Shark Island also represented the studio's expansion of research in pursuit of obscure historical figures and events. Mudd's experience was unique, but the film would demand exacting research. Lincoln was such a famous and permanent fixture in the national cinematic mind that the critics' and audiences' awareness of historical peccadilloes would be more acute. Research was crucial to meet critical expectations; even before Zanuck assigned the topic to the screenwriter, he requested a research bibliography. Johnson later admitted that he had first come up with the idea of introducing Lincoln in Richmond with his conciliatory song request after reading Lloyd Lewis's *Myths after Lincoln*.[11] Lewis's book was only one of many historical studies of Lincoln's life and death that Johnson would read in preparation for writing his original screenplay. He also read the government records of the Mudd trial, the biography of Mudd published by his daughter Nettie in 1903, and the more contemporary discussions of the Reconstruction era.[12] In Lewis's exploration of the postassassination deification of Lincoln and the consequent demonization of Booth, Mrs. Surratt, and Mudd, Johnson realized that violent nationalism had distorted popular history. Although President Andrew Johnson pardoned the country doctor in 1870, recognizing that he had simply been in the wrong place at the wrong time, the military court and

Congress never formally admitted that the charges of conspiracy were false.[13] Although government records showed the impropriety of trying a citizen in front of a military court without the ability to testify in his own defense, Johnson found that historical accounts of the assassination were tendentious, and Mudd's name was still a national byword for wrongdoing and shame. In tackling this controversial and nationally embarrassing topic, the screenwriter revealed a history of postwar injustice and the public's passionate need to condemn an innocent man merely because he was a white southerner.

Zanuck's preliminary researcher, Sidney Cook, quoted many conflicting reports and documents claiming Mudd's innocence and guilt in the conspiracy to kill Lincoln, and he warned both Zanuck and Johnson that "we must not be led astray by such perfunctory snap-shot judgments as the statement in the *Reader's Digest* for August 1934,"[14] which had first alerted Zanuck to the controversial topic.[15] Although the thorough bibliography and multiple historical perspectives intrigued Johnson, he was more interested in taking a position against the government and revising the canonical historiography that had allowed national mourning to obscure national miscarriages of justice. Cook also warned Johnson of the perils of sympathizing with a man convicted, however unjustly, of the president's murder: "If a picture is to be made in which Mudd is to be glorified as a hero-martyr, extraordinary care should be taken in the editing of the script or film to avoid the charge of distorting known historical facts in a case of involving the assassination of a most beloved president." Johnson agreed, sympathizing with both Zanuck's efforts to side with Mudd and the potential repercussions of challenging Lincoln's legacy. Initially he accomplished this by creating an elaborate foreword stressing the defeated South's grim expectations and the efforts of Lincoln, the "great and generous conqueror."[16]

For the first time since *Abraham Lincoln* six years earlier, Lincoln would play more than a national cameo. Even more unique was Zanuck and Johnson's decision to confront the consequences of his broken postwar legacy. This production also taught them the advantages of creating a well-researched original screenplay. Although research libraries were a necessary part of most major studios' production offices, it was only when a screenwriter was faced with an "original story" that he or she had to depend on the library's resources to create a dramatic but reasonably accurate and intelligent use of history. Zanuck also knew that by assigning Johnson, who was from Georgia, to write the script, he was capitalizing on the writer's zeal to exonerate a persecuted southerner. Johnson's thor-

ough research practices and willingness to confront a neglected and controversial historical topic represented a high point in the construction of
historical film scripts. With *The Prisoner of Shark Island*'s success as a
prestige picture, Johnson had proved to the head of the studio that written
craftsmanship paid off.

In the next few years, Zanuck returned to historical subjects and increasingly to biopics, such as the McKinley assassination thriller *This Is
My Affair* (1937), which told the obscure story of a naval officer hired by
McKinley to infiltrate a crime ring connected to high government officials.[17] However, these films tended to celebrate more traditional, Horatio Alger heroes, such as Irving Berlin (*Alexander's Ragtime Band*, 1938)
and Alexander Graham Bell (*The Story of Alexander Graham Bell*, 1939).
Yet as his conference notes on these projects demonstrate, Zanuck often
allowed himself to slip into a formulaic idea of biography: the story of
the great man struggling against society's myopia or outright hostility.[18]
It would take another southern screenwriter, another original historical
screenplay, and another unconventional approach to the Lincoln myth to
hone his former critical edge.

By 1938, Zanuck's growing interest in biographical-historical filmmaking led him to consider the commercial possibilities of a screen life
of Lincoln. At that time, he was overseeing the final stages of *The Story
of Alexander Graham Bell* and longed to escape from it. His latest foray
into history was becoming an increasing source of irritation. The film had
developed from Twentieth Century–Fox hack writer Ray Harris's lifelong
interest in Bell. Harris, no doubt recognizing Zanuck's taste for American
history, wrote a well-researched treatment of Bell's life from his early days
in Edinburgh, his research and teaching of elocution, and his "accidental"
discovery of the telephone. Kenneth Macgowan, a former RKO producer
who had handled many period films, including *Little Women*, supervised
Harris's work.[19] But the writer often annoyed Zanuck with his didacticism
and a persistent concentration on Bell's elocution studies, which rendered
his discovery of the telephone incidental. Zanuck had other ideas. As he
wrote to Harris in May 1938, "Our main drama lies in Bell's fight against
the world to convince them he had something great, then to protect his
ownership. . . . Despite the fact that elocution was the rage at the time,
casting a leading man of today as an out-and-out elocution enthusiast is
like asking Tyrone Power to wear lace on his underdrawers."[20]

Late in the summer, Zanuck assigned Lamar Trotti to polish the
script. Trotti had come to Hollywood several years earlier as Dudley
Nichols's writing partner, and like Nunnally Johnson, Trotti knew how

to handle Zanuck when the producer was annoyed. He agreed with Zanuck that the best character films had stories that showed the protagonist struggling against the odds for something great. However, he did like Harris's historical touches.[21] For Trotti, the historical content was simply the most effective part of the script, and by the end of the day, Trotti had convinced Zanuck that the major problem with the script was a lack of historical specificity rather than a surfeit. Zanuck now felt that "we have departed too far from the true character and events of Bell's life" and that "our script had been simplified down to a 'success story' and 'boy meets girl.'" Macgowan must have been dumbfounded by this abrupt reversal of judgment, but Trotti had succeeded in turning the producer partially away from his growing tendency to streamline history into success stories. He began to favor an elaborate foreword and even a nonlinear form of narrating Bell's life, and the new script contained a brief prologue in the 1910s showing Watson and Bell making the first transcontinental phone call. Trotti liked to experiment with historical filmmaking, and he now had Zanuck as an ally. But the writer had another reason for handling Zanuck so carefully: Trotti had just finished an outline and treatment based on the prepresidential career of Abraham Lincoln. Macgowan had been impressed by the idea, and he reminded Zanuck of Trotti's good record at Fox and his readiness to handle an original screenplay.[22] Zanuck agreed.

Young Mr. Lincoln and the Burden of American Film History

Zanuck committed himself to the Lincoln story in November 1938. Although Lincoln had appeared in many Hollywood films, including some Twentieth Century–Fox releases, there had been no biography since Griffith's ill-fated *Abraham Lincoln*. His most recent appearance was in MGM's adaptation of Bradbury Foote's *Of Human Hearts* (1938), another rural family melodrama with Lincoln in the cast. It tells the story of a young boy, brought up in poverty in the antebellum Midwest, who is ashamed of his rube preacher father and the family's hand-to-mouth existence. With the help of his mother's sacrifices, he escapes, eventually becoming an army surgeon in Washington. Over the years, he has lost touch with his mother, and she writes to President Lincoln, hoping that he will be able to locate her son in the army. The president naturally finds, chastises, and reunites him with his mother. It was another sympathetic appropriation of Griffith's "Great Heart" myth and, unlike many historical appearances by Lincoln in 1930s films, was managed without any engagement with the projected text of Civil War history. In contrast,

Robert Sherwood's new Broadway play, *Abe Lincoln in Illinois* (1938), embodied the self-conscious prestige that MGM's film lacked and was a huge success. Zanuck sensed the bankability of Trotti's original story and sent him to Washington in November to ascertain whether Sherwood could sue for plagiarism. Trotti quickly returned, utterly delighted that Sherwood's play was so different in tone and approach from his script.[23]

Zanuck hurried into production; he knew that eventually Sherwood would bring his play west for a film treatment. He watched curiously as Warner Brothers produced a short color feature, *Lincoln in the White House* (1939). The short was one of a series of educational films on American history planned by Gordon "Holly" Hollingshead and overseen by the meticulous director of the studio's research department, Herman Lissauer. Using voice-of-God narration, excerpts of Lincoln's speeches, and judiciously constructed scenes between Lincoln and William Seward, the film narrates the heroic president's life from his first inaugural address on 4 March 1861, to his recitation of the Gettysburg Address in 1863. Warner Brothers' research department used only the most expurgated sources for their construction of Lincoln, including Ida Tarbell's and John Drinkwater's biographies.[24] After all, as the narrator instructed his audience, Lincoln was the "savior of his country," not a figure struggling with historical events. Zanuck breathed again. The short educational film only smoothed the way for his historical feature. *Lincoln in the White House,* Sherwood's *Abe Lincoln in Illinois,* and E. P. Conkle's contemporaneous *Prologue to Glory* (produced in 1938 by the Federal Theater in New York) represented a nationally established and revered hero; *Young Mr. Lincoln* would be unique.

Years before, as an Atlanta reporter, Trotti had covered a trial that reminded him of one of Lincoln's defense trials. Although Trotti acknowledged the impact of the Georgia trial, he contended that his historical source was Lincoln's defense of William "Duff" Armstrong for murder in 1858.[25] On 29 August 1857, at a religious camp meeting in Virgin Grove near Old Salem, James Norris and Duff Armstrong got into a brawl with James Metzker. Later that night, Metzker collapsed, supposedly dying from the effects of the assault. Norris was tried separately and convicted of manslaughter in October, but Hannah Armstrong went to Lincoln's law offices in Springfield and pleaded with him to defend her son. Years before, the Armstrongs had provided Lincoln with a home in New Salem, and Lincoln readily agreed to help his old friends. The trial was held in the spring of 1858, and Lincoln's superb defense convinced the jury to acquit Armstrong. Lamar Trotti's script and John Ford's film changed the Armstrong family name to Clay, made the two defendants brothers, staged the "killing" at an Independence Day celebration, and dated the trial several years earlier in Lincoln's law career.[26]

If Trotti was so familiar with Lincoln's career, why did he change the name of the Armstrong family and deliberately obscure the exact date of the trial? Film historians have long considered Trotti's evident lack of historical exactitude regarding the narrative's most dramatic event—the murder trial—as just another example of Hollywood's manipulation of history in the interest of a trite narrative.[27] Both historians and film scholars have concurred that, as with any other Hollywood myth, the filmmakers reproduced an uncomplicated, heroic template, a symbolic Lincoln roughly correct in its monumental outlines. In 1970 *Cahiers du cinéma* even asserted that *Young Mr. Lincoln*'s subject was not Lincoln's youth but rather "the reformation of the historical figure of Lincoln on the level of myth and the eternal." The editors insisted that the film's premise, the murder trial, was fictitious and that the only background for it was the cycle of Depression-era Hollywood films with themes of lynching and legality.[28] According to scholarly convention, *Young Mr. Lincoln* possessed no deliberate perspective on Lincoln or American history because, like so many other classical Hollywood films, it simply reflected prevailing cultural assumptions and ideology.

Filmmakers and critics in 1939 had another perspective. Writing about *Jesse James* in 1939, Kate Cameron credited Zanuck with inaugurating a new and sophisticated cycle of American historical films that included *The Prisoner of Shark Island, Ramona,* and *In Old Chicago* (1938).[29] His investment in Trotti's screenplay was part of this commitment to American history. Trotti's Lincoln script was unique because it was not based on the writer's adaptation of one particular Lincoln biography, historical novel, or *Saturday Evening Post* potboiler, nor was it written with the help of another studio writer. Instead, like any other written biography or history, *Young Mr. Lincoln* was an original screenplay based on Trotti's extensive knowledge of and research on Lincoln's life. On this project, Trotti worked more as a traditional historian than as a screenwriter, evaluating the work of others rather than merely adapting it. Long before filming commenced, Zanuck and Ford were enthusiastic about the project, largely because they both admired Trotti's dual historical and screenwriting capabilities.[30] The cinematic alteration of the Armstrong trial represented more than just Hollywood's regression to simplified myth. Trotti liberated the film from being a reflection of the most recent treatment of Lincoln's prepresidential years, the assertively historical play *Abe Lincoln in Illinois;* or the past Hollywood eulogies, *The Dramatic Life of Abraham Lincoln* and Griffith's *Abraham Lincoln;* or the standard Lincoln cameos of the last ten years. Instead, he explored the difference between the real, "historical" Lincoln and the myth in American consciousness.

Questioning Historiography in 1939

Following the credits, the first and final stanzas of contemporary poet Rosemary Benét's "Nancy Hanks" appear.[31] The lines are engraved as if part of a marble monument or a gravestone epitaph:

> If Nancy Hanks
> Came back as a ghost
> Seeking news
> Of what she loved most,
> She's ask first,
> "Where's my son?
> What's happened to Abe?
> What's he done? [quick dissolve]
> You wouldn't know
> About my son?
> Did he grow tall?
> Did he have fun?
> Did he learn to read?
> Did he get to town?
> Do you know his name?
> Did he get on?"

Trotti's foreword for *Young Mr. Lincoln* (1939).

Young Mr. Lincoln's prologue begins with the monumental Lincoln, the man whose life is engraved in stone, yet the questions posed by the poem are simple, human ones about "Abe." The poem was originally part of a children's poetry anthology of great Americans. Its inclusion as the film's introductory title establishes a contrast between the human and monumental Lincoln that dominates the narrative. It has been argued that this opening sequence is crucial in establishing the film's mythic structure, since the questions posed in the poem generate simple binary oppositions or strict yes or no answers rather than more complicated, critical historical arguments.[32] But how are the questions visually presented? The poem is engraved in marble; the queries, this suggests, are already part of history. However, it is significant that only the questions are shown; the answers may be too long, too ambivalent, or too unsettled by historians to be set in stone. Lincoln's life and his character are perhaps too complex to be answered with a terse yes or no. The questions may be incised in our historical memory, but the answers are elusive, perhaps only partially evident in the film.

Since *Cimarron*'s full-scale deployment of text in 1931, projected historiography had become one of the American historical cycle's most recognizable attributes. Yet, although many films aligned themselves with the discourse of traditional history, text forewords were increasingly used to confine the film narrative within one dominant historical perspective. *Young Mr. Lincoln*'s prologue is rather unusual. It is tempting to attribute this innovative and complex use of text to John Ford, since no such foreword appears in *Young Mr. Lincoln* until the revised final script.[33] Ford, however, had recently vetoed a foreword for *Stagecoach* written by Dudley Nichols.[34] It seems more likely that Zanuck and Trotti developed the idea of a text foreword in the later stages of production. Yet Ford's direction and filming of Henry Fonda as Lincoln carry the text's initial contrast between the human and the monumental, the "real" and the constructed figure, throughout the film narrative.

In 1939 it was highly unusual for any Lincoln "monument" to be so unadorned and even tentative in its engraved rhetoric. Throughout the interwar era, Lincoln was the subject of countless heroic statues commemorating the various stages of his career, from the young lawyer in Urbana, Illinois (1927), to his head on Mount Rushmore, completed in 1937. The statuary had multiplied to such proportions that in 1932 Franklin Meade published a study of the imagery from 1865 onward.[35] But Henry Fonda's Lincoln does not belong to any solemn iconic study. Throughout *Young Mr. Lincoln*, the young lawyer arranges and rearranges his lanky body into a more comfortable slouch. He is shy and unpolished. In the court-room, he fidgets, often striking a pose fleetingly reminiscent of the iconic Lincoln, and then uncomfortably shifting his position. Even in the film's final sequence, Lincoln walks alone up a hill and out of the frame while the camera lingers for several seconds on the empty landscape before sev-ering the long take with a shot of Lincoln's profile on the Lincoln Memo-rial and then a low-angle frontal view of the statue. The contrast between the young, living Lincoln to the old, chiseled monument is uncomfort-able, if not shocking.

The opening shots of the engraved monument are followed by the first sequence in Lincoln's youth announced by the title, "New Salem, Ill. 1832." It has been suggested that the decision to film Lincoln's early years enabled Trotti and Ford to show the predetermined greatness of an American hero.[36] The concept of the fully formed hero implies that historical fact is subservient to the promotion of a reverent view of the protagonist and his future greatness. One might speculate that a story of Lincoln's youth would encourage embellishment, since his New Salem and Springfield years lacked the documented details of his later political life. However, Lincoln's youth was well chronicled, analyzed, and cri-tiqued by historians during the interwar period.[37] In 1936 Lincoln histo-rian Paul Angle republished an annotated version of William Herndon's definitive personal biography, correcting the author's exaggerations and supplementing the text with new research discoveries.[38]

Both Trotti's script and the film begin with Lincoln's first electoral speech, during his run for the legislature in 1832, rather than with How-ard Estabrook's original story adaptation written in 1935, which begins with Lincoln splitting rails in front of his family cabin.[39] Estabrook's script and planned opening images belong to the standard version of Lincoln filmmaking. The western frontier or folklore images of the log cabin and the youth struggling to read by the firelight figure prominently in Griffith's 1930 biopic, as well as Sherwood's 1938 play. Lincoln's obscure birth and parentage had occupied the public since his presidency and, as Lincoln historian David Donald noted, properly belong to the realm of the mythic hero.[40] Instead, *Young Mr. Lincoln* begins with a seminal and documented moment in the known life of Lincoln.

Bombastic politician John T. Stuart attacks President Andrew Jack-son's policies from a rustic storefront and then introduces a local mem-ber of the "incorruptible" Whig Party. Lincoln, sitting alone, rises, fiddles with his hands rather nervously, and then begins his speech in a high, midwestern drawl.[41] He declares his political principles, which are exact

An uncertain hero's
first speech.
(*Young Mr. Lincoln*)

intonations of the Henry Clay platform (his support of a National Bank, internal improvements, and high protective tariffs), but he individualizes them by remarking, "My politics are short and sweet, like the old woman's dance." This is a direct quotation of Lincoln's oft-cited first stump speech in 1832, as documented by biographer William Herndon.[42] Trotti and Ford chose to begin their film with a moment in Lincoln's career that was either a documented occurrence (according to Herndon) or an outright fabrication (according to one of Lincoln's other biographers). Although the lingering low-angle close-up and Fonda's grave demeanor resonate with the emblematic Civil War leader, this is a young, unknown Lincoln, a callow young man whose political principles are still developing. Fonda's nervous moments before he begins his speech, his fumbling hands and baffled smile, re-create Herndon's own description of the candidate's "awkwardness, sensitiveness, and diffidence" before a speech.[43]

Historian David Donald has written that it would be a mistake to view Herndon's more human, imperfect portrait of Lincoln as more realistic or historically accurate than the idealized biographies of Holland, Hays, and Tarbell.[44] According to Donald, both "schools" of biography created mythological portraits of Lincoln as the frontier hero and the nation's patron saint. Yet in beginning *Young Mr. Lincoln* with an event first included in Herndon's biography, Trotti was not attempting to reproduce Herndon's Lincoln. Rather, he embedded Herndon's own recorded events within a film narrative that distanced itself from the structural trappings of traditional biopics. In returning to a little-known period in Lincoln's life, *Young Mr. Lincoln* deliberately confronted national history and myth with its own obscurities. The film took aim at the most insurmountable problems in Lincoln historiography: whether historians were capable of separating the real, historical Lincoln from the mythic hero, or whether the history itself was part of the mythic foundation.[45]

The two most influential biographies of Lincoln written by Trotti's generation were Carl Sandburg's *The Prairie Years* (1926) and Senator Albert J. Beveridge's *Abraham Lincoln* (1928).[46] *Young Mr. Lincoln* shares both structural and stylistic qualities with the biographies. All three break their narratives before Lincoln's presidential career begins. Sandburg's poetic sensibility and understanding of Lincoln's western frontier background is similar to Ford's, and his biography was instantly accessible and popular with the general public.[47] However, Sandburg was not interested in the relative importance and complexity of Lincoln's mythical and historical identities. Beveridge, in contrast, pleased critics and academic historians with his command of historical evidence and footnoting. Although Beveridge shared Sandburg's and the filmmakers' penchant for humanizing Lincoln, he had no patience with idealized characterizations, and his biography mentions Lincoln's laziness, slowness, and uncouth demeanor.[48] These imperfections were unearthed and analyzed not to debunk a national hero but rather to separate history from legend. Still other historians inquired into Lincoln myths during the late 1920s and 1930s. Roy Basler focused on the differences between Lincoln legend and history and their changing perspectives in popular biography and literature.

Young Mr. Lincoln conspicuously avoids Lincoln's major claim to historical attention and one that preoccupied the other two Lincoln films of 1939: his presidential leadership during the Civil War and his role in ending slavery. Thirty years later, *Cahiers du cinéma* attributed this omission to the film's overarching, mythic "Hollywood" discourse, a discourse intent on the repression of conflict.[49] Yet the filmmakers' unique decision to avoid direct reference to Lincoln's well-documented but hopelessly heroicized Civil War administration may instead emphasize the contradiction they perceived between the historical and the mythical, the real and the monumental Lincoln. A film about the Civil War Lincoln, however touted as a historical film and supplemented with documentation, would necessarily be linked to wartime heroics and his apotheosis following the assassination. This Lincoln is innately the mythic hero. But a changing, youthful protagonist undoubtedly gave Trotti and Ford distance from America's national, emotional investment in the iconic Lincoln.

From a historical standpoint, however, young Lincoln's unexpressed opinion on slavery was also an accurate portrayal of Lincoln's known political convictions at that time.[50] Lincoln's own documented opinion of slavery years later was that of a careful politician rather than that of the Great Emancipator.[51] Only in 1862 did Lincoln decide to make the Civil War an issue of slavery by announcing the Emancipation Proclamation. Even then, as he wrote in a famous open letter to Horace Greeley in 1862, political rather than personal convictions determined his decision: "My paramount object in this struggle is to save the Union, and is not either to save or destroy slavery. If I could save the Union without freeing any slave I would do it, and if I could save it by freeing all the slaves I would do it, and if I could save it by freeing some and leaving others alone I would also do that. What I do about slavery, and the colored race I do because I believe it helps to save the Union."[52]

During the 1930s Lincoln's status as the Great Emancipator was far more prevalent in foreign countries than in the United States, where he was regarded primarily as the man who saved the Union.[53] Following the lead of Charles and Mary Beard in *The Rise of American Civilization* (1927), professional historians focused less on slavery as the primary cause of the Civil War than on the economic and cultural divisions between the North and South. Any mention of slavery in Lincoln's opening address and thereafter in the film would not belong to a historical portrait. It would be an obvious and heavy-handed attempt to show the young Lincoln as the composite hero, fully formed politically and historically and the embodiment of the Lincoln myth. Ironically, when Estabrook planned a biography of Lincoln in 1935, his adaptation emphasized Lincoln's role as the Great Emancipator; he acknowledged that his script was not bound by questions of history but would instead be a "dramatic" narrative.[54] Estabrook even wanted to keep the word "Lincoln" out of the film title, fearing that its educational implications would scare audiences away. Several years later, Twentieth Century–Fox's Darryl F. Zanuck dismissed Estabrook's concerns and discarded his version in favor of Trotti's script.

Multiple Views of the Past

Young Mr. Lincoln alluded to Lincoln's future Civil War presidency without presenting Lincoln as a prescient, mythic hero. Trotti and Ford's Lincoln is learning, changing, growing. His mature political principles are yet unknown. Compared with William Seward and Stephen Douglas, much less was known about Lincoln's political commitments prior to 1861. Although his famed debates with Douglas in 1858 made him known as an antislavery but moderate Whig, according to historian William E. Baringer (a contemporary of Trotti, Ford, and Zanuck), it was Lincoln's status as a political dark horse that enabled him to be nominated.[55] By leaving Lincoln's political makeup somewhat ambiguous, the filmmakers were able to suggest Lincoln's future political power without turning him into the mythic composite hero.

At one point in the narrative, Trotti and Ford focus specifically on Lincoln's development of moral, legal, and political principles. Lincoln lies by the Sangamon River in New Salem reading from Blackstone's *Commentaries*: "'The right to acquire and hold property . . . the right to life and reputation . . . and the wrongs are a violation of those rights.' . . . That's all there is to it—right and wrong." This study session by the river references a passage from Herndon's biography that describes Lincoln reading by the river with his feet against a tree trunk.[56] Trotti may have imagined Lincoln's thoughts as he studied, but this passage is not simply a folksy fabrication written in the simple binary language of myth. Here is a constructed moment that alludes to matters central to Lincoln history. His great constitutional struggle with the southern states in 1860 was motivated by the South's belief that the Constitution and the tenets of republican liberty sanctioned the protection of private property. Since slaves were defined as property, slavery was therefore protected by the Constitution. Lincoln's summation, "That's all there is to it—right and wrong," functions on several levels. Lincoln may see only right and wrong in reading Blackstone's unwieldy tome, but he will realize in his defense of the Clays that sometimes things can be more ambiguous. He has a better handle on the text of *Poor Richard's Almanac*. When he realizes the import of the documented moon cycles in this homely book, young Lincoln smiles, knowing that he has won the case. Later in his political life he will understand that right and wrong are not so narrowly defined. Pitted against Lincoln's ending of slavery are the unconstitutional lengths he went to in the Emancipation Proclamation, attacking the concept of private property. But most of all, this short confrontation with Blackstone demonstrates an almost ambivalent attitude toward Lincoln's Civil War policies and values. Again, *Young Mr. Lincoln* shows Lincoln learning the complexities of law and of history, rather than merely proclaiming his innate liberal principles. This presentation of a historical process is Trotti's own creation; in contrast, Herndon and other biographers depicted only the result of Lincoln's study rather than his struggle to achieve an imperfect understanding of the law.

Lincoln's skill as a mediator is tested early after he comes to Spring-

Mastering Blackstone's *Commentaries* and the common laws of *Poor Richard's Almanac. (Young Mr. Lincoln)*

field as John T. Stuart's law partner. Trotti embeds Lincoln's attempt to reconcile two irate farmers in a larger allusion to the Civil War. Each man has grievances, Lincoln admits. One owes the other money, and the other has beaten up his dilatory debtor. Lincoln ignores the fire-eaters to great comic effect while he reads through their statements of grievance. He tries to settle the dispute mathematically, but when the two are still at odds, he insinuates that he will crack their two skulls together. Historically, the confrontation may be seen as a microcosm for 1930s historians' explanations of the causes of the Civil War—economic troubles, wounded pride, and retaliation. Although Lincoln solves this dilemma in the film through subtle intimidation, he was, of course, historically unable to reconcile the North and the South years later. Lincoln suffers even more anguish as a lawyer when he realizes that it would not be morally right to force Mrs. Clay to choose which of her two sons is guilty of murder. Trotti depicts Lincoln's meetings with his clients, and as the young lawyer's understanding of the law deepens, his more complex future confrontations with war guilt hover over the narrative like uneasy ghosts. In the later stages of writing, Trotti, under the direction of Zanuck, compounded the film's reference to the Civil War by staging a lengthy Independence Day celebration following Lincoln's morning in the law office.[57] While Lincoln watches the parade with the rest of the townsfolk, he is conspicuously the first to remove his hat when the veterans from the Revolutionary War pass by. Lincoln's respect for the veterans prefigures his own role as head of the army during the Civil War. This parade, this progression in time, shows the linkage of the Civil War to America's other wars and a poignant difference—Lincoln's soldiers would be fighting their own countrymen.

The filmmakers' creation of the Independence Day celebrations indicates that they were certainly not attempting an unimpeachable document of Lincoln's early life. Ford was particularly indifferent to creating a standard eulogy. Later in the day, Lincoln takes part in a tug-of-war, according to Trotti's revised final script, but in the film, Ford has Lincoln cheat in order to win. He ties his end of the rope to a wagon, slaps the horse's rump, and causes the opposing side to be dragged through a mud puddle. Lincoln is no ideal representative of the law; the tug-of-war scene shows that he is ready to cheat when his side is in danger of losing. Trotti and Ford also create an imperfect lawgiver who knows little courtroom etiquette. Their flawed hero might have been a reaction to historian Paul Angle's research on Lincoln's early legal career, which revealed that he was not the most astute or polished lawyer.[58] However, the representation of the young Lincoln was more directly influenced by the humanizing and sometime critical trends in American biography established by Sandburg and Beveridge.

Recent historians' claims that *Young Mr. Lincoln* is laden with undocumented images, such as those of the Independence Day celebrations, and that the filmmakers' Lincoln is a symbol of the American spirit are valid, but they are deliberate choices that supplement the film's historical elements. This contrast suggests that certain Hollywood filmmakers during the classical era were generating a new approach to American historical cinema. Trotti, Ford, and Zanuck created a sense of history that did not depend on reflecting or transcribing the standard version of the past with the careful arrangement of dates and documents; rather, it attempted to compare the conflicting sources of knowledge about Lincoln's life and image. This does not make *Young Mr. Lincoln* any less of a *history* film. During the past ten years, mainstream reformed, modernist historians may have responded with fear to what they perceived to be *Young Mr. Lincoln's* collapsing of the boundaries between fact and fiction, history and ideology, by designating the film "popular history" or myth. Yet upon its release, contemporary critics hailed Twentieth Century–Fox's *Young Mr. Lincoln* as a landmark in American historical cinema.[59] Terry Ramsaye, the elder statesman of film history, commented in the *Motion Picture Herald*, "The like of this picture in the nature of its story concept has never before been offered outside the art cinemas."[60] According to Ramsaye, *Young Mr. Lincoln* achieved something unique in historical filmmaking. It did not merely record historical events or document Lincoln's life but assumed the audience's knowledge and moved beyond to a more subtle engagement with the past. Rather than unconsciously reflecting the mixture of myth and history associated with popular history, *Young Mr. Lincoln* was constructed to contrast the many Lincolns known in both history and myth. In many ways, the filmmakers' approach not only resonates with Basler's study of Lincoln myth and history but also seems to anticipate late-twentieth-century historians' interest in demystifying the discourses of history, memory, and culture.

It is worth returning to the film's final sequence, for here the filmmakers reveal their contrasting understandings of the dichotomy between the human and the monumental, the historic and the mythic Lincoln. On screen, Lincoln has won the trial and walks alone up the road. He walks out of the frame, and Ford's camera remains fixed on the empty, raining landscape for several seconds before a quick dissolve to a close-up of the Lincoln Memorial. The decisive transition from Fonda's Lincoln to a shot of the Lincoln Memorial is a deliberate reminder of the difference between the human, real Lincoln and the icon created in the years after his death. The transition from history to myth is not seamless.

Trotti and Zanuck initially saw things differently. Trotti's ending in the revised final shooting script had Lincoln actually talking to God and being shown the consequences of his future, his marriage, the Civil War, and his assassination.[61] Zanuck later eliminated this over-the-top "mystic tag." Although Zanuck was committed to preserving the film's broad historical integrity, he was not as interested in the nuances of Lincoln myth and history. In a January 1939 conference with Trotti regarding the temporary script, Zanuck, worried about its meditative and history-laden pace, complained, "We are inclined to be narrative rather than dramatic for the first part of the story." He later suggested rather desperately that Trotti consult a new book of Lincoln anecdotes to see if there was anything that could be done to enliven the script.[62] Months later, having examined the film's rushes, he felt that Ford shared Trotti's alarming tendencies and appealed to the director to brighten the film's mood and speed up the tempo.[63] Evidently Young Mr. Lincoln lacked the traditional heroic glamour associated with Twentieth Century–Fox's other Depression-era biopics.

Zanuck's insistence on narrative interest did not compromise his understanding of the complexities of creating a new Lincoln biography. Indeed, the book of anecdotes he recommended, undoubtedly Emanuel Hertz's Lincoln Talks, begins with Lincoln complaining about the repeated inaccuracies of biographers interested only in heroizing their subjects at the expense of historical truth.[64] There is some evidence that Zanuck was the one most deeply affected by Lincoln's criticism of biographers. In an early conference on Trotti's script, Zanuck had set forth his initial preference for trumpeting Lincoln's future heroic status in the final shots: "Lincoln rides off. . . . As Lincoln rides along, music swells in volume and faintly superimposed over screen we see the outline of the Lincoln Memorial. The scene of the young Lincoln riding along becomes less distinct—while the Memorial becomes clearer and clearer, finally completely obliterating the other."[65] The finished film reveals that Zanuck changed his mind. As the uncredited editor of all of John Ford's productions at Twentieth Century–Fox, the producer did add the evocative "Battle Hymn of the Republic" to the opening credits and finale. However, his editing of Young Mr. Lincoln deliberately avoided both Trotti's mythic meeting of deity and hero and his original prescribed natural transformation from living man to mythic icon. Instead, as Ford remembered years later in an interview, his "cutter" had the idea to shift abruptly from the rainy landscape to the statue, opting for a disconcerting contrast.[66] Although Zanuck's early stylistic advice suggests that he saw history and myth as naturally blending and even indistinguishable at the film's conclusion, his vision for the possibilities of historical film changed. His final mark on the film separates the real from the monumental Lincoln with a long view of a bleak, rainy landscape that relies on contrast and visual disjuncture.

Although the Abraham Lincoln articulated in Young Mr. Lincoln may be a response to trends in contemporary Lincoln historiography, the relativist exploration of historical alternatives, and the vicissitudes of historiography, the film is neither a historical text nor a simple reflection of historiographic trends. The narrative is not chronological nor, strictly speaking, a documented historical event. It is not constructed as a filmed biography to be judged on its ability to replicate the chronological details of the past. Unlike *Lincoln in the White House, Young Mr. Lincoln* made no overt claims to be a historically accurate document of Abraham Lincoln's life. It does not give serious exhortations to the camera, it does not use document cutaways, photographic allusions, or biographical sources to bolster its reputation as a historical film and to justify its script. As Ramsaye wrote, "It is the picture's presumption that the spectator really knows all about Lincoln, and to a degree of knowing that it will contribute to the implied dramatic intensity of the phrases so effectively sketched under John Ford's most artful direction."[67] Other critics in the Hollywood community, undoubtedly wearied by Robert Sherwood's didactic patriotism echoing from the East Coast, appreciated *Young Mr. Lincoln's* mature historical outlook and a narrative that showed a youthful, imperfect protagonist. The *Hollywood Reporter* added it to "filmdom's growing library of historical works," and *Film Daily* called it living history without the "mustiness or stodginess" attributed to academic history. Publicity releases in trade papers emphasized the film's unique perspective, "portraying little-known incidents in his early career": "Pictures, statues, all of history have shown him as the Great Emancipator! *But there was another Lincoln* . . . a young man, known to everybody in the backwoods town of Springfield, Ill., a jackleg lawyer whose strength was legend and wit was famous. . . . It is this other Lincoln . . . whose story has *never* been told . . . that is shown in the 20th Century–Fox picture, YOUNG MR. LINCOLN."[68]

Young Lincoln, set off between two marble monuments invoking the cumulative real and imagined burden of national memory and the Civil War, is part of American history and myth. With Zanuck's watchful, sometimes apprehensive, but ultimately supportive collaboration, Trotti and Ford juxtaposed complexity with simplicity, the real man with the monumental icon, and history with myth. In the process, they generated a new form of American historical cinema, one that meditated on many Lincoln histories and myths, rather than recording one uncontested human document.

Imitating Historiography

Young Mr. Lincoln proved that a biographical film did not need to be a success story or a deification of a national hero. Ramsaye in particular clearly hoped that the film's visual and historical discourse would generate a new development in American historical filmmaking. Yet *Young Mr.*

Lincoln lasted only two shaky weeks at New York City's Roxy Theatre, in spite of being "highly regarded" by critics and exhibitors. Competition with the World's Fair that month may have killed its New York box-office potential, but the film did "surprisingly weak" business in all the key cities.[69] Sherwood's more traditional view in *Abe Lincoln in Illinois*, released by RKO several months later, fared only slightly better at the box office, being eclipsed by Selznick's *Rebecca*; MGM's annual Clark Gable release, *Boom Town*; and even the color-saturated frontier epic *Northwest Passage*.[70] Although Zanuck could afford an occasional artistic failure and continued to employ Trotti, the screenwriter never again attained such control over an original work. RKO's gamble with writers and fancy scripts was debilitating; the $275,000 fee paid to Sherwood for the screen rights to *Abe Lincoln in Illinois* was only the beginning of the studio's red ink in 1940.[71]

Although 1939–1940 audiences ignored both films, late-twentieth-century historians traditionally preferred Sherwood's film to *Young Mr. Lincoln*. Like Warner Brothers' short educational feature, *Abe Lincoln in Illinois* makes use of iconic Lincoln images, continuing the tradition of heroicized, cradle-to-grave biopics established by *The Dramatic Life of Abraham Lincoln* and Griffith's *Abraham Lincoln*. Sherwood's film takes Lincoln from his rustic family hearth to his departure for the White House in 1861 in twelve anecdotal but chronological incidents, including his first trip down the Mississippi River to Louisiana (where he meets Ann Rutledge en route); his return to New Salem as a storekeeper, election official, and postmaster; the death of Rutledge and his first legislative term; his courtship by Mary Todd; the campaign for senator and the famed debates with Douglas; and his successful bid for the presidency. The events are sequentially arranged to point directly to his election.

Director John Cromwell filmed Sherwood's play almost exactly as it was written. The few cinematic additions to the narrative reinforce Lincoln's iconic status and the deliberate equation of the cinematic image with history. In one of these, Lincoln is shown swearing an oath as an election official in New Salem. In a solemn-faced medium close-up, with his right hand raised, he intones the pledge, evoking his future presidential oath. Unlike the more youthful Henry Fonda, Raymond Massey moves through his role at a slower pace, striking thoughtful poses and lingering portentously before the camera. At one point shortly before the presidential election, he poses for a photographic portrait with his family. Seated with his hands on his knees and with a pronounced stoop, he uncannily resembles his future Lincoln Memorial likeness. The equation of

Raymond Massey's
swearing in.
(*Abe Lincoln in Illinois*)

photographic images with the film's historical accuracy culminates when
a lantern slide, a precursor of the motion picture apparatus, displays Lincoln's image and reports his presidential victory to a cheering Springfield
crowd. The 1860 and 1940 "cameras" are functioning together, producing the same irrefutable history of Lincoln's life.

The implications of *Abe Lincoln in Illinois* as a photographic document continued outside the boundaries of the film narrative. A short
history of Lincoln's life from 1830 to 1865, published in 1940, roughly
follows the chronological format of Sherwood's play. The slim biography
is illustrated not with Lincoln's photographic portraits by Mathew Brady
and others but with motion picture stills from *Abe Lincoln in Illinois*.[72]
The photographs show Raymond Massey sitting with his hands on his
thighs or reading at his desk in poses reminiscent of Brady's photographs.
The combination of a written history of Lincoln's early life and stills from
Sherwood and Cromwell's film implies not only that Massey's performance as Lincoln was interchangeable with the real Lincoln but also that
Sherwood's play performs the same function as a traditional biography.
This was nothing new. Fifteen years earlier, when producer A. L. Rockett
released his production of *The Dramatic Life of Abraham Lincoln*, Grosset
& Dunlap published a studio biography of Lincoln illustrated with scenes
from the picture. Rockett had a rather flamboyant faith in his film's ability
to portray Lincoln's life with historical accuracy and still be successful at
the box office. Yet in his foreword to A. M. R. Wright's biography, the producer expressed his belief that the historical accuracy of a motion picture
biography of Lincoln was measured in its capacity for eulogy.[73]

Sherwood may have had a bit more finesse, but he also proclaimed his play's historical accuracy in a fifty-page addendum to the published text entitled "The Substance of *Abe Lincoln in Illinois.*" He wrote that even though a playwright's province is "feelings, not facts," when writing about "the development of the extraordinary character of Abraham Lincoln, a strict regard for the plain truth is more than obligatory; it is obviously desirable."[74] Yet in spite of his seemingly meticulous, scene-by-scene analysis of the play's historical sources and his hint to let history "speak for itself," *Abe Lincoln in Illinois* is no pure historical document unsullied by contemporary contexts.

William Herndon, the most famous biographer of Lincoln's prepresidential years, appears as a principal character in the play, but he acts less as a law partner and more like the scolding chorus of a Greek tragedy as he exhorts Lincoln to live up to his political principles. Despite his admiration for the film, even Lincoln film historian Mark Reinhart noted Sherwood's curious and historically unfounded portrayal of an unambitious Lincoln. In a scenario that extends to 1861, the political opportunist is nowhere to be seen. In the staged debate between Lincoln and Douglas, Sherwood borrowed and then pieced together extensive excerpts from Lincoln's "house divided" speech, private correspondence, and some debating texts, but his self-described obsession with documents does not acknowledge their compromised historical context in the play.[75] This use of "history" is pushed farther in the film when Lincoln gives a ten-minute exhortation to the camera, creating the illusion that the film audience in early 1940 has been transformed into Lincoln's antebellum public.

Unlike *Young Mr. Lincoln, Abe Lincoln in Illinois* focuses on Lincoln's personal and political stance on slavery. Sherwood's play contains extensive passages from the Lincoln-Douglas debates, and RKO (acting for Sherwood when the film was in production) fought Joseph Breen and the Production Code Administration (PCA) to retain the playwright's account of the debaters' historic exchange about the future possibility of whites eating with, sleeping with, and marrying black Americans. Initially, Breen believed that this historical information violated the morals clause of the Motion Picture Code (miscegenation) and would invite heavy censorship nationally and internationally. Breen later dropped the matter when RKO producer Max Gordon (who had also produced the play) protested that the studio and the PCA would invite massive criticism if Lincoln's and Douglas's own words were edited for content.[76] Yet these allusions to Lincoln's stance on slavery, which were directly avoided (or whitewashed) by Trotti and Ford in *Young Mr. Lincoln,* should not be taken as Sherwood's fusion of history and liberal politics. Sherwood chose passages from Lincoln's speeches on liberty that would appeal to the white men of the Depression era without entirely alienating the black population. Perhaps the most astonishing and memorable line Massey speaks as Lincoln is this one: "As an American, I can say—thank God we live under a system by which men have the right to strike." As historian Alfred Jones has pointed out, that speech resonated more with participants in the 1937 auto and steel workers' strikes than with mid-Victorian Americans.[77]

Sherwood relied on Herndon's biography for material on Lincoln's years in New Salem and Springfield, but he dwelled with the greatest relish on Herndon's account of Lincoln's relationships with Ann Rutledge and Mary Todd.[78] Lincoln's commitment to Rutledge, always questioned by professional historians but cherished in popular historical tradition, is central in *Abe Lincoln in Illinois* and is treated as a crucial event in Lincoln's life. Sherwood's Lincoln kneels by Ann's deathbed, holds her hand as she dies, abandons Mary Todd on the day of their wedding, and rambles around the woods of New Salem grieving for Ann. Todd (Ruth Gordon) is portrayed as a shrewish and unstable woman and the bane of Lincoln's existence. By 1948, historian David Donald had documented the biases, embellishments, and inaccuracies of Herndon's biography, particularly regarding the Rutledge and Todd episodes, but scholarship during the Depression had also begun to question Herndon's reliability.[79] For Sherwood, however, the work of Herndon and his disciple, Sandburg, was the template for the historical content and structure of the play.

In spite of his obvious debt to Herndon, the playwright cited Carl Sandburg as his true *historical* source.[80] Contemporary critics noticed the connection between the play and the enormously popular *Abraham Lincoln: The Prairie Years*.[81] Of course, Sandburg's tendency to combine history with treasured myth made Sherwood's citation of the poet-biographer as an irrefutable historical source problematic, but it enabled him to mold a mythic Lincoln. Sherwood's version of Lincoln's pre–Civil War years worked hand in glove with the Roosevelt administration's manipulation of Lincoln's image during the Depression era.[82] Both Sherwood and Sandburg saw Lincoln and Roosevelt as political twins with comparable presidential struggles. Massey was a perfect mouthpiece for Sherwood's project. In a *New York Times* interview, he called Lincoln a New Dealer and claimed, "If you substitute the word dictatorship for the word slavery throughout Sherwood's script . . . it becomes electric with meaning for our time."[83] Sherwood corroborated Massey in March 1939 when the playwright announced that he was allowing his Broadway play to be turned into a film because the international situation was too precarious for Lincoln's belief in democracy to go unheard on a large scale.

Sherwood's Lincoln intones the creed of Roosevelt's New Deal democracy. After Lincoln addresses his Springfield friends following his election, his train to Washington pulls away from the dual 1861 and 1940 audiences. Its destination is war, bloodshed, and assassination. *Abe Lincoln in Illinois* announced its ideological project, and Massey acknowledged that its reading of history was actively influenced by the author's and audience's need to solve contemporary problems such as the impending war in Europe, but Sherwood insisted on the uncompromising historical content of his play.[84] Yet on screen, *Abe Lincoln in Illinois* merely reproduces the standard eulogy and pompous history lesson expressed in Rockett's and Griffith's earlier efforts. Above all, Sherwood and Massey's Lincoln lacks the humanity, humor, and imperfection of the man portrayed by Herndon. Sherwood wanted his film, like his play, to be an impressive historical document, but it remains a document of the last antebellum days of the 1930s.

Abe Lincoln in Illinois was part of a group of prestigious historical films made in late 1939 and 1940 that capitalized on Lincoln's archetypal image as a heroic national leader and unifier, while whitewashing his role as the Great Emancipator. Lincoln justified the expansion of the transcontinental railroad in Cecil B. DeMille's *Union Pacific* (1939), and his monument inspired modern-day hick politician Jefferson Smith to fight government graft in *Mr. Smith Goes to Washington* (1939). His oral narration frames Warner Brothers' Civil War western *Virginia City* (1940), and the effects of his presidential election loom over the narrative of *Santa Fe Trail* (1940). But only in Frank Capra's *Mr. Smith Goes to Washington* do Lincoln's marble effigy and engraved rhetoric have any explicit impact on contemporary Americans. In his first trip to Washington, newly appointed Senator Smith concludes his tour of the city at the Lincoln Memorial. As a young boy reads the second inaugural address, his bespectacled grandfather (himself a boy when Lincoln was assassinated) helps the youngster decipher the text. Although his sight is failing, Lincoln's text is engraved in the old man's consciousness. An aging black man, possibly born a slave, approaches the towering script, looks upward silently, and removes his hat. No one has access to his personal translation of the text, yet in one sense, the reflected equation of the free man and the founding text of racial equality needs no elaboration. Here was the personal Lincoln connection that Sherwood failed to create. In Capra's film, Lincoln's soul and rhetoric are passed on from the last living generation to know his presidency firsthand. Unlike the remote marble figures of George Washington, Thomas Jefferson, and Alexander Hamilton (which begin Smith's Washington montage), Lincoln remains a vital memory of the country's oldest living generation.

One could make a case that in 1939 and 1940, Hollywood cinema drew on Lincoln's iconic presence to glorify the American people's survival of the Great Depression and to prepare them for the coming of another world war. In an age of poverty, Lincoln personified the hope that even the poorest American could overcome adversity. In an age of political upheaval, Lincoln stood as a reminder that tyranny could be overcome in the name of freedom. In an age of instability, Lincoln proved that America would endure. According to this argument, any Hollywood film about Lincoln made between the Depression and the Second World War could only be a nationalist panegyric for a classic American hero. Many of them were just this, regardless of their self-conscious historical pedigrees. Both *Lincoln in the White House* and *Abe Lincoln in Illinois*, along with countless other films, represent Lincoln in this celebratory mode. Occasionally, a film employed Lincoln to provoke revisionist history and to push the boundaries of established film historiography. Yet *The Prisoner of Shark Island*'s national criticism and *Young Mr. Lincoln*'s analytical counterpoint of questions, doubts, and ambivalence were soon obscured by plans for another war.[85]

PART FOUR

VETERANS OF DIFFERENT WARS

7

War in the Roaring Twenties, 1932–1939

"And it's chuck him out, the brute! But it's savior of his country when the guns begin to shoot."
— Rudyard Kipling, quoted in Samuel Taylor Moore, *America and the World War*, 1937

He was a big shot—once.
— Kansas (Texas Guinan) in *The Roaring Twenties*, 1939

Although Civil War and western histories would dominate American historical production by the end of the 1930s, the popular film biographies of bootleggers Terry Druggan, Franky Lake, and Al Capone had served as a source for Hollywood's future lives of Jesse James and George Armstrong Custer. Prompted to rework the prestige and historical iconography of *Abraham Lincoln* and *Cimarron*, ironically, *Scarface* and *The Public Enemy*'s twentieth-century controversies paved the way for safer nineteenth-century blockbusters. Howard Hughes's and Darryl Zanuck's willingness to treat Al Capone and other gangsters with the same historical tools used to film Abraham Lincoln and Alexander Hamilton certainly inflamed the censorship of the gangster cycle, but equally disturbing to contemporaries were these and other films' references to the Great War, foreign conflict, and the troublesome lives of returning veterans, soon known as "forgotten men." Not all veterans chose the violent and disruptive path of Nails Morton, but the relationship between war and crime was a popular historical explanation for the postwar era, and one that was increasingly censored in the 1930s. From 1932 to 1939, Hollywood's depictions of the Great War, the impoverishment of the war hero, and national decline revealed frustrating barriers between the American cinema's struggle for historical prestige and the antagonism of censors and critics.

Postwar Fugitives and Forgotten Men

Robert Elliot Burns began his autobiography with the war: "Discharged from the army, after the World War, a broken man, I committed petty crime in Georgia, was caught, convicted, sentenced to ten years on the Georgia chain gang."[1] Like many returning veterans in 1919, Burns had expected life in America to be as he had left it in 1917, but it was not. His former job had paid $50 per week, but a noncombatant had taken it. Try as he might, Burns could not find another that paid him even $20 per week. Employers were unsympathetic, and he grew despondent. His brother Vincent wrote that being at the front for over a year had permanently marked Robert Burns. "He was not wounded externally but he was mentally wounded—a casualty . . . a typical shell-shock case."[2] Although the government made some effort to help returning soldiers readjust, pensions were minuscule, full disability pensions were far from adequate and hard to get, and the educational programs and job networks that would be instituted after the Second World War did not exist. Vincent Burns felt that the government and the public had abandoned its veterans: "His country has rewarded him with indifference in his need, with flagrant neglect, with outright injustice."[3]

In the circumstances, it was understandable that Robert Burns would turn to crime. Nails Morton and allegedly Al Capone had turned bootlegging into a successful livelihood, but Burns's postwar fate was different. His attempt at petty theft in Georgia netted him a lengthy jail sentence to be served in a chain gang. With no money, no lawyer, and no possibility of an appeal, with little hope and an understandable bitterness toward the American judicial system, Burns escaped, changed his name, and eventually became a successful Chicago businessman before authorities recognized him and forced him to return to Georgia. Now, favorable press and a moneyed lawyer promised him a new trial, but Georgia officials incarcerated him again. Ignored by his wealthy friends and trapped in a repressive judicial system, he escaped a second time and published his harrowing autobiography, *I Am a Fugitive from a Georgia Chain Gang*. Warner Brothers quickly sought the rights to Burns's story and, betting on his need for quick cash and anonymity, paid him $12,500.[4] The film was part of Zanuck's program to make stimulating and high-profile pictures based on contemporary events, but it also fit with his historical productions that focused on the lives of important or unusual Americans.

In spite of the fact that Burns and his postwar experiences marked the deviant and declining course of twentieth-century America, Burns truly believed that he was an old-fashioned, upstanding, middle-class American war hero, struggling against the government and social injustice.[5] After his first escape, he became a prominent magazine editor in Chicago, and after his recapture, many wealthy Chicagoans and friends wrote to Georgia authorities to secure his release. But Georgia's reaction was summed up by a fellow prisoner: "'You can't edit any magazines here, Mr. Al Capone from Chicago.'"[6] Burns felt very strongly that southern prejudice against northern big-city dwellers affected his treatment. Burns had been born and raised near New York City and had redeemed himself in Chicago, the country's two richest, brashest, and most racially and culturally diverse cities. Down south, the newspapers characterized him as a "gunman" from New York and a hardened criminal, and prison officials treated him like an escaped slave. Indeed, Burns indicted "Georgia's viewpoint" and the southern penal system as evidence of still-thriving slavery and described the harsh beatings and even murders of black inmates. Burns wrote, "History will account for their prejudice against Yankees and Negroes," and he grimly acknowledged that Sherman's March to the Sea had as much to do with his brutal treatment as did his residence in New York and Chicago.[7] But like the South, Burns had been marked by war and disillusionment. His autobiography portrayed a man struggling to escape from the debilitating forces of history.

From the outset, Zanuck and his writers Sheridan Gibney and Brown Holmes followed Burns's premise—namely, that he was a patriotic solider betrayed by his country after the war. Their decision to film the injustice and corruption of the American judicial system and the public's apathy toward its veterans was unprecedented and dangerous. The filmmakers introduce Burns (renamed Allen) as a decorated U.S. serviceman, and the early scripts open on the parade grounds in France, where Allen receives a medal. After this prologue, the narrative dissolves to America, where Allen unsuccessfully attempts to find work, but his prewar job has been taken. His ex-boss and others have spent the last three years making money, and they have little sympathy for him. In his autobiography, Burns was bitter, writing, "The promises of the YMCA secretaries and all the other 'fountain-pen soldiers' who promised us so much in the name

Tray full of pawned war medals. (*I Am a Fugitive from a Chain Gang*)

of nation and the Government just before we'd go into action turned out to be the bunk." He regretted even serving in the war and blamed the government. "Is this how my country rewards its volunteers—the men who were ready and willing to sacrifice life itself that democracy might not perish?"[8] Studio writers, assisted by Burns,[9] scripted his impotent fury, and one of the most powerful sequences shows him, an unemployed veteran, seeking shelter and sleep on a park bench. A fat cop forces him out, and Allen looks eloquently from his swinging billy club to the Great War memorial partially obscured by the cop's bulk. Soon after, he tries to pawn his war medal, another empty symbol of American patriotism. The broker stares at him grimly and wordlessly pulls out a tray full of such medals.[10]

After reading these first treatments, Zanuck retained the screenwriters' searing visual prologue, which presented the disjunction between the marginalized veteran and postwar America's economic boom. But he quickly removed the more overt criticisms of profiteering American businessmen and at first objected to the cop chasing Allen out of the park.[11] This scene may have been too reminiscent of the government-authorized pension massacre outside the Capitol in 1932, where future general Douglas MacArthur ordered his men to fire on peacefully protesting, destitute veterans and their families.[12] Instead, Zanuck added a text foreword to the film, outlining in a memo that he wanted Burns's own words, quoted from his autobiography, to open the "true story."[13] He also planned a number of newspaper inserts to structurally link the narrative to contemporary history.[14] Undoubtedly hoping to prevent legal retaliation, the studios asked the Reverend Vincent Burns to authenticate the story, just as he had supplied an impressive introduction to his brother's autobiography. In the final script of the text foreword, Vincent Burns states that his brother, Robert, was "a fugitive from a chain gang" and that "the scenes in I Am a Fugitive from a Chain Gang which depict life in a chain gang are true and authentic, being based upon my brother's experience."[15] Studio publicity emphasized the film's historical nature, and Zanuck compounded this by framing it as a historical document. Yet soon after the film's release, this text foreword mired the studio in legal trouble.

Georgia sued Warner Brothers for its alleged "unfair depiction" of the state's penal system. Georgia authorities were particularly offended by Vincent Burns's text foreword and cried that his endorsement was slanderous.[16] Warner executives were treading a fine line. On the one hand, they had to insist on and prove I Am a Fugitive from a Chain Gang's historical accuracy to escape the charge of slander; on the other hand, they had to distance themselves from Burns, who was still a convicted felon on the run. In fact, Burns, who had vainly hoped that the film's impact would secure his freedom, was recaptured shortly after its general release. In 1938, when the case against Warner Brothers was still pending, writer Sheridan Gibney gave a deposition in which he cited all the original penal code sources used in preproduction research as he was constructing the script. He also claimed in a letter to the studio that he had used Burns's book only as a departure point for a modern discussion of chain gangs and social punishment.[17] Walter MacEwan, executive assistant to producer Hal Wallis, even assured the Atlanta lawyers that the foreword had been deleted from all the 1932 release prints.[18] Of course, it was a clumsy lie, but the studio won the case in October 1938, proving the hard way that an autobiography or a historical account cannot easily be charged with libel.

Despite the studio's later efforts to camouflage the film's controversial historical basis, Fugitive was marketed and received as a true story of a down-and-out veteran.[19] In fact, despite Variety's prediction of the failure of this "depressing" and "brutal" film, audiences were attracted by a press campaign that focused on the film's authenticity.[20] It was an uncomfortable but timely account of the country's neglect and abuse of its war heroes. Zanuck, encouraged by the film's critical success, injected another reference to the veteran in a much different type of Hollywood film: the musical. The Gold Diggers of 1933 was a sequel to the successful backstage Depression musical 42nd Street (1932). Gold Diggers, however, was not only set during the present Depression; the stock market crash and its aftermath were scripted as the subjects of the film's fictional stage production. When a Broadway producer decides to stage breadlines rather than a chorus line, his audience of chorus girls is dismayed. By 1933, these women had seen too much of the Depression, both offstage and on. After all, the last musical number they appeared in (and the opening number of the film, "We're in the Money") was interrupted midway by the police and angry bank agents. The film's treatment of the Depression, both onstage and backstage, is offhand and tongue-in-cheek—at least until the film's and the stage musical's final number, "My Forgotten Man." Rather than ending on a major high, like the exuberant "42nd Street" coda, Carol (Joan Blondell) concludes *Gold Diggers* singing as "The Spirit of the Depression." She is a somber-faced, cheaply dressed, bitter woman mourning in a minor blues key her country's forgotten man. As the lyrics and staging indicate, the veteran is out of work, a nameless bum on the street corner hounded by fat cops who have no respect for him or even for the medals he wears on his frayed coat. The number is a soulful appeal to remember and to honor the past, which this modern age so quickly forgets, to remember the men who were used and then condemned to poverty.

It was an unusual choice for a musical finale. The fluffy stage success stories and romances of the early sound era made little reference to the past. Instead, protagonists who were obsessed with the future drove film narratives. They lived to make a hit; getting somewhere meant leaving the past behind them. Zanuck almost single-handedly created a musical that deliberately looked backward and forced the audience to remember, even as it invoked the words "forgotten" in its main lyric and refrain. Curiously, writers James Seymour, David Boehm, and Ben Markson and director Mervyn LeRoy had originally planned to insert the Great War number in the middle of the film.[21] According to the script, "Shadow Waltz" and a reprise of "We're in the Money" were supposed to conclude the stage musical and the film. But the production was shot in sequence, and Zanuck and LeRoy left "My Forgotten Man" until the end. Was Zanuck, the Great War veteran, indulging in the same historical references he had used in *The Public Enemy* and *I Am a Fugitive from a Chain Gang*? Whatever the reasons, deploying the somber historical number at the end of the film gave it a prominence that was lacking in the script.

But according to the critics, the war was a jarring element in the modern musical. Often their reviews simply ignored the number, pointedly praising the other interludes and Dick Powell and Ruby Keeler's innocent duets. Lucius Beebe of the *Herald Tribune* thought that *Gold Diggers* was a fluffy and pleasant film except for the last fifteen minutes. He complained, "Superadded to this blithe and agreeable comedy recital, is an interlude depicting the woes of 'My Forgotten Man,' as the jazz score of the piece has it, which, although apparently inserted in the script of the film as an afterthought, tends to diminish in a very emphatic manner its effectiveness and its qualities as entertainment." Beebe singled out the number for a thorough critique, saying that it was a "stupid intrusion on its integrity" and remarking, "It is only a pity that its producers had to diminish its effectiveness by the introduction of a shabby theme of bogus sentimentality which should be no concern of a photoplay designed primarily as amusement fare."[22] In his view, *The Gold Diggers of 1933* was stepping outside its limited but charming range when it mentioned modern American history with such a definite attitude. Even Edwin Schallert of the *Los Angeles Times* and Mordaunt Hall of the *New York Times*, who enjoyed the number, called it "out of place" and a disjunctive element in a Hollywood musical.[23]

Perhaps for Americans, invoking the war in a film set during the Depression compounded too many tragedies. In recent years, films about the American involvement in the war increasingly stressed its fragmenting, bewildering experience and its disillusioning aftermath. In William Wellman's *Heroes for Sale* (1933), a returning wounded soldier becomes addicted to morphine and descends to an even more numbing existence of poverty and anonymity. At MGM, W. S. Van Dyck followed *Manhattan Melodrama*'s direct correlation between war and urban crime with *They Gave Him a Gun* (1937). Like Nails Nathan and allegedly Al Capone, the bookkeeper-turned-soldier goes to war and gets "another kind of diploma," one that will prepare him for the urban battlefields. These war stories were not accounts of national endurance and success but counterhistories of the nation's cast-off heroes. Even in John Ford's *The World Moves On* (1934), a grand, generational narrative of a successful Louisiana merchant family, the Great War splits the family emotionally and ideologically. War profiteering competes with patriotism. The actual war footage that was added to the fictional narrative acted as a further fissure, separating the seamlessly scripted Hollywood fiction of the nineteenth-century South from the disjunctive documentary cinematography of the war era.[24] Critics were appalled by the film; the war was part of a history that the public would rather forget.

During the silent era, before the onslaught of bitter war memoirs and rallies for disarmament, Hollywood romanticized the American wartime experience in France as a John Gilbert bildungsroman (*The Big Parade*, 1925) and even scripted the war as a redemptive experience for a young

Navaho brave (*The Vanishing American*, 1925). Filmmakers turned the war into comic relief (*What Price Glory*, 1926) and molded it into a classic tearjerker of thwarted love (*Shopworn Angel*, 1928). Narratives were set almost exclusively abroad; brief American prologues consisted of patriotic news headlines and the adolescent thrill of "joining up." Exotic, disillusioning, and dangerous, Europe only enhanced the isolation of America. With the advent of sound, war films acquired cynicism, but the most successful of these focused on the German and British perspectives, not the American experience. The film version of Erich Maria Remarque's *All Quiet on the Western Front* (1930) and R. C. Sherriff's *Journey's End*, filmed by James Whale in 1931, were some of the most honored films of their production years, and they reiterated the disputed nature of individual heroism and the overwhelming sacrifice of German and British youth. Their satire was new to American film audiences, who lacked Germany's and Britain's bitter literary tradition of war memoirs. Ernest Hemingway's more successful novel, *A Farewell to Arms*, became a motion picture success for Gary Cooper and Helen Hayes in 1932, but it lacked the anger, despair, and autobiographical components of its European competitors. Set entirely in Europe, the film had no American prologue, no display of cultural conflict, and no commentaries on war hysteria and indifference. In this sense, it was easy for Paramount to mold Hemingway's novel into a familiar romance of thwarted love. American soldier Hervey Allen's grueling, day-by-day account of his war experience, *Toward the Flame* (1925), employed all the horrific and bewildering images of Remarque's and Sherriff's fictions but had a fast, jumbled, confusing closeness to the noise, terror, and death that no fictional narrative could create. Curiously, Allen compared his memoir to a crippled film, bereft of its capacity for motion and vitality: "It is a moving picture of war, broken off when the film burned out."[25] War shattered both narrative form and cinematic time, burning history, memoir, and film narratives under the glare of Armageddon. History had reached its most destructive ends, and more than a decade later, in confronting that war, the American cinema came close to overexposure.

The Great War and Revisionist Historiography

Historian Michael Isenberg has argued that despite a growing cynicism toward war in 1930s Great War feature films, Hollywood set nearly all its war pictures abroad and therefore did not question American involvement. "The American cinema," he wrote, "while willing to offer its patrons an alternate version of war, was unwilling to debate issues that might transgress the nation's most sincere ideals."[26] For Isenberg, Hollywood ingenuously absorbed and glorified the democratic rhetoric of Woodrow Wilson. Yet Hollywood filmmakers consistently plumbed the failure of Wilson's dreams and interrogated the worth of national war aims in films set in postwar desolation and destitution. Just as in Preston Slosson's and Louis Hacker's institutional histories, American cinema's critical reassessment of postwar America began with the failure of the war experience—veterans' unemployment, urban crime, economic collapse. Despite Great War films' popularity with audiences and critics, they attracted fervent condemnation from censors, politicians, and special-interest groups. America's role in the war was hard to depict without recalling the nation's postwar decline. Romance and poignant loss might flourish in war-torn Europe (A Farewell to Arms), but "over here," the war was filmed from Robert Burns's perspective. Even though the war made the United States a major superpower and created a postwar economic boom, it was also responsible for the devastating agricultural depression, the rise of urban America, and the influx of crime. It contributed to the decline and disappearance of the nineteenth-century values and past that still persisted in many American lives and in Hollywood's historical films. It was the prelude to the Volstead era, Al Capone, and the Depression. It was not an event that could be credibly deployed to attract historical continuity and national patriotism. Instead, when Hollywood did mention America's part in the war during the early sound era, it was to deliberately criticize the national past, to point out the result of the "Great Crusade"—the decline of America and the rise of a new and destabilized national history.

A huge number of American histories and memoirs of the Great War were published before the armistice, but many were merely military and political defenses justifying the nation's involvement in the European conflict, texts that intoned the Wilsonian slogan, "The world must be made safe for democracy." However, these words rang hollow in the next decade, particularly with many historians who were now ashamed by their willingness to spread government-approved propaganda during the war. Many American historians felt that the profession had discredited itself, so they directed their talents at exposés of war profiteering, propaganda, and political machinations.[27] With the rise of urban crime and the ensuing Depression, an increasing number of popular and professional American historians condemned the country's involvement in the war. In 1931 historian John Maurice Clark's assessment of the war's economic effects acknowledged that although the Great War might not have caused the Great Depression, it had created the conditions for the nation's decline.[28] Clark did not credit the war with single-handedly initiating the crime spree, but he did not ignore the connection either. Veterans were exploited, the Veterans' Bureau was an economic travesty, and although veterans eventually returned to the workforce, most lost their jobs within months of the stock market crash. Clark's history was a shock to many who wanted to put the war behind them, because he showed that 1917–1918 was not a patriotic aberration without historical consequences, something that municipalities could simply commemorate with chunks of concrete and marble. The war did not make the world "safe for democracy"; it actuated postwar economic chaos and social unrest.

In 1936 former secretary of war Newton Baker published *Why We Went to War* in an attempt to counteract the effects of studies such as Clark's. Baker gallantly proclaimed that public opinion from 1914 to 1918 was "well-informed" and therefore almost exclusively anti-German and inveighed against the current revisionist bent of historiography. He complained, "Twenty years later it has become the fashion to suggest that our entry into the war was not in fact for the reasons then stated and generally accepted, but was either the result of the pressure of special interests of one sort or another, or that we were beguiled by propaganda which came from overseas."[29] Baker constructed a vindication of his dead president and attempted to present a "just and clear" picture of the wartime nation by quoting Wilson, the press, and other pillars of the establishment. Unfortunately for Baker, these establishment figures were no longer trusted by much of the public in the 1930s. In 1932, still a Wilsonian and an avid internationalist, Baker failed to obtain his party's nomination for the presidency. Instead, the aberrant voices of Tom Powers and Al Capone articulated the national mood during the post-Depression era. In his haste to defend Wilson and international intervention, Baker conveniently forgot the pre-1917 wartime press bias, Wilson's failure to halt arms supplies to the Allies when the United States was still allegedly neutral, the British violation of the neutrality of the seas and the Treaty of London, and the massive war loans that Americans such as J. Pierpont Morgan made to the British on the assumption that the American government would bail them out. In his history, Baker refused to credit the rumor that American war policy was influenced by big business or British pressure, and he condemned those "pacifist" and even "communist" persons who subscribed to such vulgar economic determinism.[30]

Others, though, continued to question any simple patriotic explanation for the government's motivation for entering the war. Samuel Taylor Moore's rebuttal followed in 1937. Rather than assuming that the nation shared Wilson's and the jingoist press's perspective, Moore's research indicated that even as war was declared, the public regarded the conflict as "unreal, a distant nightmarish dream, incomprehensible to lay America."[31] America had been pushed to war by violations of neutrality from both Germany and Britain, but Moore also called into question America's vaunted impartiality, citing the economic measures that consistently favored Britain. In 1939 historian H. C. Peterson went even further. *Propaganda for War: The Campaign against American Neutrality, 1914–1917* concentrated on the machinations of the American plutocrats and governing classes in favoring and eventually supporting the British war effort. The war was no patriotic crusade but rather the result of a successful propaganda campaign. But according to Moore, the public simply did not care. The government's and the press's legerdemain was as unimportant to the public as Wilson's democratic rhetoric was. The American war experience began in ambiguity and confusion and, for many, progressed to disillusionment and apathy. Returning soldiers faced civilian indifference and unemployment. Like Robert Burns, they soon discovered that patriotic phrases meant nothing.[32]

Hollywood films of the early sound era were some of the most powerful revisionist indictments of American involvement in the First World War, framing one of the most disjunctive national events of the twentieth century within the broken lives of war veterans, crime, destitution, and loss. Although Zanuck had initiated the cycle at Warner Brothers, he also occasionally inserted Great War interludes into otherwise pedestrian scripts to lend a critical edge to their period dramas. In 1937 he authorized screenwriters to add an Arlington National Cemetery prologue to *This Is My Affair*. When the tour guide mentions that soldiers fought the Great War to "make the world safe for democracy," there are a number of contemptuous sniggers from the crowd. A year later, *Alexander's Ragtime Band* also received some Great War historical gloss when Zanuck wedged a war montage to complicate the lives of his three protagonists. In the script, war is a baffling series of exploding shells, wire, and feet marching through mud and then the streets of New York. But for Zanuck, for the soldiers, and for Stella, the girl loved by the protagonists, there was no glory in America's fight. The war, she shudders, "was all so horrible—and useless." It would take Zanuck six years and another world war to alter his jaundiced perspective (*Wilson*, 1944). As the decade wore on, other studios were tempted by the Great War, particularly as a means of circumventing the Production Code's moratorium on gangster pictures and excessive violence. MGM's clout with Hays undoubtedly enabled it to make *They Gave Him a Gun*, which pursued Zanuck's early work in *The Public Enemy* and *I Am a Fugitive from a Chain Gang*.

Yet while some filmmakers scripted anonymous veterans and gangsters within the framework of film biography and history (repeating past successes), others took an even more unconventional view of wartime protagonists. When MGM decided to remake Paramount's 1928 silent success *The Shopworn Angel*, the filmmakers considered war from a woman's perspective. In 1938 James Stewart and Margaret Sullavan re-created the story of Private Pettigrew, a Texas recruit stationed outside New York while he waits for overseas orders. While on leave, he runs into the cynical Broadway actress Daisy (Sullavan) and gradually persuades her to fall in love with both him and the war. After Pettigrew embarks overseas, she is able to sing "Pack Up Your Troubles" with real tears in her eyes. MGM was notoriously casual about its historical films, frequently using them as unabashed backgrounds for star romances (*The Gorgeous Hussy*, 1936). Unlike other studios, MGM preferred to develop the history and the screenplay in separate compartments. Waldo Salt's script was therefore concerned with the Pettigrew-Daisy romance; he left the historical background and newspaper inserts for montage expert Slavko Vorkapich to work out with director H. C. Potter.[33]

By 1938, MGM filmmakers had to handle Great War material with extreme care. Europe was only one year away from another full-scale war, and many Americans were understandably anxious about yet another foreign entanglement. But although MGM's portrayal of Daisy's cynical ennui and ensuing romantic and patriotic transformation may have looked like subtle 1938 jingoism and standard MGM melodrama, it was actually a historically accurate presentation of many Americans' reaction to the Great War in 1917.[34] Unlike Paramount's 1928 version, which still operated under the romantic war cycle instigated by *The Big Parade* and *What Price Glory*, Daisy's initial disdain for patriotism in the remake reflects Americans' 1917 perspectives, while engaging postwar critiques of American involvement and contemporary war anxieties. Although at the end of the film, like Carol in *Gold Diggers*, Daisy becomes the singing emblem of the war, the patriotic inspiration who "smiles" through her tears, MGM's *Shopworn Angel* was not the studio's usual escapist fare. The war killed Daisy's ill-fated romance with Pettigrew, and it fissured MGM's standard pattern for a classically happy ending. But even more crucially, the armistice did not end the narrative as a means of justifying Pettigrew's death; instead, Daisy, 1917 Americans, and 1938 audiences were left to endure future defeats and a world war that had no end.

In spite of its unusual, two-edged historical continuity between 1917 and 1938 America, MGM's remake of *Shopworn Angel* resembles several other Great War films released during the early sound era and pre–World War II era. In particular, these films focus on a female protagonist who has to carry on when the male character becomes imprisoned in the past by death (*Shopworn Angel*, 1928), poverty (*Gold Diggers of 1933*), or persecution (*I Am a Fugitive from a Chain Gang*). If veterans were modern American history's victims in early sound-era war features, then women functioned as historians in a world permanently destabilized by war—just as white southern plantation mistresses were left to tell the Civil War's untold history and bitter postwar struggle for economic survival. Carol in *Gold Diggers* exhorted viewers to "remember," MGM's Daisy advised Americans to smile, yet both were fictional women existing within a constructed modern history. It was left to RKO to represent a real American woman's wartime story. *The Story of Vernon and Irene Castle* (1939) not only narrates Irene Castle's war experience but also illuminates the dialectic between women as historical protagonists and Hollywood actresses' struggle to gain a measure of power in studio-era Hollywood, often through their involvement in prestigious historical films. Irene Castle's and Ginger Rogers's stories were each uniquely impacted by their war experience and war stories.

Women in Film History

Throughout most of the 1930s, Ginger Rogers remained America's most popular adult actress.[35] Although her early Warner Brothers hoofer roles brought her increasing fame, her reputation as a star solidified as half of the Fred Astaire–Ginger Rogers dance team. Their films together from *Flying Down to Rio* (1932) and *The Gay Divorcee* (1933) to the 1938 release *Carefree* were RKO's most consistently successful productions. However, their work was never accorded serious consideration as prestige filmmaking. In 1939 film historian Lewis Jacobs pointedly ignored Astaire and Rogers in his contemporary history of American film. And although film critics such as Otis Fergusson, Frank Nugent, and Howard Barnes were often enthusiastic about Astaire's virtuosity, they dismissed the scripts and character development as trite and repetitive. Just as frequent were their attempts to marginalize Rogers's contribution and write her out of the historic dance team. According to most contemporary American critics,

Rogers merely mimicked Astaire; she certainly lacked any active role in creating their dance numbers. *Top Hat* was known as "the Fred Astaire dancing film," and the series was playfully called "Astaire's stock company." Astaire was the star; Rogers was "just a good-looking girl, speaking lines for money."[36] Forty-odd years later, she would discuss her independent contributions to Warner Brothers' *42nd Street* and *The Gold Diggers of 1933* and remember her demeaning treatment at RKO by director Mark Sandrich and Astaire: "Over the years, myths have built up about my relationship with Fred Astaire. The general public thought he was a Svengali, who snapped his fingers for his little Trilby to obey; in their eyes, my career was his creation. It just so happens that when Fred and I came together for the first time in *Flying Down to Rio*, it was his second film and my twentieth."[37] Rogers emphasized the endless rehearsals and the collaborative nature of their partnership when developing routines. However, Sandrich, who directed many of the Astaire-Rogers films, saw Rogers as "merely a clothes-hanger who could dance sometimes, sing upon occasion, and perhaps make the leading man smile." Rogers recalled, "When we finished a take, Mark came scurrying over to Fred to tell him how terrific he'd been—and wouldn't bat an eye at me."[38]

Unfortunately, RKO executives shared this shabby assessment of her work; they silenced Rogers's complaints on the set and prevented her from participating in more prestigious RKO films.[39] By 1935, Rogers was tired of this treatment and the time-consuming musicals and wanted to attempt a more challenging role in a prestige film: Queen Elizabeth in *Mary of Scotland*. Rogers felt that the only way she could escape her typecasting in fluffy, modern roles was to audition in disguise. With the help of John Ford and her agent Leland Hayward, she appeared at RKO as "Lady Ainslie" and was a strong contender for the role until RKO executives discovered her real identity.

Although it is understandable that the front office would insist on her continued participation in the successful, inexpensive, but slight dance films, studio executives were undoubtedly remiss in their failure to exploit Rogers's massive popularity by casting her in more impressive vehicles. Hollywood's most powerful American actresses all graduated to period or historical productions after successful modern roles. Barbara Stanwyck's early work with Frank Capra led to historical work at RKO and Paramount. Shirley Temple's biggest box-office successes were period films at Fox. Jeanette MacDonald, Mae West, and Irene Dunne were consistently cast in American period films. After a sensational start at RKO, David O. Selznick gave the lead in *Little Women* to Katharine Hepburn.

Newcomers Margaret Sullavan and Olivia de Havilland had received a great deal of press coverage for their American historical films. *Jezebel* and *The Sisters* represented Bette Davis's growing power at Warner Brothers. Even Claudette Colbert (*Maid of Salem*), Joan Crawford (*The Gorgeous Hussy*), Janet Gaynor (*The Farmer Takes a Wife*), and Jean Harlow (*Hells Angels, The Public Enemy, Suzy*) made historical pictures in the 1930s. Rogers, responsible for RKO's biggest grosses, was conspicuous by her absence in prestige filmmaking.

By 1938, Rogers had succeeded in raising the standard of her film vehicles, starring in Gregory LaCava's *Stage Door* and George Stevens's *Vivacious Lady*. In 1939 RKO decided to cast Astaire and Rogers in a historical film, *The Story of Vernon and Irene Castle*. Rogers was delighted because, as she remembered, she now had a role she could research at the library.[40] In her first historical film, Rogers was appropriately cast as the dance and fashion trendsetter Irene Foote Castle. The historical development in Hollywood filmmaking had become so widespread and successful that it infiltrated the most ultramodern film cycle of them all. Rogers traded the contemporary fashion of Bernard Newman for costume designer Walter Plunkett and Irene Castle's period prewar gowns. Cole Porter, George Gershwin, and Irving Berlin were replaced with the hits of twenty-five years ago, and instead of Astaire and Rogers's imported Broadway ballroom hoofing, RKO's dance coach Hermes Pan trained the team to imitate the Castles' dance innovations: the Castle walk, the fox-trot, and the tango.

A few years earlier, when RKO purchased the rights to Irene's stories, studio executives had agreed that she should act as a consultant on the film.[41] Although she had married twice since Vernon's death in an air accident during the Great War, Irene remained in the public eye mainly as the arbiter of their history as America's most famous dance and fashion team. In the 1920s she published several articles and pamphlets on her career with Vernon, including *My Husband*.[42] RKO assigned the script to Broadway librettist Oscar Hammerstein II, who had also written the screenplay for another period musical, *Show Boat*. Hammerstein drew heavily on Castle's narrative as he worked in the autumn of 1937,[43] and he emphasized both the historical period and how the Castles transformed it with their chic European style. But even as the Castles changed their era, Vernon became its victim after only a few years of international stardom. Born in England, Vernon had joined the Royal Air Force in 1915. He flew in France for several months before returning to Canada to train new recruits. Then, just before he was supposed to go home on leave to see Irene, one of his students crashed into his plane and killed him.

Hammerstein planned the war as the centerpiece of the narrative, the event that splits the historic team. He alluded to the outbreak of hostilities with an elaborate series of newspaper inserts and projected headlines, later cementing the hyperbolic textual rhetoric with Vernon's own understated explanation of why he had to return to England to fight Germany long before the Americans joined up.[44] Even as the war and Vernon's death end the Castle dance team, Irene's friend Walter reminds her and the audience that Vernon Castle's memory and impact will be more lasting than his life. The diegesis may end with Vernon's death, but Hammerstein planned to close the film with a montage of future dancing teams, all influenced by the Castles: Carl Hyson and Dorothy Dickson, Clifton Webb and Mary Hay, and the DeMarcos. And "as a wind-up to this pageant of talent and youth and gaiety," he wrote, "Mr. Astaire and Miss Rogers emerge in a series of quickly shifting eight-bar fragments from their succession of pictures, *Gay Divorcee*, *Top Hat*, *Swing Time*, establishing them as 'themselves,' the outgrowth, the modern equivalent, the symbol of rhythmic beauty and romantic appeal the Castles had for the public twenty years ago."[45] Casting Astaire and Rogers as the Castles was a smart publicity move, capitalizing on both their current popularity and the historical cycle; it also represented Hollywood's understanding of historical continuity, of the persistence of the past and its coexistence with its most modern symbols of Hollywood glamour: Fred Astaire and Ginger Rogers.

Like Rogers, Irene Castle had always been the second half of the dance team, but her memoirs served to both commemorate Vernon and describe her own active role in managing and publicizing their work. Hammerstein, with writers Dorothy Yost and Richard Sherman, followed Irene's lead by emphasizing her role in forming the dance partnership and deciding on its professional attitude and presentation. At the beginning of their careers, Vernon tries to explain their dance style to a prospective producer, but he is diffident and inadequate. "It's—sort of a dance," he says. Irene replies firmly, "It *is* a dance." The producer, old-time comedian Lew Fields, expostulates, "So when have you had any dancing ambitions?" Irene answers for Vernon, "Since he met me."[46] This was more credit than Ginger Rogers ever got for influencing Astaire, but the unique relationship between the Castles and Astaire-Rogers created an onscreen-offscreen resonance between the two pairs. It is unusual that Irene/Ginger is the one attempting to raise their careers from Vernon/Fred's usual brand of corny comedy, and it was Ginger who was most anxious to inject her career with historical prestige. As his initial treatment indicates, Hammerstein wanted to focus on the many connections between the two dance teams, and Irene's professional assertiveness, her creation of the team, and her control of its professional etiquette and public success in Europe and America say much about Rogers's often marginalized role in classical Hollywood filmmaking.

At the same time, Rogers decided to take the initiative and publicize her more active role in making the prestige film. Unfortunately, Irene Castle was not supportive of her decision. In fact, in her autobiography published twenty years later, Castle claimed that Fred Astaire had "begged her" not to let Rogers get the part and that the head office had promised to institute a nationwide search to keep Rogers from the role.[47] But Castle was not Scarlett O'Hara, and RKO was not Selznick International or MGM. Rogers felt the antagonism but thought that Castle's creative energies were misdirected. Castle seemed more proud of her influence on the fashion world than on dancing and insisted that she design Rogers's wardrobe. RKO agreed nominally, but the studio hired famed period costume designer Walter Plunkett, fresh from his work on *Gone with the Wind*, to supervise. Plunkett, the acknowledged doyen of period design, was also a close personal friend of Rogers, and the two worked secretly to alter the designs. Rogers supported Plunkett's and Castle's push for historical authenticity, but perhaps out of spite, she refused to alter her platinum pageboy for the shorter Castle bob. Historical film or not, *The Story of Vernon and Irene Castle* was also a Ginger Rogers film. By 1939, Rogers had an image that, if not exactly immutable, was well established from her days at Warner Brothers. Her decision to maintain her hairstyle was her way of asserting her own creative image, of melding her dance fame and style with Irene's. After all, there were no disagreements when Astaire did not mimic Vernon Castle's hairstyle or British accent. Irene, however, resented this competitor whose fame had already eclipsed her own.

Aside from these disagreements over sartorial and tonsorial details, both Astaire and Rogers reacted well to the script. Although several writers worked on it, each maintained a consistent historical structure, using text titles, newspaper inserts, fashion layouts and montages, shots of the film studio where Irene worked, and frequent dialogue references to the Castles' place in history.[48] But as the scripts developed, Hammerstein's final film references to the real Astaire and Rogers disappeared, and the text inserts of the First World War remained. Dorothy Yost in particular offered a fascinating approach, uniting the Castles' story with the international war crisis. Text inserts show the headlines announcing

that President Wilson will keep America out of the war, while inside the
newspaper, Irene models the "Castle bob," which sent women flocking to
their hairdressers.[49] The scripts emphasize these competitive histories in
their contrasting text inserts. The Castles' wealthy, successful lifestyle and
their impact on art and fashion represent a playful prewar innocence that
looks forward to the social revolutions of the 1920s. Yet this image-driven
entertainment history competes with the written history, the documents
of the war and its deadly toll on British and later American youth. In
the course of the film narrative, these document inserts become historical intrusions, black-and-white events to be feared by Irene. Even as they
chronicle contemporary events, they also represent the inescapable historical record. It turns out that even the Castles are not immune from the
grip of history. The war separates them (literally, in split-screen imagery),
and Vernon enlists in the Royal Air Force. Irene retreats to Hollywood to
make war pictures for Hearst's International Studios. While on the set of
one film, the director, a Cecil B. DeMille type, growls, "Let's make this
bigger than the war."[50] The film is *Patria*, soon to be Irene's most popular
film. But as Irene's cheerful disregard of these overblown films intimates,
these wartime pictures hardly aspired to be "accurate" portrayals of the
war or even masterpieces of propaganda. Soon after her sojourn in Hollywood, Vernon is killed. Instead of going on alone, making her own dance
and fashion history, the war forces Irene to become a passive receptacle
of patriotism—an instrument of the established historical event. The Castles' partnership has now been totally destroyed by the war, and the last
glimpse of them together is as ghostly wraiths gliding in the air of Irene's
imagination.

The Great War splits
the couple in *The Story
of Vernon and Irene
Castle* (1939).

Ginger Rogers as Irene
Foote Castle in *Patria*.

In the final stages of production, RKO decided to add an extra historical touch: a text foreword. "In a famous and beloved era," it began, "near
enough to be warmly remembered, two bright and shining stars, Vernon
and Irene Castle, whirled across the horizon, into the hearts of all who
loved to dance. This is their story." But director H. C. Potter, fresh from
working on *Shopworn Angel*, even included an afterword that reaffirmed
the film's historical basis while admitting that the script took liberties with
the names of other characters. Publicity and reviews made the most of
Astaire and Rogers's venture into historical filmmaking and RKO's choice
to historicize events only twenty-five years old, but it was certainly not the
first time that Hollywood gave the twentieth century the historical treatment.

The Story of Vernon and Irene Castle was also the last time that Astaire
and Rogers would dance together at RKO. Their partnership ended, fittingly, with a historical film recounting the brief but spectacular careers
of their dancing antecedents. Whereas the most important event of the
last generation, the Great War, had severed the Castles, only career ambition ended the Astaire and Rogers series. Rogers went on to fulfill her
dream of being a serious dramatic actress, winning an Academy Award
the following year for her performance in *Kitty Foyle*, a text-bolstered, self-
proclaimed "natural history" of the American woman. But after Kitty's
saga, Rogers only occasionally made historical or period films, such as
the 1920s courtroom farce *Roxie Hart* (1942) and a Dolley Madison biography, *Magnificent Doll* (1945). Just as Astaire was the epitome of the
modern man, Rogers was the essence of the modern woman, and historical films seemed inconsistent with their image. Although Frank Nugent

admired *The Story of Vernon and Irene Castle* and gave Rogers unusual top billing over her costar, he wrote, "Rogers and Astaire have been so closely identified with light comedy in the past that finding them otherwise employed is practically as disconcerting as it would be if Walt Disney were to throw Mickey to the lions."[51] But the blame, he said, lay with the conditioned audience's familiarity with thin scripts and the brittle present, not with the actors' work in a faultless and powerful historical drama. Film historians such as Arlene Croce have noted that Astaire and Rogers's foray into history may have indirectly ended their future as a team.[52] But in spite of both Nugent's worries about its unconventionality and film historians' cool reception, *The Story of Vernon and Irene Castle* was a huge box-office hit in April 1939, particularly in New York. With only *The Story of Alexander Graham Bell* and *Dodge City* for competition, the film about the Castles cleared more than $100,000 in the first week at Radio City Music Hall.[53] Rather than ending a historic partnership, *The Story of Vernon and Irene Castle* provided Ginger Rogers with the prestige to tackle RKO's biggest film of 1940: *Kitty Foyle.*

American filmmakers had placed the war and the bootlegging 1920s in the past tense since the early sound era. Perhaps it was the sudden Depression that ended the Jazz Age with such decision, or perhaps it was the new sound medium that made the silent 1920s even more remote and in need of "explanation," but Hollywood's historical interests expanded beyond the solid outlines of the nineteenth century. Yet this willingness to historicize the antebellum and postwar eras did not necessarily condemn films to standard linear narrative and academic stodginess—*Public Enemy* and *Scarface* ensured that. By 1939, however, with many filmmakers anxious to rival or exceed the work of traditional historians, they also tended to take themselves too seriously. *The Story of Vernon and Irene Castle* ended the pairing of Astaire and Rogers for a decade; something similar happened to James Cagney's career in screen crime with the release of *The Roaring Twenties.*

Mark Hellinger, American Historian

Mark Hellinger was no ordinary filmmaker, although he shared the background of some of Hollywood's most articulate screenwriters, having been a New York newspaperman and columnist and then a successful Broadway playwright and producer before heading west. His gritty *Night Court* (1932), an unproduced play, was an instant success as a film and brought him to the attention of the Hollywood studios. In spite of a few erratic story credits, by the late 1930s, Hellinger had not yet made a name for himself. But like many of his colleagues, Hellinger realized that prestige and historical films were the industry's most lucrative combination. Yet he was no DeMille; for him, the most powerful historical events were those that affected his own generation. The Great War and the aftermath of the Roaring Twenties were definitive historical periods, and Hellinger's most haunting realization was that his world had become part of the past. He selected Warner Brothers, the studio most connected with filming modern American history, and pitched his story, "The World Moves On," with the pronouncement, "This is a big picture: It is either big—or it is nothing at all." Specifically, he believed that the history made it "big" and prestigious. "For, while it deals with a specific set of humans, the background is far more important than the characters. And the background is the history of an era." Hellinger planned to film the history of postwar America, the Prohibition era. Perhaps worried that the historical aspects would seem too abstruse to Jack Warner and Hal Wallis, he defended his idea, saying that history was more exciting than fiction and that the events of twenty years ago would still appeal to audiences. He asked, even though he was too young to have fought in the Great War, "Did that spoil my enjoyment of *The Big Parade, What Price Glory, Journey's End, All Quiet on the Western Front*? Hell, no. . . . Was the earthquake too close for me to enjoy *San Francisco*? Did the fact that Ziegfeld died only a short time before, destroy the notion that *The Great Ziegfeld* was a glorious musical?"[54] On the contrary, he argued, history, particularly modern history, was more interesting than fiction.

Hellinger's efforts to persuade Warner and Wallis of the marketability of American history may have been unnecessary. The studio was in the process of making a series of highly successful and expensive western blockbusters, although it had been several years since the studio had made a large-scale gangster picture. Will Hays's 1935 moratorium still prevented the studios from rereleasing *Little Caesar* and *The Public Enemy*. In the early 1930s, Zanuck had often tried to deflect attacks on the films' morality by stressing their historical accuracy, but this was the very approach that the Production Code Administration feared. By 1939, Hellinger thought that he had solved the ban on gangster films and the critical uneasiness that accompanied Hollywood's treatment of the First World War. Historicizing the Lost Generation, placing it within the conventional historical film framework, would make it censor proof and audience safe.

Hellinger's treatment was unlike that of any previous historical film. He began with the armistice and proceeded year by year to focus on the national events and how the film would introduce and structure the history. "Always remember that the background is ever-present," he reiterated, "the Prohibition picture in the whole United States. We introduce background whenever possible, whenever logical . . . newspaper articles, copper situations, discussions, maps drawn in pencil on tablecloths, and so on." Robert Lord's short treatment took Hellinger's pronouncement on the history of Prohibition to heart. He began the script with the Senate's ratification of the Eighteenth Amendment and planned to end the film with another senator years later denouncing the effects of the Volstead Act.[55] However, it was Earl Baldwin and Frank Donohue's rough script that fully captured Hellinger's historical conception of the era. It was not enough to film from the present's omniscient perspective; the writers understood Hellinger's demand for a self-conscious structural commentary—a modern reaction to history. They constructed a foreword superimposed over a revolving globe, capturing the paradox between American national history and the challenge of international events thrust on the United States in 1914 and again in 1939. "Today, while an era crumbles beneath the heels of marching men, America has little time to remember an astounding era of her own recent history. An era which will grow more and more incredible with each passing generation—until someday, people will say it could never have happened at all." They then outlined a Great War montage of exploding shells, spitting machine guns, and waves of falling soldiers.[56] Later, writers Jerry Wald and Richard Macaulay complicated this traditional historical structure by layering a foreword over a series of images, drawing the viewer from the present of fascist armies and labor riots back to breadlines, Hoover, Coolidge, big business, Wilson, and the war. But they eschewed the traditional text foreword and turned completely to the modern visual and oral qualities of cinema and radio historiography.

The final script of *The Roaring Twenties*, as it was soon retitled, began with an oral newsreel commentary controlling the slew of images. Rather than the deliberate contrast of media and room for ambiguity and deliberate contradiction in the use of text, *The Roaring Twenties* gave an updated and assertive historical commentary. This new approach to historical credibility created total control over the images and an almost ethnographic distance between viewers and their remote and quaint past. The writers planned the voice-of-God narration to punctuate the entire narrative, from April 1918 and the war through 1919, 1920, 1922, 1924, 1927, and 1929, creating what film historian Philip Rosen considered to be the epitome of nineteenth-century historical positivism.[57] Yet in spite

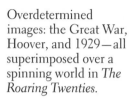

Overdetermined images: the Great War, Hoover, and 1929—all superimposed over a spinning world in *The Roaring Twenties.*

of its orally contained historical narrative, the documentary images were superimposed so quickly that they presented a rich and historically over-determined surface, a roaring complexity that no voice-over could fully restrain.

The film tells the stories of three fictional doughboys who meet during the war and return home to become a gangster, a bootlegger, and a lawyer—unobtrusively connecting Hollywood's fictional narratives to history. The technique also emphasized the veteran-gangster connection established in the early 1930s by journalists and filmmakers.[58] Curiously, Warner Brothers seemed comfortable with the script's elaborate historical structures and overt didacticism. *The Roaring Twenties* was its prestige history picture of 1939. The studio hired Raoul Walsh to direct and then cast top star James Cagney and rising players Priscilla Lane, Jeffrey Lynn, and Humphrey Bogart. Surprisingly, the studio allowed the filmmakers a great deal of time to research and assemble the opening foreword and montage, examining everything from historical texts to newspaper clippings to Hellinger's own memory.[59]

Although Hellinger had written only the story outline, Warner Brothers retained him as a reliable historical compass throughout production. Like so many other historical productions, *The Roaring Twenties* remained the writer's film. Wallis even commissioned Hellinger to write "a special narrative foreword" for the film based on the opening historical montage.[60] Hellinger's foreword did not condemn or judge the 1920s and its gangsters; instead, it said, if "we will be confronted with another period similar to the one depicted in this photoplay . . . I pray that events as dra-

actually occurred.

Bitter or sweet, most memories become precious as the years move on. This film is a memory—and I am grateful for it.

Mark Hellinger

Mark Hellinger's modern history.
(*The Roaring Twenties*)

matized here, will be remembered." Hellinger was "grateful" for his memories of the 1920s, not ashamed or horrified, as censors had once been. Although he envisioned American history from 1918 to 1939 as a time of major political movements and legislation, years dominated by presidents from Wilson to Roosevelt, Hellinger's narrative was about the rise and fall of marginal figures struggling against the establishment. Shots of FDR, Hitler, Mussolini, and Wilson may have crowded the opening prologue, but the true narrative of the Roaring Twenties belonged to anonymous ex-doughboys like Eddie Bartlett (James Cagney). Although he might adopt the structures of institutional historiography, Hellinger wanted to use that establishment voice to place the country's misfits within the trajectory of American history.

Hellinger's vision was realized. Under Wallis's supervision, Warner Brothers covered the historical highlights of the past twenty years—the war, the armistice, the Volstead Act, the crash of 1929, the repeal of Prohibition. Warner Brothers even managed to advertise the studio's own claim to national historical importance by including its great contribution to the motion picture industry, the talking *Jazz Singer* (1927), within the great events of modern American history. As Wallis remarked, he wanted the spoken foreword to sound like Henry Luce's popular newsreel series "The March of Time,"[61] blending the terse authority of contemporary news reportage with the "text" of established historiography. But this establishment voice was capable of expressing postwar cynicism, noting that in 1918, "almost a million young men are engaged in a struggle *which they have been told* will make the world safe for democracy" (emphasis added).

In the process, the film adopted an omniscient, didactic historical tone that appealed to the studio's burgeoning sense of prestige but often struck others outside the industry as pretentious. Warner executives admitted that they hoped to stave off any censor criticism at home or abroad by putting out publicity that *The Roaring Twenties* "is an historical picture," not a crime drama.[62]

Many critics admired a film so obviously conceived to impress, but curiously, Frank Nugent despised it. As the years went by, the critic grew increasingly annoyed with Hollywood's prestigious historical films. While DeMille's willfully inaccurate western epics might elicit his amused contempt, Warner Brothers' self-conscious modern history was too much. He wrote: "The Warners are presenting *The Roaring Twenties* (at the Strand) with the self-conscious air of an antiquarian preparing to translate a cuneiform record of a lost civilization. With a grandiloquent and egregiously sentimental foreword by Mark Hellinger, with employment of newsreel shots to lend documentary flavor, with a commentator's voice interpolating ultra-dramatic commonplaces as the film unreels, their melodrama has taken on an annoying pretentiousness which neither the theme nor its treatment can justify."[63] For Nugent, American history was clearly the traditional, nineteenth-century national tales rehashed and transcribed with deadly precision in school textbooks. Warner Brothers, in attempting to emulate that style of historiography for a comparatively modern subject, was guilty of an absurd "pretentiousness." Here, cinema had stopped being the harmless entertainment he loved to demean and was attempting something above its station. Nugent continued with his diatribe, hoping to deflate the film's pomposity by remarking that *The Roaring Twenties* was really just Warner Brothers' return to its profitable gangster era. Accidentally, Nugent hit on the heart of Warner Brothers' original decision to film Hellinger's history. *The Roaring Twenties* was a continuation of the early gangster films—but it was a culmination of the historical gangster pictures initiated by *Little Caesar* and *The Public Enemy*.[64] Critic Leo Miskin, though more sympathetic to Warner Brothers' attempt to narrate modern history, also remarked that the film was less a "view of that decade between 1920 and 1930" than it was "a condensed history of all those Warner gangster films."[65] Warner Brothers created a dual history—a deliberate and structured traditional history of the United States from the First World War through the Depression, and a farewell to its early gangster films now banned from circulation by the censors. Ironically, history was the only way to return to its early triumphs with historical gangster pictures and the effects of the war. But critics would not allow Warner

Brothers the right to make such a historical film. The studio had gone too far.

Although Hollywood had been producing critical historical successes since 1931, Nugent's ire and Miskin's misunderstanding resulted from the fact that Warner Brothers chose to historicize the Roaring Twenties with all the structural solemnity of a more traditional nineteenth-century historical drama. The 1920s was not a decade of national harmony, peace, prosperity, and virtue. Rather than heroic Valley Forges or poignant Gettysburgs, there was only confusing, mechanized foreign war. There were no triumphant returning heroes but disillusioned veterans and gangsters. There was no democratic freedom to return to but political and economic repression and the Volstead Act. There was crime, graft, sex, money, violence, depression, and despair. The war began the narrative of *The Roaring Twenties*; it created a fissure in American history, a deeply violent age, and the Great Depression. It was an era when small-time fellows struggled against the bewildering forces of history and lost. As the Texas Guinan–inspired character Kansas says of Eddie Bartlett (Cagney) in the final sequence of the film, "He used to be a big shot." Hollywood's historical gangsters had once been antiheroes to be proud of. Censorship silenced them, and by 1939, under a burden of history, they were defeated in the final frames of the film. It is true that Rico, Powers, and Camonte also died, but ahead of their time. Rico may be unrecognizable in death, but his name still haunts the Chicago papers. In contrast, Cagney's character in *The Roaring Twenties* is a relic through much of the film. His name is forgotten by the time he is shot.

Oddly, Nugent's choice of words in his review was apt: the postwar era was "antique" in 1939, and the gangster-veteran was a relic. But in choosing the film format of the traditional nineteenth-century epic historical narrative, Warner Brothers made critics and audiences uncomfortable. Unlike the other historical releases in 1939, including *Gone with the Wind, Drums along the Mohawk, The Oklahoma Kid*, and *Jesse James*, this was no tale of unity and patriotism or even of rebellious heroism. It was a tale of defeat and decline, initiated by the war. Hellinger's commitment to documenting recent American history, even when narrated by an omniscient personal voice, only disconcerted the public. Hollywood had examined controversial points of view before, but always from a safe historical distance. The war, bootlegging, and the Depression were too close for comfort. Hellinger focused on the war and on the historical background to such an extent that it ceased to be background, and the characters faded into pallid nothingness. Self-consciously or not, he created a historical world without heroes and without hope. The historical prologue, rather than reassuring and stabilizing the narrative, succeeded only in presenting a destabilized view of the national past.

8

The Last of the Long Hunters, 1938–1941

"York, have you ever read this?"
"History of the United States. Sure is a lot of writing . . ."
"That book's full of great men."
— Major Buxton and Alvin York, 1941

In spite of the critics' negative response to *The Roaring Twenties*, Warner Brothers continued to invest in the Great War, releasing *The Fighting 69th* in early 1940. As with its westerns and Civil War histories, it solicited the help of Herman Lissauer and the studio's expanding research library. A vast team of researchers read the military histories of the Shamrock Battalion, the Rainbow Division, the 69th Regiment, and the life of Chaplain Duffy. The studio contacted dozens of 69th veterans in the hope of collecting their obscure war memories, and there were many eager responses.[1] From the beginning, screenwriters Norman Reilly Raine, Fred Niblo Jr., and Dean Franklin took a page from *The Roaring Twenties'* script and planned to introduce the fate of Chaplain Duffy and his Irish Regiment during the last months of the Great War with an elaborate combination text and image prologue. The 69th's history, like America's, was not one of effortless glory but one of defeat, tragedy, and defensive, marginal, Pyrrhic victories: Bull Run, Fredericksburg, the Spanish-American War, and the Mexican border skirmishes of 1916.[2] Placed in the company of these other battles, World War I is less a noble fight for democracy than a bloody and unavoidable tragedy that the fighting Irish would overcome only through plain guts. By the time shooting was completed, Duffy and "Wild Bill" Donovan were the only historical characters left in the narrative, but the prologue, the hallmark of historical authority, remained intact.

Two unusual occurrences marked the film's production. Darryl Zanuck, hearing of the rival studio's project, wrote to Jack Warner demanding that Warner Brothers desist from filming Duffy's and the regiment's story, since Twentieth Century–Fox had already registered the film title *Father Duffy of the Fighting 69th* and owned the film rights to Duffy's memoirs. Zanuck complained at length to Warner that he had to "be fair about it and recognize the fact that we have the registration of the title," and he also made a point of condemning the rising practice of claim-jumping other studios' historical property.[3] Even Samuel Goldwyn, who had never been a competitor in American historical production (having spent the last few years adapting lavish contemporary American and British literary projects), was becoming a problem. The independent producer had announced earlier that year that his production company was filming the life and times of Judge Roy Bean in the upcoming *The Westerner*. In doing so, Goldwyn infringed on Zanuck's historical territory. When Fox merged with Twentieth Century in 1935, Zanuck inherited *West of the Pecos* (1934), a script and film loosely based on Bean's career as a rustic lawman with an incurable crush on British actress Lillie Langtry. Since then, the producer had successfully intimidated anyone who showed an interest in the area, including popular western historian and former silent screenwriter Stuart N. Lake. It took Lake's agents years to interest Goldwyn in "The Vinegaroon and the Jersey Lily," the basis for *The Westerner*.[4] Zanuck was furious, but powerless, as his upstart colleagues realized that entire historical periods could not be under one studio's copyright jurisdiction.

American historical filmmaking had become a business, and Zanuck now wanted regulation. Although he realized that there was nothing he could do to stop other studios from making such films, the competition for historical subjects (unlike literary adaptations and original screenplays) was so widespread that it was generating chaos in the industry. American history was not under copyright, and even if Zanuck had purchased all the biographies of Duffy and his regiment or all those of Judge Roy Bean, Warner and Goldwyn could still get away with filming the subjects. Zanuck's frustration is understandable. He spent money to purchase the definitive account of a historical period, Duffy's memoirs, and another studio preempted his subject, destroying any chance of making a profit. He was learning that purchasing historiography was not worth the expense, an attitude that would cripple the filmmaker's former regard for well-researched and innovative film histories. Yet paradoxically, Zanuck's historical innovations had saved him from other forms of interstudio exploitation; his most highly regarded historical films were original works constructed by his screenwriters Nunnally Johnson and Lamar Trotti. In 1939 the Duffy fiasco reminded Zanuck that screenwriters were his best financial investment in historical filmmaking.

At Warner Brothers, Norman Reilly Raine attempted to push the boundaries of modern screen history. In the past few years, Raine had worked on a range of historical scripts from Howard Hughes's *Scarface* to Warner Brothers' *The Adventures of Robin Hood* (1938), and he was responsible for outlining the original montage prologue for *The Fighting 69th*. But during production, he wrote to producer Lou Edelman proposing a text foreword to precede the regimental battle montage. Raine's planned foreword would not simply reflect on the historical period but also invoke contemporary patriotism directly. He wrote: "Here is a thought as to the presentation of this foreword. Instead of running it off the screen in the conventional way why not have it *spoken* by Mr. Harry Warner, a man already known nationally for the depth and sincerity of his Americanism? A medium shot of him behind his desk; behind him, not too obtrusively, the flag, and on his desk, facing the audience, his name plate. Let him speak quietly . . . making it a personal message from this studio to America. It will be an innovation."[5] Raine knew why Warner Brothers had suddenly become interested in Great War history, and he also understood the importance of the text foreword in legitimizing this interest. He outlined a studio position that claimed that any film about the First World War should be connected to a message of contemporary Americanism. Warner Brothers should not disguise its politics and program of antifascism, he argued, but declare its views and use American history in its new cause—rescuing Europe. Most remarkably, the screenwriter believed that film producers had the public confidence and clout to serve not only as historical authenticators but also as public figures. Although Raine's suggestion was not adopted, his belief in the rhetorical uses of the foreword and the impressment of American history in the interests of contemporary political ideologies would eventually dominate Warner Brothers' historical productions.

Although many American historical films had juxtaposed the past and present during the 1930s, these were often critical views that either interrogated the rhetoric of history or confronted America's defeats. But increasingly after 1938, filmmakers deliberately forced particular historical events to submit to current political demands. Hollywood's filmmaker-historians were recognizing the potential significance of the discourse of American historical cinema. Raine's plan for *The Fighting 69th*'s foreword represented a shift in the use of "historical" text and would determine the production choices for the studio's next two major prestige films, *Sergeant York* (1941) and *Yankee Doodle Dandy* (1942).

Although American historians such as Frederick Jackson Turner had embraced the connection between history and the present generation's interpretation of it, this relationship always threatened to transform historical objectivity and researched, articulate arguments into vehicles for political ideology and cultural control. More recently, historian Peter Novick located the objectivity "crisis" in the American historical profession within the wartime government's successful use of historians as wartime writers—or, in modern terms, propagandists.[6] Other historians have argued that with *Sergeant York*, Hollywood achieved something similar; Warner Brothers presented not a work of film historiography but a sublimation of 1941 war angst.[7] According to this argument, as a work of war propaganda and a plea for American preparedness, 1917 and 1918 mattered less in *Sergeant York* as a distinct historical period than as a metaphor for 1941 America. Alvin York's individual heroism in *Sergeant York* was insignificant compared with his malleability as an Everyman hero in 1917 or 1941.

But Warner Brothers' historical manipulations were not as facile as late-twentieth-century historians have claimed. The studio's panegyric to Sergeant Alvin York did not simply reflect contemporary wartime rhetoric; it drew on a whole genealogy of national metaphors, presenting York as a reincarnated revolutionary hero. Films about revolutionary America made after 1939 were also preoccupied with contemporary political and military conflicts. They were particularly anxious to manage American dissidence and resentment of Great Britain, rewriting America's war of independence as a conflict between colonials and Indians rather than one with the British army (*The Last of the Mohicans*, 1936; *Daniel Boone*, 1936; *Allegheny Uprising*, 1939; *Drums along the Mohawk*, 1939; *Northwest Passage*, 1940). Contextualizing *Sergeant York* within the escalating trend of eighteenth- and early-nineteenth-century revolutionary heritage films reveals the complexity of Warner Brothers' use of the American past and traditional wartime propaganda.

The Historical Cycle in 1941

The Fighting 69th's success in early 1940 convinced Jack Warner and Hal Wallis that Jesse Lasky's long-standing idea to film a biography of

American war hero Alvin York might not be a financial disaster. In fact, York's phenomenal capture of 132 German prisoners in the Argonne forest in 1918 seemed a perfect match for Warner's current taste for exotic wartime adventures. York's exploits needed no invention or script doctoring, unlike the comparatively pedestrian story of the 69th Regiment. The film would cement the studio's monopoly of the historical period and silence Zanuck. Although Lasky's $50,000 deal for York's exclusive story meant that Zanuck would not be writing to protest the film as a copyright violation, both of York's principal biographers, Sam Cowan (*Sergeant York and His People*, 1922) and the estate of Tom Skeyhill (*Sergeant York: The Last of the Longhunters*, 1930), would soon claim that the planned film biography plagiarized their work. Both demanded remuneration.[8] Studio executives knew that even York's vaunted autobiography had been ghost-written by Skeyhill and that, under these circumstances, Skeyhill's estate had some moral claim. York's life and reputation were worth money; Lasky and his colleagues were less interested in him as a challenging, previously unfilmed historical figure than as a salable film property—a made-to-order film hero.

Lasky first hired Harry Chandlee and Julien Josephson to write a treatment, and the two of them accompanied Lasky to Tennessee to meet York and his family. Experienced historical screenwriter Abem Finkel (*Jezebel*) soon replaced Josephson, and although Lasky and the studio were enthusiastic about their script, the producer's and the screenwriters' control over production was short-lived. Newly hired director Howard Hawks disliked the detailed, plodding narrative and thought that a simplified heroic tale, rewritten by John Huston and Howard Koch based on his dictation, would make a better film. Hawks had begun his Hollywood career as a script editor and was famous for trying to improve on writers' efforts, mostly with disastrous results. Historical screenwriter Nunnally Johnson still remembered Hawks's meddling with some irritation forty years after making *Roxie Hart* in 1942.[9] But Hawks was unusually officious when making *Sergeant York*. With Gary Cooper's support, he convinced Lasky to authorize a rewrite and cede production control to him. Production chief Hal Wallis, possibly more intimidated by Cooper (the studio had secured him from Goldwyn in exchange for Bette Davis) than by Hawks's reputation for "quitting" historical productions in the middle of shooting, also agreed to the new system.

Hawks never met York or admitted to reading any of the biographies, but he wanted all of the first historical script altered by the new year. Surprisingly, Huston and Koch's script retained and even enhanced Chandlee and Finkel's historical structures and text superimpositions. The new script began York's screen life with a conventional set of impressive text forewords, reminding audiences of his pioneer greatness and courage under fire. Wallis was wary of all the text and warned Lasky that the didacticism associated with text intertitles "will have a tendency to take the edge off the picture."[10] But Huston and Koch retained Chandlee and Finkel's lengthy representation of York's conscientious objections to the Great War and the detailed Argonne sequences. Their only significant changes to the Chandlee-Finkel script were to the opening antebellum scenes of churchgoing, hell-raising, farming, and turkey shooting in Fentress County. But Finkel, resenting his dismissal, was contemptuous of Hawks and his new writers' hackneyed and demeaning portrayals of southern mountain people and their trivialization of York's prewar life. Finkel protested to Wallis in a nine-page memo headed "The Sad Story of Sergeant York": "I have . . . long since despaired of protecting the script from the blundering stupidities of Messrs Cooper, Hawks, Huston and Koch." In Finkel's view, Hawks had forced rewrites that cast York's Tennessee mountain community as a collection of out-of-date, pioneering morons straight from "Coming 'Round the Mountain." Maintaining Alvin York's and the public's respect was important, he insisted, especially for a studio project of this magnitude, and cheapening York's prewar years jeopardized the credibility of the Great War sequences. According to Finkel, Hawks had also altered the battle sequences so that they focused on York's single-handed leadership and excluded the participation of the other men. Hawks's idea of heroism was trite and would invite public censure. But Lasky and Warner Brothers had already taken the precaution of buying the endorsements of York's compatriots before the film was released, an expensive if necessary hazard of making contemporary historical films.[11]

York's prewar mountain life, in particular his serious conversion to a fundamentalist faith, was telescoped. The film biography began in 1916, when York was drinking and carousing in the almost uniformly religious community of the Valley of the Three Forks. Actually, York's wild ways had ended several years before the advent of the European war, but due to Hawks and company's time manipulation, it looked as if the war itself was York's salvation. On film, his religious pacifism and antiwar convictions lacked the deep-rooted ideals and sense of personal development expressed in his autobiography and biography. Yet due to the writers, the historical text remained integral to the film; York's screen life was bound by both a foreword and an afterword and was punctuated with text inserts.

The writers also deployed a narrative device that first placed York in conflict and then in step with the text of American history. Although an impressive text foreword proclaims his enduring American heroism, early in the narrative, York's anonymous country life is spent ignoring the importance of the printed word, both secular and religious. He is a heathen, scorning the Bible and Pastor Pyle's sermons. But with his conversion to the word of God, York enters into a conflict with American foreign policy; his religious pacifism leads him to oppose the war and the printed text of patriotism. Newspapers from nearby Jamestown remind the isolated citizenry of Fentress County of the war in Europe and later of America's involvement and the draft. Signed documents and government letters from the draft board force York to go to France. But these hostile official texts are not truly important to him. He ignores the papers, and Hawks never shot a close-up of York reading the draft letters. The film inscribes a certain visual distance between York, the audience, and the printed text.

When he reaches Camp Gordon, York expostulates with his commanding officers, Major Buxton and Captain Danforth, about his pacifism, telling them that his life is governed by the supreme book, the Bible. In a scene reminiscent of York's memoirs, Danforth tries to counter his quotations with other passages from the New Testament advocating violence, but in vain. York outquotes his superior officer. However, the screenwriters constructed their own text metaphor central to historical filmmaking: Buxton circumvents York's religious pacifism by giving him another book to read, *The History of the United States*. When York flips through the pages, the first picture he sees is of Daniel Boone. Buxton then remarks that Boone was "one of the greatest" and tells York that "the book's full of great men" who all dreamed of defending freedom. York, intrigued, asks to borrow it, and the officers send him home on leave to think about the war. As he reads about his true kin, his pioneer ancestors, the historical text informs and changes his reading of the Bible. In finding his true text, York becomes part of history, the next generation of America's pioneer freedom fighters who learned that "the cost of this heritage is high." It is only after reading this book in conjunction with the Bible high in the mountains of Fentress County that York develops a godlike perspective on his town, a certain visual distance and understanding necessary to put his life in historical perspective. The audience never sees the text of these history books; the privilege of reading the text belongs only to York, who will make his own place in *The History of the United States* and in the 1941 history of America's canonical heroes, Dixon Wecter's *The Hero in America*.[12] Propped against the mountain face with

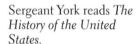

Sergeant York reads *The History of the United States.*

Alvin York: a twentieth-century Lincoln.

his faithful hunting dog at his side, York continues to read as the sun sets. Hunched over the book, his lanky frame darkens to a silhouette in the fading light. He becomes part of the mountain, the figure of a man cut in stone. Years ago, another country boy sat thus, dreaming in hills not far from Fentress: Abraham Lincoln. Lincoln's stone monuments were so numerous that in 1932 Franklin Meade published a catalog of public statuary, but by 1941, Lincoln's most famous heroic likeness was part of Gutzon Borglum's Mount Rushmore monument (completed in 1941 following Borglum's death).

Lincoln's presence had been evoked or inserted into a remarkable number of American historical films by 1941, but *Sergeant York*'s most

Revisiting old "texts": the Daniel Boone connection. (*Sergeant York*)

prominent historical analogy was between Daniel Boone and York. On his mountain hunts, York often passes a tree carved with Boone's own writing, "D Boon cilled a bar on the tree in year 1760." But he recognizes the importance of this writing, this tie of heritage and place, only after he reads Buxton's history book. Boone's name is the only one he reads aloud from the book. York's hunting expeditions, transposed to the Western Front, will make him the equivalent of an American biblical hero. In the final moments of the film, when he retreats into the wilderness with his future bride, Gracie Williams, he may turn his back on urban fame, but he becomes part of history and replays the myth of Daniel Boone.

Warner Brothers hyped the film with a reverent, four-shot text foreword and a massive publicity campaign abetted by interviews and photographs of the real Alvin C. York. Critics and audiences were captivated by the film. Although some of York's former brothers in arms wrote letters to the studio and the newspapers protesting the film's gross exaggeration of York's war exploits, audiences were not interested in the possibility of a more critical examination of heroism.[13] York's reputation as an American war hero was almost unassailable. Bosley Crowther of the *New York Times* praised it as "true Americana," and Edwin Schallert in Los Angeles claimed that *Sergeant York* was "the most biographical of movie biographies," convinced that York and his patriotic war experience represented the zenith of American historical cinema.[14]

In the years since *Sergeant York*'s release, film historians have singled it out as a masterpiece of Hollywood's wartime propaganda, a simple and direct equation between the wartime heroics and faith of Sergeant Alvin

C. York and the qualities needed to combat fascism in the Second World War.[15] Its production history seemed to corroborate this view; after all, it is well known that Lasky finally convinced the shy, reserved York to curb his pacifism and sell his life's screen rights only when the producer reminded the war hero of the duty he still owed his country. Publicity man Bill Rice proclaimed in the film's press book: "World War Two is responsible for the amazing story of America's most famous soldier hero of World War One reaching the screen."[16] The film seemed to be an explicit expression of national myth and Hollywood's manipulation of history to serve contemporary ideologies. Yet *Sergeant York* also shared many of the qualities of prewar historical filmmaking: the much publicized background research, the lavish production, the inventive structural counterpoint of text and image, and the prestigious critical reception. And although *Sergeant York* was a publicly acknowledged work of historical propaganda, it was not considered a conservative, establishment film in 1941. Whereas film theorists Jean-Luc Comolli and Jean Narboni and *Cahiers du cinéma* established the template for ideologically driven analyses of Hollywood films, asserting that most of them reinforced dominant, conservative, government-approved discourse, *Sergeant York* was conceived to oppose those views in 1941 America.[17] The isolationist contingent of Congress considered it subversive and passed Senate Resolution 152, championed by Senators Gerald Nye and Bennet Champ Clark, thus forcing Warner Brothers to remove the film temporarily from general release. On 4 July 1942, a year after its premiere, it returned to American theaters.[18]

In spite of Howard Hawks's efforts to commandeer production and rewrite the script, few critics singled him out as the principal historical filmmaker; instead, Lasky and the screenwriters received more attention.[19] But it was Gary Cooper who received the greatest praise and his first Academy Award.[20] Hollywood's highest-paid male star and 1941's most critically acclaimed actor reached the height of his career playing one of the nation's canonical heroes. Cooper's success in the film was especially fitting; throughout his early career, he had worked on large-scale American historical productions such as *Only the Brave, Operator 13, The Plainsman,* and *The Texans,* and he had first attracted attention as a doomed Great War pilot in William Wellman's Academy Award–winning *Wings* (1927).

Sergeant York represented both a continuation and an intensification of Hollywood's World War I cycle. Whereas most early references to doughboys were fictional types, unknown veterans suffering under the repressive forces of history, York was the ultimate individual hero and one of the few of his generation to enter the pages of history with a name. Although Warner Brothers had depicted Chaplain Duffy's wartime career in *The Fighting 69th*, most of the supporting cast was imaginary, and the narrative avoided portraying wartime America. *Sergeant York* was the first of these Great War films to focus exclusively on a famous American war hero, but it also depicted portions of his prewar life and his struggle with conscientious objection. Despite its scripted and publicized historical basis, Warner Brothers' biggest grosser in 1941 represented a transition for Hollywood.[21] After the massive expenditures on period historical films in the 1939 and 1940 seasons, the studios cut back on traditional prestige films and supported the war effort.[22] Although critics such as Barnes, Schallert, and Crowther applauded the film's presentation of history, they also acknowledged its use as a tool of wartime propaganda. *Sergeant York* was caught between these two modes of production.

From the time of *Sergeant York*'s release until recently, critics have reiterated its powerful applications of myth in the interest of the war effort.[23] In many ways, the film does seem to lack the critical historical perspective of its predecessors. Even though the film presented a hero torn by patriotism and conscientious objection, *Sergeant York* possessed none of the criticism of American war policy, the bitter postwar outcome, and the widespread antagonism toward the military and the government that drove so many of Zanuck's early Great War veteran features. Instead, *Sergeant York* relied on the precedents established by Alvin York and his biographers and returned to founding national myths to establish a sense of historical continuity in the unstable twentieth century. Yet this self-conscious return to pioneer ancestors was not a mere mythical regression to timeworn national symbols. *Sergeant York* and its revolutionary film precursors explored the complex and conflicted identity of the elemental patriot, the mutable public conception of "revolutionary" heroes, and the process of becoming part of the text of American history.

Pioneer Ancestors

Despite the Great War's appearance in 1920s prestige films such as *Wings* and *The Big Parade*, America's unusual and even remote relationship to the war restricted the purely American forays to elliptical examinations of wartime America and the postwar veteran's anonymous struggle for survival. With the exception of Chaplain Duffy and Alvin York (and the more obscure Robert Elliot Burns), real historical figures or heroes were almost nonexistent. As historian Dixon Wecter wrote in 1941, York was "the greatest individual hero of the war," achieving a traditional heroic status that even General John Pershing and Woodrow Wilson lacked.[24] Instead, the doughboy or veteran became an Everyman, a nameless and passive American reacting to the horrors of war and the poverty of the aftermath. In many ways, Hollywood's historical attitude toward the war concurred with contemporary reportage and postwar writings about 1917 and 1918. Heroes were extremely hard to locate in a nightmare of mechanized killing. Even Britain's T. E. Lawrence, pursued and exploited by both the American and the British press, was hardly the establishment's idea of a traditional military hero. Pershing and the American press had even more difficulty finding an American war hero. Two decades later, popular historian Samuel Taylor Moore reasoned that "it was not alone because of censorship, nor the comparative brevity of large-scale American participation that no military heroes comparable to Grant, Lee, Sherman, Stonewall Jackson, Phil Sheridan and J. E. B. Stuart emerged from the war."[25] The unprecedented scale of the battles meant that commanding officers were removed from the fighting. Instead, doughboys and their officers of the line saw the action. But the casualties were such that audacity, courage, and leadership often earned death, not lasting remembrance. Even ace flyer Eddie Rickenbacker, whose solitary aerial exploits recalled an era of individual wartime heroism, could not completely acquire the status of America's greatest war hero. In the eyes of many, his German surname and ancestry compromised his reputation, and throughout the war he was subject to persecution by anti-German warmongers and spy hunters.[26] Anglo-Saxon Sergeant Alvin York became the press's answer when they discovered that he had walked out of the Argonne forest in October 1918 with 132 German prisoners.

The public was astonished to learn that he was a Tennessee mountain man, born in a log cabin in Fentress County, largely self-educated, poor, devout, lean, lanky, and a dead shot with a long rifle. This twentieth-century Hawkeye resisted being drafted on four separate occasions, even appealing to President Wilson that his pacifism was the conviction of his church. His appeals were all denied. Eventually he would meet a Georgia-born major who attempted to convert him to the war effort with a barrage of Bible quotations. After the religious duel and a last leave in the mountains, York, transformed into a muscular Christian crusader, embarked for France. In the last days of October 1918, York was part of a detail ordered to clear a hill for the American advance. When the rest of his company was killed or wounded, he managed to capture a German machine gun company single-handedly. Imagining that the advancing

Germans were "wild turkeys," he shot the back ranks first, then the front. When he finally returned through the enemy lines, he conveyed 132 prisoners into American hands. The story leaked out slowly, but when it appeared in the *Saturday Evening Post*, York became a household name. In the closing weeks of the war, he proved that American heroism and individual action were still viable.

Curiously, though, neither York nor the army seemed anxious to capitalize on his achievements.[27] York's report was sparse and matter-of-fact. It was his commanding officer and the members of his company who endorsed his actions and spread the story. Yet the events were not widely known until George Patullo's *Saturday Evening Post* story made York a national hero in 1919.[28] In fact, Patullo claimed that General Pershing was annoyed with the article, since it publicized York and scuppered the general's attempts to highlight the heroic deeds of a professional soldier. Pershing's reluctance to publicize York's work in the Argonne forest is understandable. Americans had been fighting in Europe for months, and when an individual heroic action finally captured the public's fancy, the hero was not a professional soldier but an uneducated, uncouth backwoods sergeant, a draftee, and, to top it all, a conscientious objector. Yet from the beginning of Sergeant Alvin York's appearance in printed history, his biographers emphasized the very qualities of the reluctant citizen-soldier. In writing York into the history of the Great War, Patullo stressed his subject's simple and devout background, his mountain-man independence that linked him directly to America's canon of rugged individualists and citizen-soldiers: Daniel Boone, Andrew Jackson, Sam Houston, and, of course, Abraham Lincoln. Patullo's article connected York to the country's righteous Christian heritage, work ethic, simplicity, and modesty. He was an old-fashioned hero for a rapidly changing America, a throwback to the nineteenth- or even eighteenth-century generation of pioneers. York's life in the mountains enhanced the public view of him as a traditional American and a vanishing type in the wake of industrial and urban progress.

Sergeant Alvin C. York was not an anonymous doughboy, yet he seemed to have another quality that might have restricted his impact on the American public—namely, his modesty. From all accounts, he was a shy young man, deeply conscious and ashamed of his lack of formal education. He shunned the press. After his discharge, he returned to the quiet of his prewar existence. York might have disappeared from public view forever had it not been for Tom Skeyhill. A veteran himself, Skeyhill was an unsuccessful journalist who knew that York's story could change his fortunes. But York refused to work with him on an autobiography until Skeyhill slyly implied that proceeds from the book's publication could be used to finance a school for the underprivileged mountain children of Fentress County. In 1927 they set to work.

Skeyhill's first York publication was well timed. *Sergeant York: His Own Life Story and War Diary* was published shortly after American veteran Hervey Allen's *Toward the Flame*, but it preempted the glut of British memoirs in the late 1920s and early 1930s.[29] The book concludes with York's terse daily journal, begun shortly after his training in Georgia, but the majority of the text is a reputed narrative autobiography. Former secretary of war Newton Baker wrote the foreword and stressed the transformation of modern warfare from "pomp and parade" to "industrial" terror. But Baker was proud to point out the persistence of American heroes like Alvin York: "It is often said that the glory and the opportunity for individual exploit have all been taken out of war, but every now and then circumstances still make opportunity, and certainly one such was made when Sergeant York, with his little band, found himself surrounded by machine-gun nests in Chatel-Chelchery on October 8, 1918." For Baker, York's life was particularly relevant for modern Americans, for it taught "the priceless value of individual character and may warn us here in America from allowing our children, who have to use machines, from being themselves made into machines."[30] Skeyhill's preface also bolstered York's life story with pointed reminders of York's status as a reluctant draftee and a pure descendant of American pioneers. Although the book concludes with York's war diary, York did not write the bulk of the narrative. Advertised as York's "own life story," it is nonetheless retold by Skeyhill in an imitation backwoods dialect. Skeyhill astutely realized the importance of displaying the book as York's own, of connecting his heroic individual actions in the war with an equally autonomous autobiography. Yet as Baker indicates, York's own life was insignificant compared to the abstract principles and historical tradition he stood for.

Skeyhill corroborated this conviction, beginning the "autobiography" with chapters on the historic "long hunters" of Fentress County, Tennessee, outlining York's pioneer ancestors and "pure stock," and relating family stories of Daniel Boone. Only by chapter 14 does Skeyhill describe York's youth and boyhood. The narrative describes York's pacifism, his resistance to war and eventual conversion, his war career, and his return to Fentress. He rejected all efforts to commercialize his fame, including an offer to act in Hollywood, and he returned to the peaceful anonymity of life in the mountains. The account portrays the war as merely an interruption with no lasting effect on this old-fashioned American hero. The counterpoint between York's fame as a traditional hero and his desire to return to a pioneering past also captured the nation's own feeling about the war's effect on modern America. As historian T. J. Jackson Lears has pointed out, Americans have always maintained an antagonistic attitude toward modernity and industrial development.[31] This conflict was especially evident in the language with which the canny Skeyhill represented York.

In 1930 Skeyhill published York's official biography, tellingly subtitled *The Last of the Long Hunters*, thereby solidifying York's claim as a descendant of Daniel Boone.[32] Yet even as Skeyhill emphasized the "pure" Anglo-Saxon and pioneer blood in the Tennessee backwoodsman's veins, Skeyhill's notion of York's place in history retained the uneasily subjective quality of postwar American historiography and anticipated the tone of many Hollywood historical films. "Sergeant York's life story is one of the greatest stories in the world today," he wrote. "It is stranger than fiction, stranger than life itself, and just as intangible. Edgar Allen [*sic*] Poe, nor H. G. Wells nor Dumas would have dared to create such a character."[33] That same year, Fred Pasley, another journalist-turned-biographer, said much the same thing when attempting to summarize Al Capone's historical appeal. It was a subtle way of attributing modern events and people with an unruly and subjective power that defied the bloodless conventions of traditional historiography. For these historians, creative imagination was necessary to understand and interpret York and Capone. Yet York was not one of those modern heroes who operated in a corrupt and hostile world. It took an almost fictional imagination to conceive of him precisely because he was like a displaced pioneer hero—a part of America's legendary heritage. Skeyhill spent the bulk of his biography tracing York's pioneering ancestors and remarked in one definitive passage that "the log cabins of the pioneers were the outposts of civilization. They tell more plainly than the historian the heroic story of the conquering of the wilderness. They are distinctly, uniquely American. Many of the greatest Americans that ever lived were born within their rough-hewn walls. Abraham Lincoln, Andrew Jackson, Daniel Boone, David Crockett, and Sam Houston first saw the light of day in log cabins." As Skeyhill narrated it, York's childhood was spent with his parents telling him family stories of these pioneers "as though they still lived." For York, the past was not dead; it was literally the contemporary text on which he based his life. American history "was their patrimony."[34] York never learned this history from books; instead, he learned it orally as a family tradition.

If York's early life reads like a modern American myth where historical personages flit in and out of past and present tenses and the mountain
men live in a timeless frontier landscape untouched by industrialism or
specific dates, then Skeyhill's account of York's war experience was written as a deliberate contrast. His exploits in the Argonne forest, of such
epic proportions that "at first even the officers refused to believe it," are
examined with scrupulous and even documentary attention. Skeyhill first
quoted the "official story" from American war records and the statements
of confirmation made by members of his company; then he compared
these with York's own statement made shortly after the events. Skeyhill
quoted extensive passages, and there were no discrepancies in the documents. Having won such historic fame in Europe, with his quiet return
to Fentress County in 1919, York became part of an even more illustrious company. Fentress County, untouched by the modern world, was,
for Skeyhill, the cradle of the American pioneer: "This is the land of pioneers and of the Long Hunters. Alvin York is their lineal descendant. He
is an eighteenth-century character living in the twentieth century, and
has been fittingly referred to as 'one of our contemporary ancestors.' The
mantle of Boone and Crockett, of Houston and 'Old Hickory,' has fallen
on worthy shoulders in Alvin Cullum York, the Last of the Long Hunters."[35] Skeyhill's was a curious metaphor, linking York to James Fenimore
Cooper's most famous historical novel, *The Last of the Mohicans: A Narrative of 1757*. Whereas Cooper intended his novel to be read as a cor-
rective to traditional history, Skeyhill and others saw York's actual life as a
metaphor for one of the most hallowed traditions in American history: the
pioneer hero. Within a few short years, York was transformed into an eighteenth-century myth. York's connection to the pioneer heroes of the last
two centuries was essential to his screen biography by Harry Chandlee.
The September 1940 temporary script text foreword began, "When America was young, only the most daring pioneers—the followers of the long
hunters led by Daniel Boone—threaded these mountain labyrinths."[36]
Although the reference to Boone was later curbed, the opening foreword
still announced York as the inheritor of the pioneer's mantle, relating the
Great War story to the nation-building struggles of our ancestors.

Although a number of westerns, mainly by Warner Brothers, had
stressed the determination and toughness of the nineteenth-century American pioneers, it was Hollywood's pan-studio involvement in marshaling
the formative defensive period in America's past from the colonial era
through the Revolutionary War and the War of 1812 that truly captured
the contemporary war aims. Even in the Great War and the modern eras

of York's life, filmmakers ignored any divisive and bewildering transformations in favor of recounting the pioneer myth. Lasky and Warner Brothers' film drew on an impressive body of historical pictures that described the unification of the nation in times of oppression.

In 1936 both Daniel Boone and Hawkeye returned to American theaters. Although Boone had appeared in MGM's *The Great Meadow* in 1931, RKO's small production *Daniel Boone* was the first sound-era Boone biopic. Starring George O'Brien, the film continued RKO's economical biographical work in *Annie Oakley* and *The Arizonian*. Although it began with a lengthy text foreword declaring, "No figure in early American history stands out more heroically than Daniel Boone," the production's historical trappings covered only one episode in his life, a 1775 trek with settlers to Kentucky. Contrary to what many film historians have asserted, classical Hollywood films of this era were not solely preoccupied with great men.[37] Daniel Boone's name was not a sufficient draw for audiences, and the film had an insignificant run. Instead, audiences preferred to watch the gormandizing good-timer Jim Brady (*Diamond Jim*), the romantic escapades of Peggy Eaton (*The Gorgeous Hussy*), the wild life of San Francisco's Barbary Coast (*The Barbary Coast, San Francisco*), and the gaudy Broadway of arch-philanderer Florenz Ziegfeld (*The Great Ziegfeld*). These were hardly the professional historians' chosen national figures and events. The brand of traditional heroism would not regain filmmaking status for several years. Eighteenth-century history and pioneers were not the focus of Hollywood's prestigious historical cycle. Although *The Last of the Mohicans* was one of the most respected historical films of this period, Edward Small's production was not an ode to the fictional hero Nattie Bumpo (Hawkeye). Deeply indebted to the early traditions of historical filmmaking, Small and his filmmakers told a history of British and American relations in 1757, rather than a classic·myth of America.

Toward the end of the decade, several major American historical films focused on the eighteenth-century pioneer and his connections to the American Revolution and nation making. But films such as RKO's *Allegheny Uprising* (1939), MGM's *Northwest Passage* (1940), and Twentieth Century–Fox's *Drums along the Mohawk* (1939) were seen as vehicles for contemporary political propaganda, and the studios cut any excessive anti-British sequences. In *Allegheny Uprising*, the British government began as the colonials' enemy. After fighting for the king in the French and Indian War, they are enraged when the government ignores their appeal for help against raids. The bureaucracy is so corrupt that arms smugglers manage to sell their wares to the tribes in defiance of British law. Law has simply lost its meaning. From the moment P. J. Wolfson's screenplay shows a British officer attempting to court-martial Jim Smith (who has been a captive for several years) as a deserter, the British government proves its inept and obsolete management of the New World. Very quickly, the British become the standard against which Smith and his Black Boys pit their rebellion and the growing definition of Americanism.

The film's indictment of the British was so strong that in the 1940 rerelease and British versions, RKO ordered Wolfson to rewrite the opening foreword, whitewashing the film's new critical history. Roosevelt had strengthened ties to the former imperial governors, and by 1940, it was less advisable to show American patriotism in conflict with British interests. "This is a tale," it began, "laid in the Allegheny Mountains, of Jim Smith and his Black Boys, loyal subjects of His Majesty King George III—and their fight against the Delaware Indians in the year 1759." Unfortunately, the polite foreword did not fit the narrative, even when RKO cut several scenes of British pigheadedness and outright brutality. But the executives needed to salvage what they could of foreign profits; Britain and the empire constituted one of the few stable foreign markets left to Hollywood films in 1939, and RKO needed the overseas proceeds. With George Schaefer in charge of production, RKO had constructed a risky and expensive prestige lineup (purchasing *Abe Lincoln in Illinois* and hiring Orson Welles). RKO's policy of historical innovation was too expensive and partially succumbed to the pressures of national policy and fiscal necessity.

MGM had more success cementing American-British relations in an adaptation of Kenneth Roberts's colonial tale *Northwest Passage*.[38] In producing Roberts's popular historical novel, Hollywood's wealthiest studio avoided RKO's practice of developing untouched and potentially controversial revolutionary heroes, as well as Wolfson's predilection for rebels and lawless mavericks as the definitive American heroes. *Northwest Passage*'s setting was far enough from the Revolution to avoid any Anglo-American spats. As Indian fighter Rogers growls to his fractious Rangers, "You're not Americans and you're not British—you're Rangers." The problem with *Northwest Passage* was that it took two years and more than a dozen writers to complete the script.[39] The screenwriters' major efforts were devoted to adapting Roberts's enormous narrative, not to historical embellishments or portentous forewords; the producers simply could not agree on the basic narrative.[40] As film historian Rudy Behlmer noted, despite the considerable resources that Hollywood's wealthiest studio expended for long-term location shoots, it spent nearly as much on hiring and rehiring writers for extensive rewrites.[41] *Northwest Passage* cost twice as much as the average American historical film (nearly $3 million), and although audiences and exhibitors were relatively happy with it, was not an unusual success.[42]

It is difficult to imagine MGM's troubles affecting Darryl F. Zanuck's productions. Of all the Hollywood studios, Twentieth Century–Fox had the fewest problems when constructing a historical film. This was due in large part to Zanuck's clear vision for his studio's developing productions and, as Nunnally Johnson remarked, Zanuck's respect for screenwriters. Over the past several years, Zanuck had initiated film confrontations with America's more controversial historical figures, but by late 1939, even he was persuaded to place archetypal American heroes within a framework of historical compromise. Shortly before Margaret Mitchell published the spectacular and divisive *Gone with the Wind,* Walter D. Edmonds published his historical novel *Drums along the Mohawk,* the story of a young New York couple's repeated attempts to settle their land in the Mohawk Valley during the Revolutionary War.[43] The studio quickly purchased the screen rights, adding the story to its prestige lineup. By 1939, Zanuck was prepared to cast Henry Fonda as Gilbert Martin. Fonda's last three films for Twentieth Century–Fox — *Jesse James, The Story of Alexander Graham Bell,* and *Young Mr. Lincoln* — had cemented him as a major studio star and earned him acclaim for creating a variety of American historical roles (Frank James, Thomas Watson, and Abraham Lincoln). Gilbert Martin was to be Fonda's first fictional period role for the studio in a year, but extant production records attest that Zanuck was going through one of his periods of historical angst.

Zanuck first hired Bess Meredith to adapt the novel and then William Faulkner to write the script, but Faulkner's episodic country tale and densely dialogued script was quickly turned over to occasional historical screenwriter Sonya Levien (*In Old Chicago*).[44] Levien, no doubt familiar with the American historical bias in Zanuck's production line, read Edmonds's fictional narrative and Meredith's meticulous condensation and constructed her script as a historical document.[45] Unlike the beginning of the novel, she planned to fade in on a close shot of the opening paragraph of the Declaration of Independence and then include a lengthy expository conversation between scout Martin and General Herkheimer, commander of the rebel militia. The gist of the encounter outlines the settlers' major difficulties: the colonial government refuses to send troops west to protect the settlers and expects the impoverished farmers and militia to fight the British and the Native Americans, tend their crops, and produce enough tax money for the new government. Martin and Herkheimer are furious, and the general dictates an appropriate letter to the politicians: "The wish of our hearts is to raise enough wheat to feed our army, but if you don't help us, you can tear up the Declaration of Independence and save yourself the trouble of the Revolution because you ain't—aren't going to win. Soldiers can't fight on empty stomachs, Governor, and victory depends on us farmers!"[46] This was evidently too critical of the founding fathers for Zanuck. He crossed out the first twelve pages of Levien's prologue and directed her to begin the script with Gilbert and Lana's marriage in Albany, free of the political conflicts of the Revolution. Already Zanuck was planning to replace Levien and have Trotti or Dunne simplify the narrative. He wanted not a critical historical film but a "great simple love story of pioneers."[47] Zanuck also cut Levien's additional criticisms of the colonial government by Herkheimer, who called the legislators "dough-faced, pot-bellied war-winners," ditherers who only crippled Washington's efforts with ineffective military supply.[48] It was a curious and somewhat uncharacteristic choice for Zanuck on a historical picture—after all, he had openly courted controversy in American history throughout his career. But after reading her script, he wrote, "Wherever possible, keep British out of brutality and blame all on Indians and Tories."[49] Zanuck intended *Drums along the Mohawk* to be a patriotic romance, not a critical piece of American history.

Zanuck's vision of *Drums along the Mohawk* as a romantic period drama rather than Levien's densely documented historical screenplay was arguably closer to Edmonds's intent. Although Edmonds claimed in an author's note that a historical novelist possessed "a greater opportunity for faithful representation of a bygone time than a historian" because of his attention to the prosaic details of everyday colonial existence, he was not as interested in true historiography's preoccupation with "cause and effect" presented "through the lives and characters of 'famous' or 'historical' figures."[50] Not all historical novelists believed this. Margaret Mitchell's contemporaneous *Gone with the Wind* managed to convey the lives of southern women from 1861 to 1873 through a cause-and-effect study of the Civil War, its aftermath, and its effect on major characters from Scarlett O'Hara to Generals John B. Gordon and Nathan Bedford Forrest. Mitchell's novel, although focusing on "fictional" characters, contained extensive diegetic and nondiegetic discussion of historical events, crises, and arguments. Documents were evaluated; historical positions were criticized. Edmonds's novel, in contrast, consisted mostly of dialogue among the characters and interior monologues. Direct references to the

"damned Yankee-controlled Congress" were scarce, and Edmonds, unlike Mitchell, did not explore congressional inefficiency and corruption
with the thoughtful and direct discourse of the historian. Instead, Gilbert
and Lana witnessed paymasters defrauding militia widows of their husbands' pay and the government overtaxing the settlers even though the
army had consistently failed to protect them.[51] Broader historical issues
appeared indirectly.

Zanuck was certainly justified in seeing the novel as a romance. It
began not with a description of a historical document but with Gil and
Lana's postnuptial trip to German Flats. After cutting Meredith's and
Levien's versions, the producer hired Lamar Trotti, a screenwriter known
principally for his historical work, to plot the script. Rather than expung-
ing the historical framework, Zanuck wanted someone to manage Edmonds's indirect but potentially explosive jabs at the colonial government
and the British. Levien's script enhanced many of Edmonds's sly barbs
directed at the feckless colonial government, its neglect of the settlers, and
its early love of collecting taxes. The brash General Herkheimer and Mrs.
McKlennar articulated what Edmonds had vaguely implied. Yet Zanuck
excised these in his plan to represent early America. For the producer,
the colonial government had to remain beyond reproach, and the British
(who were rapidly becoming America's allies in the newspapers) were to
be almost nonexistent enemies. He replaced red coats and political and
military conflict with red skins and romance.

Zanuck outlined his view in a conference in April 1939: "This book
should be dramatized for the screen in the same manner that a playwright
would dramatize it for the stage. We must not let ourselves be bound by
the contents of the book—but simply retain the *spirit* of the book . . . we
are in the business TO GIVE A SHOW. . . . Were we bound by some
specific world-famous event, our problems would be more difficult—but
here we have a successful book and that is all."[52] He nonetheless wanted
the film adaptation to approximate the prestige of his last American historical films, among them *In Old Chicago*, *Alexander's Ragtime Band*,
and *The Story of Alexander Graham Bell*. In effect, Zanuck wanted the
feel of a historical period without the constraints of a major historical film.
Levien's forewords were to be dropped and the romance accelerated. In
spite of the film's latter-day reputation as a pillar of American political
ideology,[53] Zanuck specifically ordered any overt patriotic discourse to be
cut. "Whatever patriotism comes through should come from inference—
let the audience write in the flag-waving for themselves," he ordered. Yet
Zanuck was sly; he insisted that Trotti cut out any obvious gibes at the

revolutionary government in Edmonds's book and Levien's early script. When Trotti had finished, Zanuck handed the script over to John Ford, who had just finished shooting Trotti's *Young Mr. Lincoln*. In spite of his antihistorical attitude in conferences, Zanuck gave the story to a pair of proven American historical filmmakers. Yet the producer maintained a growing determination to reduce the impact of history on screen entertainment, perhaps aware that the American historical cycle was headed toward its critical and audience saturation point by 1940.

Upon its release, *Drums along the Mohawk* had two modes of cinematic responses. On the one hand, it was advertised as a "historical melodrama," a Revolutionary War epic restoring to importance the anonymous farmer-heroes of the war. Gilbert Martin, however fictional, stood for much of what the common American had endured in 1776—the derelict colonial government, the British oppression, the Indian raids. Yet in the final frames of the film, Martin's mission to find the rebel army and bring it to the besieged fort succeeds. A new flag, symbolic of the new nation, flies over the fort. On the other hand, the narrative was a collaborative invention of Edmonds and Twentieth Century–Fox filmmakers. Gil Martin is no Washington or Franklin, and his wife Lana is no Molly Pitcher or Betsy Ross, but in trying to describe the lives and fears of thousands of colonial farmers, Martin's anonymity is an affecting historical choice. And this is how the critics received the film. *Variety* wrote that *Drums along the Mohawk* narrated the tale "of pioneer American homemaking and nation-building along the colonial frontier," "telling a tale of patriotism when patriotism was a simple, elemental thing of getting down the flintlock and defending a man's house amidst the clearings, his family and his neighbors against Tory intrigue, subsidized tomahawks and flame-tipped arrows."[54] Like any prestigious historical film, the script's craftsmanship received special commendation. Zanuck's attempts to modulate the history seem to have failed, yet some reviews were distinctly weary of the theme of settlers versus Indians.[55] It had become an all-too-familiar part of Hollywood's history, principally because it was told in the same way. Perhaps the reviews would have been less indifferent had Zanuck retained Levien's or even Trotti's criticisms of the British and colonial governments. However, even Columbia's rare historical effort, *The Howards of Virginia*, which did criticize both Tories and the racially thwarted concept of American liberty, failed at the box office in 1940.[56]

A few months later, MGM's *Northwest Passage* received its jaded reviews. Its fantastic expense and floundering script recalled *The Big Trail's* reception some ten years earlier. Late in production, director King Vidor (who had replaced W. S. Van Dyke) attempted to place the film within the tradition of recently released American revolutionary productions by writing a foreword that proclaimed that American history "made simple men, unknown to history, into giants in daring and endurance."[57] However, neither author Roberts nor the public liked the film or respected its historical discourse. People were undoubtedly weary of the onslaught of pretentious historical films that celebrated a pioneer narrative formula that was already numbingly familiar in 1940.

Even Zanuck was cutting corners by 1940. In July, in a note to Kenneth Macgowan and William Koenig, Zanuck directed them to keep production costs down on *Hudson's Bay* (1940): "This means that you have to cut corners in every direction . . . from the standpoint of production, sets, costumes and locations, I want this picture to be a 'cheater.' . . . I do not want a lot of extravagant or elaborate plans made for the picture in advance that will only have to be thrown out eventually."[58] Later that month, the leader in American historical productions fumed, "The failure of *Edison the Boy*, of *Edison the Man* . . . and the only mild success of *Alexander Graham Bell* emphasizes again the fact that whenever we deal with subjects or titles of this nature there is always a grave danger of keeping people away from the theatre who are looking for entertainment instead of education, who want a show instead of enlightenment."[59] Zanuck knew that Twentieth Century–Fox's less-than-stellar gross in 1939 was due in part to the expensive American historical films he had released.[60] Knowing that MGM had also lost money by copying his biographical films did not ease the sting; MGM could afford an expensive failure or two. As *New York Times* critic Frank Nugent noted in 1940, the cycle of American historical epics was beginning to pall, mainly due to "dog-eared script[s]."[61] After observing the 1939 and 1940 Hollywood seasons, Leo Rosten, never a fan of Zanuck's, was caustic: "The producer, steeped in the Hollywood tradition, headstrong with authority, often makes decisions which are psychologically gratifying rather than economically wise. Million-dollar movies are sometimes an expression of a producer's ego rather than his business judgment. For it is profoundly satisfying to produce movies on an immense and dazzling scale. Reputations are made in Hollywood by movies, not balance sheets."[62]

By 1940, Zanuck had made his reputation; now he needed money. But he was not the only filmmaker affected by audience indifference and critical sneers. Earlier in 1938 and 1939, when Hollywood did depart from conventional historical narratives, the filmmakers were often met with resistance, revision, or incomprehension. Only *Sergeant York* met with critical and box-office success. Although Alvin York's tale was deeply linked to the tradition of American pioneer history, and in spite of the fact that Warner Brothers' filmmakers constructed his screen life with an impressive array of printed text inserts and pioneer references, York was a man dealing with twentieth-century conflicts. Since his exploits were only a generation old, he was familiar to the present generation of filmgoers. Wecter's canonical book of American heroes put him in the same category as Daniel Boone, Lincoln, and Buffalo Bill, but York, a traditional hero, still had to suffer through the twentieth century's greatest calamity. Hollywood was free to draw on Skeyhill's helpful historical metaphors without condemning the narrative to the staleness of *Drums along the Mohawk* and *Northwest Passage*. When York hunted Indians or went out on a "turkey shoot," he bagged Germans, a pastime that Americans in 1918 and 1941 could understand.

PART FIVE

HOLLYWOOD HISTORY

9

Stars Born and Lost, 1932–1937

Most history is autopsy. This one is vivisection.
—Terry Ramsaye, A Million and One Nights, 1926

In 1931 Clara Bow, arguably Paramount Studios' most famous and exploited actress, was ravaged in the rag press during a prolonged and vicious slander suit.[1] Although she returned briefly to the screen to make the successful Call Her Savage (1932) and Hoopla (1933) for Fox, Bow had lost her joy of filmmaking. And in spite of her considerable powers as an actress, her multiple public and personal battles had devastated her box-office reputation. In 1933, despite pleas from loyal friends, Clara Bow retired from the screen.

Surprisingly, one of her staunchest supporters was producer David O. Selznick, who had gotten to know Bow well a few years previously when they had both worked at Paramount for the dictatorial B. P. Schulberg. Known as one of Hollywood's toughest and most financially canny filmmakers, Selznick nonetheless defended Bow's reputation in the industry, and after he left Paramount to head production at RKO, he planned a new film for her based on her life. He cabled the New York offices, "Suggest sensational comeback for Clara Bow in a Hollywood picture titled The Truth About Hollywood. Feel very strongly any objections to Hollywood story as such have no basis whatever."[2] The film would eventually be released in 1932 as What Price Hollywood? although the price was too high for the studio to chance casting Bow. Selznick's script, developed from

Clara Bow in *Call Her Savage* (1932; with Gilbert Roland).

Adela Rogers St. Johns's original story, dealt elliptically with the events of Bow's meteoric rise to fame and her heartbreaking retirement.

Selznick's motivation was not solely his friendship with Bow and his regret about her deteriorating emotional state. He had seen before how cruel Hollywood critics, producers, directors, exhibitors, and the public could be. One of the earliest victims had been his own father, producer Lewis J. Selznick, an early silent film pioneer. The elder Selznick's profligacy and constant search for novelty and innovation had bankrupted his film company. When his principal rivals, Louis B. Mayer and Adolph Zukor, refused to help, their cutthroat competition hastened his collapse. After 1923, Selznick Sr. would never again work in the film industry. Years later, young David gritted his teeth and went to work for the very men responsible for his father's demise. His bitterness toward Hollywood executivedom, toward the town's short memory and willingness to forget the past in order to make the next picture, never left him. Many of his projects at MGM, Paramount, RKO, and Selznick International Pictures would be period films with varying degrees of historical specificity, but they were always infused with a powerful sense of nostalgia and loss (*Forgotten Faces*, 1928; *The Four Feathers*, 1929; *Little Women*, 1933; *Manhattan Melodrama*, 1934; *A Tale of Two Cities*, 1935; *The Prisoner of Zenda*, 1937; *Gone with the Wind*, 1939).

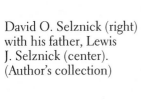

David O. Selznick (right)
with his father, Lewis
J. Selznick (center).
(Author's collection)

Yet as vice president in charge of production at RKO in 1931 and 1932, Selznick was easily bored with filming the established history of the United States. Films such as the *Cimarron* knock-off *The Conquerors* (1932), acutely conscious of its historical importance and laden with textual documentation, left him "flat."[3] His true historical interest was in Hollywood—his period, the late silent and early sound eras. He had lived through the great events of that age, but the total conversion to sound had rendered it a lost era, cut off from the demands of modern filmmaking. In Hollywood's historical parlance, the silent era was "finished," and Selznick endured the consequences of outliving it. For Selznick, even more than for contemporary film historian Terry Ramsaye, films about Hollywood history would be painful and personal vivisections, not autopsies. Although Hollywood's investment in prestigious historical films had reconstructed established, heroic periods of national history such as the Revolution (*Alexander Hamilton*, 1931), the West (*The Big Trail*, 1930; *Cimarron*, 1931), and the Civil War (*Only the Brave*, 1930; *Abraham Lincoln*, 1930), as the 1930s progressed, Selznick became more aware that he and Clara Bow were living relics of a passing era in motion picture history. In spite of cinema's relative youth as an art—a point intoned frequently by national and industrial critics—the producer was growing older in a town that forgot and reinvented its own past quite easily. He thus made an important and unique decision to remember not only Lewis J. Selznick and Clara Bow but also the lives and careers of Frank Fay and Barbara Stanwyck, John Bowers and Marguerite de la Motte, John Gilbert and Virginia Bruce, John McCormick and Colleen Moore, Marshall "Mickey" Neilan, John Barrymore, Mabel Normand, Greta Garbo, Gloria Swanson, and Jean Harlow.[4] Selznick's attitude toward the dying age of old Hollywood was not one constructed of pioneering glory and heroic careers, a historiographic frame that could fit easily over a frontier epic or a biography of Lincoln. Instead, it was a courageous attempt to face Hollywood's failures and the industry's almost historical compulsion to make obsolete relics out of its living filmmakers.[5]

Early Hollywood Histories

Selznick had worked at the two biggest and most lavish studios, MGM and Paramount, before accepting RKO's offer to head production. RKO was certainly smaller scale, but its compact operations suited Selznick and his growing obsession with complete production control at both the studio and the individual unit level. There were no rivals such as B. P. Schulberg or Irving Thalberg to take precedence; at RKO, Selznick could oversee every element of studio production: choose, develop, criticize, and leave his mark on film style. Undoubtedly thinking of Darryl F. Zanuck's early financial and critical successes with gangster films, Selznick wrote to the studio's New York office in March 1932 urging it to make *The Truth about Hollywood* and establish RKO's preeminence in a new cycle of Hollywood history films. "Reason why we are at tail end of cycles," he cabled, "is objection to departures such as Hollywood story, which story gives us opportunity to lead field."

The last prestigious films about Hollywood, Rupert Hughes's *Souls for Sale* (Goldwyn, 1923) and James Cruze's Paramount extravaganza *Hollywood* (1923), had been released nearly a decade before. Neither had been conceived as a historical film or even a thinly disguised biography of an actual star, yet both may have been planned to retrieve the scandalous reputation Hollywood had acquired in the past ten years. As Robert E. Sherwood remarked in one review, after the Fatty Arbuckle "orgy" that resulted in the death of starlet Virginia Rappe and the mysterious shooting of director Desmond Taylor, "Hollywood became the most notorious community on the face of the earth, being associated in the public mind with such historic boroughs as Nineveh, Tyre, Babylon, Sodom and Gomorrah."[6] *Souls for Sale* attempted to present a sympathetic portrait of a struggling actress's career and the sacrifices she makes in order to reach stardom. It was a formula many critics had seen ad nauseam, but Goldwyn's film used glamorous production values to obscure the contemporary "trivial" narrative. If nothing else, it was an entertaining "Cook's Tour of the empire of celluloidia."[7]

Hollywood dazzled audiences with glimpses of Douglas Fairbanks, Mary Pickford, Cecil B. DeMille, and Gloria Swanson in their own environment, but this orgy of star-spotting only added to the film's attraction as an accurate, up-to-the-minute document of the American motion picture business.[8] Frank Condon's original story broke with the traditional myth of the young actress's rise to fame; instead, it presented a more accurate tale of pretty young Angela Whitaker's repeated failure to achieve stardom. Directors ignored her, but William C. DeMille (Cecil's older brother) made her crotchety grandfather a successful character actor. Although it was a fictional story set in contemporary Hollywood, Condon's narrative, scripted by Tom Geraghty, noted the consequences of Hollywood's manufactured myths. According to Sherwood, "Angela had been fed with stories of girls like herself who had gone to this strange place and achieved instantaneous success," yet when she tried to repeat the formula, the real Hollywood rejected her.[9]

Although James Cruze would make his name as the studio's American epic filmmaker, he did not make *Hollywood* into a historical film along the lines of *The Covered Wagon* (1923) and his later successes *Pony Express* (1925) and *Old Ironsides* (1926). *Hollywood*, critics responded, was "fantasy rather than a grimly realistic drama." Even by 1928, when MGM released another major Hollywood story, *Show People*, the film industry still had not made a "Hollywood epic" with all the prestige of major historical films.[10] During the 1920s, there was very little interest and almost no need for Hollywood to reflect on its past. And yet, Selznick may well have had Cruze's film in mind when he made his disguised Clara Bow picture. One of the many cameos in *Hollywood* was made by Roscoe "Fatty" Arbuckle, whose career had been destroyed in 1921 when he was accused of the sexual assault and murder of Virginia Rappe. In *Hollywood*, he made his cameo in, of all places, a casting office. A note in the script indicates that the filmmakers hoped his presence would be unobtrusive and even poignant, but *New York Times* critic Mordaunt Hall noticed the sequence and wanted Arbuckle to stay where he belonged—off the screen and in Hollywood's past. He predicted that the film "will not whet public desire for [Arbuckle's] reintroduction to motion picture enthusiasts . . . nothing would be lost by its [the scene's] elimination."[11]

In 1932 Selznick appropriated the momentary image of the destroyed career and the finished star, but instead of repeating it as an unobtrusive cameo, he made it the center of his narrative. He was not interested in making another Hollywood Cinderella myth, a recycled narrative with nonspecific elements and characters. Instead, he wanted financial and critical prestige. In order to garner that kind of success in the early sound era, he had to follow the historical proclivities and structures of his rival Darryl Zanuck. He took events from modern Hollywood history and retained their historical specificity, memory-saturated images, and potential for instigating public controversy. His idea to cast Bow in the lead role of Adela Rogers St. Johns's story "The Truth about Hollywood" would have added a radical historical dimension to the evolving genre of American historical film.[12] St. Johns's story loosely paralleled the major events of Bow's own Hollywood career: her rise from an impoverished Brooklyn childhood to Hollywood superstardom, her sometimes pernicious mentorship by a tightfisted producer (Schulberg), her romantic involvement with a director (Victor Fleming), her sponging family and cronies, the social snubs she received from Hollywood's elite, and the public condemnation resulting from an unfounded scandal that nearly ended her career. Yet the narrative was by no means a faithful screen biography of Bow that viewers could recognize from the precedents of *Abraham Lincoln* or *Alexander Hamilton*. Even though Bow would hardly have objected to the film's sympathetic portrayal of her life or sued RKO for libel, Selznick had to realize, however reluctantly, that fans had as little desire to see Bow *in* a picture as they did to see a picture *about* her.

In producing *What Price Hollywood?* Selznick instituted a new cycle of historically minded Hollywood films, but they were by no means the rigorously structured, meticulous, somewhat pompous historical-biographical offerings that filmmakers and the public immediately associated with "prestige" and "highbrow" cinema. Often these eighteenth- and nineteenth-century epics had a distinct historical advantage over their younger imitators. It paid to be accurate when you were filming the life of a well-known figure like Abraham Lincoln or a nationally charged event like the Civil War. Historical sophistication earned far more critical and box-office accolades than public jeers. Even if some dates were fudged, the studios won anyway—libel suits were next to impossible when the subject was dead. Living subjects, be they gangsters, shyster lawyers, or drunken directors, could sue the Hollywood libelers and win. Living subjects also rankled with the censors. Many of the stories Selznick wanted to allude to more directly in the narrative, such as the collapse of the careers of Clara Bow, Mabel Normand, and Mickey Neilan, would awaken the censors and rake up memories of Hollywood's wicked past. There were drug and sex scandals; murder; and careers destroyed by alcoholism, ego, Louis B. Mayer, studio legerdemain, box-office decline, sound, and slander—all memories that Hollywood would rather forget. But Selznick wanted to remember and to record, and, by harnessing the public's appetite for modern history, he wanted to force his audience to remember too.

Like modern gang histories, Hollywood merited a different approach toward the past, a revisioning of modern history. Superimposed dates, accurate names and events, documented consequences—this was the stuff of Terry Ramsaye's and Benjamin Hampton's histories of the American cinema, of film reviews and even the interviews and production updates in *Moving Picture World*, *Photoplay*, and *Modern Screen*.[13] Coupled with Selznick's drive to remember and commemorate was the town's own reputation for artistic invention and commercial exploitation; of lies, half-truths, and exaggerations designed to forward a career; of short memories and devastating dismissals. This combination, tentatively explored in *What Price Hollywood?*, would culminate in *A Star Is Born* (1937) and the attainment of a visual and textual historical film style for Hollywood, a form that would push narratives to the point of violent death to force Hollywood and audiences to simply remember the real tragedy obscured through a screen of censorship and industrial amnesia.

St. Johns, like Selznick, also carried memories of a vanished Hollywood. Writer and publicist, it was she who had helped to invent the Latin lover mystique of Rudolph Valentino, and the fabrication of Valentino's image remains the most spectacularly successful star-making venture in Hollywood history.[14] But by 1926, it was over. Valentino died in New York of complications from appendicitis. St. Johns also witnessed the career of Clara Bow and befriended the actress briefly after interviewing her for *Photoplay* in 1927.[15] Bow's harrowing candor convinced St. Johns to print the interview in the first person. But, as Bow's biographer David Stenn noted, Hollywood and audiences did not want to hear the truth about destitution, abuse, family insanity, overwork, and loneliness.[16] Bow's truthfulness and lack of pretense ensured Hollywood's scorn and Paramount's neglect of her lucrative career. In a few years, the career of Hollywood's biggest box-office draw would be over.

With the advent of sound, the growing bureaucratization of studio production, and a new generation of less impressive stars, it was easy to understand St. Johns's view of Hollywood in the past tense. Armed with memories of Bow and other ruined filmmakers, she wrote a story, a behind-the-scenes look at Hollywood's creation of a new actress and the decline of a director. She wrote of a young Brown Derby waitress, Diane, who becomes a star under the tutelage of a fading alcoholic director named Max Carey. Although St. Johns was still the master of glamorous subterfuge and did not name names, her protagonists are shorthand for some of the industry's most powerful filmmakers. Max Carey's opinion of Hollywood, "The only thing this town respects is success," would be echoed by silent directors Charles Chaplin, D. W. Griffith, and Erich von Stroheim. By 1932, this triumvirate of directors would not or could not make a successful film in the new sound era and were pushed to the margins. There was more than one Max Carey in 1930s Hollywood.

St. Johns also embedded many subtle references to the correct procedure for "making it" in Hollywood. After Diane meets Carey, she returns to her shabby apartment and opens a fan magazine. She stares at a picture of Fox star Janet Gaynor and struggles to imitate Gaynor's wide-eyed innocence. Gaynor was Hollywood's ideal of the girl next door, a silent star who, unlike Clara Bow, made the transition to sound without fuss or scandal. Diane knew what she was doing, trying to imitate Gaynor. Yet when she does achieve stardom, Diane becomes famous as a Bow-type vamp, and she suffers the same fate as the famed party girl. Like Bow, Diane's lower-class background and vamp pictures cause social Hollywood and the Hollywood "ladies" to ignore her. Diane raves, "Either I go out with men—men—men—or I stay home. There are nice people here. Nice parties. Why don't I get invited? I'm an outsider. I hate it. I'm as good as any of them."[17]

The final script retained the young actress's imitations of Hollywood stars, but with some slight alterations. Diane, now Mary Evans (Constance Bennett), a name befitting the new homegrown simplicity in star persona, opens her magazine and sees a photo spread for a new Greta Garbo–Clark Gable vehicle. She folds away Garbo's portrait and plays a cheek-to-cheek scene with Gable before her mirror, adopting the requisite exotic Swedish accent. Mary plays a scene inspired from Garbo and Gable's most recent MGM success, ironically entitled *Susan Lennox—Her Fall and Rise*. In a curious bit of screen sleight of hand, Mary's experiences become a reversal of Susan Lennox's screen life. Unlike the standard Hollywood fictions that told of redemption and eventual success, in *What Price Hollywood?* Mary rises and falls, in the tradition of real Hollywood actors like Clara Bow. Selznick and St. Johns planned no triumphant return to the screen for Mary Evans.

However, despite the allusion to Garbo and Gable, the final script, variously worked on by Marjorie Dudley, Robert Pressnel, Gene Fowler, Roland Brown, Jane Murfin, and Ben Markson, had few of the documentary touches associated with prestige pictures. The bitter specificity Selznick had imagined in "The Truth about Hollywood" was virtually written out of the final script. But the final film looked somewhat different. In postproduction, Selznick added an opening title sequence that consists of a series of movie billboards. Each credit is quickly replaced by another, introducing a sense of restless impermanence and obsolescence in Hollywood's attitude toward the past. The film fades in on Constance Bennett's hand flipping through her fan magazine, skipping through an assembly line of images and advertisements until she comes to the real thing—Garbo and Gable in *Susan Lennox*.

Like the most prestigious films of that era, *What Price Hollywood?* employs a consistent series of text inserts. But these are Hollywood documents, both private (film call sheets and script inserts) and public (gossip columns and excerpts from *Variety*). Curiously, the text inserts seem to poke fun at Hollywood traditions and the industry's attempts at prestige. Shortly after Max Carey (played by sometime director Lowell Sherman) takes Mary to a premiere, a daily reads, "Carey in again: Max Carey stole the Brown Derby's prettiest waitress. What for? Oh, same old story. Going to put her in pictures." The Cinderella story is a rather bad joke in 1932, an old cliché used often in Hollywood films and film magazines; it is a dirty old executive's line to ensnare aspiring young actresses. But Carey does give Mary a break—a couple of lines in his new film. Its title is suggestive of the absurd lengths studios would go in the quest for glamour and sensationalism: *Purple Flame*. Soon after, as Mary rises in the publicity machine as "America's Pal," the papers document her public and private life in a series of inserts. Just as the papers write of Mary's rise, they chronicle Max Carey's decline. Too many florid failures like *Purple Flame*, too many arguments with philistine producers, too many drinks to kill his artistic ambition, have marked Carey. One of Selznick's postproduction news inserts reads, "The names on casts of current Poverty Row productions look like the *Who's Who in Filmdom* of ten years ago." Selznick's text inserts draw attention to the decline of old Hollywood, and later, as Mary is crucified in the penny press following Carey's suicide, the producer adds another clipping straight from Clara Bow's career: a note that the women's clubs of America are banning her films.

Shooting wrapped in April 1932, but Selznick's additions to the film in postproduction delayed its general release until mid-July. It was a huge success, with many critics agreeing with *Photoplay*: "Almost everything in this picture has actually happened in Hollywood."[18] Selznick started the cycle he had dreamed of, but he dallied so long with the text inserts that Columbia and Paramount were able to release their low-budget imitations later that summer. Critics paid little attention to *Hollywood*

Speaks and *Movie Crazy*, however; *Variety* dismissed *Hollywood Speaks* as a cheap, fictional glorification of the Hollywood success story.[19] *Movie Crazy* fulfilled Selznick's original intention to cast a fading star in a new sound film about Hollywood, but even with Harold Lloyd heading the cast, *Movie Crazy* lacked the necessary prestige to garner much critical attention. Despite concentrating on bumbling Howard Hall's rise as a comic movie star, there were few parallels between the film and Lloyd's own distinguished career as a writer-director-actor, nor were there text inserts to reinforce the film's historical account and the passage of time. In 1932, like many of the silent comics, Lloyd was on his way out of Hollywood, and *Movie Crazy* lacked the self-conscious importance that Selznick had given *What Price Hollywood?*

Yet both *What Price Hollywood?* and *Movie Crazy* ignored the most crucial explanation for failed careers: stars' inability to cope with the new sound era. Bow's hatred of the microphone was such that she even attacked one during a take. Lloyd's voice may not have ended his career (he went on to make several more comedies), but his association with silent comedy was so strong that neither he nor audiences could adapt. In 1931 film historian Benjamin Hampton acknowledged that none of the studios was financially crippled by the advent of sound, and theater earnings offset any drop in studio profits; yet filmmakers both above and below the title were unprepared for speech.[20] After the national frenzy for any talking picture dissipated and arguments for quality grew, the studios realized that a new medium required new producers, screenwriters, directors, and actors. The casualties of sound were too recent and painful for even Selznick to approach.

Coming to Terms with Hollywood's History

In early 1933 Selznick briefly pursued his fascination with star biographies, planning to adapt Zoe Akins's play *Morning Glory* in order to reteam Constance Bennett and Lowell Sherman. Bennett would reprise her role as a determined rising star, but Sherman would no longer play a cynical director—he would direct *Morning Glory*. However compelling it may have seemed to Selznick to continue the cycle of Hollywood entertainment histories with Bennett, he eventually assigned Katharine Hepburn to star in *Morning Glory*.[21] In many ways, she was more appropriate in the role. The script told the sentimental tale of an obscure young woman's tenacious rise to the top in Broadway. She has talent and drive, but the question remains, will she be a morning glory following her first Broadway success? With Bennett—the original hothouse Hollywood star—in the lead, the film would have possessed little of the historical resonance that Selznick attempted to pursue in *What Price Hollywood?* The script did not claim to be the unauthorized biography of Katherine Cornell or Jeanne Eagles, although one source said that Akins had modeled the character on a young Tallulah Bankhead. Hepburn's own slow start on Broadway, her eventual success, and her quirky Yankee femininity gave *Morning Glory* the necessary historical undercurrents to intrigue Selznick. Hepburn was, after all, his discovery in Hollywood. Critics also remarked on the similarities between the character and the actress, and Rob Wagner wrote, "So perfectly does the role of Eve Lovelace fit Katharine Hepburn that you'll believe it is her own life story. If it isn't, it might well have been, for this strange young lady has one of the most decisive personalities on the screen."[22] As Selznick was the first to acknowledge, in that moment, a new star was born. Selznick's most famous discovery earned her first Oscar for the role. But in spite of the film's critical and box-office success, Selznick left RKO a few months later, having accepted a more lucrative position as MGM's vice president in charge of production.

At that time, MGM was also interested in Selznick's original idea to film a barely concealed Bow biopic. The studio purchased Caroline Francke and Mack Crane's play in late 1932. *Bombshell* opens with screen star Lola Burns's secretary fielding calls about the actress's alleged "alienation of affections" case involving a disgruntled dancing teacher. Lola is the only child of an abusive, sponging father; her mother committed suicide when Lola was a child. Her director was also her lover until she suggested that they marry. Her studio exploits her sex appeal ruthlessly, and the executives never give her good scripts, only lousy publicity stunts. Lola sums up her attitude toward the studio: "I hate your guts and all your damned company with their silly lies and lousy stories! I hate the whole damn racket!" MGM story reader Vivian Moses wrote, "Lola is a Clara Bow type. In fact, one is almost tempted to think that it is Miss Bow being dramatized."[23] From the beginning, MGM knew that casting Clara Bow as Lola Burns would be too risky. Instead, it cast a young woman who had once worked with Bow as an extra—Jean Harlow. Harlow could play a "Clara Bow type," and in many ways, their careers, characters, images, and popularity were alike.

Harold Johnsrud's treatments outline an extended opening prologue documenting Lola's career in Hollywood, including shots of women studying pictures of her platinum hair in the beauty parlor and inserts of national gossip columnist Walter Winchell's prattle about her career.[24] Clara Bow's flaming red hair had inspired many of her films (*Red Hair*, 1928), and at first, MGM had marketed Harlow as another *Red-Headed Woman* (1931) before differentiating her as a *Platinum Blonde* (1932). Hair and gossip were not the only connections between them. Early treatments blended Bow's and Harlow's on- and offscreen characters, pushing the boundaries between fiction and history. These early treatments constantly referred to Lola as "the Burns (or Bow) character" or "the It Girl."[25] John Lee Mahin and Jules Furthman developed the connections, writing a scene in which Lola is forced to do retakes on *Red Dust* (Harlow's last big success for MGM). When Lola hears the news and is handed the script, she looks blank. She looks at the script of her (and Harlow's) most recent film and does not recognize it—an amusing commentary on Hollywood's notoriously short memory.[26] Yet while Mahin and Furthman helped turn Lola into a screen parallel of Harlow, they tended to obscure the original historical connections to Bow. Victor Fleming's name had originally been included in a line of Lola's dialogue; when she hears that she must return to the *Red Dust* set, she asks if Fleming will be directing. But by the time the entire script had been rewritten, Fleming's name no longer appeared. Did Clara Bow's former director and lover, her former fiancé, ask that his name be removed from a film, however disguised, about Bow's life?[27]

Producer Hunt Stromberg also capitalized on the potential to elide Lola with Jean Harlow, suggesting that they open with shots of real crowds surrounding theater marquees reading "Lola Burns in *Red-Headed Woman*," "Lola Burns in *Red Dust*," Harlow's most successful MGM films.[28] Although he was well aware of the parallels between Bow and Lola, Stromberg tended to downplay them, asserting on 7 April, "We might say that the character of Harlow might represent a composite of any and all stars who have reached for the moon and arrived there. This is how real the story must be." Yet Stromberg's reluctance to film a Bow biography did not mean that he was averse to filming a correct account of Hollywood's past. He, like Selznick, was tired of fantasy and invention: "I personally have known Hollywood since it was a vacant lot. I have known the pioneers in the business and I've known the successes and failures. The real Hollywood has never been put on screen. Someone has always gone either too far or not enough. They have tried to clown Hollywood, but Hollywood isn't to be clowned. Hollywood is a very miserable place."[29] Yet, for all his interest in filming the "real" Hollywood, of adding incidents that paralleled problems experienced by actresses such as Bebe Daniels, Constance Bennett, and Gloria Swanson, he could not transform Hollywood's history using traditional historical values associated with cinema histories.[30] Instead, Joan Crawford, Bow, Harlow—all models for Lola—became a Hollywood casting type, a component of the staple story, a cliché known to Hollywood screenwriters and producers since Mary Pickford's Biograph Company days. Stromberg was circumscribed by his view of types rather than historical figures, but he had the same ambition to give Hollywood a legitimate history on film. He wrote that Lola "is, really, to our screen story what Ethel and John Barrymore were to the stage in *The Royal Family*."[31] Like the Barrymore characters, Lola was a disguised representation of a real person—or, in Hollywood, a series of persons. In Hollywood, people's offscreen lives had as many similarities and tendencies toward cliché as Hollywood scripts did. They were all types operating within a repeated historical pattern.

Hollywood Upstages Broadway

The contemporaneous run of Broadway entertainment period films was not plagued by historical problems. Broadway success and failure stories had been the basis for a slew of moneymaking if forgettable sound films in the late 1920s, as well as the rare critical and box-office hits *Broadway Melody*, *42nd Street*, and *The Gold Diggers of 1933*. Yet with the exception of the sly Barrymore biopic *The Royal Family of Broadway*, none of these films dealt with actual or disguised historical characters from the entertainment past. Even attempts at brief historical criticism and commentary (as in *Gold Diggers'* Great War number) were met with open hostility. Yet Mae West's entertainment vignettes set in Gay Nineties New York, and West herself, escaped such criticism. In spite of the fact that many of her most popular films from 1933 to 1936 were period tales based on her original stories or scripts (*She Done Him Wrong*, 1933; *Belle of the Nineties*, 1934; *Klondike Annie*, 1936), West never played a historical character. Indeed, when screenwriters approached her about playing Lillian Russell or Lillie Langtry, she refused. West would never play a name that could compete with her own. In fact, despite their period settings, West's productions always subordinated history to her own star persona. There was no research necessary for a western or a Bowery drama; West was the arbiter of the Gay Nineties and credited herself with period films' rise in popularity.[32] Yet the studio, apparently with her compliance, added the structural devices of historical films—occasional text titles and superimposed dates.[33] Perhaps Paramount executives thought that the trappings of more respectable historical cinema would get West past the Production

Code. Whatever the reason, West consistently appropriated an American historical period as a sexual escape from contemporary life, but she never allowed her image to be trapped by the demands of history.

For several years, West's entertainers dominated the field, but in 1936, MGM decided to reexamine its success with *The Royal Family* and its competitors' increasingly daring forays into Hollywood history and American biography. As a result, MGM made the first major prestige entertainment biography. Although he was no film figure, Florenz Ziegfeld Jr. was, like the Barrymores, the property of MGM by marriage. Ziegfeld's wife, actress Billie Burke, had been a prominent MGM star for years, although she occasionally worked at other studios. In focusing on the career of Burke's recently deceased husband, MGM was honoring what Louis B. Mayer prized above all things: the power of the producer and his own property. It was no accident that the first lavish entertainment biopic, a cornerstone of anyone's assessment of Hollywood's "great man" attitude toward history, focused on the most famous producer of the twentieth century.[34] Although *The Great Ziegfeld* was no stirring tale of the rise of a Jewish junk salesman to film mogul, it gave Mayer the necessary autobiographical thrill. But in selecting Ziegfeld for a major biographical-historical release, Mayer and his associates had the unique advantage of the participation of many of the real players in Ziegfeld's life: Fanny Brice, Will Rogers, writer William Anthony McGuire (who had been with Ziegfeld for ten years), costume and set designer John Harkrider, and, of course, Billie Burke.

In the early stages of the script, screenwriter William Anthony McGuire was obviously caught up by the technical demands of a serious historical film and the possibility of commemorating many of the Ziegfeld shows he had written. McGuire planned an elaborate prologue or "Parade of Ziegfeld," chronologically highlighting Ziegfeld's work from the early *Follies* to Marilyn Miller in *Sally* and Helen Morgan in *Show Boat*. McGuire then planned to finish the prologue with a spoken foreword by Billie Burke. He envisioned her historical introduction in the tradition of MGM's foreword for *Gorgeous Hussy*; although he did not attempt to confront that film's standard of "fiction based on fact," he saw Burke indicating that *The Great Ziegfeld* did not tell "the actual facts in the proper sequence, but rather . . . used incidents in Ziegfeld's colorful career to base our story on."[35] Only MGM could have pulled it off. If Burke, scripted like an authority, a historian, had been used, the device of the historical foreword would have deconstructed its own purpose: authenticity. In the end, however, Burke did not appear in the film, and the foreword was scrapped. Instead, the filmmakers opened sedately in 1893 at the Chicago World's Fair. MGM did preserve the illusion of accuracy and followed the impresario's successes and failures through his death in 1932, even as it camouflaged his many affairs with chorus girls with spectacular production numbers.

Regardless of its attempt to include an entertainer within the growing pantheon of biographical subjects, *The Great Ziegfeld's* reinvention of historical values made it a fascinating piece of twentieth-century historiography. As film critic Otis Fergusson wrote, "We have had romanticized biographies of show people before," but the glamour, the girls, the lengthy production numbers, and the sheer fantasy are not historical foibles but "appropriate" to a study of Ziegfeld the legend. "The only other way to do such a figure," he wrote, "why and how he did it, what it took from the country and what it left—would be to do a book, to be more sober and thorough and first-causey—and inevitably to lose the principal radiance identified with the name . . . it would be rather barren to write a book."[36] As a historical figure, Ziegfeld demanded innovation and a new historical format. The stodgy values of traditional historiography would have lost the historical value of Florenz Ziegfeld's life. Even though extravagance and prestige had always been the assets of the more successful American historical productions, *Ziegfeld's* excess, music, girls, and vague or even invented historical details departed from the values of previous historical productions. Yet according to Fergusson, this departure made good history.

The studio's eulogy to the producer was the most honored film of 1936. Its historical structures, unusual cast, and huge publicity campaign proved that entertainment history could be written as successfully as any traditional historical topic. In fact, one critic felt that in filming Ziegfeld's life, Hollywood had trumped even the entertainment genius of its protagonist.[37] Later, media historian Linda Mizejewski would also observe that this canonization of the showman paradoxically diminished Ziegfeld's aura. "The irony of their Hollywood success," she wrote, "is that they eagerly absorb the musical theater milieu of Ziegfeld and flip-flop its implications, so that Hollywood cinema itself is glorified as the entertainment ideal."[38] The film had pulled off production spectacles that Ziegfeld could not have attempted on any stage. Hollywood's technical restaging of Broadway's past was another triumph for the film medium over the theater, just as its popular mastery of history represented a victory over detracting academic historians. As Hollywood historicized Broadway's great successes, some in Hollywood began to reimagine the possibility of a comparable Hollywood history or biography. But Ziegfeld's life was filled with more successes than failures, and the film repeatedly alleviated personal pain and loss with an opiate of spectacular production numbers. Hollywood's shorter history had more personal pain. In 1936 Selznick and several other filmmakers questioned whether *The Great Ziegfeld*'s triumphalism was the only mode of historical address or the most appropriate one for remembering Hollywood's history.

Selznick's Return to the Past

By 1936, Selznick had left MGM to form Selznick International Pictures (SIP). In his last years at MGM, he had indulged in the prestige of British period films with *David Copperfield* and *A Tale of Two Cities* (1935), and he continued in this lucrative vein as an independent producer (*Little Lord Fauntleroy*, 1936; *The Prisoner of Zenda*, 1937). Now the head of his own studio, Lewis J. Selznick's son wanted to return to the historical period he knew best. The Hollywood history cycle had lost its impetus in the last couple of years. *What Price Hollywood?* and *Bombshell* had begun to experiment with Hollywood's past but had not retained the historical specificity or the marked prestige he had envisioned in 1932. Although Clara Bow had retired by late 1933, the careers of many stars such as Mary Pickford, Douglas Fairbanks, D. W. Griffith, Gloria Swanson, and John Gilbert had stalled but not ended. By 1936, however, the reign of the old Hollywood elite was definitely over. Wallace Reid, Rudolph Valentino, Barbara La Marr, Mabel Normand, Lon Chaney, Lewis J. Selznick, John Gilbert, Alexander Pantages, Samuel "Roxy" Rothafel, and Marilyn Miller were all dead. No one was remembering them.

Paramount's low-budget, understarred *Hollywood Boulevard* capitalized on St. Johns and Selznick's Brown Derby locale, but it added a more poignant commentary on the recent transformation of Hollywood. Protagonist John Blakeley's Brown Derby cartoon is knocked down from the wall and left on the floor. Later at a premiere at Sid Grauman's Chinese Theatre on Hollywood Boulevard, a new star presses her feet and hands into the cement. Grauman tells her, "And now, my dear, you have left your immortal mark in Hollywood." Although it is cement and not marble, this is a startling remark for a film showman to make. Are films more forgettable than a concrete slab in the forecourt of a theatrical temple? Are they too marginal to be considered enduring historical material?

In contrast to the famous silent-era names lining the cement foyer, this young sound star is a glamour template rather than a personality.

Her name is unrecognizable, and she has no real part in film history. Beyond the red carpet, a mother explains the maze of cement monuments to her daughter, and the script calls for close-ups of the slabs belonging to Norma Talmadge, Douglas Fairbanks, and William S. Hart, "all with inscriptions of name and year."[39] John Blakeley also has one of these monuments, but neither the mother nor the little girl remembers who he was. Blakeley watches them, an anonymous figure in the crowd. Soon after this sequence, a reporter approaches Blakeley, down and out and finished in Hollywood, and asks him to consider writing and serializing his memoirs. Like Lew Ayres's doomed gangster in *Doorway to Hell*, his life truly comes to an end when someone asks for his biography. The message is that when you become "historically valuable" in Hollywood, your career is finished. But beyond these historical traces in the opening sequence, *Hollywood Boulevard* ignores Hollywood's past. There are no text inserts or other stylistic tricks of historical cinema, and following the Grauman's premiere, *Hollywood Boulevard* degenerates into a conventional murder mystery with no relation to events in the industry's sometimes lurid past.

Selznick was contemptuous of such low-budget results. He cabled his secretary Katharine Brown in September 1936, "Our feeling is that Hollywood has become identified with cheap titles of cheap pictures, and this is more true today than ever because of *Hollywood Boulevard*, which has been outstanding failure as Paramount quickie."[40] Selznick's implication was clear: his new Hollywood film would have prestige.

Both Selznick and screenwriters Robert Carson and William Wellman would claim authorship of *A Star Is Born*.[41] According to Wellman, the film's sources were things "that happened . . . things from memory."[42] Carson and Wellman's original story, "It Happened in Hollywood," exists only as a thirty-two-page rough draft of one-third of the story and the outline of the rest.[43] In this early script dated 22 July 1936, they opened in Alberta, Canada, with the screen-struck life of mountain girl Esther Smythe (later Blodgett). Only her grandmother, Lettie, supports her ambition to become an actress, and she likens Esther's potential struggles in Hollywood's wild west to her own pioneer experience years before: "When I left England to come to this country, we landed in Nova Scotia and came across the plains in prairie schooners. We didn't have enough food or water; in the summer we burned, in the winter we froze. . . . We never quit trying and we were never licked. . . . Do you think it was worth it? . . . It was! We made this country—the people out on the barren land. We made the towns and the railroads and sweated and suffered—but we were pioneers. That's a certain breed, but it's the best breed that ever was."[44]

That autumn, Dorothy Parker and Allan Campbell liked and re-tained Carson and Wellman's pioneer allusions. Nevertheless, by the time the final shooting script was complete, everyone had agreed that however charming it would be to make the heroine Canadian—like the reigning queen of Hollywood, Norma Shearer—it would be more effective to Americanize this story of old and new western frontiers. Lettie became a native easterner and not an Englishwoman, and the writers relocated the pioneer setting from Canada to the American West, specifically, North Dakota. Lettie even makes the prediction that Hollywood will be her granddaughter's wilderness to conquer; Hollywood will be the last frontier, and Esther will be the pioneer to settle and conquer it. In late 1936 and early 1937, well into production, Ring Lardner Jr. and Budd Schulberg (B. P.'s son) were hired to write intertitles, and they expanded on this theme in a series of five planned text superimpositions as Esther travels to Los Angeles:

> TITLE 1: Hollywood/A mythical kingdom in Western America.
> TITLE 2: Where the magic brilliance of the sunlight is outshown only by the aura of fame surrounding its ever-changing kings and queens.
> TITLE 3: HOLLYWOOD!/ The last frontier!
> TITLE 4: El Dorado for a new generation of pioneers.—
> TITLE 5: Pioneers in silk stockings and high heels—/Converging by a thousand obscure routes to form one mighty caravan of hope.[45]

If Selznick wanted the prestige associated with historical allusions and multiple text inserts, he had more than enough. Although not all the Lardner-Schulberg frontier texts were used, Carson and Wellman were attracted by the El Dorado and new frontier analogies, and as Esther makes her way to Los Angeles, the film provided Hollywood with its "historical foreword."

Selznick's film took many of the text and visual tools used in *What Price Hollywood?* and magnified them. There were more text inserts, more newspaper shots, more elaborate historical references. And though Selznick used a conventional historical foreword, linking Hollywood with the established history of the West, his most radical use of text within the film narrative began in the opening credits. Fading from the opening cast credits over a panoramic shot of Hollywood at night, the credits appear as pages from a shooting script. It is not a doctored script generated for the camera in postproduction, as in *What Price Hollywood?*, but a shot of the opening pages of Carson and Wellman's final shooting script. The film begins as a script, a clever studio pun for Hollywood film production. The camera zooms in on the text describing the planned opening shot in the snowy landscape of North Dakota. "As the wolf raises his muzzle and howls again, we dissolve to. . . ." The wolf howls in voice-over, and the script page dissolves to the opening shot described in the text. Selznick and Wellman's framing device (the script pages return in the final sequence) not only draws the audience into the world of Hollywood film production but also indicates the film's own status as an elaborately constructed idea, a written work mechanically grafted by the director onto the screen. But the opening sequence also reworks the standard structural device of the historical foreword. It projects text, immediately cuing the audience to the script's historical material, and combines it with Hollywood's own nontraditional way of writing its history as an acknowledged constructed text—as in *What Price Hollywood?* and *Bombshell.* This is Hollywood's historical discourse, and it is written with the textual forms (shooting scripts, call sheets) and historiographic iconography (intertitles) employed by the industry. In rare circumstances, traditional historical films (*Cimarron*) succeeded in subverting the discourse of their own projected historical text. But Selznick's construction of Hollywood history employed the motion picture industry's already complex rhetorical frames.

Screen Biography or Historical Composite?

A *Star Is Born* is a historical narrative, but it is not arranged like a chapter from Ramsaye's *A Million and One Nights* or an exclusive, effusive interview from a popular fan magazine such as *Photoplay* or *Modern Screen.* It is a self-conscious composite biography, even though most 1937 viewers associated the character Norman Maine, a fading alcoholic leading man, with actor John Gilbert, who had died of a heart attack in January 1936.[46] Gilbert had been one of the silent screen's most popular romantic leads. Earthier than Ronald Coleman, more serious than the insouciant Douglas Fairbanks, he was an American Valentino, a capable balance to Greta Garbo's European exoticism. According to 1930s Hollywood critics, the advent of sound destroyed his career, revealing his squeaky voice. His romance with Garbo ended abruptly, and his alcoholism grew out of control. His momentary happy marriage with a young screen actress named Virginia Bruce did little to slow his decline. He died in 1936, forgotten by the industry. But Gilbert had voiced another opinion, publicly blaming Louis B. Mayer for ruining his career with a slapdash, poorly recorded

```
                    A STAR IS BORN

        Scene 1

        FADE IN:

        MOONLIGHT.  LONG SHOT EXPANSE OF SNOW.

        In the foreground a wolf silhouetted in
        the moonlight.

        In the background the isolated farmhouse
        of the Blodgetts.

        As we hear the melancholy howling of the
        wolf, we

                                    DISSOLVE TO:
```

A Star Is Born: introducing the "text."

sound film. He even took a full page in *Variety* to air the truth. Mayer may have had a reputation for ruining careers, but few outside Hollywood listened; *Variety*'s obituary headlined Gilbert as "one of the first victims of talking pictures."[47] But the author disputed that his voice alone had destroyed his career and instead blamed MGM's poor screenwriting, which "failed to realize that the impassioned love scenes of the silent pictures became silly when done into speech." It was MGM's inability to adapt to sound film, not Gilbert, that was at fault. Although Selznick may have relished the chance to indict his callous father-in-law for destroying a major star, denigrating major producers was a dangerous choice for a maverick independent to make.

Instead, Selznick, Wellman, and Carson created a character and a series of limited events that paralleled Gilbert's life, leaving an unwritten, unspoken history for audiences to recall. Selznick re-created Hollywood's construction of appearance and allowed it to collapse under the weight of its historical frames. The connections between Norman Maine and Gilbert were evidently obvious enough without blaming producer Oliver Niles for Maine's decline. The romantic actor with a short temper, deep thirst, and cynical sense of humor loses his box-office appeal in *A Star Is Born*. As the director complains to Niles, "His acting is beginning to interfere with his drinking."[48] There were many similarities between Gilbert and Maine, as well as between Virginia Bruce and Esther Blodgett (Vicki Lester). It would be easy enough to methodically dissect the narrative and classify the various veiled historical allusions, but shortly after

John Gilbert and Greta Garbo
in *Queen Christina* (1933).

the film's release, Selznick was forced to do just that. At the end of 1937, insolvent French writer Charles Rudolph Ritter instituted legal proceedings against Selznick International Pictures for allegedly plagiarizing his "literary work" *L'homme sans voix*. Ritter's short story outlined the fall of a French silent screen star and the difficulties facing the Paris film industry following the conversion to sound. The star's young wife has a good voice and succeeds in the new industry, while his career fails.

Selznick International Pictures' lawyers went to work preparing the brief. Lawsuits were common in Hollywood, and although historical films were often the target of libel suits by impoverished but indignant family members, historical subjects were also easy to defend. As producers were learning, to their delight, historical events were not under copyright jurisdiction. The lawyers, Joynson-Hicks & Co., hired another set of lawyers to prepare a report on *A Star Is Born*. That report quoted *New York Times* film critic Frank S. Nugent's review, emphasizing that Selznick's film was distinctly American and about Hollywood. But the report went even further, stating that *A Star Is Born* was based on real events in Hollywood's past. "Although there are many Hollywood stories in real life which are very like *A Star Is Born* in enough ways to have suggested that picture to writers, I think that the three best known ones will suffice as illustrations."

The report then described Greta Garbo's relationship with director Mauritz Stiller, Barbara Stanwyck's failed marriage to Broadway comic Frank Fay, and John Gilbert's tragic union with Virginia Bruce. The memorandum went on to describe Hollywood's film antecedents—namely, *Hollywood, What Price Hollywood? Bombshell,* and *Hollywood Boulevard.*[49] Although the Hollywood lawyers could have mentioned that some of the Hollywood films were based on historical events and people, the studio had to demonstrate a variety of sources, historical and cinematic, even though the two were not always exclusive. Selznick could have saved himself and his lawyers time by claiming that the film was a screen biography of John Gilbert, but he might have incurred a libel suit from Virginia Bruce; or he could have formally identified the callous MGM executives and publicity agents who had helped ruin Gilbert's career. As it was, both on paper and on screen, *A Star Is Born* discreetly avoided mentioning that Maine's heyday was in silent pictures or attributing his decline to an inability to appeal to sound-era audiences. Mentioning the sound crisis would have increased the film's historical specificity, but it also would have incurred the lawsuits of many others equally attuned to Hollywood's last ten years. Still, the trace of Gilbert and the specter of sound remain with the images of *A Star Is Born.*

The producer chose to layer his film with historical allusions, many of them identifiable only to people in the industry. He had Robert Rosson film poignant shots of Grauman's Chinese Theatre (naturally advertising the current run of Selznick's flop, *The Garden of Allah*), and he has Esther look respectfully at the cement monuments to Shirley Temple, Joe E. Brown, Eddie Cantor, and Harold Lloyd.[50] These cement impressions, a shrine of modern Veronica's veils, are Hollywood's own monument to the impression of divinity and mortality. Although many of these names are part of Hollywood's recent past and present (Temple was still the country's top box-office attraction), some have become slabs. Esther also looks at Jean Harlow's message to Sid Grauman and her fans: "In sincere appreciation." This shot was rich with association for Selznick and Wellman. Born Harlean Carpenter, Harlow had been a real-life Esther Blodgett— that rare "one in one hundred thousand" who made it to superstardom.[51] Once, she had been a lonely extra in Clara Bow's films. A year after that, Wellman was directing her in *The Public Enemy.* Two years later, she was starring in the Bow-Harlow biopic *Bombshell.* A year or so after that, she was immortalized in the cement outside Grauman's. Then she merited a shot in *A Star Is Born.* Once again, her miraculous story made headlines as part of the subtext of Selznick's film. But a few weeks after *A Star Is*

Jean Harlow's memorial at Grauman's Chinese Theatre.

Born opened, she was dead at age twenty-six. As the film played late that spring in theaters across the nation, Esther's longing look became one not only of respect and delight but also of nostalgia and regret. Harlow's monument had indeed become a slab, but one that, like her films, still contained a physical impression of the figure who wrote her own name in Hollywood's history.[52]

Esther's transformation is rare and remarkable, but she is not alone. Esther may fear her screen test, but Norman reassures her with a canon of great actresses who started small: "They all had to go through this—Harlow, Lombard, Myrna Loy—and Esther Blodgett."[53] Esther's rise is not fictional. In addition to Jean Harlow, Carole Lombard, and Myrna Loy, Gary Cooper, Clark Gable, and, of course, Janet Gaynor (who played Esther) had all begun as anonymous extras pushed to stardom by chance and hard work.[54] As one reviewer wrote, *A Star Is Born* "tells a story which could happen in Hollywood, a story which in most of its elements has happened. The story of the country girl who becomes a star is no more fantastic than the story of Janet Gaynor, who plays the role, for Miss Gaynor was a theater usher and then an extra player before she became a star."[55] The press book especially capitalized on these real-life connections and historical allusions, proclaiming, "History Repeats Itself" as it advertised individual scenes in the film and hinting that Janet Gaynor was playing herself on screen. Other historical legacies haunted Gaynor's career. A recent news article had touted her as Mary Pickford's successor, a title with which America's Sweetheart concurred.[56] Gaynor's brand of sweet, homegrown innocence and vivacity reminded audiences of Pickford, and lately, Fox studios had been casting her in remakes of Pickford's silent hits, including *Tess of the Storm Country* (1935). Yet just as Pickford did not disappear with silent film (*Coquette*, 1930; *Kiki*, 1931; *Secrets*, 1933), neither did Gaynor emerge with sound; she had been working for Fox since early 1925. In fact, after a series of unsuccessful vehicles at Twentieth Century–Fox, she was in danger of becoming another Norman Maine.

Fredric March, a Broadway actor who had made a name for himself in highbrow films since the advent of sound, was spared these historical burdens in the press. Despite the endless comparisons to John Gilbert, March's portrayal of Maine no doubt borrowed elements of drunken elegance from his performance as John Barrymore (another alcoholic antecedent for Maine) in the 1930 film *The Royal Family of Broadway*. According to Wellman, it was Barrymore's own description of his detox clinic (with barred windows) that inspired Norman's dry prison in *A Star Is Born*.

Earlier in 1936, as Carson and Wellman worked out the details of the script, silent actor John Bowers committed suicide by drowning in the surf outside his Malibu house. Formerly married to Marguerite de la Motte, Bowers had been a successful boyish romantic lead in the 1920s. His suicide was a shock to many, but by the mid-1930s, many Hollywood stars had disappeared. The Production Code had made suicide a taboo topic in Hollywood productions, but Selznick wryly admitted that he seemed to have a fixation on the subject, since many of the films he produced at MGM and SIP ended with suicides (*What Price Hollywood? Anna Karenina, A Tale of Two Cities,* and *Garden of Allah*). Evoking an actual Hollywood suicide like Bowers's would hardly be welcomed by the Hollywood community or approved of by the censors, yet Selznick pushed. We see Maine make his despairing decision to end his life in order to save Vicki's career, and one of the most beautifully photographed sequences in Technicolor is of Maine wading into the Pacific as the sun sets in Malibu. Death may be cruel, but Hollywood columnists are worse. When he reads the news of Maine's death in the papers, Libby, the irascible press agent, sneers, "First drink of water he had in twenty years and even then he had to get it by accident. . . . How do you wire congratulations to the Pacific Ocean?" Libby's spin on the past may never be printed, but his remarks are part of Selznick's screen history, and they are embedded within the text of Carson and Wellman's script. Yet unlike Bowers's death, which was barely noticed in print, Maine commanded headlines and a funeral as impressive as that of MGM executive Irving Thalberg the year before.

Film historian Ronald Haver wrote of *A Star Is Born*, "The lore of the

John Bowers, ca. 1924.
(Author's collection)

town was rife with successes, has-beens, come-backs, ruined marriages and tragic deaths, and after years of retelling and being gossiped about and clucked over, these events and people took on a kind of romantic patina, becoming the authentic legends of Hollywood, making winners out of losers and giving some of them an immortality that transcended anything they might actually have done in pictures."[57] To a certain extent, this may be true. John Bowers will always be remembered as the man who inspired Norman Maine's suicide. Yet many of the Hollywood films about this era focused on the careers of the most important filmmakers in the business—Clara Bow, John Barrymore, John Gilbert, and Jean Harlow. What impelled Selznick to film these people's lives, to make an authentic history of Hollywood, was the way their stories simply disappeared from memory. There was no permanence, no sense of history in Hollywood. Selznick changed all that in 1932 and 1937. If he made Hollywood conscious of its present by having Esther imitate West, Garbo, and Hepburn at a studio cocktail party and by documenting Santa Anita and the Brown Derby in all their Technicolor glamour, he deliberately forced the industry to come to terms with its past—its willingness to forget or glamorize the uglier part of its history. As one reviewer put it, "A *Star Is Born* is not the whole story of Hollywood because that story would never be told in one picture, nor in a dozen pictures. But it does more than has ever been done before."[58]

Esther Blodgett may literally and figuratively step into Norman

Esther tries stepping
into Norman Maine's
footsteps.
(*A Star Is Born*)

Esther (played by new star
Vicki Lester) is stopped in
her tracks by the past.
(*A Star Is Born*)

Norman Maine's slab:
screened off, but not
forgotten.
(*A Star Is Born*)

Maine's shoe prints in the cement foyer of Grauman's. She may eclipse his career and inadvertently cause his despair and death, yet his footprints are too big for her; she cannot fill them. By implication, no modern star can fill the shoes of those stars who loomed larger than life and dominated, however briefly, a more intimidating, exotic era. Selznick never forgot those days. Esther will always remember: as she walks up the red carpet at Grauman's, her eyes drop to the slabs at her feet. She sees all that is left of her husband in the industry, faint cement impressions screened off at the margins, and it stops her in her tracks. A *Star Is Born* was David Selznick's attempt to film Hollywood history in all its variety, distortion, and elliptical basis in fact. Perhaps it was inevitable that the Hollywood film should adopt some of the iconography and projected discourse associated with contemporaneous historical films. In text, panoramic shots, monuments, historical allusions, and frontier rhetoric, Selznick International Pictures matched the more prestigious historical films of that era shot for shot and word for word. But the true measure of the film's commitment to the past comes from Norman Maine, as he says good-bye to his wife shortly before his suicide: "Do you mind if I take just one more look?"[59]

10

A Hollywood Cavalcade, 1939–1942

Here is something that is going to revolutionize the industry.
—Darryl F. Zanuck, 1939

In 1939 Hollywood produced an unprecedented twenty-seven major American historical films. It was a year saturated with critical and box-office successes, ranging from adaptations of the classics of English literature (*Wuthering Heights, Gunga Din*) to sophisticated comedies (*Midnight, The Women*), modern romances (*Ninotchka, Love Affair*), and musicals (*The Wizard of Oz, Babes in Arms*), but American historical films far outnumbered any other A-level genre or cycle. Darryl Zanuck produced ten of these films, even outdistancing the output of his rivals at Warner Brothers, Paramount, and MGM. Although Twentieth Century–Fox would continue to produce American historical films, the studio would never again attain the staggering output and range of historical material.[1] One of Zanuck's 1939 projects was *Hollywood Cavalcade*, the industry's first retrospective look at its own development from the silent era through the conversion to sound. Its release in theaters coincided with the publication of three major accounts of the American film business: Lewis Jacobs's *Rise of the American Film,* Margaret Farrand Thorp's *America at the Movies,* and William C. DeMille's *Hollywood Saga.*[2] Jacobs's and Thorp's contributions have endured as footnotes in ensuing accounts of American film history,[3] while DeMille's memoir and Zanuck's historical film have been forgotten. Although both are unique and crucial attempts

279

by Hollywood filmmakers to remember the industry's past, DeMille's autobiography is necessarily narrower—a memoir of his work with brother
Cecil at Paramount. Only Zanuck's historical film approaches the pan-
studio conception of Hollywood's history practiced by Jacobs and his two
predecessors, Terry Ramsaye (1926) and Benjamin Hampton (1931).[4]

Hollywood Cavalcade's connections to the more traditional, written
works of film history represent a turning point in the industry's confrontation with its past. From 1939 to 1942, Twentieth Century–Fox and later
Warner Brothers, the leading producers of American historical films, produced a group of entertainment histories and biographies that would rival
the prestige of the studios' more staid nineteenth-century subjects. The
production and critical reception of *Hollywood Cavalcade*, and its later
Broadway counterpart *Yankee Doodle Dandy* (1942), illuminate the entertainment cycle as a contested site of historical authority and narration.
In constructing the grand narrative of twentieth-century entertainment,
filmmakers created a canon of great events, stars, films, and technological innovations, but there were considerable struggles over their relative
importance in the script.

The "Evolution" of Film History

Writers, social critics, historians, and filmmakers had been conscious of
Hollywood's rapid growth and remarkable past for a long time, but the
publication of three major studies of the industry's artistic and financial
achievements in one year indicates a growing acceptance of Hollywood as
a historical entity. Terry Ramsaye's and Benjamin Hampton's film histories claimed to be thorough chronological accounts of the development of
film in the West, but they focused overwhelmingly on Hollywood, particularly after the studios' consolidation following the Great War. Ramsaye's
study was published shortly before the advent of sound, and Hampton's
1931 industrial history gave only marginal financial attention to the new
developments of 1927–1930. The cinematic achievements in sound and
the industry's slow conquest of the Depression had created another major
historical period that had yet to be formally incorporated into Hollywood's
grand narrative. The struggles since 1927 had been real, yet filmmakers
measured success in ways other than pure financial gain, and, despite
shaky box-office receipts, they continued to make dangerously expensive
historical films.[5]

Lewis Jacobs, a documentary filmmaker, followed the last ten years
with excitement and found that there were compensations for the loss

of pioneering directors such as D. W. Griffith and Erich von Stroheim and major stars such as Rudolph Valentino and Mabel Normand. For Jacobs, historical features, with their focus on the American past, proved the American cinema's emergence from "adolescence," its status as a mature medium.[6] Before Margaret Thorp's study, academics had only denigrated the movies as a province of cultural and moral decay.[7] Thorp examined the film industry as a powerful economic and social force, a social phenomenon with no equal in modern life. Rather than relying on outside censorship campaigns and public condemnations of the industry, Thorp proposed to look at Hollywood on its own ground. Studio executives, particularly at Warner Brothers and Twentieth Century–Fox, were eager to help Thorp and provided her with inside archival information and statistics about film production and exhibition. It was one of the earliest collaborations between academia and the film industry. Although Thorp's study was not a traditional, Ramsayean account of Hollywood filmmaking, she focused on developments since the sound era, thereby authenticating it as a new stage in Hollywood's history.

William DeMille—actor, writer, producer, director, and elder brother of Cecil—had been involved in filmmaking since 1913. In 1939, after over a quarter century in the business, he published a landmark memoir-history, one of the first accounts of the American film industry by a major Hollywood filmmaker. DeMille had started on Broadway, eventually following his brother—at first reluctantly, then enthusiastically—to California to film the early western *The Squaw Man* (1914). After years of watching and participating in industrial change, of reading the trade papers and his brother's publicity, he was well versed in the "pioneer" metaphors that dominated descriptions of the early film industry. In his account of Cecil B. DeMille Productions, he gloried in the transformation of a once despised entertainment medium into an industry and a new American art. He wrote, "From a Broadway point of view the Gold Rush of '49 was mere child's play compared to the present Gold Rush which has lured such a large proportion of the theatrical talent west of the Rockies in a mad scramble for the yellow metal of Hollywood. . . . It can be no small force which in twenty years has made the much derided movies an art more nationally important than the theater; which has actually subordinated the stage to the screen."[8] But while Jacobs lauded the development and current maturity of the industry, and Thorp represented contemporary Hollywood at the peak of its considerable powers, the tone of DeMille's memoir was elegiac. He described a pioneer era that he felt had utterly disappeared from 1930s Hollywood. The film industry, however efficient and powerful, had lost the ramshackle and romantic force that drove him and his brother.[9]

DeMille was certainly not alone in his nostalgia and need to historicize Hollywood—David Selznick's example has shown that the most powerful of these early histories of Hollywood were films, not written histories or memoirs. Yet the majority of the entertainment histories and biographies produced at the studios focused on William DeMille's moribund Broadway (*Diamond Jim*) and old-style New York nightlife (*She Done Him Wrong, The Bowery*). Perhaps it was understandable that filmmakers would historicize their older, more fastidious, and "finished" East Coast competitor; Hollywood, after all, prided itself on being an industry with its future and financial gains ahead of it. DeMille slyly wrote, "There are even those who proclaim that if the American stage is to be kept alive it must be subsidized by Hollywood; must be regarded largely as a proving ground for plays on their way to Broadway; a testing laboratory for actors in which the exact quantity of their sex appeal may be determined."[10] But Broadway, even on its last legs, was still capable of leeching $275,000 from RKO to produce Robert Sherwood's *Abe Lincoln in Illinois*; it could still send New York talent off to take the jobs of Hollywood's old stars.

Two years earlier, Twentieth Century–Fox screenwriters Sonya Levien and Richard Sherman had imbued their script *Falling Star* with some Broadway menace. An original story of a major Hollywood actor whose career is destroyed by vanity, talking pictures, and the exodus of more capable New York actors to Hollywood following the conversion to sound, *Falling Star* reminded 1937 Hollywood of the many silent careers lost to uppity Broadway talent.[11] Yet curiously, the script was set entirely in contemporary Hollywood and lacked any historical allusions or prologue. And unlike *Bombshell, Morning Glory*, and *A Star Is Born*, none of the characters was based on an actual star or scenario. Levien, a recent New York transplant herself, admitted that she invented freely without regard for Hollywood's past. Zanuck never made the film. He may have flinched at its hackneyed plot and lack of interesting historical referents, but he was not interested in copying Selznick.

In late 1937 Zanuck abandoned Selznick's unconventional efforts in cinematic history and turned instead to MGM's paragon of polished entertainment biography and box-office success—*The Great Ziegfeld*—and the memory of Mae West's period bawdiness at Paramount. Although *She Done Him Wrong*'s period prestige and nineteenth-century sex had garnered an Academy Award nomination for Best Picture in 1933, only a few years later, the Production Code had nearly finished West's contract with

Paramount. Zanuck, sensing the need for a cleaner entertainer, launched Alice Faye in a series of prestigious historical musical productions. Although *In Old Chicago*'s dance-hall sequences recalled the Mae West extravaganzas that were no longer possible under Hays's and Breen's eyes, Zanuck was committed to continuing his own risqué nightlife histories begun with *The Bowery* in 1934. As the years progressed, though, Faye's characters underwent remarkable changes. First she was the wholly fictitious Belle Fawcett, dwarfed by the performance of the 1871 Chicago fire; then she became a partially imagined Irving Berlin love interest in *Alexander's Ragtime Band*. By late 1938, she moved closer to historical specificity when she played a version of Fanny Brice in *The Rose of Washington Square*. By 1940, Zanuck cast her as one of the most influential entertainers in American history: Lillian Russell. That 1940 film was Zanuck's first studio biopic of an important American woman. Faye's characters had once reacted to events beyond their control; now, it seemed, a woman could receive the same historical prestige as P. T. Barnum, Samuel Mudd, Alexander Graham Bell, and Abraham Lincoln.

Zanuck, however, was growing bored with the cycle he had initiated at Warner Brothers a decade ago. Although the research and technical demands of *In Old Chicago* had excited him, too many of the narrative devices were identified in conferences by references to other films, such as *China Seas* or *Mutiny on the Bounty*, and especially scenes reminiscent of *San Francisco*.[12] *In Old Chicago*'s historical research was widely publicized in the press campaign,[13] but the narrative was explicable only through other films. History was becoming a film formula. Later in 1938, Zanuck attempted to make his fabricated Irving Berlin biopic more historically impressive with a long and bitter Great War interlude, and his major concerns about *The Rose of Washington Square*'s script centered around period details of prewar New York.[14] By the time he turned to nineteenth-century Broadway in late 1939, history had become too easy for him to manipulate. Zanuck also had little regard for Russell as a historical figure. Although Universal's *Diamond Jim* and MGM's *The Great Ziegfeld* had proved Russell's appeal as a cameo in major historical productions, and although he had hired *Ziegfeld* screenwriter William Anthony McGuire to write *Lillian Russell*, after doing some research and reading the script, Zanuck found her rather tedious. At one script conference he complained that things "just happened to her," and she reacted to historical forces rather than making decisions for herself.[15]

He nonetheless continued with the project, and McGuire tried desperately to link Russell's life to some of the more proven and impressive

events in American history. He developed an elaborate prologue emphasizing the coincidence of Russell's birth date and the beginning of the
Civil War in 1861.[16] He lent her home life and upbringing some vicarious
power by contrasting the career of her suffragette mother with her own.
But these efforts did little to dispel Zanuck's dissatisfaction with Russell's
passive relationship with the circumstances surrounding her career, and
by the middle of December 1939, he had developed an overreactive need
to control and rewrite her uneventful life. He outlined "his reasons for
wanting to take more license in the life of Lillian Russell," which were
"that the general public does not know anything about Lillian Russell,
except that she was beautiful and that Jim Brady was crazy about her."[17] In
other words, the American public knew only the history that motion pictures covered. Universal's *Diamond Jim* had introduced Russell as Brady's
girl, and as far as Zanuck was concerned, films were the public's only
historical frame of reference. Yet curiously, his efforts to cut and control
Russell's life mirrored the actress's own efforts in constructing her autobiography. In a 1922 account serialized in *Cosmopolitan*, Russell carefully
emphasized her feminist upbringing and cut two husbands and one child
out of her life. Zanuck, whether he knew it or not, reproduced Russell's
own construction of her life.[18]

Of course, focusing on a woman as a major "historical" figure also
may have violated Zanuck's sense of patriarchal historical values. Women
had never been an important component in his historical work. The following year, historian Dixon Wecter compiled a pantheon of American
heroes without including a single woman.[19] Wecter found this masculine
canon unique in Western countries, where more often a single woman
epitomized national heroism. England had Queen Elizabeth; France
had Joan of Arc. But America's Molly Pitcher, Abigail Adams, and Lucre-
tia Mott were at the margins of mainstream conceptions of the national
"hero" because, he wrote, in America, "the dominant ideal has been the
perfect lady."[20]

Yet perversely, American cinema of the 1930s made heroines out of
rebellious fictional women (Sabra Cravat, Ramona Moreno, Jo March,
Scarlett O'Hara, Julie Marston) and tried, perhaps unsuccessfully, to
make ladies out of historical nonconformists Annie Oakley and Calamity
Jane. Was historical fiction fulfilling a more compelling form of national
myth where women were concerned, or were women less malleable to
symbolic manipulation? Wecter argued the latter, stating that women
lack "the symbolic appeal" of men. Does this mean that women have
more historically resilient qualities, that their lives and careers are less

vulnerable to mythic manipulation? Zanuck's heroes, for all their connection to American myth, were deployed as a means of reconfronting and often revising traditional interpretations of the past. Samuel Mudd's little-known tale had impelled Zanuck to bring *The Prisoner of Shark Island* accurately and forcefully to the screen. Margaret Mitchell and Selznick accomplished something similar with Scarlett O'Hara, a fictional character who functioned as a composite of historical, nonconforming Confederate women. Scarlett's maverick status served as both mask and mirror for incomplete traditional histories and the more unsettling protofeminist realities expressed in the film. Could Zanuck have done for Russell what he had accomplished for Mudd? Probably not. It was not a question of whether Russell had mythic appeal or historical resilience; it was a question of where she fit in Zanuck's historical canon. For the producer, both Russell and Broadway had a tenuous hold in the text of American history.

Hollywood's history was another matter. In 1939 Zanuck's *Hollywood Cavalcade* told the story of a pioneering director who steals a promising actress from Broadway to enter the emerging film business. They head westward, and she becomes one of the silent screen's great stars. Time and distance had encouraged Zanuck to rethink Selznick's work, but Zanuck's cinematic history was remarkable in that its narrative structure, discourse, and events followed the historiographic approach of more traditional subject matter. Less inventive than *A Star Is Born,* more self-conscious and perhaps even pretentious, Zanuck's film mimicked and aspired to the historical structures of Ramsaye's *A Million and One Nights* and the biography cycle known at Fox and Warner Brothers. Surprisingly, though, while other Fox employees were excited by the possibility of filming Hollywood's past with the detail and historical structure usually devoted to a Civil War history or prestige western, Zanuck was ambivalent. Unlike Selznick, who used the strictures of censorship and industrial amnesia as a means of exploring the difficulties and impossibilities of remembering Hollywood's past, *Hollywood Cavalcade* appropriated a well-worn historical format to construct a spurious establishment history of Hollywood.

The Dream of Hollywood History

Zanuck was as adept at capitalizing on his colleagues' cinematic developments as he was at creating new cycles and trends. For the past several years he had been watching his independent rival, David Selznick, develop his Hollywood entertainment cycle. Zanuck and Selznick did not move in the same social circles, and evidence suggests that they disliked each other.[21] This is unfortunate, since their ambitious bodies of work and their impacts on the industry were so widespread and similar. Both men worked their way up from story editors to head production at major studios and then went on to create their own studios. Both had an obsession with overseeing each script and production detail of every film released by their companies. Both were tireless workers, perfectionists who blurred the border between producer and dictator. Yet here their similarities ceased. Zanuck was the only non-Jewish studio head in Hollywood. He was no one's son-in-law, whereas Selznick had cannily married his boss's daughter, Irene Mayer, in 1930. Zanuck had no family in motion pictures. When he started as a freelance screenwriter in the mid-1920s, he started alone, with no help or encouragement. Unlike Selznick, who grew up with Hollywood, Zanuck had few memories of the glamour of "old Hollywood." Working at the thrifty Warner Brothers studio was tough, and for many years, his life outside the studio was nonexistent. Having begun as a writer, he had more respect for a screenwriter's autonomy and screen sense than did Selznick, who had a reputation for going through writers as quickly as he did Benzedrine tablets. Warner Brothers taught Zanuck the benefits of economy, and unlike Selznick International Pictures, Twentieth Century–Fox remained solvent for years.

Most important, Zanuck had no qualms about the introduction of and conversion to sound. As one of the producers of *The Jazz Singer* and *The Lights of New York* (1928), Zanuck considered sound an advancement, not a death knell. Zanuck also had no sad memories of the silent era. Unlike Selznick, the past did not haunt him unduly; instead, the old days were something quaint to celebrate. Selznick had proved the salability of entertainment history, and in 1938, Zanuck authorized a thinly disguised biography of composer Irving Berlin's early career, *Alexander's Ragtime Band*.[22] That year, he developed and oversaw the production of dozens of films, yet his prestige vehicles overwhelmingly considered high-profile American historical figures or events: *In Old Chicago* (the rise of Irish immigrants, boss politics, and the Great Fire of 1871), *Kentucky* (the legacy of Civil War and Reconstruction bitterness in the horse-racing world), *Jesse James* (outlaw heroes, the rise of big business, and the Lost Cause), *Alexander Graham Bell*, *Young Mr. Lincoln*, and *Frontier Marshal* (Tombstone and the crisis of the cattle barons). But he also set aside some time for Hollywood history.

In late October 1938 he expanded on his preliminary idea, a tale to be called *Hollywood Cavalcade*. "There can be no doubt," he remarked in a story conference, "that there is a wealth of fascinating material connected with the days of early Hollywood. . . . Instead of going out of our way to contrive a story and situations from out of thin air, we should take as a pattern the composite of several of these interesting personalities and adapt them for one story."[23] Zanuck seemed to follow Selznick's approach in drawing from specific events and careers in Hollywood's past, disguising the real names, and forming composite biographies. Zanuck reasoned that too much specificity would baffle and bewilder those viewers outside the Hollywood community. Yet, it seemed logical that using Mickey Neilan's and Mack Sennett's names would only help publicize the picture. Their careers, though over, were still recent enough to be part of the memories of all but the youngest filmgoers. Yet Zanuck persisted in his view. Was he afraid of lawsuits from living filmmakers or their wives (Neilan and his ex-wife, actress Blanche Sweet, come to mind, as well as Louis B. Mayer, who had sabotaged Neilan's directorial career) and the studios and executives for whom they once worked? These were fears that filmmakers constantly faced in filming modern history.[24] But it also may have been too much for Hollywood to commemorate its past unflinchingly, particularly when being "of the past" in an industry dependent on youth and perennial success was considered "failure." Would Zanuck's decision to make a film specifically about Hollywood's washed-up and ruined stars embarrass both the audiences who forgot them and the studios who terminated their contracts?

At first, Zanuck chose to emphasize the development of the industry rather than its personal casualties. It was an interesting reversal of his habitual approach to historical filmmaking, whereby a great life or lives dominated or fought against the forces of history. In early script meetings, he planned to show "the first close-up," the move from New York to Hollywood, the development of technique (or, in Zanuck's words, "how they nailed down the cameras in those days"), and scenes depicting the age of slapstick and spectacle. But for Zanuck, the most important element in the development of motion picture history was the advent of talkies. It was sound that would most deeply affect the protagonists of *Hollywood Cavalcade*, Elinor Kirby (later Vera Dale and then Molly Adair), Michael Thurn (later John Mitchell and then Mike Connors), and Charles Barth (later Lew Brackett and then Nicky Hayden).[25] Zanuck's writers had outlined a story that in many ways represented the popular composite biographies of D. W. Griffith and Lillian Gish, Mickey Neilan and Blanche Sweet, Douglas Fairbanks and Mary Pickford, and especially Mack Sennett and Mabel Normand. Thurn is a brilliant new motion picture director who collects Broadway actress Elinor Kirby to be his new star. The stigma of being a film actress destroys her reputation as a serious stage actress as well as her marriage, and she loses custody of her son (following the life of Belasco actress Mrs. Leslie Carter, filmed as *The Lady with Red Hair* by Warner Brothers in 1940). Elinor goes west, and Thurn, inspired by her face, develops the close-up. She becomes a multiple hit, embodying Hollywood actresses' successes as the girl next door (Mary Pickford), then as the custard-pie pratfaller (Mabel Normand), and then as the bathing beauty (Gloria Swanson). When her famed director passes his career peak, she leaves him for another studio. Thurn reacts as poorly as Griffith did when Gish left him for Paramount, or as badly as Neilan did after Thalberg and Mayer forced him to leave MGM.

Zanuck liked the outline, and the Neilan overtones allowed him to get in a dig at stodgy rival Louis B. Mayer, but he demanded that the transition to sound receive special treatment.[26] Although old friends try to help the director (now called Mitchell) make a comeback film, *The Jazz Singer* appears before it can be released, making his silent epic obsolete. In spite of the odds, Mitchell adapts his old film for sound and succeeds in recapturing audience approval (unlike the real Griffith, who never made a successful transition to sound with *Abraham Lincoln*, and Neilan, whose career fizzled after he left MGM). Originally, writer Brown Holmes developed a twenty-year history of Hollywood through a two-generation tale of Elinor's early stardom and her son's budding career; however, Zanuck disliked the more complicated script in which all the major characters would have to age considerably. He worried that the two-generation format would demand fixed dates and a historical pretentiousness that would confuse the audience. He wanted a timeless, ageless fable culled from the lore on motion picture infancy, and in late 1938, he insisted that Ernest Pascal rewrite the script to focus exclusively on Mitchell, Vera Dale, and Lew Brackett.

Producer Julian Johnson objected to Zanuck's streamlined commercial vehicle (originally intended for Spencer Tracy) and pushed for the more nuanced understanding of Hollywood's past that had been present in earlier drafts. The background details — cameras and Keystone Cops — were all right, but he argued that the foreground needed a similar depth and a narrative structure that conveyed a sense of industrial change over time. For Johnson, "the showing of *two generations* in the movies — the real feeling of history and progress made at so rapid a rate that the stars of those recent 'early days' are almost unknown to the young 1939 audience" — was the film's most original idea.[27] Old stars have become minor character actors, he wrote, and Zanuck should not ignore these casualties of history. He pressed, "We have the best examples of this terrific speed of time in the movies right on our own lot: you are the most significant example of the movie's younger generation, and Tyrone Power the most prominent example of the movie second generation." Here Johnson may have gone too far. Although Zanuck did not belong to the illustrious cast of old Hollywood, the producer liked to think that he had enough knowledge and personal experience to cover Hollywood's entire history. Johnson's comments, intended as praise, may have rankled, because they implied that Zanuck, in jettisoning the two-generation format, lacked the historical sense to portion Hollywood's history in proper perspective. Although Zanuck began his career in the 1920s, he, unlike Johnson,[28] truly belonged to the sound era. More than any other filmmaker at Warner Brothers, he was responsible for the landmark *Jazz Singer*: he edited Samson Raphaelson's original story, oversaw day-to-day production, and edited the final cut.[29]

Johnson continued, evidently stirred by the topic: "These elements of *time* and *history*, which are so important, I think are greatly diminished by finishing our story with the same people who started it, once more on the topmost pinnacle of popular success." Johnson knew that Zanuck did not want to make a full-blown historical film by running clips of *The Birth of a Nation*, *The Four Horsemen of the Apocalypse*, and *The Ten Commandments*, but he still wanted to reach audiences with a sense of the remoteness of the early silent era, "not only in sets and background, but also in human beings." Johnson wanted the narrative to take place not at one imaginary studio but at a group of real studios, giving a more nuanced and accurate view of the variety of early production. He also objected to Zanuck's facile character John Mitchell, who, in the script, makes all the major discoveries in film history: the close-up, the Keystone Cops, the bathing beauties, "and just about everything else worthwhile." Johnson admitted that this shocked him because he had originally read the script as if it were a biography of Mickey Neilan—and later a combination of Neilan and Mack Sennett. For Johnson, it was more than a mistake to combine all the achievements of Hollywood style and filmmaking in one person's career; it was a travesty and a betrayal of the audience's intelligence.

Film historians hell-bent on economically determined histories of Hollywood film production have enshrined Hollywood executives' gospel of audience infallibility ("The customer is always right"),[30] but surprisingly, many filmmakers had an unconcealed contempt for the audience's mental abilities and its capacity to recognize a good film. As his frequent story conferences indicate, Zanuck thought that he knew what a lowbrow audience wanted and consented to condescend and compromise in the name of "entertainment." He had taken a lot of risks over the years in making complex American historical productions that were not all romance and wisecracks, but he knew that they were risks. He was not the only one to worry about the popular reception of prestige pictures. William DeMille knew that producers always claimed to give the public what it wanted but frequently refused: "They have listened to the voices of the clergy, the educators, even the intelligentsia, and usually with disastrous financial results."[31] Julian Johnson was not a lowbrow of the DeMille mold; groveling to the American public's imagined sluggish mentality was not always good public relations. And no audience is so stupid, Johnson reasoned, that it cannot remember the real Mack Sennett, D. W. Griffith, and Rudy Valentino. Johnson went on to outline a direct approach to Hollywood historical filmmaking, one that departed significantly from Selznick's complex allegories in its unambiguous characterizations. He wanted to have identifiable cameos of real filmmakers. "For instance," he proposed:

> A dignified elongated, rather Shakespearean-looking man who deals daringly in heroic subjects only, and is referred to by some—though never by our hero—as "the master." Under another name, of course, D. W. Griffith. I would have a short, stocky, short-spoken hustler—turning out "punch" plays in batches and superwesterns—whom the foxy ones will have no difficulty in identifying as a legitimate paraphrase of the late Tom Ince. I am not so sure that I wouldn't even have a short, elderly actor, but *not* a dialect comedian—playing a kindly, carefully non-libelous character, laying out a valley establishment called Colossal City. The audience could spot him as Uncle Carl Laemmle—if they wished. I would even venture so close to reality that I would have one rather elegant and aggressive young man who introduced megaphone and puttees to camera art, and made edifying su-perspectacles of moral nature—yet who perhaps could never be quite identified as Cecil B. DeMille. (No need to bring in the bathtubs, which would pin him sure.)[32]

Then Johnson planned to cast actors as "living re-creations" of some of the great actors and actresses of the past, including the supreme beauty Barbara La Marr, Valentino, and Wallace Reid. He even pressed to include shots of silent film classics where appropriate.

Johnson knew Zanuck's great record on American historical films; after all, he had helped Zanuck produce most of them. He timed his next argument for *Hollywood Cavalcade* well: "We have no hesitancy in recreating well-known statesmen, inventors, explorers. Why can't we be the first to bring to life again, just for quick moments and flashes, the early greats of our industry?" He resented the script's fictionalized treatment of Hollywood's early history, its gross distortions and breezy disregard for history while the Civil War and Gilded Age received more careful handling. Why this consistently remote and fantasized view of Hollywood's past? Audiences paid far more attention to the Hollywood fan magazines than to textbooks, so why shouldn't they appreciate a more mature film about Hollywood's past? In the course of his long memo, Johnson never mentioned Selznick's efforts or the recent success of *A Star Is Born*; Zanuck always liked to be the first in everything, and even mentioning his archrival in independent production would not have been politic. Yet for all its historical references, shots of familiar locales, monuments, and names, Johnson did not want *Hollywood Cavalcade* to be an imitation of *A Star Is Born*. His view of the Hollywood historical film emphasized the history, the passage of time, in a self-conscious, conventionally structured, and unequivocal way that placed it directly within the category of more traditional nineteenth- and twentieth-century historical fare. Selznick's experimentalism, which played elaborately with the notion of forgetting and distorting the past, only to evoke its most painful memories, was not Johnson's approach. He wanted Hollywood to finally give itself the respect it deserved. Most likely, Johnson's greatest regret was that the film had to be produced by a second-generation filmmaker like Zanuck, who had little understanding of the past with which Johnson was so familiar.

Zanuck's Folly

Needless to say, Zanuck was annoyed with Johnson's abnormally lengthy reader's report, and he chose to ignore most if not all of his underling's impassioned advice. He never spliced the clips of the silent classic films with the new footage; he hesitated to show any early silents because "the films were so crude at that time."[33] Cinema had advanced so far that it seemed embarrassing to remember. Zanuck never returned to the original two-generation narrative, but he did eliminate all the planned musical numbers for Alice Faye's leading lady, stating in conference that her period musicals (*In Old Chicago, Alexander's Ragtime Band, The Rose of Washington Square*) were becoming a bit of a bore.[34] Possibly he also real-

Facing custard pies from
the past: Alice Faye
and Buster Keaton in
Hollywood Cavalcade
(1939).

ized that elaborate musical numbers would be at a disadvantage in a film
set in *silent* Hollywood.

He seemed intrigued by the many possibilities for historical details
and cameos (hiring Buster Keaton, another star whose career had ended
at MGM), and initially he envisioned the film in crisp black-and-white
"documentary" cinematography to enhance the reality of the narrative.[35]
Early in production and long before Johnson's memo, he even hired Mack
Sennett to act as a script consultant, producer, and actor in the film.[36]
Zanuck probably met Sennett when the latter was briefly honored for his
contribution to motion pictures at the 1937 Academy Awards ceremony.
However, even with his admiration for Sennett's custard pies, cops, and
bathing beauties, Zanuck never planned to honor Sennett's talents as a
director by including old footage from his work in the new film. Zanuck
planned to remake and refilm Hollywood history according to his taste,
and Johnson could not change his mind. Instead, Keaton, Sennett, and
other old faces returned merely as faded cameos, displaced stars in a narrative dominated by the new names Alice Faye and Don Ameche.

Even though he persisted in giving his protagonists innocuous fictional names and refused to name his lead Mickey, Zanuck and screenwriter Ernest Pascal saw their young matinee idol Lew as a combination
of Gary Cooper and Douglas Fairbanks Jr. Zanuck insisted, "Don't mention specific time lapses,"[37] and he jettisoned the projected timeline from
1911 to 1939 so that the leads would remain young and vaguely situated
in history. But paradoxically, the producer had to define his new time
span, 1913 to 1927, when he concluded the narrative with the advent of

the talking blockbuster.[38] Even Zanuck's Hollywood had to be marked by dates. But unlike Zanuck's rigorously historical period films, none of the scripts opened with a text foreword or date superimposition. The historical structure was left until the last minute, evidence of Zanuck's often vague but self-serving attitude toward making a Hollywood "historical" film. It was certainly revealing that the only instance in the script and film where Zanuck and his team of screenwriters did not "create" the early history of Hollywood out of their own imaginations was when he recalled one of his early masterpieces, *The Jazz Singer.*

Warner Brothers' first talkie was Zanuck's first big film success without Rin Tin Tin. It was also the symbolic catalyst for an early sound era that he would dominate. When *The Jazz Singer* became a cinematic byword, Zanuck himself became part of film history. It was the only real film title mentioned in the course of *Hollywood Cavalcade*'s narrative, and in focusing on that film to the exclusion of others, Zanuck advertised and magnified his own crucial role in the development of American film. Early in production, he planned for the Neilan-Griffith main character to experience an epiphany when he wanders into a theater to see the film.[39] By the time the film ended, Zanuck planned the pioneering silent director, a former skeptic of sound cinema, to rave, "God, it was wonderful—he can't understand how he could have been so blind . . . why, you can't look at a silent picture after you've seen one—here is something that is going to revolutionize the industry . . . it's no longer going to be considered a racket . . . it's going to be a gigantic enterprise, etc., etc."[40] Here Zanuck was echoing Hollywood historian Benjamin Hampton in 1931: "*The Jazz Singer* proved to be one of the plays that have occasionally shaken the movie world like an earthquake, people crowding into houses to see it, and leaving the theatres completely converted to the talkies."[41] But as film historian Donald Crafton later pointed out, it is uncertain how big a success the film was. Critics and publicists did not faithfully report the grosses and attendance tallies (which were extremely inaccurate until the mid-1940s). What is certain is that the studios constructed *The Jazz Singer* as a spectacular box-office success.[42] But it was not only a question of Warner Brothers cannily generating a publicity screen to draw in much-needed box-office; it was a question of filmmakers and critics justifying the technological transformation as a major historical event. After a dozen years, Zanuck was simply reaffirming this discourse in another institutional work of film historiography.

Although Zanuck maintained during *Hollywood Cavalcade* story conferences that he did not want any of the other dates to be spelled out on screen, he was definite about marking *The Jazz Singer* as the advent of sound. It was to be the film's one self-consciously historical moment, and in late November 1938, he even mentioned that he was "planning to use cutouts from *Jazz Singer*, showing Al Jolson singing Mammy. . . . If we cannot use actual cutout, we will probably hire Jolson to do a scene for us."[43] Warner Brothers allowed Zanuck to use the scene, and the nostalgic clip became one of *Hollywood Cavalcade's* most memorable moments, according to Hollywood critics.[44] It was the first time that Zanuck ever pushed to add vintage footage to any historical film,[45] but *The Jazz Singer* was, after all, Zanuck's film. For him, real film history began with talking pictures.[46]

Hollywood critics, well versed in Hollywood's past and present preoccupation with invention, nonetheless praised *Hollywood Cavalcade* as an "introspective and essentially historical account of the birth and growth of the world's greatest medium of entertainment." Just as Julian Johnson had predicted, there were two types of audience responses, both of which resulted from the groups' own specific and diverse memories of Hollywood's history. "To the older generation of picturegoers, the pie-throwing slapstick, the Mack Sennett bathing beauties, the Keystone Cop of the nickelodeon days will bring chuckles and perhaps a gulp, while to the younger generation these uncouth but bellylaugh comicalities will be an entertaining prelude to the coming of the talkies which they know."[47] In spite of Zanuck's efforts to obscure many of the actual names, critics and audiences were now experienced in decoding the historiography. Johnson's predictions were accurate, but one wonders what would have occurred had Zanuck taken Johnson's notion of historical change seriously. Johnson had envisioned the possibility of filming Hollywood's own history with the same attention to detail and argument accorded to Hollywood's most prestigious films of that era. Although *Hollywood Cavalcade* probably prompted Edward Small to advertise "The Life of Rudolph Valentino" as a 1940 work in progress, the independent producer had to abandon his biopic.[48] Rudy's life did not reach the screen until 1951 (*Valentino*, Columbia).

Zanuck undoubtedly gave *Hollywood Cavalcade* the glamour treatment by casting the two Twentieth Century–Fox stars most associated with the studio's historical films: Don Ameche (*In Old Chicago, Alexander Graham Bell*) and Alice Faye (*Alexander's Ragtime Band, In Old Chicago*). He even went to the added expense of filming in Technicolor. Certainly color gave the narrative a greater physical reality; many historical films were shot in color to generate a sense of realism and obviate historical remoteness. Selznick reserved Technicolor for both *A Star Is Born* and *Gone with the Wind*. Yet for the first traditional film history of Hollywood, perhaps black-and-white cinematography would have emphasized the original "documentary" atmosphere and the memories of flickering celluloid. His one-generation format could outline and approximate but not engage with the major structural changes in filmmaking: the close-up, the eight-reeler, the slapstick comedy, the talking picture. Zanuck was invested in contemporary cinema. Unlike Selznick, Zanuck had no relationship, personal or historical, with *Hollywood Cavalcade*'s retelling of American cinema history from 1913 to 1927. The film had a fictional core, unlike *A Star Is Born*, where raw memories were not soothed by self-reflexive Hollywood gloss.

The production of *Hollywood Cavalcade* raises some major questions about the limits of historiography. Who narrates Hollywood's past? What constitutes the great story? For Zanuck and many others, Hollywood's own historical narrative was appropriately a heroic success story. In 1939 this mode accorded with the growing narrative tendency in more traditional historical film narratives and the bent of mainstream American historians who were losing their revisionist edge. Curiously, William and Cecil B. DeMille's careers in Hollywood closely approximated Zanuck's historical time span in *Hollywood Cavalcade* (1913–1927). Zanuck also shared some of William DeMille's view of Hollywood history. The story of developments in American film art was a tale of progress toward artistic maturity in the sound era. The advent of sound, although tragic for some and introducing sweeping changes, was a necessary purgative for the evolving art.[49]

Relativist doubts about progress and objectivity, whether articulated by Selznick or Carl Becker, were an increasing rarity. And yet, there was a distinct difference between the historical narratives of Zanuck and those of Ramsaye and Jacobs. Zanuck refused to acknowledge or recognize the legendary successes of D. W. Griffith and Charles Chaplin. More than any other figure, Chaplin consistently dominated the box office from 1913 to 1927. Ramsaye, Jacobs, and especially critic Gilbert Seldes considered him crucial to any discussion of Hollywood's past. Yet both Griffith and Chaplin remained committed to silent filmmaking. Both spoke out against the widespread capitulation to sound. Griffith adapted poorly and faded. Chaplin simply refused to conform, and in defiance of the talkies and production wisdom, he produced the enormously successful silent comedies *City Lights* (1931) and *Modern Times* (1936). Chaplin refused to allow Hollywood's past to be *past* and thus defied Zanuck's confident historical structure and defining historical moment, the advent of sound. Griffith and Chaplin were not part of Zanuck's Hollywood history precisely because they contradicted the notion of historical progress. Rather than progressing, Hollywood lost many of its greatest artists after 1927; the golden age was not in Zanuck's future but in Griffith's and Chaplin's past. Nevertheless, *Hollywood Cavalcade* is an important historical text, as crucial to the representation of Hollywood history as Jacobs's *Rise of the American Film*; it may be even more important because it represented a contemporary industrial view and included the visual detail and narrative invention integral to Hollywood's development.

The American film industry's fascination with entertainment history extended well beyond its own motion picture past. Just as long-standing were the industry's historical accounts of Broadway. *Alexander's Ragtime Band* (1938), *The Rose of Washington Square*, and *Lillian Russell* (1940) were all popular ways of advertising Alice Faye's voice, Fox's commitment to historical filmmaking,[50] and even the subtle but deeply cherished belief among film people that Broadway was a relic, a moribund entertainment venue and worthy of historical treatment. In 1939 William DeMille expressed this view in his memoirs. His "life" began in 1913 when Cecil persuaded him to write for the cinema rather than the theater. Neither Broadway's contempt nor Hollywood's perilous environment affected the DeMilles. They controlled one of the few early silent production companies to survive and prosper in the sound era. Both DeMilles had begun in the theater, but they had no regrets about leaving. Broadway had once dismissed the brothers and the new entertainment industry, but William DeMille had much satisfaction in remarking, "It can be no small force which in twenty years has made the much derided movie an art more nationally important than the theater, which has actually subordinated the stage to screen."[51] Hollywood had the last laugh. With the advent of sound, Broadway playwrights took up the new craft of screenwriting, and Broadway actors such as Humphrey Bogart, Henry Fonda, Clark Gable, Katharine Hepburn, Paul Muni, Barbara Stanwyck, and Spencer Tracy quickly dominated the prestige pictures of the motion picture industry.

Although Zanuck honored the great age of Broadway's past with admiring biopics of Fanny Brice, Irving Berlin, and Lillian Russell, he was just as ready to lampoon its hoity-toity condemnation of Hollywood with *The Great Profile* (1940).[52] Here, under no pressure to render an impressive history, Zanuck endorsed the similarities between the character Garrick and actor John Barrymore. Garrick, a New York actor turned film star, is kicked off the lot of his latest picture, *Macbeth*, and returns to

Broadway to do a lousy contemporary play. The implications are obvious: Hollywood has sucked up Broadway's old claims to prestige and pomposity by annexing both its actors and its plays. But Garrick, like Broadway, is "washed up and finished," according to his agent, and in 1940 he is sent back to Broadway. The parallels between Barrymore, the "Great Profile," and Garrick make this film close to biography. Barrymore had met Zanuck when the two worked for Warner Brothers in the 1920s, but after leaving Warner Brothers and MGM, the actor's career as a romantic leading man declined. In 1939, in a well-publicized move, he left Hollywood to star in a new play.

My Dear Children (1939–1940) was not comparable to Barrymore's famous productions of *Hamlet* or *Richard III*, but it was a huge touring and Broadway success. The critics called it a "trashy story" but loved it.[53] Zanuck quickly beckoned him back to Hollywood to improvise a film version. Although *My Dear Children* was conceived as a farce from the start,[54] the script of *The Great Profile* makes a deliberate strike at contemporary theater. Garrick is confronted with a pretentious, obsolete Broadway and a young female playwright infused with the need to write serious drama. He knows that his new "highbrow" vehicle is unintentionally more farce than drama. After a dismal opening night, and primed with alcohol, he turns the arty fiasco into a comic hit as he insults the play, the leading lady, and the audience onstage, swings on curtain cords, and mimics his own image with slow, sweeping presentations of his profile. In the film text, newspaper inserts herald this Brechtian tour de force as "a landmark of theatre history," and once again, Zanuck's film denigrates Broadway in order to valorize Hollywood. After all, this landmark of theatrical innovation is possible only on film.[55]

For several years, Zanuck had dominated entertainment history, and no one else was willing to historicize the industry or explore the creative tensions between film and stage. Instead, the most successful entertainment film at that time eulogized a man and the theatrical era even more carefully than *Hollywood Cavalcade*: Warner Brothers' biography of George M. Cohan, *Yankee Doodle Dandy* (1942). The film responded to many of the factors that had developed early sound-era historical filmmaking, but it also represented a transition and the end of that historical tradition. *Yankee Doodle Dandy* was Robert Buckner's final historical script for Warner Brothers. Beginning in 1943, he, like many others, made the transition from historical screenplays to Second World War adventures. That year, he wrote and produced period star Errol Flynn's first war film, *Uncertain Glory*. *Yankee Doodle Dandy* represented Warner Brothers' final large-scale historical film; although it shared Oscars with *Mrs. Miniver*, MGM's wartime resistance film was the future of prestigious Hollywood filmmaking.[56] Although Warner Brothers had produced several antifascist films in 1939 and 1940, by 1942, most of its production line was focused on war pictures. Cagney, Bogart, and Flynn were seconded from historical films to aid war production. *Yankee Doodle Dandy* was the last of these expensive and serious historical films, but a cinematic life of George M. Cohan was certainly a curious conclusion to the cycle.

Although he was of the twentieth century, with a legendary career extending through the First World War, Cohan was an authentic Victorian individualist, an old-fashioned hero straight from the pages of a Horatio Alger novel. Although he and Alvin York shared a code of individualism, perseverance, and national faith, York's life and its resonance with traditional American heroes such as Daniel Boone had to be interpreted by others. No one ever spoke for George M. Cohan. Cohan was responsible for creating his public identity, and for fifty years, both onstage and off, he exploited it. Unlike most public figures, particularly those in show business, he never adapted or reinvented his principles; although very conscious of himself as a star, he lacked the twentieth-century self-consciousness that was so incompatible with traditional heroes. Broadway's eventual vicious attack on its most famous playwright, producer, director, actor, composer, and lyricist signified a change in American values as poignant as the fate of John Gilbert and D. W. Griffith in Hollywood. By 1941, when Warner Brothers began to consider his biography, Cohan had been a national institution for nearly fifty years and a Broadway pariah for twenty. With his biopic, Hollywood had the opportunity to consider neglect, loneliness, decay, and another entertainment industry's mistreatment of a great star. However, Warner Brothers resisted any temptation to dwell on the conflict and decline of his career and instead focused on the celebratory patriotism of his music. By emphasizing the music and its recognized perennial Americanness, the historical context of Cohan's life disappeared, leaving the narrative vulnerable to wartime propaganda.

The Man Who Once Owned Broadway

George M. Cohan was born on 4 July 1878, and his most famous lyrics in *Little Johnny Jones* (1904) would never let his audiences forget it.[57] Although he first achieved stardom in 1891 with his performance as "Hennery" Peck in *Peck's Bad Boy*, Cohan's early talent did not lie in playing other writers' work but in creating his own acts and revues for himself and his family, known nationally as "The Four Cohans." As biographer John McCabe noted, before Cohan's influence, Broadway's musical theater tradition was largely derivative of British and French work; Cohan gave the stage its American identity.[58] Beginning in 1901 with *The Governor's Son*, through the runaway hit *Little Johnny Jones, 45 Minutes from Broadway* (1905), to *Broadway Jones* (1914), Cohan remade American musical theater. Yet he never wrote for the critics; in fact, most reviewers such as James Metcalf were extremely hostile to his unrepentant, "vulgar comedy." Cohan dismissed them; as he frequently said, he wrote for the people, not the critics. His characters were from the ranks of the working class: maids, jockeys, secretaries, and struggling actors. His message or tone was simple, direct, and patriotic. As Oscar Hammerstein II remembered shortly after Cohan's death in 1942, "Never was a plant more indigenous to a particular part of the earth than was George M. Cohan to the United States of his day. The whole nation was confident of its moral superiority, its moral virtue, its happy isolation from the intrigues of the old country, from which many of our fathers and grandfathers have emigrated."[59]

In many ways, Cohan's situation mirrored Hollywood's attitude toward critics and historians in the early 1940s. Undoubtedly weary of the critical responses to historical filmmaking and historians' sublime contempt for Hollywood's lucrative historical work, Warner Brothers, like many other studios, was tired of hiring popular historians as script consultants and sending screenwriters off for weeks of preliminary research before they even began writing a script. Instead, writers turned increasingly to areas of modern history where historians could not bother them with arguments or minute criticisms. Writers such as Robert Buckner consulted Mr. and Mrs. Knute Rockne's private papers for *Knute Rockne, All American* (1940), looked at newspaper accounts and personal reminiscences of Lou Gehrig for *Pride of the Yankees* (1942), and later advertised their research practices in the film credits. Twentieth Century–Fox, the leader in traditional eighteenth- and nineteenth-century historical subjects, experienced a rebuff in 1940. While producer Kenneth Macgowan was in the midst of preparing the script for *Hudson's Bay*, he wrote to historian Grace Lee Nute asking for permission to read her galleys for a new history of the Hudson's Bay Company. She huffily declined, stating that films were one thing, and serious history another. "As a professional person," she wrote, "I am naturally more concerned with my reputation as a scholar than with a few hundred dollars that might come through allowing my manuscript to be made the basis of a fictionalized account of the founding of the Hudson's

Bay Company."[60] High-profile critics such as Frank Nugent were becoming increasingly intolerant of Hollywood's forays into American history. It is therefore perfectly understandable that Warner Brothers would choose a subject untouched by previous historiography and a protagonist who openly despised critics. Cohan and Hollywood producers shared a similar viewpoint. In 1924 Cohan had introduced his autobiography: "My idea in this story is to appeal to the general public. To me, the college professor with the tall forehead is of no more importance than the ordinary buck dancer or dramatic critic. My aim is to reach all classes and to be known as the 'Mary Pickford of the literary world.'"[61]

Cohan's autobiography irritated many who hoped for a more intimate view of its author. He focused overwhelmingly on his nineteenth-century childhood, the years of poverty with his parents and sister Josie in their pursuit of Broadway respect. *Twenty Years on Broadway* might well be retitled *My Life as Peck's Bad Boy*; Cohan even concluded his narrative with a quotation from that play, "And so he snuck off, all alone by himself, and nobody didn't see him no more."[62] This was a fitting conclusion, for in 1924, many critics were gleefully convinced that Cohan was finished on Broadway. Cohan hardly touched on the reason for this: his refusal to support actors' rights to organize a union. Cohan had always loathed the left-wing labor contingent on Broadway; he knew the worst of an actor's struggles from bitter experience, and since his success at the turn of the century, he had been known as the top-paying producer in the business. He supported his own way to success—individual action and hard work—and he loved to point out the many double standards in Actors' Equity. The original charter supported only billed actors' rights and refused equal treatment to the more needy chorus and stagehands. But Broadway did not forgive him and even attempted to expunge his name from its history. There were no revivals of his plays, and he found it more difficult to find backers. Shortly after his death, Actors' Equity predictably refused to give more than a paltry sum for a statue commemorating Cohan on Broadway.[63]

Yet neither Cohan's autobiography nor Robert Buckner's script mentioned the strike and the transformation of Cohan's postwar Broadway. Warner Brothers promised Cohan the right to edit his own story, and he exercised that right, much to Buckner's chagrin. Cohan altered his libretto as if it were one of his own revues, removing his first Jewish wife from his screen biography, along with any references to the strike controversy and his subsequent blackballing. Critics from 1943 to 1980 dismissed the film as a "fairy tale" with "few actual and factual details of his personal life," but in doing so, these critics ignored the fundamental structure of the film: it was meant to be Cohan's own tale—factual or fictional, actual or invented, unrevealing or embellished. Unlike standard historical films, Buckner intended to preserve the subjective autobiographical nature of the film by eliminating impersonal text historiography or forewords and instead projecting Cohan's voice (James Cagney) to introduce and narrate the entire film. It was his reminiscence, and like his autobiography, it excised or re-created a number of details. But Buckner used this rather blunt historical construct to justify a great deal of script invention.

In the opening scenes, Buckner fabricated a patriotic prologue that showed Cohan playing Franklin D. Roosevelt in Rogers and Hart's *I'd Rather Be Right*. According to an early biography of Cohan, the entertainer despised both the show and the patrician Roosevelt, who had never had to struggle for anything. Buckner nonetheless invented a meeting between the two where Cohan tells his life story to the president. Cohan was infuriated when he read the script. The Warner Brothers screenwriter not only introduced him in one of the few productions he had starred in that was not his own (and playing his least favorite role) but also had him narrating his life to a man he disliked on principle.[64] As Buckner planned it, Cohan confesses to Roosevelt that his life has been one of constant struggle and the pursuit of success. His scrappy childhood, lack of schooling, and constant rejection and blackballing by producers who resented his Irish ego were certainly more familiar to the Depression-era American public than Roosevelt's early life of unconscious privilege and wealth. Cohan may have been born at a time of national celebration and comfortable nineteenth-century prosperity, he may have achieved great personal success on Broadway, yet he is presented as a heroic anachronism, a fragment from the past who ironically cannot understand the new motion picture lingo in *Variety*.[65] The youngsters he meets in the early 1930s have never even heard of "I'm a Yankee Doodle Dandy" from *Little Johnny Jones*. Yet, as we find out in the course of the film, there is one Cohan song that the public remembers—"Over There." As Cohan leaves the White House, people are singing it, and Americans are joining up for the Second World War. Cohan may be forgotten, but his patriotism endures. In the final sequence, he is drawn into the marching ranks and the chorus.

In spite of Warner Brothers' efforts to honor Cohan's life and give him script approval, there were frequent skirmishes over the amount of personal and professional setbacks he endured. At the end of his life, Cohan did not want to dwell on his failures and his decline, and he wrote to

Opening shot: someone else presents George M. Cohan.

Independence Day, 1878. (*Yankee Doodle Dandy*)

Remembering "Over There." (*Yankee Doodle Dandy*)

the studio complaining that Buckner gave him too much adversity to deal with. Associate producer William Cagney and Buckner replied swiftly, attempting to gloss over his objections. "The dramatization of your life, Mr. Cohan, has a great and timely importance. It is the story of a typical American boy, who grew up with a strong love of his country, its ways and institutions. His life was spent in expressing and defending an American way of life."[66] Yet Cohan recognized that this remote address, this separation between "you, Mr. Cohan," and "his life," was the studio's way of molding his life into a defense of American ideals in the face of contemporary political crises. Being George M. Cohan, he did not want his life to play second fiddle to anything, least of all Franklin Roosevelt's policies. Cagney and Buckner replied that editing or changing a historical life "is the only way in which biographical pictures can be made interesting and worthy." Cohan was annoyed, but outside events were militating against his personal commitment to "accuracy" and directly infecting the motivation for making American historical films.

When Cohan responded to Buckner's first script with his own "more accurate" version, Buckner was livid, telling Hal Wallis that Cohan's script was a mere "egotistical epic." Cohan, he said, "has told the factual, year-by-year catalogue of his life. He has cut out the family's trouble getting started on Broadway. He has cut out romance. He has no dramatized failure or setback, except a minor incident which he immediately brushed off with another sensational hit. These are the major faults. Between them Cohan has written a series of largely disconnected scenes with no continuity or purpose but to pile up personal anecdotes of 'How I succeeded on Broadway.'"[67] These savage memos may have been the result of Buckner's considerable ego as a screenwriter. The truth is that Cohan had not neglected to confront his own youthful egotism and frequent setbacks in his 1924 autobiography. For all of Buckner's vaunted "research" on the project, he apparently never consulted the primary textual source. Cohan's preeminent objections to the scripts were tied to the studio's and Buckner's evolving sense of overarching historical importance. When it made superwesterns, Warner Brothers wanted to justify and laud American expansion. Likewise, when the studio was dealing with Cohan, it was determined to subsume his individual life beneath the contemporary needs of the American public. The film's mode of presentation and narration had become more important than the content. As William Cagney wrote to Hal Wallis, "The great Americanism theme of this picture is far more important at this time than the wish of a single individual to have his life presented in a manner that is historically correct." He continued,

"Cohan should be made to realize that this is a great American message at the most crucial period in American history and he should patriotically bow to our efforts to dramatically present the story of this great American spirit."[68] Cohan wanted a historical document that dealt accurately with his own construction of his career. Curiously, Warner Brothers' declaration justified the obscuring of historical facts in order to present and preserve a compelling historical argument. Hollywood had learned the secret trick of the successful historian: to sacrifice historical details in the name of an "enlightened argument." Yet this enlightened argument was now directly linked to expressing contemporary political ideologies.

In 1938 historian Allan Nevins argued that biography is the preeminent means of influencing the public's conception of history because "it humanizes the past" and makes it more accessible.[69] Yet because of this communicative ease, the biography is often denigrated by professional history as a less complicated and less illustrious view. Its popular appeal is also its intellectual nemesis. The fact that, particularly after 1938, Hollywood often advertised historical films with biographical titles attests to this popular allure and explains the ensuing professional condemnation of Hollywood's history. Nevins, however, defended biography: "It is perfectly valid to argue that the personal element in the past is less important that the communal element; that the cultural tendencies of any period, its great economic forces, its governmental forms and traditions . . . are in general more potent than the actions of any single man or coterie. . . . But . . . those economic forces, those governmental institutions, those cultural traditions and ideas . . . are interesting to me chiefly as elements against which [great Americans] . . . achieve their victories."[70] In the past, Hollywood filmmakers had often followed both these processes, employing nominal historical figures to explore issues in American history and pitting great individuals against national norms. But as the remarks of Cagney, Wallis, and Buckner demonstrate, biography or autobiography had become not a means of exploring the events and developments in America from 1878 to 1935 but simply a way to reconfigure audiences' relationship to the present. Although American historians Frederick Jackson Turner, Carl Becker, and Allan Nevins had variously admitted the present's influence on a historian's interpretation of history (the degree of influence and its importance forming the crux of the relativist debate), in 1942, Warner Brothers' historians asserted that the past, true or fabricated, was always inferior to the demands of the present generation and must serve those ends. History was simply in poor taste; biography was "egotism."

Unlike the prestigious historical films of 1941, *Yankee Doodle Dandy* avoided text forewords and intertitles. Crucial events in Cohan's personal life, such as his sister Josie's death, were not scripted. Buckner allowed Cohan only one failure: the play *Popularity*, ironically intended as a high-brow work to gain critical praise. When the attempt to meld intellectualism with a Cohan libretto failed, it took him no more than a screen minute to recover from the shock.[71] Hollywood avoided the Broadway strike carefully, as though still wincing from the recent successes of Hollywood directors', writers', and actors' guilds. Mentioning unionism, either to defend or to condemn it, was taboo. The Cagney family, all deeply involved in the production, had an equally pressing desire to keep left-wing politics out of the film. James Cagney's labor work in Hollywood had recently led to accusations of communism. An investigation cleared his name, but only a completely union-free George M. Cohan could expunge the taint.[72] Buckner, Wallis, and Cagney had accurately gauged the public mind. *Yankee Doodle Dandy* was a spectacular success, and although critics may have understood the strident patriotic continuity between the two world wars in the script, they also praised the evocative historical background. As *Los Angeles Times* critic Edwin Schallert wrote, "It brings to mind the passing pageant of American history through its chronicle of one man's huge success in the show business."[73] Cohan and *Yankee Doodle Dandy* represented the end of an entertainment era. John Barrymore, almost as famous as Cohan on Broadway, died on the day of the Los Angeles premiere, and the papers were full of the historical resonance.[74] Two years before, Barrymore had starred in his own satirical biography.

Cohan could not attend the film's premiere; he was dying of cancer in New York, and he did not live long enough to see James Cagney win the Academy Award for his performance. However, he did manage to see an advance print of the film at home. Although it is questionable whether the film exacerbated his decline, his daughter commented that it represented "the life Daddy would have liked to live."[75] This comment has been the basis for many academic assessments of the film as a Hollywood myth, a film that eradicated controversy and reconciled Cohan's career to a story of classic American values.[76] Yet there was more at stake in Hollywood's transformation of Cohan's life to support the present war effort and cleanse Cagney's career. Although Buckner and Wallis seemed to abandon historical narrative for mythic creation, their rewriting of Cohan's life was justified by the accepted practices of American historiography. According to Buckner and Wallis, they were merely exercising the right of any historian to edit his manuscript for dramatic emphasis. Their view of history was a living one—although the past and Cohan were honored, they had to be sacrificed for present demands. History was a living force with an active role in contemporary life. Cohan may have been contemptuous of both critics and Hollywood screenwriters, but even with Warner Brothers practicing its own form of creative editing, George M. Cohan's name was in lights on Broadway for the first time in years. Unfortunately for Cohan, the only kind of Broadway theater that would accommodate him was a movie theater.

From *Land of Liberty* to the Decline and Fall of *Citizen Kane*

> Self-evidently, it was impossible for me to ignore American history.
> —Orson Welles, 1940

The year 1936 had been a peak one for high-profile American histori-cal productions, but in spite of their diversity and sheer numbers,[1] one disgruntled filmgoer complained to Will Hays and Joseph Breen that no studio had produced a comparable prestige picture about the signing of the Constitution. It was significant that lawyer George W. Nilsson wrote to the two most famous censors in America rather than to a studio head.[2] After all, the historical foci at Warner Brothers, Paramount, MGM, and Twentieth Century–Fox were the unconventional Barbary Coast, Zieg-feld's Broadway, rebels such as Samuel Mudd, and poignant mixed-race heroines such as Ramona Moreno. Warner Brothers did make a film about the Revolution (*Give Me Liberty*, 1936), but it saved this stodgy establishment fare for educational shorts produced by Gordon "Holly" Hollingshead.[3] Yet Hays and Breen sympathized with Nilsson—and no wonder: the creation and signing of the Constitution were a triumph of bureaucratic cooperation. A film on this subject offered the prestige of a grand historical film without the censorship snags that often beset productions about the Civil War, Great War, and Prohibition eras. At Hays's request, his and Breen's departments compiled a preliminary list of

Hollywood's American historical output spanning the past twenty years.[4] The list, which included A and B features, serials, and educational shorts, included *Abraham Lincoln, The Iron Horse, Maid of Salem, Operator 13, The Plainsman, The Prisoner of Shark Island, Ramona, Show Boat, So Red the Rose,* and *The Vanishing American.* Although the researchers admitted that the list was "by no means complete," the search testified to the Production Code Administration's conservative definition of American history and its interest in controlling the fastest growing cycle in Hollywood. Although the brief list demonstrated the breadth of Hollywood's historical subject matter, even more apparent were the limitations of the censors' short list. Hays and his associates excised gangster-veteran biographies such as *Scarface* (Al Capone) and *I Am a Fugitive from a Chain Gang* (Robert Burns) and postwar histories such as *Three on a Match* (1932), *Heroes for Sale* (1933), and *Only Yesterday* (1934). Although there were no twentieth-century events and people included, they ignored even biographies of famous women (*Annie Oakley*) and controversial men (*Billy the Kid* and *Silver Dollar*). Instead, they promoted more conventional eighteenth- and nineteenth-century military topics that narrated the expansion of the frontier and the coming of the Civil War. But with the controversial *Gone with the Wind* in production, it was more necessary than ever for Hays and the PCA to assert their censorious power.

While Hays toyed with the idea of sponsoring an American historical film, Cecil B. DeMille's *The Plainsman* had been raking in most of the new year's box-office profits. Encouraged by his successful return to American history, the Paramount producer-director was already preparing the research and script for *The Buccaneer* with Jeannie Macpherson. As he had dominated the sex and religion spectacles of the postwar era, so DeMille now pushed to command the spectacle of American history. But the critical response to *The Plainsman* as a "historical" film was not encouraging; would the "DeMille touch" mar one of the most promising developments in American cinema?[5] DeMille may have been more showman than craftsman to America's "highbrow" audience, and the leading producers of American historical film, Darryl F. Zanuck and David O. Selznick, may have considered him an old-fashioned dinosaur, but DeMille was Hays's and Breen's most favored filmmaker. Selznick was a well-known renegade, and Zanuck, who cherished his rebel status at Warner Brothers and then his independence at Twentieth Century–Fox, had had far too many run-ins with the censors for them to trust his discretion as a historian. In late 1938, when the World's Fair Committee approached Hays and the Motion Picture Producers and Distributors of

America (MPPDA) about the industry's exhibition entry, Hays selected DeMille to oversee the production of a major American historical film to be shown at the two fairs in New York and San Francisco.[6] Rather than face the prohibitive cost, contractual obligations, and bickering of a pan-studio original feature, Hays authorized DeMille to edit and produce a feature-length series of clips from Hollywood's most prestigious American historical films to narrate the nation's history from pre-European times to the present.

Land of Liberty's general release in 1941 constituted the first major retrospective of Hollywood filmmaking. Its memorialization of the American historical cycle, however problematic in its dismemberment and reconfiguration of film fragments and historical evidence, indicated the death of Hollywood's most complex, controversial, and expensive venture since the advent of sound. This final chapter begins with a reconstruction of this triumphant endorsement of America's past, well publicized in its time but unmentioned in current film histories. Curiously, many of the individual films chosen to complete the grand narrative did not fit the unwavering discourse of progress and development that Hays and DeMille envisioned. It was a disturbing forced fit of evidence and history. Although DeMille slashed and sutured some of Hollywood's most prestigious historical films into a triumphant narrative, the seams of this massive, even monstrous historical document showed.

Another major American historical film released that year also returned to the roots of the cycle, reconfronting both traditional historiography's assemblage of fragmentary documents and Hollywood cinema's tendency to edit nuance and development in pursuit of a clear, quickly articulated story. But Citizen Kane's News on the March sequence is only the superficial beginning of its encounter with the disjunctive relationship between American myths of success and the decline of heroic history. Citizen Kane's ensuing cinematic excavation of the past complicates the national resolution of Land of Liberty in 1941, but shortly after its release, the film's scripted historical investigation (pursued most memorably in Kane's connections to William Randolph Hearst) disappeared from critical reviews and interpretations. As the years passed, Orson Welles's stylistic innovations were used to differentiate his new, modernist sensibility from the stodgier narratives of classical Hollywood cinema. With the lionization of André Bazin, the editors of Cahiers du cinéma, and later Andrew Sarris, Welles and Citizen Kane became emblems in a crusade to legitimize American directors as auteurs.[7] Yet Citizen Kane represents neither a single auteur's masterpiece nor a violent break with the so-called classical tradition. Both *Land of Liberty*'s and *Citizen Kane*'s conflicting attitudes toward writing the American past deliberately revisit the legacy of American historical filmmaking in the 1930s. Welles's and Herman Mankiewicz's reevaluation of *Cimarron* and the American self-made man in *Citizen Kane* are as harrowing as DeMille's and Hays's violent dismemberment of Hollywood's American historical cycle.

Reconstructing the Evidence

American Cavalcade, Our America, America, or *Land of Liberty,* as it was finally known, seemed an enormous task to negotiate. Hays and DeMille agreed to hire a high-profile "historical consultant" to lend the film that extra credibility. James T. Shotwell was a Columbia University professor of international relations, chairman of the American National Committee on Intellectual Cooperation, and director of the Division of Economics and History of the Carnegie Endowment for Peace. More than any other historian of his generation, his career was directed and amplified by his close association with the Wilson government. After the war, he continued to print variations of Wilson's vision for international cooperation and peace at the Carnegie Institute, editing a staggering number of texts on the social and economic history of the Great War, world economy, modern and contemporary European history, British history, and historiography.[8] His individual works, *War as an Instrument of National Policy and Its Renunciation in the Peace of Paris* (1929) and *On the Rim of the Abyss* (1936), did an eloquent job of redeeming the wartime competence of the Wilson administration and warning the United States of the price of isolation. Shotwell was undoubtedly the most government-approved economic historian in America, having also served under Wilson as chief of the Division of History at the Paris Peace Conference. Although he had edited the series that included John Maurice Clark's critical study of the postwar era,[9] Shotwell's own accounts of the war ignored the war protests, propaganda, and draconian antiespionage tactics of the government and instead focused on the successful economic mobilization of the country and Wilson's international idealism. Shotwell knew money, he knew how to tell an *official* history, and he had the kind of establishment credentials that Hays and Breen revered. Most important, he knew how to edit. But as DeMille would soon discover, Shotwell's ideas of editing history on film did little to help the project.

Although, superficially, Shotwell's and DeMille's views of the American past seemed identical and in accord with Hays's and Breen's intentions, the filmmaker gave the historian only a nominal role in the production. Shotwell was publicized as a "historical consultant," and the two bureaucracies joined hands in the trade papers, but Shotwell did not influence the outline of the script. Shotwell sent in his first treatment and interpretive monologue in October 1938,[10] but after looking it over, production assistant Arthur DeBra wrote to DeMille that the material was not of any particular use. According to DeBra, Shotwell's film ideas resembled the early efforts of a hack writer. His overarching theme, "the American saga: the history of America was born and nurtured in romance," was even less intellectually complex than DeMille and screenwriter Jeannie Macpherson's initial delineation of territorial expansion, religious freedom, and national glory.

Macpherson's continuity outline was clearer: "The theme we are trying to bring out in this story of America is LIBERTY (governmental and individual); EQUALITY (all races, all creeds); FREEDOM (speech, personal, press); PURSUIT OF HAPPINESS (for all men)."[11] She persisted, "The slogan and watchword that we are trying to bring out in our story is 'United we stand—Divided we fall.'" Each clip from each film, placed in relentless chronological order, was to support the film's thesis of national union. Macpherson and DeMille both saw the course of American history as a progressive and magnificent struggle for greatness, and they would manipulate Hollywood's historical filmmaking to support this premise. She continued, "We hope to show at the END of this picture, that after our country has been brought into a magnificent UNION . . . that every citizen in it must fight to the death, to see that this UNION is preserved and that no disturbing outside forces whatsoever, shall be permitted to split or destroy it."[12] The massive reappraisal of American historical cinema was certainly unusual, and although many studios may have objected to DeMille's rhetoric and the undue prominence he gave to his own few films in the editing process, no one wanted to argue with Hays and Breen or to turn down free publicity for their most recent prestige efforts. Although Macpherson occasionally tried to introduce some of the American people's more brutal actions (such as the burning of Atlanta and Columbia during the Civil War), these attempts were few and were often vetoed by the community of censors.[13]

DeMille and Shotwell's first idea was to surround the edited film clips with a suitable historical prologue, one that would convey a patriotic message to audiences with a minimum of rhetoric. DeMille never thought of the film as an isolated educational subject, but rather the sum of Hollywood's most spectacular historical pictures. Even though the film was intended as a curiosity for World's Fair audiences, he kept his eye on potential box-office returns for a general release. Early in production, he wrote to Hays that it was "absolutely essential to humanize and personalize our story in order to prevent its becoming a lengthy and perhaps dull educational feature with very little mass appeal. . . . I do not say that we should sugarcoat history but that we should inject in our story . . . a personal element that will make our audience feel it is a part and that its forebears have been a part of the American Cavalcade."[14] He planned to temper the history with an early sequence showing a typical American family listening to Roosevelt on the radio and discussing history in light of contemporary events. Yet it was nearly impossible for DeMille to keep his penchant for voice-of-God narration and didacticism under control. Macpherson was familiar with both pillars of DeMille's style and approached her historical research accordingly. Throughout January 1939 she organized the major events and people in American history along the lines of their appeal to different members of an ideal American family.[15] Hence, "Grandfather's list of heroes" included great American warriors such as King Philip and Stonewall Jackson, while "Grandmother's list of thinkers" included Massosoit, William Penn, and Susan B. Anthony. The boy in the family favored Leif Erikson's voyages, while Aunt Jane preferred scenes from Valley Forge and Gettysburg. Macpherson's original outline really took the epic approach, beginning in prehistoric times and carrying through the European settlement of the continent by various peoples, emphasizing that "America thus became the Melting Pot or rather crucible in which is destined to be fused all those living and enduring interests of mankind upon which a higher civilization can be based."[16] This was the dominant historical tone and encompassed the episodes of Valley Forge, Saratoga, Yorktown, Manifest Destiny, the Civil War, the Gettysburg Address, the settlement of California, and finally "Our Inheritance," the present. She concluded, "The wilderness was conquered, the continent made one and the nation and the children of those who achieved these exploits unparalleled in the annals of civilization, found themselves faced with another task even more difficult, that of assuring justice in the distribution of the inheritance."[17] The Great War, titled with Shotwellian flourish "The Great Crusade," concluded the chapter headings. Yet despite all these momentous events, strung out laboriously in fifteen episodes, Macpherson and DeMille's work insisted on America's perennial youth.[18] History, glorious cavalcade that it was, left the core of American struggle, development, age, and decay untouched.

Even as Macpherson outlined her historical background, she and De-

Mille retold the bloodless textual records with appropriate film titles.[19] Although DeMille endorsed a "Lowell Thomas" commentator to unite the formless film history with an appropriately grand narrative, this early "Cavalcade of America" illustrated DeMille's flawed memory of Hollywood's works of history. The 1929 British imperial African adventure *The Four Feathers* was supposed to illustrate "America before the white man came." A *Tale of Two Cities* (1935) and *The Count of Monte Cristo* (1935) were to show the religious persecution in Europe that drove colonists to the New World. *So Red the Rose* was to epitomize "the settlement of Virginia," *Drums along the Mohawk* was suppposed to represent the French and Indian War, and *The Buccaneer* was going to head the "Montcalm and Wolfe" segment. DeMille's grasp of historical periods was even more confused than Macpherson's truncated appraisal of the course of American history. Curiously, while *The Prisoner of Shark Island, Operator 13*, and *Little Women* were included to represent the Civil War, *So Red the Rose* was ignored in that regard. According to DeMille's records, *Jezebel*, an antebellum feature, was going to illustrate the Reconstruction era. His associates also ignored *Cimarron*, the industry's most prestigious and acclaimed American historical film. Although RKO's complex epic covered a historical period that could have illustrated several of Macpherson and DeMille's headings, the filmmakers filed it as an "Oklahoma oil field" film.

In spite of the filmmakers' spotty recollection of history, early versions of the script by Macpherson and Jesse Lasky Jr. constructed a unique historical prologue that emphasized the disparate views Americans held about their heritage.[20] The Waynes were a typical American family listening to one of FDR's fireside chats. The president is comparing the present instability in Europe with the travail America has endured. Each of the Waynes has a different perspective on America's military glory and defense of freedom. The last war is a particularly sore point of contention between the father and grandfather. While the grandfather, of Teddy Roosevelt's generation, is proud of their work in the Great War, his son, who actually fought on the Western Front, has no heroic memories or bombastic rhetoric with which to assault his own son. "I got gassed," he says tersely to the young boy. These contrasting personal attitudes toward the Great War operate as metaphors for the disparate historical views held by Americans in the more controversial twentieth century. Should the nation look inward or outward for its national future? Was isolationism possible or safe in the late 1930s? The young son, weary of his elders' bland patriotism and commitment to isolationism in an age that he believes demands more sacrifice, feels that the Depression generation has ruined America. "You're all so color-blind from saluting the Red, White, and Blue, you can't see the plain truth in black and white."[21] The ensuing meditation on American's cherished self-sufficiency articulated an underlying conflict between contemporary national and international identities.

Yet by the spring of 1939, DeMille, Hays, and Shotwell vetoed this personal prologue, with its contrasting views of the past and present, because it conflicted with their increasingly rigid view of American history. DeMille's progressive history, his story of the development of union, had such a clearly defined, authoritative thesis that the personal elements crucial to Hollywood historical filmmaking, the images of dissent and controversy, of little-known heroes and imagined heroines, simply disappeared in the march for unity. DeMille opened instead with one voice, the establishment voice, *his* voice, narrating the undisputed historical path.[22] This opening oral foreword ignored dispute and argument and trumpeted the country's irrefutable and immutable greatness. "America's history," DeMille began, "is a saga of struggle and achievement by millions of men and women who courageously labored [on] a home for freedom wherein all, regardless of race, creed, color, or position, might continue to enjoy the priceless heritage of LIBERTY."[23] The mosaic of impressive clips followed, unified by a suitably impressive supplementary commentary. This oral narration indicated the industry's view that films could not tell the relevant historical text from revolution to expansion, from Civil War to westward nation building, without extensive oral and textual commentary. In spite of the cinematic mosaic, the images were held in thrall of an inexorable historical persuasion defined by text. Images were incomplete and fragmented, and DeMille assumed that his voice was the only means of uniting his filmmaker colleagues' long-term commitment to American history. Late in production, he decided to add a director's prologue that expanded his own personal and professional vision for American history and American filmmaking. He wrote, "By the grace of God, the sacrifice of our forefathers, we sit here in a land that's free." Later, the film commentator would echo his sentiments, remarking, "This is no story from the Arabian Nights. It is the story of our own time. The world has just begun to be civilized. Brute force gives way to intelligence. . . . No wonder, therefore that the pathway of Progress is blocked by Ignorance and the ideals of Justice and Liberty at times are dimmed. Humanity is on the march." [24]

Final continuities began with these fulsome historical forewords acclaiming "the priceless heritage of liberty and democracy." The Civil War became a tragic but necessary struggle against slavery rather than an expression of brutality and economic pressures. The nation's involvement in the Great War became "our answer when Democracy was challenged." The World's Fair release continuity, dated 20 June, was impressively titled "Land of Liberty: A Cavalcade of American History Drawn from Film Classics Produced during the Past Quarter Century."[25] Lincoln was one of the few historical figures given the opportunity to narrate his historical perspective (reciting the Gettysburg Address, of course). Yet in spite of individual American historical films' exploration of unusual historical perspectives and people, DeMille and Hays kept the conglomerate's discourse to the most traditional and textbook-bound events and figures. In their entirety, films had emphasized struggle, controversy, the voices of both men and women, and the participation of different races and ethnicities. DeMille and his team of editors cut the film texts into emblematic and manageable fragments. Iconic portraits of presidents, mythic images of anonymous gunfighters and soldiers replaced a once prominent cast of women in American historical film. Only presidential wives Mary Todd Lincoln and Dolley Madison made it to the film's program, which was headlined by such names as Patrick Henry, George Washington, Thomas Jefferson, Napoleon, Prince Albert of Britain, William Jennings Bryan, and Woodrow Wilson. American women were known only as the appendages of statesmen.

According to the program, 124 films were used in the editing process, yet many of them were not American historical films (*The Adventures of Marco Polo, Viva Villa, Victoria the Great*) or even historical films (*Dead End, The Ten Commandments*). Controversy was edited. The Native American perspective in the push westward vanished from the text; films with Native American or mestizo protagonists, such as *The Vanishing American*, never made the preliminary cut. From *Cimarron*, DeMille used only the gunfighting sequence.[26] *Ramona*, originally slated to form part of the expansionist picture, was also cut. No doubt when DeMille's team looked at the footage, they realized that *Ramona* hardly endorsed white westward expansion. *Jezebel's* only contribution was Preston Dillard's portentous comment, "On a war of commerce, the North will win." DeMille excluded the rest of *Jezebel's* pro-southern rhetoric but included Duncan Bedford's anti-Confederate sentiments from *So Red the Rose*. Lincoln's voice soothed and settled the divisions of the Civil War.

Land of Liberty represented the epitome of consensus history. It was not made by Hollywood's historical filmmakers but was culled by censors and government officials and Hollywood's most conservative showman. It was released as a fourteen-reel novelty in 1939 in San Francisco and New

York, but after substantial editing in 1940, MGM rereleased a shorter, more palatable version to accommodate the country's push toward war in 1941. In the months between the summers of 1939 and 1941, American historical filmmaking had grown to approximate the demands of the PCA and the florid patriotic style of DeMille. Although Warner Brothers made legitimate history out of *The Roaring Twenties* and George M. Cohan, Twentieth Century–Fox made its own *Hollywood Cavalcade*, and Samuel Goldwyn continued to release modern biopics such as *Pride of the Yankees* (Lou Gehrig), the majority of filmmakers repeated the success of revolutionary and frontier epics epitomized in *Land of Liberty*.

Historian Louis Gottschalk once complained to filmmaker Samuel Marx that Hollywood's historical filmmakers owed its patrons "a greater accuracy" and that "no picture of a historical nature ought to be offered to the public until a reputable historian has had a chance to criticize and revise it."[27] Although filmmakers often worked with popular historians, and although screenwriters read the most recent academic work in preparation for writing a historical script, *Land of Liberty* was the most publicized production to use an academic historian in an advisory capacity. Yet this pretentious association with an outside "professional historian" resulted not in a prestigious, pathbreaking reappraisal of American history but rather in the supreme conventionalization of the cycle.[28] According to Macpherson's extensive background research and DeMille's film resources, Shotwell looked over scripts and research but did not contribute much more than his name. As DeMille's aides pointed out, the historian was practically useless except as a liaison to the World's Fair Committee and Hays. If Shotwell's presence represented the contribution of a professional historian to American filmmaking, then it is fortunate that Hollywood screenwriters managed their own research for so long.

Shotwell oversaw a production that eschewed the recent developments in historical filmmaking, the arguments and correctives to the traditional narrative, that had motivated so many of the early sound-era historical films. He also seemed anxious to separate filmed history from the respectable form of written history, and in the 1939 World's Fair program introduction, which sounds like an apology to his colleagues, he wrote: "It is not, therefore, as a rival to the written word that this narrative is presented. . . . Rather it is a new and challenging way of evoking the past and contemplating the present, one designed to enrich and strengthen our interest in the story which historians provide."[29] The press found the film stirring and suitably serious;[30] World's Fair audiences were happy, and although the 1941 general release was not a great success, DeMille and Hays's impressment of American history in the service of contemporary war work pleased the studios. Yet Shotwell, who had been Hays's choice to lend the film some historical prestige, reaffirmed the balance of power between filmmakers and real historians. In the past ten years, American historical filmmaking *had* become traditional historiography's rival, and far from ignoring the written word, it had appropriated the old tools of historiography to form a popular and critical audience that no historian could ever hope to match. Yet, paradoxically, the cycle's success would become its nemesis.

In the years since 1930, American historical filmmaking had been transformed from an experimental and sometimes innovative prestige practice to a lucrative business. Historical periods and figures in American history could initiate battles between Darryl Zanuck and Jack Warner or Warner and David O. Selznick. It was a thriving business formula for all the studios. But *Land of Liberty*'s release suggests that the cycle was nearly finished. Its run at the World's Fair, intended to honor American history in the cinema, may have had the studios' individual cooperation, but the film was a retrospective. Had the cycle ended? Most of the filmmakers whose work was showcased in the film had left historical filmmaking. By 1940, Howard Estabrook had given up all historical screenwriting, and Nunnally Johnson was turning producer-director. Dudley Nichols was disgusted with Hollywood mediocrity and went back to Connecticut. Sidney Howard was dead. Selznick was exhausted. Zanuck approached the production of *Lillian Russell* with uncharacteristic indifference. Hal Wallis and Michael Curtiz were fed up with Robert Buckner, Errol Flynn, and the whole superwestern cycle. Jeanette MacDonald's and Mae West's careers were faltering. Henry Fonda emerged from *The Grapes of Wrath* even more determined to leave Zanuck and the historical roles that had made his reputation.[31] DeMille abandoned major American historical figures and events for the peripheral Canadian Rockies (*Northwest Mounted Police*, 1941) and a sexed-up Key West shipping saga (*Reap the Wild Wind*, 1942). Critics such as Frank S. Nugent and Howard Barnes were bored or dismissive. By 1940, *Cimarron* and its reception seemed to belong to another era.

RKO, Raising Kane in 1941

RKO's expensive 1931 bid for equality with the major studios had not ended its commitment to making historical pictures, but throughout the 1930s, those efforts were circumscribed by poor finances. The studio was always one step away from bankruptcy, and as Ginger Rogers recalled, production chiefs changed so frequently that one never knew whose name would be on the front office door.[32] RKO was not the only studio facing a bleak future; antitrust suits and the lost foreign markets filled the pages of *Variety* in 1939 and 1940. But in 1940, the new head of production, George Schaefer, ignored the industrial warnings and pushed the studio once more toward the vanguard of historical filmmaking. Just as William LeBaron had once purchased an expensive Edna Ferber novel and hired Broadway talent Howard Estabrook, Schaefer now imported Robert Sherwood to write the screen adaptation of his Pulitzer Prize–winning play *Abe Lincoln in Illinois*. Although the film received a great deal of critical praise, particularly from New York critics,[33] only a box-office miracle would have saved the expensive film from the red ink. Schaefer must have been worried, for that year he also invested in another innovative Broadway entertainer, Orson Welles.[34] During the late 1930s, Welles had tested the limits of theatrical tradition, producing the first all-black *Macbeth* and courting public controversy with *The Cradle Will Rock*. Bored and restless on Broadway, Welles accepted RKO's offer to give him complete artistic control over his next two films.[35]

It was an unprecedented deal, especially for one with no filmmaking experience and an erratic reputation. The industry was worried. As film historian Robert Carringer wrote, by giving Welles control over the final cut, "Schaefer had violated one of the most sacred canons of the industry."[36] But Schaefer, courting prestige and following the policy of his predecessor William K. LeBaron, took another exceptional chance.[37] Welles, however, continued to shock, and after his first tour of the studio, he made an offhand remark that Hollywood would never forget. Asked what he thought of the movies, Welles laughed and said, "I think it's the greatest train set a boy ever had." Whether candid or dramatically calculated, this response was ill timed. Filmmaking had become a legitimate business and serious art in the minds and words of many Hollywood filmmakers. The past ten years of historical pictures had been a crucial contribution to this advance, and many considered it a magnanimous gesture for Hollywood to allow a Broadway unknown to control his own film work as if he were a Cecil B. DeMille. Welles's dismissal of the film industry as a child's toy hardly endeared him to Hollywood's elite.

Over the next few months, Welles continued to make professional decisions that widened the rift between him and the studio. He refused to be integrated into the production system. Rather than learning to work with a Hollywood cast, he brought his Mercury Theater Company to Hollywood. His adaptation of *Heart of Darkness* went over budget and was deemed a poor box-office risk. His next adaptation, of Cecil Day-Lewis's espionage thriller *Smiler with a Knife*, failed when Carole Lombard refused to star in it.[38] Realizing that he was in trouble, Welles asked the studio to hire screenwriter Herman Mankiewicz to show him the mechanics of good screenwriting. It was an interesting partnership. Mankiewicz had been one of the first to realize the potential power of screenwriters in sound cinema. In the late 1920s he had lured some of the best writers from New York, including Ben Hecht, Nunnally Johnson, and his younger brother Joseph. Many of them became important filmmakers through their historical scripts, and Mankiewicz had doctored his share, including *The Royal Family of Broadway*, *Bombshell*, and *The Great Ziegfeld*. But having worked primarily at MGM and Paramount, Mankiewicz did not achieve the autonomy of some of his peers at RKO, Warner Brothers, and Twentieth Century–Fox. He was always one of several writers working on a script and often did not receive screen credit.

In his spare time, though, Mankiewicz wrote original screenplays. Although they were unproduced, his biographies of evangelist Aimee Semple McPherson and John Dillinger testified to the current wisdom that historical writing was the way out of hack writing.[39] He preferred writing about his generation's most controversial figures, people who achieved national status in the newspapers before becoming historical material. When Frank Capra persuaded Harry Cohn to buy Robert Riskin's 1930 play about McPherson, *Bless You Sister* (later released with Barbara Stanwyck as *The Miracle Woman*, 1931), the studio had to camouflage as many historical references as possible.[40] Several years after his death, Dillinger remained an even more dangerous topic. Although the press loved to foster rumors about an impending Dillinger biopic,[41] after *Scarface's* notorious national reception, Hays had made it nearly impossible for a biographical gangster film to reach theaters. In 1940, although Mankiewicz was at another low in his career, Welles encouraged him to write a treatment of an idea they had discussed in New York. Mankiewicz's ensuing original screenplay was a biography of a prominent newspaperman and public figure, a fusion of modern history and its journalistic counterpart. The script was no "imagined" biography, and as it developed, Welles kept publicity in check and a closed set to keep the identity of their subject a secret. In lieu of Dillinger, Mankiewicz had chosen his generation's next most controversial figure to film: William Randolph Hearst.

In an infamous 1971 article, critic Pauline Kael reasserted the centrality of Mankiewicz and William Randolph Hearst in the authorship and production of *Citizen Kane*.[42] It was a bold move at a time when academic film studies was gaining credibility by focusing on directorial style and eliminating the importance of historical content. Christian Metz's semiotic studies of film form valorized the structure of film narration, but content was an area beneath notice. In the 1960s and 1970s the study of film history had far too many connotations of the out-of-date (Terry Ramsaye's film history), the honorific (William K. Everson's film series), the sensational (Charles Higham's star biographies), and the downright filthy (Kenneth Anger's *Hollywood Babylon*). Kael's investigation of Hearst and Mankiewicz seemed to be an attack on the authorial power of Welles and an attempt to marginalize individual visual style while raising the banal contribution of Hollywood writing and gossip. The fact that Kael was not an academic but a critic for the *New Yorker* was just as irritating.

With time, the recent reconceptualization of film history, and Robert Carringer's careful study *The Making of* Citizen Kane, Hearst's presence has been admitted into canonical accounts of *Citizen Kane*.[43] But scholars often use Hearst as merely historical shorthand to explore Welles's more fascinating examinations of American isolationism (Laura Mulvey) and the mythic hero (Morris Beja).[44] Welles's complex objective versus subjective cinematic vision, visual metaphors, and spectacular parables still motivate the appraisals by James Naremore, David Bordwell, and Dudley Andrew.[45] Within this framework, the film's meditations on nostalgia, time, and the impossibility of objective vision all spring from Welles and his personally marked cinematic style. To acknowledge Mankiewicz as the "author" would seem to valorize the text, the script, and the historical precedent over the image and the creative genius of the filmmaker, so film studies continue to avoid Mankiewicz and his complex interpretation of American history. But within William Randolph Hearst's career as a journalist, within the trajectory of post–Civil War history, within Mankiewicz's original script and Welles's film lie the essential conflicts between objective and subjective accounts of the past and the struggle against American decline. For the past ten years, these layers of historical knowledge had been some of the organic components of Hollywood's American historical cycle.

Citizen Hearst

Mankiewicz and Welles's selection of Hearst as the subject of a major historical film violated many of the more recent formulas in screen biographies. "Willie" Hearst was no pioneer who made good through effort and education. It was his father, George Hearst, who was born in a poor Missouri frontier settlement and witnessed the 1849 gold strike. It was George who made the Hearst millions in silver and copper; became the good-hearted, boisterous, self-made man; and ended his life with a government career and public respect.[46] Indeed, mining colleagues of Hearst's father such as H. A. W. Tabor and leading Californians such as John Sutter became the subjects for early sound-era historical films (*Silver Dollar* and *Sutter's Gold*). In fact, considering his log-cabin birth, southern roots, Confederate sympathies during the Civil War, and longtime residence in San Francisco, it is surprising that George Hearst was never the subject of a Depression-era historical film. George Hearst had all the raw humor, shrewdness, and common sense of a Lincoln and the wealth and flamboyance of a Diamond Jim Brady.

His only son, Willie, was another matter. Born during the Civil War in San Francisco, Willie was a spoiled heir. His mother took him on his first European tour when he was ten, and before he was twenty he had been expelled from Harvard. In January 1887 George gave up on making him a steady citizen and businessman and gave Willie the struggling *San Francisco Examiner* with great misgivings. For the next fifty years, William Randolph Hearst would remain the national press's most towering and temperamental star, a man who began by attacking the corrupt California railroad industry and providing moving human-interest stories, but who ended up "inventing" news and fomenting the international disaster of the Spanish-American War. As biographer W. A. Swanberg wrote, "In truth, Hearst was not a newspaperman at all in the conventional sense. He was an inventor, a producer, and arranger. The news that actually happened was too dull for him, and besides it was also available to other papers. He lived in a childlike dream world, imagining wonderful stories and then going out and creating them, so that the line between fact and fancy was apt to be fuzzy."[47] According to his antagonistic contemporary Joseph Pulitzer and his biographer Ferdinand Lundberg,[48] Hearst cared nothing for objectivity and the discovery of news. He wanted to create his own American legend, one as different as possible from the traditional American success story that was his father's life.

His reportage of the Spanish-American War in 1898 was a turning point in his career, the moment when he forsook the crusading inspiration of his early antirailroad days for the notoriety and circulation increases of yellow journalism. One of his most notorious aphorisms was directed at artist Frederic Remington, a Hearst employee who had been assigned to Havana to cover the Cuban rebellion against Spain. Remington, seeing no prospect of war, had cabled Hearst that he wanted to return to New York. Hearst replied, "Please remain. You furnish the pictures and I'll furnish the war."[49] In an ensuing onslaught of press coverage by his papers, Hearst exaggerated the Spanish menace, fabricated eyewitness reports of imperial brutality, and championed the exclusive story of captive rebel Evangelina Cosio y Cisneros.[50] Americans learned to hate Spain, and when the *Maine* sank, Hearst's jingoism and imperial hatred increased tenfold. Yet for all his vaunted muscular democracy, Hearst's press campaign against Spain's presence in the Western Hemisphere laid the foundations for a new age of American imperialism, one founded not on spheres of trade but on spheres of frontier rhetoric. As George Hearst respresented the traditional nineteenth-century froniter hero, so William Randolph Hearst embodied the imperial corruption of the frontier ideology in the twentieth century. Historian William Appleman Williams traced the legacy of the frontier, commenting in *The Tragedy of American Diplomacy*, "When Americans *thought* that the continental frontier was gone, they advanced and accepted the argument that continued expansion in the form of overseas economic and even territorial expansion provides the best, if not the only, way to sustain their freedom and prosperity."[51]

Hearst's notoriety as a master yellow journalist eventually caused his failure in politics and his decision to spend the remainder of his father's millions on the production of motion pictures. During the Great War his International Pictures produced the xenophobic but successful serial *Patria*, and during the 1920s his wealth and friendship with Louis B. Mayer secured a merger of their film companies. Hearst's relationship with Mayer, his multiple collaborations with actress Marion Davies, and the creation of his palatial retreat San Simeon provided the base for his almost feudal social influence in the film community.[52] A surprising number of Davies's films for Hearst were period subjects (including *Little Old New York*, 1923, and *Janice Meredith*, 1924), yet only *Operator 13*, released late in the actress's career in 1934, maintained any interest in presenting a historical background independent of Davies's character. At the same time that Hearst was financing one of the new American historical films, one of his reporters, Willis J. Abbot, was remembering his years working for the Hearst papers. Abbot's book described the true yellow journalist as one who "can work himself into quite as fiery a fever of enthusiasm over a Christmas fund or a squalid murder, as over a war or a presidential campaign. He sees everything through magnifying glasses and can make a first-page sensation out of a story which a more sober paper would dismiss with a paragraph inside."[53] Curiously, Abbot's comments about Hearst's press sense resonate with contemporary censors and late-twentieth-century historians' views of classical Hollywood historical films: the preoccupation with trivia, the inaccuracies, the films of the wrong events and notorious people, the callow narratives. And although it would be difficult to justify Hearst's 1898 war coverage, his early crusades against the establishment and his desire to provide real news for real people on the streets[54] resembled the visions of filmmakers such as Darryl Zanuck, David Selznick, and even Orson Welles.

The American

Although Welles and Mankiewicz would later stake separate claims as sole author of *Citizen Kane,* and although scholars have continued to debate whether the film was entirely an auteur's masterpiece or a Hollywood collaboration, Carringer sensibly credited much of the historical content in the first script of "The American," linking Charles Foster Kane and William Randolph Hearst, to Herman Mankiewicz.[55] What Carringer neglected in his analysis of the Hearst connection was Mankiewicz's career as a part-time historical screenwriter and script doctor, his familiarity with the evolving historical cycle in Hollywood and its prestige, and the possibility that the successful application of the historical approach might save Welles's and his own reputations.[56] But as both would soon discover, selecting Hearst as the subject of a major historical motion picture could prove fatal. Although Hearst had courted public attention in his youth, since the war and Franklin Roosevelt's election, he had been the subject of increased and sometimes libelous criticism. By June 1937, he was forced to relinquish financial control of his publishing enterprises. Although he became a recluse at San Simeon, a structure later described as "one man's revolt against history,"[57] Hearst could still wield considerable power in Hollywood.

When Mankiewicz completed the treatment in April 1940, "The American" was over three hundred pages and had so many obvious references to Hearst that even Welles felt compelled to edit some of the more inflammatory contents.[58] In the beginning, Kane's parents are the poor owners of a Colorado boardinghouse, but his mother is left a fortune from a miner's claim, and the stuffy businessman Walter Thatcher, Charlie's newly appointed guardian, takes the youngster on a tour of the big cities. Mankiewicz clearly drew from Hearst's Anaconda mining inheritance, his parents' pioneer roots and upbringing, his headstrong devotion to his mother, and his own will. Mankiewicz writes of Kane's early inspired newspaper days, his young paper struggling against the entrenched reputation of the *Chronicle,* his obsession with circulation, his flagrant and cheerful use of blackmail to get stories. In this first draft, Mankiewicz even paraphrases Hearst's famous remark to Remington,[59] and with his slow abandonment of the Declaration of Principles in favor of increasing circulation and creating news, Kane falls inexorably from public figure to demagogue. As he moves into the international stage, he encounters a paradoxical sense of isolation that is salved only partially by compulsive antique buying and a younger woman. But even with his massive reputation, Mankiewicz impugns the Kane/Hearst image. He is no hero. As Thatcher writes in his diary: "Fifty years after my death, I am confident that the whole world will agree with my opinion of Charles Foster Kane, assuming that he is not completely forgotten, which I regard as extremely likely."[60] Even Kane realizes that he is not a great man in the traditional sense and can never compete with the likes of Abraham Lincoln. While courting Emily, the president's niece, on a visit to the White House, he looks at a portrait of Lincoln. "I'm afraid that if I'd been born a rail-splitter — I'd be a rail-splitter now," he says.[61]

In the second draft, Welles removed references to Hearst's (Kane's) expulsion from college, a rendering of the "stolen" election that Hearst had lost to Tammany supporters years before, gossipy tidbits about his first-nighter status in New York, and an especially dangerous reference to the death of one of Marion Davies's (Susan's) lovers while at San Simeon (Xanadu) — the mysterious death of Hollywood director Thomas Ince aboard a yacht. Instead, Welles bolstered the love triangle of Kane, Emily, and Susan. Whether he realized it or not, Welles's emendations were merely what Zanuck had done to *Drums along the Mohawk,* Selznick to *Gone with the Wind,* and Hal Wallis to *Dodge City* a year ago. Yet paradoxically, even with Welles's alterations, Kane's (Hearst's) ties to American history are unbroken and even enhanced.

After seeing the film, one of Hearst's biographers, Ferdinand Lundberg, brought suit against RKO for plagiarism. Indeed, Carringer pointed out that several facts about the dates and details of Hearst's acquisition of the *Examiner* were lifted bodily and in sequence from Lundberg's *Imperial Hearst.*[62] However, Lundberg's acerbic and even libelous biography (he accused Hearst of blowing up the *Maine* to provoke war and boost circulation) has little in common with *Citizen Kane*'s narrative beyond the major unalterable events in Hearst's life. According to Lundberg, Hearst "had no intention of sincerely fighting on the people's side" in his early crusades against the railroads, and his new human-interest stories were merely "for the delectation of gaping chambermaids."[63] In his foreword to Lundberg's biography, historian Charles Beard calls Hearst "a colossal failure," but Mankiewicz and Welles's complex narrative, with its multiple and conflicting perspectives, is not as polemical or damning. It thus seems far more likely that Oliver Carlson and Ernest Sutherland Bates's contemporaneous *Hearst, Lord of San Simeon*, which admitted the biases of any biography, was Mankiewicz's primary source. Their introduction could have been Welles's story outline: "The setting will be found in his divided inheritance of temperament and ideals, his privileged upbringing, his California background of raucous wealth, crude force, and noisy demagoguery, and in his unhappy experiences when western impudence first encountered eastern snobbishness . . . how in his imaginary world such concepts as truth and sincerity came to have no meaning; how he went from masquerade to masquerade not so much to hide himself as to find himself, always finding another mask—from journalism to politics . . . how he grew old and hardened until Hollywood revived him."[64]

In the last stages between press and general release, the rumors that *Citizen Kane* was a biography of Hearst and that the film would be suppressed were so strong that Hearst papers banned any mention of the film (and, for a time, any RKO production). Hearst's friend Louis B. Mayer attempted to purchase the negative from RKO in order to destroy it.[65] Welles even issued a statement in *Friday* magazine: "*Citizen Kane* is not about Louella Parson's boss. It is the portrait of a fictional newspaper tycoon."[66] RKO's Richard Baer was so worried about a Hearst lawsuit that he gave a deposition in May 1941 claiming the film's fictional status. These were necessary lies in the face of censorship and the possible destruction of the negative. As with *Scarface*'s backers a decade ago, Welles had a great deal of support from the non-Hearst press. But whereas *Scarface*'s champions such as Robert Sherwood had praised its honest confrontation of postwar America and its portrayal of Al Capone, many of *Citizen Kane*'s press supporters skirted the issue of history and ignored Mankiewicz's contribution to the film. Bosley Crowther of the *New York Times* would not even mention Hearst's name but called the historical connections "an uncommon fuss" and "cryptically alleged" by Kane detractors.[67] Otis Fergusson of the *New Republic* did mention Hearst but dismissed the relationship as "distinctly coincidental." He characterized the story (a Welles invention) as simply, "Once upon a time there was a man of whom certain things were remembered."[68] Their denial of the film's historical aspects and ties to the cycle were most likely intended to save Welles from a lawsuit and the film from suppression. Instead, their reviews lauded Welles as a supremely innovative filmmaker.

Crowther, eager to establish himself after Frank Nugent's departure from the *New York Times* and to forge a relationship with new filmmakers, took particular pleasure in denigrating old Hollywood and the subjects of his predecessor's reviews. For Crowther, Welles's direction had "more verve and inspired ingenuity than any of the elder craftsman have exhibited in years." Mankiewicz and the script disappeared from view in a haze of Welles coverage. In their efforts to push the film's visual innovation as a means of camouflaging its historical content, cameraman Gregg Toland gave interviews about deep-focus photography and realism and received lavish commendation.[69] Relations between Welles and Mankiewicz deteriorated, as had those between Ford and Nichols over the historical content and authorship of *Stagecoach* two years before. With the eastern press coverage, *Citizen Kane* became an artistic milestone, a cinematic experience independent of the rest of Hollywood filmmaking.

The laurels Welles received in New York may have reinforced his sense of genius, for he continued to assert his film's fictional status and his own creative powers. Although he resented Hearst and the history receiving as much attention as he did in Hollywood, Welles never denied the film's inspiration from post–Civil War American history. In another written defense, he admitted, "It was impossible for me to ignore American history."[70] Throughout production, Welles not only retained most of Mankiewicz's historical connections and biographical threads but also structured them with an elaborate system of text prologues, constructed newsreel footage, and voice-over commentary. The foreword, prologue, and newsreel, which both referenced and impugned the structural and discursive achievements of historical films of the past ten years, were hardly mentioned by the press. Like many of these earlier American historical films, *Citizen Kane*'s most controversial material was developed in the script, not by the camera. Although Pauline Kael, Robert Carringer, Laura Mulvey, and Morris Dickstein noted Welles's indebtedness to the biopic cycle, Welles's historical perspective, his dual engagement with both American history and film historiography of the past decade, has never been sufficiently acknowledged. In spite of *Citizen Kane*'s critical acclaim as a brilliant anomaly in Hollywood cinema, as the harbinger of a more mature film technique, Welles always conceived of his film as an American biography, his narrative as part of American history. From the outset, Welles was obsessed with rewriting and reconsidering America's post–Civil War past, and his film must be reconsidered as a response to

Hollywood's now fully established historical cycle and a return to the historical possibilities initiated by *Cimarron* years before. Schaefer, well aware of RKO's history, had one ambition in 1939–1940: to improve RKO's prestige output and bankability. A decade ago, William LeBaron's expensive investment in Edna Ferber ($125,000) and Howard Estabrook had briefly made RKO the leader in prestige pictures, but in the years since, the studio had been forced to cut corners and historical productions as its competitors outdistanced it with American historical films. In 1940–1941, RKO and *Citizen Kane* did more than return to the production gambles of the past; they reinterpreted the studio's most controversial and acclaimed production: *Cimarron.*

Mankiewicz, more familiar with the mechanics of historical cinema, envisioned the complete prologue in the first draft of "The American." As in *The Roaring Twenties,* a newsreel resembling Henry Luce's "The March of Time" documented the life of Welles's recently deceased protagonist, Charles Foster Kane, a major newspaper publisher and public figure. As in *Cimarron,* the film used a complex series of date superimpositions and projected text titles. The earliest draft from April 1940 has a twenty-three-page historical prologue that, like the entirety of *Cimarron,* unites the major dates in post–Civil War history to the present with the life span of one man (1865–1941). In the opening reels of the film, Welles and Mankiewicz present the establishment view of Kane, a newsreel account of his public persona and prominent roles in a series of national and international incidents from the Spanish-American War to the Great War to the rise of Adolf Hitler. The images are eclectic fragments from the past, spatially and temporally disjunctive and sutured by projected and spoken text: 1906, the year of the San Francisco earthquake and fire; 1918, the armistice; 1898, the Spanish-American War; 1910 and 1922, punctuated with documentary footage showing the oil scandals, suffrage and the Nineteenth Amendment, Prohibition, and the introduction of FDR and the Tennessee Valley Authority. Mankiewicz planned to use actual newsreel clips of William Jennings Bryan (another associate of Hearst), Stalin, Al Smith, McKinley, Landon, and Roosevelt. Kane would later be seen in the company of stage and screen performers George M. Cohan and Al Jolson. There was to be no boundary between history and journalism; even events of 1941 would be contained within the iconography and structures of historical filmmaking.

Accompanying the great story of America is the odd counterpoint and decline of Kane's influence and life. Sometimes America's and Kane's fates are intertwined. On screen, the narrator tells of Kane's support of the

Remembering the Great
War: a graveyard in
1919. (*Citizen Kane*)

Spanish-American War with a shot of Teddy Roosevelt parading through
cheering crowds. Then Kane's "opposed participation in another" war—
World War I—is shown, not with cheering crowds (which would have
invalidated Kane's antiwar stance) but with a silent shot of miles of American grave markers in Flanders. As far as the Great War was concerned
in the 1920s and 1930s, history vindicated Kane. We also are shown his
receding newspaper influence and massive wealth, the highlights of his
lurid romances and reclusive lifestyle. Mankiewicz and Welles introduce
the newsreel technique familiar to all cinemagoers. Yet as many film historians have noticed, this seemingly precise and objective account of Kane's
relationship to American history is problematic from the outset. Contrasting perspectives on his life (fascist, communist) seem to be silenced by
the text of his own words superimposed on the screen: "I am, have been,
and will be only one thing—an American." Text would seem to silence
the strident businessmen and Union Square orators, to stop the glut of
documentary images, and to unify the trajectory of his life and American
history within one personal statement. But Kane's words, silently superimposed on a black screen and lacking a voice, are also incomplete and
ambiguous.

The irony of this sequence is one that Hearst himself had to endure.
Kane, the arbiter of text who once determined the tone of American
newsprint, loses his hold over the printed word, and near the end of his
life, other newspapers are able to narrate his decline and loss of influence.
Superficially, the newsreel has the monotonous and vaunted impartiality
of DeMille's assemblage and narration in *Land of Liberty*. *Kane's* pro-

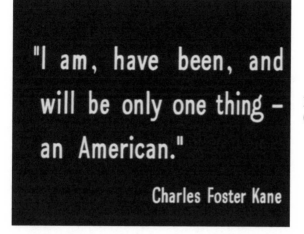

Kane's declaration.
(*Citizen Kane*)

logue also has the documentary footage and sparse prose associated with the journalistic objectivity claimed by Hearst's archrival Joseph Pulitzer. But even with the omniscient totalizing control of the voice-over and the historical text inserts, the fragmented footage subverts the illusion of textual completion. The moment the official screening ends and the lights go up in the projection room, the news editor sends a reporter in search of the "real story."

The official text, reminiscent of previous American historical prologues and forewords, is superseded by Welles's new visual history.[71] So begin the contrasting histories—the disjunctive, episodic, establishment newsreel history and the nonlinear, contradictory, personal visual history. Film theorist Garrett Stewart characterized these flashbacks as the "outtakes" of the *News on the March* film, the moments when consciousness and duration are subsumed by "the replay of history's mechanical (edited) time."[72] Welles's visual investigation of Kane's past restores what historical documentation, text, and traditional biographies have excised from historiography: a sense of time, complex development, and a personal internal acknowledgment of death and decline. One of Welles's and Mankiewicz's most evocative historical juxtapositions occurs when Thompson (the reporter) has his first encounter with Kane's past in the sepulchral Thatcher library.[73]

Shortly after watching an official biographical documentary on Charles Foster Kane, a newspaper editor sends one of his reporters off to find the real story behind Kane's life. Thompson's first stop is telling: the library and archive of Walter P. Thatcher. This young journalist-turned-

The "vault" of the
Thatcher library.
(*Citizen Kane*)

historian, a nondescript Beckeresque Everyman, has been primed with
official photographs; key public events; film footage of famous Americans; impersonal, rigid newstype; and the booming, pompous oratory of
an establishment narrator. His first encounter with the library would seem
to portend more of the same monumental images of public success and
wealth: Thatcher's library is a pharaoh's tomb, complete with a looming, larger-than-life bronze effigy, forbidding acolytes and guards, and a
cavernous reading room. Thompson enters the reading room. In its dark,
echoing center is a long table cut from above by a projected beam of light.
The attendant reverently places the text Thompson seeks within the circle
of light. In Kane's official screen biography, Thompson had viewed the
projected text of national and international news headlines and intertitles
stripped from their image contexts. Although the written memoir is also
caught within a projected beam of light, Thompson holds this historical
artifact and historical text within his grasp. Thatcher's handwritten interpretation of the past is an elemental form of historiography, or the writing
of history, that he has never encountered.

The straight and elegant Victorian script of Thatcher's journal is the
first subjective textual account on view in the film. Thompson's gaze,
aligned with the camera, is confined to the text, which recalls in detail
young Thatcher's first meeting with Charlie Kane in 1871. The camera
pans slowly in the laborious act of reading as Bernard Herrmann's score
punctuates filmic time with a quavering ticktock. Then the flowing script
and score release Thompson and the camera from the archival tomb of
the Thatcher library; the tempo accelerates into a dissolving rush of open

western landscapes and bracing snow. Here Thompson reads his way from the grim plodding of written history to the cinematic romanticism of the western past. No *News on the March* impersonal voice-over or official text could achieve such historical freedom and completeness; it is a subjective document and Thatcher's personal, written perspective that first inspire the cinema to explore and then supersede the limitations of traditional historiography. After all, it is within the cinematic flashback that we have all the answers to Thompson's historical questions: Rosebud is clutched in young Charlie's grasp, and, according to Charlie's exuberant cry, the Lincoln Republic is immortal ("The Union Forever!"). But as readers of this history, our understanding, like Thompson's, is imperfect. We do not see the complete, pristine perfection of Herman Mankiewicz's and Orson Welles's cinematic history. Perhaps more than any other sequence in *Citizen Kane*, Thompson's encounter with the text develops a counterpoint of written and visual history; through the abandonment of official, documented history and a confrontation with an acknowledged subjective text, it explores the possibility of a complete filmic writing of American history during the golden age of classical Hollywood cinema.

In many ways, *Citizen Kane* seems both sequel to and parody of the American historical film, with its *Roaring Twenties*–inspired newsreel, its public antihero (*Gabriel over the White House*, 1933), and its critical look at popular American journalism (*His Girl Friday*, 1940).[74] But its resemblance to *Cimarron* is unusual and deserves more attention than a passing item in a potential genealogy. Both film narratives build a symbiotic relationship between history and journalism from the nineteenth century

Thompson reads
Thatcher's journal.
(*Citizen Kane*)

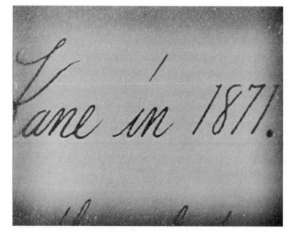

Reading from the text of history to the cinematic West. (*Citizen Kane*)

Historical completion
and "the Union forever."
(*Citizen Kane*)

through the present. Old images are imbued with documentary imme-diacy, and contemporary events are structured within the iconography of the historical text. Kane, like Yancey Cravat and Hearst, is a newspaper-man and a native westerner. Unlike Yancey, though, Kane has never had to earn his livelihood; he picks up reporting as a whim. Like Yancey and Hearst, early in his career he enjoys exposing injustice and helping the poor. He sees his work as part of the historic struggle for democracy and freedom, even going so far as to document his mission in a "Declaration of Principles" that he hopes will be as valuable as the Declaration of In-dependence and the Constitution. But in 1898, things change, and Kane stops following the heroic path established by his forebears. For both Mankiewicz and Welles, 1898 is a crucial year in Kane's development. In all the scripted text and newsreel prologues, it is the one date that disrupts the chronological order of Kane's life and the American past; the narrator moves from 1906 to 1918, and then retreats to Kane's influence on the Spanish-American War.[75]

Although *Citizen Kane*'s news prologue covers events spanning 1865 to 1941, much of what happens to Kane in the series of flashbacks occurs in 1898. Beginning with Thatcher's handwritten diary, Kane is seen insti-gating the Spanish-American War, birthing yellow journalism, luring top reporters away from the *Chronicle* to work for him, leaving for Europe, and marrying a president's niece. The advantageous but loveless marriage will be his political undoing; his willingness to sacrifice his principles in journalism prefaces his personal decay. The personal and the public become hopelessly entangled in 1898, just as American history officially turns from its self-sufficient individualism and makes an international im-perialist splash in Cuba and the Philippines. Thereafter Kane will go to Europe, rebuild a European castle in America (as unlike a log cabin as possible), flirt with Hitler and Mussolini, and destroy his Declaration of Principles as viciously as these European dictators violated treaties. In all these international excursions, Kane betrays his national heritage. Although born in a western log cabin with a strong Nancy Hanks–like mother and a weak-willed father, Kane is no new Lincoln.[76] As the pro-logue reminds us with a shot of his tombstone, Kane was born in 1865, in the year of Lincoln's death, the symbolic end of Lincoln's Republic and the dawn of the gilded industrial age of money and power without obligation. Sorties into his post–Civil War childhood become journeys into a mythic wilderness of frontier metaphors and endless winter, a lonely counterpoint to his public life.[77] The strength of American history seems to lie in its isolation; Kane's participation in events after the Spanish-American

War—the Great War, the disastrous forays into showmanship at the Chicago Opera House, the Depression—are all part of national decay, a betrayal of the western frontier "childhood" and the Lincoln Republic. As America becomes older and increasingly international in its political reach, trading the continental frontier for imperial conquests and European "crusades," Kane himself becomes more personally isolated. On the eve of America's involvement in the Second World War, he will die, unable to cope with this last historical breech, yet still clutching the emblem of his childhood—the snow globe, with its frontier landscape, a petrified historical artifact.[78]

Within Welles's more personal and complex visual history, encompassed by the multiple-flashback structure, Kane's life is not revealed in chronological order. After Bernstein remembers Kane's famous line of contempt for journalistic authenticity in 1898, the history of Kane's life is disrupted. Memories, instead of progressing to 1900, retreat further back to the 1890s and extend again chronologically through Kane's trip to Europe and his engagement to presidential niece Emily. There, he famously brings back a whole series of European sculptures and paintings, in effect, collecting a history and transporting it to the barren cultural landscape of the United States. Kane's mania for collecting is typical of the man searching for his lost past. He collects but does not create. Art becomes bric-a-brac in storage at his isolated castle Xanadu.

In *Cimarron*, 1898 is also a crucial year. The war sends Yancey, the emblem of the old West, fleeing to Cuba to pursue his empire-building fantasies, but it is an empire the film never shows. It is not part of American history. The disruptive power of 1898 is also one of *Citizen Kane's* deepest ties to Hearst. Hearst's warmongering in 1898 would transform his reputation as a newspaperman to one of corrupt yellow journalist, an inventor rather than a serious reporter or commentator. For Kane, the Cuban crisis exacerbates his megalomania and his obsession with circulation and influence. War boosts circulation. Whereas Yancey corrects the historical record, revealing the truth behind the government's manipulation of the Cherokee and Osage tribes, Kane constructs his own news, contributing to the decay of objectivity in reporting and complicating any notion of revealing historical truth. Welles incorporates this instability, this historical decline, within the very structure of his narrative, which moves from a contemporary newsreel eulogy and reporter's search back through the memories of Kane's life. *Cimarron* chronicles this same period in American history, countering the progression of time with a critical sense of loss. Yet Yancey never betrays that western heritage or the principles that make him a great American. He would rather lose a gubernatorial election than tone down his Indian rights and citizenship plank. Kane, however, loses his election through moral carelessness. As Yancey helps to "write the history of the Old Southwest," he becomes a mythic memory to the people of Oklahoma. Nostalgia concludes *Cimarron*, but *Citizen Kane* begins with a contemporary death and prefigures film history's narration of decline. American history becomes the script of decline, a death within a death that only cinema narrates with any illusion of completeness.

As *Citizen Kane* revisited RKO's early challenge to traditional American history in *Cimarron*, it also gathered myriad national confrontations and eulogies projected over a decade of American historical filmmaking. *Citizen Kane*'s engagement with the myth of the united Lincoln Republic, of the West, of rugged, self-made men, of crime and betrayal of principles in the twentieth century, of confrontations with journalism and the "shaping" of the text of history, of showmanship and theatricality, all evoke Hollywood's competing visions for American history released since the advent of sound. By contrasting *News on the March* with a series of personal flashbacks, Welles and Mankiewicz accommodate both establishment views of the past and more critical and contradictory attitudes. DeMille also had to contend with the American cinema's conflicting historical approaches, but in *Land of Liberty*, he chose to edit history for content. Welles was just as interested in history and cinema's "outtakes."

The Magnificence of the Ambersons

Welles would continue to pursue themes of American decline in his next film, but without the lurid historical gossip, his adaptation of Booth Tarkington's *The Magnificent Ambersons* was bound to fail.[79] As film historian V. F. Perkins acknowledged, even *Citizen Kane*'s huge and largely unplanned publicity did not ensure its box-office success, and Schaefer's tenure at RKO was limited.[80] Although Welles did not have the assistance of Mankiewicz on this new script, he would shortly discover that his autonomy as screenwriter-director-producer was an illusion. Things became worse in early 1942; the Hollywood elite denied Welles the critical accolades that many critics expected. Although they were willing to honor Mankiewicz and Welles by default in the screenwriting category, Academy voters gave the best picture and direction awards to Zanuck and Ford for *How Green Was My Valley*. Yet Welles's influence on his jealous colleagues was unquestionable; in 1942, when MGM attempted to turn the controversial presidential failure Andrew Johnson into another Charles Foster Kane (*Tennessee Johnson*), Welles must have enjoyed Mayer's box-office disaster. American historical films increasingly focused on declining careers and failure, and poor reviews and scant box-office returns would not only cripple Welles at RKO but also hit wealthy studios such as MGM.

Tarkington's novel was a study of an imaginary midwestern family and the waning of their power in a small industrial town, and it served Welles's interest in filming the post–Civil War decline of America. In some ways, *The Magnificent Ambersons* was *Citizen Kane*'s small-town twin. Yet Welles's scripts indicate that his interest in exploring and reworking traditional forms of historical cinema was also in decline. *Ambersons* has little of *Citizen Kane*'s self-conscious historical resonance and structure. There are no text prologues, superimposed dates, text commentary, or captions of national events.[81] The Amberson family lives apart from the rest of the country and the town. Their decline seems to stem from their inability to recognize or initiate historical change. André Bazin noted that the scenes' stillness was a stark contrast to *Citizen Kane*'s fluid sequence shots.[82] Welles chose a simple oral narration without text superimpositions, thereby abandoning the structures of historical cinema for the character of radio. "The Magnificence of the Ambersons started in 1873," he began. In 1873, the country was experiencing the first of many national financial panics and agricultural declines, yet the magnificence of the Ambersons seems to be untouched by these historical crises. They live apart from the history of American industry and are disconnected from the rest of the town. Welles narrates the charming period as if he had only a photo album or a stray issue of *Collier's* in front of him. We see and hear about old-fashioned automobiles, antiquated hats, and etiquette. Although countless other American historical films had used these basic visual differences to generate a sense of history, Welles made these qualities of fashion, design, and manners the equivalent of a historical foreword. These insubstantial visual qualities become the historical foundation of the Amberson family and perhaps account for their eventual decline.

There are no Amberson sons to carry on the line, only a daughter, Isobel. George Minafer, her son, treats everyone around him with contempt, and when the family fortunes plummet, he is unable to adapt. He becomes trapped in the magnificent wealthy heritage that supported him, existing only as a relic of a changing America. This would be Welles's last American historical film and was, in many ways, his most brilliant. Here, he broke completely with the stylistic conventions and rhetoric of traditional historical cinema and invested the narrative with a purely imagistic sense of American history. His historical cinema completely abandoned the notion of the printed and projected word and the film industry's avid exploration of historical topics, inquiry, and narrative. The Ambersons were fiction, operating far from any markers of conventional history. Ironically, as the Ambersons ignored national events and moved apart from the rest of the community, Welles also disassociated his work from the historical tradition of *Citizen Kane*. Both the Ambersons and Welles suffered in their disregard for convention. Midway through postproduction, Schaefer was replaced with Charles Koerner, and the studio, appalled by the complex story and preview audiences' baffled reactions, ordered Robert Wise to cut the film to a palatable length. By reducing it to under an hour and a half, *The Magnificent Ambersons* could fit on a double bill. Hollywood critics pointed out the many unnecessary "personal bows" Welles took in his narration of the prologue and credits and relished naming the film the year's box-office disaster.[83] RKO released Welles from his contract.

By 1942, industrial, financial, and political circumstances had seriously affected American historical filmmaking. Although *Yankee Doodle Dandy* and *Pride of the Yankees* were critically and financially successful, contemporaneous critical responses reveal that they were less popular as historical films than as wartime propaganda and baseball drama. Far more typical was the critical and popular response to Warner Brothers' biography of boxer James Corbett, *Gentleman Jim* (1942). The film did lukewarm box office, but the critics were contemptuous. Even the Hollywood periodicals, which had been consistently appreciative and increasingly tolerant over the years, condemned the studio's historical effort with disgust. According to *Variety*, the film was "so far removed from fact that it's ludicrous," and the screenplay had taken it "out of the biographical class and into fantasy."[84] Just as serious for this critic was Warner Brothers' failure to capitalize on the history of early filmmaking; after all, Corbett had been the first boxing film star, appearing in several films from the late 1890s to the early years of the twentieth century. Yet the film ended in 1892, after the Sullivan-Corbett fight and before the advent of filmmaking. Warner Brothers ignored the connection between Corbett in 1898 and 1942 and, in so doing, forfeited the one historical aspect that would have redeemed the blatant biographical inaccuracies. Having witnessed the achievements of historical cinema for over a decade, by 1942, *Variety* had lost patience.

Although several years earlier, the Gilded Age had been instrumental in popularizing the historical cycle, the response to *Gentleman Jim* and *The Magnificent Ambersons* indicated the waning taste for American history. RKO had first purchased the rights to *Ambersons* in 1932, and even Warner Brothers' writer Julien Josephson had attempted a treatment.[85] But by 1942, Welles's challenging meditations on the American past were "distinctly not attuned to the times."[86] The Second World War virtually ended the studio's interest in the cycle. Contemporary war films were far more popular and applicable, and with foreign markets gone or crippled, Hollywood simply could not afford the expense of major historical productions like *Cimarron, San Francisco, In Old Chicago*, and *Gone with the Wind*.[87] But American historical cinema's decline was not determined solely by Hollywood's finances. Beginning with *Cimarron*, filmmakers had taken chances when making historical films, whether due to controversial subject matter or new approaches to a period or a person. Without discounting the historical innovations, censorship increasingly took the edge off history in the cinema. *Land of Liberty*'s 1939–1941 production and release were not accidental. Although Zanuck and Selznick persisted (*Wilson*, 1944; *The Late George Apley*, 1947; *Duel in the Sun*, 1947; *Portrait of Jennie*, 1948), after years of fighting censors and spending money on research, it was far easier to revert to formulas and sound-stage war dramas.

The critics, the original supporters of the cycle, had grown restless and even hostile by 1940.[88] Although it is easy to argue American historical cinema reached its artistic and popular peak in the 1939 and 1940 seasons, the same golden age also killed the possibility for immediate future production. American historical film production plummeted; only MGM and Paramount seemed to have the money to spend on lavish period pieces such as *The Harvey Girls* (1945), *Magnificent Doll* (1946), and *The Perils of Pauline* (1947). However, this later work was vastly different from early sound-era cinema and consisted of period musicals and biographies of show people (*Shine On, Harvest Moon*, 1943; *The Jolson Story*, 1946; *Mother Wore Tights*, 1947; *Words and Music*, 1948; *Jolson Sings Again*, 1949). There was little preproduction research, screenwriters had less control over content, there were fewer text inserts and contrasts between visual and textual forms of history, and critics never mentioned the filmmakers' treatment of history. The age of the producer and his screenwriters was over, and the age of director auteurs had begun. As *Variety* noted, "An era . . . has passed. . . . Things just aren't what they used to be for those members of the cinema-scribbling fraternity."[89]

But in 1941, while *Sergeant York* and *Land of Liberty* trumpeted the virtues of American history in theaters and *Citizen Kane* disrupted them, and *Yankee Doodle Dandy* and *Pride of the Yankees* were still in the future, Hollywood's production of American history seemed self-possessed and secure. But nothing was sacred to Billy Wilder and Charles Brackett, and that year, the screenwriting duo managed to both manipulate the iconography of the historical film and lampoon the stodginess of professional historians and the entrenched power of Hollywood's works of history. *Ball of Fire*, their script for Sam Goldwyn, described a think tank of doddering professors disoriented by the arrival of a nightclub singer, Sugarpuss O'Shea (Barbara Stanwyck). Wilder and Brackett began the narrative with a traditional text foreword that described all that the seven wise men knew about, and then "the one thing about which they knew very little"—sex. If the screenwriters were implying that historical filmmaking needed a boost, the academics got it. Sugarpuss teaches the bumbling geriatrics to conga and the younger English professor Bertram Potts (Gary Cooper) about slang and history. "There's a lot of words we haven't covered yet," she points out. "For instance, do you know what this means: 'I'll get you on the Ameche'? . . . The Ameche is the telephone, on account of he invented it." When Potts attempts to disagree, she cuts him off, "Like you know, in the movies." Historians and academics might expostulate in vain, but Carl Becker realized long ago that popular history, regardless of whether it was more accurate, accessible, or controversial than professional history, had the public's attention.

Zanuck must have appreciated the irony of Wilder and Brackett's quip. At the time of *The Story of Alexander Graham Bell*, he had been Hollywood's biggest producer of American historical films. But in Zanuck's push for prestige and his patronage of original screenplays as potential works of film historiography, he had struggled to get around the American public's stumbling intellect: *Silver Dollar*, as he remarked to John Huston in 1934, had aimed too high; *Young Mr. Lincoln* was a box-office failure; even *Alexander Graham Bell* had been a disappointment. Yet when *The Littlest Rebel* was taking shape in a 1936 story conference, he had warned an overimaginative screenwriter not to construct Abraham Lincoln's meeting with little Virgie (Shirley Temple) as his inspiration for the Gettysburg Address, or the public "will throw rocks at us." Would Sugarpuss, the hip singer–gangster's moll, like Susan Alexander, another "cross-section of the American public," have known the difference or cared? Or was the Bell-Ameche divide between history and Hollywood's works of history now moot after a dozen years of heavy productions? The answer was as disturbing and invigorating as Sugarpuss O'Shea's introduction to the Totten Foundation household. Zanuck and his colleagues' film historiography had supplanted traditional tomes; Sugarpuss and the public's fixation on the star was simply one of the effects that Bertram Potts had to get used to and integrate into his new encyclopedia.

Hollywood filmmakers had helped create a powerful historical legacy. For over a decade, they proved that films could argue complex historical perspectives and question the formulas of traditional American history and biography. Some braved controversy, and others knuckled under the demands of censorship. Some appropriated the structures of conventional historiography, and others upended them. Hollywood's filmic writing of American history was both DeMillean cavalcade and historical hybrid. Abraham Lincoln and Al Capone were the subjects of major biographies, and the transformation of historical scholarship following the First World War gave new meaning to the term *forgotten men*. Filmmakers confronted the modern dialectic between popular biography and the decline of the traditional American hero. In high-profile adaptations of American fiction from *Cimarron* to *Ramona* to *Gone with the Wind*, women emerged not only as popular historians but also as active historical protagonists. Race, miscegenation, disunion, total war—women began to tell these powerful counterhistories on a vast public scale. Their voices reanimated American history from Sherman's march through the Great War and the decline of silent Hollywood—the narratives and lost careers of American women from Eliza Frances Andrews to Irene Castle and Clara Bow were scripted within the history of modern America.

Perhaps the cycle could not last beyond America's decade of isolation and self-reflection. American involvement in the Second World War forced Hollywood production and historical thought beyond the borders of America. And despite contemporary Hollywood's occasional high-profile forays into American history (*Glory*, 1989; *Malcolm X*, 1992; *Saving Private Ryan*, 1998), the box-office future of these films has become even more tenuous in the face of a globalized film market. How can uniquely American tales appeal to a global market? Between 1931 and 1941, American cinema pushed the borders of traditional historical discourse even as it redefined the structures of film narration. With a national cinema dependent on a deeply complex, conflicted, but culturally specific series of narratives, it was no wonder that, when confronted with new international pressures, it collapsed—like Charles Foster Kane's Declaration of Principles—in the face of American expansion.

Historical Films by Year, 1913–1950

1913   *The Battle of Gettysburg* (Ince)
1914   *In the Days of the Thundering Herd* (Selig)
       The Littlest Rebel (Photoplay Productions)
1915   *Barbara Frietchie* (Metro)
       The Birth of a Nation (Epoch)
       The Crisis (Selig Polyscope)
       Heart of Maryland (Metro)
       The Warrens of Virginia (Lasky Feature Play Company/Paramount)
1916   *Davy Crockett* (Paramount)
1917   *Betsy Ross* (World)
       The Conqueror (Fox)
       The Little Yank (Fine Arts)
       The Man without a Country (Thanhouser)
       A Mormon Maid (Friedman)
1918   *The Spirit of '76* (Continental)
1919   *Little Women* (William A. Brady)
1920   *The Copperhead* (Famous Players–Lasky)
       The Last of the Mohicans (Tourneur/Associated Producers)
1921   *The Heart of Maryland* (Vitagraph)

The Highest Law (Selznick International Pictures)
Jesse James as the Outlaw (Mesco Pictures)
Jesse James under the Black Flag (Mesco Pictures)
1922   *A California Romance* (Fox)
       Cardigan (Messmore Kendall)
       The Heart of Lincoln (Anchor Film Distributors)
1923   *The Courtship of Miles Standish* (Associated Exhibitors)
       The Covered Wagon (Paramount)
       Hollywood (Paramount)
       Jamestown (Pathe)
       Little Old New York (Cosmopolitan/MGM)
1924   *America* (United Artists)
       Barbara Frietchie (Regal)
       California in '49 (Arrow)
       The Dramatic Life of Abraham Lincoln (Rockett)
       The Iron Horse (Fox)
       Janice Meredith (Cosmopolitan/MGM)
       Secrets (Schenck/Associated First National)
       So Big (First National)
       The Warrens of Virginia (Fox)

1925   *The Big Parade* (MGM)
       The Man without a Country
           (Fox)
       The Scarlet West (First
           National)
       Tumbleweeds (William S.
           Hart/United Artists)
       The Vanishing American
           (Famous Players–Lasky/
           Paramount)
1926   *Across the Pacific* (Warner
           Brothers)
       The Flaming Frontier
           (Universal)
       Hands Up! (Paramount)
       The Last Frontier
           (Metropolitan)
       Old Ironsides (Paramount)
       The Pony Express (Famous
           Players–Lasky/Paramount)
       The Scarlet Letter (MGM)
       War Paint (MGM)
1927   *California* (MGM)
       The Frontiersman (MGM)
       Heart of Maryland (Warner
           Brothers)
       Jesse James (Paramount)
       The Rough Riders
           (Paramount)
       Uncle Tom's Cabin
           (Universal)
       Wings (Paramount)
       Winners of the Wilderness
           (MGM)
1928   *Court-marital* (Columbia)
       Kit Carson (Paramount)
       Ramona (United Artists)
       Shopworn Angel
           (Paramount)
       Show People (MGM)
       Wyoming (MGM)
1929   *The California Mail* (Warner
           Brothers)
       Evangeline (United Artists)
       The Gold Diggers of Broadway
           (Warner Brothers)
       In Old Arizona (Fox)

       The Invaders (Big
           Productions)
       Morgan's Last Raid (MGM)
       Redskin (Paramount)
       Show Boat (Universal)
       The Virginian (Paramount)
1930   *Abraham Lincoln* (United
           Artists)
       The Big Trail (Fox)
       Billy the Kid (MGM)
       Dixiana (RKO)
       Doorway to Hell (Warner
           Brothers)
       The Floradora Girl (MGM)
       The Girl of the Golden West
           (Warner Brothers)
       Moby Dick (Warner
           Brothers)
       Only the Brave (Paramount)
       *The Royal Family of
           Broadway* (Paramount)
       The Spoilers (Paramount)
       The Texan (Paramount)
       Tol'able David (Columbia)
       Tom Sawyer (Paramount)
1931   *Alexander Hamilton* (Warner
           Brothers)
       Cimarron (RKO)
       The Conquering Horde
           (Paramount)
       East Lynne (Fox)
       Fighting Caravans
           (Paramount)
       The Finger Points (Warner
           Brothers)
       The Great Meadow (MGM)
       Huckleberry Finn
           (Paramount)
       The Lash (Warner Brothers)
       Little Caesar (Warner
           Brothers)
       The Miracle Woman
           (Columbia)
       The Public Enemy (Warner
           Brothers)
       Secret Service (RKO)
       The Secret Six (MGM)

1932   *Call Her Savage* (Fox)
        The Conquerors (RKO)
        Destry Rides Again
          (Universal)
        I Am a Fugitive from a Chain
          Gang (Warner Brothers)
        Law and Order (Universal)
        The Match King (Warner
          Brothers)
        The Mouthpiece (Warner
          Brothers)
        Movie Crazy (Paramount)
        Scarface (Caddo)
        Silver Dollar (Warner
          Brothers)
        So Big (Warner Brothers)
        Three on a Match (Warner
          Brothers)
        The Wet Parade (MGM)
        What Price Hollywood?
          (RKO)
1933   *Ann Vickers* (RKO)
        Bombshell (MGM)
        Broadway to Hollywood
          (MGM)
        The Chief (MGM)
        Ever in My Heart (Warner
          Brothers)
        Frisco Jenny (Warner
          Brothers)
        Gold Diggers of 1933
          (Warner Brothers)
        Heroes for Sale (Columbia)
        I Loved a Woman (Warner
          Brothers)
        Jennie Gerhardt (Paramount)
        Little Women (RKO)
        The Man Who Dared (Fox)
        Morning Glory (RKO)
        One Sunday Afternoon
          (Paramount)
        Only Yesterday (Universal)
        The Power and the Glory
          (MGM)
        Secrets (United Artists)
        She Done Him Wrong
          (Paramount)

        The Silver Cord (RKO)
        Song of the Eagle
          (Paramount)
        Sweepings (MGM)
        The World Changes (Warner
          Brothers)
1934   *The Age of Innocence* (RKO)
        Belle of the Nineties
          (Paramount)
        Beloved (Universal)
        The Bowery (Twentieth
          Century)
        David Harum (Fox)
        Frontier Marshal (Fox)
        Judge Priest (Fox)
        Manhattan Melodrama
          (MGM)
        The Mighty Barnum
          (Twentieth Century)
        Mrs. Wiggs of the Cabbage
          Patch (Paramount)
        Now I'll Tell (Twentieth
          Century)
        Operator 13 (MGM)
        The Pursuit of Happiness
          (MGM)
        Viva Villa! (MGM)
        The World Moves On (Fox)
        You Can't Buy Everything
          (MGM)
1935   *Ah, Wilderness* (MGM)
        Alice Adams (RKO)
        Annie Oakley (RKO)
        The Arizonian (RKO)
        The Barbary Coast
          (Paramount)
        The County Chairman
          (Twentieth Century–Fox)
        Diamond Jim (Universal)
        Dr. Socrates (Warner
          Brothers)
        The Farmer Takes a Wife
          (Twentieth Century–Fox)
        The Frisco Kid (Warner
          Brothers)
        In Old Kentucky (Twentieth
          Century–Fox)

The Little Colonel
(Twentieth Century–Fox)
The Littlest Rebel (Twentieth
Century–Fox)
Mississippi (Paramount)
Naughty Marietta (MGM)
Rendezvous (MGM)
Ruggles of Red Gap
(Paramount)
So Red the Rose (Paramount)
Steamboat Round the Bend
(Twentieth Century–Fox)
Sweet Adeline (Warner
Brothers)
Way Down East (Twentieth
Century–Fox)
West of the Pecos (RKO)

1936   *Bullets or Ballets* (Warner
Brothers)
Captain January (Twentieth
Century–Fox)
Come and Get It (United
Artists)
The Country Doctor
(Twentieth Century–Fox)
*The Gentleman from
Louisiana* (Republic)
Go West, Young Man
(Paramount)
The Gorgeous Hussy
(MGM)
The Great Ziegfeld (MGM)
Hearts Divided (MGM)
Hearts in Bondage
(Republic)
Hollywood Boulevard
(Paramount)
Klondike Annie (Paramount)
The Last of the Mohicans
(United Artists)
A Message to Garcia
(Twentieth Century–Fox)
The Plainsman (Paramount)
The Prisoner of Shark Island
(Twentieth Century–Fox)
Ramona (Twentieth
Century–Fox)

Robin Hood of El Dorado
(Twentieth Century–Fox)
San Francisco (MGM)
Show Boat (Universal)
Souls at Sea (Paramount)
Sutter's Gold (Universal)
Texas Rangers (Paramount)

1937   *The Californian* (Twentieth
Century–Fox)
Captains Courageous
(MGM)
High, Wide, and Handsome
(RKO)
Maid of Salem (Paramount)
Make Way for Tomorrow
(MGM)
Marked Woman (Warner
Brothers)
Maytime (MGM)
Slave Ship (Twentieth
Century–Fox)
A Star Is Born (Selznick
International Pictures)
That Certain Woman
(Warner Brothers)
They Gave Him a Gun
(MGM)
This Is My Affair (Twentieth
Century–Fox)
The Toast of New York (RKO)
Wells Fargo (Paramount)

1938   *The Adventures of
Tom Sawyer* (Selznick
International Pictures)
Alexander's Ragtime Band
(Twentieth Century–Fox)
Boys Town (MGM)
The Buccaneer (Paramount)
Every Day's a Holiday
(Paramount)
The Frontiersman (Paramount)
The Girl of the Golden West
(MGM)
Gold Is Where You Find It
(Warner Brothers)
In Old Chicago (Twentieth
Century–Fox)

Jezebel (Warner Brothers)
Kentucky (Twentieth Century–Fox)
Of Human Hearts (MGM)
Shopworn Angel (MGM)
The Sisters (Warner Brothers)
The Texans (Paramount)
The Toy Wife (MGM)
Yellow Jack (MGM)

1939 *Allegheny Uprising* (RKO)
Destry Rides Again (Universal)
Dodge City (Warner Brothers)
Drums along the Mohawk (Twentieth Century–Fox)
The Flying Irishman (RKO)
Frontier Marshal (Twentieth Century–Fox)
Gone with the Wind (Selznick International Pictures/MGM)
Hollywood Cavalcade (Twentieth Century–Fox)
Jesse James (Twentieth Century–Fox)
Let Freedom Ring (MGM)
Man of Conquest (Republic)
Mr. Smith Goes to Washington (Columbia)
The Oklahoma Kid (Warner Brothers)
The Old Maid (Warner Brothers)
The Real Glory (United Artists)
Return of the Cisco Kid (Twentieth Century–Fox)
The Roaring Twenties (Warner Brothers)
The Rose of Washington Square (Twentieth Century–Fox)
Stagecoach (United Artists)
Stand Up and Fight (MGM)
Stanley and Livingstone (Twentieth Century–Fox)

The Star Maker (Paramount)
The Story of Alexander Graham Bell (Twentieth Century–Fox)
The Story of Vernon and Irene Castle (RKO)
Swanee River (Twentieth Century–Fox)
Union Pacific (Paramount)
Young Mr. Lincoln (Twentieth Century–Fox)

1940 *Abe Lincoln in Illinois* (RKO)
Arizona (Columbia)
Boom Town (MGM)
Brigham Young— Frontiersman (Twentieth Century–Fox)
Chad Hanna (Twentieth Century–Fox)
The Dark Command (Republic)
Edison the Man (MGM)
The Fighting 69th (Warner Brothers)
Geronimo (Paramount)
The Grapes of Wrath (Twentieth Century–Fox)
The Great Profile (Twentieth Century–Fox)
The Howards of Virginia (Columbia)
Hudson's Bay (Twentieth Century–Fox)
Kit Carson (Reliance/United Artists)
Kitty Foyle (RKO)
Knute Rockne, All American (Warner Brothers)
The Lady with Red Hair (Warner Brothers)
Lillian Russell (Twentieth Century–Fox)
Little Old New York (Twentieth Century–Fox)
My Little Chickadee (Paramount)
New Moon (MGM)

Northwest Passage (MGM)
Our Town (United Artists)
The Queen of the Mob
(Paramount)
The Return of Frank James
(Twentieth Century–Fox)
The Santa Fe Trail (Warner
Brothers)
They Knew What They
Wanted (RKO)
Tin Pan Alley (Twentieth
Century–Fox)
Virginia City (Warner
Brothers)
The Westerner (United
Artists)
When the Daltons Rode
(United Artists)
Young Tom Edison (MGM)

1941 Back Street (Universal)
Belle Starr (Twentieth
Century–Fox)
Billy the Kid (MGM)
Blossoms in the Dust (MGM)
Citizen Kane (RKO)
Gentleman Jim (Warner
Brothers)
Harmon of Michigan
(Columbia)
H. M. Pulham, Esq. (MGM)
Honky Tonk (MGM)
Kings Row (Warner Brothers)
The Lady from Cheyenne
(Universal)
Land of Liberty (MPPDA/
MGM)
The Little Foxes (Warner
Brothers)
One Foot in Heaven (MGM)
The Return of Daniel Boone
(Columbia)
Sergeant York (Warner
Brothers)
The Strawberry Blonde
(Warner Brothers)
They Died with Their Boots
On (Warner Brothers)

Western Union (Twentieth
Century–Fox)
1942 The Great Man's Lady
(Paramount)
The Loves of Edgar Allan Poe
(Twentieth Century–Fox)
The Magnificent Ambersons
(RKO)
Pride of the Yankees (RKO)
Reap the Wild Wind
(Paramount)
Roxie Hart (Twentieth
Century–Fox)
The Spoilers (Republic)
Tennessee Johnson (MGM)
The Vanishing Virginian
(MGM)
Yankee Doodle Dandy
(Warner Brothers)
1943 Dixie (Paramount)
Heaven Can Wait (Twentieth
Century–Fox)
Hello, Frisco, Hello
(Twentieth Century–Fox)
In Old Oklahoma (Republic)
Is Everybody Happy?
(Columbia)
Jack London (United Artists)
The Outlaw (Hughes)
1944 The Adventures of Mark
Twain (Warner Brothers)
Buffalo Bill (Twentieth
Century–Fox)
Meet Me in St. Louis
(MGM)
Mr. Skeffington (Warner
Brothers)
Mrs. Parkington (MGM)
Roger Touhy, Gangster
(Twentieth Century–Fox)
Shine On, Harvest Moon
(Warner Brothers)
Show Business (RKO)
The Story of Dr. Wassell
(Paramount)
Wilson (Twentieth Century–
Fox)

1945 *Captain Eddie* (Twentieth
Century–Fox)
Dakota (Republic)
The Dolly Sisters (Twentieth
Century–Fox)
Flame of the Barbary Coast
(Republic)
The Harvey Girls (MGM)
Incendiary Blonde
(Paramount)
Roughly Speaking (Warner
Brothers)
Saratoga Trunk (Warner
Brothers)
The Story of G.I. Joe (United
Artists)
A Tree Grows in Brooklyn
(Twentieth Century–Fox)

1946 *The Daltons Ride Again*
(Universal)
The Jolson Story (Columbia)
Magnificent Doll (Universal)
My Darling Clementine
(Twentieth Century–Fox)
Night and Day (Warner
Brothers)
Strange Woman (United
Artists)
Till the Clouds Roll By
(MGM)
Two Years before the Mast
(Paramount)
The Virginian (Paramount)

1947 *Duel in the Sun* (Selznick
International Pictures)
The Fabulous Dorseys
(United Artists)
The Late George Apley
(Twentieth Century–Fox)
Life with Father (Warner
Brothers)
Mother Wore Tights
(Twentieth Century–Fox)
My Wild Irish Rose (Warner
Brothers)
The Perils of Pauline
(Paramount)

The Romance of Rosy Ridge
(MGM)
The Sea of Grass (MGM)
The Shocking Miss Pilgrim
(Twentieth Century–Fox)
The Unconquered
(Paramount)

1948 *The Babe Ruth Story* (Allied
Artists)
Fort Apache (RKO)
I Remember Mama (RKO)
Isn't It Romantic (Paramount)
Portrait of Jennie (Selznick
International Pictures)
Red River (Monterey)
Streets of Laredo (Paramount)
Tap Roots (Universal)
Up in Central Park
(Universal)
Words and Music (MGM)
The Younger Brothers
(Warner Brothers)

1949 *The Great Dan Patch* (United
Artists)
I Was a Male War Bride
(Columbia)
Jolson Sings Again
(Columbia)
Little Women (MGM)
Look for the Silver Lining
(Warner Brothers)
Oh, You Beautiful Doll
(Twentieth Century–Fox)
The Sands of Iwo Jima
(Republic)
The Story of Seabiscuit
(Warner Brothers)
The Stratton Story (MGM)
Task Force (Warner Brothers)
You're My Everything
(Twentieth Century–Fox)

1950 *All about Eve* (Twentieth
Century–Fox)
Annie Get Your Gun
(MGM)
Broken Arrow (Twentieth
Century–Fox)

Cheaper by the Dozen
  (Twentieth Century–Fox)
*The Daughter of Rosie
  O'Grady* (Warner
  Brothers)
Davy Crockett, Indian Scout
  (United Artists)
The Magnificent Yankee
  (MGM)
Sunset Boulevard
  (Paramount)
Young Man with a Horn
  (Warner Brothers)

Historical Films by Studio, 1928–1950

Caddo/Hughes
Scarface (1932)
The Outlaw (1943)

Columbia
Court-martial (1928)
Tol'able David (1930)
The Miracle Woman (1931)
Heroes for Sale (1933)
Mr. Smith Goes to Washington
   (1939)
Arizona (1940)
The Howards of Virginia (1940)
Harmon of Michigan (1941)
The Return of Daniel Boone (1941)
Is Everybody Happy? (1943)
The Jolson Story (1946)
I Was a Male War Bride (1949)
Jolson Sings Again (1949)

Fox
In Old Arizona (1929)
The Big Trail (1930)
East Lynne (1931)
Call Her Savage (1932)
The Man Who Dared (1933)
David Harum (1934)
Frontier Marshal (1934)
Judge Priest (1934)
The World Moves On (1934)

MGM
Show People (1928)

Wyoming (1928)
Morgan's Last Raid (1929)
Billy the Kid (1930)
The Floradora Girl (1930)
The Great Meadow (1931)
The Secret Six (1931)
The Wet Parade (1932)
Bombshell (1933)
Broadway to Hollywood (1933)
The Chief (1933)
The Power and the Glory (1933)
Sweepings (1933)
Manhattan Melodrama (1934)
Operator 13 (1934)
The Pursuit of Happiness (1934)
Viva Villa! (1934)
Ah, Wilderness (1935)
Naughty Marietta (1935)
Rendezvous (1935)
The Gorgeous Hussy (1936)
The Great Ziegfeld (1936)
Hearts Divided (1936)
San Francisco (1936)
Captains Courageous (1937)
Make Way for Tomorrow (1937)
They Gave Him a Gun (1937)
Boys Town (1938)
The Girl of the Golden West (1938)
Of Human Hearts (1938)
Shopworn Angel (1938)
The Toy Wife (1938)
Yellow Jack (1938)
Let Freedom Ring (1939)

Stand Up and Fight (1939)
Boom Town (1940)
Edison the Man (1940)
New Moon (1940)
Northwest Passage (1940)
Young Tom Edison (1940)
Billy the Kid (1941)
Blossoms in the Dust (1941)
H. M. Pulham, Esq. (1941)
Honky Tonk (1941)
One Foot in Heaven (1941)
Tennessee Johnson (1942)
The Vanishing Virginian (1942)
Meet Me in St. Louis (1944)
Mrs. Parkington (1944)
The Harvey Girls (1945)
Till the Clouds Roll By (1946)
The Romance of Rosy Ridge (1947)
The Sea of Grass (1947)
Words and Music (1948)
Little Women (1949)
Annie Get Your Gun (1950)
The Magnificent Yankee (1950)

Paramount
Kit Carson (1928)
Shopworn Angel (1928)
Redskin (1929)
The Virginian (1929)
Only the Brave (1930)
The Royal Family of Broadway (1930)
The Spoilers (1930)
The Texan (1930)
Tom Sawyer (1930)
The Conquering Horde (1931)
Fighting Caravans (1931)
Huckleberry Finn (1931)
Movie Crazy (1932)
Jennie Gerhardt (1933)
One Sunday Afternoon (1933)
She Done Him Wrong (1933)
Song of the Eagle (1933)
Belle of the Nineties (1934)
Mrs. Wiggs of the Cabbage Patch (1934)
The Barbary Coast (1935)
Ruggles of Red Gap (1935)

So Red the Rose (1935)
Go West, Young Man (1936)
Hollywood Boulevard (1936)
Klondike Annie (1936)
The Plainsman (1936)
The Texas Rangers (1936)
Maid of Salem (1937)
Souls at Sea (1937)
Wells Fargo (1937)
The Buccaneer (1938)
Every Day's a Holiday (1938)
The Frontiersman (1938)
The Texans (1938)
The Star Maker (1939)
Union Pacific (1939)
Geronimo (1940)
My Little Chickadee (1940)
The Queen of the Mob (1940)
The Great Man's Lady (1942)
Reap the Wild Wind (1942)
Dixie (1943)
The Story of Dr. Wassell (1944)
Incendiary Blonde (1945)
Two Years before the Mast (1946)
The Virginian (1946)
The Perils of Pauline (1947)
The Unconquered (1947)
Isn't It Romantic (1948)
Streets of Laredo (1948)
Sunset Boulevard (1950)

RKO
Dixiana (1930)
Cimarron (1931)
Secret Service (1931)
The Conquerors (1932)
What Price Hollywood? (1932)
Ann Vickers (1933)
Little Women (1933)
Morning Glory (1933)
The Silver Cord (1933)
Age of Innocence (1934)
Alice Adams (1935)
Annie Oakley (1935)
The Arizonian (1935)
West of the Pecos (1935)
High, Wide, and Handsome (1937)

The Toast of New York (1937)
Allegheny Uprising (1939)
The Flying Irishman (1939)
The Story of Vernon and Irene Castle (1939)
Abe Lincoln in Illinois (1940)
Kitty Foyle (1940)
They Knew What They Wanted (1940)
Citizen Kane (1941)
The Great Man's Lady (1942)
The Magnificent Ambersons (1942)
Pride of the Yankees (1942)
Show Business (1944)
Fort Apache (1948)
I Remember Mama (1948)

Republic
The Gentleman from Louisiana (1936)
Hearts in Bondage (1936)
Man of Conquest (1939)
The Dark Command (1940)
The Spoilers (1942)
In Old Oklahoma (1943)
Dakota (1945)
Flame of the Barbary Coast (1945)
The Sands of Iwo Jima (1949)

Selznick International Pictures
A Star Is Born (1937)
The Adventures of Tom Sawyer (1938)
Gone with the Wind (1939)
Duel in the Sun (1947)
Portrait of Jennie (1948)

Twentieth Century
The Bowery (1934)
The Mighty Barnum (1934)
Now I'll Tell (1934)

Twentieth Century–Fox
The County Chairman (1935)
The Farmer Takes a Wife (1935)
In Old Kentucky (1935)
The Little Colonel (1935)
The Littlest Rebel (1935)
Steamboat Round the Bend (1935)
Way Down East (1935)

Captain January (1936)
The Country Doctor (1936)
The Prisoner of Shark Island (1936)
Ramona (1936)
Robin Hood of El Dorado (1936)
The Californian (1937)
A Message to Garcia (1937)
Slave Ship (1937)
This Is My Affair (1937)
Alexander's Ragtime Band (1938)
In Old Chicago (1938)
Kentucky (1938)
Drums along the Mohawk (1939)
Frontier Marshal (1939)
Hollywood Cavalcade (1939)
Jesse James (1939)
Return of the Cisco Kid (1939)
The Rose of Washington Square (1939)
Stanley and Livingstone (1939)
The Story of Alexander Graham Bell (1939)
Swanee River (1939)
Young Mr. Lincoln (1939)
Brigham Young—Frontiersman (1940)
Chad Hanna (1940)
The Grapes of Wrath (1940)
The Great Profile (1940)
Hudson's Bay (1940)
Lillian Russell (1940)
Little Old New York (1940)
The Return of Frank James (1940)
Tin Pan Alley (1940)
Belle Starr (1941)
Western Union (1941)
The Loves of Edgar Allan Poe (1942)
Roxie Hart (1942)
Heaven Can Wait (1943)
Hello, Frisco, Hello (1943)
Buffalo Bill (1944)
Roger Touhy, Gangster (1944)
Wilson (1944)
Captain Eddie (1945)
The Dolly Sisters (1945)
A Tree Grows in Brooklyn (1945)
My Darling Clementine (1946)
The Late George Apley (1947)
Mother Wore Tights (1947)

The Shocking Miss Pilgrim (1947)
Oh, You Beautiful Doll (1949)
You're My Everything (1949)
All About Eve (1950)
Broken Arrow (1950)
Cheaper by the Dozen (1950)

United Artists
Ramona (1928)
Evangeline (1929)
Abraham Lincoln (1930)
Secrets (1933)
Come and Get It (1936)
The Last of the Mohicans (1936)
The Real Glory (1939)
Stagecoach (1939)
Kit Carson (1940)
Our Town (1940)
The Westerner (1940)
When the Daltons Rode (1940)
Jack London (1943)
The Story of G.I. Joe (1945)
Strange Woman (1946)
The Fabulous Dorseys (1947)
The Great Dan Patch (1949)
Davy Crockett, Indian Scout (1950)

Universal
Show Boat (1929)
Destry Rides Again (1932)
Law and Order (1932)
Only Yesterday (1933)
Beloved (1934)
Diamond Jim (1935)
Show Boat (1936)
Sutter's Gold (1936)
Destry Rides Again (1939)
The Lady from Cheyenne (1941)
The Daltons Ride Again (1946)
Magnificent Doll (1946)
Tap Roots (1948)
Up in Central Park (1948)

Warner Brothers
The California Mail (1929)
The Gold Diggers of Broadway (1929)
Doorway to Hell (1930)

The Girl of the Golden West (1930)
Moby Dick (1930)
Alexander Hamilton (1931)
The Finger Points (1931)
The Lash (1931)
Little Caesar (1931)
The Public Enemy (1931)
I Am a Fugitive from a Chain Gang (1932)
The Match King (1932)
The Mouthpiece (1932)
Silver Dollar (1932)
So Big (1932)
Three on a Match (1932)
Ever in My Heart (1933)
Frisco Jenny (1933)
I Loved a Woman (1933)
The World Changes (1933)
Dr. Socrates (1935)
The Frisco Kid (1935)
Sweet Adeline (1935)
Bullets or Ballets (1936)
Marked Woman (1937)
That Certain Woman (1937)
Gold Is Where You Find It (1938)
Jezebel (1938)
The Sisters (1938)
Dodge City (1939)
The Oklahoma Kid (1939)
The Old Maid (1939)
The Roaring Twenties (1939)
The Fighting 69th (1940)
The Lady with Red Hair (1940)
The Santa Fe Trail (1940)
Virginia City (1940)
Gentleman Jim (1941)
Kings Row (1941)
The Little Foxes (1941)
Sergeant York (1941)
The Strawberry Blonde (1941)
They Died with Their Boots On (1941)
Yankee Doodle Dandy (1942)
Shine On, Harvest Moon (1944)
The Adventures of Mark Twain (1944)
Mr. Skeffington (1944)
Roughly Speaking (1945)
Saratoga Trunk (1945)

Night and Day (1946)
Life with Father (1947)
My Wild Irish Rose (1947)
The Younger Brothers (1948)
Look for the Silver Lining (1949)
The Story of Seabiscuit (1949)
Task Force (1949)
The Daughter of Rosie O'Grady
        (1950)
Young Man with a Horn (1950)

Appendix C

American Historical Films That Won
Major Academy Awards, 1927–1950

Note: Far fewer award categories existed from 1927 to 1936, and until 1940, far fewer films were nominated per category. Although American "historical" films won some awards in the 1940s, these were mostly nominations for musical score, song, and cinematography. The bulk of the major picture, directing, writing, acting, and editing awards were won from 1931 to 1942.

1927–1928 (Silent)
Wings: Best Picture and Engineering (Special) Effects

1928–1929
In Old Arizona: Best Actor; nominated Best Picture, Director, Writing, and
    Cinematography

1929–1930
No awards.

1930–1931
Cimarron: Best Picture, Screenplay, and Art Direction; nominated Best Actor,
    Actress, Director, and Cinematography
Little Caesar: nominated Best Adapted Story
The Public Enemy: nominated Best Original Story
The Royal Family of Broadway: nominated Best Actor

1931–1932
What Price Hollywood?: nominated Best Original Story

1932–1933
The Gold Diggers of 1933: nominated Best Sound Recording
I Am a Fugitive from a Chain Gang: nominated Best Picture, Actor, and Sound
    Recording

Little Women: nominated Best Picture, Director, and Adapted Story
Morning Glory: Best Actress
She Done Him Wrong: nominated Best Picture

1934
Manhattan Melodrama: Best Original Story
Operator 13: nominated Best Cinematography
Viva Villa!: Best Assistant Director; nominated Best Picture, Adapted Story, and
    Sound Recording

1935
Alice Adams: nominated Best Picture and Actress
The Barbary Coast: nominated Best Cinematography
Naughty Marietta: nominated Best Picture and Sound Recording
Ruggles of Red Gap: nominated Best Picture

1936
Come and Get It: Best Supporting Actor; nominated Best Editing
The Gorgeous Hussy: nominated Best Supporting Actress and
    Cinematography
The Great Ziegfeld: Best Picture and Actress; nominated Best Director, Original
    Story, Set Designs, and Editing
The Last of the Mohicans: nominated Best Assistant Director
San Francisco: Best Sound Recording; nominated Best Picture, Actor, Director,
    Original Story, and Assistant Director
The Texas Rangers: nominated Best Sound Recording

1937
Captains Courageous: Best Actor; nominated Best Screenplay and Editing
Every Day's a Holiday: nominated Best Set Design
In Old Chicago: Best Supporting Actress and Assistant Director; nominated
    Best Picture, Original Story, Sound Recording, and Score
Maytime: nominated Best Sound Recording and Score
Souls at Sea: nominated Best Set Design, Assistant Director, and Score
A Star Is Born: Best Original Story; nominated Best Picture, Actor, Actress,
    Director, and Screenplay
Wells Fargo: nominated Best Sound Recording

1938
The Adventures of Tom Sawyer: nominated Best Set Design
Alexander's Ragtime Band: Best Score; nominated Best Picture, Original Story,
    Set Design, Song, and Editing
Boys Town: Best Actor and Original Story; nominated Best Picture, Director,
    and Screenplay
The Buccaneer: nominated Best Cinematography
Jezebel: Best Actress and Supporting Actress; nominated Best Picture,
    Cinematography, and Score

Kentucky: Best Supporting Actor
Of Human Hearts: nominated Best Supporting Actress

1939

Drums along the Mohawk: nominated Best Supporting Actress and Color Cinematography
Gone with the Wind: Best Picture, Actress, Supporting Actress, Director, Screenplay, Set Design, Editing, and Color Cinematography; nominated Best Actor, Supporting Actress, Sound Recording, Original Score, and Special Effects
Man of Conquest: nominated Best Set Design, Sound Recording, and Original Score
Mr. Smith Goes to Washington: Best Original Story; nominated Best Picture, Actor, Supporting Actor (2), Director, Screenplay, Set Design, Sound Recording, Score, and Editing
Stagecoach: Best Supporting Actor and Score; nominated Best Picture, Director, Black-and-White Cinematography, and Set Design
Swanee River: nominated Best Score
Union Pacific: nominated Best Special Effects
Young Mr. Lincoln: nominated Best Original Story

1940

Abe Lincoln in Illinois, nominated Best Actor and Black-and-White Cinematography
Arizona: nominated Best Black-and-White Set Design and Original Score
Boom Town: nominated Best Black-and-White Cinematography and Special Effects
Dark Command: nominated Best Black-and-White Set Design and Original Score
Edison the Man: nominated Best Original Story
The Grapes of Wrath: Best Director and Supporting Actress; nominated Best Picture, Actor, Screenplay, and Sound Recording
The Howards of Virginia: nominated Best Sound Recording and Original Score
Kitty Foyle: Best Actress; nominated Best Picture, Director, Screenplay, and Sound Recording
Lillian Russell: nominated Best Black-and-White Set Design
Northwest Passage: nominated Best Color Cinematography
Our Town: nominated Best Picture, Actress, Black-and-White Set Design, Sound Recording, Score, and Original Score
They Knew What They Wanted: nominated Best Supporting Actor
The Westerner: Best Supporting Actor, nominated Best Original Story and Black-and-White Set Design

1941

Back Street: nominated Best Dramatic Score
Billy the Kid: nominated Best Color Cinematography

Blossoms in the Dust: Best Color Set Design; nominated Best Picture, Actress, and Color Cinematography

Citizen Kane: Best Screenplay; nominated Best Picture, Director, Actor, Black-and-White Cinematography, Black-and-White Set Design, Sound Recording, Dramatic Score, and Editing

The Little Foxes: nominated Best Picture, Actress, Supporting Actress (2), Director, Screenplay, Black-and-White Set Design, Dramatic Score, and Editing

One Foot in Heaven: nominated Best Picture

Sergeant York: Best Actor and Editing; nominated Best Picture, Supporting Actor, Supporting Actress, Director, Original Screenplay, Black-and-White Cinematography, Black-and-White Set Design, Sound Recording, and Dramatic Score

The Strawberry Blonde: nominated Best Musical Score

1942

Kings Row: nominated Best Picture, Director, and Black-and-White Cinematography

The Magnificent Ambersons: nominated Best Picture, Supporting Actress, Black-and-White Cinematography, and Black-and-White Set Design

Pride of the Yankees: Best Editing; nominated Best Picture, Actress, Actor, Original Story, Screenplay, Black-and-White Cinematography, Black-and-White Set Design, Sound Recording, Dramatic Score, and Special Effects

Reap the Wild Wind: Best Special Effects; nominated Best Color Cinematography and Color Set Design

Yankee Doodle Dandy: Best Actor, Sound Recording, and Musical Score; nominated Best Picture, Supporting Actor, Director, Original Story, and Editing

1943

Heaven Can Wait: nominated Best Picture, Director, and Color Cinematography

Hello, Frisco, Hello: Best Song; nominated Best Color Cinematography

In Old Oklahoma: nominated Best Sound Recording and Dramatic Score

1944

The Adventures of Mark Twain: nominated Best Black-and-White Set Design, Dramatic Score, and Special Effects

Jack London: nominated Best Dramatic Score

Meet Me in St. Louis: nominated Best Screenplay, Color Cinematography, Song, and Musical Score

Mr. Skeffington: nominated Best Actress and Actor

Mrs. Parkington: nominated Best Actress and Supporting Actress

The Story of Dr. Wassell: nominated Best Special Effects

Wilson: Best Original Screenplay, Color Cinematography, Color Set Design, Sound, and Editing; nominated Best Picture, Actor, Director, Dramatic Score, and Special Effects

1945

Captain Eddie: nominated Best Special Effects

Flame of the Barbary Coast: nominated Best Sound Recording and Dramatic
    Score

Incendiary Blonde: nominated Best Musical Score

The Story of G.I. Joe: nominated Best Supporting Actor, Screenplay, Song, and
    Dramatic Score

A Tree Grows in Brooklyn: Best Supporting Actor; nominated Best Screenplay

1946

The Dolly Sisters: nominated Best Song

Duel in the Sun: nominated Best Actress, Supporting Actress, and Color
    Cinematography

The Harvey Girls: Best Song; nominated Best Musical Score

The Jolson Story: Best Musical Score; nominated Best Actor, Supporting Actor,
    and Editing

Saratoga Trunk: nominated Best Supporting Actress

1947

Life with Father: nominated Best Actor, Color Cinematography, Art Direction,
    and Dramatic Score

Mother Wore Tights: Best Musical Score; nominated Best Color
    Cinematography and Song

My Wild Irish Rose: nominated Best Musical Score

Unconquered: nominated Best Special Effects

1948

I Remember Mama: nominated Best Actress, Supporting Actress (2), Supporting
    Actor, and Black-and-White Cinematography

Portrait of Jennie: Best Special Effects; nominated Best Black-and-White
    Cinematography

Red River: Best Original Story and Editing

1949

Jolson Sings Again: nominated Best Story and Screenplay, Color
    Cinematography, and Musical Score

Little Women: nominated Best Color Art Design and Color
    Cinematography

Look for the Silver Lining: nominated Best Musical Score

The Sands of Iwo Jima: nominated Best Actor, Original Story, Sound Recording,
    and Editing

She Wore a Yellow Ribbon: Best Color Cinematography

The Stratton Story: Best Original Story

1950

All about Eve: Best Picture, Supporting Actor, Director, Screenplay, Sound
    Recording, and Black-and-White Costume Design; nominated Best Actress

(2), Supporting Actress, Black-and-White Cinematography, Black-and-White Art Direction, Dramatic Score, and Editing

Annie Get Your Gun: Best Musical Score; nominated Best Color Cinematography, Editing, and Color Art Direction

Broken Arrow: nominated Best Supporting Actor, Screenplay, and Color Cinematography

The Magnificent Yankee: nominated Best Actor and Costume Design

Sunset Boulevard: Best Story and Screenplay, Dramatic Score, and Black-and-White Art Direction; nominated Best Picture, Actress, Actor, Supporting Actor, Supporting Actress, Director, Black-and-White Cinematography, and Editing

Appendix D

American Historical Films to Be Named the National Board of Review's and *Film Daily*'s Best Films of the Year

Note the steady waning of critical and box-office accolades for American historical films after 1942. Beginning in 1942 with *In Which We Serve*, more and more British films dominated the top-ten lists. Italian filmmakers Visconti, de Sica, and Rossellini were also prominent beginning in 1944.

1927
No American historical films made the list. *Film Daily*'s top five were *Beau Geste, The Big Parade, What Price Glory, The Way of All Flesh,* and *Ben Hur.*

1928
No American historical films made the list. *Film Daily*'s top ten were *The Patriot, Sorrell and Son, The Last Command, Four Sons, Street Angel, The Circus, Sunrise, The Crowd, King of Kings,* and *Sadie Thompson.*

1929
Of *Film Daily*'s top ten, only *Gold Diggers of Broadway* (entertainment past) and *In Old Arizona* (first talking western) made the list, at numbers 5 and 7, respectively. *Show Boat* and *The Virginian* make the "Roll of Honor." The other top ten were *Disraeli, Broadway Melody, Madame X, Rio Rita, Bulldog Drummond, Cock-eyed World, The Last of Mrs. Cheyney,* and *Hallelujah!*

1930
All Quiet on the Western Front was named the top film by both *Film Daily* and the National Board of Review poll. *Abraham Lincoln* was number 2 on *Film Daily*'s list. The only other American period film to make either list was *Tol'able David* (National Board of Review).

1931
Cimarron became the first American historical film to win top honors from both *Film Daily* and the National Board of Review. The latter's "Supplementary Ten"

361

included *The Public Enemy* and *Little Caesar*. *Film Daily's* list mentioned *Little Caesar* (11), *Royal Family of Broadway* (14), *Alexander Hamilton* (16), *The Public Enemy* (18), *Tom Sawyer* (30), *Huckleberry Finn* (38), and *Miracle Woman* (51).

1932

Greta Garbo's films led the choices of both *Film Daily* (*Grand Hotel*) and the National Board of Review (*As You Desire Me*), but *Scarface* made the top ten of both lists (numbers 10 and 7, respectively). The National Board of Review also listed *I Am a Fugitive from a Chain Gang* at number 4 (*Film Daily* included the film in its 1933 tally). *Movie Crazy* (26), *What Price Hollywood?* (39), *So Big* (42), and *Mouthpiece* (49) also made the *Film Daily* list.

1933

The British historical drama *Cavalcade* led *Film Daily* and came in at number 2 for the National Board of Review. American period films *She Done Him Wrong* (numbers 7 and 6, respectively) and *Little Women* (3) made the lists. *The Bowery* (18), *The Power and the Glory* (21), *The Gold Diggers of 1933* (28), *Silver Dollar* (30), and *Morning Glory* (14) won honorable mention from *Film Daily*.

1934

Viva Villa! made both top-ten lists: number 10 for the National Board of Review, and number 7 for *Film Daily*. Also on *Film Daily's* list were *Little Women*, *David Harum*, *Judge Priest*, and *Operator 13*.

1935

Film Daily included the following films: *Ruggles of Red Gap* (6), *Naughty Marietta* (4), *Alice Adams* (11), *Diamond Jim* (27), *Steamboat Round the Bend* (30), *The Barbary Coast* (35), *The Little Colonel* (36), *The Farmer Takes a Wife* (37), and *Mighty Barnum* (46). The National Board of Review listed *Alice Adams* (1) and *Ruggles of Red Gap* (4).

1936

Film Daily listed *The Great Ziegfeld* (3), *San Francisco* (4), *Ah, Wilderness* (honorable mention; number 12 in 1935), *The Petrified Forest* (18), *Show Boat* (20), *The Gorgeous Hussy* (27), *The Prisoner of Shark Island* (39), *Ramona* (46), and *The Last of the Mohicans* (54). The National Board of Review listed *The Prisoner of Shark Island* (9).

1937

Film Daily's choices were *Captains Courageous* (3), *A Star Is Born* (5), *The Plainsman* (honorable mention; number 20 in 1936), *Maytime* (15), *Come and Get It* (46), *Maid of Salem* (47), and *Slave Ship* (49). The National Board of Review chose *Captains Courageous* (8) and *A Star Is Born* (9).

1938

Film Daily listed *Alexander's Ragtime Band* (3), *Boys Town* (4), and *In Old Chicago*

(6) and gave honorable mention to *Jezebel* (13), *Wells Fargo* (15), *Of Human Hearts* (20), *The Buccaneer* (21), and *The Sisters* (26). For the National Board of Review, *Of Human Hearts* (3) and *Jezebel* (4) made the list, with *Alexander's Ragtime Band* and *In Old Chicago* listed as top moneymakers.

1939
Film Daily's list included *Stanley and Livingstone* (9) and *The Old Maid* (10); the National Board of Review listed *Stagecoach* (3), *Young Mr. Lincoln* (5), *Mr. Smith Goes to Washington* (8), and *The Roaring Twenties* (9). *Film Daily* also gave honorable mention to *Stagecoach* (11), *Young Mr. Lincoln* (12), *Union Pacific* (15), *Jesse James* (21), *The Story of Vernon and Irene Castle* (22), *The Story of Alexander Graham Bell* (25), *Dodge City* (32), and *Hollywood Cavalcade* (34), along with *The Roaring Twenties*, *Real Glory*, and *Man of Conquest*.

1940
Film Daily chose *The Grapes of Wrath* (2), *Abe Lincoln in Illinois* (6), and *Northwest Passage* (8). The National Board of Review chose *The Grapes of Wrath* (1) and *Gone with the Wind* (9) and also mentioned *Edison the Man* (13), *Knute Rockne, All American* (14), *Young Tom Edison* (20), *The Howards of Virginia* (21), *Destry Rides Again* (23), *The Fighting 69th* (27), *Drums along the Mohawk* (30), *Brigham Young* (34), *The Westerner* (35), *Lillian Russell* (37), and *Swanee River* (53). This year, the National Board of Review began to include three categories based on artistic merit and popular appeal.

1941
The National Board of Review cited *Citizen Kane* (1) for artistic merit and *Sergeant York* for popularity with the Motion Pictures Council. *One Foot in Heaven* and *Blossoms in the Dust* also made the top-ten popularity polls. *Gone with the Wind* still headed *Film Daily's* list as the best film in circulation in 1941, followed by *Sergeant York* (2), *The Philadelphia Story* (3), *Citizen Kane* (4), and *Kitty Foyle* (7). *The Westerner* (39), *Western Union* (43), *Strawberry Blonde* (44), *Chad Hanna* (45), *Hudson's Bay* (48), *Belle Starr* (52), and *Arizona* (58) were also mentioned.

1942
In Which We Serve and *Mrs. Miniver* topped the National Board of Review list, which also included *Pride of the Yankees* and *Yankee Doodle Dandy*. *Film Daily* listed *Kings Row* (3), *Pride of the Yankees* (5), *One Foot in Heaven* (7), *Reap the Wild Wind* (12), *The Magnificent Ambersons* (24), and *The Great Man's Lady* (43).

1943
Only *Yankee Doodle Dandy* (3) was in *Film Daily's* top ten.

1944
Film Daily listed *The Adventures of Mark Twain* (20) and *Buffalo Bill* (52). The National Board of Review cited *Wilson* (6) and *Meet Me in St. Louis* (7).

1945

The National Board of Review chose *The Story of G.I. Joe* (4) and *A Tree Grows in Brooklyn* (7). *Film Daily* listed *Wilson* (1), *A Tree Grows in Brooklyn* (2), *The Story of G.I. Joe* (7), *Meet Me in St. Louis* (13), *The Dolly Sisters* (41), *Incendiary Blonde* (50), and *Roughly Speaking* (53).

1946

Film Daily's list included *Saratoga Trunk* (6), *The Jolson Story* (19), *Harvey Girls* (29), *My Darling Clementine* (47), and *The Outlaw* (55). The National Board of Review's best artistic films were *Henry V* (Great Britain) and *Open City* (Italy). *Clementine* (7) and *Saratoga Trunk* (10) made the most-popular list.

1947

Film Daily listed *The Jolson Story* (2), *Duel in the Sun* (18), *Mother Wore Tights* (21), *Sea of Grass* (25), and *The Perils of Pauline* (37).

Appendix E

American Historical Film Output by Major Studios

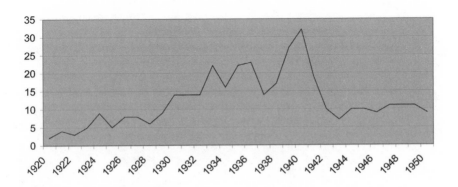

Total Number of American Historical Films, 1928–1950

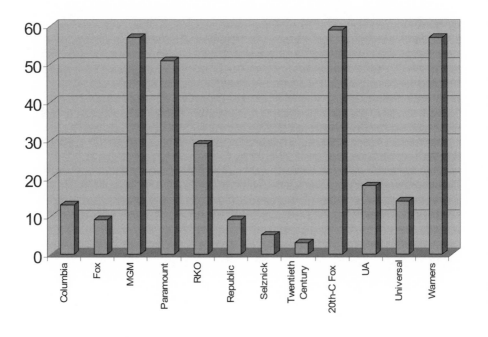

Notes

Introduction

The epigraph to this section is from D. W. Griffith, *The Rise and Fall of Free Speech in America* [pamphlet] (Los Angeles, 1916), 8.

1. Ince's feature was arguably the first major American historical film (five reels). America's only competitor in historical films, Italy, tended to produce Roman epics such as Guazonni's *Quo Vadis?* (1913) and Pastrone's *Cabiria* (1914).

2. See Fred Silva, ed., *Focus on* The Birth of a Nation (Englewood Cliffs, N.J.: Prentice-Hall, 1971), 62–105.

3. *Crisis*, May–June 1915, 40–42, 87–88; Griffith did cut 558 feet of anti-black, pro-Klan footage from the original print (Silva, *Focus*, 4); editorial, "Capitalizing Race Hatred," *New York Globe*, 6 April 1915; Francis Hackett, "Brotherly Love," *New Republic*, 20 March 1915, 185.

4. Hackett, "Brotherly Love" 185.

5. *Moving Picture World*, 13 March 1915, 1586–87.

6. Woodrow Wilson, *A History of the American People*, 5 vols. (New York: Harper & Brothers, 1902).

7. D. W. Griffith, "Reply to the *New York Globe*," *New York Globe*, 10 April 1915, and "The Motion Picture and the Witch Burners," in Silva, *Focus*, 77–79, 96–99.

8. V. F. Calverton, "Current History in the World of Fine Arts: Cultural Barometer," *Current History* 49 (September 1938): 45; Mimi White, "*The Birth of a Nation*: History as Pretext," in *The Birth of a Nation*, ed. Robert Lang (New Brunswick, N.J.: Rutgers University Press, 1994), 214–24.

9. Lillian Gish with Ann Pinchot, *Lillian Gish: The Movies, Mr. Griffith and Me* (Englewood Cliffs, N.J.: Prentice-Hall, 1969), 136.

10. Thomas J. Pressly, *Americans Interpret Their Civil War* [1954] (New York: Free Press, 1966), 265; Peter Novick, *That Noble Dream: The "Objectivity Question" and the American Historical Profession* (Cambridge: Cambridge University Press, 1988).

11. Richard Barry, "Five-Dollar Movies Prophesied," *Editor*, 24 April 1915, 409.

12. American historian Frederick Jackson Turner offered the most thorough analysis of the pivotal distinction between the work of a historian and a mere fact-finding antiquarian in his article "The Significance of History" [1891], in *Rereading Frederick Jackson Turner*, ed. John Faragher (New York: Henry Holt, 1994), 11–30.

13. Michael Rogin, "'The Sword Became a Flashing Vision': D. W. Griffith's *The Birth of a Nation*," in Lang, *The Birth of a Nation*, 250–93.

14. George Bancroft, *The History of the Colonization of the United States*, 3 vols. (Boston: Little, Brown, 1834–1841); *The History of the United States*, 9 vols. (Boston: Little, Brown, 1858–1866); *The American Revolution*, 4 vols. (Boston: Little, Brown, 1872–1874).

15. My use of the term *historiography* is based on the primary definition and etymological translation: the writing of history.

16. *New York Post*, 4 March 1915. The quote was subsequently used in the film's promotion.

17. Griffith, "The Motion Picture and the Witch Burners," 97.

18. Compare Robert Sherwood's exhaustive appraisal of *The Covered Wagon* in his *The Best Moving Pictures of 1922–1923* (Boston: Small, Maynard, 1923), 71–77, and *Photoplay*'s equally history-laden review (May 1923, 64) with reviews of *Robin Hood* (Sherwood, *Best Moving Pictures*, 37–44; *Variety*, 20 October 1922, 40), *Beau Brummel* (*Photoplay*, May 1924, 54), and *The Patriot* (Richard Watts Jr., *The Film Mercury*, 31 August 1928, 6; *Photoplay*, June 1928, 53). Reviews of these major British and European productions focused on performance and decor.

19. See Richard Koszarski, *An Evening's Entertainment: The Age of the Silent Feature Picture, 1916–1928* (New York: Charles Scribner's Sons, 1990), 33. Based on exhibitors' reports, the top box-office attraction for 1923, 1924, 1925, 1926, and 1927 was a historical film.

20. See Walter Benn Michaels, *Our America: Nativism, Modernism, and Pluralism* (Durham, N.C.: Duke University Press, 1995), 38–40.

21. The exceptions were Anita Loos and Frances Marion, who generally were not principal writers for historical productions, although Loos did write one of the major historical films of the early sound era, *San Francisco* (1936).

22. According to *Film Daily*, the major Hollywood studios produced around 350 features per year during the 1930s, along with 100 independent productions, but only about 80 of these films qualified as A-level, prestige films (e.g., *Grand Hotel*, *A Bill of Divorcement*, *Scarface*, *What Price Hollywood?* for 1932). Serials, B pictures, lower-grade "Poverty Row" productions, quota quickies for foreign markets, and documentaries made up the balance.

23. Thomas Schatz, *The Genius of the System* (New York: Pantheon, 1988), passim.

24. John Ford made only $57,000 (*Variety*, 12 April 1939, 6). At Paramount, screenwriter-producer Howard Estabrook took home $125,000.

25. See appendixes A and B.

26. Frank S. Nugent, *New York Times*, 10 December 1937.

27. See appendixes A through D.

28. André Bazin, "The Evolution of the Language of Cinema," in *What Is Cinema?* (Berkeley: University of California Press, 1967), 1:23–40.

29. Christian Metz, *Film Language: A Semiotics of the Cinema*, trans. Michael Taylor (Oxford: Oxford University Press, 1974); Metz, *The Imaginary Signifier: Psychoanalysis and the Cinema* (London: Macmillan, 1982); Jean-Louis Baudry, "Ideological Effects of the Basic Cinematographic Apparatus" [1970], reprinted in *Narrative, Apparatus, Ideology*, ed. Philip Rosen, (New York: Columbia University Press, 1986), 186–98; Baudry, "The Apparatus: Metaphysical Approaches to the Impression of Reality in the Cinema" [1975], in ibid., 299–318.

30. Hortense Powdermaker, *Hollywood: The Dream Factory* (Boston: Little, Brown, 1950).

31. Mircea Eliade, *The Sacred and the Profane* (New York: Harcourt, Brace, 1959); Northrop Frye, *The Critical Path: An Essay in the Social Context of Literary Criticism* (Bloomington: Indiana University Press, 1973); Claude Lévi-Strauss, *The Raw and the Cooked: Introduction to a Science of Mythology* (New York: Harper & Row, 1969).

32. Robert Warshow, "The Gangster as Tragic Hero" and "Movie Chronicle: The Westerner," in *The Immediate Experience* (Garden City, N.Y.: Doubleday, 1962), 127–34, 135–54; Will Wright, *Six Guns and Society: A Structural Study of the Western* (Berkeley: University of California Press, 1975); Steve Neale, *Genre* (London: BFI, 1980); Thomas Schatz, *Hollywood Genres* (Philadelphia: Temple University Press, 1981).

33. Rick Altman, *Film/Genre* (London: BFI, 1999). Altman not only outlines the history of genre and its appropriation in film studies but also, in close production studies of films such as *Disraeli* (1929) and *Frankenstein* (1931), shows how producers developed film cycles on a more idiosyncratic, case-by-case basis.

34. Schatz, *The Genius of the System*; George F. Custen, *Twentieth Century's Fox: Darryl F. Zanuck and the Culture of Hollywood* (New York: Basic Books, 1997).

35. David Bordwell, Kristin Thompson, and Janet Staiger, *The Classical Hollywood Cinema: Film Style and Mode of Production to 1960* (New York: Columbia University Press, 1985).

36. Miriam Hansen, "Mass Production of the Senses: Classical Cinema as Vernacular Modernism," in *Reinventing Film Studies*, ed. Linda Williams and Christine Gledhill (London: Arnold, 1999), 332–50. See also Jane Gaines, ed., *Classical Hollywood Narrative: The Paradigm Wars* (Durham, N.C.: Duke University Press, 1992).

37. Although Dana Benelli, "Jungles and National Landscapes: Documentary and the Hollywood Cinema of the 1930s" (Ph.D. diss., Iowa, 1992), has considered the unique production circumstances of Hollywood documentary films, the prevailing approach to "fiction" or narrative films of this period follows John O'Connor and Martin Jackson, eds., *American History/American Film: Interpreting the Hollywood Image* (New York: Ungar, 1979), and Robert Brent Toplin, *History by Hollywood: The Use and Abuse of the American Past* (Urbana: University of Illinois Press, 1996).

38. Sergei Eisenstein, V. I. Pudovkin, and G. V. Alexandrov, "Statement on

Sound" [1928], reprinted in Sergei Eisenstein, *Film Form* (New York: Harcourt, 1949), 257–60.

39. Pascal Bonitzer, "The Silences of the Voice" [1975, *Cahiers du cinéma*], reprinted in Rosen, *Narrative, Apparatus, Ideology*, 319–34, 331–32.

40. See chapters 1, 2, 3, 4, and 7.

41. Tom Gunning, "The Cinema of Attractions: Early Film, Its Spectator and the Avant-Garde" in *Early Cinema: Space, Frame, Narrative*, ed. Thomas Elsaesser with Adam Barker, (London: BFI, 1990), 56–63. My use of *excess* deliberately subverts Kristin Thompson's anti-narrative, anti-Hollywood formulation in "The Concept of Cinematic Excess" [1981], in *Film Theory and Criticism*, 6th ed., ed. Leo Braudy and Marshall Cohen (Oxford: Oxford University Press, 2004), 513–24.

42. Paul Rotha, *The Film till Now* (London: Jonathan Cape, 1930); Rotha, *Documentary Film* (London: Faber & Faber, 1936).

43. Donald Crafton, "The Portrait as Protagonist: *The Private Life of Henry VIII*," *Iris* 14–15 (fall 1992), 25–43. Crafton, though exploring Korda's visual play with objectivity and popular history, is not willing to consider Korda a historian.

44. Michael T. Isenberg, *War on Film* (London: Associated University Presses, 1981), 33.

45. George Custen's study of the Hollywood biopic (*Bio/Pics: How Hollywood Constructed Public History* [New Brunswick, N.J.: Rutgers University Press, 1992]) owes much to Isenberg's characterization of Hollywood history.

46. Frederick Jackson Turner, "The Significance of History" [1891], in *Re-reading Frederick Jackson Turner*, ed. John Faragher (New York: Henry Holt, 1994), 18.

47. Novick, *That Noble Dream*, 111–32.

48. Carl Becker, "Everyman His Own Historian," *American Historical Review* 37 (1932): 221–36.

49. Allan Nevins, "What's the Matter with History?" *Saturday Review of Literature* 19 (4 February 1939): 3–4, 16.

50. Custen, *Bio/Pics*, 8.

51. Louis Gottschalk to Samuel Marx, 18 April 1935, box 1, folder 6, Louis R. Gottschalk Papers, University of Chicago.

52. Isenberg, *War on Film*, 43.

53. Marc C. Carnes, ed., *Past Imperfect: History According to the Movies* (New York: Henry Holt, 1995); Peter C. Rollins, ed., *The Columbia Companion to American History on Film: How the Movies Have Portrayed the American Past* (New York: Columbia University Press, 2004).

54. Richard Slotkin's film analysis in *Gunfighter Nation* (Norman: University of Oklahoma Press, 1998) and Novick's study of historiography (*That Noble Dream*, 5) follow an abbreviated version of Lévi-Strauss's definition in *Structural Anthropology* (New York: Basic Books, 1963).

55. See Slotkin, *Gunfighter Nation*; Custen, *Bio/Pics*; Carnes, *Past Imperfect*; Rollins, *Columbia Companion*.

56. Editors of *Cahiers du cinéma*, "John Ford's *Young Mr. Lincoln*" [1970], reprinted in Rosen, *Narrative, Apparatus, Ideology*, 444–82.

57. In his lengthy study of the vicissitudes of Lincoln historiography, Merrill

D. Peterson included only a few paragraphs on Lincoln's cinematic representation (*Lincoln in American Memory* [New York: Oxford University Press, 1994]). See also Mark S. Reinhart, *Abraham Lincoln on Screen: A Filmography, 1903–1998* (Jefferson, N.C.: McFarland, 1998).

58. Editors of *Cahiers*, "John Ford's *Young Mr. Lincoln*," 456–58.

59. See O'Connor and Jackson, *American History/American Film*; Slotkin, *Gunfighter Nation*; Custen, *Bio/Pics*; Kenneth M. Cameron, *America on Film: Hollywood and American History* (New York: Continuum, 1997).

60. Mark W. Roche and Vittorio Hoesle, "Vico's Age of Heroes and the Age of Men in John Ford's Film *The Man Who Shot Liberty Valance*," *Clio* 23, no. 2 (1994): 131–47.

61. Alan David Vertrees, *Selznick's Vision* (Austin: University of Texas Press, 1997).

62. Isenberg, *War on Film*; Michael Birdwell, *Celluloid Soldiers: The Warner Bros. Campaign against Nazism* (New York: New York University Press, 1999).

63. Will Wright, *Six Guns and Society: A Structural Study of the Western* (Berkeley: University of California Press, 1975); Slotkin, *Gunfighter Nation*; Ian Cameron and Douglas Pye, eds., *The Book of Westerns* (New York: Continuum, 1996).

64. Warren Susman, "Film and History: Artifact and Experience," *Film and History* 15, no. 2 (May 1985): 26–36.

65. Ibid., 31.

66. Hayden White, "Historiography and Historiophoty." *American Historical Review* 93, no. 5 (1988): 1193–99.

67. Robert Rosenstone restated his position and the "separate but comparable" thesis in "Inventing Historical Truth on the Silver Screen," *Cineaste* 29, no. 2 (spring 2004): 29–33.

68. Marc Ferro, *Cinema and History*, trans. Naomi Greene (Detroit: Wayne State University Press, 1988), 161–63. Pierre Sorlin shares Ferro's view of Hollywood "historians" in his *The Film in History: Restaging the Past* (Totowa, N.J.: Barnes & Noble, 1980)).

69. Robert A. Rosenstone, *Visions of the Past* (Cambridge, Mass.: Harvard University Press, 1995); Robert Burgoyne, *Film Nation: Hollywood Looks at U.S. History* (Minneapolis: University of Minnesota Press, 1997); Steven C. Caton, *Lawrence of Arabia: A Film's Anthropology* (Berkeley: University of California Press, 1999); Natalie Zemon Davis, *Slaves on Screen* (Cambridge, Mass.: Harvard University Press, 2001).

70. Philip Rosen, "Document and Documentary: On the Persistence of the Historical," in *Theorizing Documentary*, ed. Michael Renov (New York: Routledge, 1993), 58–89.

71. Philip Rosen, *Change Mummified* (Minneapolis: University of Minnesota Press, 2001), 112–14, 147–63.

72. Philip Rosen, "Securing the Historical: Historiography and the Classical Cinema," in *Cinema Histories, Cinema Practices*, ed. Patricia Mellencamp and Philip Rosen (Frederick, Md.: University Publications of America, 1984), 17–34.

73. Crafton, "Portrait as Protagonist," 28–43.

74. This separation between the image and the word in historical cinema is not confined to late-twentieth-century scholarship but has its roots in early film critics' (e.g., Rudolf Arnheim, Sergei Eisenstein, Béla Balázs, Gilbert Seldes) qualms about and predictions for sound cinema. Although some, like Balázs, continued to articulate a basic antagonism between spoken word and image; others, like Eisenstein, believed in the possibility of an "audio visual counterpoint" ("A Dialectical Approach to Film Form," in *Film Form* [New York: Harcourt, 1977], 55). Although Eisenstein and others hoped that sound would erase the presence of projected text in cinema, their accounts of American cinema in the early sound era take up the question of word and image at its most basic level: production.

75. Pamela Falkenberg, "Rewriting the 'Classic Hollywood Cinema': Textual Analysis, Ironic Distance, and the Western in the Critique of Corporate Capitalism" (Ph.D. diss., University of Iowa, 1983).

76. See appendix A for the number of releases. After peaking in 1940 at more than thirty films, American historical filmmaking plummeted and eventually stabilized at ten films throughout the 1940s.

77. J. E. Smyth, "*Cimarron*: The New Western History in 1931," *Film & History* 33, no. 1 (2003): 9–17; Smyth, "*Young Mr. Lincoln*: Between Myth and History in 1939," *Rethinking History* 7, no. 2 (summer 2003): 193–214; Smyth, "Revisioning Modern American History in the Age of *Scarface* (1932)," *Historical Journal of Film, Radio, and Television* 24, no. 4 (October 2004): 535–63.

78. The Screen Writers' Guild was formed on 6 April 1933 and received National Labor Relations Board certification in 1938, but studio heads prevented a guild shop until May 1941. See Tino Balio, *Grand Design: Hollywood as a Modern Business Enterprise, 1930–1939* (New York: Charles Scribner's Sons, 1993), 84–85.

79. See, for example, Garth Jowett, *Film: The Democratic Art* (Boston: Little, Brown, 1976), and Thomas Schatz, *Hollywood Genres* (Philadelphia: Temple University Press, 1981).

80. Studios, particularly Warner Brothers, kept reviews on file.

81. KMG, note to DOS, 21 October 1932, box 29, folder 16, Kenneth Macgowan Collection, UCLA Special Collections.

82. Balio, *Grand Design*, 405–6; these were *Variety*'s top-grossing films.

83. See individual exhibitors' reviews in *Variety*.

84. Leo Rosten, *Hollywood* (New York: HBJ, 1941), 231.

85. Colin Shindler, *Hollywood in Crisis: Cinema and American Society, 1929–1939* (New York: Routledge, 1996).

86. See, for example, Roger Dooley's work on 1930s cinema, *From Scarface to Scarlett* (New York: HBJ, 1981); Eugene Rosow, *Born to Lose: The Gangster Film in America* (New York: Oxford University Press, 1978); John O'Connor and Martin A. Jackson, eds., *American History/American Film; Interpreting the Hollywood Image* (New York: Ungar, 1979); Thomas Pauly, "*Gone with the Wind* and *The Grapes of Wrath* as Hollywood Histories of the Depression," *Journal of Popular Film* 3 (1974): 202–18; Custen, *Bio/Pics*; Lary May, *The Big Tomorrow*:

Hollywood and the Politics of the American Way (Chicago: University of Chicago Press, 2000); Shindler, *Hollywood in Crisis*; and Balio, *Grand Design.*

87. Therefore, the historical adaptation of Cooper's *Last of the Mohicans* is a major part of chapter 3, while I ignore the adaptations of *Tom Sawyer* (1930, 1938), *Huckleberry Finn* (1931, 1939), and *Moby Dick* (1930), which do not concern themselves textually with historical events.

88. Orson Welles, "Statement on His Purpose in Making *Citizen Kane*," in *Perspectives on* Citizen Kane, ed. Ronald Gottesman (New York: G. K. Hall, 1996), 23–25.

1. The New American History

1. Robert E. Sherwood, "Renaissance in Hollywood," *American Mercury* 16, no. 64 (April 1929): 431–37, 432–33.

2. Gilbert Seldes, *An Hour with the Movies and the Talkies* (Philadelphia: J. B. Lippincott, 1929); Rudolf Arnheim, *Film*, trans. L. M. Sieveking and Ian F. D. Morrow (London: Faber & Faber, 1933); Béla Bálazs, *Der Geist des Films* [1930], in *The Theory of Film* (London: Arno, 1952).

3. Sherwood, "Renaissance in Hollywood," 433.

4. See, for instance, Robert E. Sherwood, *Life*, 13 March 1924, 26.

5. Stephen V. Benét to Rosemary Benét, December 1929, in *Selected Letters*, ed. Charles Fenton (New Haven, Conn.: Yale University Press, 1960), 197.

6. Ibid., 202–3.

7. "Weby," in *Variety*, 27 August 1930, 21; Richard Watts, *New York Herald Tribune*, 26 August 1930.

8. Mordaunt Hall, *New York Times*, 26 August 1930, 24:1.

9. Harry Alan Potamkin, "*Storm over Asia* and *Abraham Lincoln*," *New Masses* (October 1930): 16.

10. *The Virginian*, dialogue-continuity, final script, 14 May 1929, 1, Paramount Collection, Academy of Motion Picture Arts and Sciences (AMPAS).

11. Jerry Hoffman, "*The Virginian*," *Los Angeles Examiner*, 1 April 1929.

12. Mordaunt Hall, *New York Times*, 20 September 1930, 15:4.

13. Walter Noble Burns, *The Saga of Billy the Kid* (Garden City, N.Y.: Doubleday, 1925).

14. Ibid., 53–54.

15. Ibid., 68–69.

16. *Billy the Kid*, 1930 final script, UCLA.

17. Ralph A. Lynd, "*Billy the Kid*," *Glendale (Calif.) New Press*, 2 December 1930, reprinted in *The American West on Film: Myth and Reality*, ed. Richard A. Maynard (Rochelle Park, N.Y.: Hayden Book Co., 1974), 78–79; Elena Boland, "Honesty or Hokum—Which Does the Public Want?" *Los Angeles Times*, 2 November 1930.

18. *Hollywood Reporter*, 18 September 1930.

19. Sime Silverman, *Variety*, 29 October 1930, 17, 27.

20. *Photoplay*, November 1930, 52.

21. Benjamin Hampton, *History of the American Film Industry from Its Beginnings to 1931* [1931] (New York: Dover Publishing, 1970), 320.

374 Notes to Pages 32–35

22. RKO's merger also marked the first alliance between cinema and radio companies, or film and sound.

23. Jack Alicoate, ed., *The 1930 "Film Daily" Year Book of Motion Pictures* (*Film Daily*, 1930), 386.

24. In spite of her success, Ferber is all but forgotten in recent studies of American literature. One exception is Fred Pheil's "Montage Dynasty: A Market Study in American Historical Fiction," in *Another Tale to Tell: Politics and Narrative in Postmodern Culture* (London: Verso, 1990), 151–91, which recovers a sense of her widespread appeal and prestige.

25. Frederick Jackson Turner, "The Significance of the Frontier in American History," in *Rereading Frederick Jackson Turner*, ed. John Mack Faragher (New York: Henry Holt, 1994), 31–60; Theodore Roosevelt, *The Winning of the West* (New York: G. P. Putnam's Sons, 1907), 1:273–74; Charles A. Beard, "The Frontier in American History," *New Republic* 25 (16 February 1921): 349–50; John C. Almach, "The Shibboleth of the Frontier," *Historical Outlook* 16 (May 1925): 197–202; Kerwin Lee Klein, *Frontiers of the Historical Imagination* (Berkeley: University of California Press, 1997), 21; Bernard De Voto, "Footnote on the West," *Harper's* 155 (November 1927): 714–22; Carey McWilliams, "Myths of the West," *North American Review* 232 (November 1931): 424–32.

26. Gerald Nash, *Creating the West: Historical Interpretations, 1890–1990* (Albuquerque: University of New Mexico Press, 1991), 13–14; Beard, Almach, and McWilliams were some of his most prominent academic critics in the postwar era.

27. Edna Ferber, *Cimarron* (Garden City, N.Y.: Doubleday, Doran, 1930), preface. She refrained from appending her bibliography only because she thought that these historical credentials would discourage potential readers. Edna Ferber, *A Peculiar Treasure* (New York: Doubleday, Doran, 1939), 295.

28. Ferber, *Peculiar Treasure*, 339; Julie Goldsmith Gilbert, *Ferber: A Biography* (Garden City, N.Y.: Doubleday, 1978), 42.

29. Percy H. Boynton, *The Rediscovery of the Frontier* (Chicago: University of Chicago Press, 1931), v–vi, 179.

30. Dorothy Van Doren, "A Pioneer Fairy Story," *Nation*, 23 April 1930, 494. See also reviews of *Cimarron:* "In Odd Oklahoma," *Time*, 24 March 1930, 80; G. T. H., *New Republic*, 30 April 1930, 308; Stanley Vestal, *Saturday Review of Literature*, 22 March 1930, 841.

31. E. Douglas Branch, *Westward: The Romance of the American Frontier* (New York: D. Appleton, 1930), v.

32. *Hollywood News*, 12 August 1930; Edward Churchill, *Exhibitors' Herald World*, 13 September 1930, *Cimarron* clipping file, AMPAS.

33. *Cimarron* production files, RKO Collection, UCLA Arts Library Special Collections.

34. Ferber's *Show Boat*, a Broadway musical, was released in 1929 to great acclaim as a semitalking picture starring Helen Morgan, and *The Royal Family of Broadway* was released the following year.

35. Paul Powell, "Story treatment and critique," 28 June 1930, 5, *Cimarron* script collection, RKO Collection, UCLA Arts Library Special Collections.

36. William Christie MacLeod, *The American Indian Frontier* (New York: Alfred A. Knopf, 1928); Estabrook Collection, *Cimarron* research, AMPAS.

37. MacLeod, *American Indian Frontier*, vii, 366.

38. Klein, *Frontiers of the Historical Imagination*, 146–47.

39. Howard Estabrook, *Cimarron*, final shooting script, 27 August 1930, dialogue and continuity, 12 January 1931, AMPAS.

40. Sergei Eisenstein, Vsevolod Pudovkin, and Grigori Alexandrov, "Statement on Sound" [1928], reprinted in *Film Theory and Criticism*, ed. Leo Braudy and Marshall Cohen (Oxford: Oxford University Press, 2004), 370–72.

41. Fred E. Sutton and A. B. MacDonald, *Hands Up!* (New York: Bobbs-Merrill, 1927).

42. Compare "Adaptation and Structure of Screen Play," 22 May 1930; first draft, 19 June 1930, 35; and shooting script, 27 August 1930, Howard Estabrook Collection, AMPAS.

43. Elizabeth Madox Roberts, *The Great Meadow* (New York: Viking Press, 1930).

44. *The Great Meadow*, treatment by Charles Brabin, 26 May 1930; continuity, 14 June 1930; shooting script, 12 August 1930; and titles, dictated by Edith Ellis, 5 November 1930, MGM Collection, USC. Dialogue and cutting continuity dated 12 December 1930, with foreword and inserts.

45. Roosevelt, *Winning of the West*, 1:273–74.

46. Ibid., 147–48.

47. Turner, "The Significance of the Frontier in American History," 32.

48. Early drafts of the script and notes confirm that Estabrook conceived this structural practice from the beginning.

49. Zane Grey, *The Vanishing American* (New York: Grosset & Dunlap, 1925). See also *Red Skin* (Paramount, 1929), also starring Dix. See Michael J. Riley, "Trapped in the History of Film: *The Vanishing American*," in *Hollywood's Indian*, ed. Peter Rollins and John E. O'Connor (Lexington: University Press of Kentucky, 1998), 58–72.

50. He is also one of the first mixed-blood Indian characters in American literature not to be demonized as a racial monster. See Harry Brown, *Injun Joe's Ghost: The Indian Mixed-Blood in American Writing* (Columbia: University of Missouri Press, 2004).

51. Estabrook's annotated copy of Ferber's *Cimarron*, 10–11, 61, 88, Howard Estabrook Collection, AMPAS; Estabrook, "Adaptation and Structure of Screen Play," 22 May 1930, A20; first draft, 19 June 1930, 35; shooting script, 27 August 1930, A23.

52. Will Wright, *Six Guns and Society: A Structural Study of the Western* (Berkeley: University of California Press, 1975), 17–28; John G. Cawelti, *The Six-Gun Mystique* (Bowling Green, Ohio: Bowling Green University Popular Press, 1971), 35–46; Robert Warshow, "Movie Chronicle: The Westerner," in *The Immediate Experience* (Garden City, N.Y.: Doubleday, 1962), 135–54; Jim Kitses, *Horizons West* (Bloomington: Indiana University Press, 1969); and Richard Slotkin, *Gunfighter Nation* (Norman: University of Oklahoma Press, 1998), 233, all share this perspective.

53. See Rick Altman's summary in *Film/Genre* (London: BFI, 1999),19–29.

54. Slotkin, *Gunfighter Nation*, 235–36.

55. Nash, *Creating the West*, 206. *Cimarron's* commitment to urbanization

as a defining force in western history also anticipated Arthur M. Schlesinger Sr.'s academic study by two years; see *The Rise of the City, 1878–98* (New York: Macmillan, 1933).

56. Slotkin, *Gunfighter Nation*, 34.

57. Ibid., 5, 34; Peter Stanfield, *Hollywood, Westerns and the 1930s: The Lost Trail* (Exeter: University of Exeter Press, 2001), 34.

58. Slotkin, *Gunfighter Nation*, 14.

59. Ibid, 38–42.

60. Lewis Mumford, *The Golden Day* (New York: Boni & Liveright, 1926), 73.

61. David M. Kennedy, *Over Here: The First World War and American Society* (New York: Oxford University Press, 1980), 218–19; Willa Cather, *One of Ours* (New York: Alfred A. Knopf, 1922), 118.

62. Ferber, *Cimarron*, 367.

63. Jack Alicoate, ed., *The 1932 "Film Daily" Year Book* (*Film Daily*, 1932).

64. Edwin Schallert, "Pioneer Days Well Depicted," *Los Angeles Times*, 7 February 1931; Thornton Delehanty, "The New Films," *New York Evening Post*, 27 January 1931; Howard R. Barnes, "*Cimarron*," *New York Herald Tribune*, 16 January 1931; Mordaunt Hall, *New York Times*, 27 January 1931, 26:5.

65. Robert Sherwood, "The Moving Picture Album: *Cimarron*," *Hollywood Reporter*, 7 February 1931.

66. Richard Watts Jr., "*Cimarron* a Triumph for Radio," *New York Herald Tribune*, 1 February 1931, 3.

67. Carl Becker, "Everyman His Own Historian," 1931 address to the American Historical Association (El Paso, Tex.: Academic Reprints, 1960), 16–17.

68. See Patricia Limerick, *Legacy of Conquest: The Unbroken Past of the American West* (New York: W. W. Norton, 1987); Richard White, *Western History* (Washington, D.C.: American Historical Association, 1997); Valerie Matsumoto and Blake Allmendinger, eds., *Over the Edge: Remapping the American West* (Berkeley: University of California Press, 1999); Neil Foley, *The White Scourge: Mexicans, Blacks, and Poor Whites in Texas Cotton Culture* (Berkeley: University of California Press, 1997); George Sanchez, *Becoming Mexican American* (Berkeley: University of California Press, 1997).

69. Paul Rotha, *The Film till Now* (London: Spring Books, 1967), 447–48.

70. Thornton Delehanty, "The New Films," *Evening Post*, 27 January 1931.

71. Lewis Jacobs, *The Rise of the American Film: A Critical History* (New York: Harcourt, Brace, 1939), 531.

72. Ronald Haver, *David O. Selznick's Hollywood* (New York: Alfred A. Knopf, 1980), 67.

73. William A. Johnston, "Writer's Gold in Hollywood," *Graphic*, 2 May 1931, 172; Howard Estabrook, "This Amusement School of Ours," *Hollywood Reporter*, 8 May 1931.

74. Estabrook, *The Conquerors*, box 184, first draft continuity, 24 December 1931, 1–2, UCLA Arts Library Special Collections.

75. *The Conquerors*, production files, box p-40, 5-page undated memo from Vorkapich to Selznick, UCLA Library Arts Special Collections.

76. *Silver Dollar,* story file, Lucien Hubbard to Jack Warner, 25 May 1932, Warner Brothers Archive, USC.

77. Paul Green to Lucien Hubbard, 24 May 1932, Warner Brothers Archive, USC.

78. Zanuck conference notes, 9 March 1932, 11 July 1932, Warner Brothers Archive, USC.

79. Thornton Delehanty, *New York Evening Post,* 23 December 1932; Richard Watts, *New York Herald Tribune,* 23 December 1932; Mordaunt Hall, *New York Times,* 23 December 1932, 20.

80. Sherwood, "Renaissance in Hollywood," 437.

81. DFZ to Huston, *The Mighty Barnum,* story file, 5 February 1934, Twentieth Century–Fox Collection, USC.

2. Contemporary History in the Age of *Scarface,* 1932

1. *Disraeli* press book (1929), 2, Lilly Library, Indiana University.

2. Land, *Variety,* 9 October 1929.

3. Film production finished in May, and the film was released in September 1931.

4. John S. Cohen Jr., *New York Sun,* 17 September 1931; Richard Watts, *New York Herald Tribune,* 17 September 1931.

5. Rush, *Variety,* 22 September 1931, 22, 26.

6. Although Carlos Clarens occasionally cited the basis for classic gangster scripts, he was not interested in the potential of these historical adaptations. Carlos Clarens, *Crime Movies: From Griffith to* The Godfather *and Beyond* (New York: W. W. Norton, 1980), 43, 53, 66.

7. See Pierre Sorlin, *The Film in History: Restaging the Past* (Totowa, N.J.: Barnes & Noble, 1980); Philip Rosen "Securing the Historical: Historiography and the Classical Cinema," in *Cinema Histories, Cinema Practices,* ed. Patricia Mellencamp and Philip Rosen (Frederick, Md.: University Publications of America, 1984), 24–25; Rosen, *Change Mummified* (Minneapolis: University of Minnesota Press, 2001), ch. 4; Marc Ferro, *Cinema and History* (Detroit: Wayne State University Press, 1988); George F. Custen, *Bio/Pics: How Hollywood Constructed Public History* (New Brunswick, N.J.: Rutgers University Press, 1992), 3–31; Richard Slotkin, *Gunfighter Nation* (Norman: University of Oklahoma Press, 1998); Marc C. Carnes, ed., *Past Imperfect: History According to the Movies* (New York: Henry Holt, 1995).

8. Robert Warshow, "The Gangster as Tragic Hero," first published in the *Partisan Review* in February 1948.

9. Andrew Bergman, *We're in the Money: Depression America and Its Films* (New York: New York University Press, 1971); Eugene Rosow, *Born to Lose: The Gangster Film in America* (New York: Oxford University Press, 1978); and Robert B. Ray, *A Certain Tendency of the Hollywood Cinema, 1930–1980* (Princeton, N.J.: Princeton University Press, 1985), 74–77.

10. Stephen Louis Karpf, *The Gangster Film: Emergence, Variation, and Decay of a Genre* (New York: Arno, 1973), 212. See also Carlos Clarens, *Crime Movies* (New York: W. W. Norton, 1980), and Jonathan Munby, *Public Enemies,*

378 Notes to Pages 60–63

Public Heroes (Chicago: University of Chicago Press, 1999), for similar perspectives.

11. Garth Jowett, "Bullets, Beer, and the Hays Office," in *American History/American Film: Interpreting the Hollywood Image*, ed. John O'Connor and Martin A. Jackson (New York: Ungar, 1979), 57–75; Clarens, *Crime Movies*, 81; Richard Maltby, "Tragic Heroes? Al Capone and the Spectacle of Criminality, 1948–1931," in *Screening the Past: The 6th Australian History and Film Conference Papers*, ed. John Benson (Bundoora: La Trobe University, 1993), 112–19; Maltby, "Grief in the Limelight: Al Capone, Howard Hughes, the Hays Code and the Politics of the Unstable Text," in *Movies and Politics: The Dynamic Relationship*, ed. James Combs (New York: Garland, 1993), 133–81; Munby, *Public Enemies, Public Heroes*.

12. David E. Ruth, *Inventing the Public Enemy: The Gangster in American Culture, 1918–1934* (Chicago: University of Chicago Press, 1996), 1.

13. Walter Noble Burns, *The One-Way Ride: The Red Trail of Chicago Gangland from Prohibition to Jake Lingle* (Garden City, N.Y.: Doubleday, Doran, 1931); Fred D. Pasley, *Al Capone: The Biography of a Self-made Man* (Garden City, N.Y.: Garden City Publishing Company, 1930); John Bright, *Hizzoner Big Bill Thompson, an Idyll of Chicago* (New York: Jonathan Cape & Harrison Smith, 1930).

14. Preston William Slosson, *The Great Crusade and After, 1914–1928* (New York: Macmillan, 1930); Louis M. Hacker, *American Problems of Today: A History of the United States since the World War* (New York: F. S. Crofts, 1938).

15. Slosson, *The Great Crusade*, xv, 95.

16. Peter Novick, *That Noble Dream: The "Objectivity Question" and the American Historical Profession* (Cambridge: Cambridge University Press, 1988); Charles Beard and Mary Beard, *The Rise of American Civilization* (New York: Macmillan, 1927).

17. Frederick Lewis Allen, *Only Yesterday: An Informal History of the Nineteen-Twenties* (New York: Harper & Brothers, 1931), xiii.

18. Ibid., ch.10, esp. 245–63. Capone is the only figure who merited an entire chapter in Allen's history.

19. Universal's *Broadway* (1929) allegedly based two of its characters on Legs Diamond and Texas Guinan, but it received less critical attention than Zanuck's film did.

20. Pasley, *Al Capone*, 11; Burns, *One-Way Ride*, 31–32.

21. Pasley, *Al Capone*, 52–53. Nails, a twice-wounded lieutenant of the 101st Illinois Infantry, received the French Croix de Guerre.

22. Joseph Gollumb, "Meeting the Crime Wave: A Comparison of Methods," *Nation*, January 1921, 82; Fred L. Holmes, "Making Criminals out of Soldiers," *Nation*, 22 July 1925, 114; Ruth, *Inventing the Public Enemy*, 18, 58.

23. Clarens, *Crime Movies*, 53.

24. Warner Brothers Collection, USC; George F. Custen, *Twentieth Century's Fox: Darryl F. Zanuck and the Culture of Hollywood* (New York: Basic Books, 1997), 136; Clarens, *Crime Movies*, 53. Although *New York Times* reviews reveal that Griffith (*Musketeers of Pig Alley*, 1913) and Allan Dwan (*Big Brother*, 1922) hired gangsters as technical advisers, their work would have been confined to

set design on these contemporary and fictitious narratives, rather than the more historically minded film biographies of the early 1930s.

25. *Variety*, 5 November 1930; Creighton Peet, "Doorway to Hell," *Outlook*, November 1930.

26. The National Board of Review and *Film Daily* also included *The Public Enemy*. See Jack Alicoate, ed., *The 1931 "Film Daily" Year Book of Motion Pictures* (*Film Daily*, 1932), 23, 63. A year before, *Film Daily* listed *Doorway to Hell* in the "Honor Roll" of memorable pictures. Critics from 350 major newspapers, trade papers, and fan journals across America voted in these polls.

27. See press book, *Blondie Johnson* (Warner Brothers), 1933, AMPAS.

28. W. R. Burnett, *Little Caesar* (London: Cape, 1929), author's note.

29. See Leonard J. Leff and Jerold L. Simmons, *The Dame in the Kimono: Hollywood, Censorship, and the Production Code* (Lexington: University Press of Kentucky, 2001).

30. Burns, *One-Way Ride*, 29–30.

31. Ibid., 164–65.

32. Pasley, *Al Capone*, 20–21.

33. Ibid., 29–30.

34. Novick, *That Noble Dream*, 111.

35. Ibid., 345–46.

36. *Little Caesar*, final script, 5, 14, 54, 77, 121, AMPAS.

37. Burns, *One-Way Ride*, 31.

38. Bright, *Hizzoner Big Bill Thompson*, 120–21.

39. A threatened lawsuit allegedly brought him to Hollywood.

40. Warner Brothers Collection, State Historical Society, Madison, Wis., cited in Roger Dooley's *From Scarface to Scarlett* (New York: HBJ, 1981), 254. See also Henry Cohen, "An Ordinary Thug," introduction to *The Public Enemy* (Madison: University of Wisconsin, 1981), 16–17.

41. Letter from DFZ to Jason Joy, 6 January 1931, PCA files, AMPAS.

42. Letter from August Vollmer to Will Hays (script review), 20 April 1931, PCA files, AMPAS.

43. Henry Cohen noticed these revisions in his introduction to the screenplay ("An Ordinary Thug," 11–33) but called them "adaptations of reality" (17).

44. Ibid., 14.

45. See Warner Brothers script, 18 January 1931. Zanuck's production of *Three on a Match* (1932) would also structure the past (1919–1931) with a similar use of dates, headlines, and newsreel footage, but its tale of three women in the 1920s, perhaps inspired by Frederick Lewis Allen's *Only Yesterday*, was not based on actual persons.

46. Sid, "The Public Enemy," *Variety*, 29 April 1931, 12.

47. This foreword is not in any of the existing scripts and was therefore added in postproduction, most likely at the insistence of the producer.

48. William Boehnel, "*Public Enemy* a Strong Talkie," *New York World-Telegram*, unmarked press clipping, *Beer and Blood* story file, Warner Brothers Archive, USC.

49. Morton was thrown from his horse while riding in Lincoln Park in the spring of 1923. His associates avenged his death in the traditional manner—ex-

cept this time, Two-Gun Louis Alterie shot the horse. Kenneth Allsop, *The Boot-leggers: The Story of Chicago's Prohibition Era* (New Rochelle, N.Y.: Arlington House, 1968), 230.

50. Production reports, 26 February 1931; final shooting script, 18 January 1931, Warner Brothers Archive, USC.

51. Letter to DFZ from Jason Joy, 26 January 1931, PCA files, AMPAS.

52. Walter Noble Burns, *The Saga of Billy the Kid* (Garden City, N.Y.: Doubleday, 1925).

53. Bright also emphasized the corrupt mayor's frontier background (*Hizzoner Big Bill Thompson*, 10–12).

54. Burns, *One-Way Ride*, 1.

55. Ibid., 19. Burns was not the only one to make this connection. See O. O. McIntyre, "Bad Man," *Cosmopolitan*, February 1931, 52–53.

56. David E. Ruth, *Inventing the Public Enemy* (Chicago: University of Chicago Press, 1996), 32.

57. Pasley, *Al Capone*, 113, 263. See also Fred Pasley's own informal history of the postwar rackets, *Muscling In* (New York: Ives Washburn, 1931), where he again likens the growth of crime to a Western Front battle (15).

58. John Landesco, *Organized Crime in Chicago* (1929; reprint, Chicago: University of Chicago Press, 1968), 221.

59. See Irvin G. Wyllie, *The Self-made Man in America: The Myth of Rags to Riches* (New York: Free Press, 1963); Herbert A. Leibowitz, *Fabricating Lives: Explorations in American Autobiography* (New York: Alfred A. Knopf, 1989).

60. Pasley, *Al Capone*, 9, 7–8, 142–43.

61. Ibid., 336.

62. See John McCarty, *Hollywood Gangland: The Movies' Love Affair with the Mob* (New York: St. Martin's Press, 1993).

63. Excerpts from *Scarface*, entitled "Gun Girl," were serialized in *Underworld Magazine* from April to July 1929 and were probably the first thing to catch Hughes's eye. The book was later published as *Scarface* in 1930.

64. See William MacAdams, *Ben Hecht* (New York: Charles Scribner's Sons, 1990), 124–26.

65. Armitage Trail, *Scarface* [1930] (London: Bloomsbury, 1997).

66. Ibid., 37.

67. Ibid., 41, 44.

68. Robert E. Sherwood, "Moving Picture Album: *Scarface*," *Hollywood Citizen-News*, 2 April 1932, mentions Pasley as a collaborator. Also a memo from Hawks to Rosson, 28 March 1931, mentions that Pasley associates helped with historical data (Hawks Collection, Brigham Young University [BYU]).

69. After further censorship, Colisimo was changed to Costillo, and Bannon became O'Hara.

70. *Scarface*, Miller typescript, folder 6, p. 3, undated, Hawks Collection, BYU.

71. Joy's resume of film, 7 March 1931, folder 1, PCA files, AMPAS.

72. Joy to Hughes, 1 May 1931, folder 1, PCA files, AMPAS; emphasis added.

73. Telegram from Hays, 10 December 1931 and Joy reply to Julia Kelly describing Hughes's refusal, 19 December 1931, folder 1, PCA files, AMPAS.

74. Letter from publicity director Lincoln Quarberg to Hughes, February 1932, Lincoln Quarberg Collection, AMPAS.

75. Todd McCarthy, *Howard Hawks* (New York: Grove Press, 1997), 151.

76. *Variety*, 24 May 1932, 29.

77. Sherwood, "Moving Picture Album." A syndicated column, it also appeared in *Pawtucket Times*, 2 April 1932.

78. D. W. Griffith's *Abraham Lincoln* was released to mixed reviews in 1930.

79. Letter from Joe Breen to Louis B. Mayer, 6 March 1934, PCA files, AMPAS.

80. Clarens, *Crime Movies*, 76.

81. *Manhattan Melodrama*, advertising manual by Howard Dietz, no date, 35–36, MGM Collection, AMPAS.

82. Compare 5 December 1933 script (35) to 1 February 1934 script, MGM Script Collection, AMPAS.

83. Dana Benelli, "Jungles and National Landscapes: Documentary and the Hollywood Cinema in the 1930s" (Ph.D. diss., University of Iowa, 1992), 1–2; Munby, *Public Enemies, Public Heroes*, 19, 84.

84. *Variety*, 28 April 1934, 29 May 1934. See USC outline (n.d), and scripts, 26 January 1934 and 5 February 1934.

85. Mary McCall's version, 28 May 1935 (2) substantially reworked by Finkel and Erickson, 11 June 1935, Warner Brothers Archive, USC.

86. Dillinger's name never appears in the *Dr. Socrates* scripts by Cain, Abem Finkel, and Carl Erickson or in the press books advertising the film (Warner Brothers Archive, USC). Barton MacLane as Red Bastion, the Dillinger stand-in, is merely referred to as "Public Enemy No. 1 of the screen."

87. *Little Caesar*, *Public Enemy*, and *Scarface* were refused licenses from the Hays office, and in 1949 Joe Breen refused to allow Hughes exhibition rights (folder 3, PCA files, AMPAS). See also letter to Warner from Joe Breen, 24 August 1936, *Little Caesar*, PCA files, AMPAS,.

88. *New York Times*, 27 May 1936, 27:1.

89. Compare 28 April 1939 long synopsis by Lewis Morton (17, 64) to Johnson's 13 July 1939 script (26–27, 149), both Fox Collection, USC, which eliminates references to Pretty Boy Floyd and Tom. The film also has no historical foreword or superimposed text.

3. Competing Frontiers, 1933–1938

1. See Robert Warshow, "The Movie Chronicle: The Westerner," in *The Immediate Experience* (Garden City, N.Y.: Doubleday, 1962); John G. Cawelti, *The Six-Gun Mystique* (Bowling Green, Ohio: Bowling Green University Popular Press, 1971); Will Wright, *Six Guns and Society: A Structural Study of the Western* (Berkeley: University of California Press, 1975).

2. Peter Stanfield, *Hollywood, Westerns and the 1930s: The Lost Trail* (Exeter: University of Exeter Press, 2001).

3. *Alexander Hamilton* (1931, Warner Brothers), *Silver Dollar* (1932, Warner Brothers), *The Mighty Barnum* (1934, Twentieth Century–Fox), and *Sutter's Gold* (1935, Universal).

4. Custen, *Bio/Pics: How Hollywood Constructed Public History* (New Brunswick, N.J.: Rutgers University Press, 1992).

5. *Annie Oakley*, story report, 22 April 1935, RKO production files, UCLA.

6. Courtney Ryley Cooper, *Annie Oakley: Woman at Arms* (New York: Duffield, 1927).

7. RKO production files, UCLA Arts Library Special Collections.

8. There is no foreword in the revised final shooting script (15 August 1935), but there was one in the cutting continuity (n.d.), RKO Script Collection, UCLA Arts Library Special Collections.

9. Estimating script, 13 July 1935, 53, 61.

10. Estimating script, 84; revised shooting script, 96.

11. "Advance Info on *Annie Oakley*," RKO publicity (1935), 3, AMPAS.

12. See Richard Dyer, *Stars* (London: BFI, 1979); Custen, *Bio/Pics*, 46–47.

13. "Advance Info on *Annie Oakley*," 4.

14. Joy S. Kasson, *Buffalo Bill's Wild West: Celebrity, Memory, and Popular History* (New York: Hill & Wang, 2001).

15. Jill Watts, "Sacred and Profane: Mae West's (re)Presentation of Western Religion," in *Over the Edge: Remapping the American West*, ed. Valerie Matsumoto and Blake Allmendinger (Berkeley: University of California Press, 1999), 50–64.

16. David Todd to Lake, 25 November 1936, box 2, folder 30, Stuart Lake Papers, Henry E. Huntington Library, San Marino, Calif.

17. The historical setting was the first element mentioned by the critics.

18. John Balderston, *The Last of the Mohicans*, notes and treatment, 7 March 1935, Edward Small Collection, USC.

19. See especially Richard Slotkin, *The Fatal Environment: The Myth of the Frontier in the Age of Industrialization, 1800–1890* (Norman: University of Oklahoma Press, 1985), 81–106.

20. Richard Slotkin, *Regeneration through Violence: The Mythology of the American Frontier, 1600–1860* (Middletown, Conn.: Wesleyan University Press, 1973), 6.

21. Slotkin's argument remains the same throughout his trilogy (1973–1992), but his most direct address of the opposition between myth and history is in *Gunfighter Nation: The Myth of the Frontier in Twentieth-Century America* (Norman: University of Oklahoma Press, 1998), 5–6. For a similar argument, see Martin Barker and Roger Sabin, *The Lasting of the Mohicans* (Jackson: University Press of Mississippi, 1995).

22. James Fenimore Cooper, *The Last of the Mohicans: A Narrative of 1757* [1826] (New York: Penguin, 1986), 1. Subsequent references are to the 1986 edition, unless otherwise noted.

23. Ibid., 12–13, 20–21, 30, 54–56, 120–23, 179.

24. John McWilliams, "The Historical Context of *The Last of the Mohicans*," in *The Last of the Mohicans*, ed. McWilliams (Oxford: Oxford University Press, 1990); James F. Beard, "Historical Introduction," in *The Last of the Mohicans*, ed. James F. Beard, James A. Sappenfield, and E. N. Feltskog (Albany: State University of New York Press, 1983); William Kelly, *Plotting America's Past: Fenimore Cooper and the Leatherstocking Tales* (Carbondale: Southern Illinois University Press, 1983).

25. James Fenimore Cooper, *The Last of the Mohicans: A Narrative of 1757*, 2 vols. (Philadelphia: Carey & Lea, 1826). The date is even emphasized with shadowed type. Compare this with the 1864 edition (New York: James Gregory) and any of the many contemporary editions.

26. Cooper, *Last of the Mohicans*, 11–14.

27. Ian K. Steele, "Cooper and Clio: The Sources for 'A Narrative of 1757,'" *Canadian Review of American Studies* 20 (winter 1989): 121–35, 123. Thomas Mante's *The History of the Late War in North America* (London, 1772) is the best-known defense by a British historian of Montcalm's conduct.

28. Cooper, *Last of the Mohicans*, 180.

29. Ibid., 31, also 117.

30. Ibid., 11.

31. Kelly, *Plotting America's Past*, 49–50.

32. Cooper, *Last of the Mohicans*, 102–3, 169–70.

33. See Steele, "Cooper and Clio"; Terence Martin, "From Atrocity to Requiem: History in *The Last of the Mohicans*," in *New Essays on* The Last of the Mohicans, ed. H. Daniel Peck (Cambridge: Cambridge University Press, 1992), 47–66; Robert Lawson Peebles, "The Lesson of the Massacre at Fort William Henry," in ibid., 115–38.

34. Susan Fenimore Cooper, *Papers and Pictures from the Writings of James Fenimore Cooper* (New York: W. A. Townsend, 1861), 129–30. Some of his sources were Charlevoix, Penn, Smith, Lewis and Clark, Colden, and Lang. He found Chateaubriand's *Atala* an imaginary bore (130).

35. Cooper, *Last of the Mohicans*, 249.

36. Ibid., 303–5.

37. See Cassandra Jackson, *Barriers between Us: Interracial Sex in Nineteenth-Century American Literature* (Bloomington: Indiana University Press, 2004).

38. Balderston, notes and treatment, 7 March 1935; see also Barker and Sabin, *The Lasting of the Mohicans*, 62–73.

39. Balderston was once the London correspondent for the *New York World*, then a successful playwright.

40. Balderston, *Last of the Mohicans*, first screen continuity, 22 March 1935, Edward Small Collection, USC.

41. Ibid. Recent historical interpretations of the reaction to the massacre at Fort William Henry also emphasize its impact in forging American and British unity during the French and Indian War. See Fred Anderson, *The Crucible of War: The Seven Years' War and the Fate of Empire in British North America* (New York: Alfred A. Knopf, 2000).

42. Dunne later complained that an unnamed script polisher (actually Paul Perez and Daniel Moore) had been hired by the studio at the last minute, removing much of the "authentic" historical background and rendering it a "pallid ghost" of its original self. Philip Dunne, *Take Two: A Life in Movies and Politics* (New York: McGraw-Hill, 1980), 35.

43. See Mary Duncan Carter, "Film Research Libraries," *Library Journal*, 15 May 1939, 404–7, which gives a history of the development of the research library. In 1936 Warner Brothers was in the process of building a separate facility for its research materials and hiring a staff to tend to them. By the end of the

384   Notes to Pages 102–111

decade, it would have a card catalog and a set of stacks as extensive as those of any city library.

44. Lambert, *Last of the Mohicans*, research notes, October 1935, Edward Small Collection, USC.

45. Carter, "Film Research Libraries"; Frances Cary Richardson, "Previous to Previews," *Wilson Bulletin for Librarians* 12, no. 9 (May 1939): 589–92.

46. Helen Hunt Jackson, *A Century of Dishonor* (New York: Harper, 1881).

47. See A. C. Vroman's introduction to Helen Hunt Jackson's *Ramona* (Boston: Little, Brown, 1913).

48. C. C. Davis, *The True Story of Ramona* (New York: Dodge Publishing Company, 1914), 15. See also A. C. Vroman and T. F. Barnes, *The Genesis of the Story of Ramona* (Los Angeles: Press of Kingsley-Barnes & Neuner, 1899).

49. Davis, *True Story of Ramona*, 33–42.

50. Scholars are divided as to whether Ramona's mixed status truly affected readers' perceptions of the novel and nineteenth-century California history. See David Fine, *Los Angeles: A City in Fiction* (Albuquerque: University of New Mexico Press, 2000); Dydia DeLyser, *Ramona Memories: Tourism and the Shaping of Southern California* (Minneapolis: University of Minnesota Press, 2005).

51. Ibid., 88.

52. George Bancroft, *History of the United States, from the Discovery of the American Continent* (Boston: Little, Brown, 1834–1875).

53. Davis, *True Story of Ramona*, 34.

54. Ramona pageant program, 1936, 13–14, Henry E. Huntington Library.

55. *Ramona* (1916), directed by W. H. Clune, reviewed for *Film Daily*, 16 April 1916, and *Ramona* (1928) with Dolores Del Rio, directed by Edwin Carewe for United Artists, reviewed 20 May 1928, both silent.

56. Trotti would be nominated for his original script, *Young Mr. Lincoln*, in 1939 and would win for Zanuck's "last gasp" at American historical cinema: *Wilson* (1944).

57. Trotti, *Ramona*, story outline, 25 April 1935, Twentieth Century–Fox Collection, USC.

58. Ibid., 1.

59. Ibid., 10.

60. Trotti and Fox, *Ramona*, 26 June 1935, 1, Twentieth Century–Fox Collection, USC.

61. *Ramona*, final script, 6 May 1936, 1, USC.

62. Darryl F. Zanuck to Neil McCarthy, 28 April 1936, in *Memo from Darryl F. Zanuck*, ed. Rudy Behlmer (New York: Grove Press, 1993), 10.

63. *Time*, 5 October 1936, 28.

64. *The Plainsman*, story department notes, 12 September 1935, box 526, folder 7, DeMille Collection, BYU. See also "List of Books Used in Research," undated, box 526, folder 6, 163 entries.

65. "List of Books Used in Research."

66. After shooting, DeMille altered the final phrase from the final script (20 May 1936, AMPAS), changing "characterizes this breed of men" to the cited wording.

67. Box 5, folder 54, Stuart Lake Papers, Henry E. Huntington Library.

68. Box 9, folder 78, ibid.

69. Stuart N. Lake, *Wyatt Earp, Frontier Marshal* (Boston: Houghton Mifflin, 1931), esp. 33–44, 48–56, 87, 89, 117–18, 192–93, 212–13.

70. Max Hart Agency, William S. Gil to Lake, 18 December 1930 and 22 December 1930, box 4, folder 28; Collier Agency's list of current properties, 1932, box 2, folder 27, Lake Papers, Huntington Library.

71. Josephine Earp to Lake, April 1931, box 3, folder 36; Merritt Hurlburd to Lake, 21 December 1933, box 10, folder 86, ibid.

72. Lake to Lamar Trotti, 6 June 1933, and to Dudley Nichols, 25 June 1933, box 8, folder 83; Trotti to Lake, 9 June 1933, and Nichols to Lake, 30 June 1933, box 11, folder 56, ibid.

73. Julian Johnson to Lake, 24 January 1933, and Nichols to Lake, 1 October 1933, ibid.

74. Letter to Ira Rich Kent, 5 July 1929, box 7, folder 9, suggests that the book be called "Wyatt Earp: Gunfighter." Kent has Lake change it to "Frontier Marshal;" Lake agrees, 23 September 1929. Harrison Leussler had already suggested the change in March (ibid.).

75. Box 14, folder 15, ibid.

76. Letter to Fred Black, 20 April 1940, box 5, folder 79; letter to Roth Collier, 10 October 1936, box 6, folder 5; letter to G. W. Wickland of Wells Fargo, 21 May 1937, box 9, folder 35, ibid.

77. Letter to Ruth Collier, 18 April 1937, box 6, folder 5, ibid.

78. Letter from Lake to Jane Hardy of Robert Thomas Hardy Agency, 25 June 1935, box 4, folder 25, ibid.

79. Letter to Lloyd, 12 August 1937, box 7, folder 81, ibid.

80. Letter to William LeBaron, 7 December 1937, ibid.

81. Clipping file, AMPAS.

82. Lloyd on *Wells Fargo, Pony Express Courier*, December 1937.

83. *Variety*, 8 December 1937, 16.

84. *Hollywood Reporter*, 3 December 1937, 3.

85. *Motion Picture Herald*, 11 December 1937, 40.

86. *New York Times*, 20 December 1937, 15:2. Paramount's publicity machine was mammoth, however, and managed to push the film in key cities as *The Plainsman*'s successor. In early 1938 exhibitors were very happy with attendance, and *Wells Fargo* had no competition until Zanuck's *In Old Chicago* blew every film off the charts (*Variety*, 5 January 1938, 13; 12 January 1938, 8–9). The latter film lasted twelve weeks at the Astor Theater in New York.

87. Frances Taylor Patterson, "The Author and Hollywood," *North American Review* 244, no. 1 (autumn 1937): 77–89.

4. The Return of Our Epic America, 1938–1941

1. Frank S. Nugent, *New York Times*, 3 March 1939, 21; Nugent, "A Sixty Day Note," *New York Times*, 12 March 1939, X5.

2. Both these films made use of historical details and intertitles.

3. Some of the best known among the Ford-Nugent collaborations were *Fort Apache* (1948), *She Wore a Yellow Ribbon* (1949), *The Quiet Man* (1952), and *The Searchers* (1956).

4. André Bazin, "The Evolution of the Western," in *What Is Cinema?* ed. and trans. Hugh Gray (Berkeley: University of California Press, 1972), 2:149–57; Nick Browne, "The Spectator-in-the-Text: The Rhetoric of *Stagecoach*," in *Film Theory and Criticism*, 6th ed., ed. Leo Braudy and Marshall Cohen (Oxford: Oxford University Press, 2004), 118–33; Richard Anobile, *Stagecoach* (New York: Avon Books, 1975); Edward Buscombe, *Stagecoach* (London: BFI, 1992), 88; Tag Gallagher, *John Ford: The Man and His Films* (Berkeley: University of California Press, 1986), 147; Tino Balio, *Grand Design: Hollywood as a Modern Business Enterprise, 1930–1939* (New York: Charles Scribner's Sons, 1993); Richard Slotkin, *Gunfighter Nation* (Norman: Universitiy of Oklahoma Press, 1998), 303.

5. See Jack Nachbar, ed., *Focus on the Western* (Englewood Cliffs, N.J.: Prentice Hall, 1974), and other titles in the bibliographical note in ch. 3 of that book. For more on John Ford's mythic West, see Andrew Sarris, *The John Ford Movie Mystery* (Bloomington: Indiana University Press, 1975); Peter Bogdanovich, *John Ford* (Berkeley: University of California Press, 1978); Lindsay Anderson, *About John Ford* (London: Plexus, 1981); Peter Stowell, *John Ford* (Boston: Twayne, 1986); Gallagher, *John Ford*; Slotkin, *Gunfighter Nation*; William Darby, *John Ford's Westerns* (Jefferson, N.C.: McFarland, 1996); and Ian Cameron and Douglas Pye, eds. *The Book of Westerns* (New York: Continuum, 1996).

6. Rudy Behlmer's comparison of the Ernest Haycox short story, the script, and the film ignores Nichols's historical perspective and the connection to earlier historical westerns: Behlmer, *Behind the Scenes* (Hollywood: Samuel French, 1990), 104–18.

7. Only recently have authors begun to explore Zanuck's and Nichols's dominant roles in "Ford" films; see George Custen, *Bio/Pics: How Hollywod Constructed Public History* (New Brunswick, N.J.: Rutgers University Press, 1992); *Twentieth Century's Fox: Darryl F. Zanuck and the Culture of Hollywood* (New York: Basic Books, 1997); Charles Maland "'Powered by a Ford'? Dudley Nichols, Authorship, and Cultural Ethos in *Stagecoach*," in *John Ford's* Stagecoach, ed. Barry Keith Grant (Cambridge: Cambridge University Press, 2003), 48–81.

8. Leo Rosten, *Hollywood* (New York: HBJ, 1941), 325–26.

9. Gilbert Seldes in *The Movies Come from America*, 74, quoted in Rosten, *Hollywood*, 302.

10. Ernest Haycox, "Stage to Lordsburg," *Collier's*, 10 April 1937, reprinted in Stagecoach: *A Film* (New York: Simon and Schuster, 1971), 5–18.

11. Edward Buscombe, *Stagecoach* (London: BFI, 1992), 14–15. See also Peter Stanfield's *Hollywood, Westerns and the 1930s: The Lost Trail* (Exeter: University of Exeter Press, 2001), which claimed that the historical western went out of circulation from 1932 to 1938.

12. Selznick to Messrs. Whitney and Wharton, 29 June 1937, in *Memo from David O. Selznick*, ed. Rudy Behlmer (New York: Viking, 1972), 116–17.

13. The script is at Yale University's Beinecke Library (WA Mss. S-1610, box 46, f. 339). The other known copy is deposited at the Lilly Library, Indiana University.

14. Only Warner Brothers' studio archives retain any records of their production research bibliographies.

15. Paul Wellman, *Death in the Desert: The Fifty Years War for the Great*

Southwest (New York: Macmillan, 1935). See also Woodworth Clum, *Apache Agent: The Story of John P. Clum* (Boston: Houghton Mifflin, 1936); Frank C. Lockwood, *The Apache Indians* (New York: Macmilllan, 1938).

16. Britton Davis, *The Truth about Geronimo: Life with the Apache Scouts* (Oxford: Oxford University Press, 1929); Anton Mazzanovich, *Trailing Geronimo* (Hollywood: A. Mazzanovich, 1931). Mazzanovich's popular book had been reissued twice by 1931, and since it had been published in the author's adopted home, Hollywood, it was certainly known to Nichols. Mazzanovich had many friends in the entertainment industry, some of whom he thanked in his preface for inspiring him to write the book.

17. Mazzanovich, *Trailing Geronimo*, 148.

18. Davis, *Truth about Geronimo*, xvi.

19. Ibid., xvii.

20. Geronimo's autobiography as told to S. M. Barrett (New York: Duffield, 1906) was not cited in ensuing popular histories of the Southwest Apache wars.

21. See Richard White, *Western History* (Washington, D.C.: American Historical Association, 1997).

22. Dudley Nichols, *Stagecoach*, November 1939, John Ford Collection, Lilly Library, Indiana University. Nichols's 1977 publication ("*Stagecoach*," in *Twenty Best Film Plays*, ed. Dudley Nichols and John Gassner [New York: Garland, 1977], 995–1038) reads "untamed American frontier." A typographical error in the latter text records the foreword's date as 1855. Other references in this version read 1885 and are in accord with the original studio copy of the final shooting script, which refers to all *Stagecoach* dates as 1885.

23. Dudley Nichols, *Stagecoach*, rough draft 10–23 October 1938, 1, Lilly Library, Indiana University.

24. Ibid., 19.

25. Nichols, "*Stagecoach*," 1029.

26. Geronimo's most famous portrait was taken by A. Frank Randall in 1886 and showed him kneeling and clutching a rifle. Reed and Wallace's series of photographs, also taken in 1886, were widely circulated as postcards and souvenirs.

27. Nick Browne, "The Spectator-in-the-Text: The Rhetoric of *Stagecoach*," in *Film Theory and Criticism*, ed. Leo Braudy and Marshall Cohen (Oxford: Oxford University Press, 2004), 118–33.

28. Buscombe, *Stagecoach*, 66–67.

29. Nichols, "*Stagecoach*," 1030.

30. Bosley Crowther, "John Ford vs. *Stagecoach*," *New York Times*, 29 January 1939; *Hollywood Reporter*, 3 February 1939, 3; *Film Daily*, 15 February 1939, 7; Welford Beaton, *Hollywood Spectator*, 18 February 1939, 5–6; *Life*, 27 February 1939, 31–35.

31. Nichols to Ford, undated letter, likely March 1939, John Ford Collection, Lilly Library.

32. *Variety*, 8 February 1939, 17; *Film Daily*, 15 February 1939, 7.

33. *Life*, 27 February 1939, 31–35.

34. John Huston (*Jezebel*) and Preston Sturges (*Sutter's Gold*) would also take this route.

35. Dudley Nichols, "Film Writing," *Theatre Arts* (December 1942): 770–74, 773.

36. John Gassner, "The Screenplay as Literature," in Nichols and Gassner, *Twenty Best Film Plays*, xxi.

37. According to *Variety's* reports of key cities (8 February 1939, 10), *Jesse James* played well for several weeks; its only competitor in February was RKO's *Gunga Din*.

38. Helen Gilmore, "The Bad Men Are Coming Back," *Liberty*, 31 December 1938, 20–21.

39. *Jesse James* treatment, 6 May 1937, Twentieth Century–Fox Collection, USC.

40. Jesse James Jr., *Jesse James, My Father, the First and Only True Story of His Adventures Ever Written* (Independence, Mo.: Sentinel Printing Co., 1899), 194.

41. T. J. Stiles, *Jesse James* (New York: Simon & Schuster, 2002), 211–25.

42. *Sioux City Journal*, 23 July 1873, cited in Stiles, *Jesse James*, 236.

43. John Rosenfield, "Jesse James Hero of Epic Melodrama," *Dallas Texas News*, 22 January 1939; *Time*, 23 January 1939; Nugent, *New York Times*, 8 January 1939, IX, 4:1, 14 January 1939, 13.

44. Zanuck conference, 14 May 1937, Twentieth Century–Fox Collection, USC.

45. *Variety*, 11 January 1939, 12; *Motion Picture Herald*, 14 January 1939.

46. *Union Pacific*, script notes, box 540, folder 1, Cecil B. DeMille Collection, BYU.

47. Letter from Lasky to DeMille, 21 February 1938, box 540, folder 10, ibid.

48. Communication, 10 July 1938, box 540, folder 2, folder 4, ibid.

49. Pamela Falkenberg, "Rewriting the 'Classic Hollywood Cinema': Textual Analysis, Ironic Distance, and the Western in the Critique of Corporate Capitalism" (Ph.D. diss., University of Iowa, 1983), 193–94.

50. Ibid., 200.

51. *Variety*, 27 April 1939, 3; *National Box Office Digest*, 8 May 1939, 7, and 22 May 1939, 5. See also Robert S. Birchard, *Cecil B. DeMille's Hollywood* (Lexington: University Press of Kentucky, 2004), 306.

52. Letter to DeMille, 16 May 1939, and response, 23 May 1939, box 549, folder 19, BYU.

53. Bosley Crowther, "DeMille Checks Facts," *New York Times*, 7 May 1939, X, 5.

54. Birchard, *DeMille's Hollywood*, 293. *The Plainsman* would gross over $2 million domestically.

55. Mary Duncan Carter, "Film Research Libraries," *Library Journal*, 15 May 1939, 406.

56. *New York Herald Tribune*, 6 November 1938.

57. Research log, 9 August 1938, Warner Brothers Archive, USC.

58. *The Oklahoma Kid*, treatment, 8 July 1938, ibid.

59. Buckner, temporary script, 9 September 1938, and Duff, 4 October 1938, ibid.

60. Memo, B. F. to Casey, 2 November 1938, *Oklahoma Kid* story file, ibid.

61. Memo, 11 July 1938, 2, story file, ibid.

62. *The Oklahoma Kid*, script, 9 September 1938, 149, ibid.

63. *Variety*, 15 March 1939, 16.

64. Howard Barnes, *New York Herald Tribune*, 11 March 1939, 8.

65. *Variety*, 5 April 1939, 2. By the end of May, *Variety* (31 May 1939, 6) reported that *Dodge City* would easily outgross $2.5 million domestically.

66. Memo, 30 March 1938, *Dodge City*, story file, Warner Brothers Archive, USC.

67. Memo, 25 January 1938, ibid.

68. Buckner, script treatment, 30 March 1938, ibid.

69. *Dodge City*, scripts, 14 May 1938 and 27 September 1938, final script dated 14 October 1938, ibid.

70. Wallis to McCord, story file, 12 February 1940, ibid.

71. Howard Barnes (*New York Herald Tribune*) and Frank Nugent (*New York Times*) both wrote about *Dodge City* on 8 April 1939; Nugent reviewed *Virginia City* in *New York Times*, 23 March 1940, 16.

72. Wallis to Curtiz, story file, 4 December 1939, Warner Brothers Archive, USC.

73. Zanuck wanted to substitute a montage of newspaper headlines to prepare the largely fictional account of Frank James's revenge, but the final film includes the clip. See treatment, 2 December 1939; note from Johnson, 4 December 1939; conference with Zanuck, 6 December 1939, 7; and shooting script, 23 February 1940, Twentieth Century–Fox Collection, USC.

74. Vera Dika, *Recycled Culture in Contemporary Art and Film: The Uses of Nostalgia* (Berkeley: University of California Press, 2003).

75. *Daily Variety*, 23 May 1941; *Hollywood Reporter*, 23 May 1941.

5. Jezebels and Rebels, Cavaliers and Compromise, 1930–1939

1. See Edwin Granberry, review, *New York Evening Sun*, 30 June 1936, and Mitchell's response, letter, 8 July 1930, in Margaret Mitchell, *Margaret Mitchell's "Gone with the Wind" Letters, 1936–1949*, ed. Richard Harwell (New York: Macmillan, 1976), 27–30; Donald Adams, *New York Times Book Review*, 5 July 1930, and Mitchell's response, letter, 9 July 1936, 30–34.

2. Hershel Brickell, review, *New York Evening Post*, 30 June 1936, and Mitchell's response, letter, 7 July 1936, in *Mitchell's "GWTW" Letters*, 19–21.

3. *R. E. Lee* won the Pulitzer Prize for biography in 1935.

4. *Mitchell's "GWTW" Letters*, 77–78, 104, 289–91; Douglas Southall Freeman, *The South to Posterity* (New York: Charles Scribner's Sons, 1939), introduction.

5. Freeman, *The South to Posterity*, 201–2.

6. Kate Cummings, *Journal of Hospital Life in the Confederate Army of the Tennessee from the Battle of Shiloh* (Louisville, Ky., 1866); Judith W. McGuire, *Diary of a Southern Refugee during the War* (Richmond, Va., 1889); Mrs. D. Giraud Wright, *A Southern Girl in '61: The War-Time Memories of a Southerner's Daughter* (New York: Page, 1905); Eliza Frances Andrews, *The War-Time Journal of a Georgia Girl* (New York: D. Appleton, 1908); *Journal of Julia LeGrand*, ed. Kate Mason Rowlands and Mrs. Morris LeGrand Croxall (Richmond, Va.,

1911); Sarah Morgan Dawson, *A Confederate Girl's Diary*, ed. Warrington Dawson (New York: Houghton Mifflin, 1913); *Women of the South in War Times*, comp. Matthew Page Andrews (Baltimore: Norman, Remington, 1920); *The Diary of Susan Bradford through Some Eventful Years* (Macon, Ga., 1926); and Mary Chesnut, *Diary from Dixie*, ed. Isabella D. Martin and Myrta Lockett Avary (New York: Peter Smith, 1929).

7. Freeman, *The South to Posterity*, preface, xi.

8. Malcolm Cowley, "Going with the Wind," *New Republic*, 16 September 1936, reprinted in both *Mitchell's "GWTW" Letters*, 66, and Darden Asbury Pyron, ed., *Recasting:* Gone with the Wind *in American Culture* (Miami: University Presses of Florida, 1983). Bernard De Voto also attacked Mitchell, but his condemnation of her "sentimental romance" was virulently misogynist; see "Fiction Fights the Civil War," *Saturday Review*, 18 December 1937, 16.

9. Darden Asbury Pyron, "The Inner War of Southern History," in Pyron, *Recasting*, 185–201, ix, 2; Anne Jones, "'The Bad Little Girl in the Good Old Days': Sex, Gender, and the Southern Social Order," in ibid., 105–15. Elizabeth Young, *Disarming the Nation* (Chicago: University of Chicago Press, 1999), also notes that although Mitchell's novel is undoubtedly racist, its romance contains unstable racial conflicts that "darken" Rhett and transform Scarlett into a masculine belle. Yet Young claims that these racial complexities are unconscious on Mitchell's part. See also Diane Roberts, *The Myth of Aunt Jemima: Representations of Race and Region* (London: Routledge, 1994), 171–81.

10. Gerald Wood, "From *The Clansman* and *The Birth of a Nation* to *Gone with the Wind*: The Loss of American Innocence," in Pyron, *Recasting*, 123–36; and especially Kenneth O'Brien, "Race, Romance, and the Southern Literary Tradition," in ibid., 153–66.

11. Young, *Disarming the Nation*, 236–73; Catherine Clinton, *Tara Revisited: Women, War, and the Plantation Legend* (New York: Abbeville, 1995).

12. Tara McPherson, *Reconstructing Dixie: Race, Gender, and Nostalgia in the Imagined South* (Durham, N.C.: Duke University Press, 2003), 54.

13. Sarah Gardner, *Blood and Irony: Southern White Women's Narratives of the Civil War, 1861–1937* (Chapel Hill: University of North Carolina Press, 2004).

14. Margaret Mitchell, *Gone with the Wind* (New York: Macmillan, 1936), 58.

15. Ibid., 172.

16. Ibid., 210–12, 233, 279, 295.

17. Drew Gilpin Faust, *Mothers of Invention: Women of the Slaveholding South in the American Civil War* (New York: Vintage, 1996); Gardner, *Blood and Irony*, 235.

18. Young, letter to Mitchell, 14 September 1936, in *Stark Young: A Life in the Arts, Letters, 1900–1962*, ed. John Pilkington (Baton Rouge: Louisiana State University Press, 1975), 707–9; Mitchell to Young, 29 September 1936, in *Mitchell's "GWTW" Letters*, 65–67.

19. Henry Steele Commager, *New York Herald Tribune Books*, 5 July 1936, 1–2.

20. Pyron, *Recasting*, 204–5.

21. Mitchell, letter to Harold Latham (Macmillan), 1 June 1936, in *Mitchell's "GWTW" Letters*, 9–12.

22. Mitchell, letter to Mrs. Julia Harris, 28 April 1936, ibid., 2–3, 5.

23. See *Mitchell's "GWTW" Letters*, especially her letters to Harry Stillwell Edwards, 18 June 1936, 13–15; to Julia Collier Harris, 8 July 1936, 26–27; and to Stephen V. Benét, 9 July 1936, 36.

24. Mitchell, letter to Adams, 9 July 1936, ibid., 31.

25. J. G. Randall, *Civil War and Reconstruction* (Boston: D. C. Heath, 1937).

26. Eliza Frances Andrews, *The War-Time Journal of a Georgia Girl* (New York: D. Appleton, 1908), 12–13.

27. Mitchell, letter to Julia Peterkin, in *Mitchell's "GWTW" Letters*, 41.

28. Mitchell, *Gone with the Wind*, 479.

29. Mitchell, letter to K. T. Lowe of *Time*, 29 August 1936, in *Mitchell's "GWTW" Letters*, 55–56.

30. As time passes, fewer histories mention this episode. It is no myth. Sherman's aide Henry Hitchcock gleefully recounted the Yankee pillaging, but he left this out. General W. P. Howard's official report to Governor Joseph Brown, 7 December 1864, recounts the horrors of the cemetery (Archives, University of Georgia at Atlanta).

31. Henry Hitchcock, *Marching with Sherman, Passages from the Letters and Campaign Diaries of Henry Hitchcock, November 1864–May 1865*, ed. M. A. DeWolfe Howe (New Haven, Conn.: Yale University Press, 1927), 53–75.

32. Randall, *Civil War and Reconstruction*, 558–64.

33. Faust, *Mothers of Invention*.

34. Gardner, *Blood and Irony*, 2–6.

35. Francis Butler Simkins and James Welch Patton, *The Women of the Confederacy* (Richmond, Va.: Garrett & Massie, 1936), 243, 240–41, 260.

36. Ibid., 260.

37. Mitchell, *Gone with the Wind*, 439–40.

38. Faust, *Mothers of Invention*, 200; Joseph T. Glatthaar, *The March to the Sea and Beyond: Sherman's Troops in the Savannah and Georgia Campaigns* (New York: New York University Press, 1985), 73–74.

39. Mitchell, *Gone with the Wind*, 745–46.

40. Chesnut, *Diary from Dixie*, 5 March 1865 entry, 359.

41. Selznick, letter to Sidney Howard, 6 January 1937, 2, *GWTW* Collection, Harry Ransom Research Center, University of Texas, Austin.

42. Mitchell, letter to Katharine Brown, 6 October 1936, in *Mitchell's "GWTW" Letters*, 71–73, 71.

43. Howard wrote to Mitchell on 18 November 1936 asking for help with the "darkie" dialogue and offering to show her what he had written. Mitchell replied on 21 November that she had "made it very plain that I would have nothing whatsoever to do with the picture" (*Mitchell's "GWTW" Letters*, 92–94).

44. Ibid., 94.

45. Agnes Brand Leahy and Edward E. Paramore Jr., *Only the Brave*, Paramount Production files, final script, 9 December 1929, seq. A-2, release dialogue, 5, 6 February 1930, AMPAS.

46. *Little Women*, revised estimating script, 20 June 1933, 1, Lilly Library, Indiana University.

47. See *Operator 13*, final cutting continuity, 6 June 1934, MGM Script Collection, AMPAS.

48. Zanuck, note to Griffith, 8 August 1935, USC.

49. Ibid., 47–65.

50. See Walter Benn Michaels's illuminating discussion of the historical divide between Page and Dixon in *Our America: Nativism, Modernism, and Pluralism* (Durham, N.C.: Duke University Press, 1995), 16–23.

51. David Roediger, *The Wages of Whiteness: Race and the Making of the American Working Class* (New York: Verso, 1991).

52. Mitchell, *Gone with the Wind*, 722.

53. Robert Buckner, *Jezebel*, temporary script, 30 April 1937, 11, Warner Brothers Archive, USC.

54. Letter, 8 March 1938, *Jezebel* production files, ibid.

55. Buckner, *Jezebel*, first draft, 30 April 1937, ibid.

56. For a basic production history and contextualization of *Jezebel* within Davis's career, see Thomas Schatz, "'A Triumph of Bitchery': Warner Bros., Bette Davis, and *Jezebel*," in *The Studio System*, ed. Janet Staiger (New Brunswick, N.J.: Rutgers University Press, 1995), 74–92.

57. See Warner Brothers research "bible" and research log, Warner Brothers Archive, USC.

58. Press book, 4, ibid.

59. Owen Davis, *Jezebel* [1933], studio typescript, story file, ibid.

60. Goulding, *Jezebel* production notes, 7 July 1937, 3, ibid.

61. W. E. B. DuBois, *Black Reconstruction* (New York: Harcourt, Brace, 1935); C. Vann Woodward, *Tom Watson: Agrarian Rebel* (New York: Macmillan, 1938).

62. Olivia de Havilland, letters to the author, 2000–2001.

63. Mitchell, *Gone with the Wind*, 426.

64. Lasting well over a minute, the darkened close-up rivals the length of the final shot of *Queen Christina* (1933).

65. Although Linda Williams described this sequence in both novel and film, she ignored the biracial rebirth and connections to southern history and instead focused on it as a moment when Scarlett is realigned with her father's immigrant Irish philosophy. See Williams, *Playing the Race Card* (Princeton, N.J.: Princeton University Press, 2001), 207.

66. Howard, "Preliminary Notes to a Screen Treatment of *Gone with the Wind*," 14 December 1936, 1, David O. Selznick Papers, Harry Ransom Research Center, University of Texas, Austin.

67. Howard, "Preliminary Notes to a Screen Treatment of *Gone with the Wind*," 14 December 1936, 1, ibid.

68. Selznick, letter to Howard, 6 January 1937, 5, ibid.

69. W. Gordon Ryan to Will Hays, 20 July 1939, PCA files, AMPAS.

70. Mitchell, *Gone with the Wind*, 521; Claude G. Bowers, *The Tragic Era: The Revolution after Lincoln* (Cambridge, Mass.: Houghton Mifflin, 1929); Arthur Schlesinger quoted in Peter Novick, *That Noble Dream: The "Objectivity Question" and the American Historical Profession* (Cambridge: Cambridge University Press, 1988), 231. Historian Arthur Schlesinger wrote that this definitive if

openly racist history was equally popular with academics and the public during the 1930s and represented the dominant national view of the period.

71. Howard, outline, 41, David O. Selznick Papers.

72. Selznick, letter, 6 January 1937, 6, 7, ibid.

73. Phillis Wheatley (YWCA of Washington, D.C.) to Selznick, 10 June 1939, ibid.; Thomas Cripps, "Winds of Change: *Gone with the Wind* and Racism as a National Issue," in Pyron, *Recasting*, 137–52.

74. Howard, *GWTW*, final script, 16 January 1939, formerly Kay Brown's, Lilly Library, Indiana University.

75. Rudy Behlmer, ed., *Memo from David O. Selznick*, (New York: Viking, 1972), 214.

76. Matthew Bernstein, "Selznick's March: The Atlanta Premiere of *Gone with the Wind*," *Atlanta History* 43, no. 2 (summer 1999): 7–33.

77. See Mitchell's letter to Col. Telamon Cuyler, 17 February 1939, in Susan Myrick, *White Columns in Hollywood: Reports from* Gone with the Wind *Sets* (Macon, Ga.: Mercer University Press, 1982), 16.

6. The Lives and Deaths of Abraham Lincoln, 1930–1941

1. Cameron Rogers, story outline, 2, Twentieth Century–Fox Collection, USC.

2. Julian Johnson, memo, 30 January 1939; Zanuck, 31 May 1940 conference; Zanuck, 21 June 1940 conference, ibid.

3. See Mark S. Reinhart, *Abraham Lincoln on Screen: A Filmography, 1903–1998* (Jefferson, N.C.: McFarland, 1998).

4. James G. Randall, "Has the Lincoln Theme Been Exhausted?" *American Historical Review* 41, no. 19 (1936): 270–94.

5. Compare *Ruggles's* 16 June 1934 script and 25 June 1934 script (yellow) to the 3 November 1934 script (white), in which the scene finally appears (C-8 through C-11), Paramount Collection, AMPAS. Scripts by Walter Deleon and Harlan Thompson, adaptation by Humphrey Pearson.

6. Zanuck to Raymond Griffith, 8 August 1935, Lilly Library, Indiana University.

7. *Hollywood Reporter*, 2 February 1935, and *Daily Variety*, 19 November 1935.

8. Mordaunt Hall, *New York Times*, 9 August 1935, 21:2; *Hollywood Reporter*, 13 August 1935, 15; *Variety*, 14 August 1935, 15.

9. Edwin Burke, first draft, 18 January 1935, 55–58. The scene is basically unchanged in the final continuity and dialogue, 21 June 1935, 52, USC.

10. Thornton Delehanty, *New York Evening Post*, 21 July 1935, Janet Gaynor scrapbook, Gaynor Collection, Boston University.

11. Tom Stempel, *Screenwriter: The Life and Times of Nunnally Johnson* (New York: A. S. Barnes, 1980), 52–55.

12. Sidney Cook, research report, 9 February 1935, USC.

13. Elden C. Weckesser, *His Name Was Mudd* (Jefferson, N.C.: McFarland, 1991).

14. Cook, research report, 1935, USC.

15. Zanuck and his staff first noticed the topic as a condensed version of George Allan England's *Isles of Romance* (New York: D. Appleton-Century, 1929) in "His Name Was Mudd," *Reader's Digest*, August 1934, 74–76.

16. First draft screenplay, 27 April 1935, USC.

17. Zanuck dictated this story himself, 14 May 1936, Macgowan Papers, UCLA. Allen Rivkin adapted it.

18. Although George Custen's concept of Zanuck's historical discourse is limited and inflexible, Zanuck's notes of the period reveal that on less important projects, he was willing to make "streamlined" historical pictures.

19. Macgowan would later become a prominent faculty member in UCLA's film department.

20. Zanuck, memo to Harris, 21 May 1938, USC.

21. In particular, Trotti liked the sequence where Bell meets the emperor of Brazil at the exposition and later introduces Queen Victoria to the thrills of intimidating her cabinet ministers via phone.

22. Memo from Macgowan to Zanuck, 2 November 1938, USC.

23. Straight wire to Jason Joy and Trotti from Zanuck, 10 November 1938, box 28, folder 1, Macgowan Papers, UCLA. Unfortunately, Robert Sherwood did not agree, campaigned against *Young Mr. Lincoln* from the pages of *Variety*, and even tried to prevent Zanuck from using "Lincoln" in the film title. "Sherwood's 'Lincoln' Would Enjoin 20th-Fox's Use of 'Abe' Title in Film," *Variety*, 12 April 1939, 7; see also George Wasson memo to William Goetz, Julian Johnson, and Macgowan, 8 April 1939, box 35, folder, 10, Macgowan Papers, UCLA.

24. Herman Lissauer, "Bibliography for picture" (1938), *Lincoln in the White House*, Warner Brothers Archive, USC.

25. Merrill D. Peterson, *Lincoln in American Memory* (New York: Oxford University Press, 1994), 95. See also Trotti's "Lincoln Trial Story," dated 17 January 1938, in which he compares a contemporary Georgia trial he covered as a reporter to Lincoln's own trial, Twentieth Century–Fox Collection, USC.

26. Ford's intellectual and emotional investment in Lincoln is well documented. See Tag Gallagher, *John Ford: the Man and His Films* (Berkeley: University of California Press, 1986), 162n. Zanuck, writing to Ford about the upcoming project, gloated that his screenwriter Lamar Trotti was "practically an authority on Lincoln," 3 December 1938, John Ford Papers, Lilly Library, Indiana University.

27. Mark E. Neely, "The Young Lincoln: Two Films," in *Past Imperfect: History According to the Movies*, ed. Mark C. Carnes (New York: Henry Holt, 1995), 124–27; Peterson, *Lincoln in American Memory*; Reinhart, *Abraham Lincoln on Screen*; George F. Custen, *Bio/Pics: How Hollywood Constructed Public History* (New Brunswick, N.J.: Rutgers University Press, 1992), 135.

28. Editors of *Cahiers du cinéma*, "John Ford's *Young Mr. Lincoln*" [1970], reprinted in *Narrative, Apparatus, Ideology*, ed. Philip Rosen, (New York: Columbia University Press, 1986), 451.

29. Kate Cameron, "Wild James Boys Come to Life in Film," *New York Daily News*, 14 January 1939.

30. Zanuck, memo to John Ford, 3 December 1938, Lilly Library, Indiana University.

31. Rosemary and Steven Vincent Benét, *A Book of Americans* (New York: Farrar & Reinhart, 1933), 65.

32. J. A. Place, "*Young Mr. Lincoln,*" *Wide Angle* 2, no. 4 (1978): 28–35.

33. See Trotti, final shooting script, *The Story of Alexander Graham Bell*, 1, Lilly Library, Indiana University. Compare Trotti's temporary script for *Young Mr. Lincoln* (13 January 1938) and the final shooting script (27 January 1939) to the revised final script (27 February 1939).

34. See Dudley Nichols, *Stagecoach*, temporary script, 10–23 October 1938, and final shooting script, 14 November 1938, John Ford Papers, Lilly Library, Indiana University.

35. Franklin B. Meade, *Heroic Statues in Bronze of Abraham Lincoln* (Fort Wayne, Ind.: Lincoln National Life Foundation, 1932).

36. Custen, *Bio/Pics*, 51.

37. Thomas P. Reep, *Lincoln and New Salem* (Peterburg, Ill.: Old Salem Lincoln League, 1927); Paul Angle, "Abraham Lincoln: Circuit Lawyer," *Lincoln Centennial Association Papers* 5 (1928): 19–44; Paul Angle, *Lincoln, 1854–1861* (Springfield, Ill.: Abraham Lincoln Association, 1933).

38. See William H. Herndon and Jesse Weik, *Herndon's Life of Lincoln* [1889], ed. Paul Angle (New York: Albert & Charles Boni, 1936), where Angle adds to the authors' original recollections of Lincoln as a lawyer with new evidence provided by Lincoln's former law partner, Stephen T. Logan (209). For more on Herndon's influence on Lincoln scholarship, see David Donald, *Lincoln's Herndon* (New York: Alfred A. Knopf, 1948).

39. Lamar Trotti, temporary script, 13 January 1939, final shooting script, 27 January 1939, revised final script, 27 February 1939; Howard Estabrook, adaptation, "The Young Lincoln," 22 July 1935.

40. David Donald, "The Folklore Lincoln," in *Lincoln Reconsidered: Essays on the Civil War Era* (New York: Alfred A. Knopf, 1956), 149.

41. Fonda's own high, thin voice supposedly resembled Lincoln's; he did not possess the resonant voice of a traditional orator.

42. Herndon and Weik, *Life of Lincoln*, 86.

43. Ibid., 331–32.

44. Donald, *Lincoln's Herndon*, 371–73.

45. Roy Basler's *The Lincoln Legend* (Boston: Houghton Mifflin, 1935) and Lloyd Lewis's *Myths after Lincoln* [1929] (New York: Readers Club, 1941) inaugurated this question, but Merrill D. Peterson cites James G. Randall's address at the fiftieth anniversary meeting of the American Historical Association as the moment when historians seriously began to separate Lincoln myth from historical fact; see Peterson, *Lincoln in American Memory*, 292.

46. Carl Sandburg, *Abraham Lincoln: The Prairie Years* (New York: Harcourt, Brace, 1926); Albert J. Beveridge, *Abraham Lincoln* (Boston: Houghton Mifflin, 1928).

47. Peterson, *Lincoln in American Memory*, 276.

48. Beveridge, *Abraham Lincoln*, 68, 116, 132, 277.

49. Editors of *Cahiers*, "John Ford's *Young Mr. Lincoln*," 453, 456–57.

50. David Donald, *Lincoln* (New York: Simon & Schuster, 1995), 165–66.

51. Lewis, *Myths after Lincoln*, 89; Basler, *The Lincoln Legend*, 207–11.

52. Abraham Lincoln, *The Collected Works of Abraham Lincoln*, ed. Roy Basler (New Brunswick, N.J.: Rutgers University Press, 1953), 5:388.

53. Basler, *The Lincoln Legend*, 203.

54. Howard Estabrook, "Lincoln Trial Story," 7–8, Twentieth Century–Fox Collection, USC.

55. William E. Baringer, *Lincoln's Rise to Power* (Boston: Little, Brown, 1937), 330–37.

56. Herndon and Weik, *Life of Lincoln*, 91.

57. After a series of conferences with Zanuck on the state of his script, Trotti changed the scene of the murder from a traveling circus to an eclectic series of Independence Day–Illinois Day celebrations. Compare pages 26–36 of the final script and the revised final script.

58. Angle, "Abraham Lincoln."

59. Among many, *Film Daily*, 1 June 1939; *Hollywood Reporter*, 3 June 1939; *Variety*, 3 June 1939; *Motion Picture Herald*, 3 June 1939; *Variety*, 7 June 1939.

60. Terry Ramsaye, "Young Mr. Lincoln," *Motion Picture Herald*, 3 June 1939, 36. Ramsaye's *A Million and One Nights* (New York: Simon & Schuster, 1926) is one of the earliest comprehensive histories of the American film industry.

61. Trotti, *Young Mr. Lincoln*, revised final script, 144–47, USC.

62. Conference with Mr. Zanuck, 23 January 1939, on temporary script of 13 January 1939; conference with Mr. Zanuck, 20 February 1939, on final script of 27 January 1939, 3.

63. Memo from Darryl F. Zanuck to Ford, 22 March 1939, Lilly Library, Indiana University.

64. Emanuel Hertz, *Lincoln Talks: A Biography in Anecdote* (New York: Viking, 1939).

65. Conference with Mr. Zanuck, 23 January 1939, on temporary script of 13 January 1939, 6, USC.

66. In an interview for Mel Gussow's *Don't Say Yes until I Finish Talking: A Biography of Darryl F. Zanuck* (Garden City, N.Y.: Doubleday, 1971), Ford admitted that Zanuck often cut his pictures at Fox (162). In an unpublished interview with Dan Ford (Lilly Library, Indiana University), Ford credited Zanuck with creating the ending sequence of shots and deciding on their relative duration.

67. Ramsaye, "Young Mr. Lincoln," 36.

68. *Motion Picture Herald*, 27 May 1939, insert between 30 and 31.

69. See *Variety*, 7 June 1939, 7–10, and 14 June 1939, 7–9.

70. *Abe Lincoln in Illinois* played only two weeks at Radio City and was considered "weak," "mediocre," and "a big disappointment" by exhibitors in Philadelphia, Brooklyn, and other key cities (*Variety*, 28 February 1940, 9; 13 March 1940, 11).

71. In addition to the steep cost of the screen rights, RKO gave Broadway producer Max Gordon a costly two-year contract (*Variety*, 22 March 1939, 2). See Neely, "The Young Lincoln"; Reinhart, *Abraham Lincoln on Screen*; Peterson, *Lincoln in American Memory*.

72. H. E. Barker, *Abraham Lincoln: His Life in Illinois* (New York: M. Barrows, 1940).

73. A. M. R. Wright, *The Dramatic Life of Abraham Lincoln* (New York: Grosset & Dunlap, 1925), vii.

74. Robert E. Sherwood, *Abe Lincoln in Illinois* (New York: Charles Scribner's Sons, 1939), 189–90.

75. Reinhart, *Abraham Lincoln on Screen*, 27–28.

76. Joseph I. Breen to Max Gordon, 9 July 1939, and Max Gordon to Joseph I. Breen, 18 July 1939, *Abe Lincoln in Illinois*, PCA files, AMPAS.

77. Alfred Jones, *Roosevelt's Image Brokers* (Port Washington, N.Y.: Kennikat Press, 1974), 43.

78. Herndon and Weik, *Life of Lincoln*, 105–15, 166–79.

79. Donald, *Lincoln's Herndon*, 353–57; Basler, *The Lincoln Legend*, 149–60.

80. Sherwood, *Abe Lincoln in Illinois*, 191.

81. E. van Rensselaer Wyatt, "Abe Lincoln in Illinois," *Catholic World* 148 (December 1938): 340.

82. Sherwood would become one of Roosevelt's speechwriters shortly after the completion of the film version of his play. See Jones, *Roosevelt's Image Brokers*, 3–4; Donald, "The Folklore Lincoln."

83. *New York Times*, 30 October 1938, XI:3.

84. See Frank Nugent, "Robert Sherwood on Historical Accuracy," *New York Times*, 25 February 1940, IX, 4:2, and his review, 23 February 1940, 19:2.

85. By 1942, the number of American historical films had dropped from the highs of 1939 (27), 1940 (32), and 1941 (19) to a mere 10 films.

7. War in the Roaring Twenties, 1932–1939

1. Robert E. Burns, *I Am a Fugitive from a Georgia Chain Gang* (New York: Grosset & Dunlap, 1932), foreword, 5.

2. Ibid., 11.

3. Ibid., 35.

4. John E. O'Connor, ed., *I Am a Fugitive from a Chain Gang* (Madison: Wisconsin Center for Film and Theater Research, 1981), 12.

5. Burns, *I Am a Fugitive*, 14, 93–94.

6. Ibid., 146.

7. Ibid., 79, 196–97.

8. Ibid., 38–39.

9. Ralph Lewis to I. Howard Levinson, 5 February 1938, legal file, Warner Brothers Archive, USC, reprinted in Rudy Behlmer, ed., *Inside Warner Brothers* (New York: Simon & Schuster, 1985), 6.

10. Undated temporary script, 1–5, Warner Brothers Archive, USC.

11. Zanuck memo, 7 July 1932, USC. Zanuck eventually let the cop sequence stand.

12. Paul Dickson and Thomas B. Allen, *The Bonus Army: An American Epic* (New York: Walker, 2004).

13. Zanuck memo, 7 July 1932.

14. Zanuck's conference notes, 7 July 1932, Warner Brothers Archive, USC.

15. Script, 19 July 1932, 1, ibid.

16. See story file, ibid.

17. Sheridan Gibney, deposition and letter, 23 March 1938, ibid.

18. Letter, 15 April 1932, ibid.

19. Thornton Delehanty's *New York Evening Post* review mentions Burns's autobiography.

20. *Variety*, 15 November 1932, 19; see press book, Wisconsin Center for Film and Theater Research, and Wilton A. Barrett's review in *National Board of Review*, November 1932.

21. See revised final script, 8 February 1933, 53, 142–43, Warner Brothers Archive, USC. Production files note that "Forgotten Man" rehearsed and finished 6–9 February.

22. Lucius Beebe, *Herald Tribune*, 8 June 1933, 18. The studio kept a copy of this review (production files, Warner Brothers Archive, USC).

23. Edwin Schallert, *Los Angeles Times*, 3 June 1933, 7; Mordaunt Hall, *New York Times*, 8 June 1933.

24. William Troy, "The Unregenerate Art," *Nation*, 19 September 1934, 336, viewed the film as "pretentious" and turgid.

25. Hervey Allen, *Toward the Flame* (New York: George H. Doran, 1925), viii.

26. Michael Isenberg, *War on Film* (London: Associated University Presses, 1981), 140–41.

27. Peter Novick, *That Noble Dream: The "Objectivity Question" and the American Historical Profession* (Cambridge: Cambridge University Press, 1988), 111–32. See Warren I. Cohen, *The American Revisionists: Lessons of Intervention in World War I* (Chicago: University of Chicago Press, 1967).

28. John Maurice Clark, *The Costs of the World War to the American People* (New Haven, Conn.: Yale University Press, 1931), 285–88.

29. Newton Baker, *Why We Went to War* (New York: Harper & Brothers, 1936), 4.

30. Ibid., 124–27.

31. Samuel Taylor Moore, *America and the World War* (New York: Greenberg, 1937), 2, 16–60. For other critical contemporary perspectives on American war aims and neutrality, see Charles C. Tansill, *America Goes to War* (Boston: Little, Brown, 1938), and Charles Seymour, *American Neutrality, 1914–1917* (New Haven, Conn.: Yale University Press, 1935).

32. H. C. Peterson, *Propaganda for War: The Campaign against American Neutrality, 1914–1917* (1939; reprint, Port Washington, N.Y.: Kennikat Press, 1968); Moore, *America and the World War*, 305–6.

33. See *Shopworn Angel*, 23 March and 17 July 1938 scripts, AMPAS.

34. See Robert Zieger, *America's Great War: World War I and the American Experience* (Lanham, Md.: Rowman & Littlefield, 2000).

35. *Variety* polls placed her third after Temple and Deanna Durbin in the latter half of the 1930s.

36. Don Herold, *Life*, November 1935, 50; Sid, *Variety*, 4 September 1935, 14.

37. Ginger Rogers, *Ginger: My Story* (New York: HarperCollins, 1991), 147.

38. Ibid., 150.

39. Ibid., 170–75.

40. Ginger Rogers, foreword to Irene Castle, *Castles in the Air* [1958] (New York: Da Capo, 1980), 5–6.

41. RKO Collection, Production Records, UCLA Arts Library Special Collections. The studio paid $20,000.

42. Irene Foote Castle, *My Husband* (New York: Scribner's, 1919).

43. *The Story of Vernon and Irene Castle*, script, 6 October 1937, RKO Collection, UCLA Arts Library Special Collections.

44. Ibid., 46.

45. *The Story of Vernon and Irene Castle*, treatment, 6 October 1937, 58, ibid.

46. *The Story of Vernon and Irene Castle*, revised final script, 8 November 1938, 50, ibid.

47. Castle, *Castles in the Air*, 246.

48. See Dorothy Yost's script, 10 June 1938, passim, RKO Collection, UCLA Arts Library Special Collections.

49. *The Story of Vernon and Irene Castle*, revised outline, 15 June 1938, 76, ibid.

50. *Patria*, script, 8 November 1938, 125, ibid.

51. Frank Nugent, *New York Times*, 31 March 1939, 19:2.

52. Arlene Croce, *The Fred Astaire and Ginger Rogers Book* (New York: Outerbridge & Lazard, 1972), 155–57; Edward Gallafent, *Astaire and Rogers* (New York: Columbia University Press, 2002), 100.

53. *Variety*, 5 April 1939, 9, 15. In the second week, it made a remarkable $110,000 (*Variety*, 12 April 1939, 9).

54. Hellinger outline, n.d., 1–2, Warner Brothers Archive, USC.

55. Lord, short treatment, n.d., ibid.

56. *The Roaring Twenties*, script, 20 January 1939, 1–2, ibid.

57. Philip Rosen, "Securing the Historical: Historiography and the Classical Cinema," in *Cinema Histories, Cinema Practices*, ed. Patricia Mellencamp and Philip Rosen (Frederick, Md.: University Publications of America, 1984), 17–34.

58. This was more fully expressed by Humphrey Bogart's doughboy–future gangster when he looks at his machine gun and says, "I think I'll take it with me."

59. Letter from Wallis to Hellinger, 16 August 1939, Warner Brothers Archive, USC.

60. Walter MacEwan to associate producer Sam Bischoff, 6 September 1939, ibid.

61. Wallis to Levinson, 4 October 1939, ibid.

62. A memo to Wallis from MacEwan, 1 August 1939, mentions that the British censors' objections to crime films might be stopped if they put out advance information that the film "is an historical picture in a sense."

63. Frank Nugent, *New York Times*, 11 November 1939, 12.

64. In an appropriate epitaph for the cycle, Jerry (Cagney) is shot to death on the steps of a massive public building, just as Rico (Edward G. Robinson) had murdered one of his former gang members in *Little Caesar*.

65. Leo Miskin, *Morning Telegraph*, 11 November 1939, 2.

400 Notes to Pages 225–235

8. The Last of the Long Hunters, 1938–1941

1. Consult *Sergeant York*, research files, Warner Brothers Archive, USC.

2. Norman Reilly Raine, outline, 27 July 1939; revised final script, 18 September 1939, ibid.

3. Zanuck to Jack Warner, 13 July 1939, ibid.

4. See Stuart N. Lake Papers, Henry E. Huntington Library, San Marino, Calif.

5. Raine to Lou Edelman, 22 November 1939, memo file, Warner Brothers Archive, USC.

6. Peter Novick, "Historians on the Home Front," in *That Noble Dream: The "Objectivity Question" and the American Historical Profession* (Cambridge: Cambridge University Press, 1988), 111–32.

7. Michael T. Isenberg, *War on Film* (London: Associated University Presses, 1981), 94–96; Robert Brent Toplin, *History by Hollywood: The Use and Abuse of the American Past* (Chicago: University of Illinois Press, 1996), 81–102; Michael E. Birdwell, *Celluloid Soldiers: The Warner Bros. Campaign against Nazism* (New York: New York University Press, 1999).

8. Sam Cowan, *Sergeant York and His People* (New York; Funk & Wagnalls, 1922); Tom Skeyhill, *Sergeant York: The Last of the Long Hunters* (Philadelphia: John C. Winston, 1930); Cowan, 6 November 1941 to WB, legal folder 2; Skeyhill, legal 1 and 2, 11 July 1942, Lasky to Fanny E. Holzmann, Warner Brothers Archive, USC.

9. Nunnally Johnson, interviews with Dan Ford, John Ford Papers, Lilly Library, Indiana University.

10. Wallis to Lasky, 24 April 1941, Warner Brothers Archive, USC.

11. See story files for release forms, ibid.

12. Dixon Wecter, *The Hero in America* (New York: Charles Scribner's Sons, 1941), includes chapters on both Boone and York.

13. Letter to the editor of an unknown paper, 14 July 1941, legal file 2, Warner Brothers Archive, USC.

14. *New York Times*, 3 July 1941, 15:3; *Los Angeles Times*, 19 September 1941, 13; *Variety*, 2 July 1941, 12.

15. Isenberg, *War on Film*, 94–96; Toplin, *History by Hollywood*, 81–102; Birdwell, *Celluloid Soldiers*.

16. Press book, "The Private Life of a Motion Picture," n.d., Warner Brothers Archive, USC.

17. Jean-Luc Comolli and Jean Narboni, "Cinema/Ideology/Criticism" [1971], reprinted in *Film Theory and Criticism*, 6th ed., ed. Leo Braudy and Marshall Cohen (Oxford: Oxford University Press, 2004), 752–59.

18. Birdwell, *Celluloid Soldiers*, 129.

19. Todd McCarthy, *Howard Hawks* (New York: Grove Press, 1997), 315.

20. He also won the New York Film Critics' Award. See Crowther's review, *New York Times*, 3 July 1941, 15:3.

21. Jack Alicoate, ed., *The 1942 "Film Daily" Year Book of Motion Pictures* (*Film Daily*, 1941); *Variety*, various issues; Birdwell, *Celluloid Soliders*.

22. See appendixes.

23. Isenberg, *War on Film*, 95.

24. Wecter, *The Hero in America*, 409.

25. Samuel Taylor Moore, *America and the World War* (New York: Greenberg, 1937), 259.

26. Ibid., 65. With York as a precedent and a German American as the most famous general of World War II, Rickenbacker's biography was filmed in 1945 (*Captain Eddie*, Twentieth Century–Fox).

27. David Lee, *Sergeant York: An American Hero* (Lexington: University Press of Kentucky, 1985), 53; Skeyhill, *Sergeant York: Last of the Long Hunters*, 221–22.

28. George Patullo, "The Second Elder Gives Battle," *Saturday Evening Post*, 26 April 1919, 3–4, 71–74.

29. Tom Skeyhill, *Sergeant York: His Own Life Story and War Diary* (Garden City, N.Y.: Doubleday, Doran, 1928); Hervey Allen, *Toward the Flame* (New York: George H. Doran, 1925).

30. Skeyhill, *Sergeant York: His Own Life Story*, vix, xi.

31. T. J. Jackson Lears, *No Place of Grace: Antimodernism and the Transformation of American Culture, 1880–1920* (Chicago: University of Chicago Press, 1981).

32. Skeyhill, *Sergeant York: Last of the Long Hunters*.

33. Ibid., 17.

34. Ibid., 62, 88.

35. Ibid., 196, 240.

36. Harry Chandlee, *Sergeant York*, temporary script, September 1940, 1, Warner Brothers Archive.

37. Isenberg, *War on Film*, 33; George F. Custen, *Bio/Pics: How Hollywood Constructed Public History* (New Brunswick, N.J.: Rutgers University Press, 1992), introduction.

38. Kenneth Roberts, *Northwest Passage* (New York: Doubleday, Doran, 1938).

39. According to the numerous scripts in the Vidor and MGM Collections at USC, Laurence Stallings, Talbot Jennings, Conrad Richter, Robert E. Sherwood, Frances Marion, Jules Furthman, Noel Langley, Bruno Frank, Jack Singer, Sidney Howard, Jane Murfin, Richard Schayer, Elizabeth Hill, and King Vidor all produced treatments and variations on the script.

40. See USC script files, King Vidor Collection, which are all about adaptation.

41. Rudy Behlmer, "To the Wilderness for *Northwest Passage*," *American Cinematographer* 68, no. 11 (November 1987): 38–47.

42. See Howard Strickland Collection, *Northwest Passage* Production Costs ($2.67 million), AMPAS. See *Variety* for exhibitors' reports: 28 February 1940, 9–11; 6 March 1940, 9–11; 13 March 1940, 9; 20 March 1940, 12).

43. Walter D. Edmonds, *Drums along the Mohawk* (Boston: Little, Brown, 1936).

44. The only copy of Faulkner's script, dated 3 July 1937, has no text foreword or inserts; it is in folder HM58704, Levien Papers, Henry E. Huntington Library.

45. *Drums along the Mohawk*, script, 2 December 1938, Twentieth Century–Fox Collection, USC.

46. Ibid., 5.

47. Script, first draft (with Zanuck's notes on title page), Lilly Library, Indiana University.

48. Ibid., 84.

49. Copy of wire from Zanuck, 1939, box 29, Sonya Levien Papers, Huntington Library.

50. Edmonds, *Drums along the Mohawk*, vii.

51. Ibid., 305–6, 430–32, 487–91, 585. For an assessment of Edmonds's approach to historical fiction, see Robert M. Gay, "The Historical Novel: Walter D. Edmonds," *Atlantic Monthly* 165 (May 1940): 656, and Arthur B. Tourtellot, "History and the Historical Novelist," *Saturday Review of Literature* 22 (20 August 1940): 3.

52. Conference notes, 15 April 1939, Twentieth Century–Fox Collection, USC.

53. John E. O'Connor, "A Reaffirmation of American Ideals," in *American History/American Film*, ed. John E. O'Connor and Martin Jackson (New York: Ungar, 1979), 97–119; Robin Wood, "*Drums along the Mohawk*," in *The Book of Westerns*, ed. Ian Cameron and Douglas Pye (New York: Continuum, 1996), 174–80.

54. *Variety*, 8 November 1939, 14.

55. See, for instance, *Hollywood Reporter*, 2 November 1939.

56. O'Connor, "Reaffirmation of American Ideals," 115, 119.

57. *Northwest Passage*, cutting continuity, 24 January 1940, Vidor Collection, USC.

58. Note from Darryl Zanuck to Kenneth Macgowan and William Koenig, 3 July 1940, box 29, folder 3, Macgowan Papers, UCLA Special Collections.

59. Darryl F. Zanuck to Sidney Kent, 15 July 1940, box 29, folder 3, Macgowan Papers, UCLA Special Collections.

60. In 1939 and 1940, Zanuck easily outdistanced his colleagues, with nine productions per year. However, Twentieth Century–Fox's percentage change in net earnings declined by 42.8 percent (versus MGM-Loew's decline of only 3.8 percent from the 1938 season). See Leo Rosten, *Hollywood* (New York: HBJ, 1941), 376, 377.

61. Frank Nugent, "*The Fighting 69th*," *New York Times*, 27 January 1940, 9:2.

62. Rosten, *Hollywood*, 248.

9. Stars Born and Lost, 1932–1937

1. For an assessment of the case and its effect on Bow's career, see David Stenn, *Clara Bow: Runnin' Wild* (New York: Doubleday, 1988), 209–34.

2. Teletype to RKO in New York, 4 March 1932, in *Memo from David O. Selznick*, ed. Rudy Behlmer (New York: Viking Press, 1972), 45.

3. See Selznick's comments on Howard Estabrook's scripts, *The Conquerors*, story file, RKO Collection, UCLA Arts Library Special Collections.

4. Although the connections between the character Norman Maine and the actors John Gilbert, John Barrymore, and John Bowers were publicly noted back

in 1937 and restated more recently by Gene D. Philips, "A *Star Is Born,*" *Films in Review* 40, nos. 8–9 (August–September 1989): 445, and David L. Smith, "John Bowers: This Is the Real Norman Maine," *Films of the Golden Age* 35 (winter 2003–2004): 68–77, critics have been silent on Selznick's documented interest in these other filmmakers.

5. Critical analyses of Hollywood's films about the film industry have never examined these films as historical views of Hollywood; instead, they characterize the pre–*Sunset Boulevard* (1950) productions as naive, modern-day, "film-as-mirror" clichés embedded with the mythic discourses of "Cinderella." See Patrick D. Anderson, *In Its Own Image: The Cinematic Vision of Hollywood* (New York: Arno, 1978); James Robert Parish and Michael R. Pitts, *Hollywood on Hollywood* (Metuchen, N.J.: Scarecrow Press, 1978); Christoper Ames, *Movies about the Movies: Hollywood Reflected* (Lexington: University Press of Kentucky, 1997).

6. Robert E. Sherwood, "*Hollywood,*" in *The Best Moving Pictures of 1922–1923* (Boston: Small, Maynard, 1923), 78–85.

7. Frederick James Smith in *Photoplay,* June 1923, 65.

8. Frank Thompson, *Lost Films: Important Movies that Disappeared* (New York: Citadel, 1996), 104–13.

9. Sherwood, "*Hollywood.*"

10. Welford Beaton, "*Show People,*" *Film Spectator,* 5 January 1929, 8.

11. *Hollywood* script files, AMPAS; Mordaunt Hall, *New York Times,* 30 July 1932, 11:4.

12. Studio typescript, 3 March 1932, box 195, RKO Collection, UCLA Arts Library Special Collections.

13. Terry Ramsaye, *A Million and One Nights* (New York: Simon & Schuster, 1926); Benjamin Hampton, *A History of the Movies* (New York: Covici-Friede, 1931).

14. Ben-Allah, *Rudolph Valentino: A Dream of Desire* (London: Robson, 1998); Emily Leider, *Dark Lover: The Life and Death of Rudolph Valentino* (New York: Farrar, Straus & Giroux, 2002).

15. Clara Bow as told to Adela Rogers St. Johns, "My Life Story," *Photoplay* (February–April 1928).

16. Stenn, *Clara Bow,* 122.

17. St. Johns, "The Truth about Hollywood," 32, *What Price Hollywood?,* UCLA Arts Library Special Collections.

18. *Photoplay,* August 1932, 51. See also *Variety,* 19 July 1932, 24.

19. Rush, *Variety,* 16 August 1932, 13.

20. Benjamin Hampton, *History of the American Film Industry* [1931] (New York: Dover, 1970), 388–89, 405–7. Robert Allen and Douglas Gomery, *Film History: Theory and Practice* (New York: Random House, 1985), and Donald Crafton, *The Talkies: American Cinema's Transition to Sound* (New York: Scribner's, 1997), would also point this out later.

21. Anne Edwards, *A Remarkable Woman: A Biography of Katharine Hepburn* (New York: William Morrow, 1985), 105–6.

22. Robert Wagner, *Rob Wagner's Script,* 2 September 1933, 9–10.

23. *Bombshell,* story report, 25 October 1932, MGM Script Collection, AMPAS.

24. *Bombshell*, treatments, 23 January 1933, 30 January 1933, MGM Script Collection, AMPAS.

25. Johnsrud, 30 January 1933, 2; Graham Baker and Gene Towne, treatment, 8 March 1933, 18. Famed Hollywood designer Max Adrian is mentioned as a character in the script.

26. Mahin and Furthman, preliminary script, 8 July 1933, AMPAS.

27. Mahin and Furthman, script, 25 July 1933, 33. Fleming was also assigned at one point to direct but was replaced for unknown reasons.

28. Stromberg, "Production Notes," 25 January–29 June 1933, MGM Collection, USC.

29. Stromberg, notes, 7 April 1933.

30. Ibid., 8 April 1933.

31. Ibid, 25 May 1933.

32. Mae West, *Goodness Had Nothing to Do with It* (New York: McFadden, 1970).

33. Compare Paramount scripts, which often contain rewrites of titles or none at all, with the finished films.

34. George F. Custen, *Bio/Pics: How Hollywood Constructed Public History* (New Brunswick, N.J.: Rutgers University Press, 1992), 119; Linda Mizejewski, *Ziegfeld Girl: Image and Icon in Culture and Cinema* (Durham, N.C.: Duke University Press, 1999), 145, 155.

35. William Anthony McGuire, *The Great Ziegfeld*, script, 21 September 1935, 1, Henry E. Huntington Library, San Marino, Calif.

36. Otis Fergusson, *"The Great Ziegfeld," New Republic*, 13 May 1936, 18.

37. Wagner, *Rob Wagner's Script*, 25 April 1936, 12.

38. Mizejewski, *Ziegfeld Girl*, 145.

39. *Hollywood Boulevard*, final script, A5-A7, box 1095, UCLA Arts Library Special Collections.

40. Selznick to Brown, 28 September 1936, in Behlmer, *Memo from Selznick*, 105.

41. Selznick to Daniel O'Shea, deposition, 28 June 1938, box 2499, David O. Selznick Papers, Harry Ransom Center, University of Texas, Austin.

42. Quoted in Ronald Haver, *David O. Selznick's Hollywood* (New York: Alfred A. Knopf, 1980), 192.

43. Carson and Wellman, 18 September 1936, box 1053, David O. Selznick Papers, HRC.

44. Carson and Wellman, "It Happened in Hollywood," 22 July 1936, 17, ibid.

45. Text superimpositions, 12 January 1937, box 513, David O. Selznick Papers, HRC.

46. Unmarked press clippings, Janet Gaynor Collection, Boston University.

47. Gilbert obituary, *Variety*, 15 January 1936.

48. As if there were not enough Hollywood ironies in the script, Selznick had Owen Moore play the director, Casey. Moore was a notorious drunk and the has-been ex-husband of Mary Pickford. He was better suited to play Maine than one critical of Maine's thirst.

49. Report by Cohen, Cole, Weiss & Wharton of New York City, particularly Memorandum B, box 2500, David O. Selznick Papers, HRC.

50. *A Star Is Born*, final script, 16 October 1936, Robert Carson Papers,

Mugar Memorial Library, Boston University, has her look at Norman Maine's slab but not those of the other real stars. These shots were obviously added later at Wellman's or Selznick's request.

51. See press book, Lilly Library, Indiana University.

52. Jean Harlow died 7 June 1937; *A Star Is Born* premiered 20 April 1937 at Grauman's Chinese Theatre.

53. *A Star Is Born*, final script, 42.

54. Both Cooper and Harlow owed their early recognition as extras to Clara Bow.

55. Unmarked press clipping, Gaynor scrapbook, Gaynor Collection, Boston University.

56. Frederick L. Collins, "Where Are Those Second Mary Pickfords?" 20–21, 113–14, unmarked press clipping, ibid.

57. Haver, *Selznick's Hollywood*, 191.

58. Unmarked review, Gaynor scrapbook, Gaynor Collection, Boston University.

59. *A Star Is Born*, final script, 110.

10. A Hollywood Cavalcade, 1939–1942

1. The number of American historical films would peak in 1940 at thirty-two, but curiously, Twentieth Century–Fox's production declined to nine and then sunk to two films in 1941, 1942, and 1943. With the exception of *Wilson* (1944) and *Captain Eddie* (1945), Zanuck's historical output consisted of period musicals and biographies of musical figures. Although Warner Brothers maintained a diverse production line in 1940 and 1941, by the mid-1940s, it too had moved into musical biopics.

2. Lewis Jacobs, *The Rise of the American Film* (New York: Harcourt, Brace, 1939); Margaret Farrand Thorp, *America at the Movies* (New Haven, Conn.: Yale University Press, 1939); William C. DeMille, *Hollywood Saga* (New York: E. P. Dutton, 1939).

3. Charles Altman, "Towards a Historiography of American Film, *Cinema Journal* 16, no. 2 (1977): 1–25; John Belton, "American Cinema and Film History," in *The Oxford Guide to Film Studies*, ed. John Hill and Pamela Church Gibson (Oxford: Oxford University Press, 1998), 227–37.

4. Terry Ramsaye, *A Million and One Nights* (New York: Simon & Schuster, 1926); Benjamin Hampton, *History of the American Film Industry from Its Beginnings to 1931* [1931] (New York: Dover, 1970).

5. In 1939 William DeMille warned against the "million dollar failures" that represent producers' attempts at prestige and at educating increasingly "general" audiences (*Hollywood Saga*, 306).

6. Jacobs, *Rise of American Film*, 531.

7. William J. Perlman, ed., *The Movies on Trial* (New York: Macmillan, 1936).

8. DeMille, *Hollywood Saga*, 19.

9. Ibid., 27–28.

10. Ibid., 19.

11. *Falling Star*, revised treatment by Richard Sherman and Sonya Levien, 28 December 1937, box 4, folder HM55710, Levien Papers, Henry E. Huntington Library, San Marino, Calif.

12. Conference notes, 25 January 1937, USC.

13. See 1938 press book, Lilly Library, Indiana University.

14. See Zanuck's penciled script notes, 3 December 1938, temporary script, Lilly Library.

15. Conference on script, 16 October 1939, 7–8, USC.

16. First draft continuity, 11 October 1939, ibid.

17. Conference notes, 22 December 1939, ibid.

18. See Parker Morrell, *Lillian Russell: The Era of Plush* (New York: Random House, 1940).

19. Dixon Wecter, *The Hero in America* (New York: Charles Scribner's Sons, 1941).

20. Ibid., 477.

21. Although Selznick had attended Zanuck's parties while the latter was still at Warner Brothers (letter to Irene, 16 March 1933), he became increasingly jealous of Zanuck after the intrepid formation of Twentieth Century productions (letter to L. B. Mayer, 14 June 1933) and blamed Mayer for "the dissuasion from my plans" to form an independent studio of his own. Zanuck had beaten him to the punch, and it rankled (Rudy Behlmer, ed., *Memo from David O. Selznick* [New York: Viking, 1972], 60, 63–69).

22. The song was Berlin's first big hit, perennially identified with his and singer Al Jolson's careers.

23. Story conference, 21 October 1938, 1, USC.

24. DeMille, *Hollywood Saga*, 131–32.

25. Curiously, Zanuck's view of Hollywood history from youth to adolescence (1914–1928) to maturity (sound to present) mirrored William DeMille's characterization of the trajectory of film style and narration. Yet DeMille, being primarily a writer, believed that the silent film's development could be measured by the length and complexity of its intertitles (*Hollywood Saga*, 250).

26. Conference notes, 21 October 1938, USC.

27. Johnson, script memo to Zanuck, 12 December 1938, ibid.

28. Johnson had been in the business for some years before Zanuck, and when Terry Ramsaye dedicated his landmark American film history, *A Million and One Nights*, he thanked Julian Johnson.

29. George F. Custen, *Twentieth Century's Fox: Darryl F. Zanuck and the Culture of Hollywood* (New York: Basic Books, 1997), 94–107.

30. Michael Wood, *America in the Movies* (New York: Delta, 1975); Garth Jowett, *Film: The Democratic Art: A Social History of the American Film* (Boston: Little, Brown, 1976); Thomas Schatz, *Hollywood Genres: Formulas, Filmmaking, and the Studio System* (Philadelphia: Temple University Press, 1981); Gorham Kindem, ed., *The American Film Industry: The Business of Motion Pictures* (Madison: University of Wisconsin Press, 1982); Douglas Gomery, *The Hollywood Studio System* (New York: St. Martins Press, 1986); Ethan Mordden, *The Hollywood Studios* (New York: Alfred A. Knopf, 1987); Thomas Schatz, *The Genius of the System* (New York: Pantheon, 1988).

31. DeMille, *Hollywood Saga*, 23.

32. Johnson, memo to Darryl F. Zanuck, 12 December 1938, 2, USC.

33. Conference memo, 25 November 1938, 3, ibid.

34. Conference memo, 15 May 1939, ibid.

35. Ibid.

36. Conference memo, 21 October 1938, ibid.

37. Conference on revised treatment, 20 December 1938, 14–15, ibid.

38. Script, 1 April 1939, 151–52, ibid.

39. Ibid.

40. Ibid. William DeMille experienced a similar epiphany with talking pictures, but as he recalled, it was not Zanuck's *Jazz Singer* that caught his attention but Warner Brothers' *Glorious Betsy* (1928), with Conrad Nagel and Dolores Costello (*Hollywood Saga*, 268–70). It may have been competitive spite, but Zanuck is nowhere in DeMille's personal history of Hollywood.

41. Hampton, *History of the American Film Industry*, 387.

42. Donald Crafton, "*The Jazz Singer*'s Reception in the Media and Box Office," in *Post Theory*, ed. David Bordwell and Noel Carroll (Madison: University of Wisconsin Press, 1996), 460–81. The film grossed a very impressive $3 million.

43. Conference, 10 November 1938, 1, 12, USC.

44. *Variety*, 4 October 1939, 12.

45. He would later okay the use of old footage from *Jesse James* to introduce *The Return of Frank James* (1940).

46. Curiously, although Lewis Jacobs honored *The Birth of a Nation*, *The Four Horsemen of the Apocalypse*, and *The Ten Commandments* as peaks in film achievement in his 1939 film history, he barely mentioned *The Jazz Singer*.

47. *Variety*, 4 October 1939, 12.

48. Jack Alicoate, ed., *The 1939 "Film Daily" Year Book of Motion Pictures* (*Film Daily*, 1940), 122.

49. Although no research records exist for *Hollywood Cavalcade*, it is likely that DeMille's book inspired some of the story ideas and details. One must also bear in mind that DeMille told the history of only DeMille productions, while Zanuck, lacking specificity, attempted to negotiate the entire Hollywood spectrum.

50. Each of these films had text forewords and intertitles and was reviewed as historical material.

51. DeMille, *Hollywood Saga*, 18.

52. Original screenplay by Milton Sperling and Hilary Lynn, directed by studio hack Walter Lang, with Ray Griffith assisting Zanuck in production. Although not set in the past and by no means accorded the prestige of Zanuck's other releases, the film begins with an extended news montage of the stage and screen career of star Garrick, "The Great Profile."

53. Brooks Atkinson, quoted in Alma Power-Waters's *John Barrymore* (New York: J. Messner, 1941), 260.

54. Power-Waters, *John Barrymore*, 224–38.

55. The film also represented the first major biography of Barrymore and the only one completed before his death in 1942 (with the exception of his 1926 autobiography and Power-Waters's *John Barrymore*).

56. After *Yankee Doodle Dandy*, Warner Brothers made only five films set in the American past from 1942 to 1945: *Shine On, Harvest Moon* (1944), a period musical; *The Adventures of Mark Twain* (1944); *Mr. Skeffington* (1944, starring Bette Davis); *Roughly Speaking* (1945); and Edna Ferber's *Saratoga Trunk*. In contrast, its usual output had been five per year in 1939, 1940, and 1941. Of the wartime films, only Davis's film and *Saratoga Trunk* received critical and box-office attention, but reviews and publicity focused on star performances, not history.

57. *Little Johnny Jones*'s "Yankee Doodle Dandy," 1903.

58. John McCabe, *George M. Cohan: The Man Who Owned Broadway* (Garden City, N.Y.: Doubleday, 1973), 50.

59. Ibid., 51.

60. Macgowan persisted through 1937 and 1938, but see especially his letters dated 24 May 1937 and 29 June 1937, and from Nute to Macgowan, 25 July 1937, *Hudson's Bay* (1940) correspondence, box 29, folder 3, Macgowan Papers, UCLA Special Collections.

61. George M. Cohan, *Twenty Years on Broadway* (New York: Harper & Brothers, 1925), 6.

62. Ibid., 269.

63. Actors' Equity offered only $200, mentioning that it was the sum of Cohan's missed years of equity dues. Oscar Hammerstein returned the check with a stinging reply.

64. Cohan note, 5 August 1941, Warner Brothers Archive, USC.

65. The bizarre headline "Stix Nix Hix Pix," pans small-time rural films and endorses the coming of major prestige films such as *Yankee Doodle Dandy*.

66. Letter to Cohan, 29 August 1941, Warner Brothers Archive, USC.

67. Memo, Buckner to Wallis, 27 September 1941; Buckner to Wallis, 13 August 1941, ibid.

68. Memo, William Cagney to Wallis, 27 August 1941, ibid.

69. Allan Nevins, *The Gateway to History* (New York: D. Appleton-Century, 1938).

70. Ibid., 320.

71. Final script, 25 November 1941, 88, ibid.

72. James Cagney, *Cagney by Cagney* (Garden City, N.Y.: Doubleday, 1976), 104.

73. Edwin Schallert, *Los Angeles Times*, 13 August 1942, 12.

74. *Hollywood Reporter*, 1 June 1942.

75. McCabe, *George M. Cohan*, 265–66.

76. George F. Custen, *Bio/Pics: How Hollywood Constructed Public History* (New Brunswick, N.J.: Rutgers University Press, 1992).

Conclusion

1. Twenty-three films appeared in 1936 (see appendixes).

2. Hays was head of the Motion Picture Producers and Distributors of America and later ceded day-to-day control of the Production Code Administration to Joseph Breen.

3. Warner Brothers' 1936 educational short won an Academy Award. In 1938 its two-reel *Declaration of Independence* won another award, and in 1939 *Sons of Liberty* won in the two-reel category.

4. Report for Will Hays and Joseph Breen, 29 January 1937, PCA Collection for *Show Boat* and *So Red the Rose*, AMPAS.

5. Frank Nugent, Edwin Schallert, and Howard Barnes considered it juvenile entertainment; see reviews in chapter 4.

6. Rudy Behlmer, "Land of Liberty, a Conglomerate," *American Cinematographer* 72 (March 1991), 34–40, 34–35; see also A. W. Palmer, "Cecil B. DeMille Writes America's History for the 1939 World's Fair," *Film History* 5, no. 1 (March 1993): 36–48.

7. André Bazin, "The Evolution of the Language of Cinema," in *What Is Cinema?* (Berkeley: University of California Press, 1967); Bazin, *Orson Welles: A Critical View* [1978] (Los Angeles: Acrobat Books, 1991); Andrew Sarris, *The American Cinema, Directors and Directions, 1929–1968* (New York: Dutton, 1968); Peter Wollen, "Introduction to Citizen Kane," *Film Reader* 1 (1975): 9–15.

8. James T. Shotwell, ed., *The Economic and Social History of the World War* [1922–1936] (New Haven, Conn.: Yale University Press, 1936); *Studies in World Economy* (New York: Carnegie Endowment for International Peace, 1931); *Modern and Contemporary European History, 1815–1922* (Boston: Houghton Mifflin, 1922); *The History of History* [1922] (New York: Columbia University Press, 1939).

9. See chapter 7.

10. Shotwell, treatment and interpretive monologue, box 550, folder 6, Cecil B. DeMille Collection, Brigham Young University.

11. "Note Outline for Continuity—American Cavalcade," 23 November 1938, box 550, folder 7, ibid.

12. Ibid.

13. "Outline for Continuity—American Cavalcade," 30 November 1938, box 550, folder 8, ibid.

14. Telegram to Hays, October 1938, box 551, folder 9, ibid.

15. "Outline for Continuity—American Cavalcade," 6, 11, 17, 20, 25 January 1939, box 550, folder 3, ibid.

16. Ibid., undated, folder 4, 11.

17. Ibid., 32.

18. Ibid., 37.

19. "The Cavalcade of America: Suggested Treatments of the General Subject Matter of the Highlights of American History," undated, box 550, folder 5, ibid.

20. Outline script, 23 February 1939, box 550, folder 9, ibid.

21. Temporary script, 10 April 1939, A7–8, ibid.

22. Script, 8 May 1939, ibid.

23. Submitted by Frances S. Harmon, 8 May 1939, ibid.

24. Director's prologue, box 550, folder 15, ibid.

25. Release continuity, box 551, ibid.

26. Projection room notes, 21 May 1939, box 551, folder 5, ibid.

27. Louis Gottschalk to Samuel Marx, 18 April 1935, box 1, folder, 6, Louis R. Gottschalk Papers, University of Chicago.

28. Allen W. Palmer, "Cecil B. DeMille Writes America's History for the 1939 World's Fair," *Film History* 5, no. 1 (March 1993): 36–48, argued without evidence that *Land of Liberty* was Hollywood's first relationship with a historian and that Shotwell helped make American history "more real."

29. *Land of Liberty* program, June 1939, AMPAS.

30. Frank Nugent, *New York Times*, 16 June 1939, 27:3; 18 June 1939, IX, 3:1.

31. Henry Fonda, *Fonda: My Life* (New York: New American Library, 1981).

32. Ginger Rogers, *Ginger: My Story* (New York: HarperCollins, 1991), 124.

33. See especially Nugent's review, *New York Times*, 23 February 1940, 19:2.

34. *Variety*, 3 July 1940, 16.

35. Contract signed 21 July 1939; Robert L. Carringer, *The Making of Citizen Kane* (Berkeley: University of California Press, 1985), 1, 151.

36. Ibid., 2.

37. Betty Lasky, *RKO: The Biggest Little Major of Them All* (Englewood Cliffs, N.J.: Prentice-Hall, 1984), 160–64.

38. For the false starts before *Citizen Kane*, see Carringer, *Making of Citizen Kane*, 1–15.

39. Pauline Kael, "Raising Kane" [1971], in *Raising Kane and Other Essays* (London: Marion Boyars, 1996), 159–266, 200.

40. *The Miracle Woman*, like many other controversial historical features, did not recoup its cost. See Frank Capra, *The Name above the Title* (New York: Macmillan, 1971), 129–31.

41. Warner Brothers' 1939–1940 program of pending productions advertised in *Variety* included "John Dillinger, Outlaw" (22 March 1939, 14). *Time*, 29 May 1939, 51, noted that Warner Brothers, the "pacemaker in gangster films and biographies, is now the spearhead of Hollywood's biographical thrust." *Time* also mentioned that Cagney was due to star in a biopic of John Paul Jones and Dillinger.

42. Kael, "Raising Kane,"

43. See also Laura Mulvey, *Citizen Kane* (London: BFI, 1992); Morris Dickstein, "The Last Film of the 1930s: Nothing Fails Like Success," in *Perspectives on Citizen Kane*, ed. Ronald Gottesman (New York: G. K. Hall, 1996), 82–93.

44. Mulvey, *Citizen Kane*; Morris Beja, "'A Really Great Man': Myth and Realism in *Citizen Kane*," in *Perspectives on Orson Welles*, ed. Morris Beja (New York: G. K. Hall, 1995), 253–59.

45. James Naremore, "On *Citizen Kane*" [1978, 1989], in Gottesman, *Perspectives on Citizen Kane*, 268–94; David Bordwell, "*Citizen Kane*," in *Film Comment* (summer 1971): 38–47; Dudley Andrew, "Echoes of Art: The Distant Sounds of Orson Welles," in *Film in the Aura of Art* (Princeton, N.J.: Princeton University Press, 1984), 152–71.

46. W. A. Swanberg, *Citizen Hearst* (New York: Charles Scribner's Sons, 1961).

47. Ibid., 60.

48. Ferdinand Lundberg, *Imperial Hearst* (New York: Equinox, 1936).

49. James Creelman, *On the Great Highway* (Boston: Lothrop, 1901), 177–78.

50. Swanberg, *Citizen Hearst*, 120–30.

51. William Appleman Williams, *The Tragedy of American Diplomacy* (1959; reprint, New York: W. W. Norton, 1988), 23. See also Paul T. McCartney, *Power and Progress: American National Identity, the War of 1898, and the Rise of American Imperialism* (Baton Rouge: Louisiana State University Press, 2006).

52. Louis Pizzitola, *Hearst over Hollywood* (New York: Columbia University Press, 2002).

53. Willis J. Abbot, *Watching the World Go By* (Boston: Little, Brown, 1933), 207–8.

54. Swanberg, *Citizen Hearst*, 51.

55. Carringer, *Making of* Citizen Kane, 23. However, Carringer also pointed out that Welles had quite an impact on later versions of the script.

56. Morris Dickstein ("Last Film of the 1930s") placed *Citizen Kane* within a more general tendency of Depression-era Hollywood cinema to consider failed lives, the bizarre rich, and the newspaper industry, but he ignored the presence of a contemporaneous historical cycle and *Kane's* relationship to it.

57. Swanberg, *Citizen Hearst*, 462.

58. See Mankiewicz's "The American," 16 April 1940, and compare it with the next draft, 9 May 1940, and the "final," dated 18 June 1940, Orson Welles Collection, Lilly Library, Indiana University.

59. "The American," 16 April 1940, 58, box 14, folder 29, Lilly Library.

60. Ibid., 35.

61. Ibid., 119–20.

62. Carringer, *Making of* Citizen Kane, 21–23. Although most historians in this situation lost in and out of court, Lundberg's case resulted in a hung jury, evidence of a particularly strong case for plagiarism

63. Ferdinand Lundberg, *Imperial Hearst, a Social Biography* (New York: Equinox Cooperative Press, 1936), 74, 36, 53.

64. Oliver Carlson and Ernest Sutherland Bates, *Hearst, Lord of San Simeon* (New York: Viking Press, 1936), xiv.

65. Swanberg, *Citizen Hearst*, 497.

66. Orson Welles, "*Citizen Kane* Is Not About Louella Parson's Boss," *Friday* 2 (14 February 1941): 9.

67. Bosley Crowther, *New York Times*, 2 May 1941, reprinted in Gottesman, *Perspectives on* Citizen Kane, 33–37.

68. Otis Fergusson, *New Republic*, 2 June 1941, 760–61, reprinted in Gottesman, *Perspectives on* Citizen Kane, 41–43.

69. Crowther, *New York Times*, 2 May 1941; Gregg Toland, "How I Broke the Rules in *Citizen Kane*," *Popular Photography Magazine*, June 1941, 55.

70. Welles, undated statement, possibly 1941, Lilly Library, Indiana University.

71. Morris Dickstein claims that the *News on the March* sequence reproduces the discourse of the Hollywood biopic ("Last Film of the 1930s," 87), but these abbreviated, colorless fragments, though using some of the structural tricks of historical prologues, do not coincide with the humanizing, personal film narratives of even the most illustrious American heroes and heroines.

72. Garrett Stewart, *Between Film and Screen* (Chicago: University of Chicago Press, 1999), 164–76.

73. In spite of its brevity, this is one of the most discussed sequences in the film. Bruce Kawin devoted an entire article to the library-boardinghouse sequence ("*Citizen Kane:* The Boardinghouse Scene," in Gottesman, *Perspectives on Citizen Kane*, 465–503), but his only interest in the camera's encounter with Thatcher's script is a vague comparison between the text and what purports to be an objective view of events (but is actually Thatcher's subjective point of view) and the camera's independent narration (466–67). Frank Tomasulo ("Narrate *and* Describe? Point of View and Narrative Voice in *Citizen Kane*'s Thatcher Sequence," in ibid., 504–17) is in favor of multiple narration but ignores the text's relationship to historiography, its significant difference with the *News on the March* sequence, and Welles's provision for visual historiography.

74. See Dickstein, "The Last Film of the 1930s," 82–93.

75. See all *Kane* scripts from "The American" to the final draft. The film preserves something of this disjunction in newsreel (beginning with his death and then 1898, 1919, and back to his marriage in 1916), but it is more evident in the structure of the flashbacks.

76. Ironically, in 1906, Hearst purchased Lincoln's farmstead in Springfield, Illinois (Swanberg, *Citizen Hearst*, 243).

77. Recall that on the lonely night he accidentally and disastrously meets Susan, he is on his way to view his mother's things, stored in a Westside warehouse.

78. The snow globe also functions as an artifact from Hollywood's past and further establishes Welles's connection to Hollywood cinema rather than his circumvention of it. In several of the industry's top 1940 releases (*Kitty Foyle* [RKO] and *All This and Heaven Too* [Warner Brothers]), snow globes appear as childlike emblems that eventually thwart the illusion of the protagonists' "perfect" memories and Hollywood's complete, linear narratives. Both *Kitty Foyle* and *All This and Heaven Too* rely on the problems of subjective narration, history, personal loss, and a complex use of flashbacks.

79. Booth Tarkington, *The Magnificent Ambersons* (New York: Doubleday, 1918).

80. V. F. Perkins, *The Magnificent Ambersons* (London: BFI, 1999), 1–14.

81. See *Ambersons* scripts, Welles Collection, Lilly Library.

82. André Bazin, *Orson Welles: A Critical View* [1978] (Los Angeles: Acrobat Books, 1991), 64–82.

83. *Variety*, 1 July 1942, 8.

84. *Variety*, 4 November 1942, 8.

85. Story file, box 112, folder 1, RKO Collection, UCLA Arts Library Special Collections.

86. *Variety*, 1 July 1942, 8.

87. *Variety*, 3 July 1940, 5, 19; 14 August 1940, 16; and 27 November 1940, 7.

88. See, for example, *Variety* on Kit Carson's big Denver premiere and exploitation and *Variety*'s mini-review, 28 August 1940, 16: "Just a western . . . full of action, short on story."

89. *Variety*, 21 August 1940, 5.

Selected Bibliography

Archival Sources

Bacon, Lloyd. Papers. Margaret Herrick Library, Academy of Motion Picture Arts and Sciences, Beverly Hills, Calif.

Benét, Stephen Vincent. Papers. University Archives, Yale University, New Haven, Conn.

Carson, Robert. Papers. Mugar Memorial Library, University Archives, Boston University.

Cukor, George. Papers. Margaret Herrick Library, Academy of Motion Picture Arts and Sciences, Beverly Hills, Calif.

Curtiz, Michael. Papers. Warner Brothers Archive, University of Southern California, Los Angeles.

Davis, Bette. Papers. Mugar Memorial Library, University Archives, Boston University.

De Havilland, Olivia. Letters to the author, 2000–2001.

DeMille, Cecil B. Papers. University Archives, Brigham Young University, Provo, Utah.

Dunne, Philip. Papers. University Archives, University of Southern California, Los Angeles.

Ford, John. Papers. Lilly Library, Indiana University, Bloomington.

Gaynor, Janet. Papers. Mugar Memorial Library, University Archives, Boston University.

Gottschalk, Louis R. Papers. Joseph Regenstein Library, University of Chicago.

Hawks, Howard. Papers. University Archives, Brigham Young University, Provo, Utah.

Hepburn, Katharine. Papers. Formerly Fenwick, Old Saybrook, Conn. Courtesy of Steve Hansen, New York, N.Y.

Howard, Sidney. Papers. University Archives, University of California, Berkeley.

Howard, W. P., General. Official Report to Governor Joseph Brown, 7 December 1864. University Archives, University of Georgia, Atlanta.

Hunt, Marsha. Recorded interviews with the author, 2001.

Johnson, Nunnally. Papers. Mugar Memorial Library, University Archives, Boston University.

King, Henry. Papers. Margaret Herrick Library, Academy of Motion Picture Arts and Sciences, Beverly Hills, Calif.

Lake, Stuart N. Papers. Henry E. Huntington Library, San Marino, Calif.

LeRoy, Mervyn. Papers. University Archives, University of Southern California, Los Angeles.

Levien, Sonya. Papers. Henry E. Huntington Library, San Marino, Calif.

Macgowan, Kenneth. Papers. University Archives, UCLA.

Metro-Goldwyn-Mayer Studios. Papers. Mayer Library, American Film Institute, Los Angeles.

Motion Picture Production Code Administration. Files, 1934–1942. Margaret Herrick Library, Academy of Motion Picture Arts and Sciences, Beverly Hills, Calif.

Motion Picture Reviews. Collection. Margaret Herrick Library, Academy of Motion Picture Arts and Sciences, Beverly Hills, Calif.

Nichols, Dudley. Papers. Beinecke Library, Yale University, New Haven, Conn.

Nugent, Frank. Papers. Mugar Memorial Library, University Archives, Boston University.

Paramount Studios. Papers. Margaret Herrick Library, Academy of Motion Picture Arts and Sciences, Beverly Hills, Calif.

Quarberg, Lincoln. Papers. Margaret Herrick Library, Academy of Motion Picture Arts and Sciences, Beverly Hills, Calif.

RKO Studios. Script Collection. University Archives, UCLA; Lilly Library, Indiana University, Bloomington.

Rutherford, Ann. Interviews with the author, 2001.

Scripts. Western Americana Collection, Beinecke Library, Yale University, New Haven, Conn.

Selznick, David O. Papers. Harry Ransom Research Center, University of Texas, Austin.

Selznick International Pictures. Papers. Harry Ransom Research Center, University of Texas, Austin.

Small, Edward. Papers. University Archives, University of Southern California, Los Angeles.

Strickland, Howard. Papers. Margaret Herrick Library, Academy of Motion Picture Arts and Sciences, Beverly Hills, Calif.

Turner, Frederick Jackson. Papers. Henry E. Huntington Library, San Marino, Calif.

Twentieth Century–Fox Studios. Papers. University Archives, University of Southern California, Los Angeles; University Archives, UCLA; Lilly Library, Indiana University, Bloomington.

United Artists Film Corporation. Papers. State Historical Society of Wisconsin, Madison; Margaret Herrick Library, Academy of Motion Picture Arts and Sciences, Beverly Hills, Calif.

Universal Studios. Papers and Scripts. Margaret Herrick Library, Academy of Motion Picture Arts and Sciences, Beverly Hills, Calif.; Lilly Library, Indiana University, Bloomington.

Warner, Jack L. Papers. Warner Brothers Archive, University of Southern California, Los Angeles.

Warner Brothers Studios. Papers and Scripts. Warner Brothers Archive, University of Southern California, Los Angeles.
Welles, Orson. Papers. Lilly Library, Indiana University, Bloomington.
Zanuck, Darryl F. Papers. Lilly Library, Indiana University, Bloomington.

Primary Sources

Abbot, Willis J. *Watching the World Go By.* Boston: Little, Brown, 1933.
Adams, James Truslow. *America's Tragedy.* New York: Charles Scribner's Sons, 1934.
Alicoate, Jack, ed. *The "Film Daily" Year Book of Motion Pictures.* New York: Film Daily, 1922–1950.
Allen, F. L. *Only Yesterday: An Informal History of the Nineteen-Twenties.* New York: Harper & Brothers, 1931.
———. *Since Yesterday.* New York: Harper & Brothers, 1940.
Almach, John C. "The Shibboleth of the Frontier." *Historical Outlook* 16 (May 1925): 197–202.
Andrews, Eliza Frances. *The War-Time Journal of a Georgia Girl.* New York: D. Appleton, 1908.
Andrews, Matthew Page, ed. *The Women of the South in War Times.* Baltimore: Norman, Remington Co., 1920.
Angle, Paul. "Abraham Lincoln: Circuit Lawyer." *Lincoln Centennial Association Papers* 5 (1928): 19–44.
———. *Lincoln, 1854–1861, Being the Day-by-Day Activities of Abraham Lincoln from January 1, 1854 to March 4, 1861.* Springfield, Ill.: Abraham Lincoln Association, 1933.
———. *"Here I Have Lived": A History of Lincoln's Springfield, 1821–1865.* Springfield, Ill.: Abraham Lincoln Association, 1935.
Bachellor, Irving. *Father Abraham.* Indianapolis: Bobbs-Merrill, 1925.
Baker, Newton. *Why We Went to War.* New York: Harper & Brothers, 1936.
Baringer, William E. *Lincoln's Rise to Power.* Boston: Little, Brown, 1937.
Barker, H. E. *Abraham Lincoln: His Life in Illinois.* New York: M. Barrows, 1940.
Barnes, Howard. Selected reviews. *New York Herald Tribune,* 1936–1941.
Basler, Roy P. *The Lincoln Legend.* Boston: Houghton Mifflin, 1935.
Beard, Charles A. "The Frontier in American History." *New Republic* 25 (16 February 1921): 349–50.
———. *The Myth of Rugged American Individualism.* New York: John Day, 1932.
———. "Historical Relativism." In *The Varieties of History.* Edited by Fritz Stern. New York: Meridian, 1956.
Beard, Charles A., and Mary Beard. *The Rise of American Civilization.* New York: Macmillan, 1927.
Becker, Carl. "Detachment and the Writing of History." *Atlantic Monthly* 106 (October 1910): 524–36.
———. *Everyman His Own Historian: Essays on History and Politics.* New York: F. S. Crofts, 1935.
———. "Everyman His Own Historian." *American Historical Review* 37 (1932): 221–36. Reprint, El Paso, Tex.: Academic Reprints, 1960.

Behlmer, Rudy, ed. *Memo from David O. Selznick.* New York: Viking, 1972.
————. *Inside Warner Brothers.* New York: Simon & Schuster, 1985.
————. *Memo from Darryl F. Zanuck: The Golden Years at Twentieth Century–Fox.* New York: Grove Press, 1993.
Benét, Stephen V. *Selected Letters.* Edited by Charles Fenton. New Haven, Conn.: Yale University Press, 1960.
Beveridge, Albert J. *Abraham Lincoln.* 2 vols. Boston: Houghton Mifflin, 1928.
Bowers, Claude G. *The Tragic Era: The Revolution after Lincoln.* Cambridge, Mass.: Houghton Mifflin, 1929.
Boynton, Percy H. *The Rediscovery of the Frontier.* Chicago: University of Chicago Press, 1931.
Branch, E. Douglas. *Westward: The Romance of the American Frontier.* New York: D. Appleton, 1930.
Brickell, Hershel. *"Gone with the Wind."* *New York Evening Post,* 30 June 1936.
Browder, Earl. *Lincoln and the Communists.* New York: Workers Library Publishers, 1936.
Buel, James W. *The Border Bandits: An Authentic and Thrilling History of the Noted Outlaws Jesse and Frank James.* Chicago: Donohue Henneberry, 1893.
Burke, Kenneth. *Attitudes toward History* [1937]. Berkeley: University of California Press, 1984.
Burnett, W. R. *Little Caesar.* London: Cape, 1929.
Burns, Robert E. *I Am a Fugitive from a Georgia Chain Gang.* New York: Grosset & Dunlap, 1932.
Burns, Walter Noble. *The Saga of Billy the Kid.* Garden City, N.Y.: Doubleday, 1925.
————. *Tombstone: An Illiad of the Southwest.* Garden City, N.Y.: Doubleday, Doran, 1928.
————. *The One-Way Ride: The Red Trail of Chicago Gangland from Prohibition to Jake Lingle.* Garden City, N.Y.: Doubleday, Doran, 1931.
Capra, Frank. *The Name above the Title: An Autobiography.* New York: Macmillan, 1971.
Carlson, Oliver, and Ernest Sutherland Bates. *Hearst, Lord of San Simeon.* New York: Viking Press, 1936.
Carnegie, Dale. *Lincoln the Unknown.* New York: Century, 1932.
Carter, Mary Duncan. "Film Research Libraries." *Library Journal* 64 (15 May 1939): 404–7.
Castle, Irene. *My Husband.* New York: Scribner's, 1919.
————. *Castles in the Air* [1958]. With a foreword by Ginger Rogers. New York: Da Capo Press, 1980.
Chesnut, Mary Boykin. *Diary from Dixie.* Edited by Isabella D. Martin and Myrta Lockett Avary. New York: Peter Smith, 1929.
Churchill, Edward. Selected reviews. *Exhibitors' Herald World,* 1928–1936.
Clark, John Maurice. *The Costs of the World War to the American People.* New Haven, Conn.: Yale University Press, 1931.
Cohen, Henry, ed. *The Public Enemy.* Madison: Wisconsin Center for Film and Theater Research, 1981.
Cohen, John S., Jr. Selected reviews. *New York Sun,* 1930–1933.

Commager, Henry Steele. *"Gone with the Wind." New York Herald Tribune Books*, 5 July 1936, 1–2.

Conant, A. J. "Personal Recollections of Abraham Lincoln." *New York Times*, 4 December 1888.

Cooper, Courtney Ryley. *Annie Oakley: Woman at Arms*. New York: Duffield, 1927.

———. "The Story of William Frederick Cody." *Elks Magazine* (May 1927).

Cooper, James Fenimore. *The Last of the Mohicans: A Narrative of 1757*. 2 vols. Philadelphia: Carey & Lea, 1826. Reprint, New York: Penguin, 1986.

Cooper, Susan Fenimore. *Papers and Pictures from the Writings of James Fenimore Cooper*. New York: W. A. Townsend, 1861.

Cowan, Sam. *Sergeant York and His People*. New York: Funk & Wagnalls, 1922.

Cowley, Malcolm. "Going with the Wind." *New Republic*, 16 September 1936, 161–62.

Craven, Avery. *The Repressible Conflict, 1830–61*. University, La.: Louisiana State University Press, 1939.

———. *The Coming of the Civil War*. New York: Charles Scribner's Sons, 1942.

Creelman, James. *On the Great Highway*. Boston: Lothrop, 1901.

Crowther, Bosley. Selected reviews. *New York Times*, 1939–1942.

Cummings, Kate. *A Journal of Hospital Life*. Louisville, Ky.: John P. Morgan, 1866.

Davis, Britton. *The Truth about Geronimo: Life with the Apache Scouts*. Oxford: Oxford University Press, 1929.

Davis, Carlyle Channing. *The True Story of Ramona*. New York: Dodge Publishing Company, 1914.

Dawson, Sarah Morgan. *A Confederate Girl's Diary*. Edited by Warrington Dawson. New York: Houghton Mifflin, 1913.

Dedmon, Emmett. *Fabulous Chicago*. New York: Random House, 1933.

Delehanty, Thornton. Selected reviews. *New York Evening Post*, 1930–1936.

DeMille, Cecil B. *The Autobiography of Cecil B. DeMille*. Edited by Donald Hayne. Englewood Cliffs, N.J.: Prentice-Hall, 1959.

DeMille, William C. *Hollywood Saga*. New York: E. P. Dutton, 1939.

De Voto, Bernard. "Footnote on the West." *Harper's* 155 (November 1927): 714–22.

Dunne, Philip. *Take Two: A Life in Movies and Politics*. New York: McGraw-Hill, 1980.

———. "Darryl from A to Z." *American Film* 9, no. 19 (July–August, 1984): 47.

Dunning, William A. "The Truth in History." *American Historical Review* 19 (January 1914): 217–29.

Edmonds, Walter D. *Drums along the Mohawk*. Boston: Little, Brown, 1936.

England, George Allan. *Isles of Romance*. New York: D. Appleton-Century, 1929. Excerpted in *The Reader's Digest*, August 1934, 74–76.

Estabrook, Howard. "This Amusement School of Ours." *Hollywood Reporter*, 8 May 1931.

Ferber, Edna. *Cimarron*. Garden City, N.Y.: Doubleday, Doran, 1930.

———. *A Peculiar Treasure*. New York: Doubleday, Doran, 1939.

Fergusson, Otis. Selected reviews. *New Republic*, 1936–1941.

Film Daily. Selected reviews, 1931–1942.

Fletcher, John Gould. *The Crisis of the Film*. Seattle: University of Washington Chapbooks, 1929.

Fonda, Henry, with Howard Teichmann. *Fonda: My Life.* New York: New American Library, 1981.

Freeman, Douglas Southall. *R. E. Lee.* 4 vols. New York: Charles Scribner's Sons, 1934–1935.

———. *The South to Posterity: An Introduction to the Writing of Confederate History.* New York: Charles Scribner's Sons, 1939.

Freeman, Joseph. "Biographical Films." *Theater Arts* 25 (December 1941).

Gilmore, Helen. "The Bad Men Are Coming Back." *Liberty* (31 December 1938): 20–21.

Gish, Lillian, with Ann Pinchot. *Lillian Gish: The Movies, Mr. Griffith and Me.* Englewood Cliffs, N.J.: Prentice-Hall, 1969.

Gollumb, Joseph. "Meeting the Crime Wave: A Comparison of Methods." *Nation* 112 (January 1921): 82.

Grattan, C. Hartley. *Why We Fought.* New York: Vanguard Press, 1929.

Grey, Zane. *The Vanishing American.* New York: Grosset & Dunlap, 1925.

Griffith, D. W. *The Rise and Fall of Free Speech in America* [pamphlet]. Los Angeles, 1916.

Hacker, Louis. *American Problems of Today: A History of the United States since the World War.* New York: F. S. Crofts, 1938.

Hall, Mordaunt. Selected reviews. *New York Times,* 1923–1935.

Hampton, Benjamin B. *History of the American Film Industry from Its Beginnings to 1931* [1931]. New York: Dover, 1970.

Haycox, Ernest. "Stage to Lordsburg." *Collier's,* 10 April 1937.

———. *Troubleshooter.* Garden City, N.Y.: Doubleday, 1937.

Herndon, William, and Jesse Weik. *Herndon's Life of Lincoln: The History and Personal Recollections of Abraham Lincoln* [1889]. Edited by Paul Angle. New York: Albert & Charles Boni, 1936.

Hertz, Emanuel, ed. *The Hidden Lincoln.* New York: Viking Press, 1938.

———. *Lincoln Talks: A Biography in Anecdote.* New York: Viking Press, 1939.

Hitchcock, Henry. *Marching with Sherman.* Edited by M. A. DeWolfe Howe. New Haven, Conn: Yale University Press, 1927.

Hollywood Reporter. Selected reviews, 1928–1942.

Holmes, Fred. L. "Making Criminals out of Soldiers." *Nation* 121 (22 July 1925): 114.

Huettig, Mae D. *The Economic Control of the Motion Picture Industry.* Philadelphia: University of Pennsylvania Press, 1944.

Isaacs, Edith, ed. "Artists of the Movies." *Theatre Arts* 23 (June 1939): 424–28.

Jackson, Helen Hunt. *A Century of Dishonor.* New York: Harper & Brothers, 1881.

———. *Ramona.* Boston: Roberts Brothers, 1884.

———. *Ramona.* With an introduction by A. C. Vroman. Boston: Little, Brown, 1913.

Jacobs, Lewis. *The Rise of the American Film.* New York: Harcourt, Brace, 1939.

James, Jesse, Jr. *Jesse James, My Father, The First and Only True Story of the Adventures Ever Written.* Independence, Mo.: Sentinel Printing Co., 1899.

Johnson, Alva. "The Wahoo Boy." *New Yorker,* 10 November 1934, 25.

Johnston, William A. "Writer's Gold in Hollywood." *Graphic,* 2 May 1931, 172.

Kauffmann, Stanley, and Bruce Hentsell, eds. *American Film Criticism: From the Beginnings to Citizen Kane.* New York: Liveright, 1972.

Kendrick, Benjamin Burks, and Alex Mathews Arnett. *The South Looks at Its Past*. Chapel Hill: University of North Carolina Press, 1935.

Lake, Stuart. *Wyatt Earp: Frontier Marshal*. Boston: Houghton Mifflin, 1931.

Landesco, John. *Organized Crime in Chicago* [1929]. Chicago: University of Chicago Press, 1968.

Leigh, Frances Butler. *Ten Years on a Georgia Plantation since the War* [1875]. London: Richard Bently & Son, 1883.

Lewis, Lloyd. *Myths after Lincoln* [1929]. New York: Press of the Readers Club, 1941.

Life. Selected reviews, 1937–1941.

Lincoln, Abraham. *The Collected Works of Abraham Lincoln*, 9 vols. Edited by Roy P. Basler. New Brunswick, N.J.: Rutgers University Press, 1953.

Lundberg, Ferdinand. *Imperial Hearst, a Social Biography*. New York: Equinox Cooperative Press, 1936.

MacLeod, William Christie. *The American Indian Frontier*. New York: Alfred A. Knopf, 1928.

Macgowan, Kenneth. *Behind the Screen: The History and Techniques of the Motion Picture*. New York: Delacourt Press, 1965.

Margaret Mitchell and Her Novel "Gone with the Wind." New York: Macmillan, 1936.

Marion, Frances. *How to Write and Sell Film Stories*. New York: Covici-Friede, 1937.

Massey, Raymond. *A Hundred Different Lives*. Boston: Little, Brown, 1979.

Mathews, John Joseph. *Wah'Kon-Tah: The Osage and the White Man's Road*. Norman: University of Oklahoma Press, 1932.

———. *The Osage: Children of the Middle Waters*. Norman: University of Oklahoma Press, 1961.

Mazzanovich, Anton. *Trailing Geronimo*. Hollywood: A. Mazzanovich, 1931.

McIntyre, O. O. "Bad Man." *Cosmopolitan* (February 1931): 52–53.

McWilliams, Carey. *The New Regionalism in American Literature*. Seattle: University of Washington Book Store, 1930.

———. "Myths of the West." *North American Review* 232 (November 1931): 424–32.

Meade, Franklin B. *Heroic Statues in Bronze of Abraham Lincoln*. Fort Wayne, Ind.: Lincoln National Life Foundation, 1932.

Meserve, Frederick Hill, and Carl Sandburg. *The Photographs of Abraham Lincoln*. New York: Harcourt, Brace, 1944.

Miller, Walter. *The Road to War*. New York: Houghton Mifflin, 1935.

Mitchell, Margaret. *Gone with the Wind*. New York: Macmillan, 1936.

———. *Margaret Mitchell's "Gone with the Wind" Letters, 1936–1949*. Edited by Richard Harwell. New York: Macmillan, 1976.

Mitgang, Herb, ed. *The Letters of Carl Sandburg*. New York: Harcourt, Brace & World, 1968.

Moore, Samuel Taylor. *America and the World War*. New York: Greenberg, 1937.

Motion Picture News Blue Book. New York: *Motion Picture News*, 1928–1942.

Motley, John Lothrop. *The Causes of the American Civil War*. New York: D. Appleton, 1861.

Mudd, Nettie. *The Life of Dr. Samuel A. Mudd.* New York: Neale, 1906.

Mumford, Lewis. *The Golden Day.* New York: Boni & Liveright, 1926.

Myrick, Susan. *White Columns in Hollywood: Reports from* Gone with the Wind Sets. Macon, Ga.: Mercer University Press, 1982.

Naumburg, Nancy. *We Make the Movies.* New York: W. W. Norton, 1937.

Nevins, Allan. *The Gateway to History.* New York: D. Appleton-Century, 1938.

———. "What's the Matter with History?" *Saturday Review of Literature* 19 (4 February 1939): 3–4, 16.

———. *Allan Nevins on History.* New York: Charles Scribner's Sons, 1975.

Nichols, Dudley. "Film Writing." *Theatre Arts* 26 (December 1942): 770–74.

———. "Writing and the Film." *Theatre Arts* 27 (October 1943): 591–602.

———. "*Stagecoach.*" In *Twenty Best Film Plays* [1943]. Edited by Dudley Nichols and John Gassner, 995–1038. New York: Garland, 1977.

Nichols, Dudley, and John Ford. *Stagecoach: A Film by John Ford and Dudley Nichols.* New York: Simon & Schuster, 1971.

Nugent, Frank S. Selected reviews. *New York Times,* 1936–1941.

O'Connor, John, ed. *I Am a Fugitive from a Chain Gang.* Madison: Wisconsin Center for Film and Theater Research, 1981.

Pasley, Fred D. *Al Capone: The Biography of a Self-made Man.* Garden City, N.Y.: Garden City Publishing Co., 1930.

———. *Muscling In.* New York: Ives Washburn, 1931.

Patterson, Frances Taylor. "The Author and Hollywood." *North American Review* 244, no. 1 (autumn 1937): 77–89.

Patullo, George. "The Second Elder Gives Battle. *Saturday Evening Post.* 26 April 1919, 3–4, 71–74.

Paxson, Frederic L. *The Last American Frontier.* New York: Macmillan, 1910.

———. *When the West Is Gone.* New York: Henry Holt, 1930.

Perlman, William J., ed. *The Movies on Trial.* New York: Macmillan, 1936.

Peterson, H. C. *Propaganda for War: The Campaign against American Neutrality, 1914–1917* [1939]. Port Washington, N.Y.: Kennikat Press, 1968.

Photoplay. Selected reviews, 1922–1942.

Pitkin, Walter C. "Screen Crime vs. Press Crime." *Outlook,* 29 July 1931.

Potamkin, Harry Alan. "*Storm over Asia* and *Abraham Lincoln.*" *New Masses* (October 1930): 16.

Powers-Waters, Alma. *John Barrymore.* New York: J. Messner, 1941.

Ramsaye, Terry. *A Million and One Nights.* 2 vols. New York: Simon & Schuster, 1926.

———. "*Young Mr. Lincoln.*" *Motion Picture Herald,* 3 June 1939, 36.

Randall, James G. "Lincoln's Task and Wilson's." *South Atlantic Quarterly* 29, no. 4 (October 1930): 349–68.

———. "Has the Lincoln Theme Been Exhausted?" *American Historical Review* 41 (1936): 270–94.

———. *Civil War and Reconstruction.* Boston: D. C. Heath, 1937.

Reep, Thomas P. *Lincoln and New Salem.* Petersburg, Ill.: Old Salem Lincoln League, 1927.

Richardson, Frances Cary. "Previous to Previews." *Wilson Bulletin for Librarians* 12, no. 9 (May 1939): 589–92.

Roberts, Elizabeth Madox. *The Great Meadow*. New York: Viking Press, 1930.

Roberts, Kenneth. *Northwest Passage*. New York: Doubleday, Doran, 1938.

Rogers, Ginger. *Ginger: My Story*. New York: HarperCollins, 1991.

Roosevelt, Franklin D. *The Public Papers and Addresses of Franklin D. Roosevelt*. New York: Macmillan, 1941.

Roosevelt, Theodore. *The Winning of the West*. 7 vols. New York: G. P. Putnam's Sons, 1907.

Rosenfield, John. "Jesse James Hero of Epic Melodrama." *Dallas Texas News*, 22 January 1939.

Rosten, Leo. *Hollywood*. New York: HBJ, 1941.

Rotha, Paul. *The Film till Now: A Survey of the Cinema* [1930]. London: Spring Books, 1967.

Sandburg, Carl. *Abraham Lincoln: The Prairie Years*. 2 vols. New York: Harcourt, Brace, 1926.

Schallert, Edwin. Selected reviews. *Los Angeles Times*, 1932–1941.

Schlesinger, Arthur M., Sr. *The Rise of the City, 1878–98*. New York: Macmillan, 1933.

Seldes, Gilbert. *The Seven Lively Arts*. New York: Sagamore Press, 1924.

———. *An Hour with the Movies and the Talkies*. Philadelphia: J. B. Lippincott, 1929.

———. *The Movies Come from America*. New York: Scribner's Sons, 1937.

Seymour, Charles. *American Neutrality, 1914–1917*. New Haven, Conn.: Yale University Press, 1935.

Sherwood, Robert E. Selected reviews. *Hollywood Reporter*, 1922–1936.

———. "Renaissance in Hollywood." *American Mercury* 16, no. 64 (April 1929): 431–37.

———. "The Moving Picture Album: *Cimarron*." *Hollywood Daily Citizen*, 7 February 1931.

———. "The Moving Picture Album: *Scarface*." *Hollywood Citizen-News*, 2 April 1932.

———. *Abe Lincoln in Illinois*. New York: Charles Scribner's Sons, 1939.

Simkins, Francis Butler, and James Welch Patton. *The Women of the Confederacy*. Richmond, Va.: Garrett and Massie, 1936.

Skeyhill, Tom. *Sergeant York: His Own Life Story and War Diary*. Garden City, N.Y.: Doubleday, Doran, 1928.

———. *Sergeant York: The Last of the Long Hunters*. Philadelphia: John C. Winston, 1930.

Slide, Anthony, ed. *Selected Film Criticism, 1896–1960*. 6 vols. Metuchen, N.J.: Scarecrow Press, 1982–1985.

Slosson, Preston W. *The Great Crusade and After, 1914–1928*. New York: Macmillan, 1930.

Sullivan, Edward D. *Look at Chicago*. Chicago: Bles, 1930.

Sutton, Fred E., and A. B. MacDonald. *Hands Up!* New York: Bobbs-Merrill, 1927.

Swanson, Neil Hamilton. *The First Rebel: Being a Lost Chapter of Our History*. New York: Farrar & Reinhart, 1937.

Tansill, Charles C. *America Goes to War*. Boston: Little, Brown, 1938.

Tarbell, Ida. *The Early Life of Abraham Lincoln*. New York: S. S. McClure, 1896.

————. *Life of Abraham Lincoln*. New York: Macmillan, 1917.

————. *In the Footsteps of the Lincolns*. New York: Harper & Brothers, 1924.

Thomas, Benjamin P. *Lincoln's New Salem*. Springfield, Ill.: Abraham Lincoln Association, 1934.

Thorp, Margaret Farrand. *America at the Movies*. New Haven, Conn.: Yale University Press, 1939.

Time. Selected reviews, 1936–1942.

Toland, Gregg. "How I Broke the Rules in *Citizen Kane*." *Popular Photography Magazine* 8 (June 1941): 55.

Trail, Armitage. *Scarface* [1930]. London: Bloomsbury, 1997.

Turner, Frederick Jackson. *Rereading Frederick Jackson Turner*. Edited by John Mack Faragher. New York: Henry Holt, 1994.

Van Doren, Dorothy. "A Pioneer Fairy Story." *Nation* 130 (23 April 1930): 494.

Variety. Selected reviews, 1928–1942.

Vestal, Stanley. "*Cimarron*." *Saturday Review of Literature* 6 (22 March 1930): 841.

Vroman, A. C., and T. F. Barnes. *The Genesis of the Story of Ramona: Why the Book Was Written, Explanatory Text of Points of Interest Mentioned in the Story*. Los Angeles: Press of Kingsley-Barnes and Neuner, 1899.

Waples, Dorothy. *The Whig Myth of James Fenimore Cooper*. New Haven, Conn.: Yale University Press, 1938.

The War of the Rebellion: A Compilation of the Official Records of the Union and Confederate Armies. Washington, D.C.: Government Printing Office, 1893, 1895.

Watts, Richard, Jr. Selected reviews. *New York Herald Tribune*, 1930–1934.

Wecter, Dixon. *The Hero in America: A Chronicle of Hero Worship*. New York: Charles Scribner's Sons, 1941.

Wellman, Paul. *Death in the Desert: The Fifty Years War for the Great Southwest*. New York: Macmillan, 1935.

West, Mae. *Goodness Had Nothing to Do with It*. New York: McFadden, 1970.

Whitney, Henry Clay. *Life on the Circuit Court with Lincoln*. With an introduction by Paul Angle. Caldwell, Ind.: Caxton Printers, 1940.

Wilson, Woodrow. *A History of the American People*. 5 vols. New York: Harper & Brothers, 1902.

Wilstach, Frank J. *Wild Bill Hickok—Prince of Pistoleers*. New York: Doubleday, Page, 1926.

Wright, A. M. R. *The Dramatic Life of Abraham Lincoln*. New York: Grosset & Dunlap, 1925.

Wright, Louis B. "American Democracy and the Frontier." *Yale Review* 22 (1930): 349–65.

Wyatt, E. Van Rensselaer. "*Abe Lincoln in Illinois*." *Catholic World* 148 (December 1938): 340.

Young, Stark. *So Red the Rose*. New York: Charles Scribner's Sons, 1934.

————. *Stark Young: A Life in the Arts, Letters, 1900–1962*. Edited by John Pilkington. Baton Rouge: Louisiana State University Press, 1960.

Secondary Sources

Abramson, R., and R. Thompson. "*Young Mr. Lincoln* Reconsidered: An Essay on the Theory and Practice of Film Criticism." *Ciné-Tracts* 2, no. 1 (fall 1978): 41–9, 50–62.

Allen, Robert C., and Douglas Gomery. *Film History: Theory and Practice.* New York: Random House, 1985.

Allsop, Kenneth. *The Bootleggers: The Story of Chicago's Prohibition Era* [1961]. New Rochelle, N.Y.: Arlington House, 1968.

Altman, Charles F. "Towards a Historiography of American Film." *Cinema Journal* 16, no. 2 (1977): 1–25.

Altman, Rick. *Film/Genre.* London: BFI, 1999.

Ames, Christopher. *Movies about the Movies: Hollywood Reflected.* Lexington: University Press of Kentucky, 1997.

Anderson, Christopher. "Jesse James, the Bourgeois Bandit: The Transformation of a Popular Hero." *Cinema Journal* 26, no. 1 (fall 1986): 43–64.

Anderson, Fred. *The Crucible of War: The Seven Years' War and the Fate of Empire in British North America.* New York: Alfred A. Knopf, 2000.

Anderson, Patrick D. *In Its Own Image: The Cinematic Vision of Hollywood.* New York: Arno Press, 1978.

Andrew, Dudley. *Film in the Aura of Art.* Princeton, N.J.: Princeton University Press, 1984.

———. "Film and History." In *The Oxford Guide to Film Studies.* Edited by John Hill and Pamela Church Gibson, 176–89. Oxford: Oxford University Press, 1998.

Appleby, Joyce, et al. *Telling the Truth about History.* New York: W. W. Norton, 1994.

Balio, Tino. *Grand Design: Hollywood as a Modern Business Enterprise, 1930–1939.* New York: Charles Scribner's Sons, 1993.

Barker, Martin, and Roger Sabin. *The Lasting of the Mohicans: History of an American Myth.* Jackson: University Press of Mississippi, 1995.

Barr, Charles. "*Dodge City.*" In *The Book of Westerns.* Edited by Ian Cameron and Douglas Pye, 181–88. New York: Continuum, 1996.

Barthes, Roland. *Mythologies.* New York: Hill & Wang, 1975.

Baxter, John. *Hollywood in the Thirties.* New York: Barnes, 1968.

———. *The Gangster Film.* London: A. Zwemmer, 1970.

Bazin, André. "The Evolution of the Language of Cinema." In *What Is Cinema?* vol. 1. Edited by Hugh Gray. Berkeley: University of California Press, 1967.

———. "The Evolution of the Western." In *What Is Cinema?* vol. 2. Edited by Hugh Gray. Berkeley: University of California Press, 1972.

———. *Orson Welles: A Critical View* [1978]. Los Angeles: Acrobat Books, 1991.

Beck, Philip. "Historicism, Historicity, and Film Historiography." *Journal of Film and Video* 37 (winter 1985): 5–17.

Behlmer, Rudy. "To the Wilderness for *Northwest Passage.*" *American Cinematographer* 68, no. 11 (November 1987): 38–47.

———. *Behind the Scenes.* Hollywood: Samuel French, 1990.

———. "*Land of Liberty,* a Conglomerate." *American Cinematographer* 72, no. 3 (March 1991): 34–40.

Beja, Morris, ed. *Perspectives on Orson Welles.* New York: G. K. Hall, 1995.

Belton, John. "American Cinema and Film History." In *The Oxford Guide to*

Film Studies. Edited by John Hill and Pamela Church Gibson, 227–37. Oxford: Oxford University Press, 1998.

Benson, Susan Porter, et al. *The New American History.* Philadelphia: Temple University Press, 1997.

Bergman, Andrew. *We're in the Money: Depression America and Its Films.* New York: New York University Press, 1971.

Bernstein, Matthew. "Selznick's March: The Atlanta Premiere of *Gone with the Wind.*" *Atlanta History* 43, no. 2 (summer 1999): 7–33.

———, ed. *Controlling Hollywood: Censorship and Regulation in the Studio Era.* New Brunswick, N.J.: Rutgers University Press, 1999.

Bernstein, Matthew, and Gaylyn Studlar, eds. *John Ford Made Westerns.* Bloomington: Indiana University Press, 2000.

Birchard, Robert S. *Cecil B. DeMille's Hollywood.* Lexington: University Press of Kentucky, 2004.

Birdwell, Michael E. *Celluloid Soldiers: The Warner Bros. Campaign against Nazism.* New York: New York University Press, 1999.

Bonitzer, Pascal. "The Silences of the Voice" [1975, *Cahiers du cinéma*]. Reprinted in *Narrative, Apparatus, Ideology.* Edited by Philip Rosen, 319–34. New York: Columbia University Press, 1986.

Bordwell, David. *On the History of Film Style.* Cambridge, Mass.: Harvard University Press, 1997.

Bordwell, David, Kristin Thompson, and Janet Staiger. *The Classical Hollywood Cinema: Film Style and Mode of Production to 1960.* New York: Columbia University Press, 1985.

Bourget, Jean-Loup. "Social Implications of the Hollywood Genres" [1973]. Reprinted in *The Film Genre Reader II.* Edited by Barry Keith Grant, 50–58. Austin: University of Texas Press, 1995.

Braudy, Leo. *Frenzy of Renown: Fame and Its History.* New York: Oxford University Press, 1986.

Braudy, Leo, and Marshall Cohen, eds. *Film Theory and Criticism,* 6th ed. Oxford: Oxford University Press, 2004.

Brown, Harry. *Injun Joe's Ghost: The Indian Mixed-Blood in American Writing.* Columbia: University of Missouri Press, 2004.

Browne, Nick. "*Cahiers du cinéma*'s Rereading of Hollywood Cinema." *Quarterly Review of Film Studies* 3, no. 3 (summer 1978): 405–16.

———. "The Spectator of American Symbolic Forms: Rereading John Ford's *Young Mr. Lincoln.*" *Film Reader* 4 (1979): 180–88.

———. "The Spectator-in-the-Text: The Rhetoric of *Stagecoach.*" In *Film Theory and Criticism,* 6th ed. Edited by Leo Braudy and Marshall Cohen, 118–33. Oxford: Oxford University Press, 2004.

Bruns, Roger. *The Bandit Kings: From Jesse James to Pretty Boy Floyd.* New York: Crown, 1995.

Burgoyne, Robert. *Film Nation: Hollywood Looks at U.S. History.* Minneapolis: University of Minnesota Press, 1997.

Buscombe, Edward. *Stagecoach.* London: BFI, 1992.

Cameron, Ian, and Douglas Pye, eds. *The Book of Westerns.* New York, Continuum, 1996.

Cameron, Kenneth M. *America on Film: Hollywood and American History.* New York: Continuum, 1997.

Carnes, Mark C., ed. *Past Imperfect: History According to the Movies.* New York: Henry Holt, 1995.

Carringer, Robert L. *The Making of* Citizen Kane. Berkeley: University of California Press, 1985.

Caton, Steven C. *Lawrence of Arabia: A Film's Anthropology.* Berkeley: University of California Press, 1999.

Cawelti, John G. *The Six-Gun Mystique.* Bowling Green, Ohio: Bowling Green University Popular Press, 1971.

Clarens, Carlos. *Crime Movies: From Griffith to* The Godfather *and Beyond.* New York: W. W. Norton, 1980.

Clinton, Catherine. *Tara Revisited: Women, War, and the Plantation Legend.* New York: Abbeville Press, 1995.

———, ed. *Half-Sisters of History: Southern Women and the American Past.* Durham, N.C.: Duke University Press, 1994.

Cohen, Paula Marantz. *Silent Film and the Triumph of the American Myth.* New York: Oxford University Press, 2000.

Comolli, Jean-Luc, and Jean Narboni. "Cinema/Ideology/Criticism" [1969]. Reprinted in *Film Theory and Criticism,* 6th ed. Edited by Leo Braudy and Marshall Cohen, 812–19. Oxford: Oxford University Press, 2004.

Cormack, Mike. *Ideology and Cinematography in Hollywood, 1930–1939.* London: Macmillan, 1994.

Crafton, Donald. "The Portrait as Protagonist: *The Private Life of Henry VIII.*" *Iris* 14–15 (fall 1992): 25–43.

———. *The Talkies: American Cinema's Transition to Sound, 1926–1931.* New York: Charles Scribner's Sons, 1997.

Cripps, Thomas. *Slow Fade to Black: The Negro in American Film, 1900–1942.* New York: Oxford University Press, 1977.

———. "Winds of Change: *Gone with the Wind* and Racism as a National Issue." In *Recasting:* Gone with the Wind *in American Culture.* Edited by Darden Asbury Pryon, 137–52. Miami: University Presses of Florida, 1983.

———. *Hollywood's High Noon: Moviemaking and Society before Television.* Baltimore: Johns Hopkins University Press, 1997.

Croce, Arlene. *The Fred Astaire and Ginger Rogers Book.* New York: Outerbridge & Lazard, 1972.

Cullen, Jim. *The Civil War in Popular Culture: A Reusable Past.* Washington, D.C.: Smithsonian Institution Press, 1995.

Custen, George F. *Bio/Pics: How Hollywood Constructed Public History.* New Brunswick, N.J.: Rutgers University Press, 1992.

———. *Twentieth Century's Fox: Darryl F. Zanuck and the Culture of Hollywood.* New York: Basic Books, 1997.

Davis, Natalie Zemon. "'Any Resemblance to Persons Living or Dead': Film and the Challenge of Authenticity." *Yale Review* 76, no. 4 (summer 1987): 457–80.

———. *Slaves on Screen.* Cambridge, Mass.: Harvard University Press, 2001.

DeLyser, Dydia. *Ramona Memories: Tourism and the Shaping of Southern California.* Minneapolis: University of Minnesota Press, 2005.

Denning, Michael. *The Cultural Front*. New York: Verso, 1997.

Dickson, Paul, and Thomas B. Allen. *The Bonus Army: An American Epic*. New York: Walker, 2004.

Dippe, Brian. *Custer's Last Stand: The Anatomy of an American Myth*. Lincoln: University of Nebraska Press, 1994.

Donald, David. *Lincoln's Herndon*. New York: Alfred A. Knopf, 1948.

———. *Lincoln Reconsidered: Essays on the Civil War Era*. New York: Alfred A. Knopf, 1956.

———. *Lincoln*. New York: Simon & Schuster, 1995.

Dooley, Roger. *From Scarface to Scarlett: American Films in the 1930s*. New York: HBJ, 1981.

Duff, John J. A. *Lincoln: Prairie Lawyer*. New York: Rinehart, 1960.

Dyer, Richard. *Stars*. London: BFI, 1979.

Editors of *Cahiers du cinéma*. "John Ford's *Young Mr. Lincoln*" [1970]. Reprinted in *Narrative, Apparatus, Ideology*. Edited by Philip Rosen, 444–82. New York: Columbia University Press, 1986.

Edwards, Anne. *A Remarkable Woman: A Biography of Katharine Hepburn*. New York: William Morrow, 1985.

Eliade, Mircea. *The Sacred and the Profane*. New York: Harcourt, Brace, 1959.

Elsaesser, Thomas, with Adam Barker, eds. *Early Cinema: Space, Frame, Narrative*. London: BFI, 1990.

Falkenberg, Pamela. "Rewriting the 'Classic Hollywood Cinema': Textual Analysis, Ironic Distance, and the Western in the Critique of Corporate Capitalism." Ph.D. diss., University of Iowa, 1983.

Faust, Drew Gilpin. *Mothers of Invention: Women of the Slaveholding South in the American Civil War*. New York: Vintage, 1996.

Ferro, Marc. *Cinema and History*. Translated by Naomi Greene. Detroit: Wayne State University Press, 1988.

Fine, David. *Los Ángeles: A City in Fiction*. Albuquerque: University of New Mexico Press, 2000.

Fine, Richard. *Hollywood and the Profession of Authorship, 1928–1940*. Ann Arbor: University of Michigan Press, 1985.

Foner, Eric. *Reconstruction, 1863–77: America's Unfinished Revolution*. New York: Harper & Row, 1988.

French, Philip. *Westerns*. New York: Viking Press, 1973.

Gaines, Jane, ed. *Classical Hollywood Narrative: The Paradigm Wars*. Durham, N.C.: Duke University Press, 1992.

Gallafent, Edward. *Astaire and Rogers*. New York: Columbia University Press, 2002.

Gallagher, Gary, and Alan T. Nolan, eds. *The Myth of the Lost Cause and Civil War History*. Bloomington: Indiana University Press, 2000.

Gallagher, Tag. *John Ford: The Man and His Films*. Berkeley: University of California Press, 1986.

Gardner, Sarah. *Blood and Irony: Southern White Women's Narratives of the Civil War, 1861–1937*. Chapel Hill: University of North Carolina Press, 2004.

Gehring, Wes D. *Populism and the Capra Legacy*. Westport, Conn.: Greenwood Press, 1995.

Gilbert, Julie Goldsmith. *Ferber: A Biography*. Garden City, N.Y.: Doubleday, 1978.

Glatthaar, Joseph T. *The March to the Sea and Beyond: Sherman's Troops in the Savannah and Georgia Campaigns*. New York: New York University Press, 1985.

Glover, Susan. "Battling the Elements: Reconstructing the Heroic in Robert Rogers." *Journal of American Culture* 26, no. 2 (June 2003): 180–87.

Gomery, Douglas. *The Hollywood Studio System*. New York: St. Martin's Press, 1986.

Gottesman, Ronald, ed. *Perspectives on* Citizen Kane. New York: G. K. Hall, 1996.

Grant, Barry Keith, ed. *The Film Genre Reader II*. Austin: University of Texas Press, 1995.

———. *John Ford's* Stagecoach. Cambridge: Cambridge University Press, 2003.

Gussow, Mel. *Don't Say Yes until I Finish Talking: A Biography of Darryl F. Zanuck*. Garden City, N.Y.: Doubleday, 1971.

Hamilton, Ian. *Writers in Hollywood, 1915–1951*. New York: Harper & Row, 1990.

Handlin, Oscar, et al. *The Harvard Guide to American History*. Cambridge, Mass.: Harvard University Press, 1954.

Hansen, Miriam. "Mass Production of the Senses: Classical Cinema as Vernacular Modernism." In *Reinventing Film Studies*. Edited by Linda Williams and Christine Gledhill, 332–50. London: Arnold, 1999.

Haver, Ronald. *David O. Selznick's Hollywood*. New York: Alfred A. Knopf, 1980.

Hitt, Jim. *The American West from Fiction (1823–1986) into Film (1909–1986)*. Jefferson, N.C.: McFarland, 1990.

Isenberg, Michael T. *War on Film*. London: Associated University Presses, 1981.

Issel, William, and Robert V. Cherny. *San Francisco, 1865–1932: Politics, Power, and Urban Development*. Berkeley: University of California Press, 1986.

Jewell, Richard A., with Vernon Harbin. *The RKO Story*. New York: Arlington House, 1982.

Jones, Alfred H. *Roosevelt's Image Brokers*. Port Washington, N.Y.: Kennikat Press, 1974.

Jones, Gordon L. "*So Red the Rose*: Atlanta's *Gone with the Wind* That Wasn't." *Atlanta History* 43, no. 2 (summer 1999): 45–67.

Jowett, Garth. *Film: The Democratic Art: A Social History of the American Film*. Boston: Little, Brown, 1976.

———. "Bullets, Beer, and the Hays Office." In *American History/American Film*. Edited by John O'Connor and Martin A. Jackson, 57–75. New York: Ungar, 1979.

Kael, Pauline. *Raising Kane and Other Essays*. London: Marion Boyers, 1996.

Karpf, Stephen Louis. *The Gangster Film: Emergence, Variation, and Decay of a Genre*. New York: Arno, 1973.

Kasson, Joy S. *Buffalo Bill's Wild West: Celebrity, Memory, and Popular History*. New York: Hill & Wang, 2001.

Kelly, William. *Plotting America's Past: Fenimore Cooper and the Leatherstocking Tales*. Carbondale: Southern Illinois University Press, 1983.

Kennedy, David M. *Over Here: The First World War and American Society*. New York: Oxford University Press, 1980.

Kennett, Lee. *Marching through Georgia: The Story of Soldiers and Civilians during Sherman's Campaign*. New York: HarperCollins, 1995.

Klein, Kerwin Lee. *Frontiers of the Historical Imagination*. Berkeley: University of California Press, 1997.

Kreuger, Miles. *Show Boat*. Oxford: Oxford University Press, 1977.

Landy, Marcia. *Cinematic Uses of the Past*. Minneapolis: University of Minnesota Press, 1996.

———, ed. *The Historical Film: History and Memory in Media*. New Brunswick, N.J.: Rutgers University Press, 2001.

Lang, Robert, ed. *The Birth of a Nation*. New Brunswick, N.J.: Rutgers University Press, 1994.

Lasky, Betty. *RKO: The Biggest Little Major of Them All*. Englewood Cliffs, N.J.: Prentice-Hall, 1984.

Lawson-Peebles, Robert. "The Lesson of the Massacre at Fort William Henry." In *New Essays on* The Last of the Mohicans. Edited by H. Daniel Peck, 115–38. Cambridge: Cambridge University Press, 1992.

Lears, T. J. Jackson. *No Place of Grace: Antimodernism and the Transformation of American Culture, 1880–1920*. Chicago: University of Chicago Press, 1981.

Lee, David E. *Sergeant York: An American Hero*. Lexington: University Press of Kentucky, 1985.

Leff, Leonard J., and Jerold L. Simmons. *The Dame in the Kimono: Hollywood, Censorship, and the Production Code*. Lexington: University Press of Kentucky, 2001.

Leibowitz, Herbert A. *Fabricating Lives: Explorations in American Autobiography*. New York: Alfred A. Knopf, 1989.

Leuchtenburg, William E. *Franklin D. Roosevelt and the New Deal, 1932–40*. New York: Harper & Row, 1963.

Lévi-Strauss, Claude. *The Raw and the Cooked: Introduction to a Science of Mythology*, vol. 1. New York: Harper & Row, 1969.

Limerick, Patricia Nelson. *Legacy of Conquest: The Unbroken Past of the American West*. New York: W. W. Norton, 1987.

MacAdams, William. *Ben Hecht*. New York: Charles Scribner's Sons, 1990.

Maltby, Richard. "Grief in the Limelight: Al Capone, Howard Hughes, the Hays Code and the Politics of the Unstable Text." In *Movies and Politics: The Dynamic Relationship*. Edited by James Combs, 133–81. New York: Garland, 1993.

———. "Tragic Heroes? Al Capone and the Spectacle of Criminality, 1948–1931." In *Screening the Past: The 6th Australian History and Film Conference Papers*. Edited by John Benson, 112–19. Bundoora: La Trobe University, 1993.

———. "A Better Sense of History: John Ford and the Indians." In *The Book of Westerns*. Edited by Ian Cameron and Douglas Pye, 34–49. New York: Continuum, 1996.

Marsden, Michael T., John G. Nachbar, and Sam L. Grogg Jr., eds. *Movies as Artifacts*. Chicago: Nelson-Hall, 1982.

Martin, Terence. "From Atrocity to Requiem: History in *The Last of the Mohicans*." In *New Essays on* The Last of the Mohicans. Edited by H. Daniel Peck, 47–66. Cambridge: Cambridge University Press, 1992.

May, Lary. *The Big Tomorrow: Hollywood and the Politics of the American Way.* Chicago: University of Chicago Press, 2000.

McCarthy, Todd. *Howard Hawks.* New York: Grove Press, 1997.

McCartney, Paul T. *Power and Progress: American National Identity, the War of 1898, and the Rise of American Imperialism.* Baton Rouge: Louisiana State University Press, 2006.

McCarty, John. *Hollywood Gangland: The Movies' Love Affair with the Mob.* New York: St. Martin's Press, 1993.

McElvaine, Robert S. *The Great Depression: America, 1929–1941.* New York: Times Books, 1984.

McPherson, James. *Battle Cry of Freedom.* New York: Oxford University Press, 1988.

McPherson, Tara. *Reconstructing Dixie: Race, Gender, and Nostalgia in the Imagined South.* Durham, N.C.: Duke University Press, 2003.

Michaels, Walter Benn. *Our America: Nativism, Modernism, and Pluralism.* Durham, N.C.: Duke University Press, 1995.

Mizejewski, Linda. *Ziegfeld Girl.* Durham, N.C.: Duke University Press, 1999.

Moses, L. G. *Wild West Shows and the Images of American Indians, 1883–1933.* Albuquerque: University of New Mexico Press, 1996.

Mulvey, Laura. *Citizen Kane.* London: BFI, 1992.

Munby, Jonathan. *Public Enemies, Public Heroes: Screening the Gangster from Little Caesar to Touch of Evil.* Chicago: University of Chicago Press, 1999.

Nachbar, Jack, ed. *Focus on the Western.* Englewood Cliffs, N.J.: Prentice-Hall, 1974.

Nash, Gerald D. *Creating the West: Historical Interpretations, 1890–1990.* Albuquerque: University of New Mexico Press, 1991.

Neely, Mark E., Jr. "The Young Lincoln: Two Films." In *Past Imperfect: History According to the Movies.* Edited by Mark C. Carnes, 124–27. New York: Henry Holt, 1995.

Novick, Peter. *That Noble Dream: The "Objectivity Question" and the American Historical Profession.* Cambridge: Cambridge University Press, 1988.

O'Connor, John. "A Reaffirmation of American Ideals: *Drums along the Mohawk.*" In *American History/American Film: Interpreting the Hollywood Image.* Edited by John O'Connor and Martin A. Jackson, 97–119. New York: Ungar, 1979.

O'Connor, John, and Martin Jackson, eds. *American History/American Film: Interpreting the Historical Image.* New York: Ungar, 1979.

Palmer, Allen W. "Cecil B. DeMille Writes America's History for the 1939 World's Fair." *Film History* 5, no. 1 (March 1993): 36–48.

Parish, James Robert, and Michael R. Pitts. *Hollywood on Hollywood.* Metuchen, N.J.: Scarecrow Press, 1978.

Parks, Rita. *The Western Hero in Film and Television: Mass Media Mythology.* Ann Arbor, Mich.: UMI Research Press, 1982.

Pauly, Thomas H. "*Gone with the Wind* and *The Grapes of Wrath* as Hollywood Histories of the Depression." *Journal of Popular Film* 3, no. 3 (1974): 202–18.

Peck, H. Daniel, ed. *New Essays on* The Last of the Mohicans. Cambridge: Cambridge University Press, 1992.

Pells, Richard. *Radical Visions and American Dreams.* New York: Harper & Row, 1973.

Perkins, V. F. *The Magnificent Ambersons.* London: BFI, 1999.

Peterson, Merrill D. *Lincoln in American Memory.* New York: Oxford University Press, 1994.

Pheil, Fred. *Another Tale to Tell: Politics and Narrative in Postmodern Culture.* London: Verso, 1990.

Philips, Gene D. "*A Star Is Born.*" *Films in Review* 40, nos. 8–9 (August–September 1989): 445.

Pizzitola, Louis. *Hearst over Hollywood.* New York: Columbia University Press, 2002.

Place, J. A. "*Young Mr. Lincoln.*" *Wide Angle* 2, no. 4 (1978): 28–35.

———. *The Non-Western Films of John Ford.* Secaucus, N.J.: Citadel Press, 1979.

Powdermaker, Hortense. *Hollywood: The Dream Factory.* Boston: Little, Brown, 1950.

Pyron, Darden Asbury, ed. *Recasting:* Gone with the Wind *in American Culture.* Miami: University Presses of Florida, 1983.

Ray, Robert B. *A Certain Tendency of the Hollywood Cinema, 1930–1980.* Princeton, N.J.: Princeton University Press, 1985.

Reinhart, Mark S. *Abraham Lincoln on Screen: A Filmography, 1903–1998.* Jefferson, N.C.: McFarland, 1998.

Renov, Michael, ed. *Theorizing Documentary.* New York: Routledge, 1993.

Riley, Glenda. *The Life and Legend of Annie Oakley.* Norman: University of Oklahoma Press, 1998.

Riley, Michael J. "Trapped in the History of Film: *The Vanishing American.*" In *Hollywood's Indian.* Edited by Peter C. Rollins and John O'Connor. Lexington: University Press of Kentucky, 1998.

Roberts, Diane. *The Myth of Aunt Jemima: Representations of Race and Region.* London: Routledge, 1994.

Roche, Mark W., and Vittorio Hoesle. "Vico's Age of Heroes and the Age of Men in John Ford's Film *The Man Who Shot Liberty Valance.*" *Clio* 23, no. 2 (1994): 131–47.

Roddick, Nick. *A New Deal in Entertainment: Warner Brothers in the Thirties.* London: BFI, 1983.

Roediger, David. *The Wages of Whiteness: Race and the Making of the American Working Class.* New York: Verso, 1991.

Rollins, Peter C., ed. *The Columbia Companion to American History on Film: How the Movies Have Portrayed the American Past.* New York: Columbia University Press, 2004.

Rollins, Peter C., and John E. O'Connor, eds. *Hollywood's Indian.* Lexington: University Press of Kentucky, 1998.

Roman, Robert C. "Lincoln on the Screen." *Films in Review* (February 1961): 87–101.

Rosen, Philip. "Securing the Historical: Historiography and the Classical Cinema." In *Cinema Histories, Cinema Practices.* Edited by Patricia Mellencamp and Philip Rosen, 17–34. Frederick, Md.: University Publications of America, 1984.

———. *Change Mummified: Cinema, Historicity, Theory.* Minneapolis: University of Minnesota Press, 2001.

Rosenstone, Robert A. *Visions of the Past: The Challenge of Film to Our Idea of History.* Cambridge, Mass.: Harvard University Press, 1995.

———. "Inventing Historical Truth on the Silver Screen." *Cineaste* 29, no. 2 (spring 2004): 29–33.

———. *History on Film/Film as History.* New York: Longman/Pearson, 2006.

Rosow, Eugene. *Born to Lose: The Gangster Film in America.* New York: Oxford University Press, 1978.

Ruth, David E. *Inventing the Public Enemy: The Gangster in American Culture, 1918–1934.* Chicago: University of Chicago Press, 1996.

Sarris, Andrew. *The American Cinema, Directors and Directions, 1929–1968.* New York: E. P. Dutton, 1968.

———. *The John Ford Movie Mystery.* Bloomington: Indiana University Press, 1975.

Schatz, Thomas. *Hollywood Genres: Formulas, Filmmaking, and the Studio System.* Philadelphia: Temple University Press, 1981.

———. *The Genius of the System.* New York: Pantheon, 1988.

———. "'A Triumph of Bitchery': Warner Bros., Bette Davis, and *Jezebel.*" In *The Studio System.* Edited by Janet Staiger, 74–92. New Brunswick, N.J.: Rutgers University Press, 1995.

———. *Boom and Bust: American Cinema in the 1940s.* Berkeley: University of California Press, 1997.

Shindler, Colin. *Hollywood in Crisis: Cinema and American Society, 1929–1939.* New York: Routledge, 1996.

Silva, Fred, ed. *Focus on* The Birth of a Nation. Englewood Cliffs, N.J.: Prentice-Hall, 1971.

Sklar, Robert. *Movie-Made America: A Cultural History of American Movie Making.* New York: Random House, 1975.

Slotkin, Richard. *Regeneration through Violence: The Mythology of the American Frontier, 1600–1860.* Middletown, Conn.: Wesleyan University Press, 1973.

———. *The Fatal Environment: The Myth of the Frontier in the Age of Industrialization, 1800–1890.* Norman: University of Oklahoma Press, 1985.

———. *Gunfighter Nation: The Myth of the Frontier in Twentieth-Century America.* Norman: University of Oklahoma Press, 1998.

Smith, David L. "John Bowers: This Is the Real Norman Maine." *Films of the Golden Age* 35 (winter 2003–2004): 68–77.

Smith, Henry Nash. *Virgin Land: The American West as Symbol and Myth.* New York: Viking, 1950.

Smyth, J. E. "*Cimarron:* The New Western History in 1931." *Film & History* 33, no. 1 (2003): 9–17.

———. "*Young Mr. Lincoln:* Between Myth and History in 1939." *Rethinking History* 7, no. 2 (summer 2003): 193–214.

———. "Revisioning Modern American History in the Age of *Scarface* (1932)." *Historical Journal of Film, Radio, and Television* 24, no. 4 (October 2004): 535–63.

Sorlin, Pierre. *The Film in History: Restaging the Past.* Totowa, N.J.: Barnes & Noble, 1980.

————. "Cinema: An Undiscoverable History?" *Paragraph* 15, no. 1 (March 1992): 1–18.

Spatz, James. *Hollywood in Fiction: Some Versions of the American Myth.* Brussels: Mouton, 1969.

Stanfield, Peter. *Hollywood, Westerns and the 1930s: The Lost Trail.* Exeter: University of Exeter Press, 2001.

Steele, Ian K. "Cooper and Clio: The Sources for 'A Narrative of 1757.'" *Canadian Review of American Studies* 20 (winter 1989): 121–35.

Stempel, Tom. *Screenwriter: The Life and Times of Nunnally Johnson.* New York: A. S. Barnes, 1980.

Stern, Jerome. "*Gone with the Wind:* The South as America." *Southern Humanities Review* 6 (winter 1972): 5–12.

Stewart, Garrett. *Between Film and Screen: Modernism's Photo Synthesis.* Chicago: University of Chicago Press, 1999.

Stiles, T. J. *Jesse James.* New York: Simon & Schuster, 2002.

Strout, Cushing. *The Pragmatic Revolt: Carl Becker and Charles Beard.* New Haven, Conn.: Yale University Press, 1958.

Susman, Warren I. "The Thirties." In *The Development of an American Culture.* Edited by Stanley Cohen and Lorman Ratner. Englewood Cliffs, N.J.: Prentice-Hall, 1970.

————. "Film and History: Artifact and Experience." *Film and History* 15, no. 2 (May 1985): 25–36.

Swanberg, W. A. *Citizen Hearst: A Biography of William Randolph Hearst.* New York: Charles Scribner's Sons, 1961.

Tatum, Stephen. *Inventing Billy the Kid: Visions of the Outlaw in America, 1881–1981.* Albuquerque: University of New Mexico Press, 1982.

Thompson, Frank. *Lost Films: Important Movies that Disappeared.* New York: Citadel Press, 1996.

Thompson, John. *Closing the Frontier: Radical Response in Oklahoma, 1889–1923.* Norman: University of Oklahoma Press, 1986.

Trachtenberg, Alan. *Reading American Photographs: Images as History, Mathew Brady to Walker Evans.* New York: Hill & Wang, 1989.

Tuska, Jon. "The American Western Cinema: 1903–Present." In *Focus on the Western.* Edited by Jack Nachbar, 25–44. Englewood Cliffs, N.J.: Prentice-Hall, 1974.

Vertrees, Alan David. *Selznick's Vision: Gone with the Wind and Hollywood Filmmaking.* Austin: University of Texas Press, 1997.

Warshow, Robert. *The Immediate Experience: Movies, Comics, Theatre & Other Aspects of Popular Culture.* Garden City, N.Y.: Doubleday, 1962.

Watts, Jill, "Sacred and Profane: Mae West's (re)Presentation of Western Religion." In *Over the Edge: Remapping the American West.* Edited by Valerie Matsumoto and Blake Allmendinger, 50–64. Berkeley: University of California Press, 1999.

Weckesser, Elden C. *His Name Was Mudd.* Jefferson, N.C.: McFarland, 1991.

White, Hayden. "Historiography and Historiophoty." *American Historical Review* 93, no. 5 (1988): 1193–99.

White, Richard. *Western History.* Washington, D.C.: American Historical Association, 1997.

Williams, Linda. *Playing the Race Card.* Princeton, N.J.: Princeton University Press, 2001.

Williams, William Appleman. *The Tragedy of American Diplomacy* [1959]. New York: W. W. Norton, 1988.

Wish, Harvey. *The American Historian: A Social-Intellectual History of the Writing of the American Past.* New York: Oxford University Press, 1960.

Wood, Robin. "*Drums along the Mohawk.*" In *The Book of Westerns.* Edited by Ian Cameron and Douglas Pye, 174–80. New York: Continuum, 1996.

Woodward, C. Vann. *Tom Watson: Agrarian Rebel.* New York: Macmillan, 1938.

Wright, Will. *Six Guns and Society: A Structural Study of the Western.* Berkeley: University of California Press, 1975.

Young, Elizabeth. *Disarming the Nation.* Chicago: University of Chicago Press, 1999.

Zieger, Robert. *America's Great War: World War I and the American Experience.* Lanham, Md.: Rowman & Littlefield, 2000.

Index

Abbot, Willis J., 322–23
Abe Lincoln in Illinois (1938), 175, 242, 318
Abe Lincoln in Illinois (1940), 189–94, 282
Abraham Lincoln (1930), 28–29, 169, 172, 177, 189, 253, 256, 288, 308
Adamson, Ewart, 91
Adventures of Robin Hood, The (1938), 227
Age of Innocence, The (1934), 91
Alexander Hamilton (1931), 14, 21, 57–59, 84, 253, 256
Alexander's Ragtime Band (1938), 173, 207, 245, 283, 286, 294, 296
All Quiet on the Western Front (1930), 62–63, 204, 217
Allegheny Uprising (1939), 228, 241–42
Allen, Frederick Lewis, 61–62
Allen, Hervey, 204
Almach, John C., 33
Altman, Rick, 8
Ameche, Don, 292, 294
America (1924), 28
Anderson, Eddie, 164
Andrews, Eliza Frances, 141, 147–48, 165, 340
Angle, Paul, 179, 185

Annie Oakley (1935), 17, 91–94, 107, 109, 114, 241, 308
Arbuckle, Roscoe "Fatty," 255
Arizonian, The (1935), 20, 118, 241
Arliss, George, 57–58, 95
Astaire, Fred, 209–10
auteur criticism, 8, 17, 116–18, 309–10, 319–20, 325–26
Autry, Gene, 89

Baer, Richard, 325
Baker, Newton, 206, 238
Balderston, John, 91, 95, 99–100
Baldwin, Earl, 218
Ball of Fire (1941), 339
Bancroft, George, 4
Bankhead, Tallulah, 261
Barnes, Howard, 136–37, 209, 317
Barrymore, John, 253, 262, 274–75, 305
Barthes, Roland, 15
Basler, Roy, 181, 186
Bates, Ernest Sutherland, 325
Battle of Gettysburg, The (1913), 1
Bazin, André, 8, 309
Beard, Charles, 12, 33, 61, 65, 146–47, 182, 325
Beard, Mary, 146–47, 182
Becker, Carl, 12–13, 23, 50, 65, 295, 304

Becky Sharp (1935), 107
Beebe, Lucius, 202–3
Behlmer, Rudy, 242
Belle of the Nineties (1934), 93, 263
Belle Starr (1941), 167–68
Benét, Rosemary, 177
Benét, Stephen Vincent, 28–29, 34
Bennett, Constance, 258–60, 262
Beveridge, Albert J., 14, 168, 181, 185
Big Parade, The (1927), 203, 208, 235
Big Trail, The (1930), 20, 31, 36, 37,
    89, 109, 217, 246, 253
Billy the Kid (1930), 31, 36, 138, 308
Billy the Kid (1941), 138
Birth of a Nation, The (1915), 1–5, 28,
    36, 95, 109, 150, 162–63
biography and biopics, 13–14, 57–59,
    63–64, 74–82, 91–94, 167–94,
    197, 255–57, 264–65, 267, 304,
    326
Blondell, Joan, 202
Boehm, David, 202
Boehnel, William, 71
Bogart, Humphrey, 135, 219, 296, 298
Bombshell (1933), 261–63, 266, 272,
    282
Bonitzer, Pascal, 10, 11
Bonney, William, 14, 31, 111
Bonus Army, 200
Boone, Daniel, 237–41
Bordwell, David, 8–9, 10, 11
Bow, Clara, 53, 251–53, 255–63, 266,
    272, 275, 340
Bowers, Claude, 58, 158, 163
Bowers, John, 253, 274–75
Bowery, The (1935), 105, 170, 282
Boynton, Percy, 34
Brabin, Charles, 37
Brackett, Charles, 339
Branch, E. Douglas, 34
Brice, Fanny, 264, 283
Brickell, Hershel, 141–42
Bright, John, 59, 60, 71, 118

Broadway: historical films, 263–66,
    298–306; history of decline,
    280–84, 296–97
Broadway Melody (1929), 263
Brown, Katharine, 150, 267
Brown, Roland, 258
Bruce, Virginia, 253, 269–70, 272
Buckner, Robert, 117, 118, 134–37,
    155–56, 297, 300–301, 303–5,
    317
Bullets or Ballots (1936), 84
Burke, Billie, 264–65
Burke, Edwin, 170
Burnett, W. R., 63, 65–66, 76–77
Burns, Robert Elliot, 198–201, 205
Burns, Walter Noble, 14, 23, 31, 35,
    60, 62, 64–65 73–74, 77, 111, 207
Buscombe, Edward, 118
Bush, W. Stephen, 2

Cagney, James, 62, 69, 134, 216,
    219–20, 222, 298, 301, 305
Cagney, William, 303
Cahiers du cinéma, 16–17, 176, 181,
    234, 309
Call Her Savage (1932), 14, 20, 53
Campbell, Allan, 268
Capone, Al, 14, 60–64, 68, 73–74,
    197–99, 206, 235, 325, 340;
    and ethnicity, 66; and *Scarface*,
    75–82; as self-made man, 74–75;
    as veteran, 62
Capra, Frank, 193–94, 319
Captain January (1935), 170
Cardinal Richelieu (1935), 101
Carlson, Oliver, 325
Carringer, Robert, 318, 320, 323–24,
    326
Carson, Robert, 267–69, 274
Castle, Irene, 210–16, 340
Castle, Vernon, 210–16
Cather, Willa, 47–48
Caton, Stephen C., 18

Cawelti, John, 89
censorship and historical films, 2,
    19–20, 68, 71–73, 80–81, 89, 128,
    152, 162, 191–92, 200–201, 220,
    222, 242, 325
Chambers, Robert W., 152
Chandlee, Harry, 229–30
Chaplin, Charles, 258, 295–96
Chesnut, Mary, 149, 165
Cimarron (1929), 14, 32–34, 48–49,
    134
Cimarron (1931), 14, 19, 20, 21, 22,
    23, 34–53, 63, 69, 89–90, 92,
    94–95, 99, 101, 103, 108, 109,
    111–14, 121, 135–36, 170, 178,
    253, 269, 313, 315, 327, 331–35,
    338, 340
cinematography as historical tool, 69,
    154–62, 186–87, 190, 214, 295,
    331–33
Citizen Kane (1941), 11, 21, 309–10,
    317–37
Civil War, 1–4, 137, 141–65; and
    historiography, 2–4, 141–48; and
    women's history, 142–49
Clark, John Maurice, 205–6, 310
classical Hollywood cinema, 8–10, 17,
    18, 23–24, 59–60, 122–23, 143,
    160–62, 309–10
Clinton, Catherine, 143
Cody, William F. (a.k.a. Buffalo Bill),
    92–93, 109–10, 118
Cohan, George M., 298–306
Colbert, Claudette, 211
Commager, Henry Steele, 144–45
competition over historical material,
    155, 226–27
Condon, Frank, 255
Conkle, E. P. (*Prologue to Glory*), 175
Conquerors, The (1932), 20, 51–53,
    91, 119, 253
Cook, Sidney, 172
Cooper, Courtney Ryley, 35, 91, 110

Cooper, Gary, 30, 150–52, 229, 234,
    273, 292, 339
Cooper, James Fenimore, 90, 95–99,
    146, 241
Count of Monte Cristo, The (1935), 313
Covered Wagon, The (1923), 5, 17, 28,
    31, 32, 36, 90, 95, 255
Cowan, Sam, 229
Cowley, Malcolm, 143–44, 165
Crafton, Donald, 17–19
Crane, Mack, 261
Crawford, Joan, 211, 263
crime histories, 62–85
Cripps, Thomas, 164
Cromwell, John, 189
Crowther, Bosley, 133, 233, 325–26
Cruze, James, 254–55
Custen, George F., 13

Daily Variety, 169
Daniel Boone (1936), 228
Daniels, Bebe, 262
Davies, Marion, 151, 322
Davis, Bette, 154–57, 211, 229
Davis, Britton, 119–20
Davis, Natalie Zemon, 18
Davis, Owen, 154, 156
DeBra, Arthur, 311
De Havilland, Olivia, 211
De la Motte, Marguerite, 253, 274
Delehanty, Thornton, 51, 54, 134,
    170
DeMille, Cecil B., 53, 90, 108–10,
    113–16, 118, 131–33, 255, 281,
    290, 295–96, 308–18, 328, 335
DeMille, William, 255, 279, 281–82,
    290, 295–96
Depression: and historical film-
    making, 21, 48–49, 52, 89–90,
    202, 220, 222; and effect on
    studio production, 21, 32, 51, 89,
    192–93, 194
Destry Rides Again (1932), 89, 138

Destry Rides Again (1939), 138
Diamond Jim (1935), 282, 283
Disraeli (1929), 57–58
Dillinger, John, 83–84, 319
Dix, Richard, 40, 53
Dixon, Thomas, 1, 153
documentary films, 10, 11
documentary footage inserts, 5, 10,
     69–70, 203, 218, 327
Dodge City (1939), 136–37, 216, 324
Donald, David, 179–80, 192
Donohue, Frank, 218
Doorway to Hell (1930), 59–60,
     62–63, 267
Dr. Socrates (1935), 83–84
*Dramatic Life of Abraham Lincoln,
     The* (1924), 5, 29, 177, 189–90
Druggan, Terry, 68, 72, 197
Drums along the Mohawk (1936),
     243–45
Drums along the Mohawk (1939),
     222, 228, 241, 244–46, 324
DuBois, W.E.B., 158
Dudley, Marjorie, 258
Duel in the Sun (1947), 338
Duff, Warren, 134
Dunne, Irene, 41, 210
Dunne, Philip, 100
Dunning, William, 158

Edelman, Lou, 227
Edmonds, Walter D., 243–45
educational features, 7, 307
Eisenstein, Sergei, 9–10
Ellis, Edith, 37
entertainment cycle. *See* Hollywood,
     history of; Broadway
establishment history, 3–4, 113–14,
     131–38, 218–21, 234, 285, 291,
     310–17, 327, 329
Estabrook, Howard, 20, 22, 30, 34–37,
     40–41, 46, 47, 50–53, 91, 108,
     112–14, 182, 317–18, 327

European versus American historical
     filmmaking, 5
expansion, critiques of, 103–8,
     128–31, 134–35, 333–34

Fairbanks, Douglas, 255, 266, 267,
     269, 287
Falkenberg, Pamela, 17, 19, 131–33
Falling Star (1937), 282
Farewell to Arms, A (1932), 204–5
Farmer Takes a Wife, The (1935), 170,
     211
Faulkner, William, 243
Faust, Drew Gilpin, 144, 148–49
Fay, Frank, 253, 272, 294
Faye, Alice, 283, 291–92, 296
Ferber, Edna, 14, 23, 32–35, 40, 48,
     49, 90–91, 95, 108, 134, 146, 152,
     318, 327
Fergusson, Otis, 209, 265, 325
Ferro, Marc, 18, 19
Fields, Joseph, 91
Fighting 69th, The (1939), 23, 225–28
film critics and historical cinema, 2–3,
     7, 21, 113–14, 115–17, 125–26,
     136, 170, 188–89, 221–22, 265
Film Daily, 32, 63, 188
film studies: approaches to historical
     cinema, 15–17, 319–20
filmic writing of history, 4, 18, 19,
     23–24, 329–31
Finger Points, The (1931), 65
Finkel, Abem, 229, 230
First World War, 47–48, 55, 72, 73,
     77, 197–223, 225–27; and Ameri-
     can versus European experiences,
     204–5; and disillusionment, 12,
     55, 65, 198, 203, 205–6, 225–26,
     313, 328
Fitzgerald, F. Scott, 164
Fleming, Victor, 30, 160, 170, 256,
     262
Floyd, "Pretty Boy," 85

Flynn, Errol, 297–98
Fonda, Henry, 170, 178, 243, 296, 317
Ford, John, 16–17, 30, 89, 106,
    115–26, 178, 181, 183, 185, 189,
    203, 210, 326
forewords, 36, 71, 100–101, 107,
    109–10, 120–22, 127–28, 131–32,
    134, 164–65, 177–78, 201, 215,
    219, 223, 225, 227–28, 230, 233,
    242–44, 259, 264–65, 293
Forgotten Faces (1928), 252
forgotten man, 197, 202–3
42nd Street (1932), 201–2, 210, 263
Four Feathers, The (1929), 252, 313
Fowler, Gene, 258
Fox, Paul Hervey, 106–7
Francke, Caroline, 261
Franklin, Dean, 225
Freeman, Douglas Southall, 141–42,
    145–46
Frontier Marshal (1934), 89, 111, 138
Frontier Marshal (1939), 138
frontier myth, 34, 47, 267–68, 281,
    333–34
Furthman, Jules, 262

Gable, Clark, 258, 273, 296
Gabriel over the White House (1933),
    331
gangster genre, 7, 59–60, 218–23; and
    the First World War, 72–74, 77,
    83, 219–20; and popular biogra-
    phies, 60, 62–64, 68, 77, 83; and
    western myths, 73
Garbo, Greta, 253, 258, 269, 272
Gardner, Sarah, 143–44
Garrett, Oliver H. P., 164
Gassner, John, 126–27
Gaynor, Janet, 170, 211, 258, 273–74
genre, 8, 17, 21, 42, 59–60, 89–90,
    108
Gentleman Jim (1942), 337
Geraghty, Tom, 255

Geronimo, 119–22
Gibney, Sheridan, 199, 201
Gilbert, John, 203, 253, 266, 269–70,
    272, 275, 298
Girl of the Golden West, The (1915),
    109
Girl of the Golden West, The (1930), 30
Girl of the Golden West, The (1938),
    21, 93
Gish, Lillian, 3, 287–88
Give Me Liberty (1936), 307
Glasgow, Ellen, 148
Glasmon, Kubec, 59, 68, 71
Gold Diggers of 1933, The (1933), 22,
    201–3, 208–10, 263
Gold Is Where You Find It (1938), 134
Goldwyn, Samuel, 226, 339
Gone with the Wind (1936), 14,
    141–50, 153–54, 159–60, 164–65
Gone with the Wind (1939), 14, 17,
    19, 20, 143, 149–50, 155, 158–65,
    213, 222, 252, 295, 308, 324, 338,
    340
Gorgeous Hussy, The (1936), 208, 211,
    241, 264
Goulding, Edmund, 158
Grapes of Wrath, The (1940), 85, 317
Great Meadow, The (1931), 37, 109,
    241
Great Profile, The (1940), 296–97
Great Ziegfeld, The (1936), 20, 217,
    241, 264–66, 283
Great War films and historiography.
    See First World War
Grey, Zane, 40
Grierson, John, 18
Griffith, D. W., 1–7, 11–12, 23, 27,
    28–29, 60, 150, 162–63, 169,
    174, 258, 266, 281, 287–88, 290,
    295–96, 298
Gunning, Tom, 10

Hackett, Francis, 2

Hall, Mordaunt, 29, 54, 203, 255

Haller, Ernie, 160, 165

Hammerstein, Oscar, II, 211–13, 300

Hampton, Benjamin, 257, 260, 280, 293

Hansen, Miriam, 9

Harlow, Jean, 211, 261–63, 272–73, 275

Harris, Ray, 173

Hart, William S., 35, 267

Harvey Girls, The (1945), 338

Haver, Ronald, 274

Hawks, Howard, 14, 76, 78, 229–30, 234

Haycox, Ernest, 118–20, 131

Hays, Will, 71, 80–81, 162, 307–9; and moratorium on gangster films, 83–84, 208, 217

Hearst, George, 321

Hearst, William Randolph, 309, 319–33

Hecht, Ben, 60, 76–77, 118, 164–65, 319

Heerman, Victor, 151

Hellinger, Mark, 216–21

Hells Angels (1930), 34, 75

Hemingway, Ernest, 204

Hepburn, Katharine, 210, 260–61, 296

Herndon, William, 179–80, 183, 191–93

Heroes for Sale (1933), 203, 308

heroism, 12, 29, 74–75, 284–85

Hertz, Emmanuel, 187

His Girl Friday (1940), 14, 331

historians' attitudes toward historical films, 4, 11–12, 14–17, 34, 110–12, 120, 299–300, 316–17

historical cycle, beginning of, 54; end of, 21, 283, 297–98, 309, 317–18, 337–40

historical fiction, 5, 10–11, 18, 90–91, 95–99, 244–45; and women, 13–14, 143–49

historical film: criteria, 4–5, 9–11, 13–14, 17, 21–24, 54, 234, 263

historiography, 1–5, 10, 11–13, 14, 18, 49–51, 96–98, 120, 144–49, 218, 265–66, 311–14, 329

Hitchcock, Henry, 147

Hollingshead, Gordon "Holly," 175, 307

Hollywood (1923), 254–55, 272

Hollywood, history of, 14, 280–83. *See also* silent era

Hollywood Boulevard (1936), 266–67, 272

Hollywood Cavalcade (1939), 11, 14, 22, 279–80, 286–97, 316

Hollywood Reporter, 113, 138, 169, 188

Hollywood Speaks (1932), 259–60

Holmes, Brown, 199, 288

Howard, Sidney, 150, 152, 159–60, 162–65, 317

Howards of Virginia, The (1940), 246

Hudson's Bay (1940), 247, 299–300

Hughes, Howard, 34, 60, 75–76, 80, 84, 197, 227

Hughes, Rupert, 254

Huston, John, 55, 118, 229–30, 339

I Am a Fugitive from a Chain Gang (1932), 22, 198–202, 208–9, 308

ideology, 8, 15–17, 18, 45, 234, 303–4

imperialism, 44–45, 322

In Old Chicago (1938), 20, 243, 245, 283, 286, 294, 338

Informer, The (1935), 117–18

intertitles, 2, 5–7, 9–10, 36–38, 41–42, 43–44, 48, 52–53, 69, 92, 109–10, 112, 121, 127–29, 134–36, 136, 151–52, 162–65, 177–78, 200, 212–14, 218, 230–31, 259, 263, 268–69, 293, 297, 326–28. *See also* forewords

interracial heroes/heroines in American literature, 97–99, 103–5, 153–54, 159–60; in classical Hol-

lywood cinema, 19–20, 40–41,
    50, 53, 99–100, 105–8, 158–62
Intolerance (1916), 109, 118
Iron Horse, The (1924), 30, 90, 115,
    118, 308
Isenberg, Michael, 11–12, 204–5

Jackson, Helen Hunt, 90, 103–8, 146
Jacobs, Lewis, 209, 297–81, 295
James, Jesse, and Frank James, 84,
    128–30, 135
Jazz Singer, The (1927), 11, 220, 286
    288, 293–94
Jesse James (1939), 11, 14, 22, 119,
    127–30, 222, 243, 286
Jezebel (1933), 154, 156
Jezebel (1938), 14, 20, 23, 153–58,
    211, 313, 315
Johnson, Julian, 138, 288–91
Johnson, Mary, 153
Johnson, Nunnally, 6, 20, 85, 108,
    118, 126–31, 163, 171–73, 227,
    243, 317, 319
Johnsrud, Harold, 261–62
Jolson Sings Again (1949), 338
Jolson Story, The (1946), 338
Josephson, Julien, 229, 338
journalism and history, 14, 60, 66, 82,
    327, 329–30
journalists as screenwriters, 68, 76,
    127, 175, 216; as popular histori-
    ans, 62–77, 142, 145–46, 237–38
Journey's End (1931), 204, 217

Kael, Pauline, 319–20, 326
Keaton, Buster, 292
Keeler, Ruby, 202
Kitty Foyle (1940), 215–16
Klein, Wally, 134
Klondike Annie (1936), 93, 263
Knute Rockne, All American (1940), 299
Koch, Howard, 229–30
Koenig, William, 247

Korda, Alexander, 18
Ku Klux Klan, 2, 129, 162–63

Lady with Red Hair, The (1940), 288
Lake, Franky, 68, 197
Lake, Stuart, 94, 110–13, 136, 226
La Marr, Barbara, 290
Lambert, E. P., 101–2
Land of Liberty (1939, 1941), 308–17,
    328, 335, 338
Lardner, Ring, Jr., 268
Lasky, Jesse, 228–9, 234
Lasky, Jesse, Jr., 131, 314
Last Gangster, The (1937), 6–7
Last of the Mohicans, The (1826), 90,
    95–100
Last of the Mohicans, The (1909), 99
Last of the Mohicans, The (1920), 6, 99
Last of the Mohicans, The (1936), 22,
    99–103, 114, 152, 241
Last Parade, The (1931), 73
Late George Apley, The (1947), 338
Law and Order (1932), 89
Lawrence, T. E., 236
lawsuits and slander, 53, 55, 256–57,
    271–72. *See also* censorship
Leahy, Agnes Brand, 151
Lears, T. J. Jackson, 239
LeBaron, William, 20, 34, 51,
    112–13, 131, 318, 327
Lee, Robert N., 63
LeRoy, Mervyn, 202
Lévi-Strauss, Claude, 15, 42
Levien, Sonia, 118, 243–44, 282
Lewis, Lloyd, 171
Lights of New York, The (1928), 286
Lillian Russell (1940), 283–85, 296,
    317
Lincoln, Abraham, 53–54, 131, 137,
    163, 167–94, 232, 237, 256, 315,
    324, 333, 339–40; assassination,
    171–72; biographies and biop-
    ics, 169–71, 174–94; early life,

16, 179–80; and Civil War, 16, 168, 181; historiography, 16, 29, 167–69, 180, 186–87; monuments, 179–80, 232
Lincoln in the White House (1939), 175, 188, 194
Lissauer, Dr. Herman, 7, 133, 175, 225
Little Caesar (1931), 59–60, 63–64, 66, 76–77, 84, 92, 217, 221
Little Women (1933), 91, 151, 173, 252, 313
Littlest Rebel, The (1935), 152–53, 169, 339
Lloyd, Frank, 91, 110, 112–14, 118
Lloyd, Harold, 260, 272
Lockwood, Frank, 110
Long, Hal, 128
Loos, Anita, 94, 118
Lord, Robert, 218
Luce, Henry, 220, 327
Lundberg, Ferdinand, 321, 324–25

Macaulay, Richard, 218
MacDonald, Jeanette, 93–94, 210, 317
MacEwan, Walter, 136–27, 201
Macgowan, Kenneth, 20, 173–74, 247, 299
MacKenzie, Aeneas, 136–37
MacLeod, William Christie, 35, 119
Macpherson, Jeannie, 108, 118, 131, 308, 311–13
Magnificent Ambersons, The (1942), 335–37
Magnificent Doll (1945), 215, 338
Mahin, John Lee, 262
Maid of Salem (1937), 211, 308
Man Who Dared, The (1934), 106
Manhattan Melodrama (1934), 82–83, 203, 252
Mankiewicz, Herman, 310, 319–35
March, Fredric, 274

Markson, Ben, 202, 258
Marxist cultural criticism, 16, 17, 132–33
Mary of Scotland (1936), 210
Mason, Sarah Y., 151
Massey, Raymond, 189–90, 192–93
Mayer, Louis B., 51, 76, 80, 252, 256, 264, 269–70, 287–88, 322
Mazzanovich, Anton, 119–20
McCormick, John, 253
McCrea, Joel, 114
McDaniel, Hattie, 164
McGuire, William Anthony, 264, 283–84
McPherson, Tara, 143
McQueen, Butterfly, 164
McWilliams, Carey, 33
Meredith, Bess, 243
mestizas, 103–8
Metro-Goldwyn-Mayer (MGM Studios), 6–7, 83, 94, 118, 208, 242–43, 247, 264–65, 270
Mighty Barnum, The (1934), 21
military history, 145–46
Miller, Marilyn, 264, 266
Miller, Seton I., 77, 118
miscegenation, 19–20, 152
Misejewski, Linda, 265
Miskin, Leo, 221–22
Mitchell, Margaret, 14, 23, 141–50, 152–55, 158–60, 164–65, 243–45, 285; research by, 141–42, 146
mixed-race Americans, 40–41, 95–96, 98–101, 105, 107–8
Moore, Colleen, 253
Moore, Samuel Taylor, 197, 207, 236
Morning Glory (1933), 260–61, 282
Morton, Samuel J. "Nails," 62, 71, 77–78, 197–98
Moses, Vivian, 261
Mother Wore Tights (1947), 338
Motion Picture Herald, 130
Mouthpiece, The (1932), 53, 55

Movie Crazy (1932), 260
Mr. Everyman (Becker), 12–13, 50, 330
Mr. Smith Goes to Washington (1939), 193–94
Mudd, Samuel, 84, 127, 171–72
mulattas, 98–99, 154–58
Mumford, Lewis, 47
Munby, Jonathan, 59, 76
Muni, Paul, 77, 84, 296
Murfin, Jane, 258
myth, 8, 15, 16–17, 49, 89–90, 95–96, 116, 178, 284–85; and classical Hollywood cinema, 8–10, 16–17

Nash, Gerald, 44
Native Americans, 5, 40, 47, 97–99
Naughty Marietta (1935), 93–94
Neilan, Marshall "Mickey," 253, 256, 287–89
Nevins, Allan, 13, 14, 304
New Western History, 50–51, 120
New York Times, 114, 115–17, 133
Niblo, Fred, Jr., 225
Nichols, Dudley, 17, 20, 105, 111, 115–27, 178, 317, 326
Nilsson, George W., 307
1920s. *See* postwar era, history of
Normand, Mabel, 253, 256, 266, 281, 287–88
Northwest Passage (1940), 21, 189, 228, 241–43, 246
Novick, Peter, 228
Now I'll Tell (1934), 83–84
Nugent, Frank S., 7, 84, 115–17, 129–30, 133, 135, 137, 209, 215–16, 221–22, 247, 271, 317, 326
Nute, Grace Lee, 299–300

Oakley, Annie, 91–93, 118
O'Bannion, Dion, 64, 68
objectivity, 2–3, 11–12, 15, 64–66, 73, 110, 128, 228, 320, 328

Of Human Hearts (1938), 174
Oklahoma Kid, The (1939), 22, 23, 134–36, 222
Oklahoma: land rush of 1889, 39–40, 44
Old Ironsides (1925), 255
Only the Brave (1930), 150–51, 234, 252
Only Yesterday (1934), 308
Operator 13 (1934), 151–52, 234, 308, 313, 322
original screenplays, 171–73, 283–98, 323–28
Osage tribes, 47

Page, Thomas Nelson, 153
Paramore, Edward E., 134, 151
Paramount Studios, 94, 108–9, 111, 251–52
Parker, Dorothy, 268
Parkman, Francis, 116–17
Pascal, Ernest, 288, 292
Pasley, Fred, 14, 60, 65, 74–77, 235
Patterson, Frances Taylor, 89, 114
Patton, James Welch, 148
Patullo, George, 237
Paxton, Frederic, 117
Perils of Pauline, The (1947), 338
Perkins, V. F., 335
Pershing, General John, 236–37
Peterson, H. C., 207
Petrified Forest, The (1936), 84–85
Phillips, Ulrich, 3, 158
Photoplay, 257, 259, 269
Pickett, LaSalle Corbell, 148
Pickford, Mary, 255, 263, 266, 273–74, 287–88
Plainsman, The (1936), 109–10, 113–14, 127, 132–33, 234, 308
plantation epics and myth, 143, 153
Plunkett, Walter, 159, 165, 211, 213
Polk, Oscar, 164
Pony Express (1925), 255

popular historians, 13–14, 31, 61–62, 108–13, 119–20, 131
Portrait of Jennie (1948), 338
postwar era, history of, 55, 59–61, 65–67, 71, 198–203, 216–23
Potamkin, Harry Alan, 29
Potter, H. C., 208, 215
Powdermaker, Hortense, 8
Powell, Dick, 202
Powell, Paul, 34–35
press books, 68, 156, 234, 273
Pressnel, Robert, 258
Pride of the Yankees (1942), 299, 316, 337–38
Prisoner of Shark Island, The (1936), 14, 22, 118, 127, 163, 171–73, 285, 308, 313
Prisoner of Zenda, The (1937), 252, 266
Private Life of Henry VIII, The (1933), 18
Production Code Administration (PCA), 19–20, 68, 76, 80–82, 191, 208, 263–64, 274, 282, 308
Prohibition, 55, 71, 82, 205, 220. *See also* postwar era, history of
propaganda, 205–7, 227–28, 233–34, 248
Public Enemy, The (1931), 14, 19, 22, 59, 68–73, 75–77, 82–84, 197, 208, 211, 217, 221, 272
publicity campaigns, 20, 63, 80, 93, 112, 125–28, 136, 156–57, 188, 201, 221, 233, 234, 273, 283, 315–17, 326
Pulitzer, Joseph, 321
Pyron, Darden Asbury, 145

Quarberg, Lincoln, 80

race: and American history, 1–5, 12, 20; and Civil War, 143
racial ambiguity and cinema, 20, 103, 107, 143, 153–58. *See also* mulattas and mestizas

Raine, Norman Reilly, 118, 135, 225, 227
Ramona (1884), 103–8
Ramona (1936), 14, 17, 20, 22, 103–8, 114, 116, 152, 308, 315, 340
Ramsaye, Terry, 186, 188, 251, 257, 269, 280, 285, 295, 320
Randall, James G., 146, 148, 168–69
Raphaelson, Samson, 289
reception, box office, 21, 54–55, 189, 216
reception, critical. *See individual critics*
Reconstruction, 1–4, 128–29, 161–65, 171; and historiography, 1–4, 163–64
Red Skin (1929), 40
Reid, Wallace, 290
relativism, 12–13, 65, 295
remakes, 138
research bibliographies, 20, 35, 102, 109, 112, 156, 171–72, 187, 225; libraries, 5–7, 101–3, 112, 114, 133–34; techniques, 101–2, 114, 225, 230, 299–300
Return of Frank James, The (1940), 11, 138
reuse of old footage, 11, 138, 292, 294, 327–28
revisionist history, 24, 33, 35, 50–51, 53–54, 66, 114, 119, 207, 220–21, 257, 315
revolutionary heroes, 228, 232–33, 235–48
Richardson, Frances, 101
Ritter, Charles Rudolph, 271
RKO Studios, 20, 22, 32, 48–49, 91, 94, 111, 210, 252–53, 317–18, 327
Roaring Twenties, The (1939), 18, 197, 217–23, 225, 316, 331
Roberts, Kenneth, 242
Robinson, Edward G., 6–7, 54, 75, 84

Rockett, A. L., 190
Rogers, Cameron, 167
Rogers, Ginger, 209–16, 318
Rogers, Will, 105, 264
Roosevelt, Franklin D., 220, 301
Roosevelt, Theodore, 38–39, 42, 46, 110
Rose of Washington Square, The
    (1939), 283, 296
Rosen, Philip, 17–18, 218
Rosenstone, Robert A., 17–19
Rosten, Leo, 21, 118, 247
Rotha, Paul, 11, 51
Rothstein, Arnold, 83
Rough Riders, 45
Roxie Hart (1942), 215, 229
Royal Family of Broadway, The (1930),
    263–64, 274
Ruggles, Wesley, 35–37, 42, 46, 47,
    49, 51, 113, 118
Ruggles of Red Gap (1935), 169
Russell, Lillian, 263, 283–84

Salt, Waldo, 208
San Francisco (1936), 93–94, 116,
    217, 241
Sandburg, Carl, 168, 181, 185, 192
Santa Fe Trail, The (1940), 137, 193
Sarris, Andrew, 309
Sayre, Joel, 91
Scarface (1932), 14, 17, 19, 59, 75–82,
    83, 197, 227, 308, 325
Scarlet Pimpernel, The (1935), 14
Schaefer, George, 20, 242, 318, 327,
    337
Schallert, Edwin, 203, 233, 305
Schatz, Thomas, 8, 23
Schulberg, B. P., 251, 254, 256
Schulberg, Budd, 268
screenwriters and historical cinema,
    6–7, 19, 112, 117, 169–70; in
    1930s, 6–7, 20, 117–18, 125–27,
    286, 338; during silent era, 5–6,
    22

Second World War propaganda, 234,
    241–42, 244–45, 303–6
Secret Six, The (1931), 83
Seitz, George B., 118
Seldes, Gilbert, 20, 27, 118
self-reflexivity, 42
Selznick, David O., 6, 20, 22, 23,
    51, 52, 119, 143, 150, 152, 155,
    158–65, 251–53, 255–62, 266–77,
    282, 285–87, 291, 308, 317, 324
Selznick, Lewis J., 252–53, 266
Selznick International Pictures, 252,
    266, 271
Sennett, Mack, 287–88, 290, 292
Sergeant York (1941), 17, 20, 228–35,
    338
Seymour, James, 202
She Done Him Wrong (1933), 93,
    263, 282
Shearer, Norma, 268
Sherman, Lowell, 259–60
Sherman, Richard, 212, 282
Sherman, William T.: and March to
    Sea, 147–48, 159, 199
Sherwood, Robert, 5, 27, 28, 49, 54–
    55, 81–82, 84–85, 168, 188–89,
    191–94, 254–55, 318, 325
Shine On, Harvest Moon (1943), 338
Shopworn Angel (1928), 34, 204
Shopworn Angel (1938), 209–9
Shotwell, James T., 309–12, 314,
    316–17
Show Boat (1929), 27
Show Boat (1936), 152, 211, 308
Show People (1928), 255
silent era: historical filmmaking, 1–6,
    22, 203–4; histories of, 251–77
Simkins, Francis Butler, 148
Silver Dollar (1932), 20, 53–54, 308,
    321, 339
Sisters, The (1938), 211
Skeyhill, Tom, 229, 237–40
Slave Ship (1937), 127

Slosson, Preston William, 60–61

Slotkin, Richard, 15, 42, 45–46, 96

Small, Edward, 90, 95, 241, 294

So Red the Rose (1935), 21, 152, 308, 313, 315

Souls for Sale (1923), 254

sound and historical filmmaking, 6–7, 8–10, 28–29, 36, 60, 76, 260

Spanish-American War, 44–45, 321–22, 328, 333–34

Squaw Man, The (1931), 109, 281

St. Johns, Adela Rogers, 252, 256–58, 266

Stagecoach (1939), 17, 20, 89, 115–27, 178, 326

Stanfield, Peter, 90

Stanwyck, Barbara, 93, 210, 253, 272, 296, 319

Star is Born, A (1937), 20, 257, 266–77, 282, 291, 295

Stenn, David, 257

Stewart, Garrett, 329

Stiller, Mauritz, 272

Story of Alexander Graham Bell, The (1939), 21, 173–4, 216, 243, 245, 286, 294, 339

Story of Vernon and Irene Castle, The (1939), 209–16

Stromberg, Hunt, 262–63

structuralism and poststructuralism, 8–9, 12, 320

Sullavan, Margaret, 208, 211

superwestern, 21, 90, 117, 133

Susan Lennox—Her Fall and Rise (1931), 258

Susman, Warren, 17–18

Sutter's Gold (1936), 21, 321

Swanberg, W. A., 321

Swanson, Gloria, 253, 255, 262, 266, 288

Sweet, Blanche, 287

Tabor, H. A. W. (Yates Martin), 53

Tale of Two Cities, A (1935), 253, 266, 313

Temple, Shirley, 6, 152–53, 169, 210, 272

Tennessee Johnson (1942), 21, 336

Texans, The (1938), 234

text superimpositions. *See* intertitles

Thalberg, Irving, 254, 274, 288

That Certain Woman (1937), 85

Thew, Harvey, 53–54, 68

They Died with Their Boots On (1941), 137

They Gave Him a Gun (1937), 203, 208

This Is My Affair (1937), 173, 207

Thompson, Kristin, 8, 10

Thorp, Margaret Farrand, 279, 281

Three Bad Men (1926), 115

Three on a Match (1932), 308

Time, 108, 129, 147

Tracy, Spencer, 288, 296

Trail, Armitage, 76–77

Trotti, Lamar, 17, 20, 91, 105–8, 111, 150, 168, 173–88, 227, 244–45

Tumbleweeds (1925), 35

Turner, Frederick Jackson, 12, 18, 33, 38–39, 42, 44, 46, 50, 117, 228, 204

Tuska, John, 89

Twentieth Century–Fox, 6, 17, 91, 101, 117, 169–70, 279–80

Twist, John, 91

Uncertain Glory (1942), 297

Uncle Tom's Cabin (1903), 168

Underworld (1927), 76

Union Pacific (1939), 19, 114, 131–33, 193

Valentino, Rudolph, 257, 281, 290

Van Doren, Dorothy, 34, 49

Van Dyke, W. S., 203

Vanishing American, The (1925), 5, 36, 40–41, 204, 308, 315

Variety, 29, 32, 57, 69, 201, 246, 259–60, 270, 337–38
veterans: and Depression, 55, 198–205, 219
Virginia City (1940), 137, 193
Virginian, The (1914), 109
Virginian, The (1929), 30, 31, 34, 36
voice-over narration, 10–11, 218–19, 301, 314, 316
Von Stroheim, Erich, 258, 281
Vorkapich, Slavko, 53, 208

Wald, Jerry, 218
Wallis, Hal B., 20, 117, 134, 138, 158, 201, 217, 219–20, 304, 317, 324
Walsh, Raoul, 32, 37
Wanger, Walter, 119
Warner Brothers Studios, 6–7, 23, 57, 85, 117, 133–34, 156–57, 219–23, 226, 280, 289, 297–99, 303–4
Warner, Harry, 227
Warner, Jack, 84, 137, 154–55, 217, 226
Warshow, Robert, 59
Watts, Richard, 20, 29, 49, 54, 58
Wecter, Dixon, 231, 235, 284–85
Weiss, Hymie, 64, 68
Welles, Orson, 23, 307, 309–10, 318–37
Wellman, Paul, 119
Wellman, William, 52–53, 69, 72–73, 203, 267–70, 272
Wells Fargo (1937), 21, 22, 95, 110–14, 116, 127
West, Mae, 90, 93–94, 210, 263–64, 282
Westerner, The (1940), 226
western history, 33–34, 35, 41, 50
westerns, 29–30, 31–32, 42–43, 89–114, 115–38; and myth, 30–31, 89–90, 116
West of the Pecos (1934), 226
What Price Glory (1926), 204, 208, 217

What Price Hollywood? (1932), 251, 254, 256–60, 266, 268, 272
White, Hayden, 18, 19
Wilder, Billy, 339
Williams, William Appleman, 322
Wilson (1944), 207, 338
Wilson, Woodrow, 2, 4, 205–6; public disillusionment with policies of, 204–8
Wister, Owen, 29
Wolfson, P. J., 242
women: and biography, 91–95, 283–84; and historical cinema, 13–14, 91–95, 209–16, 315; and opposition to Civil War, 144; and the West, 48; as historians, 103–5, 142–48
Woodward, C. Vann, 158
Words and Music (1948), 338
World Moves On, The (1934), 11, 203
Wright, Will, 89, 116
Wyler, William, 158

Yankee Doodle Dandy (1942), 228, 280, 297–306, 337–38
yellow journalism, 321–23, 334
York, Alvin, 229, 235–40, 298
Yost, Dorothy, 212–13
Young, Loretta, 107
Young, Stark, 144, 152
Young Mr. Lincoln (1939), 14, 15–17, 19, 21, 174–89, 191, 193–94, 241, 246, 286, 339

Zanuck, Darryl F., 6, 14, 17, 20, 22, 23–24, 53–55, 57, 68, 69, 73, 75, 84–85, 90–91, 101, 105–8, 117, 127–31, 133, 135–37, 150, 152–53, 167–89, 199–202, 207–8, 226–27, 229, 235, 243–46, 254, 256, 279, 282, 283–98, 308, 317, 324
Ziegfeld, Florenz, 264–66, 282